AFTER GREAT PAIN

THE INNER LIFE OF

EMILY DICKINSON

AFTER GREAT PAIN

THE INNER LIFE OF

EMILY DICKINSON

John Cody

THE BELKNAP PRESS OF

HARVARD UNIVERSITY PRESS

CAMBRIDGE, MASSACHUSETTS

1971

To C.W.L. — a Saturniid among Geometridae

ACKNOWLEDGMENTS

Many helpful and encouraging people have seen me through the writing of this book. Of a few, considerable forebearance and sacrifice were asked and cheerfully given—I allude to my family who often starved their own interests to insure me the needed leisure and peace. To my wife, Dorothy, I am especially grateful for this and for her criticism, her loving willingness to undertake innumerable chores, and for her professional insight as a pediatrician.

I am also indebted to: Ranice Birch Crosby for generous and valuable services; Drs. Otto and Paulina Kernberg for their critical examination of my hypothesis and for their unflagging enthusiasm; Dr. and Mrs. Karl Menninger for their support and encouragement; Dr. Herbert Modlin for reading parts of the book and for helpful suggestions; and Dr. Donald B. Rinsley who helped overcome my initial diffidence and who was a never-failing source of stimulation, ideas, and moral support.

My gratitude goes also to Barbara Warme and Judith Caprez for their careful critiques of the manuscript; to ophthalmologists Dr. Harry Watts and Dr. David Paton for suggestions concerning Emily Dickinson's eye disorder; and to my uncomplaining and overworked secretaries: Helen Baier of Larned, Iris Knoll of

Victoria, and Bertha Steele, Alberta Shanely, Janet Hays, and Dee Blackwood of Hays.

I also wish to thank the staff and readers of Harvard University Press for their considerable assistance, in particular Mrs. Dennis Clemente.

Part of Chapter II appeared originally as an article, "Emily Dickinson and Nature's Dining Room," *Michigan Quarterly Review* (October 1968) 249-254. Portions of Chapter IX were published as "Emily Dickinson's Vesuvian Face," *American Imago*, 24 (Fall 1967), and "Watchers upon the East," *Psychiatric Quarterly*, 42 (July 1968) 548-576. A sketch of the book appeared as "Mourner Among the Children," *Psychiatric Quarterly*, 41 (January and April 1967), 12-37 and 223-263, from which I have borrowed passages. This material is used with the permission of these journals.

Selections from Emily Dickinson's poems are reprinted by permission of the publishers and the Trustees of Amherst College from Thomas H. Johnson, editor, *The Poems of Emily Dickinson*, Cambridge, Mass.: The Belknap Press of Harvard University Press, copyright 1951, 1955 by the President and Fellows of Harvard College. By permission of Little, Brown and Co., from Thomas H. Johnson, editor, *The Complete Poems of Emily Dickinson*, the following poems are reprinted in whole or in part: numbers 63, 305, 310, 1247, 1598, 1670, 1677, copyright 1914, 1942 by Martha Dickinson Bianchi; numbers 100, 257, 355, 379, 396, 398, 413, 425, 443, 534, 546, 601, 618, 624, 725, 745, 752, 753, 754, 761, 766, 965, 1225, copyright 1929, 1957 by Mary L. Hampson; numbers 236, 240, 261, 378, 388, 393, 404, 410, 420, 430, 474, 485, 544, 591, 643, 646, copyright 1935 by Martha Dickinson Bianchi, © renewed 1963 by Mary L. Hampson.

Quotations from Emily Dickinson's letters are reprinted by permission of the publishers and the Trustees of Amherst College from Thomas H. Johnson and Theodora Ward, editors, *The Letters of Emily Dickinson,* Cambridge, Mass.: The Belknap Press of Harvard University Press, copyright by the President and Fellows of Harvard College.

Excerpts are reprinted from: *The Years and Hours of Emily Dickinson* by Jay Leyda by permission of the Yale University Press; *Emily Dickinson's Poetry: Stairway of Surprise* by Charles

CONTENTS

CONTENTS

AFTER GREAT PAIN

THE INNER LIFE OF

EMILY DICKINSON

INTRODUCTION

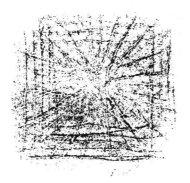

Psychoanalysis is not alone among sciences in providing a means whereby the existence of what is not directly perceptible can be inferred. Thus, the psychoanalytic interpretation of the life of a historical figure is in certain respects comparable to the reassembling of a fossil skeleton. And when the life under consideration has been rent by a psychological cataclysm, the interpretive reconstruction is not unlike the piecing together of the fragments of an aircraft that has exploded in flight.

In the first instance the paleontologist dovetails the scattered bones according to the laws of comparative anatomy: the progression of vertebrae, for example, have a known and more or less constant relationship to each other throughout the animal kingdom. In the second example, the engineer assembles the shattered metal of the aircraft on a scaffold corresponding to the known dimensions of the type of plane to which the wreckage belongs; when all the available pieces are laid out in this way, a sequence of stresses becomes discernible whose concentric waves lead back to and establish the point of origin of the explosion. In either example, what provides the gestalt and guides the interpretation placed on each discrete particle is a body of general knowledge—the laws of bone structure in the one case, the structural blueprints in the other. In my reconstruction of the psychological processes of Emily Dickinson's life, the body of theory and knowledge according to which the biographical remnants are interrelated is psychoanalytic. Through deep exploration of many lives, psychoanalysis has discovered conflicts and motivations that are assumed to be operant to some degree in all lives.

Thus, the configurations of gaps in the record become discernible when the biographical data are organized and understood psychoanalytically, much as the shape of a missing fragment of wing or fuselage becomes apparent when the surrounding interlocking pieces are correctly arranged. Psychoanalytic inferences are likewise comparable to the plaster bones that are employed to complete the reconstructed fossil skeleton when all the genuine structures are unavailable. Such piecing together with these generalized forms, which are essentially composites drawn from observation of many individuals, makes it easier to perceive the true relationships among the authentic fragments. One such "plaster bone" in the present study is the assumption that early in Emily Dickinson's life she experienced what she interpreted as a cruel rejection by her mother. Many of her statements, her choice of certain recurring metaphors and symbols, and the entire course of her life, viewed psychoanalytically, argue for the truth of this assumption. However, there exists no record of any concrete instance in which Mrs. Dickinson took such an attitude toward her daughter. Nevertheless, knowledge gained from the clinical study of patients who bear scars similar to Emily Dickinson's is persuasive evidence for the existence in the poet's life of damaging experiences comparable to theirs.

The use of such "plaster bones" is, in psychoanalytic biography as in paleontology, I submit, a legitimate device for bridging the hiatus left by the disappearance of authentic fragments. In fact it is the only way one can recreate the original relationships lying latent in a pile of discrete facts—that is, by arranging the facts according to an underlying ordering principle.

It is important, however, that psychoanalytic explorations not overstep their inherent limits. They cannot explain talent, much less genius. Psychoanalytic methodology also cannot establish *concrete* facts—for example, the identity of Emily Dickinson's presumptive lover. That is the function of the historian. The unique contribution of the psychoanalytic biographer is to generate a deepened insight into personality by making explicit the unconscious emotional connections among events. I make this definition of my goals for the benefit of the reader who, upon detecting the bland surface of plaster where he expects the texture of bone, concludes that the psychoanalytic biographer–paleontologist has not done his job. Or worse: not realizing the impossibility of rendering clearly the proportions of the original structure without this stopgap, he concludes that a hoax is being perpetrated and that in all likelihood no such creature as the one under contemplation ever existed. If, in the reconstruction of the data, there is a disproportionate amount of speculation, with a paucity of historical fact, or if authentic and relevant historical material has not been included, the reader has reason to complain. Fortunately, Emily Dickinson has left an ample record of much of her inner life. Naturally though there are lacunae— spaces which only a scientific hypothesis can span.

At this point one can anticipate that a reader temperamentally adverse to pathographic delving into the private corners of an admired author's psyche may have some uneasiness. His questions on the propriety and usefulness of the effort might go something like this: Suppose one assumes for the sake of argument that Emily Dickinson's psychiatric problems can be diagnosed, their development traced, and their probable causes defined. Suppose one also grants that they had a modulating effect on her creativity and that this influence can be demonstrated, and suppose further that the poems do contain allusions to psychic conflicts. The question is what has any of this got to do with literature? Can such investigations lead to a greater appreciation of the poems or help define Emily Dickinson's stature as a poet? That is, after all, what really matters.

The answer must be that a psychological exposition of the poetry and of its author's life will always be of more significance for some readers, will contribute more to their understanding and admiration, than it will for others. Ultimately, therefore, the answer depends on one's conception of the nature of art, and this involves certain perennial considerations. For example, to what extent should a work of art be considered a complete, insular entity whose full excellence can be apprehended without reference to anything outside itself? For some the art work is a

3

closed system. Its "meaning" is entirely contained within the formal relationships of its constituent elements; it is primarily a design. From this standpoint the finest appreciation is contaminated when it concerns itself with extrinsic factors and relationships, including the psychological vicissitudes of the artist. For others the art work is a reflection of society. It is an epitome of the artist's life and era. This view assumes that the value and meaning of a poem is derived to some extent from its relationship with the larger world, including the author's social and emotional interaction with it, and that the poetic elements are representatives and symbols of extra-poetic realities which must themselves be understood if one is to appraise the art justly.

It appears to be a matter of individual taste to what extent one inclines toward either of these extreme positions. Of equal importance is the character of the art in question. Certain of Emily Dickinson's poems lend themselves to evaluation by more or less absolutist standards while others resist it. It all appears to depend on her subject matter, which ranges from abstract philosophical pronouncements to highly personal disclosures of concrete exerience. There are those who tend not to regard the latter as capable of poetic stature because these poems depend for their intelligibility upon specific knowledge of the poet's life. Consistent with this view is the rejection of the proposition that psychological probing of the author's personality deepens appreciation of the art; such a study is seen as seducing one's attention away from a proper regard for literary values through an inquisitiveness about personalia.

Whatever one's point of view on these matters, it seems important to *read* a poem carefully before rejecting it as too narrowly personal. There exist critical denunciations of Dickinson poems where it is apparent that the major shortcoming is that of the critic, who simply missed the meaning. It may be that this sometimes occurs because the psychological atmosphere of the poem has repelled the critic before he could come to grips with the message. It would seem sensible then to resist the initial irritation and impatience evoked by a given poem in order to examine it carefully and fairly. Surely each poem is worthy of this consideration, if only because the author has composed other poems that are undisputed masterpieces. If one grants this, the logical step is to delve deeply enough into the substance of the poem to grasp its complete significance, *including all its psychological implications*. Only then is one in the proper position to render a judgement on the universality and esthetic quality of the poem. To remain unaware of or to evade central psychological issues in a work of art must weaken the appreciation of esthetic beauties, if not render such appreciation impossible. Where content and form are inseparable, then surely the content, including all its psychological ramifications, must be understood for a fair appraisal of the work. The deepest study of the works of at least some artists therefore requires investigation of the life situation of the artist.

It must be acknowledged that the psychoanalytic biographer works at a disadvantage in comparison with the psychoanalyst. The psychographer must content himself with records that are necessarily incomplete; the psychoanalyst has before him a living patient. Critics hostile to psychography never tire of pointing out this discrepancy. Yet the psychographer may have certain advantages over the psychoanalyst which are less well recognized.

The average person in psychoanalysis is young, generally not past his thirties. This means that he has yet to encounter some of those stages of life which are so revelatory of personality. For example, he may not yet have married, had children, achieved the peak of his career, experienced the deaths of parents, and so on. Neither the analyst nor the patient knows how the patient will react to these events. Thus, certain aspects of the patient's personality may remain inaccessible for purposes of examination and understanding. But the subject of the psychographer has lived his entire life and has met death. Not only the development and mid-stages of his life are available for inspection but also its ultimate unfolding and final resolution. This means that in discovering the dominant psychological themes of his subject's emotional evolution the psychoanalytic biographer has at his disposal a broader spectrum of behavior through more decades of life than has the analyst with a living patient.

Another prerequisite for successful psychoanalysis is that the patient be "psychologically minded." This means that he must be able to reflect upon the inner workings of his consciousness, must be aware of his various emotional reactions and be able to distinguish nuances of feeling. In addition he must have a capacity for fantasy. And he needs also the ability to put his thoughts, feelings, and fantasies into words so that they are transmittable to the therapist. In order to do this he must in most cases be of above average intelligence with a certain verbal facility. So important for a successful analysis are these abilities that patient-candidates are rejected for treatment if they do not possess them in sufficient degree and are advised to seek other forms of therapy. The psychographer has a wider choice than the psychoanalyst. He may choose as his subject a person who is not only above average in intelligence but of surpassing brilliance, not only psychologically minded but preternaturally discerning, not only capable of fantasy but a master at imaginative invention. His "patient" need have no mere capacity to utter his thoughts—he may be a poet. Emily Dickinson, surely, possessed a greater capacity for the perception and discrimination of psychological processes and a greater ability to find appropriate words to express her inner experiences than any patient who has ever been psychoanalyzed. From this standpoint she is the psychoanalysand par excellence.

Her poems appear to have afforded her emotional relief from her psychic pain, but they were more than a mere vehicle for its expression. They possessed also an analytic and documentary function. With penetrating self-observation and unnerving intuition she anticipated the major discoveries of psychoanalysis. She was on almost familiar terms with the unconscious and realized its role as a potent motivating force. She also grasped the existence and function of repression and a host of other ego defenses. She was vividly aware of the phenomena of identification and transference. She probably has more to tell us regarding the mysterious processes of sublimation than we are yet in a position to understand fully. One suspects that the ultimate elucidation of certain of her more obscure psychological poems awaits further advances in our scientific knowledge of personality.

Her poetry also describes a vast array of psychological symptoms, each sharply observed and exactly characterized. From the evidently chaotic flux of her inner experience she was able to pluck out and transfix the most elusive and transitory sensations and dynamisms. Freud had an army of patients to observe, examine, and compare and a more or less systematic theory to guide

6

his investigations. Emily Dickinson took only herself as subject. And, through unaided insight, without benefit of schema or system, she traveled freely in a domain whose shores Freud was not to approach for another half century. All the so-called psychopathology he encountered in his patients she discovered within herself. Her life and work reveal the awful price she paid for such self-knowledge. Freud traveled a relatively safe and, as he said, "royal" road to the unconscious through the analysis of dreams. Emily Dickinson sought no such road; the unconscious came to her, breaking in without warning.

The objection has been made, with considerable validity, that the biggest obstacle to posthumous psychoanalysis is the fact that it is impossible to get the subject's free associations, by means of which, in actual psychoanalysis, the therapist comes to understand the purport of the patient's private language. That is to say, in the case of the famous dead how can one hope to comprehend the significance of the symbols that appear in the subject's fantasies and to interpret the aura of metaphor with which unconscious forces have invested his behavior? When an actual patient dreams, for example, of a particular object, he conveys to the analyst all the images and verbal fragments that cluster in his mind around the periphery of this symbol. After accumulating enough of these contiguous associations, one can fix the symbol in the cosmology of the patient's emotional universe and thereby approach its meaning for that particular individual. Psychography, of course, suffers from the lack of this cooperative effort on the part of its remote subjects.

A partial answer to this objection, insofar as it pertains to Emily Dickinson, can be found in a consideration of her use of symbols. Unlike many poets, she tended to use the same symbols over and over again in many different poems and in varying contexts. The sun, the sea, night, the eye, the bee, noon, winter, summer, and a host of others recur many times throughout her poetry. To cite a few examples: the word "sun," for instance, occurs 170 times, "sea" 122 times, and "noon" 76 times.

These words are used frequently enough in a symbolic sense to gather around themselves a complex atmosphere of associated ideas and images. Moreover, the density of this atmosphere is further augmented by the poet's letters, in which the same symbolic words are employed in a way that clearly relates them to

7

current situations in her life. It therefore seems justifiable to consider that cross-referencing and analysis of the poet's habitual symbolic words, which appear in her verse and letters through a span of thirty or more years, do constitute a reasonably satisfactory substitute for the free associations of a living patient. It is with this rationale that the underlying meaning of the poet's eye affliction and her preoccupation with blindness is elucidated in Chapter IX through an examination of her use of the sun symbol.

Increasingly frequent in the expanding volume of commentary on Emily Dickinson are forays into the area of psychodynamics by authors whose major interests and training qualify them to concentrate on other aspects of the poet's life and work. As I shall have occasion to point out, this tendency has produced hypotheses that to a psychiatrist are untenable. As the life of Emily Dickinson exemplifies, the biographer commonly finds himself confronted with behavior that appears deviant, sometimes to a striking degree. When this occurs, he is faced with the task of integrating into his conception of the personality as a whole whatever in conduct or thought appears at first glance to be inconsistent, inappropriate, strange, or bizarre. Ordinarily, biographical interpretations of behavior are made on a commonsense, nonscientific basis, that is, they are derived from the commentator's own lifelong and day-to-day interpersonal experiences. Yet anyone's spontaneous, unorganized, and adventitious observations of human behavior are necessarily limited by the scope of his social transactions and the extent to which his own emotional perspective modifies and filters what he perceives. Whether such a personal and unsystematic psychology is fully sufficient for purposes of biography depends, perhaps, on many factors, among which would seem to be the degree to which the biographer is able to call on his own reactions and experiences to elucidate the feelings and responses of his subject. Probably the greatest difficulty arises when there exist in the life under consideration traces of disturbed psychological functioning of which the biographer has scant personal experience. In such instances the personality characteristics of the subject approximate those encountered commonly and intensively in psychiatric practice, where they are susceptible to observation and study to a degree not afforded by ordinary social interchange.

Here the biographer finds himself in the field of the psychiatrist. It is likely that unless he has considerable firsthand knowledge of the origins, genesis, and dynamics of the psychopathology which confronts him, he will unwittingly misrepresent, exaggerate, or minimize it, depending on his feeling for his subject. Sometimes biographers, duly appreciative of the "sanity" (that is, the social relevance) of their subject's life work, feel they must rationalize away evidence of behavioral and emotional aberration; or they miss such evidence altogether and conclude that their subject was entirely "normal."

The psychological hypotheses of Dickinson scholars have usually been based on genuine insight, sometimes distorted, however, by overconcentration on one facet of the problem at the expense of others. This has led to narrowly specific formulations which are overextended to explain everything—the consequence, one suspects, of academic theorizing which has never been brought down to earth by experience with real patients. Some of the studies along these lines have been ingenious, but one has reservations about their applicability to a real human being. One cannot explain Emily Dickinson's orientation to life solely on the basis of a postulated homosexuality, or her possible envy and fear of men, or a father-fixation, or a traumatic childhood incident. Though each of these theories may contain a measure of truth, they are all misleading because they are fragmentary. They do not encompass the breadth and complexity characteristic of real persons and they lack the genetic roots that would make comprehensible the poet's behavior in each of these neurotic predicaments. One or two of the theories are too specialized—too exotic —to account for the multiform, but by no means unusual, problems that appear to have beset Emily Dickinson.

The book begins with a review of those writers and Dickinson specialists who have had interpretive comments to make on the symptomatic aspects of Emily Dickinson's life. Included in this first chapter also are some arguments for the usefulness of such an analysis as mine. Following this is an examination of the probable early roots of Emily Dickinson's relationship with her mother and father and their ramifications in her later life. The following chapter presents a reconstruction of Emily Dickinson's years of latency and her transactions with school chums. Through these early chapters an attempt is made to establish the nature of Emily Dickinson's psychological imbalance and to set the stage for the series of inner struggles that were set in motion by her brother's courtship. The succeeding chapters present in some detail the phenomenology and dynamics that ushered in Emily Dickinson's breakdown and the processes by which she entered upon this catastrophe a competent poet and emerged an inspired one. The role played by Emily Dickinson's "lover" in her psychological economy (regardless of his identity, which is outside the power of psychoanalytic exploration to establish) is the theme that follows. The book concludes with some observations on the aftermath of the psychological crisis and some of the deeper reverberations of her inner life as they manifested themselves in her poetry.

The book contains a great many quotations from Emily Dickinson's letters and poems—the authentic "osseous" basis of my argument. Since Emily Dickinson's own words so often make my case for me, I have quoted liberally. This was done in the belief that the reader will be more likely to accept what she tells him directly of the subterranean motions of her inner life than my paraphrases of these insights. Of course Emily Dickinson, like all geniuses, was not always aware of the full implications of her utterances. When this is the case her words are given along with my inferences as to their unconscious import.

It should be clear that this book both includes more and leaves out more than a conventional biography. It is concerned primarily with Emily Dickinson's inner life and occupies itself mainly with those aspects of her milieu that are directly relevant to her psychosexual development. Its primary focus throughout is on the personal emotional undercurrents at the core of her personality, not on her intellectual evolution or her poetic achievement, except insofar as these are rooted in her emotional life. Nowhere have I attempted literary criticism. Though it might seem desirable for the sake of comprehensiveness to explore fully other aspects of Emily Dickinson and her environment, to do so would be to attempt to repeat what others far more qualified than I in this regard—Richard Chase, Millicent Todd Bingham, Thomas H. Johnson, to name a few—have already done thoroughly and well. Therefore I have been careful to confine my approach to those areas for the elucidation of which my training and experience have prepared me.

One more point—as a practicing psychiatrist in a community-supported mental health clinic I am very aware of the misunderstanding patients endure through the general public's ignorance of the manifestations and course of emotional and mental disturbances. It is my aim, in this presentation of my belief that Emily Dickinson was a woman who became disturbed to the point of collapse, not to remove her to the realm of the psychologically alien but on the contrary to bring her closer to us. And I would do this without divesting her of the attractiveness and humanity that were assuredly hers. If one can be induced to stare unflinchingly for a moment into the psychic hell that for a time overwhelmed her, one sees that the "psychotic" are not necessarily mindless and absurd—in fact they are far more frequently preternaturally aware of their deeper psychic processes, hypersensitive, and gentle. And in those rare instances when unusual artistic talent, adequate technical skills, and high intelligence combine in them, their mental and emotional perturbations may become the vehicle through which genius is kindled.

Chapter I THE MYTHS OF AMHERST

I must tell you about the *character* of Amherst. It is a lady whom the people call the *Myth*. She is a sister of Mr. Dickinson, & seems to be the climax of all the family oddity. She has not been outside of her own house in fifteen years, except once to see a new church, when she crept out at night & viewed it by moonlight . . . She dresses wholly in white, & her mind is said to be perfectly wonderful. She writes finely, but no one *ever* sees her. Her sister . . . invited me to come & sing to her mother sometime . . . People tell me that the *myth* will hear every note—she will be near, but unseen.
　　　　　　　　　—Mabel Loomis Todd to her parents, November 6, 1881[1]

Emily Dickinson nowhere maintained that her anxiety-ridden personality and her seclusive way of life were normal or appropriate to her circumstances. Wherever she mentions her dread of face to face encounters with those outside her family or her fear of leaving the sheltering walls of her parents' home, she does so with the clear implication that she considers herself the victim of irrational and inflexible aberration. Her open and bewildered admission that to her these reactions were phenomena that lay outside the normal and comprehensible range of behavior contrasts strongly with the views of her biographers and commentators. Conceiving of psychological function and behavior in overly dichotomous terms of "sane" and "insane," as they strongly tend to do, these writers are eager to perceive and present the poet as an essentially sound and well-proportioned personality.

At one time it was the impulse of editors and publishers to "improve" and regularize Emily Dickinson's poetry. By removing what were then considered blemishes and crudities due to technical incompetence and carelessness, they hoped to make the "inspired" elements of the poems more accessible and easier to appreciate. Today, in deference to Emily Dickinson's now unquestioned poetic stature, her every spelling, syntactical, and punctuational eccentricity has been rendered sacrosanct. But the same impulse to normalize and harmonize still operates, now, however, in relation to the poet's life. The pressure exerted in present-day efforts to place Emily Dickinson's behavior within the confines of the acceptably normal appears to exceed T. W. Higginson's early desire to conventionalize the poetry. After all, he only tried at first, as he says, "a little,—a very little—to lead her in the direction of rules and traditions; but I fear it was only perfunctory." And he expressed a view toward the poetry that modern critics have yet to accept with regard to the life: "she interested me more in her—so to speak—unregenerate condition."[2] By contrast, Millicent Todd Bingham established the position of most contemporary critics when she said of her book *Emily Dickinson's Home* that one of its major objectives was to "replace queerness with reasonableness as an explanation of Emily Dickinson's conduct."[3] Since then most writers have taken Mrs. Bingham's approach and have devoted themselves to smoothing the rough and searching for sensible reasons for the seemingly irrational. Emily Dickinson is thereby being gradually reduced to the dimensions of the "well adjusted" by a process of minimizing or expunging all that is contorted and grotesque in her life.

An interesting poem (no. 1067; semifinal draft) indicates that the poet herself would have resisted this dwarfing rehabilitation. "To normalize me is to miss my real stature" seems to be her implicit warning:

> Except the smaller size –
> No Lives – are Round –
> These – hurry to a Sphere –
> And show – and end –

The Larger – slower grow –
And later – hang –
The Summers of Hesperides
Are long –

Hugest of Core
Present the awkward Rind –
Yield Groups of Ones –
No Cluster – ye shall find –

But far after Frost –
And Indian Summer Noon –
Ships – offer these –
As West-Indian –

In this identification of human psychological growth with the processes of ripening, Emily Dickinson observes that those men and women who have undergone hypertrophy of the inner life (those who are the "Hugest of Core") are overtly peculiar, strange, forbidding, and discomforting (they "Present the awkward Rind"). Yet they are the rare and highly prized few whose achievements survive travail and death to be disseminated far beyond their place of origin ("Ships" bear them to foreign ports "far after Frost"). The normal, smooth, well-balanced, socially integrated, and ingratiating personality is necessarily of "smaller size." Such commonplace persons are known for the short duration of their span of life, after which they vanish into oblivion (they "hurry to a Sphere – And show – and end –").

To trim and smooth and polish the awkward rind of Emily Dickinson's tortured life until it takes on the complacent roundness of the cluster may well be doing as great a disservice to the complexity of her personal individuality as the earlier urge to regularize did to the subtlety and originality of her poetry. For the hugeness of core of her life seems intimately connected with the undeniable awkwardness of its rind, both qualities being products of the disturbed emotional evolution that it is the purpose of this book to examine.

The outward configuration of the life of the woman Yvor Winters considered "one of the greatest lyric poets of all time,"[4] though far removed from well-rounded symmetry and balance, can be sketched in a few pages.

Emily Elizabeth Dickinson was born in Amherst, Massachusetts, December 10, 1830, and died there fifty-five years later,

never having attained literary recognition. Her great poetic gifts remained concealed and unsuspected throughout her century; and incredible as it seems, even the parents in whose home she spent nearly every day of her life went to their graves unaware that their daughter was a gifted writer.

In those days the little village of Amherst was a remote Puritan outpost, a long day's journey from anywhere. Set apart by the surrounding Pelham Hills, the town in summer was green and torpid—aptly described by a visitor as late as 1870 (almost two decades after the introduction of the railroad) as "unspeakably quiet."[5] Though the surrounding countryside was most pleasant, the town itself was commonplace, full of solidly built but unprepossessing dwellings. Its central common, surrounded by a crude fence, was unkempt and full of weeds, and the streets were untidy and littered with debris. With winter its isolation deepened almost to inaccessibility; the town grew bleak and numb, its unpaved streets clogged with snow. Temperatures persistently near zero encouraged those who could to stay indoors, close to their stoves.

The Dickinsons were a distinguished, respected, and long-established New England family. Through many generations in the New World (Emily's was the eighth) the Dickinson men were conspicuous for the intensity of their dedication to public causes and for their sense of responsibility to the community. They were also exacting and unbending, and imbued with a joyless, Calvinistic religiosity. Samuel Fowler Dickinson, Emily's grandfather, a lawyer, was responsible almost single-handedly for the founding of Amherst College, conceived by him as a religious stronghold for the defense and promulgation of the faith. To this cause he dedicated himself heart and soul, contributing in addition, to the point of bankruptcy, all he possessed in the way of material resources.

Edward Dickinson, Emily's father, was Samuel's oldest child, the forerunner of four brothers and four sisters. He attended Yale, where he distinguished himself, graduating as valedictorian of his class. Then, following in Samuel's footsteps, he became a lawyer through apprenticeship in his father's office and a year's attendance at the Northampton Law School. Though as tireless as Samuel in his exertions for the common good, Edward learned a lesson from his father's reckless and self-immolating altruism, and took care that he never let his concern for the community impinge on his own economic security.

After two years of practice and his admission to the bar, Edward, at the age of twenty-five, married Emily Norcross of nearby Monson. By this time he had already developed a forceful and dominating personality. His wife, by contrast, was passive and submissive. These qualities were perhaps her chief attractions as far as Edward was concerned; at any rate no others come to light from the extant biographical data. Emily Norcross had been sent to Connecticut to boarding school, returned at the age of nineteen, and lived at home for five years until her marriage to Edward when she was twenty-four. Like her husband, she was one of nine children. Unlike Edward's family, however, whose circle of siblings was left unbroken by death until he was almost fifty (when his sister Mary and his brother Timothy died), Emily's family was much ravaged, several siblings having died in childhood or as young adults. Emily was the third child and oldest girl.

Edward and Emily Norcross Dickinson had three children, Austin, Emily, and Lavinia ("Vinnie"). Austin was a toddler of twenty months when Emily was born. Lavinia arrived twenty-seven months later. Mrs. Dickinson recovered only very slowly from the strain of Lavinia's birth; the baby likewise did not thrive during those first months.

Early in Mrs. Dickinson's pregnancy with Emily the couple bought and, together with their young son, moved into one half of Edward's father's house, the purchase having been made in part, apparently, to bolster Samuel's precarious financial situation. Edward chafed at these restricting quarters and found the proximity of his plaintive mother trying. After Lavinia's birth Samuel, pressed for funds, accepted a new job, sold the house to David Mack, and moved with his family to Cincinnati. For the next ten years or so, Edward continued to rent his half of the house from the new landlord.

The Dickinson house on Main Street was a drafty brick building built by Samuel in 1813, when he still possessed a fortune. It had classical columned entrances and servants' quarters in the rear. The neighbors called it a "mansion," apparently on the basis of its having more than two chimneys. It possessed an aloof and forbidding mien enhanced by large elms which overshadowed it and screened it from the street. There was nothing sumptuous about it except its size (some twenty-odd rooms). It was difficult to heat and of course devoid of plumbing.

The Dickinson children first attended the local primary school (Amherst Academy) and later were sent away to neighboring towns for the equivalent of high school—Austin to Williston Seminary in Easthampton, Emily to Mount Holyoke Female Seminary in South Hadley, and Lavinia to Wheaton Seminary in Ipswich. Thus both girls acquired under strict religious auspices an education that, considering the standard of the day for women, was unquestionably superior.

Emily attracted attention at school by her wit and humor and by her scholastic excellence and the originality of her themes. She seems to have been popular with her classmates. She impressed her teachers as gifted but physically delicate and nervous.

When she was ten years old and she and Lavinia were just beginning their studies at Amherst Academy, the family, cramped for space, moved to another house, where they lived until Emily's twenty-fourth year, at which time Edward Dickinson, whose law practice had become lucrative, was able to buy back the entire "mansion" lost by his father. The house on Pleasant Street, now no longer standing, held some pleasant associations for Emily; neither she nor her mother was willing to move back to the somber Main Street house, though of course Edward had decided the matter and they had no choice.

Edward's political career began when Emily was six years old, at which time he served in the state legislature. When she was ten, he was elected to the state Senate and when she was twenty-one he became a congressman. As his political responsibilities and aspirations grew, he was forced to spend more and more time away from his family, leaving his children in the care of his timid and dependent wife.

Emily's attendance at Mount Holyoke was marked first by an eagerness to enlarge her horizons and a real enthusiasm for living away from home. Soon, however, this attitude gave way to severe homesickness and an urge to return to the sheltering ambiance of her family. Her scholastic career, both at the Academy and at Mount Holyoke, was punctuated by frequent withdrawals for reasons of health. In her fourth year at the Academy, when she was thirteen, she became depressed following the death of a school friend and consequently missed two months of school. The following year she stayed home for the fall semester and felt "down-spirited."[6] The following July, because of "general debility,"[7] a cough, and low spirits, she again was forced to withdraw from school. She did not go back until the following December. The next year she was at Mount Holyoke, where she stayed about six months, her health continuing to be poor throughout most of that time. Apparently she still retained her cough, and her letters speak frequently of depression and tears. By August 1848, when she was age seventeen, she had finished her formal schooling.

Sometime in 1842 or 1843 Emily experienced a religious conversion that temporarily brought her great peace of mind. Gradually, however, her "old habits returned" and she "cared less for religion than ever." Then, beginning in the winter of 1845 and continuing throughout her stay at Mount Holyoke, a great religious revival spread throughout New England. During this time Emily avoided going to revival meetings, feeling "I dared not trust myself";[8] she believed that she was overly susceptible to the excitement generated at these impassioned rallies and feared being led again into spiritual self-deception. However, during her sojourn at Mount Holyoke she was unable to avoid her teachers' exhortations to "accept Christ." The pressure exerted by these pious evangelists upon their captive "congregations" was relentless and merciless—humiliation, threats, indignation, seductive persuasion, and histrionics were all used in turn and in combination to bring the "sinful" and "hard-hearted" young girls to their knees. The experience was extremely painful for Emily, who nevertheless proved impervious to her teachers' pleas that she save her soul. All of her immediate family, with the significant exception of herself, eventually joined the Congregational Church, although being a member seems to have been more important to her mother than to the others. Edward Dickinson resisted the sermons of numerous revivalists well into middle age before he finally allowed himself to be taken into the fold. Emily never joined a church.

Following his studies at Williston, Austin went on to Amherst College and the following year obtained his law degree at Harvard. Emily and Lavinia, when their schooling was completed, remained at home. It is only a slight exaggeration to say that all three of the Dickinson children spent the rest of their lives within a stone's throw of the house in which they were born.

In his late twenties Austin, teetering on the verge of emancipation, contemplated moving to Chicago with his new wife, Susan Gilbert. Ultimately he capitulated to the wishes of his father, who, by way of persuasion, built for him a house next door to the homestead, which Austin and his family occupied until their deaths. For reasons which are not readily apparent, Austin's marriage was not a happy one.

In their youth the girls made a few modest excursions. In addition to her schooling at South Hadley, Emily—before she was thirty and never afterward—was away from home about a half dozen times on what were essentially pleasure trips. In her early thirties she traveled on two occasions to Cambridgeport for treatment of an eye disorder. There she boarded with her cousins, was treated by her physician as an out-patient, and each time stayed approximately six months.

Neither Emily nor Lavinia married. As they grew into middle age, their tendency to social insecurity and retreat, always discernible beneath the surface of their wry humor and youthful friendliness, gradually asserted itself as a dominant characteristic. Emily particularly, in the eyes of the town, became strange and incomprehensible. Finally, she withdrew from its unsympathetic gaze altogether and became a recluse concealed within her parents' house. There she surrounded herself with an atmosphere of dramatic eccentricity which stimulated endless speculation among the community she left outside, who referred to her in time as the "Myth."

The myth of Amherst, though posthumously enlarged upon, has a firm basis in fact. As early as her twenty-second year Emily Dickinson was going out of her way to avoid meeting people. A year later she wrote that she was going to church early to avoid having "to go in after all the people had got there."[9] By the time she was twenty-eight it was a fixed "custom"[10] for her to run whenever the doorbell rang. By the age of thirty she was retreating to her room when old friends called and listening to their voices from upstairs. The next year she inaugurated the habit of dressing exclusively in white that she was to maintain for the rest of her life. The same year she begged her Boston cousins to take her place at a commencement tea at her home because she felt too "hopeless and scared"[11] to face the visitors. Eventually she retreated indoors altogether, and for the last fifteen years of her life the neighbors knew she was there by faith alone. To the end of their lives she and her sister still dressed and groomed themselves in the fashions of their youth.

When her sister left home on a visit, Emily felt unprotected. On one of these occasions, during a spell of hot weather, she wrote her cousins saying that at night she felt compelled to keep every window locked, that she dissipated the darkness by keeping the gas jets lit and, because she feared the front door might admit a "prowling 'booger,'" shut herself up in her no doubt stifling room. Her fears, she told them, gave her "a snarl in the brain which dont unravel yet."[12]

When her home was filled with visitors for her father's funeral services, she saw no one save a beloved friend, Samuel Bowles. When Mr. Bowles died, she of course did not accompany her brother and sister to his funeral, and arrangements were made to have a portion of the musical accompaniment repeated in her home while she listened out of sight. Sometimes she could not bear to see her brother's wife, Sue, who lived next door, giving as her reason that she loved her too much: "it is idolatry, not indifference."[13] She could not adjust her reactions to a negro servant who consulted her about his duties: "everytime he presents himself, I run."[14] A knock at the door while she was cooking, "necessitating [her] flight from the Kettle,"[15] would result in the food's being spoiled. During her mother's funeral services, conducted in the home, she listened from upstairs and said the students' singing seemed to be coming from another life. She could not wrap and address packages and often got members of her family to address her letters for her. On the rare occasions when she consented to visit with old friends, she and the visitor conversed from opposite sides of a door left slightly ajar. She would not allow a physician to examine her during an illness, and he was expected to arrive at his diagnosis from a glimpse of her, fully clothed, as she walked past a doorway.

All these apparent expressions of thwarted and pent-up feeling and signs of irrational fear increased and became more incapacitating as she grew older.

The impression of scholars that Emily Dickinson's life and art reflect an essentially normal personality is contradicted by T. W. Higginson's famous report of a face-to-face confrontation with her. Colonel Higginson did not meet Emily Dickinson until 1870, at which time she was thirty-nine years old. The visit took place more than eight years after the beginning of their correspondence, inaugurated by Emily when she sent Higginson four poems and asked his opinion of them.

Their short encounter had an almost overwhelming impact on Higginson, but his reaction was mixed. Though impressed with her profundity, he was awed by her strangeness. Higginson, who was a more than ordinarily sensitive and perceptive man, found the tension of their interview oppressive and concluded that this effect arose from some unsatisfied need in Emily, urgent and obscure. What he told his wife of Emily Dickinson caused her to refer to Emily as "insane,"[16] and he himself wrote that he considered her "partially cracked."[17] Emily opened their conversation with an apology for her obvious fearfulness, explaining that "I never see strangers and hardly know what I say."[18] Higginson was not invigorated by the interview: "I never was with anyone who drained my nerve power so much," he wrote; "without touching her, she drew from me. I am glad not to live near her."[19] This remark has been taken to mean that the swiftness and brilliance of Emily Dickinson's thought overtaxed Higginson and threatened his conventionally masculine sense of superiority. Another interpretation is suggested in an article he wrote twenty years later. Here he remarks that some undefined need in Emily's personality forced itself upon their relationship and prevented him from establishing an atmosphere of simple and relaxed interchange. The sense of voracious need, of being sucked dry, that Higginson implies exhausted him recalls a common clinical phenomenon. A certain kind of patient clings in desperation to the therapist as to a life-preserver—such men and women hunger for approval and support with a vehemence and insatiability that evokes the fantasy that one is in danger of being consumed alive by them. The same craving for affection which smolders throughout the poetry and letters of Emily Dickinson seems to have driven Higginson from her presence, relieved that he lived a safe hundred miles distant.

Higginson also found her "enigmatical," possibly meaning indirect and evasive and defensive—"an instinct told me that the slightest attempt at direct cross-examination would make her withdraw into her shell." He concluded: "The impression undoubtedly made on me was that of an excess of tension, and of an abnormal life."[20]

Higginson's imputation of striking queerness with regard to Emily Dickinson's life and behavior, though not accepted by her biographers, was corroborated by the observations and conclusions of some of her contemporaries and neighbors who were aware of her, not as a major poet of course, but simply as a human being and fellow inhabitant of Amherst. To them she appeared pathetically withdrawn, eccentric or insane.

In spite of her odd and sequestered life, Emily Dickinson knew a surprising number of prominent, and even famous, men and women. Most of them were writers of one kind or another and she became acquainted with them either through her peripatetic father or through her brother and his wife Susan, who carried on an active social life. Among her friends were: Samuel Bowles, a political figure of nationwide reputation and editor of the Springfield *Republican;* Josiah Holland, a physician turned poet, novelist, historian, lecturer, and journalist, coeditor with Mr. Bowles of the *Republican* and later head of *Scribner's Monthly*— also a man of considerable fame; Helen Hunt Jackson, a world-famous novelist, poet, and authority on Indians; Daniel Chester French, the sculptor; and Thomas Wentworth Higginson, essayist, poet, and critic. She could have met Emerson, if she had been so inclined, when he was a house guest at her brother's home next door. The list above is not exhaustive and would include many more celebrated and influential acquaintances if one counts all the political figures and educators her father and brother brought to the house—men who in their day were widely known, though their names would not be familiar to the present-day reader. Any view of Emily Dickinson's life which casts her in the role of unpolished rustic infinitely removed and cut off from the mainstream of nineteenth-century cultural activity is erroneous.

But Emily Dickinson's associations with her friends and acquaintances followed the strict rules she laid down. If they wished to see her, they must come to her home. And even then they could not be certain of an audience. As she grew older ordinary direct interviews became increasingly rare.

Within the old house Emily spent her middle years reading incessantly and keeping up more than her share of a voluminous correspondence with a small circle of friends, her special devotees. She wrote poems in private, often late at night, and hid many hundreds of them in neat packets in her dresser drawer, where they were discovered by Lavinia after Emily's death. Emily supervised the gardening, tended the greenhouse, and helped Lavinia with the household chores. She also did some cooking and baking—not the routine staples, for which the Dickinsons employed domestics—but fancy and delicate specialties. An exception to this was her bread making. This, in her father's opinion, was her great gift in which no one excelled her, and it was her assigned responsibility to provide daily supplies for him.

When Emily was forty-three, her father died suddenly, and a year later her mother was paralyzed with a stroke, lingering seven years and requiring continuous nursing care. Emily outlived her mother by only four years, dying in 1886 at the age of fifty-five of the complications of a chronic renal disorder designated in the Amherst death records as "Bright's disease."

The profoundly disordered undercurrent one senses in the life moves also through the poetry. Desolation, hopelessness, and a fierce and frustrated longing arise from nearly every page. The following poem (no. 341)—a threnody to a vanquished ego and to a paralyzed emotional life—is an example of Emily Dickinson's self-observation at its most clinical and chilling:

> After great pain, a formal feeling comes –
> The Nerves sit ceremonious, like Tombs –
> The stiff Heart questions was it He, that bore,
> And Yesterday, or Centuries before?
>
> The Feet, mechanical, go round –
> A Wooden way
> Of Ground, or Air, or Ought –
> Regardless grown,
> A Quartz contentment, like a stone –
>
> This is the Hour of Lead –
> Remembered, if outlived,
> As Freezing persons, recollect the Snow –
> First – Chill – then Stupor – then the letting go –

How is it possible to believe that the poet did not undergo the terrible prostration that she appears here to commemorate? There are many other poems which as trenchantly convey aspects of a similar psychic devastation. By what creative magic could she, high on the safe shore of normality, plumb such depths of suffering? The simplest answer is apparently the least generally acceptable: the poems are the distillation of actual circumstances. They portray faithfully the terror of a mind collapsing under pressures that exceed its endurance. The mind is Emily Dickinson's own.

When one turns from Emily Dickinson's writings, impressed as was her "preceptor" Colonel Higginson by her "excess of tension" and her "abnormal life," and consults her critics and explicators for clarification, one is faced with a variety of interpretations. Each writer places his own construction on facets of the poet's unusual behavior, and one is struck by the number and divergence of explanations assigned to each oddity of conduct. It is therefore all the more provocative that the question which, in one form or another, all Dickinson scholars feel constrained to answer—whether Emily Dickinson was "mad" or "sane"—should meet with the unanimous conclusion that she was "sane."

In support of this judgment certain writers have invented what almost amounts to a new syndrome. The characteristics of this hitherto unrecorded condition revolve around a preternatural hypersensitivity and overresponsiveness of the emotions. Thomas H. Johnson seems to have been the first exponent of this view. He avers that Emily Dickinson retreated from all direct contact with other human beings because she became overstimulated in their presence. He says, "her refusal to see old friends was determined by the fact that the nervous drain . . . had become exhausting beyond her power to cope with them."[21] And again, "the fact seems clear that she was possessed to a most uncommon degree by emotional responses so acute as to be painful to herself and others."[22] John Crowe Ransom, following Johnson's lead, expressed it this way: "Her sensibility was so acute that it made her excessively vulnerable to personal contacts. Intense feelings would rush out as soon as sensibility apprehended the object, and flood her consciousness to the point of helplessness."[23] Theodora Ward gives another version of the same view: "She lived so close to the center of her being, to the mainsprings of the life of the spirit, that she brought to every contact an emotional charge and an enhanced awareness that made extraordinary demands on her store of vital energy."[24] It is difficult to determine in what way such a state differs from a condition of poor emotional control and intense inner conflict. Emily Dickinson, one supposes, could not be said to have had a more sensitive nervous organization than, say, Mozart. Nevertheless Mozart, whatever personal problems he might have had, did not find it necessary to shrink from all contact with others.

In a sense, though, all the statements above are probably valid descriptions of Emily Dickinson's reactions. What makes the condition these writers portray a new syndrome is their insistence that her intense responses were normal for her and unrelated to any psychological maladjustment in her interpersonal relationships. They believe that her exhaustion following a visit from a friend, the pain of those interviews, and the overwhelming of her consciousness with emotion "to the point of helplessness" were inborn and a reflection only of her delicate nervous constitution. It must be granted that this view of her personality is the only one consistent with their opinion that her seclusion was not a manifestation of a psychological disturbance.

Logically, then, Johnson has concluded that Emily Dickinson's puzzling and sometimes bizarre entrances and exits were deliberate "stratagems" which were "once thought to be eccentric."[25] And Charles R. Anderson has made the observation that "the stages by which she became a recluse were so gradual . . . as to take much of the eccentricity out of such behavior."[26] Now it is a fact that even the most extreme phobias, delusional systems, and schizophrenic withdrawals frequently arise from small beginnings and build gradually over the course of decades. Therefore, one wonders where Anderson derived his idea that the slow onset of a modification of behavior is evidence of its normality. He goes on to say, "Perhaps modern theorizers, forgetful of village customs a century ago, have failed to take into account the fact that maiden ladies then were not considered eccentric because they stayed at home."[27] Here he is clearly fudging. If Emily Dickinson had merely been a recluse and had evinced no other evidence of her instability, we would not still be discussing the matter. Besides, there is abundant evidence to the effect that the neighbors a century ago, whatever they might have thought of other spinsters who stayed at home, considered Emily Dickinson outstandingly odd. Along the same lines as Anderson's comments, Richard Chase says that he would like to "modify the myth of her life . . . in the light of the persuasive idea that the course of her life was 'natural,' " and he quotes William Dean Howells, who expressed the opinion that Emily Dickinson's life probably "turned . . . in upon itself [because] this was its natural evolution, or involution, from tendencies inherent in the New England, or Puritan, spirit."[28]

Thus, her inexorable shutting away of herself and the limitation of practically all her relationships to epistolary transactions are purged of eccentricity and declared "natural." Yet we have the word of Emily Dickinson's closest woman friend, her sister-in-law, Susan, that the poet's panic-stricken retreats and disappearances were not "stratagems." "She hated her peculiarities," Susan wrote, "and shrank from any notice of them as a nerve from the knife." The goal of Emily Dickinson's profoundest yearnings, according to Susan, was a normal life: "She as deeply realized that for her, as for all of us women not fame but 'Love and home and certainty are best.' " And Susan added, "I find myself always saying 'poor Emily'."[29]

Allen Tate, however, remarked, "all pity for Miss Dickinson's 'starved life' is misdirected. Her life was one of the richest and deepest ever lived on this continent." Note that Tate says "life" not "fantasy life." He then quotes another eminent authority: " 'It is apparent,' writes Mr. Conrad Aiken, 'that Miss Dickinson became a hermit by deliberate and conscious choice.' " Tate expresses his complete agreement with this assertion and calls it "a sensible remark that we cannot repeat too often."[30]

Not only is Emily Dickinson's seclusion in this way rendered normal and justified but it is described by Millicent Todd Bingham as the only "sane" thing the poet could have done under the circumstances. According to Mrs. Bingham, "her gradual withdrawal is seen to be a natural response to her surroundings, the only sane response—given her genius—which she could have made to a world in which, as she said, there was so much matter-of-fact. The book [Mrs. Bingham's] will, it is hoped, replace queerness with reasonableness as an explanation of Emily Dickinson's conduct."[31]

Mrs. Bingham's conviction that there was nothing queer about

Emily Dickinson is probably a reflection of the influence of her mother, Mabel Loomis Todd, the poet's first and posthumous editor. Mrs. Todd was never privileged to lay eyes on Emily Dickinson, though she was frequently invited by Lavinia Dickinson to the mansion during the last years of Emily's life. Here Mrs. Todd would sing and play the piano to the applause of an invisible audience. Mrs. Todd's first reaction to Emily's invariable habit of hiding behind doors or secluding herself on the upstairs landing during these recitals was naturally to consider the behavior very strange indeed. After Emily's death, however, several forces seem to have conspired to cause her to rationalize her first impressions. One such factor was Lavinia's insistence upon her sister's normality. Another was Mrs. Todd's growing familiarity with, and admiration for, the poems, which, in their precision and control, she could not conceive as having sprung from disordered psychological soil. One other strong and practical inducement existed for both Mrs. Todd and Lavinia to deemphasize as much as possible anything that would cause the public to question the soundness of Emily's mind. This spur to reticence involved their apprehensions (quite justified as it turned out) that the poetry itself, in its defiance of accepted nineteenth-century norms of rhyme and grammar, might possibly meet with critical misunderstanding, hostility, or even ridicule. Introduced as the expressions of an eminently sound and stable, if rather shy, poet, the verse might stand a chance of being taken seriously and its irregularities might be regarded as evidence of original genius. Too great frankness with regard to the peculiarities of Emily's style of life might invite critical rejection of the work on the basis that the poet was not in full possession of her faculties. The prudent thing, so Lavinia and Mrs. Todd probably thought, was to find logical explanations for all of Emily Dickinson's oddities and to deemphasize anything in the way of symptomatic behavior that could possibly prove prejudicial to the poetry. Therefore, motivated by the high esteem in which she held the poetry and her eagerness to insure the success of the first volume of Emily Dickinson's poems, Mrs. Todd traveled about the country giving lectures on the newly discovered poet which stressed and overstressed the health and integration of her personality. As Mrs. Bingham says, "My mother used every opportunity—in everything she wrote, in every lecture she gave—to explain that it [the poet's seclusion] was 'a perfectly normal blossoming' of Emily's spirit."[32] Thus, following a lecture to the alumni of Boston College in which Mrs. Todd devoted herself to erasing the idea that there was anything strange about Emily Dickinson, a listener wrote "Mrs. Todd corrected certain impressions regarding the author's life. Those ideas, that made of Miss Dickinson a woman eccentrically dressed, an invalid, an irreverent woman, or a victim of a love tragedy, were explained away, and she was shown to have had a strong dislike for the shams and trivialities of life, which united with shyness to keep her confined to her home."[33] And following a similar occasion, another member of Mrs. Todd's audience wrote, "I had hardly thought of it before, but now I see that her peculiar life so far from being incongruous or strange, was one of the most simple, natural, congruous lives that were ever lived."[34] Yet, in spite of the fact that Mrs. Todd was able to convince those who attended her lectures that there was nothing amiss in the poet's life, she seems to have retained some uncertainties of her own. When she began her work of editing Emily's letters, she wrote, "There was something akin to dread, almost fear, as I approached them critically, lest the inner and hitherto inviolate life of Emily might be too clearly revealed."[35]

Until the present day, the deference with which Mrs. Todd and Mrs. Bingham are regarded by Dickinson specialists for the excellence of their scholarship has extended to their opinions regarding the question of the poet's psychological normality. Today many writers would still agree with the following summary of Mrs. Bingham's: "But if a broken heart is not the answer, the reader may retort that her withdrawal from the world was abnormal, a sign of morbidity. As a matter of fact, Emily was a recluse in the sense only that she withdrew from the limitations of village life in order to investigate things that interested her more."[36]

And it is only a step from Allan Tate's comment regarding the "richest and deepest life ever lived on this continent," which perhaps does not exclude the richest and deepest of mental suffering, to a view of Emily Dickinson which sees in her isolation a compensation for everything she may have missed in the way of love, recognition, marriage, children, freedom, and comfortable and rewarding human relationships. Speaking from this sanguine perspective, Thomas Johnson says: "in a truer sense she was not retreating from life, but living it with an exuberance few people experience so incessantly."[37] In another place he remarks: "The exuberance of living overwhelmed her."[38] No doubt Emily Dickinson's art gave her deep and abiding gratification. Yet she wrote (poem no. 985), "The missing All, prevented Me From missing minor Things." One must conclude that her "exuberance" can only have been a narrow and rigidly channeled ecstasy, derived perhaps from her artistic triumphs and her enjoyment of nature.

I do not mean to create the impression that all writers are in complete agreement. John Malcolm Brinnin does not share Mr. Johnson's view and wonders what "emotional disaster it was that drove her to elect and finally to covet a life of obscurity."[39] And Clark Griffith says: "There is the retreat backward into childhood, which is the crucial fact about Emily Dickinson's seclusion."[40] These opinions are obviously quite a different thing from those that see in the poet's behavior a mature decision to withdraw in order to find the time and peace to write.

If one grants that Emily Dickinson's renunciation of the ordinary rewards of life was more than made up for by her awareness that she had become an accomplished, though unknown, poet, how does one interpret the great cries of pain that emanate from the poems? And when Emily Dickinson says in a poem (no. 280, referring to herself): "And then a Plank in Reason, broke" (that is, rational faculties gave way to psychosis), why should we not believe her? Certain biographers have circumvented such disturbingly direct poetic confessions. For example, David T. Porter believes that Emily Dickinson is not describing her own experiences in the poetry. He calls the "I" of the poems her "speaker"—a "supposed person," to use her own disclaimer. He takes to task other writers for assuming that the poems are fundamentally autobiographical. "Like Whicher, in her assessment of the general tendency of Emily Dickinson's poetic expression, Mrs. Ward works from the assumption that the poems somehow chronicle the poet's struggle to overcome a personal problem."[41] In the preface to his book he makes the statement clearer: "We need not be troubled by wonder or frustration at the refusal of the *life* to explain the *poetry*."[42] Combining this view of the poems as a kind of fiction with the one that sees in the poet's withdrawal a normal response to the circumstances of her life obviates the possibility as well as the need for a psychological exploration of either the poems or the life. However, it is perhaps difficult for many readers to understand how Emily Dickinson could portray psychological states that she never experienced. When Porter reminds us that the *Red Badge of Courage* was a novel about war written by a man who had never been to war, the analogy does not seem entirely applicable to Emily Dickinson. The psychological poems have no plot upon which to hang transposed and transmogrified emotions. In fact, they express reactions to events that in themselves are undisclosed. However, as has been indicated, most writers do not go as far as Porter in divorcing the art from the artist.

When one accepts the emotional roots of the poetry as more or less a reordered outcry from the poet's experience, as the majority of writers have done, one is confronted with unmistakable revelations of psychological turmoil. But because, apparently, of a commitment to the view that nothing good or creative can emerge from a person who has been "insane," it has been the practice of some scholars to accept the fact that Emily Dickinson had a *nearly* prostrating emotional experience without, however, despite her own admissions, acknowledging that this experience involved a loss of reality contact and the disruption of rational thought processes. Therefore they say in their various ways that Emily Dickinson *came close* to having a nervous collapse and that she hovered *near the brink* of "insanity."

Part of the difficulty inheres in the all or none character of the question of "sanity" versus "insanity." It leads to the reduction: if Emily Dickinson is "sane" then all her behavior is rational—thus the poems are descriptions of normal feelings; if she is "insane" then both the life and the poetry are meaningless. Given this choice any critic in *his* right mind would be forced to choose the former alternative. Because it appears that Emily Dickinson produced great, communicative poetry at the height of her emotional travail, scholars have concluded that she must therefore never have departed from a state of complete "sanity." It is interesting to see how, with this premise, various writers have grappled with the apparent paradox of a "mad" artist and a "sane" art.

Here is how Henry Wells alternatingly commits her and

rescues her from the stigma of "insanity": "it remains apparent that she did become both abnormal and strange . . . to fail to recognize grave abnormality . . . constitutes a serious omission." Wells speaks of "her tragic frustrations, the grave and almost fatal struggles within her own psyche, and her intense neuroticism," but later he asks, "Was she sane or mad? Neither of the direct answers proves satisfactory." So far so good. Unfortunately he goes on to muddy the picture: "She was mad in this world but sane in eternity." It is clear in his book that Wells feels considerable anxiety lest Emily Dickinson's talent be attributed even partly to her psychic disorders. He is also painfully aware of what he considers a contradiction: evidence of "madness" in a writer of eminently "sane" verse. His conclusion: "Emily Dickinson outlived and outfought her madness."[43]

Mrs. Ward also is torn between her recognition of grave psychological disorder and her need to keep the poet within the confines of the acceptably normal. She points out Emily Dickinson's tendency to go to emotional extremes of rapture and deepest gloom in her 1861 poems: "She wrote voluminously, on many subjects and in many moods, living perhaps, on several levels . . . of her psychic house, while the foundations began to shake underneath . . . Such extremes are danger signals pointing to a serious imbalance." Then the rescue: "she did not pass beyond the border of sanity, for the insane cannot explain themselves; but there must have been a period when it was only with the greatest difficulty that she could withstand the disintegrating forces that assailed her."[44] Mrs. Ward here propounds a popular misconception regarding mental illness, that is, that the psychotic person cannot convey his experiences to others. But we know from many firsthand accounts how eloquently gifted patients have been able to convey the thoughts and terrors of a psychosis, sometimes even from the midst of the state itself.

Mrs. Bingham, in her scholarly and solid books, deals with most of Emily Dickinson's idiosyncrasies by ignoring them— concentrating heavily on the healthy aspects of the poet's personality. Only occasionally does she speak of "the inner turmoil which beset her [the poet] throughout life,"[45] and then she describes it as an appropriate emotional response to uncongenial external circumstances. That it is in itself symptomatic that Emily Dickinson remained in an environment inimical to her happiness when she had the opportunity to escape it is not emphasized by Mrs. Bingham. As a young woman, Emily's sister-in-law to be, Susan Gilbert, moved to an unfamiliar town to teach school. Nothing but intrapsychic factors could have prevented Emily from following suit.

Some writers get themselves caught in what come close to being contradictions. Richard Chase, quoted earlier to the effect that Emily Dickinson's seclusion was "natural," says on the other hand that "the motions of neurosis and insanity were alive in her soul"[46] and that the poet "considered sanity . . . to be just barely possible."[47] Such remarks cannot but be provocative to a psychiatric clinician. Though they contain a genuine depth of understanding, Mr. Chase leaves it at that, never considering further the implications of his insight. The idea that the "motions of neurosis and insanity" can occur without precursers and dissipate without leaving a trace, like a subclinical infection which spontaneously resolves itself, is at odds with what is known of the nature of psychiatric syndromes and the complex genesis of these breakdowns.

Even Johnson, who called her life "exuberant" and who says that one of the predominating qualities of her nature was a "zest for living," says that her "attachments to her family and her home had become . . . compulsive by the time she was twenty-one . . . Obviously by her late twenties the compulsion was obsessive."[48] Yet later he makes the seemingly irreconcilable statement: "the straight path to her seclusion she deliberately chose, the better to enable her to participate in the common experiences of all mankind."[49] One impressed through acquaintance with patients with the suffering attendant upon neurotic clinging to home and family would see that it was incompatible with pervasive enjoyment of life. When Emily Dickinson told Higginson, "I find ecstasy in living,"[50] it did not blind him to her obvious distress; she could only have been referring there to isolated ecstatic episodes. If her "compulsion" to shut herself up in her parents' home was "obsessive," as Johnson thinks, it is difficult to see how she could also have been "living with an exuberance few people experience so incessantly."

Johnson does show that he feels some uncertainty in this position; in another place he confesses: "one is tempted to find in the total retreat of her later years an element of the neurotic."[51] Unlike most temptations, this one, it sometimes appears, has in general been admirably resisted. Ultimately, though, in discussing the poet's relationship with Colonel Higginson, Johnson says that Higginson "provided a release from the tensions [brought about by her renunciation of her beloved] and preserved her sanity."[52] The implication is that the poet's "sanity" was precariously balanced. These would appear to be strong words for one who feels that Emily Dickinson's personality contained only "an element of the neurotic" and that she lived a life of practically unrelenting exuberance.

The conclusion of Higginson, embarrassing to biographers, that Emily Dickinson was "partially cracked" has its counterpart in an observation of another of her contemporaries, Joseph Lyman, a close friend of the Dickinson family and onetime sweetheart of Emily's sister Vinnie, a man who knew Emily Dickinson well. According to Richard Sewall in *The Lyman Letters,* Lyman wrote his fiancée: "Emily Dickinson I did like very much and do still. But she is rather morbid and unnatural."[53] In Sewall's interpretive comments one may sense the pain with which he passes these lines on to us in his eagerness to explain that by "morbid" and "unnatural" Lyman did not mean what we might think he meant by them. "His use of the adjectives, one should hasten to add," Sewall writes, "is distinctly pre-Freudian. His next sentence makes his meaning clear enough: 'Vinnie's kisses were very very sweet . . .' that is, Emily's 'morbidness' lay in her peculiar reserve and her refusal to fit Joseph's concept of the romanticized ideal."[54] That there is an implied contrast here between the sisters seems a legitimate reading of the lines— Vinnie's erotic responsiveness versus, perhaps, a strange and disturbing sexlessness on Emily's part. But to propose that Freud's discoveries altered the essential meaning of the words "morbid" and "unnatural" here again betrays the impulse to rescue.

It is significant that writers who do not accord Emily Dickinson great stature as a poet find it easier to take a severe view of her personality. One of these, R. P. Blackmur, writes: "We cannot say of this woman in white that she ever mastered life . . . she made a protection, a carapace of white cotton, even of brocade, so that raw life could not sack the emptiness within."[55] John Malcolm Brinnin, though more admiring than Blackmur, seemingly takes a similar position; he speaks of Emily Dickinson's "persistently disconsolate mind" and he refers to her poems as "the comparatively sane statements of a spirit half-surrendered to madness."[56] William Robert Sherwood, however, takes a firm stand against abnormality. It is only necessary, he says, to rearrange the sequence of the 1862 poems as given by her editor "To defend Emily Dickinson's integrity—and hence her sanity —and to show that her sensibility was a coherent and consistent one." This reordering, Sherwood concludes, "reveals that in 1862 Emily Dickinson did not have a crack-up . . . but a conversion."[57] Of the poet's idiosyncratic habit of dress he says, "her practice of dressing in white was a product not of willful or hysterical eccentricity but of a decision to announce . . . her private secession from society through the assumption of a worldly death that paradoxically involved regeneration."[58] So impelling is Mr. Sherwood's apparent dedication to the defense of Emily Dickinson's normality that he is seemingly persuaded to confess, then deny his own psychological insights, as the following passage shows:

A critic alert to the implications of modern psychology might suspect that such arguments [as Emily Dickinson's assertion that she cultivated deprivation because only thereby could she savor the full value of possession] disguised a deeper masochistic impulse to cultivate suffering for its own sake, a product of romanticism gone sour in New England air, of the feminine sensibility, *per se,* or of the introjection of passions and resentments forbidden to find an outlet. And the elements are there: the stern father whose children could not break loose from his domination; the mother, submissive, self-effacing, and dull; the subject a recluse with nearly two thousand poems, her sister, a suspicious, sharp-tongued old maid with nearly a dozen cats. The words *repression* and *sublimation* come the more easily to mind when one recalls that in the case of the first man Emily picked love was inseparable from sin, that the second, Judge Otis Lord, a family friend of long standing, was the most forbidding judge on the Salem bench, and that both were nearly old enough to be her father.

But Mr. Sherwood brushes all these "implications of modern psychology" aside. "It fits," he says, "but only if the critic does not appreciate the demands of the religious life to which in 1862 a merciful God allowed Emily Dickinson to commit herself. What the skeptic might call rationalizing and the psychiatrist neurotic self-deception the devout would understand as the apprehension of the position death, suffering, and tantalizing uncertainty occupy in God's beneficent plan".[59] Thus, not only is Emily Dickinson saved from the clutches of neurosis, she is snatched from the devil as well.

Clark Griffith comes close to the opinion that Emily Dickinson experienced a psychosis. He says: "There is considerable evidence that at least once or twice during her life Miss Dickinson came close to the sort of mental crisis which her poetry describes." And again: "Both these incidents have the sound of complete nervous exhaustion and perhaps even a brush with crack-up."[60] The answers to questions raised by certain stanzas he says "are overlain by a poem that is too distraught to be expressive—a poem put together on the outskirts of sanity, and at a time when the poet's sense of sequence had ravelled perilously close to the breaking point." But he makes the reservation that Mrs. Ward made: A breakdown, he says, "could produce only collapse and incoherence."[61] For this reason he retreats from his former position and joins those writers who insist on Emily Dickinson's essential soundness.

Emily Dickinson's lifelong and avid interest in deaths, obituaries, funerals, and so forth was not abnormal according to Johnson: "From first to last," he says, "her concern with death was [not] morbid."[62] Albert J. Gelpi, however, disagrees, saying, "there are poems of Dickinson . . . whose necrophilic preoccupation outdoes everybody except perhaps Poe . . . this morbidity [cannot] be ascribed completely to popular taste."[63] A perhaps more important question, which neither writer discusses, involves the psychological meaning of death to Emily Dickinson and the emotional processes that motivated her abiding absorption in the subject. It seems almost a play on words to argue whether her death-watch was "morbid" or not.

In sum, the critics find that Emily Dickinson's seclusion was natural, sensible, and noneccentric and also that it was regressive ("a retreat backward into childhood"), "neurotic," and anxiety ridden. We are told that her life was rich, deep, exuberant, and zestful as well as tumultuous, disconsolate, empty, and frustrated. Among the divergencies and contradictions only one matter is agreed upon: *she was sane.* She went to the "outskirts of sanity," she had a "brush with crack-up," she "half surrendered" to psychosis, she considered sanity "barely possible," the foundations of her psychic house were shaken, she "outfought her madness," the struggles within her psyche were grave and "almost fatal," she underwent an "emotional disaster," her emotions overwhelmed her "to the point of helplessness," she was "abnormal and strange," "obsessive" and "compulsive"—but: hard-pressed as she must evidently have been at times, she managed to stay "sane," that is to say (probably), *one of us.*

Clearly the diagnosis of "insanity" is not made lightly by these authors, and something within them blocks their attempts to face the full implication of the evidence. They want to get at the truth about Emily Dickinson but to admit to the existence of "insanity" is irreconcilable with their respect for her great gifts and brilliant intelligence. Besides, as Archibald MacLeish has admitted, "most of us are half in love with this dead girl."[64] Given the all or none concept of mental illness implied in their writings, it is understandable that these authors should shrink from imputing it to Emily Dickinson. No one could bear to acknowledge such a madness in a person with whom one is even half in love.

Are respect and affection for the poet and misunderstanding of mental illness, then, the total explanation for this tacit "conspiracy" of present-day authors to fix Emily Dickinson within the sphere of normality? The imputation of mental illness, or rather its popular stereotype, alienates one as an object of empathy from the rest of humanity. But it is not the only thing that can remove a person from the field of our sympathetic interest: overidealization may render him equally inhuman and equally remote. To answer the question: the readiness of commentators to deny the existence of Emily Dickinson's psychological symptoms appears to have been greatly reinforced by their determination to explode the *second* myth of Amherst, the one perpetrated by the poet's niece Martha Dickinson Bianchi. Mme. Bianchi's worshipful version of her aunt's personality was itself intended as a corrective of the original "myth"—the view of the neighbors that Emily Dickinson was weird and outrageous, an incomprehensible object of curiosity and even amusement. Mme. Bianchi, however, overshot the mark and created an image with which no adult with a knowledge of people could possibly identify. Emily Dickinson "was not daily bread," she writes, "she was star dust,"[65] a Tinker Bell who never walked but instead "flitted,"[66] who engaged in "girlish banditry,"[67] and "madcap escapades,"[68] "always with a flower in her hand."[69] Here is how Emily Dickinson is supposed to have reacted to the news that Susan had surreptitiously contrived to have one of her poems published: "the little white moth being almost fluttered to death, all a-tremble and ready to die of the experience and be found on the floor next morning a mere hint of winged dust!"[70]

Mme. Bianchi had carried sentimental fantasy much too far and what has been called the cult of "Our Emily" threatened to engulf the poet's reputation in cake-frosting. The inevitable reaction, as exemplified by most of the authors cited in the foregoing pages, was to insist upon an Emily Dickinson more closely resembling themselves and with whom they could empathize. In this, the painstaking research of Mrs. Bingham, Johnson, Leyda, and others succeeded brilliantly, and their reconstructions afford a view of Emily Dickinson that, as far as her strengths and virtues are concerned, is truly believable.

With the exception of one or two tentative excursions, however, there has been almost no attention paid to the "underside" of her "Divinity" (poem no. 576), and the rationalizations with regard to her psychological distress are not enlightening. When the fairies went, the phobias unfortunately went too.

Along with them also went a due consideration of those scourges of psychic pain, wrath, envy, and aggression that are the lot of all human beings, do with them what we will. Even Mme. Bianchi was willing to quote Samuel Bowles's observation that Emily Dickinson was "part angel, *part demon*" (italics added).[71] And Bowles once wrote to Austin, "I have been in a savage, turbulent state for some time—indulging in a sort of [illegible word] disgust at everything & everybody—I guess a good deal as Emily feels."[72] These quotations suggest the need for a more comprehensive view of Emily Dickinson. So also do the five poems (nos. 175, 601, 1677, 1705, and 1748) which speak of human nature as a volcano whose misleadingly calm exterior conceals appalling potentialities for destruction. Recall also that it was Emily Dickinson who associated an acute and omnipotent bliss with the concept of "murder" (poem 379).

It is time for a systematic exploration of these dark and smoldering reaches of Emily Dickinson's personality, and of that "savage, turbulent state" of which Bowles spoke. In the following chapters I shall search out the sources of Emily Dickinson's fear and anxiety and of the strange deathlike inertia that, according to poem no. 341, succeeded her suffering. And—a matter of greater importance—I shall try to show how these feeling-states were related to her creative life. For symptoms alone did not flow from Emily Dickinson's anguish: "After great pain" also came poetry.

Chapter II   EARTH'S CONFIDING TIME

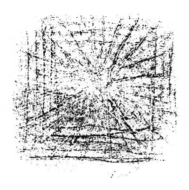

"Affection is like bread," wrote Emily Dickinson, "unnoticed till we starve, and then we dream of it, and sing of it, and paint it."[1] The observation reflects the profound and primitive identification of food with love and reveals perhaps the most powerful undercurrent of the poet's personality, a ravenous search for affection. Emily Dickinson seems always to have craved love; indeed she dreamed of it and she sang of it in her poems. Her insatiable love needs and their frustration saturate the poetry and the letters, and one finds her forever deriving new images of emotional want and fulfillment from the basic metaphor of food and drink.

Love and nourishment are simultaneously introduced by the mother into the lives of human beings immediately after birth. Thereafter, through early childhood at least, a constant supply of both is a condition of survival. Without a certain minimum of food the infant dies in a few days; and similarly with love—if the supply is too grossly inadequate, he lives only a little longer. When the quantity of these essentials falls below the optimum, but not to such a degree that the consequences are fatal, there result physical and emotional impairments that leave lasting scars upon the body and spirit. Emily Dickinson never suffered from a lack of food, but she expressed the pain attendant upon other kinds of deprivation as if she had. At some period in her early emotional unfolding it would seem that an awareness of the mortal need for alimentary replenishment became fused in her mind with a dread of dissolution through lovelessness. The depth and pervasiveness of Emily Dickinson's sense of emotional impoverishment and its unrelenting expression in what in psychoanalytic terminology would be called "oral" images impels one to question the adequacy of her mother's maternal capacities. For it is in the months of infancy and incipient childhood, when the mother is the all-important source of both food and affection, that the apprehension of a dearth of one nutriment—love— may, in the unconscious, most readily and forcibly be translated into a dearth of the other—food.

It has always been evident that the poet's relationship with her mother was not ideal. Emily Dickinson, the greatly gifted daughter, and Emily Norcross Dickinson, her undistinguished mother, spent most of their lives together in close physical proximity. Because the daughter never married, never sought employment outside the home, routinely helped with certain domestic chores, and pursued her literary and gardening interests in her mother's immediate ambience, one can only conclude that the lives of the two women were more closely and continually mingled than is usual. Physical proximity is not to be identified with emotional rapport, of course, and Dickinson scholars consider the long association to have been a superficial and mildly uncongenial one. The poet in her middle age appraised the relationship with blunt acerbity and concluded, "I never had a mother."[2] The remark can be taken as expressive of a superior woman's arrogance. The most frequently drawn inference is not only that Emily Dickinson did not have a mother worth reflecting upon, but that she managed very well without one.

For another view, consider the following poem (no. 959):

> A loss of something ever felt I –
> The first that I could recollect
> Bereft I was – of what I knew not
> Too young that any should suspect

A Mourner walked among the children
I notwithstanding went about
As one bemoaning a Dominion
Itself the only Prince cast out –

Elder, Today, a session wiser
And fainter, too, as Wiseness is –
I find myself still softly searching
For my Delinquent Palaces –

And a Suspicion, like a Finger
Touches my Forehead now and then
That I am looking oppositely
For the site of the Kingdom of Heaven –

This poem would seem to place Emily's bitter remark in another light. It tells of a nameless something of great magnitude and value whose early loss has generated a dimly apprehended and lifelong bereavement. It is a lamentation arising from some obscure sense of inner impoverishment. May not the poem be speaking metaphorically of a child's pain and hunger for love in the face of maternal inaccessibility? Had Mrs. Dickinson in her capacity as mother been in some critical way a failure? Might she not have been emotionally unavailable to the poet during early childhood, when the child's need for maternal warmth and tenderness was at its height? If such a primal deprivation can be accepted as the first premise in the poet's psychological constitution many of the enigmas and oddities of her adult behavior can be rendered comprehensible. In retracing the labyrinth of Emily Dickinson's emotional evolution throughout the rest of this book, this hypothesis will serve as the guiding thread.

Many practical or commonsense explanations for Emily Dickinson's seclusion from the world have been based on the assumption that she possessed an essentially "healthy" personality. Thus, she is said to have retreated:

(1) because of a frustrated love affair;[3]
(2) to conserve energy and have time to write;[4]
(3) to ponder "a metaphysical quandary";[5]
(4) as a stratagem to dramatize a drab existence;[6]
(5) to protect her vulnerability to overstimulation;[7]
(6) as a social protest and to avoid conformity;[8]
(7) to control and regulate her personal relationships;[9]

(8) as a reaction to her repressive schooling;[10]

(9) to spite her father or because of his dependence on her;[11]

(10) because of her plain looks.[12]

In contrast, it is the hypothesis of this study that both the failure of Emily Dickinson to achieve complete fulfillment socially and sexually and the anxiety and ambivalence which subverted her ambition to reach the reading public she merited are ultimately traceable to psychological determinants rooted in her transactions with her mother.

Emily Dickinson afforded a terrible insight into her childhood when she wrote in a letter, "I always ran Home to Awe as a child, if anything befell me. He was an awful Mother, but I liked him better than none."[13] And her older brother Austin, in a confidence to his fiancée, suggested that his sister's experience was not unique: "Tenderness has not been so common a thing to me . . . I have never *before* received *any*—from any *body* . . . towards no other have I ever felt tenderness."[14]

The lost "Dominions," "Kingdoms," and "Palaces" of the poem "A loss of something ever felt I" therefore may be symbols unconsciously related in the poet's mind to her having been shut out at an early age from the heaven of maternal affection through some emotional unresponsiveness or incapacity on the part of her mother. In the poetry of the mature woman the child speaks, still grieving for a source of sustenance that had been lacking or withdrawn—the tenderness and shelter of a mothering woman.

A reading of the letters of Emily Dickinson and those of her family evokes distinct impressions of the personality of Emily Norcross. One catches glimpse after glimpse of an habitually complaining woman, subject to depression and hypochondria. She appears emotionally shallow, self-centered, ineffectual, conventional, timid, submissive, and not very bright. There is no doubt that her figure as she appears in the correspondence is characterized to a greater extent by the virtues she lacked than by any she might have possessed. Perhaps for this reason, biographers tend to deemphasize her importance and overlook the fact that she must, of necessity, have exerted a steady, formative pressure upon the unfolding character of her famous daughter: whatever a mother's strengths and defects, virtues and vices, for better or worse, she is never a nonentity to her child.

That the blighted relationship between Emily Dickinson and her mother had far-reaching implications for the poet's life and art is eminently believable. It behooves us, therefore, to search out and scrutinize the origins of this troubled interaction, for within it there may be found one of the keys to the poet's eventual rejection of marriage and her election of a life of fantasy and loneliness. Emily and her mother seem never to have known an easy companionship. Except for the last few years of the mother's life, when circumstances brought about a radical alteration in their transactions with each other, the poet, by her own admission, felt no affection for the woman who gave her birth and with whom she spent her entire life. That, with respect to her own lifelong emotional needs and personal standards, she regarded her mother as hopelessly disappointing is clear from the bitter comments quoted. The first objective of this chapter is to indicate the extent to which Emily Dickinson retained the characteristics of the emotionally starved child. One can conservatively surmise from the evidence that some disturbance unsettled the early mother-daughter relationship, that the mother continued to be emotionally inaccessible as the girl matured, and that this lapse embued the daughter's emotional life with a craving for affection which she obsessively expressed in images of alimentary deprivation.

To obtain the fullest possible understanding of the enigmatic adult personality of Emily Dickinson, it is necessary to examine all that is known regarding the personality of her parents. Her father, the vivid and relatively accessible Edward Dickinson, has been more fully considered by biographers than has his protectively colored little wife. In the following pages, an effort will be made to redress this imbalance by attempting a closer look at the mother's elusive personality. First, however, it might be well to substantiate with some additional material the prevalence of the "oral" element in the poet's affective life which links her frustrations to her mother.

When writing to the cousins who cared for her in Cambridgeport at the time of her eye treatments, Emily Dickinson alludes to their kindness thus: "You have so often fed me."[15] She inquires of a friend if the friend feels sufficiently loved in these words: "Do you find plenty of food at home? Famine is unpleasant."[16] Again, writing to a woman friend upon the return home of her husband after a long trip, she says, "Am told that fasting gives to food marvellous Aroma, but by birth a Bachelor, disavow Cuisine."[17] Later in her life, after her friend Judge Otis P. Lord had apparently importuned for marriage or sexual favors and had been repulsed, she wrote by way of softening the rejection, "It is Anguish I long conceal from you to let you leave me, hungry, but you ask the divine Crust and that would doom the Bread."[18] And again she identifies food with love in the following: "The ravenousness of fondness is best disclosed by children . . . Is there not a sweet wolf within us that demands its food?"[19]

Her poems also offer frequent testimony to the oral derivatives of her yearning for affection. Poem 579 begins, "I had been hungry, all the Years" and goes on to tell of "The Crumb / The Birds and I, had often shared / In Nature's-Dining Room." She depicts her life as a constant observing of others whose affectional needs are amply fulfilled in contrast to her own, and she expresses the feeling of being shut out in the cold, "When turning, hungry, Home / I looked in Windows, for the Wealth / I could not hope – for Mine."

Poem 612 presents the theme explicitly:

> It would have starved a Gnat –
> To live so small as I –
> And yet I was a living Child –
> With Food's necessity
>
> Upon me – like a Claw –
> I could no more remove
> Than I could coax a Leech away – . . .

In poem 801, she remarks that she sometimes feels that her lot in life is "Too hungry to be borne" and in poem 1125, after glimpsing the possibility of gratification, she says, "Twill never be the same to starve / Now I abundance see."

In poem 1282, she declares that her years of deprivation have made fulfillment, now tardily offered, seem inferior to her accumulated desire:

> Art thou the thing I wanted?
> Begone – my Tooth has grown –
> Supply the minor Palate
> That has not starved so long –
> I tell thee while I waited
> The mystery of Food

Increased till I abjured it
Subsisting now like God —

In poem 726, the infant's nursing and the consolations to the
mortally ill of cooling water sucked from fingers reinforce the
oral image. Heaven, characteristically, is expressed in oral terms:

We thirst at first – 'tis Nature's Act –
And later – when we die –
A little Water supplicate –
Of fingers going by –

It intimates the finer want –
Whose adequate supply
Is that Great Water in the West –
Termed Immortality —

The identification of heaven with a bountiful breast is rendered
almost explicitly in poem 121, in which a "Beggar" gains his
paradisial reward through "thirsty lips to flagons pressed."

There is probably little profit in further multiplying examples
from the verse. The foregoing expressions of a persisting lust for
affection phrased in the images of hunger and thirst are typical
and are profusely embedded in the poet's writings from all periods of her life.*

Similar metaphors are not uncommonly found in the work of
other poets, and this may have been one of the observations that
led A. A. Brill to his formulation that poets as a group tend to be
"oral personalities." As such, they are gratified more than are
most people with sounds formed and modulated by the mouth,
lips, and tongue. On reviewing his psychoanalyses of persons
"who showed poetic talent . . . and who were recognized as poets
by the world,"[20] Brill concluded that this aspect of their art was a
sublimation of strong love needs never fully satisfied in the early
months of infancy and childhood, when sensual comfort and
security exist only as states of feeling in the ambience of the
child's relationship with his mother. The mother's feeding of the
poet-to-be is his earliest tangible proof of her love, and later the
ingestive process becomes a symbol for the entire mother-child

* The following is a partial listing of poems in which affection or the longing for
it are expressed in oral terms: nos. 67, 119, 121, 132, 135, 159, 167, 211, 214, 230, 239,
296, 313, 319, 335, 460, 490, 579, 588, 612, 640, 690, 717, 726, 771, 773, 791, 801, 815,
953, 1125, 1262, and 1282.

relationship. Food, therefore, in poetry, painting, in dreams and even in ordinary social life, is basically and unconsciously associated with maternal solicitude and the receiving of love.

Even Emily Dickinson's life itself may be seen as a reflection of the same insatiable need to be looked after, accommodated, and "fed." Its many famous eccentricities have as a common element an exorbitant, demanding dependency. Emily Dickinson was born and died in her parents' house. Her agoraphobia and fear of strangers made it impossible for her to leave it, and everything she needed had to be arranged for through others and brought to her. If an aged seamstress who claimed to have made dresses for Emily can be believed, she did not dine with her family in later life but had her meals carried to her room. Finally she became incapable of the slightest transaction with persons outside the family. The clothes she wore had to be fitted to her sister because she could not face the seamstress. When she was ill, medical consultations were arranged by her worried family and executed by proxy because she would not see the physicians. Her letters and packages were mailed by her family, who sometimes were even required to address them. Though the proper maintenance of the flower garden was probably of greater concern to her than to the others, she ran from the gardeners when they required instructions. On one occasion when a vendor came to the door, she could not buy a watering can she wanted for her conservatory and asked her sister to purchase it. Perhaps because her life appeared so monotonous and lonely, her relatives felt obliged to arrange for certain diversions for her—musicians would be invited to sing and play in the parlor while she remained in solitude upstairs, overhearing. It was obviously not easy to include her in family functions while at the same time making allowances for her anxious shrinking from all direct interpersonal contact. Even funeral services were held in the home, to enable her to take her small part within the rigid limits her withdrawal imposed.

It is perfectly true that, as if in reaction to this abject physical dependency, she was possessed of an astonishing independence of thought and fantasy. And, seemingly with an equally compensatory firmness, the verbal skills that raised her poetic talent to the pitch of art were acquired by means of a solitary dedication to poetry, pursued with a self-reliance that was truly heroic. That her intellectual and esthetic gifts were fiercely unsubservient must not, however, be allowed to obscure the fact that in practical life she exhibited helplessness, vulnerability, and *infantile* dependence. Studying her behavior and her explicitly expressed attitudes, one is led to conclude that all her life there smoldered in Emily Dickinson's soul the muffled but voracious clamoring of the abandoned child. Although she herself was apparently never more than dimly aware that her compulsive self-entombment in the safe family mansion and her feeling that her mother had left her emotionally unsheltered were in any way related, it is certainly plausible that the life style and the sense of loss and hunger are opposite faces of the one monolithic bereavement. The question to be answered, then, is: What factors made Mrs. Dickinson an inadequate mother?

A simple listing of the births and deaths in Mrs. Dickinson's family during her childhood and of events during the early days of her own motherhood suggests many contributing causes for her later unassertiveness, fearfulness, and self-absorption.

Emily Norcross was one of nine children. At the age of seven she was the middle child and only girl in a family of five. Then her baby brother died. Psychological injuries to the girl caused by such a disruption of this particular constellation of siblings are almost inevitable and may be of various kinds and degrees of severity, some of which undoubtedly contributed to the frailty of her adult character.

A year later a formidable rival was born to her probably still grieving mother—a second girl. And after the two younger boys and the second younger sister were born, Emily Norcross, once the center of a retinue of four brothers, necessarily lost her former special status.

The death of the first brother was succeeded by other deaths that crowded thick and fast. When Emily Norcross was twenty her older brother Austin died, as did, in the same year, her youngest sister, Nancy, then six. Five years passed leaving the family unscathed. By this time Emily Norcross had married Edward Dickinson and was pregnant with her own first child, Austin. The next year death struck again. Her only remaining brother died—Hiram, three years her senior. Of the four brothers who surrounded her when she was a child of seven, three were now dead. The birth of her son Austin may have been some solace, restoring, in a sense, the infant's lost namesake. But it would strain one's credulity to think that any new baby, however deeply wished for, could assuage the ultimate loss of the first year of Mrs. Edward Dickinson's motherhood—the death of her own mother at the age of fifty-one. The impact of five family deaths in eighteen years on a young woman of only twenty-five cannot fail to have inflicted deep psychic wounds. Such wounds, whose labyrinthine complexity and mortality I have only begun to suggest, are here advanced as a partial explanation of the failure of Mrs. Edward Dickinson to be the kind of mother her children felt they needed.

But to explore in depth at this point the probable deformative effects of these events on her adult personality is perhaps to digress too much. Suffice it to say that it cannot tenably be maintained that the failure of Mrs. Dickinson's maternal functions had no understandable genesis and was the result simply of a deliberate withholding of love and a conscious rejection of her offspring. There can be little doubt that Mrs. Dickinson had ample reason, at least for a time, to be *unable* to love.

Under the circumstances of her brother's and mother's deaths it is not difficult to see why she would have been unable to give the infant Austin the sense of loving security that he required for healthy psychological development. But my primary concern here is not with Austin. What I should like to do is attempt to establish the quality of the emotional atmosphere at Emily's birth and early infancy.

No doubt a residue of depressive and guilt feelings, mourning reactions, and lack of confidence in her maternal capacities lingered and affected Mrs. Dickinson's relationship with Emily, born about one and one half years after Austin. Several other factors may also be of importance. When Mrs. Dickinson was in the third trimester of her pregnancy with Emily, the family moved into the Main Street house occupied by Edward Dickinson's parents. Her mother-in-law was a self-pitying and demanding woman described by Edward's sister as "not apt to form acquaintances or attachments."[21] There is no indication that Edward's mother and his wife were ever friendly, and it becomes abundantly clear in later years, when Emily's family moved back into the Main Street house after having lived ten years elsewhere, that it did not hold fond memories for some of them. In fact, upon returning, Emily Dickinson's mother seems to have fallen into an immediate depression from which she recovered only after several years.

Whether or not Emily's mother found the close association with her mother-in-law worrisome, certain other events that occurred during this second pregnancy undoubtedly disturbed her. One was the death of her sister-in-law's baby girl three months before Emily was born. Certainly this would have increased her anxiety regarding her own child and tend to make her tense in anticipation of her confinement. A perhaps more disturbing situation developed just four days before Emily's birth, when Mrs. Dickinson was informed that her father was to remarry in about one month. That this was unwelcome and undoubtedly upsetting news to her is suggested by the reaction of her brothers and sisters. Not one of them attended the wedding and her sister Lavinia wrote to her: "what shall I call her? Can I say Mother[?] O that I could be far away from here."[22] In later years, the poet, her brother Austin, and sister Lavinia clearly indicated that they did not accept their grandfather's second wife. After one of her visits, Lavinia wrote: "Another *job* over for the season."[23] One may reasonably suppose they were negatively influenced by their mother's attitude.

Thus Emily Dickinson, like her brother Austin, came into the world unpropitiously and at a time when stressful circumstances weighed heavily upon their mother. Surely Mrs. Dickinson's longing for her own mother, her reaction to the death of her sister-in-law's baby, and the unwelcome announcement of her father's impending marriage induced a state of mind inimical to the mood of relaxed, primitive, happy absorption in the new baby which we are now aware is so critical for the emotional well-being of the baby.

Mrs. Dickinson also underwent another kind of psychological travail during the first months of her daughter's life. This fact is indicated in a letter written by her sister Lavinia. One of many religious revivals was in progress in Amherst at that time, and it is clear that Lavinia is strongly urging Mrs. Dickinson to join the church: "But must you be enemies to that Savior who has suffered so much for you & Me."[24] Lavinia must have touched a nerve, for two months later Mrs. Dickinson underwent the necessary conversion experience and joined the church. That she held out for two months in the face of the extreme emotional pressure exerted in those days by the pious on the unconfirmed is remarkable in view of her palpable need for multiple sources of support. Viewed altogether, Emily's infancy was a turbulent time for Mrs. Dickinson.

We know little about Emily Dickinson's early childhood, but what little evidence there is supports the idea that her needs for maternal warmth could not altogether have been supplied even then. For example, when she was barely more than two years old, her sister Lavinia was born. Mrs. Dickinson did not recover normally from this birth, and it was many weeks before she was well enough to resume regular activities. It is possible that she suffered a postpartum depression. Baby Lavinia did not thrive as a newborn, which is commonly the case when the mother is depressed. That Mrs. Dickinson was vulnerable to depressions of more than ordinary magnitude is revealed by the fact that twenty years later she suffered a very severe and protracted one. Whether her illness was depressive or not, the family felt it best to send Emily away to her Aunt Lavinia's home in nearby Monson until Mrs. Dickinson recuperated. It must have seemed to the young child that she was being displaced by the new sister. The evidence suggests that she may have responded with a kind of numb shock that later became her characteristic response to overwhelming situations. According to the aunt, Emily did not cry; instead, throughout the journey by stagecoach from Amherst, she maintained an unusual and suspect composure, even appearing (to us) blunted in her reactions to an accompanying violent thunderstorm.

Observations of young children separated from their mothers reveal that where the mother-child relationship is a close and loving one, protracted separation produces severe depression in the child. Such depressions are characterized by listlessness, withdrawal, loss of appetite, and regression to more infantile modes of behavior. However, the child who has never experienced an emotionally fulfilling relationship with his mother does not undergo this striking alteration. Superficially he seems to bear the separation better than the child who desperately misses the mother who has meant so much to him. The impression one receives from reading the letters of Emily's aunt during and after the child's visit with her is that Emily most closely resembles the child whose mother has failed in her mothering functions. Rather than becoming depressed, Emily seems to have blossomed under the care of the loving aunt. That her amiability contrasted strongly with her behavior at home is suggested by one of the aunt's letters to Emily's mother: "She [Emily] is very affectionate & we all love her very much—She dont appear at all as she does at home—& she does not make but very little trouble . . . she is so happy here."[25] The implication is that Emily was unaffectionate, troublesome, demanding, and unhappy at home—characteristics of the unsatisfied and love-starved child.

Conversely, while Emily prospered, the baby, Lavinia, did poorly, and Mrs. Dickinson was full of self-pity and anxiety. The aunt wrote: "So take courage some are worse than you."[26] Emily continued to be "perfectly contented" and, perhaps significantly, mentioned missing only her brother Austin. The aunt became very fond of Emily, indulged her ("any thing she wants I shall get"[27]), and when Emily returned home (after a stay of five or six weeks), the aunt wrote: "I cant tell you how lonely I was—it seemed so different & I wanted to weep all the time."[28] The aunt had developed the custom of lying beside Emily when she took her nap—a practice evidently foreign to Mrs. Dickinson. In reference to this demonstration of affection, the aunt wrote Mrs. Dickinson, "I suppose she did not forget it after she went home." And, "She thought everything of me—when any thing went wrong she would come to me."[29] The comfort Emily derived from her aunt contrasted sharply with her experience at home. Recall her childhood reminiscence of running home only to "Awe" when she was frightened by something. At Aunt Lavinia's she apparently found a warmer emotion than "Awe."

In sum, the strain and self-preoccupation attendant on Mrs. Dickinson following the birth of Lavinia widened the breach between herself and Emily, who may accordingly have felt rejected. Then there followed for Emily a halcyon interval during which she became an affectionate and responsive child under the influence of her aunt's loving personality. But, by so much as the visit fulfilled her emotional needs, the return home was a plunge into coldness again.

It may also be that home had suffered a further impoverishment for her while she was away from it. Just a month after Lavinia's birth, Emily's grandfather, his wife, and their two youngest daughters, who had shared the house with the Edward Dickinsons, moved away from Amherst forever. Emily of course knew these relatives and it is plausible that she was fond of some of them. Whether she realized they were gone after she was returned home is impossible to say. It is conceivable that she missed them, and after Aunt Lavinia's, the meager warmth of home was reduced not only by contrast but in an absolute sense as well.

The hungering for love that permeates Emily Dickinson's poems and her belittling of the importance of her mother represent the two sides of the poet's ambivalence. That she survived infancy at all proves her mother gave her something—enough love, at least, to whet an appetite that was thereafter insatiable. The poet was equally ambivalent about her home—a symbol, like the "Delinquent Palaces"—of mother. She could not bear to give it up, yet she felt it to be an entombment. Biographers have tended to emphasize the positive pole of this contradictory attitude, yet many of her comments indicate how she longed to escape to a more satisfying life. She vividly expressed this aspect of her reaction to the suffocating confinement of the parental home in the following lines (no. 77):

> I never hear the word "escape"
> Without a quicker blood,
> A sudden expectation,
> A flying attitude!
>
> I never hear of prisons broad
> By soldiers battered down,
> But I tug childish at my bars
> Only to fail again!

In her remarks to Colonel Higginson, the question preceding the announcement that she "never had a mother" was "Could you tell me what home is[?]";[30] This juxtaposition suggests the closeness of the linkage in her mind of the ideas of home and mother. Later, when Higginson married, she wrote, "It is very sweet and serious to suppose you at Home," meaning a state of fulfillment in love. She then made a poignant oral reference to her own longing: "I have read of Home in the Revelations— 'Neither thirst anymore.' "[31]

The young girl who experiences her mother as cool and distant, meager in love, withholding of comfort and nonreassuring when the child is troubled, is bound, from the dawn of awareness, to sense that an ingredient vital to her healthy survival is lacking. Uncertainty and fear quickly follow upon this realization and the child's personality takes on a quality of timidity. Without unquestioning assurance of her mother's constant backing, the child tends to shrink from contact with the world outside the home, overwhelmed by a sense of her own weakness and vulnerability and of the coldness and incomprehensibility of the world. Close upon the heels of these feelings of insecurity comes resentment toward the withholding mother. As I shall attempt to show subsequently, nineteenth-century New England mores directed that anger—especially on the part of children—be subjugated and denied. The frustration and consequent rage one may reasonably assume Emily Dickinson felt toward her mother would have to be suppressed. Though in Emily Dickinson's case the culture happened to encourage this maneuver, the psychodynamics of any child in such a predicament would tend in this direction. The child who feels inadequately loved often dares not risk a further loss of affection through expressions of bad temper. A safer course is to become compliant. The suppression of retaliatory and destructive impulses in Emily Dickinson was to bring on a congeries of neurotic symptoms.

The frequent or constant provocation to fear and anger, which latter must be rigidly controlled, is a severe enough handicap for a developing child but seems not to have been the worst aspect of the situation in which Emily Dickinson found herself as she was growing up. If Mrs. Dickinson had merely been mourning, self-absorbed, and rejecting, with no other serious shortcomings, the daughter might have managed to adjust to her lot better than in actuality she did. But Mrs. Dickinson was, for the most part and in addition, unadmirable. In this respect she presented, perhaps, a more formidable psychological obstacle to her daughter's maturation than she would had she been strong, capable, talented —and unloving. Poor Mrs. Dickinson was obsequious, self-abnegating, plaintive, fussy, uninterested in ideas or art, dependent, and subject to profound spells of lassitude and discouragement. She was also entirely subservient to her husband and in time even relinquished whatever authority she had had in the running of her own household to her daughter Lavinia. Emily, with her constitutional thoughtfulness and imaginativeness and her highly active and superior mind, found it difficult to accept or understand her mother. One may assume that it pained her to observe her mother catering to Edward Dickinson's every whim, submitting to his irritability, and allowing herself to be treated like a child who could not decide for herself the simplest matters or assume the least responsibility. Almost from infancy Emily must have noticed the discrepancies in power, freedom, and importance between her parents and regretted that she was a female like her mother. The inability to applaud the way in which her mother executed the woman's role in the family would certainly have blighted any nascent leanings on the part of the daughter to play such a role herself some day.

The female child learns, in the most profound sense of the word, what it is to be a woman through her perception of her mother (as the boy, of course, does through his father). It is imperative for the stability of the girl's future self-concept as a female that from her earliest childhood she hold her mother in a feeling of positive regard. She must first love her mother and she can do that only if she feels that her mother loves her. Second, she must admire her mother and want to be like her. The normal process of building up a sense of sexual identity starts with admiration and then imitation of the parent of the same sex. The little girl consciously apes her mother's mannerisms, her tone of voice, her characteristic responses to situations, her relationship to the father. In time the imitation becomes increasingly ingrained and automatic, and the resemblances between the deportment and habits of mother and daughter become ever more subtle and pervasive. Conscious imitation gives way to unconscious identification; the girl's wish to be like mother is supplanted by the bedrock conviction that she and her mother are fundamentally equivalent. When this process proceeds undisturbed, it results in an adult personality of unshakable inner certainty with regard to the woman's gender role and sexual orientation vis-à-vis other men and women.

The girl who despises her mother, for whatever collection of personal shortcomings, has nevertheless, of course, to accept the reality of her anatomical sex, no matter how loath she is to being like her mother. The processes of identification then proceed, as it were, against the girl's will, which constantly battles to reject the uncongenial identification. Feelings of dismay and self-disgust accompany her awareness that the qualities she scorned in her mother are inexorably becoming part of herself. Every bit of evidence to the effect that physically and psychologically she is growing to resemble her mother is repudiated. Her hobbies, attire, speech, and outlook take on an exaggerated masculine quality in a seemingly desperate and last-ditch struggle to evade her sexual destiny. She is convinced through intimate observations that to be a female is to be secondrate. In the case of a girl in Emily Dickinson's circumstances, in which the mother-model cuts a ludicrously inferior figure in relation to the father, real acceptance of a feminine identity may never come about. Her predicament is thus twofold: first, she is driven to seek a substitute mother who will give her the love she failed to receive from her natural mother; and second, she must search for a more acceptable model upon which to pattern her development. If she is not fortunate enough to have consistently available a woman warmer and stronger than her mother to fulfill this function, she may at last be driven to pattern herself on a masculine model. Unlike the superficial tomboyism of prepuberty, which arises from the little girl's envy of a boy's greater freedom, such an assumption of masculinity represents a deep commitment. However, it temporarily relieves the pressure, that is, the psychodynamics of imitating and later identifying herself with a masculine prototype who impresses her in a positive way, and enhances the girl's feeling of strength and self-esteem. In this way the process reinforces itself. Anxiety diminishes and the psychic structures of a sexual identity at variance with the girl's anatomical sex insidiously attain increasing solidity and rigidity. Despite the fact that cultural pressures may stifle the external expression of a girl's masculinity, when adolescence arrives such a girl is in deep psychological trouble.

This is the dilemma into which the psychological forces of her environment pushed Emily Dickinson as a growing child. The elements of repudiation of femininity and covert hostility toward her mother which made her relationship with her mother so ambiguous and unsettled appear to have foredoomed her to an agonizing and protracted adolescence and an almost insurmountable crisis in sexual identity.

Really to understand what it meant to Emily Dickinson to have a mother like Emily Norcross Dickinson, one must also have a clear picture of the man she married and of the child-rearing philosophy of the times. Mrs. Dickinson's inadequacies notwithstanding, many of the vicissitudes and crises of Emily's maturation would have been less painful, damaging, and tumultuous had her father been a simpler and more integrated personality and had the culture, insofar as children are concerned, been a more comforting one.

Emily Dickinson once said that her entire experience of the world was mediated through her father. Certainly there was something oversize about the character of Edward Dickinson (Emily once likened him to a "Roman General, upon a Triumph Day"[32]), and it is therefore remarkable that this puritan warrior attempted to play out his heroic drama among actors and sets designed, as it were, for a period piece. The little town of Amherst was palpably too small for the scope of his political ambitions. Edward Dickinson aspired to (and achieved) greater than local eminence, but he so encumbered himself with avoidable domestic burdens by choosing a helpless and dependent wife and having three children that in the end one can only feel that he died disappointed and unfulfilled. Mrs. Dickinson, as a provincial woman of narrow horizons and, as Emily said, "unobtrusive faculties,"[33] was clearly a liability to Edward in his pursuit of statewide power and influence.

Edward Dickinson seems frequently thus to have foredoomed his goals by the means and circumstances through which he chose to pursue them. This lapse between overt design and objective result was not, however, a manifestation of deviousness or indecisiveness. How then does one explain this paradoxical effect? The answer appears to lie in this: Edward Dickinson is a prime example of a personality in which consciously conceived objectives are influenced, deflected, and sometimes thoroughly subverted through the operation of unconscious opposing motivations.

His friend Samuel Bowles said of him: "His failing was he did not understand himself; consequently his misfortune was that others did not understand him."[34] The man who does not understand himself is most frequently the man who is surprised at his own behavior, who puzzles at his own motivations, and who fails to recognize the source of his own actions. In short, a man in the grip of unconscious forces. There is evidence for believing that Edward Dickinson was such a man and that hidden determinants molded his life and the lives of his children.

He was the eldest of nine children, a born leader and protector. Trained at Yale, he became an energetic and ambitious lawyer, not great in his calling but painstaking and laborious. In the course of his life he amassed a modest fortune. It was said of him that whatever he undertook was "prosecuted with an industry and perseverence excelled by none."[35] At twenty-five he was a major in the militia, of which he later said: "I was afraid to go a grade higher, lest I should get too strong a thirst for military glory,"[36]—an early indication that he had an inkling of propensities that could dominate him if in their incipient stages they were not tightly reined in.

Edward's father, Samuel, was an idealistic and intensely evangelical Calvinist who exhausted himself and his fortune with far greater regard for the advancement of noble religious and educational causes than for the comfort and security of his large family. He died, a venerated failure, when Edward was in his mid-thirties, leaving the son a substantial debt. Throughout his life, Edward too supported causes he felt were worthy ones; however, he donated primarily his time and energy, prudently reserving his financial resources for his own purposes. He belonged to and held office in many civic organizations dedicated to the maintenance or advancement of town safety, education, economy, and morality. At thirty-four he enlarged his sphere of activity and served in the Massachusetts legislature (1837-1839). Three years later he spent over a year as a state senator, and when he was forty-nine he was elected to the United States House of Representatives, where he stayed for two years. He continued to play a role in politics for the rest of his life, representing the interests of western Massachusetts on the New England or national scene. Though he was without doubt Amherst's most prominent and influential citizen, and though he poured his time and energy into numerous enterprises for the town's advancement, he was more admired than liked. The Reverend J. L. Jenkins, in a sermon preached after Edward Dickinson's death likening him to the prophet Samuel, observed that "men are not known by contemporaries . . . alienations are so frequent that perfect concord is impossible." Like Samuel, Edward Dickinson was a man "whom a whole village feared, in whose appearance there was that which terrified." According to the Reverend Mr. Jenkins, he was in reality gentle, though he hid his gentleness "so carefully" and "so unwisely."[37]

For the most part Edward Dickinson concealed his softer side even from his children. Emily remembered him thus: "His Heart was pure and terrible and I think no other like it exists."[38]

Though Edward Dickinson could be vocal and aggressive when he was debating an abstract issue, socially he tended to be aloof and cold, perhaps owing to a certain shyness and reserve. It was this side of him that caused Colonel Higginson to remark: "I saw Mr. Dickinson this morning a little—thin dry & speechless—I saw what her [Emily's] life has been."[39] At other times his irascible temper, frequently triggered by some indisposition, no doubt produced a disagreeable effect on others. Emily describes his mood on one such occasion: "Father has been shut up with the rheumatism . . . the rest of us are as well as could possibly be expected! . . . father's frame of mind is *as usual* the Happiest," she says, underscoring the irony, "developing itself in constant acts of regard, and *epithets of tenderness!*"[40] He could be most uningratiating with visitors. On this same occasion, when a man called at the house, her father's mood caused Emily to be "frightened almost to death" and "terrified beyond measure" at what he might do or at what he might say to the hapless caller. On another occasion, Lavinia notes in her diary, "Father slightly *ill, trimmed* Dr. Brewster."[41]

On rare but impressive occasions Edward Dickinson's irritability under provocation erupted. At such times one glimpses a usually latent ferocity and pent-up frustration breaking through into violent behavior. "Oh! dear!" writes Lavinia, "Father is killing the horse . . . he is whipping him because he didn't look quite '*umble*' enough this morning."[42] On one occasion Emily stayed out longer than expected. Later she wrote Austin: "[I] arrived home at 9—found Father in great agitation at my protracted stay—and mother and Vinnie in tears, for fear that he would kill me."[43]

As a pillar of the community, Edward Dickinson was well aware of his merit: at times his self-appraisal was inflated and pretentious. Once when he arrived at the station after the train had left, he is said to have remarked, no doubt indignantly, "That conductor knew that I was going."[44]

According to Emily, her father "never played,"[45] which we may take to mean that the child in him was completely overlaid, perhaps smothered, by the adult—that he could never relax, let down his guard, retreat even momentarily from the rigors of his authority. Perhaps because of his need to maintain an austere control over his family, he found it difficult to grant his children (and wife) the privilege of being anything but children. He thought nothing of intruding into their affairs when they were well into their twenties and seems never to have realized that they might have a need or right to privacy. For example, he had to know what Austin wrote Emily: "He [Father]," Emily tells Austin, "reads all the letters you write as soon as he gets, at the post office, no matter to whom addressed."[46]

Though "Father" never played, was entirely practical and engrossed in "real life," his three children remained young beyond their years, secretly rebellious, fanciful and romantic. Thus they safeguarded their emotional lives by keeping them at a vast remove from his, though, in their eyes, he was always in the background, a stern and reproving deity. "I dont love to read your letters all out loud to father," Emily tells Austin. "It would be like opening the kitchen door when we get home from meeting Sunday, and are sitting down by the stove saying just what we're a mind to, and having father hear. I dont know why it is, but it gives me a dreadful feeling."[47]

Though their father's presence gave them a sense of protection, it also increased the tension in the house and the children seem to have been relieved when he was gone; Emily, for one, rarely said she missed him. "Father went away," she writes Austin at age twenty-two, "bidding us an affectionate good bye yesterday morning, having business in Springfield which would detain him all day, and perhaps until the next day, and returned at dinner time, just as the family were getting *rather busy*—Of course, we were delighted to be together again! After our long separation!"[48] And Lavinia writes to her brother: "Mother has been sick for two days & Father 'is as he is,' so that home has been rather a gloomy place, lately."[49]

Very rarely a lighter side of Edward Dickinson showed itself. At such times he could be lively, vivid, and humorous (usually in a satirical vein), and then his children took a surprised delight in him. One such episode is alluded to in a letter Emily wrote in 1853. The occasion was a sermon the Dickinsons thought "perfectly ridiculous." "We spent the intermission in mimicking the Preacher," she writes Austin, "and reciting extracts from his most memorable sermon. I never heard father so funny . . . I know you'd have died laughing. Father said he didn't dare look at Sue—he said he saw her bonnet coming round our way, and he looked 'straight ahead.' "[50]

Edward Dickinson was slow to praise, but when he did— usually economically and with restraint—his words had impact. When Emily's cousin married, he made just such a mild comment to the new bridegroom about the bride, who later wrote: "Not fulsome flattery, surely, but coming from this man, and crowned, as it was, with the beautiful and rare smile we all felt it a success to win, it was a benediction on my new life."[51]

Edward Dickinson was the supreme authority in his family; the regulations he imposed held them together, provided material security, and largely established the nature of their relationships with the community. His wishes, according to Emily, were "orders from head-quarters."[52] They were to be followed unquestioningly, for, as his daughter said, "What father *says*, 'he means.' "[53]

From the beginning of his marriage to Emily Norcross, one senses the great disparity that existed in intelligence, vitality, and strength of personality between husband and wife. No doubt bolstered by his position as eldest son in a large family and by his later military experiences, his determination to dominate led him to select as wife a woman who presented no threat to his aggressive propensities. But Mrs. Dickinson was no challenge whatever. It seems as though Edward, at the time of his marriage, was not entirely sure of his capacity to impose his will upon others and needed domestic reassurance of his complete mastery. Alas, he achieved this status all too easily with regard to his wife, whose shrinking disposition and helplessness soon made her a millstone. As one examines the early circumstances and transactions of this curiously matched couple, one also catches glimpses of a multitude of other factors deterring Edward from the achievement of his ambitions for far-reaching power and influence.

There is little doubt, for example, that his younger siblings expected him to provide for their aged mother and father. When his father died unexpectedly, his sisters Catherine and Mary expressed their guilt to their mother. Catherine wrote: "It only remains for us to *regret* that we did not do our duty better . . . the fact that the ingratitude of *many* of his children has weighed down his spirits—is enough to break my heart";[54] and Mary wrote: "He has done much for his children—they nothing for him."[55] Although Edward is not specifically designated in these remarks as among the negligent, it is significant that as the one in the best position to have been helpful he is not singled out by the sisters as a shining exception.

His aging mother's entreaties for care seem to have aroused in him only impatience and almost callous resistance. Through his immersion in a thriving law practice, his position as treasurer of Amherst College, and his duties as a member of the state legislature, he seems to have insulated himself from her constant complaints of ill health and her worries about who was to look after her. Less than a year before her death she wrote imploringly: "I do not know what to do [about a place to live] . . . it would be best I do not ask to go to your house for I know it is not convenient . . . I know my complaints trouble you but what can I do I have no one to look to *but* my Children."[56] Two months later, in desperation, she wrote again, and it is apparent that no arrangements had been made in the meantime for her care, for she is still living alone. She tells Edward of having "turns" which she feels threaten her life and says, "it would be a satisfaction to be with some of my Children when these seasons occur." It is pathetically clear that the old woman feels rejected; she says bitterly that she cannot stay with her daughter Catherine because "her Husband does not like *Old Folks* it is likely the same reason operates throughout the family . . . [parents] must be set aside because they are old it looks too much like heathenism."[57]

It is possible that this last plea did not fall on deaf ears. Three months later, plans were under way for Edward and his family to move to larger quarters, perhaps with a view to providing accommodations for his ailing mother. They did not occupy their new home, however, for at least another month or two, and shortly after Edward's mother died. The extent to which Edward allowed his thoughts and emotions to be swallowed up in his political concerns is suggested in a letter declining an invitation to address a convention to be held on the day of his mother's funeral in support of presidential candidate William H. Harrison. First he advances the "sad offices of respect" to be held for his mother as the reason for his inability to attend the meeting; then his enthusiasm takes over: "Allow me, Sir, in conclusion, to congratulate you all, upon the glorious prospect before us. The sky is now clearing up—the Harrison seed has taken deep root—is already waving in the breeze, and will soon invite to a golden harvest . . . Please assure the whigs of Franklin, that my heart is with them . . . our triumph is sure."[58] The glorious prospects, the clearing sky, and the anticipation of a triumphant harvest—these imply sentiments curiously divergent from thoughts of funeral rites and Mrs. Dickinson's lonely and unattended corpse. The main point is not Edward Dickinson's obvious lack of prostrating grief at his mother's death but the vigor of his extrafamilial interests and his need to resist even the most urgent demands of his family.

Just as he did not allow his father's and mother's deaths to divert him substantially from his path, he did not submit to his wife's pleas for the emotional security and material protection his constant presence at home might have afforded.

Edward's intention to refuse to allow his wife or the confines of Amherst to determine the extent of his mobility was made manifest before he had been married a year. He encouraged male students at Amherst Academy to room and board at his home for his wife's protection when he was away, and one of them, Ebenezer Bullard, wrote his brother: "Esq, [Edward Dickinson] and the rest of the family, were anxious to have me stay with them this winter as he was to be from home, & the folks did not like to be without some one in the house, as *a guard* Esqr said . . . Esq. D—— has been at home but two, or three days since, and is now in Boston at court."[59] A few years later, while babysitting during one of his wife's rare visits to Boston, Edward states his position unequivocally: "I am dissatisfied that I did not go [to Bangor, Maine] when I wanted to & was ready—in spite of everything—this waiting & taking advice, I find, is poor business for a man who is in the habit of giving advice to others—I must make some money in some way, & if I don't speculate in the lands, at the 'East,' I must at the 'West'—and when the fever next attacks me—nothing human shall stop me from making one desperate attempt to make my fortune—To be shut up forever 'under a bushel' while hundreds of mere Jacanapes are getting their tens of thousands & hundreds of thousands, is rather too much for my spirit—I must spread myself over more ground—half a house, & a rod square for a garden, won't answer my turn."[60]

Emotionally, husband and wife seem to have drifted increasingly further apart. Mrs. Dickinson rarely accompanied her husband on his business trips. Her staying at home was partly the result of the need of her children to be looked after, though Mrs. Dickinson probably used her maternal duties as an excuse for avoiding a wife's obligations to support her husband's career when these obligations involved activities for which she had a temperamental aversion. Certainly it is clear that long before the children could be said to have hampered her mobility she evinced an unwillingness to leave an environment in which she felt secure. For example, in 1829, when Austin was six months old—a good age for traveling—Edward's sister Mary writes that she would very much like to see his little son and adds somewhat tartly that she realizes that the Dickinsons' visiting her is probably *"out of the question"* (underlined by Mary for emphasis): "I know Emily is not fond of travelling."[61] And before she married Edward Dickinson, Emily Norcross exhibited a similar reluctance to leave her parents' home. Two weeks before her marriage she wrote her fiancé, "I have many friends call upon me as they say to make their farewell visit. How do you suppose this sounds in my ear [?]"[62] Clearly the answer to her question is: frightening. Emily's relatives sensed her timidity and feelings of apprehension at parting with her familiar life and even shared to some extent her view of it as a painful sundering. Her cousin Albert wrote to her of "that last walk that I had with you, little did I think at that time that it was the last time I should walk with you."[63] Likewise, her sister Lavinia wrote, "I think news from home must always be desirable especially to one who is so homesick . . . do not your thoughts dwell on the pleasures of home occasionally?"[64]

How Edward Dickinson, by contrast, must have chafed under the obligations of home life! One catches an early glimpse of what seems to have become a fixed attitude in a comment made by his sister Catherine after she visited Amherst; at that time

Edward's third child, Lavinia, was two years of age, and the responsibilities of fatherhood must by then have become pressing. Catherine writes: "I found Emily [Mrs. Edward Dickinson] & the children quite well & expecting me . . . Edward seems very sober & says but little."[65] And years later Emily tells Austin that her father is as uneasy without him as a fish out of water and that "when you *first* went away he came home very frequently . . . *now* he is more resigned—contents himself by fancying that 'we shall *hear* [from Austin] today.' "[66] These frequent visits home from the office not only indicate the degree to which he missed his son but also suggest that he felt a man ought to be in residence—that women alone could not see to it that things ran well. He was caught in a conflict of interests. Clearly he was at times weighed down with a sense of family obligations not fully met.

Edward, unlike his wife, exulted in the bustle and freedom of large cities. Two years after his marriage he writes his wife from New York: "I find every thing here, which I have seen, grand & magnificent." He remarks that he was forced to tour the city in his slippers because he had got blisters on his feet when sightseeing, and reassures his perhaps scandalized wife that this is acceptable because "they are not so particular here as they are in little villages." New York, he says, is "just what I like." The next day he adds: "I like travelling,"[67] and lest she think him inordinately pleased to be away from his family, piously declares that wherever he is his family is uppermost in his thoughts.

His family's wishes do not appear to have been the paramount consideration when he decided to buy the Main Street mansion the year after he lost his seat in Congress, and it seems likely that the move to the large, imposing house was motivated by concern for his career. It was possible to entertain two hundred people in its parlors and library, and Edward did indeed hold "commencement teas" there every year, at which time the dignitaries of the region and the college were his guests. We know that Emily disliked this house in which she spent the first ten years of her life, and, as has been mentioned, Mrs. Dickinson, upon her arrival there for the second time, suffered a depressive breakdown of at least four years' duration.

Even when the exigencies of his law practice and political

commitments allowed him to reside in Amherst for relatively long periods, he was always hurrying somewhere and rarely stayed at home. When not on one of his frequent trips to Boston, he was usually attending local meetings. His presence at home in the evening was rare enough to cause comment. Thus in the fall of 1851, his daughter writes her brother: "Father is staying at home the evening is so inclement."[68]

There is a suggestion in Edward Dickinson's early letters to his wife that his feelings about the increased responsibilities attendant upon fatherhood were not altogether unmixed. As Mrs. Dickinson, harassed by bad news from her family, entered upon the last months of her first pregnancy, Edward began to voice new complaints. Shortly after Austin's birth Mrs. Dickinson visited her family to show the child off, leaving Edward at home. It was at *this* time that her husband took the opportunity to confide: "my health is far from being good—I must confess that I have not been as well as usual for, two or three months past [that is, since Austin's birth, April 16, and the month or so preceding it] . . . I am convinced that my languor & weakness which has rendered me so lifeless this Spring, has a bad cause, & it ought to be removed." He does not regard as the source of his depressive symptoms his suppressed resentment at his wife for leaving him to fend for himself while she devotes herself to his new dependent. He blames his "lifelessness" on physical causes (his teeth), though he admits that he is "not pleased at all, with the life of a widower." Clearly he is attempting to make her feel guilty for leaving him in poor health, a condition rendered suspect through his having until now kept it to himself. His concealed anger at his wife for forsaking him leads him to remark on a stingy neighbor who makes *his* wife ride in an *"old shackling waggon, without cushion* or *Buffalo-skin,"* and he asks her: "How would you like that way?"[69] In effect, what he seems to be saying is: you see how much better I am to you and yet look how you neglect me.

Apparently the offending teeth were ultimately extracted, for the next month Mrs. Dickinson's sister writes: "I fancy he [Edward] has not exercised much patience in his sufferings but he has the consolation that the teeth so painful will never vex him more."[70] It is perhaps not unreasonable to infer from these passages the existence in Edward Dickinson of a sense of self-pitying possessiveness toward his wife that on a subliminal level caused him to regard the new baby as a threat to both his physical comfort and his career. Of course, such feelings were incompatible with the manly adequacy he insisted upon and would necessarily be repressed. Also his ideal for himself—as set forth in a letter to his wife prior to their marriage in these words: "May we be virtuous, intelligent, industrious and by the exercise of every virtue, & the cultivation of every excellence, be esteemed & respected & beloved by all"[71]—left no room for such ignominious but human self-seeking and dependency. A certain acceptance of one's frailties and a tolerance of one's baser motives is necessary if the wish to be rid of the encumbrances of paternal responsibility is to persist in consciousness. The same is true with accepting one's disinclination to share a wife's attentions with offspring. Edward Dickinson could never accept the darker and weaker aspects of himself. It is typical of him that even at the time of his conversion and acceptance into the church he found it difficult to put aside his proud defensiveness. His pastor said to him: "You want to come to Christ as a *lawyer*—but you must come to him as a *poor sinner*—get down on your knees."[72]

What I am now prepared to suggest is that both Edward Dickinson's urgent desire to do himself credit in the masculine arenas of the courthouse and the political assembly and to prove himself a self-reliant and ultra-responsible member of the community were to some degree a compensation and denial of his own dependent need to be sheltered and cared for. The fact that he "never played," went to God as a lawyer rather than as an abject sinner, displayed a "pure and terrible heart" without softness, and hid his gentleness "so carefully" and "so unwisely" all appear to be the result of a fear of seeming unmanly. His strong drive for masculine ascendency, his self-centered irritability and attention-demanding impatience when he was ill, and his need to marry a weak and easily subjugated wife all betray this other side of Edward Dickinson. Unconsciously he recognized and repudiated a strong inclination to be the preferred, controlling, and indulged child. We of course know nothing of the intimate side of his relationship with his wife. Perhaps here Mrs. Dickinson's "unobtrusive faculties" became significant in providing a haven for her peripatetic warrior. It is a strong possibility, not to be minimized, that one of the causes of Mrs. Dickinson's inadequacies as a mother was that Edward's demands for attention monopolized her maternal functions to such an extent that she had little energy left to devote to her children.

That she did not meet his needs entirely, however, is apparent. Being so much his intellectual inferior, she could offer him no real companionship and little beyond physical comfort, if indeed she could provide that. Once when he was ill, Emily wrote to her cousins that "the sight of his lonesome face all day was harder than personal trouble."[73] Though he was at home with his wife at this time, it was nevertheless his loneliness that impressed his daughter. And after Edward's death, she wrote to T. W. Higginson in the same vein, speaking of "Father's lonely Life and his lonelier Death."[74]

Her conception of a father's reaction to the loss of a daughter through marriage is conveyed in her letter to the newly-wed Emily Fowler Ford: "I thought he [Mrs. Ford's father] looked solitary. I thought he had grown old. How lonely he must be— I'm sorry for him."[75]

Emily seems to have been less touched by her mother's loneliness in the face of her father's repeated absences, although there are indications that she was aware of such feelings. In an appalling letter written when she was twenty-one, she presents her views of the relationship between wives and their husbands and speaks of "the *wife forgotten*" who looks back upon the single state longingly as one "dearer than all others in the world." Wives are like "sweet flowers at noon with their heads bowed in anguish before the mighty sun [their husbands] . . . [which] scorches them, scathes them; they have got through with peace."[76] In view of her limited experience, her interpretation of the married state as one in which the "forgotten" wife is utterly subject to the merciless demands of the domineering male can only have been derived from her responses to what she observed in her home. A woman more adequate than Mrs. Dickinson might have contrived to mother such a husband (without mobilizing his masculine defense that *she* was to rely on *him*) while at the same time maintaining sufficient stamina and resources to fulfill her own needs and to provide for the emotional needs of her children.

But there was little in Emily Norcross' personality to shake

Edward's security in his supremacy. On the contrary, Mrs. Dickinson needed a great deal of protection and encouragement herself, and at times Edward was forced to take an almost parental role with her. He soon learned not to demand much of her; in the sixth year of their married life he wrote: "take care of yourself & the dear little children, if you do nothing else."[77] When Mrs. Dickinson wrote telling of her loneliness and tears, saying "perhaps you will say you think me weak and childish,"[78] he replied with his familiar refrain, thus affirming the truth of her supposition: "Let the children be careful to avoid getting hurt, or taking colds, or being out in the winds, Lavinia must be guarded against croup—& above all, take the best care of yourself—don't be nervous—Let not your anxiety overcome you—be calm—don't overdo—get along as easy as you can," and so forth.[79] Mrs. Dickinson even needed reassurance that her letters were acceptable to her husband; in response to her self-doubts he wrote: "I find you always have something to say, & it is very easy for you to say it."[80]

The full extent of Edward's lack of confidence in his wife is highlighted by contrasting his attitude toward leaving her alone in the house with his attitude toward leaving the eleven-year-old Lavinia in similar circumstances. Though he invariably arranged to have someone stay with Mrs. Dickinson, he felt comfortable in leaving Lavinia to her own devices: "Mother & I are going to Northampton to-day," he wrote Emily, who was visiting an uncle in Worcester, "and leave Lavinia to keep house— She can get a good dinner, alone."[81]

Nor was Mrs. Dickinson satisfied to have a college student as watchman and protector; she wanted her husband at home. However, she was not the kind of woman to issue ultimatums, and Edward Dickinson would not have tolerated the faintest suggestion of henpecking. Therefore, the only maneuver available to her for limiting her husband's involvement in extra-familial interests was to emphasize her own helplessness and timidity. In this way she might hope, by engendering guilt feelings, to induce him to pay increased attention to the family. Initially, however, she avoided this approach, perhaps because she had learned from the experience of her mother-in-law that her husband could resist a martyrly attitude; and while becoming not a whit less dependent and needful, she assumed a tolerant and self-abnegating posture designed to convey that she would cheerfully make the best of the situation. As the years wore on and Edward Dickinson, guilt feelings or no, continued to spend most of his time out of the house, she became "plaintive."[82] Early in the marriage, however, she seems not to have protested much, though she did speak, however weakly, for increased domesticity whenever the opportunity to do so arose. For example, when Edward wrote from Boston that he hoped a particular issue being debated in the legislature would soon be settled so that he might return home in a week, his wife replied: "My dear I can not but rejoice that you are happy in your home, & that you do not seek the honors of a public life May it ever be so."[83]

That Edward was uneasily aware of his neglect of his wife and children is suggested by his constantly reiterated reassurances to Mrs. Dickinson that despite his multiple and far-flung activities he would much prefer to be home. He wrote in 1838: "I know that it is a great deal for you to be left alone with the little children, in the winter, and I have, from the first, felt it deeply—this . . . has made me pass many sober hours."[84] To this, his wife replied, smiling, as it were, through her tears: "I have evry thing provided for my comfort and I know my dear husband does not leave me except from a sense of duty . . . I get along better than I expected with them [the children] without your aid. Still I should truly be happy of a little of your assistance."[85] Edward answered: "You need not be assured again, that I want to see you all . . . [I] wonder why I could suffer myself to be sent here: If I once more get home, & get through, here, I shall stay. I hope to be of some service to the College—this is all that induces me to be willing for a day, to stay here." These protestations about his longing to be "in my own family circle, & enjoy the sweets of domestic intercourse" notwithstanding, in the same letter he says with obvious satisfaction that he has made his first speech in the House, and "I find it no terrible thing, after all."[86] And in 1842 (four years later) he again went to Boston, this time as a state senator.

Lest his wife not be sufficiently convinced of his sincere desire to return to the hearth, he followed up his previous assurances in his next letter: "Our separation increases the affection which has ever existed between us . . . Home is the place for me—& the place of all others to which I am most attached." He continued, in an obvious attempt to placate and flatter, "and I need not tell you what constitutes its chief attraction—or what makes it so desirable."[87] The constant stress on his domesticity suggests that he had a need to convince himself as well as his wife.

Mrs. Dickinson relied on religious consolation to a greater degree than any other member of her family, and she prayed for her husband's conversion. Edward, on the other hand, was relatively indifferent to church, an attitude reflected in his surprise when a sermon he heard in Boston engaged his favorable attention: "As little regard as I have for such things, I was really charmed."[88] He was tactful, however, in expressing his appreciation of his wife's prayers for him, as his pious words indicate: "Were I a Christian, my dear, it would give me great pleasure in anticipating the happy time, when you and I should be spending that eternal Sabbath of enjoyment, in company, which is promised to all who are redeemed—May it ever be so? Can we ever be separated? And have the end of our lives here, be the last we shall ever be permitted to see & enjoy each other's society? Can it be that we cannot continue to enjoy these precious interviews which give us such pure & unalloyed pleasure? You know my whole heart so well, that you can not but believe that it would be the greatest cause of rejoicing if I were what I so much wish & hope to be [that is, a Christian]."[89] Is it possible that the prospect of spending an eternity of Sabbaths with his wife could conceivably have had something to do with his putting off joining the church for another twelve years?

Occasionally Mrs. Dickinson invoked the children as a persuasion for his return: "[Emily] speaks of her Father with much affection. She sais she is tired of living without a father."[90] In his answering letter Edward seems to have forgotten his protestation that only a sense of obligation to the college keeps him in Boston, and it is obvious that he is thoroughly enjoying his job. "I find many gentlemen here, with whom I am much pleased," he wrote his wife, "& form new acquaintances, every day", and he proceeded to tell her of the arduous preparations he must make to do justice to the "subjects [which] come up in which I am interested." He concluded the letter with an apology: "My family is the object of my thoughts, & my exertions—and without them, there would be little to prompt me to make exertion."[91]

As might be expected of so unassertive a woman, Mrs. Dickinson seems to have had difficulty in disciplining her children, and there is indication that Austin, in particular, was quite restive as a child. A letter to Edward from his sister-in-law regarding a possible visit by Austin, then five years old, reads: "Perhaps Austin will think it is his turn next—but I do not dare to have him under my care yet."[92] One gets the impression that Austin had totally escaped Mrs. Dickinson's feeble authority. Later, when Austin was thirteen and living at boarding school, his father wrote him: "I sent you there to improve."[93] It is perhaps indicative of Edward Dickinson's recognition of his wife's religiosity and his appraisal of her ability to manage her children that he purchased *The Mother at Home* sometime during her third pregnancy. This tract, written by the Reverend John S. C. Abbott of Worcester, Massachusetts, was published in 1833. Subtitled *The Principles of Maternal Duty,* it is, in the author's words, a manual of "practical utility" for mothers "looking eagerly for information regarding the government of their children."[94]

This 177-page evangelical tour de force attempts to impress upon mothers the enormity and importance of their responsibility toward their children. The point is made and elaborated that the obligation to insure the piety of the child and therefore the ultimate heavenly reward of that piety devolves upon the mother primarily and is a matter that she must take seriously. The author lays down certain basic rules to be followed to incline the child to God. The measures he advocates, regardless of what one may think of their impact on the emotional well-being of the child and the mother, were no doubt effective in achieving their proximate purpose—the obedience of the child. He proves himself a knowledgeable practical psychologist: "There are fundamental principles," he says, "in operating upon the human mind, as well as in any other science."[95] Blandly, he proceeds to help the mother apply these principles in a systematic and, from our viewpoint, sometimes ruthless way.

The Reverend Mr. Abbott thus provides us with the flavor of common parental attitudes and the extrapersonal atmosphere that prevailed throughout the poet's childhood. It cannot be proved beyond all doubt that Edward Dickinson, merely by purchasing this book for his wife, necessarily expected her to follow its every precept. Nevertheless, a study of the available biographical material strongly suggests that the poet's parents were in sympathy with its general tenor and most probably studied it and let themselves be guided by it.

For example, one of Emily Dickinson's earliest experiences with death perhaps reflects a strange inconsistency on the part of her parents that *The Mother at Home* helps to resolve. The facts are that at the age of thirteen Emily made frequent visits to the bedside of a playmate of her own age, one Sophia Holland, who was slowly dying of "brain fever"—presumably some form of meningitis or encephalitis. Later, after the child died, Emily was allowed to gaze at the corpse, had to be led away, could not weep, and ultimately gave way to a "fixed melancholy,"[96] a depressive reaction that lasted almost two months. It is clear that the impact this experience had on Emily was profound and, by present-day standards, far from salutary. When death is presented to children as a natural and not always regrettable process, without emphasis on the dreadful possibility of eternal damnation and torment following in its wake, it is usually possible for them to accept the fact with relative equanimity. However, when death is tightly linked with ideas of guilt, retribution, eternal torment, and a wrathful Father in heaven, the occurrence of death may assume the aspect of a terrifying reminder of one's own wickedness and vulnerability.

The elder Dickinsons, through Abbott, may well have had something to do with Emily Dickinson's overreaction to her friend's death. Both parents were scrupulously attentive to the well-being of their children. Surely, therefore, they would not have encouraged or allowed their daughter's repeated presence in Sophia's sickroom had Emily's exposure to a potentially contagious and fatal disease been the only factor they took into consideration. What does seem likely is that they may have deliberately precipitated their daughter into these painful circumstances for what the Reverend Mr. Abbott had persuaded them was a compensatory and higher good beyond considerations of mere bodily danger; or that if Emily did slip over to see Sophia, she did so at least partly because they, following Abbott, had already developed in her an unusual interest in and vulnerability to death scenes. Abbott says of such critical events as the death of friends, "One of the most important duties of the mother is to *watch for these occasions and diligently to improve them.*[97] He then provides several examples of occasions so "improved." Here is one:

> A child in the neighborhood dies. Your daughter accompanies you to the funeral. She looks upon the lifeless corpse of her little companion. And shall a mother neglect such an opportunity to teach her child the meaning of death? When your daughter retires to sleep at night, she will most certainly think of her friend who has died. As you speak to her of the eternal world to which her friend has gone—of the judgment seat of Christ—of the new scenes of joy or woe upon which she has entered, will not her youthful heart feel? And will not tears of sympathy fill her eyes? And as you tell your daughter that she too soon must die; leave all her friends; appear before Christ to be judged; and enter upon eternal existence; will not the occurrence of the day give a reality and an effect to your remarks which will long be remembered?

And with the assurance of one who has thus terrified many little children, he adds, "There are few children who can resist such appeals."[98]

If Edward Dickinson or his wife took Emily aside following the death of her little friend and told her, "You too, Emily, must soon die and like Sophia leave your family and all your friends and be judged by Christ," it is hardly surprising that this hypersensitive and imaginative girl responded to Sophia's death with terror and depression. The effects of such a confrontation, as the good minister well knew, would be to "produce an impression upon the mind, which all future years cannot remove."[99]

It appears probable, then, that if the Dickinsons did not actually use Abbott's book as a handbook for the raising of their children, as the incident of Sophia Holland's death suggests they did, they at least shared the same cultural outlook as John Abbott—his book was popular, and a further printing was called for as many as twenty years after its first appearance. We might, therefore, safely assume that some features of Emily Dickinson's adult personality in addition to her obsession with mortality can be illuminated by an examination of this book as an influence on her childhood. Certainly the interaction of her parents' personalities as molded by the child-rearing philosophy of the times is reflected in *The Mother at Home.*

Neither Emily nor her brother Austin nor her sister Lavinia, for example, ever quite succeeded in outgrowing childhood dependency on their father. As I have pointed out, Edward Dickinson's first objective as a married man, and even earlier as the obsequious Emily Norcross's fiancé, was to establish himself as the absolute and unquestioned authority in his household. He remained so until his death, when his children were well into middle age. It is said that even after his death his daughters were afraid to do anything that would have displeased him. In the externals of speech and behavior their subjugation was complete, and there is evidence in the poet's writings to suggest that even in the privacy of thoughts and fantasies, when they rebelled and defied him, his children suffered the pangs of outraged conscience.

The Mother at Home provides a method whereby a parent can establish just such a stranglehold on the lives and characters of his children. The infant Emily Dickinson as the woman-in-embryo must have partaken of the paradox the poet later became —a preternaturally sensitive and vulnerable creature with an inflexible core. The same kernel of stubborn persistence and independence of viewpoint that made her a unique poet may have given at least Mrs. Dickinson pause as she read Mr. Abbott's dicta: "The first thing therefore to be aimed at is to bring your child under perfect subjection."[100] And again: "Let it be an immutable principle in family government, that your word is law";[101] and, "The very first appearances of insubordination must be checked."[102] As one is led to assume from the evidence of emotional constriction in their children's later lives (for which at least one of them was able to compensate in fantasy), the Dickinson parents very likely took such sayings to heart, and Edward Dickinson probably did his best to help his gentle wife make them the keystone of her "family government."

One need not imagine the effect on a precocious child of the inevitable clashes, precipitated by Mr. Abbott's precepts, between the parental will and the self-assertive efforts of the child as the parents attempt to put the minister's advice into practice, for he provides us with a vivid example of such a contest:

A father asks his four-year-old son, John, to read the letters of the alphabet to him. The son, not for the moment in the mood for such an exercise, pretends he does not know the letters. The father insists and the child becomes increasingly stubborn. After each of John's failures to cooperate, the father spanks the child with increasing vehemence, "as severely as he dared to do it." The child continues to resist "with his whole frame in agitation." The father, though he "had already punished his child with a severity which he feared to exceed," is willing nevertheless to go further to establish his mastery over the boy. "The mother sat by, suffering of course, most acutely, but perfectly satisfied that it was their duty to subdue the child, and that in such a trying hour a mother's feelings must not interfere." Finally the child, his spirit broken, submits and recites the letters.

"'What letter is that my son?' said the mother.

"'A,' said John. He was evidently perfectly subdued. The rest of the children were sitting by, and they saw the contest, and they saw where was the victory. And John learnt a lesson which he never forgot—that his father had an arm too strong for him. He learned never again to wage such an unequal warfare. He learned that it was the safest and happiest course for him to obey ... It is by no means impossible that upon the decisions of that hour depended the character and happiness of that child for life, and even for eternity."[103]

It is a sad irony that in viewing Emily Dickinson's life one can hardly quarrel with Abbott's conclusion that a series of such encounters may decide the character and happiness of a child for life. The characteristic features of such a parent-child relationship, if they pervade all the child's communications with his parents throughout his formative years, would of necessity give an ineradicable stamp to all further intercourse with other human beings. The relevance of this fact to the poet's habit of keeping her views to herself and writing them down in private is clear, and also illuminates her resistance to having her work published during her lifetime. She could write her dissenting "letter to the world" (poem 441), but she had been deprived of the boldness to defy the world face to face.

Besides exercises in parental tyranny, *The Mother at Home* recommends other measures that the Dickinsons may well have adopted, and these also would assuredly have fostered Emily's eventual timidity and insecurity. For example, Mr. Abbott prompts the parent to set himself up as invincible and omnipotent; then, when he is firmly established on this throne in the mind of the child, he is to confess, at the very moment when the child could benefit from his strength, that he is powerless to offer him any protection. And not only from death, which was a constant marauder of childhood in nineteenth-century New England, but from many other external dangers which one might expect the parents to guard against.

Here are Mr. Abbott's recommendations for comforting a child during a "dark and tempestuous night." For the full effect of this passage one should bear in mind the immense gloom of that mansion in Amherst in the gaslight era.

> The rain beats violently upon the windows. The wind whistles around the corners of the dwelling. All without is darkness and gloom. The mind of the child is necessarily affected by this rage of the elements. You embrace the opportunity to inculcate a lesson of trust in God. "My son," you say, "it is God who causes this wind to blow, and the rain to fall. Neither your father nor I can cause the storm to cease, or increase its violence. If God wished, He could make the wind blow with such fury as to beat in all the windows and destroy the house. But God will take care of you, my son, if you sincerely ask Him. No one else can take care of you. I hope that you will pray that God will protect you, and your father, and me, tonight."[104]

The slender reassurance the child got from this sermon would have been negligible if on the stormy day the child had been naughty, a circumstance Abbot instructs the mother to deal with as follows: "Just before leaving him for the night, she tells him in a kind but sorrowful tone, how much she is displeased, and how much God must be displeased with his conduct. As usual she hears him say his prayers, or kneels by the bedside, and prays that God will forgive him. She then leaves him to his own reflections and to sleep. He is thus punished for his fault."[105]

One imagines that the gentle Mrs. Dickinson would have preferred this disciplinary approach to the kind of pitched battles John had with his father, which, one suspects, must at times have been indulged in by Edward Dickinson. Mrs. Dickinson would have expressed her displeasure in "a kind but sorrowful tone." Now the child who is spanked, even if with undue severity, has one advantage over the one who is made to feel that he has hurt his soft and harmless mother by his misbehavior. The former child can secretly regard his abusive parent as a bully who uses his advantages of size and strength unfairly to bring the child to submission. The child can express his anger and hatred with little compunction, if not openly at least in the form of sadistic fantasies of what he promises himself will take place when he is grown up and strong and the tables are turned. But the child whose mother "frowned with a smile,"[106] who takes the child's misdemeanors very much to heart as an additional cross that she must bear, and who reacts to misbehavior, though deeply saddened, by asking God's mercy—not for herself but for the unworthy culprit—this child is condemned to protracted and painful guilt. He cannot look forward, as can the other child, to redress in a brighter future. He can only hope that God will not inflict some dreadful punishment upon him for his having been so bad—for causing his innocent mother to grieve.

It is not difficult to see why the infliction of a sense of guilt upon the young Emily Dickinson might have been an effective way to get her to obey. Because she resented her mother to begin with, her conscious attitude was itself guilt-inducing. The woman who tells a stranger "I never had a mother" is planting thorns of conscience in her own flesh, even though the admission may afford some temporary relief of pent-up bitterness. That Emily Dickinson as a child would have dared to be this outspoken in her resentment seems unlikely. She probably felt revolted by her helpless and ineffectual mother and consequently suffered pangs of conscience. She thus would have been particularly vulnerable to this most insidious of Mr. Abbott's manipulations.

Consider another passage: "Before he falls asleep, you will remind him of his sin. Show him how wicked it was, and how displeased God must be. Tell him that when he is asleep he will die, unless God keeps him alive."[107] Unnervingly, the experienced molder of children adds, "Under such instructions, almost every child would desire to ask forgiveness."

If Mrs. Dickinson, herself so much acquainted with death through the loss of three brothers, one sister, and her mother, told the erring child, "When you sleep you will die unless God keeps you alive," we can readily appreciate with what terrible conviction the warning would have been conveyed and accepted. Emily Dickinson's later fears and obsessions, like a gathering stream, took their origin in many psychological springs, but we can well believe that the direction they would flow was partly determined by the training provided by her parents.

To refer to the excerpt above again: "how much she is displeased, and how much God must be displeased." Here the price of pleasing God is total subjugation to the parents. It seems not to matter whether in a given instance what the parents demand may appear unjust to the mind of the child—God is on their side. It appears likely that if the parents are perceived as arbitrary or unfeeling by the child or, worse, as deriving a covert satisfaction from their child's humiliation, the preachments may go awry and fail to produce their intended effect. The parents' hope, of course, is to bolster their authority by allying themselves with God. But what happens if the parents are not able to temper their severity with a sufficiently generous outpouring of love is that God is subsequently reduced for the child to the stature of a tyrant like them. In this way the child's faith is undermined and his inner rebellion is extended to include the deity. Thus the child brought up with so much piety, who sees his parents pray, attend church, pay tithes, and set up all manner of other "good" examples, is torn with religious conflicts and is unable—in the words applied to Emily Dickinson—to "accept Christ."

Readers of Emily Dickinson are familiar with the lifelong dismay with which she struggled to keep in repair a faith that was constantly crumbling. With every loss, her faith in a benign God suffered a dislocation and had to be re-regulated. Her agitated vacillations from doubt to belief and back to doubt again were not the cool and skeptical cerebrations of a philosopher free to play with the problem as an intellectual issue. Emily Dickinson was desperate to resolve the question once and for all, and the overwhelming need of her consciousness was to believe. The extremity of her exertions and her failure to achieve a stable resolution suggest strongly that the issue had a hidden core. It may be that one of the reasons that she could not accept the religion of her family was that in doing so she would be pleasing them too much, especially her mother: when parents are sternly authoritarian or seductively guilt-inducing, they inevitably confound their children, who consequently do not go out of their way to gratify them.

In nineteenth-century New England, however, the *direct* expression of anger was not tolerated in women and children, and it is vehemently condemned by Abbott. According to him, it is not only wickedness but "temporary insanity."[108] If Emily Dickinson had come to feel resentful toward her parents, she could only have discharged her irritation circuitously. One unconscious way she seems to have avenged herself on her mother was to find herself unable to experience conversion to the religion so dear to Mrs. Dickinson. The slight interest she took in political and community issues and her total physical withdrawal from society was a way of covertly repudiating her public-spirited father. Moreover, the ascetic life style the poet later adopted and her apparent lack of any real fulfillment undoubtedly afflicted her parents far more poignantly than any open defiance.

The idea that such subtle expressions of anger by the child toward the parents would be effective is supported by Abbott, who assures the mother that when a child is lost to heaven the fault usually lies with her. He promises that the Christian family will be reunited in heaven: "A gentleman was once asked if he had *lost* any of his children. 'No,' he replied, 'I have two in heaven, but have *lost* none.' "[109] To the elder Dickinsons it must have seemed that in Austin and Lavinia they had two they might meet again in heaven, but in Emily they had surely lost one.

Are there any further hints in Abbott's book as to the means by which Emily's mother, with the full support of her culture, may have exacerbated her daughter's feelings of resentment? Harsh discipline, even when meted out by an occasionally intemperate man like Edward Dickinson, if combined with sufficient love and regard for the child's needs as an individual, does not ordinarily provoke an undying grudge. *The Mother at Home,* taken in conjunction with certain biographical facts, suggests a vehicle of provocation subtler than punishment. One childhood pang characteristic of the puritan culture which Emily Dickinson must have felt keenly was a consequence of the idea that it was salutary to confer only niggardly praise for any accomplishment except conformity to the prescribed moral requirements. The poet as a child and adolescent surely hungered for parental approbation and encouragement of her stunning imaginative talents. But if Edward Dickinson and his wife adhered closely to the mores as interpreted by Abbott, they grudged their approval to a degree that made it a negligible factor in their daughter's motivation to be a poet. When one thinks of the odds against which Emily Dickinson fought to bring her poetic talent to fruition and how unnecessarily difficult and lonely the effort was, Abbott's advice seems tragically inappropriate. Making no allowances for the child who is truly superior, he says, "Guard against the possibility of [the child's] supposing that he says remarkable things, and is superior to other children."[110] He believes it is a parent's "duty to approve children when they do right, and to disapprove when they do wrong,"[111] but for intellectual or artistic effort he provides no such incentive. The danger lies in the child's "little heart being puffed up with vanity"; and he declares, "How few persons are there who can bear praise!"[112] With this advice (and her own intellectual limitations) Mrs. Dickinson, regardless of any inclination to foster her daughter's talent, would have been paralyzed.

Of course, far more serious and more likely to stimulate an elemental frustration was her emotional inaccessibility and inability to comfort and "mother" her young children. Naturally her inadequacies in this regard, exacerbated by her husband, were no fault of Abbott's. Yet Abbott may have bolstered her lack of warm involvement with her children by providing Mrs. Dickininson with a basis for rationalizing her deficiency as a virtue conducive to good "family government": Abbott held that even the expression of maternal tenderness and compassion was suspect and best curtailed if there was any tendency for it to border on indulgence.

Abbott says that under no circumstances should a mother defend her child against the righteous wrath of the father, and he refers to such interventions as "wicked sympathy and caresses." He calls such a mother "the most cruel and merciless enemy her child can have" because she allows "maternal feelings to influence [her] to neglect painful but necessary acts of discipline."[113] In another place he goes so far as to assert that a child pampered by its mother is in danger of becoming insane through ungoverned passions that soon become ungovernable. Certainly, solacement and softness were dangers to be guarded against.

It is appropriate to wonder just how effective Abbott's advice as employed by them was for the Dickinson parents. Apparently Abbott's various techniques for inducing fear and guilt were not enough to subdue Austin in the absence of his father. Even with his father at home Austin was not overly submissive. As we know from Emily's letters, in his twenties he was not too intimidated to "fisticuff" (undoubtedly mild verbal sparring) with his father whenever they were together. Emily and Vinnie, however, seem to have been easier for Mrs. Dickinson to manage, perhaps because any failure of her discipline would eventually be backed up by her husband, and both girls quailed before his withering eye and intense temper. However, where Mrs. Dickinson was most effective was in all probability not in the crisis of the moment but in the long stretch. Guilt and insecurity in the end are probably more powerful motivators than periodic aggressions in the name of discipline. Guilt feelings tend to become incorporated into the personality, where they exert their steady undermining influence even in the absence of the disciplinarian. Abbott seems to have provided a vehicle whereby Mrs. Dickinson was enabled to transmit these characteristics of her personality to Emily and, to some extent perhaps, to Lavinia also.

It is apparent that the precepts advanced in *The Mother at Home* were not new. The Reverend Mr. Abbott's purpose was to provide parents with a formula for setting up and reenforcing certain convictions and responses in the minds of their children. Among these were: a sense of guilt, a highly developed and rigid conscience, the repression of anger, the supremacy of the parents as God's representatives (especially the father, who as final authority was endowed almost with omnipotence), a sense of the impermanence and brittleness of life, the fear of death and judgment—all of which were an accepted part of nineteenth-century New England culture. Abbott, in his capacity as guide to mothers, was an agent of this tradition, and as such he exerted a molding force on the children of the era. Yet we have only one Emily Dickinson. Obviously one can overestimate the formative influence of the prevailing cultural patterns on the personality of a given child.

The culture defines the roles of parents and children, but it does not, of course, confer on either their essential individuality. The general culture and the specific social structures within it delineate a circumscribed area of behavior within which parents and children can interact and relate. It determines the acceptable limits to which either side can go in its intercourse with the other and it prescribes the general transactional style. These aspects of nineteenth-century Amherst are well documented in *The Mother at Home.* Possible within the rigid limits imposed, however, are widely dissimilar relationships, depending on the constitutional make-up as well as the psychodynamics of the individuals involved.

In Emily Dickinson's time, the "average" parent in rearing the "average" child produced something not far from the New England stereotype. However, when an atypical parent found his own inner emotional needs at odds with the conscience he shared with the culture, distortions inevitably occurred, and pious admonitions such as Abbott's were likely to be subverted or to take on an intensity they were not intended to have. In such a case the deviant impulses would be forced to find an outlet in seeming conformity with the collective standards of behavior as set forth in his book and elsewhere. This is true because psychological reactions, including those we call symptomatic, are always to some degree adaptive, even in their most extreme forms. They are hence not only expressions of the various kinds of conflicts within the individual but, in a wider sense, expressions of the culture and social structures in which they arose.

For example, a mother today who, for whatever reason, is struggling to suppress unconscious hostility toward her child might express her destructive feelings through overpermissiveness. In thus failing to impose reasonable limits to her daughter's behavior, she exposes her to various dangers, and if her misdeeds get too far out of hand, to the retributions of society. Such an aggressive outlet in a mother would have been rare in Emily Dickinson's milieu, which, as has been noted, equated permissiveness with reprehensible negligence.

In contrast, a nineteenth-century Amherst mother with similar covert impulses would probably vent her animosity in seeming conformity with John Abbott's formulas. Accordingly, she would make her child feel unduly guilty for minor misdeeds and frighten her with the insecurity of life and the wrath of God. Both the nineteenth-century and twentieth-century women, however, would be able to convince themselves that they were "good" mothers acting with the sanction of the prevailing norms.

Similarly, fathers who secretly regard their offspring as irksome encumbrances express their unconscious rejection in various more or less subtle ways. Abbott invites the father to take out his aggression in the most primitive way possible—physically—

the only stipulation being that it must be for the child's spiritual good. He says, "[the parent] inflicts real pain—pain that will be remembered." And he tells the parent, "all you have to do is cut off its source of enjoyment, or inflict bodily pain, so steadily and so invariably that disobedience and suffering shall be indissolubly connected in the mind of the child."[114] The contest with John over the reading of his letters is a good example of the way puritan culture urged and sanctioned the direct expression of parental aggression under the guise of morality.

For Abbott the obedience of the child—even if bought at the price of fear, a sense of sin and unworthiness, and the suppression of natural impulses—is the mother's highest achievement. No matter that the child withdraws from her, only reluctantly participates in the mother's domestic activities, appears disdainful of the mother's friends, seems uninclined to share the mother's feminine interests, and in every other way indicates unmistakably the depth of their emotional estrangement. If the child is deeply enough concerned with her own wickedness and sufficiently fearful of death and its consequences, these "salutary" reactions promise a happy outcome, and the mother can rest comfortably in Abbott's reassurance that she has served her purpose well.

If I appear to be concentrating on the gloomy side of Emily Dickinson's childhood it is because the brighter side is overstressed by most of her biographers. The relatively humane aspects of Abbott's book are no more relevant here than were the sleigh rides, maple sugar parties, excursions to Mount Vernon, and other such pleasant occasions of Emily Dickinson's youth. *They* did not cause her to fear strangers and shut herself away. There is no doubt that she did have some good times, that she had a gift for satire and a delightful sense of humor; and there is no doubt also that when the three of them were together—Austin, Emily, and Vinnie—and father and mother were at some remove, they enjoyed themselves hugely, had many jokes, shared their reading experiences with one another, and took pleasure in one another's achievements. Without these benefits, Emily's life might have been literally unbearable. But basically daily life in the mansion appears to have been unhappy, even though, decade after decade, from the viewpoint of the neighbors, the old brick house stood unremittingly placid. Inside, there seems to have been little real contentment; Emily and her sister and brother speak of being troubled from their earliest years. The major sources of their discontent have now been presented, but certain threads still need to be drawn together.

Some pages back I attempted to demonstrate two interrelated dynamisms of Edward Dickinson's subsurface personality that were not distinctly evident to his contemporaries, who, we are told, misunderstood him. These two motive forces are (1) the unconscious need to deny any and all feelings of dependency and weakness; and (2) an urgent and essential need to substitute for these passive and receptive impulses a countervailing striving for power, influence, and mastery over others. Because of the former characteristic he "never played," rarely softened, never relented in his independence and self-sufficiency. He suffered, accordingly, from estrangement from his contemporaries, from loneliness, and from lack of the capacity to accept the emotional sheltering of those who loved him. His children also suffered from this need of his for emotional distance. Lavinia is said to have remarked: "[Father] never kissed us good night in his life—He would have died for us, but he would have died before he would have let us know it!"[115] And similarly, Austin, at his father's funeral, kissed the corpse and murmured, "there, father, I never dared do that while you were living."[116] His father's sternness and remoteness cast a blight on Austin's childhood which there is no doubt the son bitterly resented. In a letter to his future wife, Sue, full of romantic reminiscences of the pastoral harmonies of boyhood, his father is included among the few sour notes. "I loved loved loved everybody," he writes, "*only* Edward Wheelock . . . all the girls—but Cynnithy Hubbard . . . all the men but father & the school teacher & the minister."[117] Austin's decision to enter his father's profession did more than a little to diminish the gulf between them, Edward Dickinson reacting to his son's choice of career with touching pleasure and taking it as proof, no doubt justifiably, of his son's respect. The sudden rapprochement appears, understandably, both to have pleased and to have discomforted Austin. He informs Sue of a visit with his father in words that reveal the distance the two men have had to traverse to approach each other. "He seems very happy . . . to have me with him," he writes, "has been pleasanter & more familiar & fatherly towards me in his visit this time than I ever knew him . . . he has found so much happiness in me—& thinks so much more of me—talked so familiarly & frankly—& seemed so much more to love to have me with him. He would hardly let me come back to Cambridge Wednesday evening & wanted me to stay with him all night—but I thought it wouldn't help to get *too* affectionate—all at once—so I stayed with him as long as I could & got aboard the half past eleven train for Cambridge & waved him Good bye."[118]

Even Emily, for all her intuitive grasp of her father's loneliness, is quoted by her cousin as once having remarked: "I am not very well acquainted with father."[119] The extent to which Edward Dickinson regarded any expression of his repudiated "gentleness" as incompatible with his position is clear from a remark of Austin made to his future wife: "I have always been brought up to the idea that it was not a man's part to *show* any one a tenderness unless in sore distress."[120]

The second characteristic—Edward Dickinson's driving ambition and overcompensatory self-reliance—gratified his pride and enhanced his sense of virility and manly adequacy, but his almost desperate need to secure them impaired the emotional life of his children. What I have been postulating as characteristic psychological functioning in Edward Dickinson is the ego defense mechanism of *reaction-formation*; that is, he contained those of his impulses that were incongruous with his self-concept and injurious to his self-esteem, first, through repression from consciousness and, second, through transforming them with great vigor into their self-reassuring opposites.

If Edward Dickinson secretly regarded the needs of his wife and children, their forcing on his attention continuing domestic and paternal responsibilities, as threats to his habitual defense of masculine overstriving, his spontaneous response to such a menace would be anger and a wish to escape the encumbering claims. But Edward Dickinson was not the man to allow himself resentful impulses toward responsibilities that he incurred voluntarily, especially those involving his family. The same conscience that made him Amherst's most dependable lawyer and the same idealistic zeal that made him, as one Amherst contemporary said, "one of the firmest pillars of society, education, order, morality and every good cause"[121] would have rendered such feelings intolerable to him, and consequently he would inevitably have repressed them. But repressed urges seek expression in accordance with the structure of the particular personality in which they operate. Because in Edward Dickinson's make-up reaction-formation played such a conspicuous part, one should expect that any resentful, hostile, or destructive impulses toward his wife and children would be converted into their opposite—that is, an excessive concern for their health, welfare, and safety, and an excessive preoccupation with circumventing the real and imagined evils that might befall them.

The magnitude of Edward Dickinson's anxiety for the welfare of the family he so persistently left behind is strikingly conveyed in the letters he wrote to his wife when the children were small. He writes: "My *positive injunction* is, that *you do not* go into the *vestry,* on *any account,* for *any purpose,* in my absence. Now don't disregard this. I shall find it out, if you do. It is a most dangerous place."[122] Again he writes: *"You must not go into the yard, yourself,* on any account—there is no necessity for it, and you *must not do it."*[123] And again: "Keep your doors all safely locked, nights—which I presume, you will not forget, tho' nothing is going to hurt you."[124] (The "nothing is going to hurt you" reassurance, as any dentist or physician well knows, is invariably interpreted by the recipient in an exactly opposite sense and arouses only increased fright.) Again he assures her, "I hope you will get along comfortably nights—don't feel timid, or nervous—but conclude that nothing will hurt you—be careful about fire—above all things."[125] And in another letter: "Do not overdo —nor exert yourself too much—don't go out, evenings, on any account—nor too much, in the afternoon. It is better for you, in cold weather, to stay at home . . . Don't let Austin be out too much in cold, stormy weather. Emily must not go to school, at all. Keep Lavinia from croup & fits—be careful of the state of her system—if any of you are unwell, *let me know it*—don't keep it secret from me. *This I insist upon."*[126]

On one occasion Mrs. Dickinson writes that Emily and Lavinia have been ill and she has been worried and called the physician: "Whilst reading your letter last evening," she tells her husband, "I could not suppress the rising tear, I did wish so much to see you, I felt as though I must fly to you . . . it is wrong for me to endulge such feelings."[127] Edward's reply combines guilt feelings about being away with what seem to be clearly identifiable unconscious death wishes: "It grieves me that you should be so troubled & broken of your rest," he writes, "while I am where I can render you no assistance, let what will, befal you. I do feel almost guilty to be absent from my little family . . . and blame myself for it . . . I know the sacrafice you make in having me absent, is not small—with your natural timidity, & your strong reliance on your husband in time of trouble, I can imagine your suffering . . . I fear [the children] all will get the Canker-rash, which prevails all over the Country. If either of them should have it, write me immediately, and I shall go home. If one of them should be taken away, & you did not let me know that it was sick, beforehand, I should never forget it."[128] He then mentions some gifts that he is sending his wife and children, perhaps as balm to his stricken conscience. Over and over he cautions his wife to warn Austin "to be careful about the cattle hooking or hurting [him]";[129] and he also warns Austin: "Austin, be careful, & not let the woodpile fall on you."[130] To Lavinia, age five, he writes: "You must not go out to stay, in the cold—if you do, you will have the *croup*."[131] And to Emily, "You must not go to school, when it is cold, or bad going—You must be very careful, & not get sick."[132] He tells Austin to "Take good care of Emily . . . & not let her get hurt."[133] And he admonishes Emily, when she was thirteen and in Boston, "be careful about wetting your feet or taking cold—& not get lost";[134] and "When you come home—be careful, & get out of the Cars at *Palmer*—dont fall, keep hold of something all the time, till you are safely off—lest they should start, & throw you down."[135]

In one letter he seems preoccupied with death and relates this directly to his family: "Life is a mere preparatory state for another period of existence . . . I need not tell you that no day passes without my having some reflections on this subject, in connection with you, & our dear little children."[136] This passage is in the letter from Boston in which he tells of making new acquaintances in the state legislature and of his determination to perform well for the public good.

Even more revealing of his secret wish to be rid of his family is his mention of a repeated dream he had on awakening on two consecutive mornings: "I thought there was a great fire devouring my friends in Amherst."[137] This he wrote in response to a letter from his wife telling of a fire that might have destroyed their whole neighborhood had it occurred on a windy night.[138] A later indication of Edward Dickinson's concern with death is found in a letter Emily wrote in answer to T. W. Higginson's request for her photograph: "It often alarms Father—He says Death might occur, and he has Molds [that is, photographs] of all the rest."[139] His worrying about the well-being of his family continued until the end of his life. Less than six months before his death he wrote Austin from Boston: "Should like to receive a note every morning to know how you all are at home."[140]

These obsessive fears that some calamity would befall his family reveal his inner conflict. Consciously, of course, he wished to be a good husband and father. But the need to be a worldly success was evidently a stronger wish, augmented in importance by its role as defense against repudiated and shamefully "unmanly" urges to be dependent and cared for. When it seemed that the demands of his family would preclude the longed-for professional and political triumphs necessary to his self-esteem, the unconscious wish to obliterate the domestic encumbrance became pressing.

Edward's vacillation with regard to his political intentions betrays the conflict of family versus ambition. For example, in 1843 he made up his mind to decline the Whig nomination for state senator, then allowed friends to dissuade him and was ultimately elected. In 1844 he offered a thousand acres of land he owned in Michigan for sale or exchange for local farm lands as if he expected to settle in Amherst for the rest of his life. But eight years later one finds him in Washington, a member of the U.S. House of Representatives.

He was not reelected to this position, perhaps because of what a newspaper called his "truancy" and his neglect of duties for "private business or pleasure."[141] Given his great conscientiousness, however, this surely cannot have been the case. The most likely reason for his frequent absences from Congress is his attempts to meet his responsibilities to his family in Amherst.

That he was torn between competing loyalties there can be little doubt. Ambition beckoned from afar and promised great rewards, family clung tenaciously and worked to confine and immobilize him. Both carried a sense of obligation and duty, but he was driven into the first on waves of inner affirmation and pulled back to the second under the sting of conscience. His imagination, stimulated by disavowed impulses to rid himself of his domestic burden and thus solve his conflict definitively, conjured up disasters of fire, illness, and accident threatening to overtake his family. The unthinkable (to him) aggression underlying these fantasies peopled Amherst for him with miscreants, ready to pounce on his wife and children, and allowed the primitive state of disease prevention and public health measures to spawn a fantasy-plague of family illnesses and early deaths.

It is not difficult to appreciate the effect of all this on his children. The menacing world of his fears tended to become for them the real world. "Father takes care of the doors," Emily writes Austin facetiously, "and mother of the windows, and Vinnie and I are secure against all outward attacks."[142] She says this lightly, but not many years after these lines were written we find her afraid to leave the house and locking herself in her room in fear of an intruder's breaking in. In addition, Edward Dickinson impressed on his wife and children the idea that he was their only bulwark against all the villainy and calamity in the world. Thus, when a dog bit Vinnie's thumb, Emily writes Austin: "this was when father was gone, and of course it frightened us more."[143] And a year after his death, she thanks a friend for an expression of affection, saying: "It helps me up the Stairs at Night, where as I passed my Father's Door—I used to think was safety."[144] And three years later, she writes friends that she was "accustomed to all through Father."[145]

I have already mentioned that a parent harboring concealed hostility toward his offspring will frequently give in to the child's demands, all the while frankly acknowledging that what the child wants is inimical to his welfare. An example of this confusing behavior on the part of Edward Dickinson is recorded in a letter Emily wrote to T. W. Higginson. "He [Father] buys me many Books," she tells Higginson "but begs me not to read them—because he fears they joggle the Mind."[146] When one considers that this letter was written after Emily had manifested some severe psychiatric symptoms and when one takes into account that in the nineteenth century the reading (and writing) of poetry was seriously considered to be an important cause of "insanity," the full incongruity of buying her unsettling books and begging her not to read them becomes apparent. It is reminiscent of the nursery rhyme:

"Mother, may I go out to swim?"
"Yes, my darling daughter.
Hang your clothes on a hickory limb,
But don't go near the water."

Such contradictory communications leave one in doubt as to their exact intent and confront one with the full impact of the other person's ambivalence. According to some observers, the excessive use of such "double bind" admonitions is characteristic of the so-called schizophrenogenic family. A similarly contradictory, though nonverbal, message must have been conveyed to the Dickinson children each time Edward, a militant prohibitionist and one-time member of the West Parish Temperance Association, served sherry and champagne at home. For himself and sometimes for his immediate family—as in this case—ordinary obligations were strangely unbinding. It must have been impossible for the young Emily and her brother and sister to grasp the principles that governed their father's moral determinations. Later in life, each of them had the tendency to conclude that being a Dickinson was to be a law unto one's self; and such a belief, however free and enviable it might seem in theory, is in practice a shaky and anxiety-riddled guide to behavior.

When Edward Dickinson died at seventy-one, his son and daughters were well into middle age. Yet his death was like the collapse of a windward coverture—as if a wall of the mansion had fallen away, leaving them exposed and vulnerable to the world whose menace he had so emphasized. Not surprisingly, he died away from home—of the combined effects of a sudden stroke and a hypersensitivity reaction to morphine. Lavinia bore the loss better than her brother or sister. By tending to the funeral arrangements herself, she spared her brother, who was so overcome that he was in a near stupor. The whole village came to pay its last respects, and Lavinia "denied herself to no one in the hours that succeeded [her father's] death, could weep with those who wept, and tried in gentlest ways to ease the burden."[147] A neighbor observed that "Austin is apparently the most shocked, stunned by the loss of her father."[148] His daughter Martha was indelibly impressed by her father's reaction: "I remember my grandfather's funeral . . . most of all by my terror at my father's grief. The world seemed coming to an end." Unlike Vinnie, who could express her feelings openly and who did not isolate herself

from others, Emily mourned in a constricted, intensely introverted solitude, unable to give of herself in any practical way.
According to Martha, "she stayed upstairs in her own room with
the door open just a crack, where she could hear without being
seen."[149] Her agoraphobia and fear of those outside her family
precluded her attending the church service, though even if this
had not been so her response to her loss was itself so disturbed as
to prevent her participation. Martha's comments on Emily's condition at this time reveal her aunt's derangement. If Emily actually whispered to her, as Martha says she did, "Where is he?
Emily will find him!"[150] one is almost forced to conclude that her
father's death at least for a time unsettled her reason. In a letter
written to her cousins, probably in the following month, Emily
writes of her constant weeping and says, "You might not remember me, dears. I cannot recall myself . . . I cannot write any more,
dears. Though it is many nights, my mind never comes home."[151]

Edward's children mourned their father for years, Austin
doing his best to look after his female relatives and Emily and
Vinnie shut up in the large house with all the blinds drawn. Two
years after Edward's death, Emily writes her cousins: "I dream
about father every night, always a different dream, and forget
what I am doing daytimes, wondering where he is."[152] And five
years later the pain is still not assuaged: "[I] have known little
of Literature since my Father died," she writes Higginson, ". . . To
see you seems improbable, but the Clergyman says I shall see my
Father."[153] If the concept of heaven had any validity at all for
Emily Dickinson, it conveyed a state in which severed relationships could be reestablished and rendered permanently secure. Her
constant dreaming of her father indicates how unready she was
to part with him and suggests the extent of her need to preserve
him alive within her. To dream of him *every night* for two
years—what an extremity of tenacious loyalty and desperate dependency is conveyed in this admission! The reaction would be
less remarkable in a young girl, prematurely denied the support
of a father and not yet at the brink of investing her emotional reserves outside the family. But Emily Dickinson was forty-three at
the time of her father's death. And Edward himself, at seventy-
one, in a century in which the average life expectancy had already
been exceeded by his children, had reached a truly venerable age.
Moreover, Emily had been aware of her father's declining health

for several years. Therefore, although his death was sudden, the family should not have been entirely unprepared. Emily's catastrophic reaction to his death is therefore not to be explained solely on the basis of its precipitousness or untimeliness. Rather, the persistence and vehemence of her mourning was a reflection of the welter of psychological forces that bound her to her father and kept her in a state of uneasy, hostile equilibrium with her mother.

Now, with the diverse elements of the children's interaction with the elder Dickinsons examined, let me attempt a synthesis of these observations with a view to deepening our understanding of the offspring of this curiously mismatched couple. What was the probable total impress of the emotional struggles and marital disharmonies of Edward Dickinson on his famous daughter?

Perhaps the best place to begin is with the most obvious meaning Edward had for Emily: he was an object of her affection. Her strong love for him was peculiarly mingled with respect, admiration to the point of overestimation, amusement at his foibles, exasperation at his rigidity, pity for his loneliness, and a profound, humiliating dependence. Evidence for the existence of all of these aspects of her attachment is readily accessible on the surface of her letters and evident from all other biographical sources. It is possible to regard these attitudes and feelings, which she consciously accepted, as reflective of the stresses of a normal love relationship between a girl and her father, though the overestimation and dependency are exaggerated. But it would be a grave error not to recognize the manner in which her relationship with him modified her understanding of the nature of masculinity and the ways in which it affected her relationship with other men. The quality of Emily Dickinson's love for her father determined (as it does to some degree with all women) the limits of her capacity later to love other men. The fact that her later masculine love objects tended to be fatherly suggests that her attachment to her father was more intense and exclusive than is usual.

Still, all this may be regarded as the affections and attachments of the normal, positive, oedipal situation. If Emily Dickinson had been able to accept her mother as a suitable model of femininity, and thus to accept herself as a female, she would have developed a less conflicted personality. But she rejected her mother as a model for identification. Her mother's actual inadequacies may have been only partly to blame for this response. It probably was also encouraged to a significant degree by Edward Dickinson's attitude toward his wife and toward women in general. For Edward Dickinson, women were distinctly inferior beings. He appears to have held the common nineteenth-century masculine view that they were incapable of serious thought, could not understand what the world of affairs was all about, and were, except for the performance of a very circumscribed assortment of domestic chores, helplessly dependent on masculine strength, foresight, organization, and direction. For him a woman's place was in the home, and her mind, if she had one, was in appropriate use only when she was using it to make her husband's domestic life comfortable. Emily's view of a wife as a supine flower beaten to the ground by the merciless energy of the sun-husband is undoubtedly a distorted reflection of her father's attitudes toward his wife. Naturally enough, in view of her native endowment of high intelligence and emotional vitality, this posture did not suit her.

From the mother-father-daughter triangle there seemed to be only two other routes open to her to resolve the tensions of this configuration of relationships. One was to outdo mother as a superior female—prove that to be a female was not the abject thing her mother's whole demeanor and deportment said it was. This maneuver tends to displace the mother and put the daughter in the mother's place vis-à-vis the father. The other route is to exclude the question of femininity altogether as unworthy of consideration. In this case, one denies that one is female at all, patterns one's self after the admired father and takes on, as far as this is possible, his attributes of authority and dominance and his masculine perspective on life. Characteristically, Emily Dickinson, as a creature who pursued her existence suspended as it were between alternatives, seems to have made no definitive choice. Ramifications of both paths—the competition with the mother for the father's love and the identification with father as a "man" among men—are to be observed in her life and poetry. Her devotion to Edward Dickinson, her protracted disconsolation following his death, her conviction of his uniqueness and irreplaceability, her doting appreciation of his merits, her tendency to form deep attachments to "father figures" such as Judge Lord—in all these one is confronted with the residuals of the positive oedipal attachment to her father. From this also stem certain facets of her devotion to Austin, the parent-child element and also the pain and conflict evinced in the letters to "Master" (otherwise unidentified) and to Judge Lord and in the love poems addressed to a beloved and unattainable man.

We see her competition with her mother in her implicit comparisons of her own merits with her mother's shortcomings. "Mother does not care for thought [as I do],"[154] she says. Mother's faculties are "unobtrusive," but of herself she says as early as age fourteen, "My abilities . . . are neither few nor small."[155] To be with her father alone she has only to "invent an absence for mother,"[156] and Mrs. Dickinson is off on some needless errand or engaged in the performance of some trivial chore. To the same point, Emily's niece Martha wrote that Mrs. Dickinson's "gentle reign" had been "increasingly enfeebled in spite of herself by the dominating daughter."[157] All of these aspects of Emily Dickinson's life are based on a foundation of positive oedipal love for her father, from which flows all that is heterosexual in her as well as some of her inhibitions with regard to this side of her nature.

The other path equally taken and equally abandoned before the end is marked by many indications of her identification with her father. Emily Dickinson had a strongly masculine side derived from her conviction that she was in reality more her father's equal than her mother's, that she possessed much of his intensity of mind and spirit and little of her mother's flaccid and petty domesticity. The psychodynamics of the ocular disorder (see Chapter IX) that afflicted her in her middle thirties reveals another kind of residual of her deeply ingrained sense of masculine identity. Traces of it also appear in her relationships with her girl friends, especially Susan Gilbert, with whom Emily adopted certain features of the role of ardent and pursuing lover. Most significant for American literature, the acceptance of her identification with her father unleashed her active, creative potential and helped her become a poet. Chapter IX examines in detail the poem "My Life had stood — a loaded Gun," which greatly illumines the relationship between Emily Dickinson's creativity and her awareness of a masculine component in her emotional make-up.

The large number of legal terms in her poetry suggests that she took more than a passing interest in her father's and brother's professional discussions and that she found elements of their thought congenial to her and appropriated them for her own uses. The tone of peremptory command so characteristic of Edward Dickinson's letters and, no doubt, his conversation can be heard throughout Emily's early correspondence. Compare Edward's bossiness toward his wife with Emily's toward her brother. In diction and attack the latter is a perfect echo of the former. Here is the father speaking: "It is better for you, in cold weather, to stay at home, pretty much. If you will ride to meeting, send Austin to ask Mr. Frink or Bartlett to carry you. I choose to have you do it."[158] Compare Emily's admonitions to Austin: "You must not stay with Howland after the studies cease—We shall be ready for you, and you must come home from school, not stopping to play by the way!"[159] One cannot imagine the self-effacing Mrs. Dickinson adopting such a military and authoritarian tone.

Besides being the evocator of his daughter's devoted affection and the model for her unconscious imitation, Edward Dickinson contributed greatly to her overconcern with death. Encouraged by Abbott, he habitually pointed out over and over again every possible danger into which his family could fall, inducing in them the view that their hold on life was tenuous. Some basis for this feeling existed in the prevalence of potentially fatal disease untreatable by nineteenth-century medicine, but Edward Dickinson made the world far more frightening than was justified even by the high mortality rates. Compared with ours their lives *were* precarious, but certainly not to the extent Edward Dickinson would have it, with woodpiles crushing small boys and trains throwing down young girls and attackers lurking in church vestries.

But the image he created of a menacing universe was a facade behind which lay concealed a deeper menace—the father himself and all his aggression toward them. The covert hostility beneath the exaggerated protectiveness of his reaction-formations oppressed his family, engendering in them an anxiety all the more disturbing because its real origin remained obscure. They knew that they stood in the way of his achievement of goals that were vitally important to him. They had reason to assume from his reaction to his mother's death that should they die in some fire or epidemic, Edward Dickinson would have mourned them for a time and then thrown himself into his political affairs with an enhanced and liberated enthusiasm. Thus, his transformed "death wishes" would have produced in them a pervasive and dimly conscious fear that he, their only bulwark against a malignant creation, might abandon them.

To appreciate the terrible nature of such a fear, one has only to conjecture the probable plight of Emily Dickinson, with her inordinate dependency and incapacity for practical life, should her father have died before Austin was able to take over the economic support of his mother and sisters. She was too fearful of strangers to teach school or run a shop, too uncertain of her attractiveness and too fearful of heterosexuality to consider marriage. What would have become of her? The question must have occurred to her often; she was aware of the thinness of the ice on which she walked. She would not literally have died, or course; relatives would have made some provision for her. But enforced modifications of habits are catastrophic for rigidly neurotic personalities—as witness, recall Emily's and Mrs. Dickinson's reactions to their simple removal to another house. For this reason, the shakiness of the foundations of Edward Dickinson's loving concern and paternal protectiveness, as betrayed in his recurring dreams and fantasies of the injury or death of his family, undoubtedly had a substantial part in transforming Emily's preoccupation with death into the overriding obsession it eventually became.

As Edward Dickinson's own concern with death was related to unconscious resentment toward his family, so, by the same mechanism, Emily's preoccupation with death was intensified by anything that provoked an anger that could not be openly allowed. Her father's attitude toward femininity in general and toward his wife in particular provided two such provocations.

Edward Dickinson seems clearly to have favored Austin over his daughters. Though the two males clashed frequently, he missed Austin greatly when the son was away from home, overpraised his accomplishments, and was moved to the depths when Austin decided to become a lawyer like himself. Because Emily's relationship with her mother was so unrewarding, the love and esteem of her father took on a special value for her; yet in her father's eyes she had nothing like the importance of his son. Fathers who favor their sons in this way at the expense of their daughters not surprisingly produce hurt and resentful daughters. A girl depreciated for being a girl is powerless to do anything about it and feels strongly the unfairness of her position. She may entertain many hostile feelings toward the favored brother and also toward the father, who she feels has devalued her.

A more serious provocation to anger can be seen in Edward Dickinson's condescending attitude toward his wife. As a young child, Emily would not have cared if her mother were intelligent or not, but she would have been sensitive as all children are to the esteem in which her father held his wife. No doubt Edward Dickinson's poor opinion of his wife's competence added to the difficulties Emily had in accepting her mother. He made it difficult for Emily to admire her through his own lack of admiration. Sometimes it must have seemed to Emily that *he* had deprived her of a mother.

To appreciate the rage he may have provoked in this way consider the intensity of Emily's search for a more suitable mother image upon which to pattern herself. She strove incessantly to find outside her home in more gratifying mother figures, such as her Aunt Lavinia, some of her teachers, and Mrs. J. G. Holland, those womanly virtues that she felt her mother lacked. And her passionate admiration of women authors like Charlotte and Emily Brontë, Elizabeth Browning, George Sand, and George Eliot cannot be based solely on their literary qualities, which she praised extravagantly. One cannot escape the conclusion that it was partly because they were admirable *women* that Emily almost worshipped them. "I am sorry I smiled at women. Indeed, I revere holy ones,"[160] she once said, thereby expressing her contempt for all women except these remote exceptions. Undoubtedly they represented the kind of woman Emily deeply wanted to be, the kind she longed to have as guide, preceptor, and friend. No matter that, in reality, several of these gifted women appear to have been profoundly uncertain of their own femininity. For Emily they no doubt symbolized the kind of assertive, lively, effective, talented, ardent woman she would have liked her mother to be. It seems quite clear that Edward Dickinson's inability to admire and respect his wife contributed largely to Emily's inability to

97

accept her mother. Edward Dickinson therefore had much to do with undermining the status of femininity, and one would be surprised if his daughter did not deeply resent it.

She learned not to express such feelings, however, no doubt realizing that to do so would not make her more lovable to her father or better able to compete with Austin for his affection. Therefore, she thrust the unacceptable and dangerous anger underground, leaving it to find an outlet in one devious way or another. Edward Dickinson unwittingly provided a model for his daughter here also. He turned his hostile wishes into excessive concern for his family's welfare. Emily did the same. Her constant worry that death would take those she loved is one indirect expression of her anger.

In still another way her father may have stimulated rage responses in Emily Dickinson that augmented her obsession with death. Edward Dickinson was a difficult love object indeed. Unable to express his gentleness, remote and forbidding, he must continually have thwarted his children's desire for his warmth and tenderness. He held himself apart and denied them access to his inner life. He was impatient with their bids for his attention. "I did not like to ask Father," Emily says in an 1853 letter to Austin, "because he's always in such a hurry."[161] In another place she characterizes the domestic atmosphere as one of problems to solve and responsibilities to meet rather than one primarily of human relationships. "Was it not crisis all the time," she asks, "in our hurrying Home."[162] Earlier she had told Higginson, "Father [is] too busy with his Briefs—to notice what we do."[163] To a girl who had never experienced a close relationship with her mother, this inattention on the part of her father must have been doubly tormenting. The love needs of children are voracious; the hungry infant screams in rage. The love-starved child has a similar reaction. One cannot be surprised that Emily Dickinson at times thought of herself as a volcano full of suppressed destructiveness. Much of this potential violence seems to have been a reaction to a sense of affectional deprivation, for which both parents, in different ways, were responsible.

It is frequently observed in psychiatric practice that parents indirectly and covertly encourage in their children the expression of impulses whose outlet they deny in themselves. Edward Dickinson seems to have been such a parent. He preached (and practiced) self-reliance, independence, self-assertion, practicality, and responsibility with a rigor that allowed no relaxation from these strenuous virtues. Yet he overprotected his children, directed their lives until they were well beyond maturity, and exercised little tolerance of their differing opinions. The consequence was that they were hampered in their efforts to emancipate themselves and gain adulthood. They tended to withdraw deeper into whatever security the family offered and to retain many of the characteristics of children. Unlike their father, they "played"—Austin with his jokes, his collecting of oil paintings, and his landscaping; Emily with her Shakespeare, her poems, and her flowers; Lavinia with her music, her burlesques of the neighbors (her "take-offs"), and her cats. The father repudiated "reveries" and fantasy life, and his offspring indulged theirs. Clearly he achieved vicarious satisfaction through these "impractical" interests of his children, but the price he paid was high. Through his need to remain free himself of these reprehensible indulgences, he further alienated his children. In effect, they were fated through the quirks of their father's personality to live out what was unfulfilled in him. Moreover, the effort to achieve the emotional support not forthcoming from their parents forced the sisters and brother to turn toward one another with a mutual devotion and interdependence that extended beyond the bounds of healthy affection, isolating them from others. Thus Emily, at the age of twenty-two, writes to Austin, "The Newmans seem very pleasant, but they are not *like us*. What makes a few of us so different from others?"[164] And again, "We're all unlike most everyone, and are therefore more dependent on each other for delight."[165] The full extent to which they were led to meet one another's needs is revealed in Emily's comment about Lavinia, "She has no Father and Mother but me and I have no Parents but her,"[166] a statement especially remarkable because it was made when both of the elder Dickinsons were still living. Accordingly, we find Lavinia in later life devoting her entire attention to sheltering Emily from the least intrusion of the outer world, and Austin, during the bitter years when his marriage foundered, turning to his sisters for consolation to such a degree that Emily could say of him, "My Brother is with us so often each Day, we almost forget that he ever passed to a wedded Home."[167] Emily's reluctant leave-taking of childhood was partly her fear of adulthood but also partly her nostalgia for the comfort she had found in her brother and sister.

Genevieve Taggard, in *The Life and Mind of Emily Dickinson,* made a case for a so-called father-fixation as *the* key to understanding Emily Dickinson's spinsterhood and retreat beneath the paternal roof. And although this explanation alone is insufficient, it is inescapable that Emily Dickinson's relationship with her father and her view of him impaired severely her ability to evolve conflict-free relationships with other men.

She stood in awe of his pure and terrible heart. That is to say, in purpose and standards no other man could be the equal of Father. There may be men who are more charming, or more brilliant, but all are inferior in these particular qualities. To this extent, any prospective suitor, compared with her father, would necessarily fall short. It has been mentioned that Emily Dickinson was moved to deep feelings of affection by men older than herself. The corollary, therefore, to the difficulties a man would have in measuring up to those idealized aspects of the father image is the ambivalence and discomfort she herself would feel upon experiencing erotic feelings for a man who called her father to mind. It is obvious that to some degree Emily Dickinson thought of Judge Lord as a paternal, benign, loving parent. He, however, did not regard her primarily as a daughter. When, in his seventies, he asked Emily, then forty-four, to marry him, she demurred. Not satisfied, he followed up his declaration of love and his offer with a request for some explanation of her refusal, and she answered him in an obscure letter full of the deepest anguish. "Don't you know you are happiest while I withhold and not confer?" she asks him. "If I felt the longing nearer—than in our dear past, perhaps I could not resist to bless it, but must, because it would be right The 'Stile' [that is, the access to sexual encounter] is God's . . . For your great sake—not mine—I will not let you cross—but it is all your's, and when it is right I will lift the Bars, and lay you in the Moss . . . it is Anguish I long conceal from you to let you leave me, hungry, but you ask the divine Crust and that would doom the Bread."[168] Since Mrs. Lord was dead, it seems clear that Emily is merely invoking a pretext to explain her refusal to consider the judge's proposal. Yet she acknowledges also her frigidity, or at least her lack of interest in sexuality: "If I felt the longing nearer *perhaps* I could not resist." In a later letter she makes it clear that in her view a platonic relationship is preferable. "I have a strong surmise," she tells the judge, "that moments we have *not* known [that is, moments of sexual expression] are tenderest to you. Of their afflicting Sweetness, you only are the judge, but the moments we had, were very good—they were quite contenting."[169] She could not bring herself to marry the judge because the thought of sexual union with him apparently was abhorrent to her; he was too like Father: a lawyer, a close friend of Edward Dickinson, a man she had known since childhood—marriage with him would be like committing incest. Yet her letters reveal the depth of her love for him—a love no doubt encouraged by his paternal qualities and association with her father.

In conclusion, as one reviews the many psychodynamic factors operant in the relationship between Emily Dickinson and her parents, one sees that their impact was multiform and of almost incalculable formative influence. Her mother was inadequately loving and nurturing; this deficiency resulted in the daughter's developing a predominantly "oral" personality characterized by clinging to home, dependency, and voracious love-hunger. Moreover, the maternal deficiency caused the daughter to reject the mother as a model on which to pattern herself. Consequently, the devalued mother, hurt by her daughter's disdainful and disparaging attitude and unable, because of cultural proscriptions, to express her anger openly, induced in the daughter the growth of fear, insecurity, and guilt. In this she was guided and encouraged by her husband and the prevailing child-rearing sanctions as outlined by Abbott. Thus, Emily Dickinson as a child found only "Awe" at home to comfort her, some of the substance of "Awe" no doubt being her mother's baleful religious admonitions.

With these privations and stresses of the infantile period still unappeased and unameliorated, Emily Dickinson limped into childhood, at which time her father became important. For convenience, let me schematize the major psychodynamic transactions:

(A) Her father generated anxiety in Emily Dickinson:
    (1) By exaggerating the malignity of the world.
    (2) By infantalizing her, encouraging her dependency, and producing in her a feeling of inadequacy regarding the practical demands of life.

(3) By the "death wishes" he expressed in reaction-formations of exaggerated concern for her welfare, which undermined the security she derived from his love.

(B) He increased her own preoccupation with death by evoking in her inexpressible rage reactions:

   (1) Through his being a frustrating love object—aloof, formidable, and stern.

   (2) Through his disparagement of femininity, which entailed her continuing rejection of herself as a female.

   (3) Through his depriving her of pride in her mother, which further hampered a feminine identification.

(C) Her relationship with her father interfered with the orientation of her sexuality toward other males:

   (1) Because by overestimating her father she made it impossible for other men to compete with him.

   (2) Because the father-daughter bond induced in her an inability to love any but father images, with consequent incest anxiety.

   (3) Because the identification with her father as a superior male tended to masculinize her.

Those dynamisms subsumed under heading A above, which produced anxiety, were more or less direct responses to certain personality characteristics of the father. Those under heading B, related to the generation of anger, produced their characteristic symptoms primarily through the standards of the culture (as reflected in *The Mother at Home*), which condemned the outward discharge of aggressive and angry impulses, especially in females, and unwittingly encouraged the utilization of indirect, devious, or pathological outlets. The complications listed under heading C represent one unsuccessful attempt to resolve certain oedipal conflicts. Here, the inadequacies of the mother and the disparity in congenital endowment between mother and daughter, both of which interfered with a comfortable feminine identification, represent the vacuum into which flowed all the exaggerated positive emotions associated with the father.

Though Edward Dickinson propelled and deflected the many tormented currents of his daughter's development, the original imbalance began with the mother. The peculiar strength and bias of Edward Dickinson's personality then perpetuated and reproportioned, after its own characteristics, the existing disequilibrium. Finally Emily Dickinson relinquished all hope of easing her sense of affectional deprivation or establishing her sexual identity through her parents. Though the parents ultimately failed her, the residuals of these early attachments determined the profoundest depths of her personality. Her frustrations drove her, over the years, to wider ranging and ever more untenable efforts to achieve love and stability, but her emotional energies were never significantly detached from their roots in these blighted primordial relationships. Traces of her longing for her mother and father pervade the poetry. Her deep interior linkage to Edward Dickinson, though blocking her completion as a woman, stimulated her to use her mind. A warmer relationship with her mother would probably have made her a housewife. A colder one combined with a less distant and more seductively tender relationship with her father could have made her a homosexual. Instead of leading to these commonplace resolutions, the suffering and sorrow that arose from her unsatisfying experiences with both parents, acting upon her congenital intelligence and sensitivity, helped make her a great poet and, in large part, determined the kind of poet she became.

Chapter III OF SHUNNING MEN AND WOMEN

Of "shunning Men and Women"—they talk of Hallowed things, aloud
—and embarrass my Dog—He and I dont object to them, if they'll exist their
side.
                                        —Emily Dickinson to T. W. Higginson, August 1862

Adolescence, so frequently the most painful and faltering of transitional processes, was for Emily Dickinson markedly so. The ambiguity of her sense of sexual identity, the result of the unusual fears and awes, attractions and repulsions of her early childhood, found her ill prepared for friendship and love outside her family. Her school mates admired her intelligence and wit, but something obscure in her inevitably arose and troubled her deeper friendships with these girls. She was formal and uncomfortable with boys. Adults apparently liked her and she had one or two close friendships with young men considerably older than herself. But among her age-mates she was more frequently than not, for reasons unclear to her or her contemporaries, a misfit. An understanding of Emily Dickinson's ultimate withdrawal from society requires an examination of the pain and confusion of her first transactions with society—the friendships and loves of adolescence.

Her leavetaking of childhood was undergone reluctantly and

was agonizingly protracted. In a sense she never did depart from it, never allowed herself to experience anything resembling a true adolescence, if one takes the term to mean the ordinary psychological developments and adjustments which usher in maturity. Rather, Emily Dickinson, in the interval between her eleventh year, at which age she introduces herself to us in her letters, and the two or three years preceding her brother's marriage, at which time she appears to have undergone a cataclysmic transformation, retained much of the character of the grade school child. Conspicuous in her letters, for example, are the following latency age* and prepubescent attitudes: She continued to seek the company of her own sex almost exclusively and tried to perpetuate girlhood relationships with female school chums. She tended to "hero-worship" other women—usually girls who were older and more attractive, or women teachers. Though she never explicitly said so, she wanted to believe that women were superior; she tended to ignore or avoid males, and her ostensible indifference toward them was tinctured with disparagement, covert hostility, and, occasionally, rivalry. At a time when most girls are allowing awareness of the other sex to occupy an increasing portion of consciousness, Emily remained absorbed in her lessons and hobbies and in her correspondence with her chums. While her friends apparently were embracing the feminine role, even its outward trappings had to be urged upon Emily by her family. She repudiated housecleaning, cultivated an ignorance of dressmaking, disliked sewing, and was content to leave most of the kitchen duties to others.

In the years prior to Emily Dickinson's fourteenth birthday, the center of her social life was the little band of school chums she fondly referred to as the "five." In addition to Emily, the group consisted of Abiah Root, Abby Wood, Harriet Merrill, and Sarah Tracy. In the letters of her fifteenth year it becomes clear that the emotional adhesive that cemented these juvenile relationships was already loosening. The interests the girls held in common were no longer sufficiently compelling to bind them as tightly together as formerly, and the circle was undergoing the process of dissolution that adolescence inevitably imposes on all such prepubescent societies.

* Latency is the period between age six (at the culmination of the oedipal crisis) and the beginning of adolescence. In Europe and America (especially among the middle and upper classes) it is an interval in which sexual urges are usually repressed and latent.

To be included among the "five" had obviously been a treasured experience for Emily Dickinson—her initial venture in friendship building. It represented her first steps as a person in her own right, her first venture beyond the compass of her parents' home. The group's passionate solidarity and exclusiveness, characteristic of the clubs and cliques of late childhood, no doubt gave her a taste of the warmth of belonging and relatedness that she was to search for desperately and vainly later in her life. In the face of ample evidence that the other girls were finding new interests and were clearly defecting from the group, Emily held fast to the illusion that the relationships were still as precious and inviolable to them as they were to her. Her emotional needs dictated that the circle of friends remain intact, and not merely for years, but indefinitely.

And there were numerous other girls, though not members of the original "five," who came to occupy similar niches in the temple of Emily's affections. Jane Humphrey and Emily Fowler, for example, became the recipients of letters that embodied the same emotional extravagance that characterized her letters to Abiah Root (and presumably to Abby Wood, Harriet Merrill, and Sarah Tracy, although these letters have been lost). In their compulsive insistence on the friends' ineffable preciousness to Emily and her reiterated foreboding that death might part them at any moment, the letters, despite their surface charm, ring with shrill overtones. They assert and project a kind of passionate and desperate empathy—almost an urge for fusion with the friend that in itself may have prematurely alienated the earliest defectors, Harriet Merrill and Sarah Tracy. Emily's letters offer eternal devotion and by implication exact in recompense a reciprocal devotion. They do this with a gilded demandingness that is palpable throughout and that at times must have been suffocating for those less feverishly committed to the relationship than Emily.

The question arises as to the psychological significance of this clinging to childhood and of these floridly ardent attachments to other girls. What emotional needs are they an attempt to fulfill? Perhaps it will be helpful to hypothesize that Emily with the "five" and subsequent recruits to her circle achieved a kind of emotional plateau in her relationship to others, that she became blocked or arrested in some way and remained at a psychological standstill that persisted for years—in fact well into her twenties.

One must return to her letters for documentation of this view and trace out the frequently unobtrusive strokes of self-revelation that lie scattered throughout. One may then discover that if these findings are related to a psychological context there emerges from obscurity the gestalt of what must have been for Emily Dickinson an agonizing crisis in the establishment of her sexual identity.

An intense and objective interest in many facets of the world around her and in the enjoyment of learning for its own sake is typical of the latency-age girl (or boy) and is perhaps the dominating fact of her consciousness. With puberty and adolescence a new subjectivity is introduced, and the former interests, shared largely with her own sex—in hobbies, mastering skills, making collections, and so forth—yield in significant measure to a new focus of attention: sex consciousness and a preoccupation with one's relationship to one's peers as a budding woman. Evidence of an awareness and anticipation of impending womanhood is conspicuously rare in Emily Dickinson's letters, while the latency-age interests still occupy a large share of center stage. At eleven, appropriately enough, she writes to Jane Humphrey, "I have a great deal to tell you about school matters";[1] at fourteen she is exchanging school compositions with other girls. The same year she devotes a good portion of her letters to Abiah Root to her studies, her collection of plants, her observations of nature, her teachers, and her piano lessions. She writes, "I have been working a beautiful book mark to give to one of our school girls," and she tells Abiah that she is pressing wild flower specimens for "all the girls."[2] The next year she tells of her German and music lessons and of her continuing interest in her plants. At sixteen she mentions these same interests in her letters to Austin, and it is clear that they are still occupying a large portion of her time. Even at seventeen she is writing about them to Abiah and in addition showing increased enthusiasm for sharing remarks about the books she has been reading. And so on. There is nothing remotely strange or abnormal about any of this, of course. By itself it is merely indicative of an active intelligence. What occasions wonder, however, is the fact that with all the time and space devoted to school, hobbies, books, and so forth, there is no sign of a developing interest in boys. That comes only late, when Emily is nineteen, and then rather strangely.

In contrast, her earliest attitude toward her girl friends is

one of warmth and possessiveness. In this respect there is little
difference between the letters she wrote to Jane Humphrey when
she was eleven, which are clearly expressive of the love of one's
latency-age chums, and the letters of her early twenties to Emily
Fowler, except that the warmth and possessiveness gather vehemence as the years pass.

At eleven she writes to Jane Humphrey: "I miss you more and
more every day, in my study in play at home indeed everywhere
I miss my beloved Jane."[3] At fourteen she writes to Abiah Root:
"I keep your lock of hair as precious as gold";[4] and later she tells
Abiah that Sarah Tracy "is a noble girl, and I love her much."[5]
At fifteen she writes to Abiah: "I long to see you once more, to
clasp you in my arms."[6] At nineteen she writes to Emily Fowler:
"I dreamed about you . . . I cannot wait to be with you."[7] The
same year she writes Jane Humphrey again in the effusive vein
of eight years before: "I can tell you how dearly I love you . . .
I have been much with you since you first wrote me, *always* with
you, but *more* since *then,* for the last few days you have been *very*
near, very dear *indeed,* and I have wished, and prayed to *see* you,
and to *hear* you, and to feel your warm heart beating near me
. . . I have dreamed of you, and talked of you, and wished for you,
and have almost thought I should see you, it has seemed that
some way would help me, and a providence would bring you,
and yet you have not come, and I am so very tired of waiting."[8]
The next year she writes to Emily Fowler again: "it may be
foolish in me but I love you so well sometimes . . . When I am
as old as you [Emily Fowler was four years her senior] and have
had so many friends, perhaps they wont seem so precious . . . I
cant find many so dear to me as you."[9] At twenty-two, following
Emily Fowler's marriage, Emily writes to her: "Dear Emily, we
are lonely here . . . I knew you would go away, for I know the
roses are gathered, but I guessed not yet, not till by expectation
we had become resigned . . . And now five days have gone,
Emily, and long and silent, and I begin to know that you will not
come back again. There's a verse in the Bible, Emily . . . 'I can
go to her, but she cannot come back to me.' I guess that isn't
right, but my eyes are full of tears."[10]

The reader is bound to ask himself: Is there something abnormal in these effusions, and if so, what? One senses here more

than the usual nineteenth-century extravagance. Because of their female objects they may, ipso facto, be designated as "homosexual." But to affix this label does not advance one's understanding much. What remains to be determined is the extent to which these avowals of love can be considered only anachronistic continuations of the so-called normal homosexuality of latency and prepubescent relationships. The prepubescent child typically has little awareness of specific desires and focused erotic urges in relation to either sex. Emily Dickinson's early, uninhibited protestations of love to Jane Humphrey are assuredly of this nature, and they seem identical in character to later endearments expressed to Abiah Root and Emily Fowler. Because these outbursts of affection toward one girl or another repeatedly occur throughout the years until the poet is well into her twenties, with little if any apparent change in their essential emphasis, one is inclined to conclude that they are symptomatic of an abnormally prolonged period of sexual latency. The letters to Sue Gilbert in the years immediately preceding her marriage to Austin, on the other hand, appear significantly different from the rest and are complicated by the poet's relation to her brother. For this reason they will be discussed in another chapter.

Emily Dickinson's unwillingness to relinquish her hold on individual girl friends comes through clearly enough in all her early letters. It is instructive, moreover, to notice that it was in the context of a *group* that these relationships had to be maintained if they were to meet her needs; therein lies the element so strongly indicative of her tenacious grasp on the outmoded ways of latency. Individual, exclusive attachments are mostly an adolescent or adult pattern.

At the age of fourteen, for example, she writes to Abiah, referring to her school chums: "How happy we all were together that term we went to Miss Adams. I wish it might be so again, but I never expect it."[11] And in a following letter: "Oh Abiah. If Sarah, Hatty and yourself were only here this summer what times we should have."[12] The next year, when Miss Adams, the beloved teacher, returned to Amherst, Emily writes Abiah: "Oh, you cannot imagine how natural it seems to see her happy face in school once more. But it needs Harriet, Sarah and your own dear self to complete the ancient picture."[13] Three months later she continues the theme: "Abby & I talk much of the happy hours we used to spend together with yourself, Sarah, and Hatty Merrill. Oh! What would I give could we all meet again."[14]

After her seventeenth birthday Emily tells Abiah of a "candy scrape" where "there was quite a company of young people assembled," though she fails to mention any boys. She then tells of her return to school: "There are many sweet girls here & dearly do I love some new faces, but I have not yet found the place of a *few* dear ones filled."[15] She is referring of course to Abiah and the "five."

Three months later, after not having heard from Abiah for five months, she writes: "I feel more reluctant to lose you from that bright circle, whom I've called *my friends*."[16] And just after her nineteenth birthday she writes to Jane Humphrey of several parties, sleigh rides, walks, music, conversation, suppers, and late hours—all in mixed company—and says: "I would gladly exchange them all for one evening's talk with the friends I love."[17] Just before turning twenty she asks Abiah what she is thinking and doing "and whether she [Abiah] still remembers the loves of 'long ago,' and sighs as she remembers, lest there be no more as true."[18]

Later the next year Emily saw Sarah Tracy again: "Isnt it remarkable," she writes Abiah, "that in so many years Sarah has changed so little—not that she has stood still, but has made such *peaceful* progress—her thots tho' they are *older* have all the charm of youth—have not yet lost their freshness, their innocence and peace—she seems so pure in heart . . . I have not seen her much —I want to see her more . . . I hope no change or time shall *blight* these loves of ours, I would bear them all in my arms to my home in the glorious heaven and say 'here I am my Father, and those whom thou hast given me.' " Here Emily, almost twenty-one, is still clinging to the girl friends of ages eleven, twelve, and thirteen. She wants their relationships never to change, the links of their associations never to be broken. When she dies she wants to have the same girlhood circle of friends accompanying her to heaven. She cherishes the fiction that Sarah is the same and is still "fresh," "innocent," "peaceful," and "pure in heart," that is, that sexuality has not touched her either.

Early in the next year she writes to Abiah, saying that she hopes Abiah will not get less pleasure from receiving Emily's letter than Emily had in sending it, and exclaims: "Oh, I do know it will not, if school-day hearts are warm and school-day memories precious!" and she speaks of "the links which bind us to each other, and make the very thought of you, and time when I last saw you, a sacred thing to me."[19]

With the passing of years Emily became more lonely. When she was most depressed, she thought of the happy days when the "five" were loving companions. Thus, at twenty-one, we find her writing to Susan Gilbert that she wishes they "might ramble away as children . . . and forget these many years, and these sorrowing cares, and each become a child again."[20]

In her last known letter to Jane Humphrey, written in her twenty-fourth year, she writes: "Only the loss of friends and the longing for them . . . I keep thinking and wishing, and then I think and wish, till for your sakes, who stray from me, *tears* patter as the rain."[21]

It is not surprising that the expression of needs so great at times overwhelmed the other girls, who did not share Emily's need to stop the passage of time. As early as age eleven, Emily was beginning to experience what no doubt seemed to her like rejection but what was really a reflection of the propensity of the other girls to live more exclusively than she in the present. Thus, she writes to Abiah: "Dont you wish Jane Kim [illegible letters] would come back. I cant bear to think she is so far away. I have sent her a letter and a catalogue since she went away, and I dont know whether she ever received them or not."[22]

By September 1845, when Emily was almost fifteen, it should have been clear to her that Harriet Merrill did not share her view that the circle of five had a sacrosanct inviolability. Since leaving for Hartford over four months before, Harriet had sent Emily one note and one paper; in return Emily had sent two letters, two papers, and a bookmark she had made herself and that she considered "beautiful." After about three more months have passed, Emily writes to Abiah that she had heard no word from Harriet or Sarah Tracy: "I send them a paper [possibly a composition] every week on Monday, but I never get one in return."[23]

In another month Emily still has had no word from either Harriet or Sarah. She writes to Abiah: "I shall write them both soon."[24] It is striking that there is no mention of boys at a time when Emily is writing voluminously to girl friends who do not respond.

Seventeen months after she last heard from Harriet, she is still concerned about her and asks Abiah: "Have you yet heard from Dear Harriet? I have not."[25]

After twenty-two months Emily sends Harriet a paper and writes to Abiah: "There is a mystery about her silence to me."[26] Readers who remember their own adolescence will probably not be mystified.

And faithful Abiah, faltering at times in her epistolary loyalty, was even less able to meet the emotional demands Emily placed on her in face to face confrontation. After an unusual five-month silence Abiah visited Amherst but neglected to seek out her friend. Later Emily writes to her: "At our Holyoke Anniversary, I caught one glimpse of your face, & fondly anticipated an interview with you, & a reason for your silence, but when I thought to find you search was vain . . . Why did you not come back that day, and tell me what had sealed your lips toward me? . . . if you dont want to be my friend any longer, say so."[27] Three years later, Abiah, in Amherst again for the commencement proceedings, did much the same thing. She met Emily briefly, had a short talk with her, and to Emily's intense disappointment left town again without seeing her. Emily afterward wrote expressing her pique, informing Abiah that she would have "improved" her bit of the visit more if she had known that it was all she was to have.[28]

Jane Humphrey too sometimes defected, and Emily at age nineteen writes telling her how much she misses her: "I have dreamed of you, and talked of you, and wished for you, etc.," a passage already quoted in another context. There is a great deal of depression in the letters of this time, and Emily may have begun to realize that she could not prevent her friends from slipping away from her. In the same letter to Jane Humphrey she says: "How lonely this world is growing, something so desolate creeps over the spirit."[29]

Emily's friendship with Abby Wood, who lived in Amherst, did not always go smoothly either. Emily writes Abiah: "I often see Abby—oftener that at sometimes when friendship drooped a little."[30] It may be that at times Abby felt a need to establish a little distance between herself and Emily's hot breath.

By her early twenties Emily was slowly coming to the realization that her efforts to prolong her childhood by means of tireless retrenchment of its associations was doomed to failure, though she continued to be bewildered that this should be so. After a difference with Sue, she indirectly acknowledges the fact that her original "five" and their replacements have not proved the bulwark against isolation that she had hoped. "You need not fear to leave me," she tells Sue, "lest I should be alone, for I often part with things I fancy I have loved,—sometimes to the grave, and sometimes to an oblivion rather bitterer than death."[31] The "oblivion bitterer than death" would seem to represent her pain at being forgotten and rejected by Harriet Merrill, Sarah Tracy, and her other friends.

Sometimes Emily groped for some way of comprehending what seemed to her to be gratuitous defections. She would give herself one reason for the seeming disloyalty of her friends and then discard it for a different one later. In her more intuitive moments she seemed to realize that part of the trouble was that her friends were outdistancing her on the path to maturity. For example, of Abby Wood she remarked: "I see but little of Abby . . . Our lots fall in different places . . . We take different views of life, our thoughts would not dwell together as they used to when we were young—how long ago that seems! She is more of a woman than I am, for I love so to be a child."[32]

But at other times it seems to her that the explanation must reside in some deficiency in her capacity to love: "when the loved are here," she wrote Jane Humphrey, "[I] try to love *more,* and *faster, dearer,* but when all are gone, seems as had I tried *harder,* they would have stayed with me."[33] Yet there remained the possibility that her essential failing was not some deficiency after all, but rather an excess of some kind. Thus, she wrote to Sue: "Few have been given me, and if I love them so, that for *idolatry,* they are removed from me . . ."[34] None of these explanations really satisfied her, however. All she was sure of was that she was incessantly lonely; why this should be so continued to baffle her.

It is difficult to convey, through excerpts from Emily Dickinson's letters, her attitude toward the young men who were frequent visitors to the Dickinson home. As one reads of her absorption in the lives of the young female population of Amherst, one finds that what she fails to say about its masculine counterpart

speaks more eloquently of her estrangement from it than do any
of her actual statements. When she does speak of men, she almost
always makes a simple, factual, emotionally neutral statement.
For example: "Chauncey Russell, Frank Pierce, and George
Cutler are somewhere on the coast catching fur and fishes."[35]
When she thus, without warmth or enthusiasm, refers to young
men, what she says has usually been prompted by some remark
or question on the part of her correspondent. In a letter to Abiah
Root written when she was fourteen, she takes a lofty and somewhat mocking attitude: "Your *beau idéal* D. I have not seen
lately. I presume he was changed into a star some night while
gazing at them."[36] In a letter of that same year Abiah apparently
made some reference to Abby Wood's interest in a boy, and
Emily seems thrown off stride and answers awkwardly: "I do
not understand your hints in regard to Abby taking so much interest in Deacon Macks family. Now Sarah is absent, I take it
William is the member of the family whom you allude to. But I
did not know as Abby had any partiality for him" and with regard to a possible romantic interest of Abiah herself Emily decides to treat it lightly: "I dont know about this Mr. Eastcott
giving you concert tickets. I think for my part it looks rather
suspicious. He is a young man I suppose. These Music teachers
are always such high souled beings that I think they would
exactly suit your fancy."[37] Obviously there is in Emily's response
little of the avid interest in romantic details typical of the adolescent girl. About five months later Emily again mentions the
young music teacher to Abiah: "I suppose you are getting along
finely in music. I had forgotten to ask after your adorable Mr.
Eastcott." Perhaps this slightly disdainful attitude has a note of
jealousy in it, and the rest of the letter is full of complaints that
Emily's girl friends, not excluding the generally faithful Abiah,
are not answering her letters: "Now if you dont answer this
letter soon I shall—I shall do something dreadful." In the same
letter Emily indicates that she is depressed and that "the New
Year's Day was unusually gloomy to me, I know not why."[38]
Further on she says that she has had no word from Harriet
Merrill (who has not written now for about seven months) or
from Sarah Tracy. There is a great deal of local news in this
letter, all of it involving older people and girls. It seems a reasonable inference that Emily's interests and her friends' are diverging

as her friends are turning their attention to boys and that this accounts partly for the frequent references to loneliness and low spirits in the letters of these years.

At age seventeen, in a short letter to her brother, Emily characteristically asks that "much love" be given to the family and to "Mary and Abby"; then she adds indifferently: "Also remember me to your room mate if you please to do so."[39] The same year, when an older friend of Austin, Elbridge Bowdoin, delivered some notes to her at school, she makes fun of his laconic conversation: "Bowdoin, tells me of no news, excepting the following," and she mentions the ripening cherry crop and the fact that there had been a party of the college seniors, "both of which facts, were received by me, with proper resignation."[40]

When Emily at nineteen writes to Jane Humphrey, she remarks about a young tutor at the college who is evidently suffering from an unrequited attraction to Jane: "Tolman I do not see— guess he is pining away—and cant say I blame him in view of the facts in the case. I shant tell you what ails him—for it is a *private* matter—and you ought not to know!" Then she adds gleefully: "How could you be so cruel Jane—it will certainly be the death of him."[41]

Any humbling of the alien and envied male affords a delicious gratification to the self-esteem of the latency-age girl; Emily's sadistic relish of the tutor's discomfort is reminiscent of this attitude. Later the same year she asks Abiah if there is any affection left over from Abiah's friendships with males: "Where are you now Abiah, where are your thoughts, and aspirings, where are your young affections, not with the *boots,* and *whiskers*."[42] It seems she could hardly have chosen a figure of speech having fewer sympathetic connotations than this synecdoche of boots and whiskers. It makes men seem heavy, lumbering, scratchy, unkempt, and uncongenial to anything feminine.

At times Emily clearly implies that she fears men as her rivals. At twenty she writes to Emily Fowler: "I know I cant have you always—some day a 'brave dragoon' will be stealing you away."[43] And in a letter to Sue the next year she expresses the same sentiment in similar language: "I told Mattie this morning, that I felt all taken away, without her, or Susie, and indeed I have thought today of what would become of me when the 'bold Dragon' shall bear you both away, to live in his high mountain

—and leave me here alone; and I could have wept bitterly over the only *fancy* of ever being so lone."[44] And again she writes Sue: "I hardly dared to sleep lest some one steal you away."[45]

At times Emily could take comfort in the indifference she presumably shared with her friend toward this or that young man. When Henry Root was indicating his interest, unavailingly, in Sue, Emily wrote to Sue: "I do think it's wonderful, Susie, that our hearts dont break, *every day,* when I think of all the whiskers, and all the gallant men, but I guess I'm made with nothing but a hard heart of stone, for it dont break any, and dear Susie, if mine is stony, your's is stone, upon stone."[46]

One wonders if Emily Fowler's new husband felt a bit excluded when, a few months after his marriage, his wife was told by Emily: "I miss you always, dear Emily, and I think now and then that I can't stay without you . . . But another spring . . . and nobody can take you away, for I will hide you and keep you—and who would think of taking you if I hold you tight in my arms?"[47]

In what is possibly her last letter to Jane Humphrey, written when she was twenty-four, Emily remarks lightly that Jane has told her nothing of the many suitors Jane must have spurned since she moved to Ohio—"how many knights are slain and wounded . . . is to me unknown". Then she advises Jane to "Keep a list of the conquests, Jennie, this is an *enemy's* Land!"[48] In some sense then, as in the days of latency, for Emily Dickinson men were still the enemy.

This statement is in need of some qualification, though. In contrast to her usual tepid or cool attitude toward most of her male acquaintances, she did hold warmer feelings toward at least two of them: Benjamin F. Newton and Henry V. Emmons, and possibly George Gould also. It seems clear, however, that the relationship that meant the most to her—that with Newton— resembled most closely that of a girl to a beloved older brother or to a venerated male teacher, and it would put a considerable strain on the evidence to see anything conventionally romantic in their relationship. Shortly after leaving Amherst, while still on the best of terms with Emily, Newton married a woman twelve years older than he. This in itself is suggestive of the unlikelihood of his ever having regarded the four years younger Emily as the answer to his sexual and emotional needs. Suffice it to say here that her high estimation of Newton seems comparable to the comradely devotion that budding adolescent girls frequently exhibit toward their fathers. Viewed in this light, her friendship with Newton may be seen as an essentially oedipal echo in which sexual undertones are strongly repressed. Her warmth toward, and possibly even infatuation with, Emmons and Gould was of still a different order and will be examined later.

Throughout her adolescent years Emily Dickinson from time to time made certain tentative efforts, all essentially abortive, to be more like other girls. She observed their interest in boys with a mixture of lofty disdain and envy tinged with a sense of inferiority. Generally, their heterosexual preoccupations seem to have dismayed her and made her feel estranged from them. Occasionally, however, she achieved with one of them a simulacrum of that degree of identification with another female that she failed to gain from her relationship with her mother, and this would temporarily mobilize in her a sense of her own femininity. At such times she was on the threshold of entering a new phase—the door to a life of psychosexual maturity seemed to be opening up for her, a chance to leave behind the obsolete stages of latency and prepuberty. But the door was guarded by too many chimeras, and ultimately she failed to cross the threshold. Before it closed forever, however, she had a glimpse of the world outside sufficient to imbue her fantasy life with the coloring of adult experience.

The first hint one gets in reading the letters of Emily Dickinson that she yearns for the "peaceful progress" that she ascribed to Sarah Tracy and that seems to be coming so naturally to the other girls occurs in a letter to Austin in which she speaks of valentines. She wrote it from school in her seventeenth year. She says: "I suppose you have written a few & received a quantity of Valentines this week . . . Many of the girls have received very beautiful ones & I have not quite done hoping for one. Surely *my friend* THOMAS, has not lost all his former affection for me. I entreat you to tell him I am pining for a Valentine . . . Probably, Mary, Abby & Viny have received scores of them from the infatuated wights in the neighborhood while your *highly accomplished & gifted elder sister* is entirely overlooked."[49] It is clear that Emily does not care who sends her a valentine. The important thing to her is that she be like the other girls and that they not think her a wallflower. Perhaps it can be questioned if this is anything but a superficial imitation of the feminine role —what is involved may be mostly a matter of pride.

It is not until 1850, when Emily Dickinson was in her twentieth year and deriving emotional support from her deepening identification with Susan Gilbert, that any evidence appears that Emily was capable of summoning up even the rudiments of a tender impulse toward a young man.

Susan Gilbert returned to live in Amherst in late 1848, when she and Emily were almost eighteen, and by August of the following year Austin had already become interested in his future wife. It is clear from the first letter we have from Emily to Sue, written about this time, that Sue had become important to Emily also. She expresses some alarm at the prospect of Sue's sister Martha joining Sue and possibly displacing her: "Dont forget all the little friends who have tried so hard to *be* sisters, when indeed you *were* alone."[50] A point I would make here is that Emily's growing intimacy with Sue obviously antedated this first letter and probably had been evolving throughout the previous year or longer—that is, concurrently with Emily's first detectable heterosexual stirrings.

One of the important aspects of Emily's relationship with Sue was that it emboldened her to reject a little her anxiety-ridden and exclusive commitment to the "innocence" of childhood. In other words, it freed Emily for a time to begin to think of herself as a human being with sexuality—a woman. In Sue's aura Emily discovered that young men occasionally might have an attractiveness of their own, and she found herself daring to date a little and to entertain a few tentative fantasies involving the opposite sex. There is a great deal of evidence that this identification with Sue in time grew unwholesomely intense, almost to the point of pathological fusion; this is epitomized by the observation on their relationship Emily made years later: "Where my Hands are cut, Her fingers will be found inside."[51] But early in the friendship Sue's effect on Emily seems mostly to have been salutary and to have turned her face for once toward the future.

Thus, in May 1850 Emily writes Abiah that she has felt obligated to remain at home to help her mother, who is ill with neuralgia. Almost for the first time she seems to be accepting a womanly role: "I have always neglected the culinary arts, but attend to them now from necessity, and from a desire to make everything pleasant for father, and Austin." Then she goes on to say that just as she removed the bread from the oven, "I heard a well-known rap, and a friend I love *so* dearly came and asked me to ride in the woods . . . I wanted to exceedingly . . . he wanted me very much—then the tears came into my eyes, tho' I tried to choke them back, and he said I *could,* and *should* go."[52] The friend has never been certainly identified, but she thought highly of George Gould, an Amherst senior at this time, and it seems plausible that the letter refers to him.

The friend's identity is not of importance here, however: what is pertinent is the documentation of a change in Emily's orientation toward herself and toward a male friend.

Two years later, her sense of closeness to Sue has superseded all her attachments to other girl friends. At times Emily thinks of Sue almost as the sheltering mother for whom she has sought so long: "Oh Susie, I would nestle close to your warm heart, and never hear the wind blow, or the storm beat, again."[53] It is at this time of heightening identification with Sue that Emily took brief notice of Henry Emmons, a student at the college. In February 1852 Emily writes to Austin: "I have been to ride twice since I wrote you . . . and last evening with *Sophomore Emmons,* alone; will tell you all about it when I write again."[54] The same month she writes Sue: "Then I've found a beautiful, new, friend, and I've told him about dear Susie, and promised to let him know you as soon as you shall come."[55] As with her earlier wish that Austin get somebody to send her a valentine, Emily seems enabled to speak of boys through identifying herself with another girl or girls, although even with Emmons part of her motivation may reside in a need to prove to Sue that she too can attract men.

In June 1852 Emily again writes to Austin: "I went to walk with Emmons,"[56] almost as if she were dutifully reporting that she was doing what Austin expected of her. But she is beginning to experience strong anxiety, and it does not surprise one, after reading of her fears of sexuality as she expressed them to Sue this same month, that the relationship with Emmons quickly fades. As Emily takes long walks with Emmons she has second thoughts, confided to Sue thus: "to the *wife,* Susie, sometimes the *wife forgotten,* our lives [that is, as unattached girls] perhaps

seem dearer than all others in the world; you have seen flowers
at morning, *satisfied* with the dew, and those same sweet flowers
at noon with their heads bowed in anguish before the mighty
sun; think you these thirsty blossoms will *now* need naught but
—*dew?* No, they will cry for sunlight, and pine for the burning
noon, tho' it scorches them, scathes them; they have got through
with peace—they know that the man of noon, is *mightier* than
the morning and their life is henceforth to him . . . It does so
rend me, Susie, the thought of it when it comes, that I tremble
lest at sometime I, too, am yielded up."[57] The "man of morning,"
exemplified by Emmons, is the deferential, courting admirer.
The "man of noon" who "scorches" and "scathes" must therefore
be the sexually overpowering husband who causes his flower-
wife to be "bowed in anguish." No wonder, therefore, that in
her next letter to Sue Emily writes that she wishes she and Sue
"might ramble away as children . . . and each become a child
again."[58] And the next year she writes to Austin: "I wish we were
children now. I wish we were *always* children, how to grow up
I dont know."[59]

Emily had insight enough to recognize that her dating and
being romantic about a man became possible only through her
imitation of and identification with Sue and that when Sue departed Emily's heterosexuality would go too. She acknowledges
to Sue that "you sketch my pictures for me, and 'tis at their
sweet coloring, rather than this dim real that I am used, so you
see when you go away, the world looks staringly, and I find I
need more vail." A few lines further on she expresses the same
idea somewhat differently: "To be sure your life is warm with
such a sunshine [this is the year of Austin's and Sue's engage-
ment], helps me to chase the shadows fast stealing upon mine."
That Emily now fears that the only sexual fulfillment she can
possibly have is a vicarious one through her identification with
Sue is made explicit toward the end of this letter: "I want to
have you gather more sheaves of joy—for bleak and waste, and
barren, are most of the fields found here, and I want you to *fill*
the *garner*."[60]

As has perhaps been evident throughout this chapter, the abnormal prolongation of latency experienced by Emily Dickinson really represents an inability to resolve the problems of the

oedipal period. This dilemma, in turn, was founded on an earlier severe conflict in the oral sphere involving the maternal-deprivation syndrome, which was explored at length in Chapter II. It is mentioned here only as a reminder that underlying all the frustrated yearning for maturity and the clinging to childhood that characterize Emily Dickinson's adolescent and young adult years is always this deeper problem, which made the failure of her hopes for a normal life unavoidable.

Emily Dickinson disowned and tried to evade the awareness of her own femininity because it was derived through identification with her mother. Because of an obscure sense that her mother had robbed her of the capacity to take pride in being a woman and because of her deeply rooted conviction that her mother had never really loved her, Emily was afflicted with feelings of loneliness, resentment of her mother, depression, and loathing of herself as a woman. To be a woman was necessarily to be like her mother—this had to be the conclusion reached and preserved on the infantile substrate of her personality. And to be like her mother was to be eternally anxious and dissatisfied, shrinking, fearful, dependent, in need of constant care and protection from others, and subject to depression. The later course of the poet's life, the years when her several phobias kept her from venturing outside the confines of her father's house, reflects the ultimate triumph of this malign female identification that she tried so desperately in her earlier years to evade.

As has been indicated in the preceding chapter, one option sometimes available to the girl who can not brook any resemblance to her mother is to pattern herself after her father or, if he is not accessible, an older brother.

Theodora Ward in *The Capsule of the Mind,* a somewhat Jungian interpretation of Emily Dickinson's psychology, cites a poem, "I have a King, who does not speak," and expresses the view that the poet here reveals her awareness of the degree to which her creative life is dominated by the masculine archetype—Jung's *animus.* On this point, I largely agree with Mrs. Ward, except that I read the poem as testifying to Emily's identification with the males in her family, which Emily to a degree welcomed, in contrast to feminine identification, which she repudiated. The poem tells of a "King" whose regular appearance in Emily's dreams causes her to wish the days away and to look forward eagerly to sleep, at which time, if she is fortunate, she may, by means of dreaming, "peep / In parlors, shut by day" (no. 103). The poet says that when this occurs she wakens the following morning thrilling with an emotion of portentous triumph. On the other hand, when she does not have this dream the next day finds her unresponsive to the beauties of nature and feeling rebellious toward God. Mrs. Ward says of this poem: "The mysterious silence of the dream king and the happiness brought by a vision of him suggest that the figure is purely symbolic. Under his domination daily life becomes meaningful, but she can maintain contact with him only in the unconsciousness of sleep." After quoting the poem in full, Mrs. Ward continues: "The dreamer's allegiance now goes to an inner authority, whose claims are recognized as of greater force than those of the human father or the father God of whom he is the representative. In the new symbol . . . Emily instinctively acknowledges the power within herself of the masculine principle, which in complementing [displacing?] her own femineity is to play a leading role in her development as woman and poet."[61]

Mrs. Ward cites another poem, the one beginning "We don't cry – Tim and I," and in her explication she identifies "Tim" quite plausibly with an aspect of the poet's own personality here taking the form of an imaginary companion of the opposite sex. Here is the poem (no. 196) in full:

> We dont cry – Tim and I,
> We are far too grand –
> But we bolt the door tight
> To prevent a friend –
>
> Then we hide our brave face
> Deep in our hand –
> Not to cry – Tim and I –
> We are far too grand –
>
> Nor to dream – he and me –
> Do we condescend –
> We just shut our brown eye
> To see to the end –
>
> Tim – see Cottages –
> But, Oh, so high!
> Then – we shake – Tim and I –
> And lest I – cry –

Tim – reads a little Hymn –
And we both pray –
Please, Sir, I and Tim –
Always lost the way!

We must die – by and by –
Clergymen say –
Tim – shall – if I – do –
I – too – if he –

How shall we arrange it –
Tim – was – so – shy?
Take us simultaneous – Lord –
I – "Tim" – and – Me!

Mrs. Ward says of this poem: "Tim's little figure seems still
alive in her memory as she writes of how he shares the terror that
has driven her into solitude."[62] In the separateness of "Tim" and
the dream king from the poet, one sees the split-off masculine
identification which the poet is not quite willing to accept consciously as a part of herself. It is explicit in the latter poem, however, that "Tim" and Emily reside in the same body and share
the same face, hand, eye, feelings, and mortality.

A greater and more complex poem than the two cited by Mrs.
Ward, "My Life had stood – a loaded Gun" (no. 754), rewards
close study by providing an insight into the relationship between
Emily Dickinson's masculine identification and her creativity.
The poem will be fully explicated in Chapter IX.

Her letters also evince this tendency to a masculine sense of
herself. In 1852, when she writes to Sue while the rest of the
family are at church, she describes the sense of luxurious freedom
her solitude produces in her: "I have the old *king feeling*."[63] To
Mrs. Holland in 1856 she writes: "Love me if you will, for I had
rather *be* loved than to be called a king in earth, or a lord in
Heaven."[64] No doubt if it had felt psychologically right to her,
she could have conveyed this idea by using nouns connoting
feminine royalty in place of "king" and "lord." In 1861 she
writes an unidentified correspondent: "He [God] built the heart
in me—Bye and Bye it out grew me—and like the little mother
with the big child—I got tired holding him."[65] The lines are obscure, but whatever they mean there is no doubt that here Emily's
"heart" is masculine ("I got tired holding *him*"). In 1866 she
refers jokingly to herself as "Uncle Emily,"[66] and in 1871, as

"Brother Emily."[67] In several different places, for example in an 1878 letter to her nephew, Ned Dickinson, she speaks of her childhood as her boyhood: "Mother told me when I was a Boy."[68] As a young adult, and therefore doubtlessly as an adolescent, she felt embarrassed in fancy clothes, and in later years dressed very plainly. Great reserve in the choice of wearing apparel is frequently a characteristic of girls who, for reasons that may be unclear to them, feel awkward and almost fraudulent in the furbelows of femininity. "I never wear Jewels,"[69] Emily Dickinson tells Higginson.

As Emily Dickinson approached her mid-twenties she found herself at an impasse. Most of the maturational milestones and obstacles ordinarily left behind and surmounted in the course of adolescence still remained before her. She was prepared for no vocation—the only one in which she may have been making any progress at all was poetry writing, and even in this she had a relatively late efflorescence. Her intellectual brilliance notwithstanding, she was so incapacitated by her accumulating phobias that she would probably not have been able to earn her living had she been called on to do so. The same phobias would have crippled her ability to respond to the ordinary pressures the community exerts on adult citizens by expecting them to assume certain civic responsibilities. Though such opportunities for service were for the women of Amherst at the time limited enough, one has only to recall her panic in the face of the "commencement teas" her father held over the years to see how little she was prepared to meet any of them. Marriage and parenthood, because of her sexual anxiety and uncertain self-image as a woman, were of course out of the question. She had made no progress in emancipation from her family; on the contrary, her needs for protection and security became more overriding with time and she looked increasingly to her family to meet these needs. She seems not to have been able to imagine herself in the role of an adult. She knew what childhood was and she could anticipate senescence and "immortality" with some hope that with a little assistance she could adjust to these states. But she dreaded adulthood as other mortals dread death. In 1847 she writes to Austin: "Did you think that it was my birthday—yesterday? I dont believe I am *17*. Is. Jacob. Holt any better[?]"[70] Jacob Holt was undergoing his terminal illness when she wrote this letter. Note the sequence of association: thoughts of her "advanced" age immediately lead her to thoughts of dying. Maturity, for her, was, as she once said of death, "a wild Night and a new Road."[71]

It appears that she would have been amenable to skipping adulthood altogether if she could, plunging immediately from prepuberty into old age. At nineteen she writes to Abiah: "We are not so young as we once were . . . I seem to be quite submissive to the thought of growing old."[72] And two years later she writes to Sue: "Vinnie and I have been talking about growing old . . . I tell her I don't care if I am young or not, had as lief be thirty . . . ar'nt there days in one's life when to be old dont seem a thing so sad . . . I feel it would be a comfort to have a piping voice, and broken back."[73] Childhood and second childhood—what do they hold foremost in common? Legitimate dependency and the absence of sexuality.

There were, then, many psychological difficulties mitigating against Emily Dickinson's maturation. Just as there were conflicts that blocked her progress, so there were seeming benefits to be gained through the perpetuation of certain obsolete modes of adjustment. By holding fast to latency-age patterns Emily sought to provide herself with the following: (1) a bulwark against loneliness—there seemed no alternative to surrounding herself with her female chums because of the dysphoric feelings evoked in her by males; (2) a source of love—by enfolding herself in the beloved group of "five" and subsequent additions she could feel loved (identification with a narcissistic love object); (3) a limited but legitimate expression of homosexual trends—by remaining fixated in the ascetic, prepubertal pattern, she could suppress the physical expression of these impulses while sanctioning the emotive and erotic elements; (4) a sense of normality. The relative freedom from conflict characteristic of latency and Emily's acceptance by the group would produce this reassurance. As long as she could successfully encourage the other girls to feel as she did—to remain loyal to each other and to avoid girl-boy attachments—she could continue to think of herself as normal.

However, given her intelligence and insight, the realization was inevitable that the pursuit of these assurances led nowhere— that "to feed upon the Retrograde – Enfeebles the Advance" (poem 904).

Thus, as with all fixations, the untenability of her position in time became obvious to her, and the illusory advantages evaporated, leaving her lonely, loveless, and feeling that she was different after all from the others: at twenty she thought of herself as "quaint [and] old-fashioned."[74]

Her needs dictated that, to be acceptable, an alternative orientation must not only provide for the gratification she was losing, but also meet the more recent demands arising from the fact that she was physically no longer a child. Altogether, any new stance had to embody certain possibilities. It must promise: (1) a source of "maternal" love (the fulfillment of a primordial sense of deprivation); (2) a source of self-esteem (the gratification of a narcissism injured by a sense of maternal rejection and by her consequent self-hatred as a woman); (3) sexual gratification (an outlet for the sexual tensions of physical maturity); (4) an ultimately attainable love object (a sexual partner not proscribed by fears, conflicts, or conscience and preferably one sanctioned by her culture).

How could these emotional stipulations best be met? Confining the problem to the choice of love object, there existed for her three possibilities: the acceptance of a heterosexual orientation, the acceptance of a homosexual orientation, or the renunciation of instinctual gratification through either.

Loving a *man* involved the following difficulties:

(1) Emily Dickinson's view of heterosexuality appears to have been based on the idea that the man subjugates, humiliates, and assaults the woman; consequently she was fearful of men.

(2) Because men had prerogatives she lacked and could steal away her beloved girl friends, she also envied and, on a certain psychic level, hated men.

(3) Her clearly expressed need was for a love that was maternal in character. (A tender and passive husband could have provided such love if, at the same time, he would not have had, as he inevitably would, to bear comparison with her image of her very adequate and active father.)

(4) Her rejection of her mother entailed rejection of her own femininity, and it is very difficult for a woman who does not feel herself to be a woman to love a man.

On the other hand, how much of a possibility was a homosexual orientation? It involved these difficulties:

(1) Emily Dickinson possessed a puritan super-ego derived from the very moralistic culture in which she lived and from her church-going and conventionally high-principled parents. It would be remarkable if she had not therefore regarded homosexuality as depraved and reacted to the mere thought of it with abhorrence.

(2) Homosexuality would have discredited the family. Emily and her sister and brother had been made acutely aware that they were *Dickinsons* and that each was a representative of the rest. Whatever one did or failed to do reflected credit or blame on all the others.

(3) Unless the ego organization is strong, choosing a lesbian as love object involves the danger of regression to utter dependence on and psychological fusion with the "mother," a situation which has ushered in many a psychosis. Emily Dickinson at one time expressed fears of insanity, and in a poem says that once "a Plank in Reason, broke" (poem 280). She may, therefore, have been aware of significant weaknesses in her own ego structure. Probably the danger for her in a homosexual relationship was deeply apprehended and would have been a source of prohibiting anxiety.

(4) Sooner or later, because Emily Dickinson did not really respect women and would tend to identify the beloved woman with her despised mother, the homosexual relationship would inevitably become deeply troubled. Evidence is not lacking that Emily Dickinson possessed insight into her covert distrust of women.

Of the two positions it appears that the homosexual may have been slightly more open to her than the heterosexual. The homosexual perspective could promise the following psychological "advantages" lacking in the other:

(1) "Maternal" affection is more easily found in women and is not commonly regarded, as it is in men, as a sign of weakness.

(2) The homosexual orientation is a "logical" extension of the latency-age pattern and does not require as great a maturation of personality. Also it is commonly adopted gradually through modifications of these previously existing attitudes, the process being accomplished with a degree of denial and self-deception regarding what one is really doing sufficient, for a time, to circumvent the inevitable guilt feelings.

(3) Self-love receives a powerful, albeit temporary, impetus when a woman chooses as her beloved another woman. Emily Dickinson's self-esteem had been damaged by the troubled relationship with her mother, and she found it hard to accept her own femininity via mother-identification. A homosexual relationship might have appeared to her to hold out a chance for correcting this.

As one reviews all these considerations the following conclusions seem tenable. A heterosexual adjustment involved almost insuperable psychological obstacles. Except for super-ego considerations, a homosexual orientation would certainly have been more easily achievable for Emily Dickinson; the particular vicissitudes of her development and her resulting personality structure would have predisposed her more strongly to this resolution than to a heterosexual one. However, in the judgment of nineteenth-century New England, to pursue such a course was to perpetuate an abomination of the most vile dimensions, and Emily Dickinson's views on what was allowable must, of necessity, have had much in common with the conscience of her place and era. For this reason *overt* homosexual impulses, that is, *physical* ones as opposed to merely affective ones, would most likely have been forcibly repressed. Thus, both heterosexuality and homosexuality as a way of life appear to be ruled out. The manner in which later, the poetry facilitated a sublimated expression of some of these impulses will be discussed in another context.

Most of the theories brought forth by biographers to explain Emily Dickinson's spinsterhood assume that there existed some set of external circumstances which set up an insuperable blockade against the fulfillment of her longing for sexual love and marriage. For example, the poet supposedly capitulated to the alleged demands of her father, who is seen, according to this interpretation, as a fanatically possessive man who would not brook his daughter's leaving his side and who was prepared, if necessary, to drive prospective suitors from the house by force.[75] Perhaps the most popularly accepted explanation, supported by occasional suggestions in the poetry, is that unspecified moral considerations presented obstacles to the consummation of the poet's love affair. The proponents of this view, each identifying a different man as the renounced lover, attribute the heartache and frustration found in the poems to the circumstance that the man they advance as Emily Dickinson's lover was already married.

Now it cannot be denied that overwhelming inimical environmental factors may certainly prevent even the most resourceful and perisistent from achieving a cherished goal. Nevertheless, psychoanalytic experience engenders a wariness toward explanations that invoke extrinsic factors as the sole determinants in such failures. Upon close examination, in the case of patients, it is frequently found that concealed beneath the parade of misfortunes, adversities, and obstacles that "explain" the patient's lack of success there lies some unacknowledged and powerful inhibition or conflict of inclinations that contributes as much or more to the frustration of the ostensible wishes. It is this inner shrinking back, the deep-seated fear or revulsion, that may cause one to pursue goals that are safely unattainable. It is this internal prescription that invokes the external difficulties for purposes of self-deception when, for motives such as pride or conscience, one dreads to concede the true state of one's feelings.

That Emily Dickinson was possessed of uncertainties and reservations regarding her status as a woman is clear from her youthful letters. Equally evident is her insecurity and anxiety in the face of male sexuality; she apparently found it difficult to develop a social role congenial to her personality as a whole that would enable her to relate to males in a spontaneous and comfortable way. It should occasion no surprise, therefore, if this tentativeness and self-doubt should have come to the fore in any increasingly intimate love relationship in the form of fears and revulsions of sufficient force to render precarious, at the very least, the continuation of the relationship. That Emily Dickinson fled sexuality because spinsterhood appeared a less dreadful fate, and not solely because the only men that ever interested her were hopelessly committed elsewhere, she seemingly confesses in two very interesting and highly symbolic poems: no. 609, "I Years had been from Home," and no. 579, "I had been hungry, all the Years." The texts of the poems follow:

> I Years had been from Home
> And now before the Door
> I dared not enter, lest a Face
> I never saw before

Stare stolid into mine
And ask my Business there –
"My Business but a Life I left
Was such remaining there?"

I leaned upon the Awe –
I lingered with Before –
The Second like an Ocean rolled
And broke against my ear –

I laughed a crumbling Laugh
That I could fear a Door
Who Consternation compassed
And never winced before.

I fitted to the Latch
My Hand, with trembling care
Lest back the awful Door should spring
And leave me in the Floor –

Then moved my Fingers off
As cautiously as Glass
And held my ears, and like a Thief
Fled gasping from the House –

I had been hungry, all the Years –
My Noon had Come – to dine –
I trembling drew the Table near –
And touched the Curious Wine –

'Twas this on Tables I had seen –
When turning, hungry, Home
I looked in Windows, for the Wealth
I could not hope – for Mine –

I did not know the ample Bread –
'Twas so unlike the Crumb
The Birds and I, had often shared
In Nature's – Dining Room –

The Plenty hurt me – 'twas so new –
Myself felt ill – and odd –
As Berry – of a Mountain Bush –
Transplanted – to the Road –

Nor was I hungry – so I found
That Hunger – was a way
Of Persons outside Windows –
The Entering – takes away –

It is immediately apparent that though the poems employ different symbol complexes the emotional condition with which they commence seems to be identical and the poems thereafter run parallel courses. Both establish their points of departure in the first line, which conveys an atmosphere of prolonged deprivation—one through images of hunger, the other with suggestions of exile and lonely wandering from "Home." The initial stanzas depict a situation in which it has become possible to satisfy the longing of many years. In no. 579 a table is set with "Curious Wine" and "ample Bread," and the poet is free to appease her pent-up hunger. In no. 609, after years of managing without a "Life" she had left behind her, she has returned "Home" to claim it as her own. The middle stanzas convey the poet's unsettling reservations about the long-awaited consummation of her desires. In no. 579 she is dismayed to find that the meager supplies on which she has subsisted until now have not prepared her for the large meal. The new food seems foreign, surfeiting to the point of uncomfortable engorgement. The poet feels "ill – and odd" and out of her element. In no. 609, standing before the door of "Home," she is afraid to knock. She fears that the occupant will tell her that she has no business there. She procrastinates, wonders at her own hesitation, and dreads the second when the door will open and let her in. In no. 579 she loses her appetite and observes that "Hunger"—that is, a positive attitude toward "food"—is maintained only if one remains "outside Windows" and does not enter the "house" and "dining room." In no. 609 the poet feels she is better off to avoid the possible gratification that entering the "House" might provide. In no. 579 she feels "transplanted" (that is, in a situation in which she does not naturally belong), and in no. 609 she flees the situation "like a Thief" (that is, as one trespassing on property to which one has no legal or moral right).

For the sake of easier comparisons I list the points of similarity in the two poems:

	no. 579	no. 609
Duration of deprivation:	"Years"	"Years"
Nature of deprivation:	Lack of food ("I had been hungry, all the Years")	Lack of warm, loving shelter ("I Years had been from Home")
Proximity of gratification:	"My Noon had Come – to dine"	"And now before the Door" (of "Home")
Nature of gratification:	"Noon" meal, "Curious Wine," "ample Bread"	The regaining of a "Life" left behind
Approach to participation:	Partaking of food and drink	Fitting the "Latch" to her hand
Emotional reaction:	"Trembling"; dismay at the difference between surfeit (the "ample Bread") and minimal sustenance ("the Crumb" shared with the "Birds"); painful engorgement ("The Plenty hurt me"); strangeness (" 'twas so new"); sensations of illness; feeling "odd"; loss of appetite; feeling of being out of natural element: a mountain berry transplanted to a road	"Trembling care"; fear ("I dared not enter," "I could fear a Door"); dread of encountering something foreign and hostile where one might expect warmth and familiarity ("lest a Face / I never saw before / Stare stolid"); procrastination and feelings of weakness and inadequacy ("I leaned upon the Awe," i.e., the poet sought strength by withdrawing momentarily from the immediate situation, by becoming absorbed in her own surprising reactions and reflections on the past—"I lingered with Before"); feeling "like a Thief," i.e., not entitled to enter "house"
Denouement:	She sickens and loses her appetite; concludes that desire is superior to gratification	She dares not take her chances in entering the house; flees in panic

Although sexual love is not directly specified in these poems, it is difficult to imagine that the sequence of need → partial gratification → anxiety → renunciation that constitutes the emotional essence of both of them could refer as readily to any other experience. Both poems were written in the same year; it seems likely, therefore, that in view of their similarity they commemorate the same event. One supposes that Emily Dickinson, in writing these poems, was seeking to purge herself of a painful recollection or to grapple with some emergent disposition within herself that she could not fully understand. Comparison of the two "versions" affords a rarely obtainable insight into the creative use of metaphorical language: they evidently represent the end products of the poet's weighing of alternative images in her search for one strong enough to evoke something of the force of her original experience. She seems to have selected two—food and "Home"— capable of suggesting its basic, elemental character. Unable or unwilling to decide between them, she elaborated each one separately, developing each one's inherent expressive possibilities, the overall configuration in both cases necessarily conforming, in my view, to the sequence of real happenings of which the poems are figurative representations.

What intrinsic qualities do food and home share that would make them emotionally equivalent, more or less interchangeable, metaphors? What special meaning do food and home have in the psychology of Emily Dickinson? Following an attempted answer to these questions the further question arises: What actual situations might have evoked such strange and powerful reactions as those described in these poems and what is their meaning?

At the risk of stating the obvious, I should like to emphasize how important it is that "Home" in no. 609 be seen to be fully as much a metaphor as "food" is in no. 579; Emily Dickinson no more wandered from the parental mansion than she suffered from a scarcity of groceries. An extensive familiarity with the poet's biography is not necessary to be firmly convinced of this.

The equation food = love, with its roots in early infancy, is as nearly universal an identification as exists; it is readily grasped by and probably meaningful to most human beings. The reader will recall from Chapter II that Emily Dickinson rendered the connection explicit when she wrote: "Affection is like bread, unnoticed till we starve, and then we dream of it, and sing of it and paint it."[76] Again, in writing to her friend Mrs. Holland, she compared a husband's return home from a long lecture tour to feast after famine: "Am told that fasting gives to food marvellous Aroma, but by birth a Bachelor, disavow Cuisine."[77] Here there seems little doubt that consciously or otherwise the metaphor refers not only to love in general but specifically to sexual love. That for Emily Dickinson the symbol may encompass sexual love is evident from her letter to Judge Lord rejecting his advances in the language of food: "It is Anguish I long conceal from you to let you leave me, hungry, but you ask the divine Crust and that would doom the Bread."[78] In Chapter II many instances were cited in which the symbolic meaning of food for Emily Dickinson is clearly love, and these are so thickly distributed throughout the letters and poems that the interested reader will have no trouble finding other examples.

One cannot claim for the metaphor "Home" the same near-universality that characterizes the identification of love with food. But it is abundantly clear from Emily Dickinson's use of the word in numerous different contexts that for her the two symbols food and home are practically interchangeable.

"Home" seems to have accumulated gradually its symbolic resonance for the poet. In her youth she employed the word frequently in her letters. She used it literally then, but in a manner that increasingly invested it with a strong emotional aura adumbrating its later use as a symbol. Thus, at sixteen she writes: "Never did Amherst look more lovely to me & gratitude rose in my heart to God, for granting me such a safe return to my *own* DEAR H O M E."[79] The next month, writing from school, she says: "Home was always dear to me & dearer still the friends around it, but never did it seem so dear as now. All, all are kind to me but their tones fall strangely on my ear & their countenances meet mine not like home faces."[80] In a letter to her brother Austin about the comforts of home, written when she was twenty, one can detect certain tentative extensions beginning to cluster around the word: "Oh Austin, it is wrong to tantalize you so while you are braving *all things* in trying to fulfill duty. Duty is black and brown—home is bright and shining, 'and the spirit and the bride say *come,* and let him that' wandereth come—for 'behold all things are ready!' "[81]

By the time she had made herself a poet, the word was firmly established as a habitual symbol, not only in the verse but in her prose utterances as well. Examples: During a visit from T. W. Higginson when she was almost forty and a confirmed recluse, she inquired of him: "Could you tell me what home is[?]"[82] And the year before she had expressed to him in a letter a related idea: "You noticed my dwelling alone [she actually, of course, lived with her parents and sister]—To an Emigrant, Country is idle except it be his own."[83] It is clear from these self-revelations that "Home" represents a congenial atmosphere, a situation in which one has a sense of belonging, an emotional field shared with others who are sympathetic and understanding and who have certain fundamental characteristics (analogous to a common "Country") similar to one's own. At the time she made these remarks the parental mansion in Amherst evidently seemed alien and ill-fitting, and obviously was not to be identified with the ideal state of being "Home." Later, after her father's death, she wrote to her friend Higginson: "Home is so far from Home, since my Father died";[84] and later, "I often go Home in thought to you."[85] The first statement adds the notions of emotional fullness, completeness, perhaps safety and security (qualities provided by her father) to the idea of "Home"; and the second establishes again the idea that "Home" is where one is appreciated and feels accepted. And as has previously been pointed out, when Higginson took a new bride after the lonely interval following the death of his first wife, the poet wrote: "It is very sweet and serious to suppose you at Home . . . I have read of Home in the Revelations—'Neither thirst anymore.'"[86] Here "Home," like heaven, is a state in which one's thirst for affection is gratified; thus "food" and "home" are in this passage overtly linked.

The poems have more to add to this multifaceted concept. In them "Home" may be equivalent to "heaven" in the conventional religious sense (nos. 79, 319, 335, 499, 625); it may indicate an environment which is sympathetic and appreciative (nos. 413, 1727); it may refer to a relationship of rapport and tenderness with a sheltering person (nos. 84, 154, 725, 775, 944, 1573); and it may signify erotic love.

Strong erotic overtones accrue to the symbol in poem 190, the first stanza of which is:

> He was weak, and I was strong – then –
> So He let me lead him in –
> I was weak, and He was strong then –
> So I let him lead me – Home.

From the foregoing considerations does it not seem justifiable to conclude that the symbol "Home" in "I Years had been from Home" (no. 609) involves connotations of happiness, belonging, sheltering love, erotic love, and sexuality? Let us see.

Some speculations about the nature of the real experience that underlies the poem now seem in order. The following represents a very tentative reconstruction of that elusive event.

I Years had been from Home

Stanza I

> I Years had been from Home
> And now before the Door
> I dared not enter, lest a Face
> I never saw before

The poet appears to be telling us that she had once felt loved (perhaps in early childhood), but then a protracted interval ("Years") of lovelessness followed. Now the opportunity for a tender fulfillment is at hand but she feels afraid—she senses something unknown and just out of sight that intimidates her ("a Face / I never saw before"). The symbol "face" needs amplification. When Emily Dickinson wrote Judge Lord, "How could I long to give who never saw your natures Face,"[87] she was clearly responding to his inquiry about the cause of her failure to respond to him sexually. It appears that his "natures Face" is his masculine passion expressed genitally. And in the poem "My Life had stood – a loaded Gun" (no. 754), in which both sensuality and explosive aggression are the characteristics of a "Vesuvian face," the poet seems to have used "face" to express her own genital desire and arousal. Though Emily Dickinson did not use "face" symbolically as extensively as she did "home" and "food," these few instances strongly suggest its meaning. And given the poem's awe and panic it seems warranted to interpret "face" as a sexual symbol here. Therefore, what in this stanza prevents the poet from achieving the longed-for shelter and tenderness of "Home" is the specter of sexuality.

Stanza 2

Stare stolid into mine
And ask my Business there –
"My business but a Life I left
Was such remaining there?"

These lines seemingly represent the poet's dialogue with herself—she is uncertain of the permissibility of sexual gratification for herself and projects the doubt to her partner, who she fears may ask with bland hostility what she thinks she is doing at the portals of sex. She replies that her "Life" lies within these gates (meaning probably the *affective* life of tender mutual caring, intimacy, and support). Her implication here is that sexual gratification is not what she seeks. The difficulty is that the tender love she wants can be had only in conjunction with sexuality.

Stanza 3

I leaned upon the Awe –
I lingered with Before –
The Second like an Ocean rolled
And broke against my ear –

With the possibility of sexual consummation immanent she hesitates. She withdraws into introspection and self-observation; she marvels at the strangeness and awfulness of the elemental natural force that grips her and also, presumably, her lover. (This appears to be the approximate meaning of "I leaned upon the Awe"). She considers next the course of their relationship before the onset of complications of sexuality. In her anxiety, tension, and suspense the seconds seem almost infinite to her; they buffet her in turbulent waves of feeling.

Stanza 4

I laughed a crumbling Laugh
That I could fear a Door
Who Consternation compassed
And never winced before.

Her composure shatters, she marvels at her collapse and con-

137

trasts it with the strength she had been able to summon in the face of other, but different kinds of, dangers (perhaps her steadiness in the confrontation of death).

Stanza 5

I fitted to the Latch
My Hand, with trembling care
Lest back the awful Door should spring
And leave me in the Floor –

She makes a faltering and terrified sexual gesture – she touches the "Latch." Suddenly we are here confronted with that ambiguity of images so characteristic of Emily Dickinson. A seemingly unconscious bisexuality pervades her symbolism. Is the latch a masculine phallic symbol? If so, it is incongruous for it to be adjacent to an "awful Door" which threatens to provide a sudden passage into which the poet feels in danger of being propelled. The "latch" certainly is more fittingly a female phallus—the clitoris suspended above the vaginal vestibule. One is tempted to conclude that the sexual threat that stands between the poet and the tender love she craves is in this instance at least a homosexual one. The function that she futilely imagines for herself and that she fears, disowns, and unconsciously desires is a penetrative one—the masculine role.

Stanza 6

Then moved my Fingers off
As cautiously as Glass
And held my ears, and like a Thief
Fled gasping from the House –

The poet, in a frozen panic, shrinkingly withdraws, finds her mobility, and flees the object of temptation, overwhelmed with guilt ("like a Thief").

In the face of a poem like this, apparently reflecting deep-seated inhibitory attitudes, considerations of the marital commitments of the poet's various male acquaintances appear irrelevant and remote. One wonders if even the most felicitously timed appearance of a suitably disposed and eligible male genius could have made any real difference in Emily Dickinson's life.

An examination of the second poem, "I had been hungry, all the Years," serves to support the impression. Before commencing an explicatory sketch, a word should be said regarding the religious allusions contained in the poem.

The "Curious Wine" and the "ample Bread" impose upon the scene of sexual temptation depicted in "I Years had been from Home" the additional connotation of a sacrament. Here the relationship between the lovers takes on the aura of a holy communion—a partaking of "body and blood," a sacrifice. The Victorian need to spiritualize sexuality by overstressing its sacredness seems to have been a compensatory reaction to the conviction that in reality sex was gross and shameful; Emily Dickinson's weaker love poetry provides numerous examples of her attempts to idealize and sentimentalize sexuality. In this poem, however, the pious euphemisms constitute a transparent screen through which is discernible the genuine primitive need that links the partaking of love with the processes of ingestion.

We know that Emily Dickinson's religious doubts and reservations prevented her from availing herself of the social and emotional reassurance that joining the church seems to have afforded all the other members of her family. While they participated in Sabbath services and imbibed the bread and wine, she, with not a few guilty misgivings, attempted to wrest comfort from her solitary communion with nature, through which "God speaks"—sometimes. It seems plausible to suppose that some of the chronic feelings of exclusion and separateness that brought about and flowed from her failure to participate in the religious life of the community were echoed in the sphere of her interpersonal relations and that this helped bring about the association in her mind—as manifested in this poem—between her estrangement from religious solace and her starving for another's tender solicitude. To pursue the nexus of Emily Dickinson's religious ruminations any further here would, however, constitute too extensive a digression. Instead I shall focus on a less consciously elaborated and less intellectualized area of mental operations—the level at which love and food (including the eucharistic elements) are synonyms.

I had been hungry, all the Years

Stanza 1

I had been hungry, all the Years –
My Noon had Come – to dine –

I trembling drew the Table near –
And touched the Curious Wine –

After years of protracted and unsatisfied yearning for love, the poet at last finds herself in circumstances capable of ushering in the consummation of her desire. Her "Noon had Come to dine"; "Noon" is another repeatedly employed symbol in the poet's writings—with the sun at the zenith it is the ultimate intensity of light and, by analogy, love at full flood. The next lines imply that the lover is assenting and that there are no obstructing external circumstances standing in the way of the poet's complete gratification. Her reaction is to be unsure, frightened, and cautious, although the first overture is hers. Her choice of metaphor necessarily casts her in the active or conventionally masculine role, since bread and wine can hardly be anything but passive. The "Wine" is experienced as "Curious," that is, what in the situation stimulates and intoxicates is strange and unfamiliar; perhaps the image "Wine" represents the quickening effects of a caress.

Stanza 2

'Twas this on Tables I had seen –
When turning, hungry, Home
I looked in Windows, for the Wealth
I could not hope – for Mine –

The poet realizes that her present intimacy with her beloved constitutes a fulfillment identical to that granted others, which previously had evoked in her envy and which she had despaired of attaining herself.

Stanza 3

I did not know the ample Bread –
'Twas so unlike the Crumb
The Birds and I, had often shared
In Nature's – Dining Room –

Though insufficiently supplied with love in the past, she had learned to subsist on small tokens of affection ("Crumbs")— tendernesses devoid of the massive sensuality ("the ample Bread") that now disquiets her with its unfamiliarity.

Stanza 4

The Plenty hurt me – 'twas so new –
Myself felt ill – and odd –
As Berry – of a Mountain Bush –
Transplanted – to the Road –

Her imbibing of physical affection quickly becomes a glut and overwhelms her painfully. The experience is novel in an uncongenial way and causes her to sicken and feel strange. She feels that sexuality is too common a territory for her (a "Road"), because she is acclimated to an unfrequented and lofty habitat. (She comes of a "Mountain Bush" and feels out of place, perhaps degraded, in the "Road"; one senses in this word unpleasant connotations of too easy accessibility, prosaic purposes, dustiness, and commercial transactions.)

The images in this stanza appear to resonate along an additional symbolic level, parallel but deeper. In a poem apparently devoted to the poet's emotional responses to some kind of sexual encounter, the images may perhaps be legitimately related to each other also in a more concrete way. It is a commonplace that a woman's introduction to sexual intimacies may be frightening and disappointing. The bruising of delicate membranes may draw blood. Thus, the line "The Plenty hurt me – 'twas so new" may refer not only to the overpowering emotion generated by her own and another's passion but also to the overwhelming and painful effects of physical force. The transplanted berry may be the hymeneal blood (the first color commonly associated with berries is red); the "Mountain Bush," the mons veneris; and the "Road," the vagina. We cannot imagine that Emily Dickinson was unaware of these anatomical facts. Perhaps the episode revealed so obliquely in the poem did not progress this far (although the poem suggests it did); perhaps Emily Dickinson had in mind no such associations as these to pain, mountain bush, berry, and road. It is possible that, because she considered sex frightening, she repressed such disturbing details. In this case one may conclude that one set of determinants for these particular symbols was rooted in unconscious sexual preoccupations. On the other hand, as a thoughtful artist she did not choose her symbols carelessly, although she apparently chose many of them because of their linkage to thought processes of which she was only dimly aware. However they were chosen—deliberately or unconsciously—these images appear related along sexual lines with an aptness that seems unlikely to have been fortuitous. For example, it is difficult to see why the idea of being in an unsuitable and alien situation (conveyed by the word "transplanted") should involve the symbol "Berry" when so many other objects in the natural world are susceptible of being transported to unaccustomed and uncongenial environments. And why precisely a berry from a "Mountain Bush"? Emily Dickinson has for so long been thought of as an ethereal other-worldly creature that few have been willing to recognize that she was a living flesh-and-blood woman who, Victorian age notwithstanding, was well aware that whether she liked it or not she had no choice but to share the physiological reactions of the rest of humanity.

Stanza 5

Nor was I hungry – so I found
That Hunger – was a way
Of Persons outside Windows –
The Entering – takes away –

The sexual episode ends in profound disillusion. The love yearned after for so many years is, in this one shattering actual experience, exposed as a fantasy. The poet realizes that the reality has an excessiveness (the hurtful "Plenty") and grossness (the "Road") that she had not reckoned on. What once seemed equivalent to the mystical sustenance of the tabernacle has proven on closer acquaintance to be made of dust. The erotic dream is dissipated. The poet's appetite is gone.*

Details of the specific concrete circumstances at which these two poems merely hint are of course irrecoverable. It is even

---

* William Robert Sherwood believes that the theme of "I had been hungry, all the Years" is the reception by the poet of the grace of God, that is, that the poem commemorates the experience of religious conversion. He says, "these references to bread and wine denote a spiritual sustenance not found in the natural world" (*Circumference and Circumstance: Stages in the Mind and Art of Emily Dickinson* [New York, Columbia University Press, 1968], p. 158). The poem, however, states that the eucharistic substances caused surfeit, pain, illness, and loss of appetite—consequences that would seem to be the opposite of what would flow from the bestowal of God's precious gift. The "Curious Wine" and "ample Bread" surely, therefore, cannot refer literally to the sacramental bread and wine or to the grace they embody, but must be interpreted symbolically along quite different lines.

possible that the poems portray a fantasy only, the actual experience being one that the poet anxiously took pains to see never came about. If, however, the poems do commemorate a real event, it is hard to escape the conclusion, repugnant to those who have a need to see Emily Dickinson as an innocent, cloistered, secular nun, that the experience she found so odious and insupportable was an actual sexual encounter. Moreover, in either case—fantasy or reality—if the person symbolized by the bread and wine in the one poem and by "Home" in the other was a *man,* the poet's psychological disposition is clearly evident: ordinary sexuality to her is abhorrent. Therefore, that she lead a lonely, yearning life is not to be explained solely on the basis of unavailability of presentable, congenial bachelors. Her emotional inclination must be taken into consideration as an obvious factor of great, if not preponderant, importance.

Earlier, I observed that as Emily Dickinson approached maturity she underwent a crisis of sexual identity. Estranged almost from infancy from her own mother, she had difficulty accepting the femininity in herself. Rejecting the characteristics of her mother's role as a woman—the submissiveness, ineffectuality, superficiality, and triviality of her existence—the poet strove to assemble some image of womanliness to which she could conform willingly, and she did this through assiduous cultivation of other females who had the admired qualities her mother lacked. Such piecemeal feminine identifications, however, are inevitably unstable. For example, in the case of her devotion to her sister-in-law Susan, the borders between Sue's function as identification model and her function as frank love object become very blurred indeed. It is never quite clear to the reader of Emily Dickinson's letters, much less, one suspects, to the poet herself, whether Emily is assigning Sue the role of surrogate mother or whether Emily, her masculine identification to the fore, is asserting a possessive and erotic love.

To oversimplify greatly for purposes of brevity, these appear to be the essentials of Emily Dickinson's dilemma: to become a woman was to resemble her despised mother and fall victim (as she saw it)[88] to masculine callousness and exploitation; to embrace fully her masculine identification, in view of her lifelong hunger for an adequate "mother," was to move perilously close to a homosexual orientation, which her conscience and her culture regarded as an abomination. Moreover, the feminine position, besides involving the dreaded sexual subjugation to a man, meant giving up the masculinity which subserved her creativity—doubtless the most precious aspect of her life. Thus, with both heterosexuality and homosexuality proscribed for different reasons, she gave up not a married male lover—as the legends say—but interpersonal sexuality *in toto*. Sometimes, when seemingly she could not bear the full implications of her renunciation, she clung to the hope that what was lost on earth would be regained in heaven. At other times she appears to have given in to the delusion—thereby providing a basis for the legends—that she had had the best part of love—the spiritual joy of her masculine beloved's recognition despite the insuperable external barriers to their union. Thus she wrote of the "Soul": "I've known her – from an ample nation – / Choose one – / Then – close the Valves of her attention – / Like Stone" (poem 303). Emily Dickinson seems to have become a recluse partly because she had no adult role to play with either men or women. It was therefore less agonizing to slam the door on the world, pursue her writing, remain a child with Sue next door as occasional mother, and for the rest "Close the Valves of her attention – Like Stone."

Before the valves closed forever, however, there occurred the traumatic crisis that underlies "I Years had been from Home" and "I had been hungry, all the Years"—an event at the heart of Emily Dickinson's most turbulent decade and one that can be supposed to have tipped the scales in favor of her retreat from the external world. That the allusions in these poems are to erotic and physical temptations to which the poet reacted with fear and revulsion has been advanced as an explanation of Emily Dickinson's retreat from marriage. One must, however, consider the possibility that the ardor and embrace from which she fled in horror were offered not by a man but by a woman. How is one to decide the matter?

Emily Dickinson wrote many love poems in which the lover is explicitly male. Other love poems do not specify the sex of the lover, but in view of the former group it has naturally been assumed that in these also the beloved is male. A third group, smaller than the first two, involves a passionate and painful relationship with another woman; these poems have received little comment by most Dickinson scholars.

Let us consider a poem (no. 190) in the first category, in which the sex of the lover is given as male:

> He was weak, and I was strong – then –
> So He let me lead him in –
> I was weak, and He was strong then –
> So I let him lead me – Home.
>
> 'Twas'nt far – the door was near –
> 'Twas'nt dark – for He went – too –
> 'Twas'nt loud, for He said nought–
> That was all I cared to know.
>
> Day knocked – and we must part –
> Neither – was strongest – now –
> He strove – and I strove – too –
> We did'nt do it – tho'!

What is the nature of the transaction depicted here between the two lovers? The wording so clearly and startlingly implies sexual intercourse that one must pause and consider: is this the poet's unconscious thought inadvertently disclosing itself or are the allusions conscious and deliberate? If unconscious, what then does the poem convey on the level of awareness? Is the poem an erotic fantasy or the record of an actual happening? None of these questions is easy to decide, though there are some strong clues.

The first stanza says the man was "weak," but weak in what sense? Uncertain that a sexual union under the circumstances was morally right? Simply fearful of consequences? Indecisive? The poet says that she was strong and that the man "let me lead him in." In where? Into the house? Into her room? Or to an even more intimate chamber? Now the poet weakens and the man becomes the stronger, and she says: "So I let him lead me – Home." "Home" signifies, as has been pointed out, utter contentment, peace, completeness, and rightness. It might not be too farfetched to say that it may mean also sexual fulfillment: her partner is now strong and aggressive, and she is "weak," meaning, possibly, rendered passive. The next stanza says: " 'Twas'nt far – the door was near –/ 'Twas'nt dark – for he went – too." It is hard to escape the sexual implications of the "door" (compare "I Years had been from Home") through which the poet led herself and her lover "Home." The third stanza begins "Day knocked," implying that the lovers spent the night together.

Could this scene with a man have actually occurred? Was not Emily Dickinson's life too sheltered? Was she not forever "under the constant direct scrutiny of her family? Some authors have taken this view. Probably the episode could *not* have taken place with a man—but not because a male lover could not have found access to the poet. After all, the "mansion" was a large house, Emily's father, brother, and sister were frequently away from home, and everyone was used to Emily's late hours, for she often stayed up writing after the others had gone to bed. Sometimes she even took solitary nocturnal walks, if we are to believe a letter she wrote to Sue: "it breaks my heart sometimes, because I do not hear from you . . . I miss you, mourn for you, walk the Streets alone—often at night."[89] The only thing that would have effectively prevented the scene in the poem from being a reality was the poet's crippling fear of heterosexuality, for the existence of which there is abundant evidence.

It is the second group of poems—those in which the sex of the lover is not clearly given—that most frequently are found on close examination to embody the ambiguity of imagery mentioned previously with regard to the "Latch" and the "Door" in "I Years had been from Home." One of these poems (no. 322), "There came a day – at Summer's full," describes, in religious imagery, a crisis in a relationship. The poet and another person are parting. They pass the short time they have together in silent agony. The present meeting is their last (and perhaps their first) opportunity to "commune": "Each was to each / The Sealed Church, / Permitted to commune – this-time." The couple attempt to hold on to the present moment: "So / faces on two Decks, look back, / Bound to opposing lands." Ultimately "when all the time had leaked / Without external sound / Each bound the Other's Crucifix – / We gave no other Bond." The poem concludes with an affirmation of faith; after death they will achieve "that new Marriage, / Justified – through Calvaries of Love."

Though a small point perhaps, it is a fact that in psychoanalytic experience the symbol of the church is very rarely masculine. The poem says that each person was with regard to the other a "Sealed Church." Of course, in a superficial sense, a man constrained by the moral strictures of marriage from entering upon a relationship with another woman could be considered a "Church"—that is, the visible sign and representative of the holy rituals and sacred obligations pertaining to his married state. A church also is where one offers praise to God. It was in this sense that Emily Dickinson held her love for Judge Lord. "While others go to Church, I go to mine, for are not you my Church . . .?"[90] she wrote him. However, in the context of a passionate renunciation, the image of two "Churches" identically sealed to penetration from each other fails to evoke strong psychological reverberations conducive to visualizing one of the persons as a male. On the level of sexual metaphor, the association of a sealed church with masculinity is incongruous. However, it is a perfectly just and vivid symbol for a woman who is taboo as a sexual object. One concludes, therefore, that the poem suggests either: (1) that Emily Dickinson's deep need for a mothering person caused her unconsciously to endow a complaisant male with the qualities of a sheltering woman; or (2) that the person Emily Dickinson tore herself from so reluctantly in this poem was another woman.

In the third and smaller group of poems, dealing with the poet's troubled attachment for a person explicitly designated as female, one of the most interesting is poem 458, beginning: "Like Eyes that looked on Wastes." Here the theme is frankly stated as a hopeless devotion between two women. The poem says that the poet stared despairingly into the face of another woman and that neither could believe in anything "But Blank – and steady Wilderness – / Diversified by Night – / Just Infinities of Nought." The poet says she was unable to comfort the other woman "Because the Cause was Mine – / The Misery a Compact / As hopeless – as divine." It is difficult not to see in this poem the mutual renunciation, by two women who love each other, of a relationship that has taken on a forbidden sexual character.

Now to return once more to the questions raised by "I Years had been from Home" and "I had been hungry, all the Years." The tools of psychoanalytic inquiry, fashioned as they are for purposes of identifying psychological patterns and dispositions and establishing the relationships among them, can only in rare instances reconstruct the concrete specific details of historical events. To the question whether these poems commemorate a crisis of revulsion toward a heterosexual encounter or toward a homosexual one, the answer must be that the resources of psychoanalysis combined with an exhaustive study of Emily Dickinson's letters, poems, and life are not sufficient to yield a firm answer. All the evidence supports the conclusion that Emily Dickinson would have responded in very much the same way to a proposal of physical intimacy by a member of either sex. It is not possible to say from which contingency she would have recoiled more. What is clear is that in the case of a man the motivation for her recoil would necessarily have had a different psychodynamic basis than in the case of a woman, though the intensity of her reaction might not differ in the two situations. The former involves mostly her dreadful conception of the relations between the sexes; the latter, super-ego considerations, including fear of censure by those around her, and the psychological dangers inherent in regression to the "mother." This conclusion is bound to be disappointing to those who prefer decisive answers, and it is admittedly at odds with popular opinion, which holds that a person is either homosexual or he is not. Emily Dickinson apparently was never able to establish for herself a stable sexual orientation, either "normal" or "abnormal," or to assume a consistent adult social role. Consequently she vacillated anxiously in a state of unresolved bisexual potentiality, like a pre-oedipal child, vulnerable from every side.

At first glance Emily Dickinson's more conventional love lyrics seem to indicate that, however excessive the emotionality of her attachments to her own sex, her specifically *sexual* orientation was "normal." Rebecca Patterson, one of the few writers to consider seriously the evidence of strong homosexual propensities in the poet, concluded that all of these poems are disguised affirmations of love for a woman—that the poet regularly substituted masculine pronouns for feminine ones.[91] To reconcile the apparent discrepancies this way, however, entails maintaining that the artistic conscience of Emily Dickinson (that is, her sense of integrity as an illuminator of the inner emotional life) was such as to enable her to write erotic verse which dissimulated her actual feeling. Thus, according to this view, she could write poems reflecting her passionate attachment to another woman and present it in the guise of a heterosexual relationship, which, as a reality, would have been psychologically repugnant to her. Surely, such a practice would have conjured up alien images sufficiently offensive to her sensibilities to severely inhibit the emotional spontaneity necessary to creativity.

There is one other obvious difficulty with this dissimulation theory. If the poet took the pains to disguise her lover's sex in some poems, why did she not do so in all of them? A poem such as no. 458, "Like Eyes that looked on Wastes," unequivocally designates a woman as the lover—or at least as a peculiarly and excessively cherished friend. Another poem (no. 518) begins: "Her sweet Weight on my Heart a Night / Had scarcely deigned to lie – / When, stirring, for Belief's delight, / My Bride had slipped away." The directness is startling, and one must lean over backward not to suspect at least a homosexual *trend* in these lines. It has been said that the love poems in which the poet's beloved is presented as a man represent the poet's need to conventionalize in order to render the poems publishable. The alternate theory is that she feared the discovery of her dreadful secret and disguised the real experience with masculine pronouns. Poem 518, however, causes one to doubt that either of these propositions can be true. The poem was copied into a packet of fair copies in presumably final form despite the daring words "My Bride." If the poet were guarded enough to change the pronoun from "she" to "he" in other poems, she might be expected to disguise this one, which is far more explicitly erotic than many in which the beloved is male. In her letters to Sue she did not attempt to conceal the passionate nature of her affection; poem 518 offer evidence that in her poems also she could dare to express without disguise what she felt.

Some readers may be offended at these observations and find them incompatible with their image of Emily Dickinson. One suspects that the often heated rejection which greeted Mrs. Patterson's *Riddle of Emily Dickinson* was based only partly on her provocative style and the weaknesses of her argument; her sound insights may have been crucial for the response. Indicative of this is the fact that the Reverend Charles Wadsworth has been readily and widely accepted by many Dickinson specialists as the important love of the poet's life. Yet if one takes all the evidence for this view and compares it with that for Mrs. Patterson's, it may be seen that the former in no measure outweighs the latter. This suggests that the bias indulged by most readers is that Emily Dickinson should be considered "normal" if at all possible.

But if one keeps in mind Emily Dickinson's strong aversion to sexuality, no explaining away of either group of poems appears really to be necessary. There seems no valid reason not to regard as fervently sincere the poems of vehement attachment to a male lover, provided one understands their function in the poet's psychology. The crisis of passionate homosexual renunciation, most clearly discerned in "Like Eyes that looked on Wastes," likewise can be accepted without doing violence to what we know of the laws of human responses. All the evidence, if one really looks at it, impels one to the conclusion that Emily Dickinson attempted to remain sexually ambiguous and uncommitted. Her early letters point to this conclusion; so does her "shunning men and women" and her eventual reduction to epistolary contact only of almost all her relationships, with males and females alike. And the puzzling shifting of attitudes and objects in the poems and her use of bisexual symbols, in the light of her psychological history, is not really incomprehensible. Psychiatric experience attests to the fact that a woman's intensely passionate and sustained preoccupation with a member of her own sex—especially when it is accompanied by an attitude of conscious revulsion and rejection toward the physical concomitants of such an attraction—may be entirely compatible with a rapt, romanticized absorption in a man. The man, however, must be safely unattainable and the danger of sexual involvement with him must be remote, for on an unconscious level the woman rejects him. The relationship between the two psychodynamic constellations is this: the forbidden attraction (in Emily Dickinson's case, to Sue and other women) may bring about the establishment of the conventionally acceptable attitude (that is, the heterosexual one) as a defense, a channel of discharge for the illicit excitations.

No doubt it is possible in some forms of literature for emotion of homosexual origin to be conventionalized into its opposite for purposes of obtaining a wider audience and of personal concealment. Though some readers of Emily Dickinson's more conventional poems have sensed a curious shallowness in some of them, few, if any, except Mrs. Patterson, would be prepared to insist that she never experienced a conscious erotic attraction to a male.

The semiautobiographical, intensely introspective lyrics of Emily Dickinson have an immediacy and impact that seem intrinsically incompatible with such deliberate manipulation. One concludes, therefore, that the agonies of renunciation that permeate Emily Dickinson's life and writings had multiple sources in hopeless, incomplete attachments to members of both sexes. In place of real love relationships she apparently evolved disembodied, and therefore nonthreatening, fantasies whose only bridge to their distant and perhaps astonished objects was her poems and letters.

Because both the erotic impulses evoked in her relationships with men and those evoked in her relationships with women forbode terrifying and destructive consequences, flight remained Emily Dickinson's only option. Flight from one's instinctual life involves a firm denial of the extent of one's erotic needs and a tight control over all emotional relations with others; otherwise these needs and relations may lead to libidinal stimulation in one's self, which is experienced as a dreaded, anxiety-laden pleasure. If these first-line defenses of denial and avoidance are insufficient in the face of too much opportunity and temptation, repression from consciousness of sexual and aggressive feelings may be called for as reenforcement. But any attempt at total repression of such basic drives severely threatens the stability of one's mental processes and is, in the long run, probably impossible. The repudiated impulses will probably be channeled into a plague of neurotic symptoms (note Emily Dickinson's fear of strangers, preoccupation with death, agoraphobia, and so forth) each one accompanied by its own quantum of anxiety. This anxiety, moreover, may be all the more incapacitating and distressing because its connection with the repressed impulses has been obscured and it therefore takes on the character of something bizarre and incomprehensible, before which the rational components of one's mind are helpless.

Whatever one wishes to call it—a protracted latency with clinging to childlike patterns of interpersonal exchange or a long adolescence attenuated by a relative shutting out of heterosexual interests—the position in which Emily Dickinson found herself in her early twenties was untenable, and one senses her trembling intuition that a psychological crisis was underway. Her state demanded, at the price of sanity if need be, that some channel be opened to the future. Thus, before her ultimate renunciation, after which her upstairs room became her hermitage—her work-shop, her cell, and eventually almost her mausoleum—the pri-mordial drives of love and aggression propelled her one last time toward the living world. The oedipal dilemma, never resolved in her infancy, exhumed itself from limbo. For the second time it moved into the foreground of Emily Dickinson's unconscious psychic life. This time the other two points of the triangle, in place of father and mother, were Austin and Sue.

In March 1852 Emily writes Austin: "It's a glorious afternoon —the sky is blue and warm—the wind blows just enough to keep the clouds sailing, and the sunshine, Oh *such* sunshine, it is'nt like gold, for gold is dim beside it . . . I only only wish you were here. Such days were made on purpose for Susie and you and me."[92] Unaware of the contradictions inherent in her dream of a lifetime of happiness together—Emily, Austin, and Sue—Emily tries to hurry the days away until Austin's marriage. So begins the long overdue final phase of Emily Dickinson's adolescence.

Chapter IV THE BRIGHT BEE

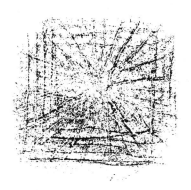

In the oedipal situation the primary question each child must settle is: With whom shall I identify? That is, shall I be a man like father and therefore love woman as he does, or shall I be a woman like mother and consequently love men? As I have attempted to demonstrate in the previous chapter, Emily Dickinson failed to resolve the matter on the first go-around, when her actual mother and father were the two other points of the triangle. In happier circumstances than existed for her, where the issues are less complicated by excessive awes and antipathies and where discrepancies of constitutional endowment between the child and the parent of the same sex are less glaring, the problem is ordinarily settled by the time the child is six. Thereafter, until adolescence, he enjoys, in the latency period, a half dozen or so relatively tranquil years more or less unruffled by sexual urgency, during which he has an unconscious and profound sense of the appropriateness of the gender role assigned to him by his parents.

For many persons and for various reasons the matter cannot be disposed of in childhood so finally and comfortably. In this event, which invariably involves disturbed parent-child relationships, the physiological onslaught of puberty again brings the issue up. Now, however, the problem is critical; the hormonal fires press for a definitive resolution and the young man or woman must make a choice. The young woman, with her more diffuse erotic sensations and slower genital awakening, may more easily than her male age-mate postpone any definite awareness of the character of her sexual orientation. Nature seemingly grants the girl more leeway. However, eventually a definite commitment to a sexual role is essential and just as crucial for her as for the male if she is to fulfill her potentialities as an adult in relation to other human beings. Sooner or later her tentative and beclouded status in the face of environmental demands produces anxiety and the need to take an unequivocal stand. There comes a critical point when the neutrality of latency will no longer do; the various possibilities of the oedipal constellaton again come up for review, as it were, and a choice is demanded. Such a crisis is frequently precipitated when circumstances bring about a simulacrum of the original oedipal triangle, this time, however, with new personalities in the roles formerly played by the father and mother.

For Emily Dickinson the belated opportunity to consolidate the inharmonious factions of her personality and to confirm and stabilize her uncertain femininity came in the form of her brother's love affair. It was an opportunity that Emily Dickinson very badly misused to her own near destruction—or perhaps it would be fairer and more accurate to say that the triangle—Austin, Susan, Emily—was in reality no opportunity at all. The emotional needs of all three protagonists rendered the situation such as to embody no real and lasting corrective. She realized this fact too late, however, and only after the stresses of their complex and tortured relationship had all but torn her apart.

Before examining Emily Dickinson's role in Austin's long and troubled courtship of Susan, which will be reserved for the following chapter, it is important to try to understand the many aspects of her attachment to her brother. This important relationship, evolved throughout their childhood and youth, evinced no outward turbulence before Susan came to revolutionize the scene.

The essential elements of Emily Dickinson's relationship to Austin are all evident in their youthful correspondence. Though in the main only her letters survive, they hold sufficient reflection of the brother's thought and feeling to establish the nature and intensity of the bonds that had developed between them since childhood.

The mass of letters of these indefatigably faithful correspondents date from their teens and early twenties and were composed during the only protracted separations they ever had to bear. The earliest of these unwelcome partings occurred when first one, then the other, was sent away to boarding school. Later, while Emily remained at home, Austin taught in elementary schools in nearby Sunderland and then in Boston, these experiences consuming altogether about two years. Finally, before returning to Amherst for the rest of his life, he attended Harvard Law School for a year, graduating and completing his bar examinations at the age of twenty-five. During his professional training he exchanged almost weekly letters with Emily.

Though the interpersonal involvement in these letters is unvaryingly intense, there exists, as in all complex relationships, a diversity of attitudes, a gamut of affective nuances and fluctuations. To understand the vital role assigned to Austin in the deepest currents of his sister's mind, it is helpful to distinguish a cluster of predominating leitmotifs around which the various minor themes revolve.

Once, when Emily Dickinson sought assistance in her development as a poet, she let her preceptor Higginson know that her need was a matter of life or death and she begged him not to withhold his criticism out of regard for her feelings. "I had rather wince, than die," she said, and observed that "Men do not call the surgeon, to commend—the Bone, but to set it . . . and fracture within, is more critical."[1] The guidance she sought consciously from Higginson with regard to art she appears to have sought blindly and gropingly from Austin with regard to her emotional life. Underlying many of the unconscious manipulations and campaigns detectable in her letters to him was an expectation that through her brother she might somehow palliate the "fracture within" of which she was vaguely, but disturbingly, aware.

One way she attempted this palliation was to conjure up an atmosphere of maternal concern beyond what her mother could supply. The measures she persistently employed to this purpose in her letters rise to the surface of expression occasionally. At a time when Emily was writing to Austin every four or five days she remarks, "Mother was much amused at the feebleness of your hopes of hearing from her—She got so far last week once, as to take a pen and paper and carry them into the kitchen."[2] At this point, Mrs. Dickinson was interrupted by visitors and, as was apparently usual, her letter was never written.

On another occasion Emily tells Austin: "Mother sends her love, and says she thinks very often she shall certainly write to you, but she knows that we write so often she thinks we say all there is, and so she recollects you, but says nothing about it."[3] Many years later, Austin's daughter Martha, writing along the same lines, noted that Mrs. Dickinson's "gentle reign" had been "increasingly enfeebled in spite of herself by the dominating daughter [that is, Emily]."[4]

These straws indicate the direction of the wind and tell us almost directly what can be perceived as an undercurrent throughout the correspondence. Emily here is outdoing her mother, has relegated her to an inferior position, and is working at proving herself to be a more loving and attentive mother to Austin than their own mother is able to be. The psychological meaning of this position will be discussed later.

If one has a powerful need to demonstrate one's superior motherliness, it is necessary that there be available a sufficiently dependent object upon which to exercise this function. The kind of possessive maternalism that cripples a child's striving for self-reliance, undermines his confidence in being able to fend for himself, and encourages a clinging dependency has long been recognized as a characteristic of certain unhappy women. These women want to be recognized as loving and motherly, although it is readily apparent to even a casual observer, as it is apparent on a deeper level to themselves, that they are grossly deficient in these feminine attributes. The smothering affection they bestow on their offspring (or on the neighbors' children, if they are fortunate enough not to have children of their own, or on their husbands, or their pets, or even their plants) is clearly recognizable as an activity designed primarily to satisfy a hunger within themselves. Only secondarily, if at all, are the real needs of the "mothered" taken into consideration.

If, as is postulated here, Emily Dickinson had a need to play this role in relation to Austin, we should expect to find in her correspondence with him a continuous chipping away at the foundations of his manly adequacy so that he would tend to rely on her more and more as a major source of emotional support. This is precisely what we do find.

As early as age eleven, Emily already shows a keen interest in Austin's emotional stamina away from home, a foreshadowing of her later attempts to bind him to Amherst. Austin, then thirteen, was sent away to Williston Seminary, and Emily writes: "Aunt Montague—has been saying you would cry before the week was out."[5] Of course such a statement to a boy Austin's age would only strengthen his resolve to show his relatives how brave he could be, but a girl of eleven may not have realized the fact.

At sixteen, Emily, now herself away at school, rejoices in a letter to a friend that without her at home Austin and Vinnie are lonesome: "How happy it made me to hear them say that 'they were *so lonely.*' "[6]

Four years later, when Austin takes up his post as schoolmaster in Boston, Emily writes: "I'm glad you are so well pleased [with the school], I am glad you are *not* delighted, I would not that *foreign* places should wear the smile of home."[7]

Not only Emily, who is their spokesman, but apparently the entire Dickinson family felt that perils lay in wait on every side of Austin in a strange city. One must continually keep in mind that Austin was only a hundred miles away and doing nothing more dangerous than teaching school. Here is how Emily voices her own concern: "I hope you're very careful in working, eating and drinking when the heat is so great—there are temptations there which at home you are free from—beware the juicy fruits, and the cooling ades, and cordials, and do not eat *ice-cream,* it is so very *dangerous* [Emily is afraid Austin will contact typhoid fever]—the folks think much about you, and are so afraid you'll get sick by being rash or imprudent—for our sakes Austin wont you try to be careful?"[8] The admonition itself is perfectly sensible, of course. What is significant is that it is conveyed by the young man's younger sister and with a parade of seasoned maternal wisdom and experience.

While Austin is trying his best to stand on his own feet, Emily emphasizes the fact that such arrangements are transitory and almost unnatural: "I should think you'd be tired of school and teaching and such hot weather, I really wish you were *here* and the Endicot school where you *found* it . . . [When Austin returns] We shall enjoy brimfull everything *now* but *half* full, and to have you home once more will be like living *again*!"[9]

Austin, as might be expected, sometimes resented this solicitude, and seems to have replied that his relatives need not concern themselves so much with his welfare—that he was surviving adequately in Boston. Such a show of independence did not go over well at home, however, as witness this reply from Emily: "You say we must'nt trouble to send you any fruit, also your clothes must give us no uneasiness. I dont ever want to have you say any more such things. They make me feel like crying. If you'd only *teased* us for it, and declared that you *would* have it, I should'nt have cared so much that we could find no way to send you any, but you resign so cheerfully your birthright of purple grapes, and do not so much as *murmur* at the departing peaches, that I hardly can taste the one or drink the juice of the other."[10]

Emily keeps suggesting to Austin how lonely he must be away from them all, but at the same time, she points out the benefits of not forming attachments away from home: the ensuing loneliness will enrich home relationships when at last they are renewed. "[I know] how much you feel the need of a companion there . . . but if you talk with no one, you are amassing thoughts which will be bright and golden for those you left at home."

The following quotation from the same letter indicates the way Emily fails to strengthen Austin in his resolve to be self-sufficient: "Sometimes, I am afraid it will hurt you to stay there. I'm afraid the year you teach will become so embittered that all this blessed country cannot wash it away . . . your being where you are is a *mutual* trial—both yourself, and us, are for the time bereaved— yet your lot is the hardest, in that while *four anticipate,* in *your* case there's but one—we can gather together and say we are very lonely, and it would be so happy if we were all at home—yet one sustains the other—Vinnie and I console and comfort father and mother—I encourage *Vinnie,* Vinnie in turn cheers *me*—but one and alone, you are indeed dependent, in any pensive hour, dependent on *yourself* too, the very one of *all* least likely to sustain you."[11] The chief message is perfectly clear: one cannot rely on oneself.

Emily continues to emphasize the dangers of the seasons. Now that the summer heat has disappeared, she admonishes Austin to beware of autumn's chill. "Dont get sick these cool days when fevers are around!"[12]

When Austin actually complains of illness or merely appears not to be in top condition, Emily's eternal watchfulness merges into parental anxiety: "he [father] thinks you are not very well, and I feel so anxious about you that I cannot rest until I have written to you and given you some advice . . . I would not spend much strength upon those little school boys—you will need it all for something better and braver, after you get away. It would rejoice my heart if . . . you'd turn the schoolroom key . . . and walk away to freedom and the sunshine here at home."

Apparently these undermining tactics are beginning to persuade Austin that a life of independence is, after all, an undesirable thing. Emily continues: "Father says all Boston would not be a temptation to you another year—I wish it would not tempt you to stay another day." At this point Emily seems on the verge of realizing that she may be luring Austin into the dependency that is also insidiously trapping her: "Oh Austin," she suddenly exclaims, "it is wrong to tantalize you so while you are braving *all things* in trying to fulfill duty."[13] But then she returns to her major theme and concludes that, after all, duty is a gloomy thing compared with the joys of home.

After Austin made a brief visit home, Emily writes: "It may seem long to *you* since you returned to Boston—how I wish you could stay and never go back again . . . Oh I am so lonely!"

Later in the same letter she expresses concern for Austin's eyes, which have been troubling him, and then says: "I wished so many times during that long evening [on which Austin returned to Boston] that the door would open and you come walking in. Home is a holy thing—nothing of doubt or distrust can enter it's blessed portals. I feel it more and more as the great world goes on and one and another forsake, in whom you place your trust." Those who are forsaking, it should be recalled, are mainly those girl friends who are disengaging themselves from Emily and turning to friends of the opposite sex. She continues, still referring to home: "Here seems indeed to be a bit of Eden which not the sin of *any* can utterly destroy."[14] It is perhaps too obvious to need emphasizing that in the traditional view the biblical Eden was destroyed by the transgression of sex. The "bit of Eden" to be found in the Dickinson home, therefore, is a realm from which sex is excluded. What she seems to be saying to Austin is: "Austin, come home and we will love each other forever—we will each be tender, solicitous parents to the other—and be each other's beloved child; this way the stresses of adult sexuality need never disturb us." Lest this interpretation be considered far-fetched, it should be recalled that Emily said of her sister, "She has no Father and Mother but me and I have no Parents but her,"[15] a statement made at a time when both of the elder Dickinsons were still living. One might add that she could as well have formulated one aspect of her relationship to Austin in the same manner: in a sense she regarded her function toward Austin as a maternal one.

As would any healthy child before his instincts are subverted, Austin struggled to emancipate himself, but despite his protests Emily keeps insisting that he must be lonely: "a *single word* may be of comfort to you . . . It should be a word big and warm and full of sweet affection . . . Oh it should fill that room [Austin's room in the city], that small and lonely chamber."[16] After another brief visit from Austin, she writes: "I often tho't of you in the midnight car, and hoped you were not lonely. I wished . . . that you were *here,* soundly asleep and adream."

Her conscious intention seems to have been to increase Austin's sense of inner security by reiterating how much he was loved and missed at home, but the way she went about expressing these sentiments can only have undermined it. Observe how she begins by encouraging him and how, seemingly against her will, she ends by asserting her own need to keep him a dependent child: "I wish I could imbue you with all the strength and courage which can be given men—I wish I could assure you of the constant remembrance of those you leave at home—I wish, but Oh how vainly, that I could bring you back again, and never more to stray! You are tired *now* Dear Austin, with my incessant din, but I cant help saying any of these things."[17]

When Austin gives indications that he is beginning not to find Boston intolerable after all and is even cultivating a woman friend, Emily is clearly disconcerted. Notice the prim and covertly reproving tone of her answering letter. In this reply one senses not only the secret jealousy of the possessive mother in the face of her son's girl friend but also the familiar devious evocation of guilt through a martyrly assertion on the part of the mother of her own selfless and contrasting fidelity: "I am glad you like Miss Nichols," Emily says, dissembling her real feelings, "it must be so pleasant for you to have somebody to care for, in such a cheerless place—dont shut yourself away from anyone whom you like, in order to keep the faith to those you leave behind! Your friends here are much happier in fancying *you* happy, than if in a pledge so stern you should refuse all friendliness." Apparently not satisfied that she has stated her case convincingly enough, she repeats: "Truth to the ones you leave does not demand of you to refuse those whom you find, or who would make your exile a less desolate thing in their cheerful circles." For Emily Dickinson this is very labored writing indeed. She plods on: "On the contrary, Austin, I am very sure that seclusion from everyone there would make an ascetic of you." Then, after telling him not to feel guilty for enjoying himself with a new friend, she emphasizes in the next breath her own superior faithfulness: "We miss you more and more, we do not become accustomed to separation from you. I almost wish sometimes we need'nt miss you so much . . . and then again I think that it is pleasant to miss you if you must go away, and I would not have it otherwise, not even if I could."[18] So much for your peccadilloes, Austin Dickinson!

Toward the end of the year, no doubt in Emily's view through divine retribution, Austin is stricken with neuralgia. Emily's hovering mother element comes again to the fore: "I'm afraid that dreadful pain will keep you wide awake all this dreary night . . . Hav'nt you taken cold, or exposed yourself in some way, or got too tired, teaching those useless boys?—I am so sorry for you . . . Dont try to teach school at all, until you get thoroughly well! The committee will excuse you, I *know* they will, they *must*."[19]

The strain of being away from home and being constantly reminded of the fact plus the discords in his relationship with Susan, of which I shall have occasion to speak at length later, seem to have induced in Austin a preoccupation with his health. A month after the previous letter we hear that in addition to his eye difficulty and his neuralgia he is now troubled with palpitations—almost certainly an anxiety symptom.

Emily writes him: "we do need you at home, and since you have been sick and are away from us, the days seem like *ages,* and I get tired of ever hoping to see you again. It seems to me it would do you a great deal of good to leave school a few days, and come home . . . Cant you, Austin? I do wish you would; never mind the boys [Austin's pupils]; if they cant fill your place for a week, let it be *un*filled."[20]

To Austin's credit he was able to resist these blandishments, and a week or so later he seems to have been better. Emily then writes: "I hope you will be very careful and not get sick again, for it seems to me you've had so much miserable health since you have lived in Boston; if it dont ruin your constitution, I shall be very glad";[21] and in a letter written the following spring she repeats the advice: "Above all things, take care of yourself, and dont get sick away, for it would be very lonely for you to be sick among strangers, and you're apt to be careless at home."[22]

And again: "Dont work too hard Austin, dont get too tired, so that you cannot sleep."[23] The maternal solicitude is incessant: "Was'nt you very tired when you got back to Cambridge?" she wants to know after Austin concluded another short visit home; "I thought you would be, you had so much to do, the morning you went away. I hope you do not cough mornings . . . If you do, go to see that Apothecary who gave you something before, and get something to cure it . . . We all love you very much—wont you remember *that* when anything worries you, and you wont care then."[24]

And still again, after an apparently minor indisposition of Austin's: "I will tell you first how glad I am you are better, and are not going to be sick, as I was afraid when you wrote me. Do be careful, very careful, Austin, for you are from us all, and if anything happens to you, we cannot find it out and all take care of you as we can when you're at home. I dont think you'd better study any for a day or two, until you feel perfectly well . . . just come home the moment whenever you are sick, or think you are going to be sick, and you shall have Vinnie and me and Somebody [meaning Susan, not Mrs. Dickinson] nearer than either of us to take care of you, and make you well."[25]

The theme of concern for Austin's well-being approaches an obsession: "Take care of your lungs, Austin—take that [medicine] just as I told you, and pretty soon you'll be well."[26] Although it was her habit to keep late hours herself, she writes Austin: "I would'nt sit up late, if I were you, or study much evenings."[27]

Constantly repeated also is her insistence upon Austin's being lonely: "Did'nt you find it very lonely, going back to Mrs. Ware's? [Austin's landlady] . . . I hope you wont be lonely in Cambridge—you must think of us all when you are. And if the cough troubles you follow my prescription . . . It seems pretty still here, Austin, but I shant tell you about it, for twill only make you lonely."[28]

Obviously, Austin's emotional condition is as much her concern as his physical health. "Take care of yourself Austin," she writes in another letter, "and dont get melancholy."[29]

That she is melancholy without him, however, she freely admits. "All the busy things work on as if the same [since Austin returned to Cambridge]," she tells him, "They do not miss you, Child, but there is a humming bee [that is, Emily] whose song is not so merry."[30]

Perhaps because his mother rarely wrote and because his father's letters were terse and businesslike, Austin fed on the debilitating emotionalism of these letters. As he said to Emily and Vinnie: "Girls—write often letters are meat & drink."[31] In addition to whatever verbal sustenance she provided (Vinnie claimed Emily fed her brother on air), Emily packaged and forwarded to Austin a constant stream of fruit and other edibles from the Dickinson gardens and orchards—grapes, peaches, apples, maple sugar, and so on. Once she got the notion to send Austin a pound of peanuts, but Vinnie's mockery dissuaded her. If one recalls the preeminent importance of food to Emily Dickinson, as evidenced in the reiterated use of images of nutriment in her poetry as symbols for love, one can see in her feeding of Austin another aspect of her cultivated self-image as a good mother to him. She was eager to know if he appreciated her offerings and asked him if he missed these edible luxuries that were always available at home. "Have you had any maple molasses," she inquires, "or any Graham Bread, since you have been away? Every time a new loaf comes smoking on to the table, we wonder if you have any where you have gone to live. I should love to send you a loaf, dearly, if I could."[32]

And so the theme of maternalism with regard to Austin runs through the correspondence, letter after letter. This is the first point to be made about the underlying currents of the poet's relationship with her brother. He was, in this sense, her property— he belonged to her; he was her child. She lavished her love and tenderness, her concern and her consideration upon him, and in doing so, she became in a sense his mother. Mrs. Dickinson's inadequacies left a vacuum in the family. Emily's emotional hungers drove her to seize the opportunity this provided, and she rushed in to fill the roles left vacant.

To achieve a realistic perspective on Emily's solicitude for Austin, which seems so genuinely maternal, we must recall the actual circumstances of her existence. She herself, during the entire interval in which these letters were written—in fact, for the rest of her life—was utterly dependent on her parents for literally everything necessary for her survival. The shelter she offered Austin was her father's house. The food she fed him, the fruit and sugar from his orchards. There was nothing with which she could provide him through her own efforts save the products of her cerebration. Even her letters arrived through the courtesy of Edward Dickinson, via his stationery, ink, and franking privilege. As she grew increasingly phobic about leaving the house, it would gradually have become impossible for her to run some little local errand for Austin had he requested this of her. Her protestation that she would do anything for her brother, that she was his to command, involved a complete denial of her essential powerlessness. One is reminded here of her later habit of indulging in extravagant offers of assistance to relatives and neighbors in difficulty. For example, in 1873, she wrote her cousin: "I am troubled for Loo's eye . . . Can I help her? She has so many times saved me."[33] Now, what exactly could she have done? She was by then an entrenched recluse who saw nobody and went nowhere. In 1882, she wrote a neighbor, Mrs. Stearns, on the death of a daughter: "Affection wants you to know it is here. Demand it to the utmost."[34] If Mrs. Stearns had asked her to cross the street and babysit for five minutes, Emily could not have complied. And again in 1884, when Austin's brother-in-law was ill, Emily wrote Sue: "Love for your suffering Brother, whose I am each moment, could I in any way refresh him and for each in the loved Home— Tell me any service and my Heart is ready."[35] It certainly must have been difficult for Sue to think of some way Emily could be helpful since, by this time, she was not even crossing the lawn to her brother's home. Of course, she wanted to be helpful, to be needed by someone, to be a "good mother." It must have been, to some extent, the very intensity of this need that drove her to play the grand game of ask and it shall be yours. The similarity between the foregoing offers of assistance and her earlier hovering readiness to care for Austin's every need seems clear.

There were other important facets in Emily's relationship with Austin, however.

The next to be considered is her vicarious participation in his virility and assertiveness, which, to some extent, she seems to have envied. In this aspect of her attachment the mother-child relationship and the competition with Mrs. Dickinson have small part. Here, Austin is apprehended primarily as a companion, an admired guide, and as a model for her own psychological development.

As we have seen it was difficult for Emily Dickinson to identify herself wholeheartedly with either of her parents. Her mother failed miserably to meet her standards; her fear and even awe of her father plus his own stiff and uneasy reactions impeded, though it did not entirely preclude, her identification with him. Thus was partially arrested the development of Emily Dickinson of that heightened feeling of closeness which is necessary for the profound inner adjustment involved in the process of identification whereby one's status as a male or female becomes a secure and inner certainty. No such insurmountable obstacles blocked her relationship with Austin. He had certain qualifications her parents lacked which made him, if not an ultimately appropriate vehicle, at least a temporarily plausible and available model for the maturation of his sister's self-image. Austin had (to a lesser degree undoubtedly) many of his father's positive and admirable characteristics. Besides, unlike his father, he was spontaneous, playful, and approachable. Moreover, he had his father's attractive prerogatives and privileges. These assets, arising simply from his status as a male, loomed very large in the estimation of a sister who thoroughly despised the obsequious posture of her mother. In her earliest surviving letter, written when she was only eleven, her admiration for Austin is clearly evident: "We miss you very much indeed you cannot think how odd it seems without you there was always such a Hurrah wherever you was."[36]

Ten years later we find her making almost the same comment: "I miss your big Hurrahs, and the famous stir you make."[37] Apparently Austin did not change in this regard during his teens and early twenties. In another letter, Emily tells a girl friend: "Austin was reading Hume's History until then—and his getting it through was the signal for general uproar."[38] Thus Austin, because he was a male, seems to have been granted by both parents a relative freedom of expression denied his more repressed sisters. "You always did what you wanted to," Emily told him admiringly, "whether 'twas against the law or not."[39] As a youth he developed a boisterousness of personality and a love of fun and jokes that constituted the brightest spot in the generally prevailing gloom and sobriety of the household. Emily admired him unreservedly, appropriated as her own whatever interested him, and missed him intensely when he was away at school. The letter mentioned above, written when Emily was eleven, speaks excitedly of his chickens and roosters in what was obviously a shared enthusiasm.

At the age of thirteen, she writes him that a meeting to be held in the Dickinson home might possibly prove to be a pleasant occasion, but "If you was at home it would be perfectly sure."[40]

Austin had a sense of humor that the whole family enjoyed, though Emily and her father seem to have been his most appreciative audience. She writes to him: "we *laughed some* when each of your letters came—your respected parents were *overwhelmed* with glee";[41] and again: "Received your note last evening, and laughed all night till now . . . Susie was here when the note arrived, and we just sat and screamed. I shall keep the letter always."[42] Also: "When I know of anything funny, I am just as apt to cry, far *more* so than to *laugh*," she writes him, "for I know who *loves jokes best*."[43] And again: "Your letters are very funny indeed—about the only jokes we have, now you and Sue are gone."[44] A year later she writes much the same thing: "I rose at my usual hour . . . and missed you very much in the lower part of the house—you constituting my principal society, at that hour of the day . . . [at breakfast] Mother and Vinnie were quite silent, and there was nobody to make fun with me at the table."[45]

In addition to this infectious buoyancy and capacity to lead others to see the comic side of things, Austin had a *presence*—as a friend of his remarks admiringly: "there was something in him which always made *folks mind*—when Austin was at home Austin was *in town*."[46] He had a kind of hauteur, an unselfconscious and unquestioned sense of his own superiority, but it was not vanity, for it attracted others, which vanity does not. Emily was as caught up as anyone in this personal magnetism of Austin's. The characteristic of personal forcefulness, of having an impact on others through one's mere presence, must have seemed to her in her formative years to be an enviable and exclusively masculine endowment. Her father's air of intrinsic authority affected everyone, though not, as in the case of Austin, necessarily positively. To repeat a remark already quoted, it was once said of him that like the prophet Samuel he was a man "whom a whole village feared, in whose appearance there was that which terrified."[47] It would be surprising, in view of such vivid and powerful masculine examples in the family, if Emily Dickinson had preferred to emulate not them but her vacuous mother. The loveless relationship with her mother was, then, only one source of Emily's aversion to identification with her; here, in the attractiveness of the male role, and also in Emily's own vividness, we may see less basic, but nevertheless formidable, inducements to abandon her femininity.

Austin's masculine eminence cast its spell over his sister, "I think of that 'pinnacle' on which you always mount, when anybody insults you, and that's quite a comfort to me."[48] And by the time she was seventeen, the image of Austin was firmly associated in her mind with the accouterments of royalty. From school she wrote him: "Viny told us, you were coming this week & it would be very pleasant to us to receive a visit from *your highness* if you can be absent from home long enough for such a purpose."[49] Of course, she is being mock-subservient here and making fun of Austin's self-importance, just as years later Samuel Bowles was to do the same with her, calling her the "Queen Recluse."[50] The same tinge of ridicule toward what she perceives as Austin's superior station occurs in a letter written two years later, when she chides him for not writing home: "Suppose [Austin] should doff his crown, and lay down his lofty sceptre ... Permit me to tie your shoe, to run like a dog behind you ... you shall be 'Jove' a sitting on great 'Olympus' ... Oh, 'Jupiter'! fie! for shame! *Kings* sometimes have fathers and mothers."[51]

This exalted view of Austin was of course supported by her family. Edward Dickinson, not one to praise overgenerously, nevertheless expressed his great pleasure at any indication that Austin agreed with him, shared his views, or championed his causes. For example, it happened that Edward Dickinson was annoyed at the apparently universal agreement regarding the excellence of Jenny Lind's singing—an opinion that he did not share. When Austin had occasion to attend a Lind concert in Boston, he wrote home about his negative reactions. Emily replied: "Father perused the letter and verily for joy the poor man could hardly contain himself—he read and read again, and each time seemed to relish the story more than at first." Mr. Dickinson declared he would have published Austin's "review" in the paper if it had arrived in time "to tell [to quote Emily again] this foolish world that one man living in it dares to say what he *thinks.*" Emily continues: "So soon as he was calm he began to proclaim your opinion . . . encomium followed encomium—applause deafened applause."[52]

Almost two years later she comments in similar vein: "Father takes great delight in your remarks to him—puts on his spectacles and reads them o'er and o'er as if it was a blessing to have an only son . . . He remarked in confidence to me this morning, that he 'guessed you saw through things there' [in the Cambridge courts] . . . I'm sure he designed to compliment you very highly . . . I believe at this moment, Austin, that there's no body living for whom father has such respect as for you."[53]

The next month she writes again: "[Father] seemed to feel so happy to have you interested in what was going on at Cambridge—he said he 'knew all about it—he'd been thro' the whole, it was only a little specimen of what you'd meet in life.' "[54] There is no evidence to suggest that Edward Dickinson took such delight in Emily's views when they happened to coincide with his own, and it seems unlikely that he would have encouraged his daughter in such an identification with himself. Though denied her father's praise, Emily certainly never worked at obtaining her mother's, and since acquiring some sort of approval is a human necessity she had to seek approbation elsewhere. What in all probability she did was to make Austin's triumphs her own vicariously, the identification with him, then, to a degree safeguarding her own self-esteem. Still, vicarious achievements are just that, and one wonders if there was not some element of envy in Emily's praise of Austin's successes. This would account for the tone of mockery and burlesque frequently found in her letters conveying to Austin the approval of others.

Once Austin criticized Emily for the obscurity of some of her high-flown language, and she replied generously enough, but in a way suggesting a measure of competition. "I like it [Austin's letter] grandly—very—because it is so long, and also it's *so* funny —we have all been laughing till the old house rung again at your delineations of men, women, and things. I feel quite like retiring, in the presence of one so grand . . . you say you dont comprehend me, you want a simpler style . . . I strove to be exalted thinking I might reach *you*."[55]

Her father's high opinion of Austin's letters impressed her, and she frequently conveyed his approval to Austin, usually with deflating exaggeration: "Father says your letters are altogether before Shakespeare, and he will have them published to put in our library."[56]

When others expressed approval of Austin, she was quick to pass the compliment on to him: "Lizzie [a cousin] says 'Miss Lyman thinks there never *was* such a fellow [as Austin],' and the girls admire her so much, that they think you must be most perfect—so to have won her regard."[57] And of a servant boy she remarked: "Austin—there's nothing in the world that Jerry wont do for you. I believe he thinks you are finer than anybody else, and feels quite consequential to think of serving you."[58]

Everyone apparently missed Austin when he was away: "They all allude to you as to a missing Saint . . . none of them speak of you, or of your noble acts, without plentiful tears."[59]

Austin was flattered by his sister's high estimation, which in turn increased his regard for her, sometimes to the point where Vinnie felt left out. Recall that when Austin and Vinnie were at home and Emily away at school she mentioned happily that he had told her that home seemed like a funeral without her.

Aided by the vivid capacity for fantasy that was hers apparently from birth, Emily at times developed the uncanny sense that Austin was physically near her, though in actuality he was living in a distant city. Experiences of this kind suggest that there was evolving within her a feeling of profound inner blending of her own being with that of Austin. Thus, she writes to him: "I wish you were here dear Austin—the dust falls on the bureau in your deserted room . . . I dont go there after dark whenever I can help it, for the twilight seems to pause there and I am half afraid, and if ever I have to go, I hurry with all my might and never look behind me for I know who I should see."[60] What is impressive here is the atmosphere of menace she projects. It is as though she senses the danger to her femininity inherent in too close an identification with this vivid and appealing male while, at the same time, she fears that to dissociate this identification from the core of her personality altogether would disrupt her contact with reality: it is clear that her reason for never looking behind her in the dark of Austin's room is that she fears that she will see Austin—that is, that she will hallucinate his presence.

That her awareness and fear of her susceptibility to this kind of psychic cleavage was not confined to this one occasion is indicated in a letter written four months earlier than the one previously quoted. She says: "Speaking of *getting up* . . . I miss 'my department' mornings . . . Your room looks lonely enough—I do not love to go in there—whenever I pass thro' I find I 'gin to whistle, as we read that little boys are wont to do in the graveyard."[61] It is apparent that Emily's sense of her own emerging individuality was closely interwoven with, and patterned after, her intuitive perception of Austin's personality. Implied in this process is the profound unconscious acceptance that one is already like the person imitated and will become increasingly like him. On still deeper levels of the personality there may even develop the conviction that one has truly become that person.

It is important not to overlook the fact that in certain characteristics Emily's personality was distinctly feminine. Paradoxical as it may sound, she apparently became feminized partly through her identification with Austin. For example, her superior intelligence for the most part remained at the service of her intuition, introspection, and subjectivity. Her father was nonintuitive, practical, and uninterested in his own or anyone else's fantasy life. She, therefore, did not develop these qualities through her identification with him. Austin, on the other hand, was a softer, less aggressive, and warmer person than his father. As an adult, he wrote verse, "doted"[62] on Elizabeth Barrett Browning, collected oil paintings with the enthusiasm of a child, and loved nature. His childhood relationship with his mother may have been benign compared with Emily's and he seems not to have resisted identifying to some extent with her, for in the main he was secure in his masculinity and had no doubts that his path was to follow in his father's footsteps. It would appear, then, that those positive qualities which existed in Mrs. Dickinson's personality became available to the daughter through the medium of the son. Unconscious hatred and resentment, and conscious depreciation of the mother, prevented their being appropriated directly.

It was the feeling of being so much like Austin and so little like her mother and sister that caused Emily, in referring to her childhood, to employ the phrase "when a Boy."[63] The same implication is evident in the poem "A loss of something ever felt I" (no. 959), where she speaks of being the "only *Prince* cast out." Her describing herself as "by birth a Bachelor"[64] and referring to her heart as "him"[65] speak to the same point. So also do her calling herself her nephew Ned's "Uncle Emily"[66] and her signing a letter to her cousins "Brother Emily."[67]

It is important, though, to bear in mind that Emily Dickinson never settled into a thoroughgoing and "mature" masculine identification and to remember that she continually sought outside the home more gratifying mother figures, such as Aunt Lavinia, some of her teachers, and certain older women friends, all of whom possessed those virtues which she felt her mother lacked. And recall also her adoration of female authors, her reverence for these "holy ones."[68] But these piecemeal identifications at a distance, indispensable as they are if one is hard enough pressed for an appropriate psychological model, are tenuous structures needing constant attention and repair. One is much more likely to be pulled into the magnetic aura of a less suitable flesh and blood personality who is consistently present. This is what seemed to be happening more and more with Emily Dickinson and Austin.

There was another significant way in which Emily felt closer to Austin than to anyone else. She revealed this aspect of her identification with him explicitly in a letter to Mrs. Holland written when she was twenty-three: "The minister . . . preached about death and judgment, and what would become of those, meaning Austin and me, who behaved improperly—and somehow the sermon scared me . . . I longed to come to you, and tell you all about it, and learn how to be better."[69]

Recall that Emily's mother, following the vigorous and persistent exhortations of her sister, joined the church in 1831, when

Emily was six months old. Also, her father, Vinnie, and Susan Gilbert were all converted during the fever of evangelism that swept through Amherst in 1850, when Emily was nineteen. And by that time all of her girl friends were professed Christians. The point is that here again she and Austin were allied. At twenty, she had only his support; of all their circle in Amherst only she and Austin remained outside the church.

Secure in Austin's sympathy, she could write to him of a Sunday: "I am at home from meeting on account of the storm and my *slender constitution,* which I assured the folks, would not permit my accompanying them today."[70] The tone is clearly one of shared conspiracy; she is free to acknowledge to Austin that she employed the ruse of ill health and bad weather to avoid going to church.

On another Sunday she writes: "I will write while they've gone to meeting, lest they stop me, when they get home. I stayed to Communion this morning, and by that way, bought the privilege of not going this afternoon, and having a talk with you, meanwhile."[71] The implication again is that church is a tedious affair but that it is worthwhile to suffer through a part of it if by doing so one can escape the rest.

She can even engage in a little mild blasphemy with Austin: "I was just this moment thinking of a favorite stanza of your's," she says ironically, " 'where congregations ne'er break up, and Sabbaths have no end.' That must be a delightful situation, certainly, quite worth the scrambling for!"[72]

What she could not share with Austin, however, was her guilt about these matters. Austin was full of intellectual arguments, "quibbles"[73] one of his pious friends called them, which may have caused him to appear to Emily to be quite secure in his unregenerate condition. She herself felt profoundly guilty. Part of her deeply wished to believe as the rest of her family and friends believed. What held her back and united her with Austin was, in her own view, a conviction of being evil. As she wrote to Abiah Root: "She [her friend Abby Wood] has told you . . . how the 'still small voice' is calling, and how the people are listening, and believing, and truly obeying—how the place is very solemn, and sacred, and the bad ones slink away, and are sorrowful . . . *I* am one of the lingering *bad* ones, and so do *I* slink away."[74] As is clear from another letter to Abiah Root, she was unable to discuss her religious doubts with her family; the others would preach, and Austin, perhaps, would laugh. "I have neglected the *one thing needful* when all were obtaining it," she tells Abiah, referring to the revivals and campaigns of exhortation carried on at school which resulted in the conversion of most of her schoolmates. "I regret that last term," she continues, "when that golden opportunity was mine, that I did not give up and become a Christian . . . [Abby] is sober, and keenly sensitive on the subject, and she says she only desires to be good. How I wish I could say that with sincerity, but I fear I never can. But I will no longer impose my own feelings even upon my friend. Keep them sacred, for I never lisped them to any save yourself and Abby." She gives various reasons for her dereliction. One of these is that "it is hard for me to give up the world."[75]

In the earliest of her existing letters in which she discusses religion, written when she had just turned fifteen to Abiah, she says, "I was almost persuaded to be a christian. I thought I never again could be thoughtless and worldly . . . One by one my old habits returned and I cared less for religion than ever . . . I am continually putting off becoming a christian. Evil voices lisp in my ear—There is yet time enough . . . I feel that life is short and time fleeting—and that I ought now to make peace with my maker."[76] It appears clear that Emily has strong feelings of guilt and sinfulness and that she despairs of ever being able to divest herself of some obscure wickedness. Never does she advance as a reason for her holding back the intellectual reservations that Austin professed to have. She simply says: "I am sinful."

Once she had a brief interval of hope, but it was soon dashed: "I think of the perfect happiness I experienced while I felt I was an heir of heaven as of a delightful dream, out of which the Evil one bid me wake & again return to the world & its pleasures . . . the world allured me & in an unguarded moment I listened to her syren voice . . . I had rambled too far to return . . . now I have bitterly to lament my folly . . . I feel that I am sailing upon the brink of an awful precipice, from which I cannot escape & over which I fear my tiny boat will soon glide if I do not receive help from above."[77]

Later, in a letter to Jane Humphrey notable for the bitterness of her description of her life, she writes: "The path of duty looks very ugly indeed—and the place where *I* want to go more ami-

173

able—a great deal—it is so much easier to do wrong than right—
so much pleasanter to be evil than good . . . They say you . . .
are happy—then I know you are good—for none *but* the good are
happy—you are out of the way of temptation—and out of the
way of the tempter [Emily herself]—I did'nt mean to make you
wicked—but I was—and am—and shall be—and I was with you
so much that I could'nt help contaminate . . . Is it wicked to talk
so Jane—what *can* I say that isn't? Out of a wicked heart cometh
wicked words."[78]

At seventeen she writes to Abiah: "*God* is sitting here, looking
into my very soul to see if I think right tho'ts. Yet I am not
afraid, for I try to be right and good, and he knows every one of
my struggles."[79] What are the *wrong* thoughts that Emily is
struggling with here—the thoughts that cause her to feel herself
to be a sinner, a contaminator, a tempter, one who is wicked, subject to the sinful allurements and pleasures of a siren world? One
thing is clear; her sinful proclivities constitute another link with
Austin—recall her fear, expressed to Mrs. Holland, of "what
would become of those, meaning Austin and me, who behaved
improperly."[80]

The letter to Abiah that begins with talk of God sitting beside
her looking into her soul suggests a tentative answer to these questions. It is probably the most fantastic and wildest letter that
Emily Dickinson ever wrote. She was suffering from a severe
cold at the time of its composition. In view of the manic mood
that is sustained throughout this long letter—the extreme looseness of her associations and the occasional bizarre, arbitrarily introduced, and seemingly irrelevant images in which it abounds
—it may be that she was feverish at the time she wrote it. Examination of the letter suggests the presence of a mild degree of
delirium: the sequence of thoughts is reminiscent of the overstimulated flight of ideas and the loosening of rational control
that occur in that and similar states. Perhaps though, bored with
being confined alone to the house, she was simply entertaining
herself—letting her imagination go. In any case, her verbal ebul-
lience betrays certain underlying preoccupations which appear to
be escaping repression.

The letter is too long to quote in its entirety, so I shall quote
only the sections relevant to the present discussion. Emily tells
Abiah that she is alone except for God and Abiah, both of whom

she can imagine very vividly as sitting there with her. She tells of having a cold, and at the end of the letter makes the observation: "Colds make one very carnal and the spirit is always afraid of them." She personifies the cold—it is a "dear creature" who came unaccompanied and lonely from the Alps with "neither husband—protector—nor friend." The cold pounced on her shawl, while she was out taking a walk, and rode home with her. When she got into the house and took off her shawl "out flew my tormentor, and putting both arms around my neck began to kiss me immoderately, and express so much love, it completely bewildered me. Since then it has slept in my bed, eaten from my plate, lived with me everywhere . . . I think I'll wake first, and get out of bed, and leave it, but . . . it is dressed before me, and sits on the side of the bed." After talking of the cold's attributes—its pocket-handkerchief and red nose—her willingness to forward the cold to Abiah, and her own loud sneezing, Emily says: "but this is a wicked story, it [the cold] can tell some *better* ones. Now my dear friend, let me tell you that these last thoughts are fictions—vain imaginations to lead astray foolish young women. They are flowers of speech, they both *make,* and *tell* deliberate falsehoods, avoid them as the snake, and turn aside as from the *Bottle* snake, and I dont *think* you will be harmed. Honestly tho', a snake bite is a serious matter, and there cant be too much said, or done about it. The big serpent bites the deepest, and we get so accustomed to it's bite that we dont mind about them. 'Verily I say unto you fear *him.*' Wont you read some work upon snakes—I have a real anxiety for you! *I* love those little green ones that slide around by your shoes in the grass—and make it rustle with their elbows—they are rather my favorites on the whole, but I would'nt influence *you* for the world! There is an air of misanthropy about the striped snake that will commend itself at once to your taste, there is no monotony about it—but we will more of this again. Something besides severe colds, and serpents, and we will try to find *that* something. It cant be a garden, can it, or a strawberry bed, which rather belongs to a garden—nor it cant be a schoolhouse, nor an Attorney at Law—Oh dear I dont know *what* it is! Love for the absent dont *sound* like it, but try it, and see how it goes."[81]

Clearly, the train of associations here is not dictated by rational connections. She seems to have been playing with words, writing down whatever popped into her head, flouting logical sequence. On the level of ordinary communication the passage means nothing; it is wild, spontaneous nonsense, written solely to amuse herself and Abiah. The impression one gets throughout the entire letter is one of relatively free association. One might roughly schematize the chain of ideas and images thus: religious struggles to think right thoughts→the imagined presence of God and Abiah→a feminized cold that clings, embraces, kisses immoderately, expresses a bewildering quantity of love, sleeps in her bed, dresses before her, and sits beside her bed→wicked stories, vain imaginations to lead young women astray→avoidance of some snakes→big snakes that bite deep to which one gets accustomed→pleasant little snakes→gardens and strawberry beds→schoolhouse→attorney at law.

The erotic imagery here glimmers at varying depths, gliding almost on the surface of consciousness in the references to the cold and dipping deeper but still remaining visible in the passages about snakes. Can there be any doubt that Emily Dickinson is unconsciously struggling here with sexual impulses, problems of sexual identification and sexual morality?

Choosing the most probable meaning of the symbols in these passages, one comes up with the following relationships:

The cold:	A girl or woman. Since Emily explicitly tells us that it has no "husband," she must have thought of it as feminine. Also, it is from the "Alps"—cf. "the siren Alps" in poem 80; mountains are almost invariably feminine in Emily Dickinson's poems.
The cold's behavior:	The relationship with the cold is erotic, suggestive of a sexual attachment.
Vain imaginations, deliberate falsehood:	The lie here may be Emily's pretense that she is a male. This follows from her behavior with the feminine cold. Thus she divulges her unconscious seductive feelings toward Abiah.
The big serpent with the bite one grows accustomed to:	Sexual intercourse with a man. This is what she warns Abiah against.

The pleasant little snakes around one's shoes:	The small, harmless female phallus—the clitoris. The shoe is a common vaginal symbol.
Garden, strawberry bed:	The female genitals—the garden is as universal a feminine symbol as the snake is a phallic one.
Schoolhouse:	The dwelling into which Austin penetrates daily (at this time he was teaching school in Sunderland). The symbol may refer to the rightful sexual object of her brother, that is, a woman.
Attorney at law:	Edward Dickinson, the only lawyer important in Emily Dickinson's life at this time.

To condense the schema still further, the train of associations in these passages seems to be: moral struggles→homosexual impulses→men→father and brother. But why should homosexual impulses lead to thoughts of Austin and father? There seem to be two explanations for this, each pertaining to a different psychic level.

First, intimations of her own homosexual impulses are linked through the one thing her male relatives and she have in common—identical love objects, that is, women. One determinant of Emily Dickinson's inability to accept the religion of her mother resided in her identification with "bad" Austin. The sister, like her brother, was one of the "lingering bad ones" who, like snakes, "slink away." Some of her sexual impulses, therefore, were like his (and also of course like her father's), that is, oriented toward females.

Emily seemingly encouraged Austin in impulses whose expression she would like to have indulged in her own behavior. This way she could vicariously enjoy an outlet for her own inclinations without awakening her conscience. For example, in many of her letters to Austin she seems to advocate strongly Austin's acquaintance with any girl in whom she herself was interested. This tendency is apparent in her earliest letters but reaches fullest expression in letters referring to Martha and Susan Gilbert. At eleven she writes to Austin: "If you could I wish you—would send Sabra a paper she would be so pleased with it . . . I will put in her respects because I know she would send them if she knew I was agoing to write."[82] At twenty she writes: "Susie asks in every letter why she dont hear from you . . . I hope if you have not written, you *will* do very soon, for Susie is so far off, and wants so much to have you. Martha wants to see you very much indeed, and sends her love to you."[83] And again: "Martha becomes far dearer to me with every week and day—her's is a spirit as beautiful and pure as one will seldom meet in a world like our's, and it is all the lovelier because it is so *rare*. Martha inquired for you, as she never comes *without* doing, and sends the weekly love which I always bring."[84] And later: "Mat sends her love to you . . . I think it would make Mat very happy to have a letter from you."[85]

It may be argued that in thus encouraging Austin to care for these girls and to be pleased when she sends him their "love" Emily is merely taking an ordinary sisterly pleasure in the fact that her brother approves of her friends and that they admire him. Yet one gets the feeling that there is the covert implication: I cannot possess my friends as fully as I would like, and so I will tie them to myself through sharing them with you, who will appreciate them as I do. An attitude such as this could cause guilt sufficient to prohibit her from partaking of the consolations of religion. Yet it is entirely possible that she was unaware of the exaggerated intensity of her emotional investment in her friends. Consciously, her struggles may have been focused on something as innocent and simple as a resistance to falling into autoerotic practices.

But the juxtaposition of homosexual thoughts with thoughts of her male relatives is probably not to be explained solely on the basis of identical love objects. The second and deeper explanation resides in the hidden link between a defense and the impulse being defended against—in Emily's case the defense being the homosexual thought and the impulse defended against being erotic feelings toward Austin and her father, who were also, on another level, love objects. The bite of the big serpent that one gets so accustomed to, of which Emily seems to be warning Abiah, may therefore be regarded as representative of these heterosexual, incestuous temptations.

Emily's longing for Austin, not as a child but as a man, comes through in occasional flashes in her letters. After she visited him in Boston when she was twenty-one, she wrote: "it is very lonely here—I have tried to make up my mind which was better—home, and parents, country; or city, and smoke, and dust, shared with the only being I can call my Brother . . . so far as I can judge, the balance is in your favor."[86] Recall that in anticipation of his next visit home she wrote: "We shall enjoy brimfull everything *now* but *half* full, and to have you home once more will be like living *again!*"[87] Another time: "how I wish you could stay and never go back again . . . Oh I am so lonely;"[88] Once she recounted a dream in which she received a letter from him and just as she was breaking the seal she dreamt that her father rapped at the door and woke her up.[89] In a letter written to him when she was twenty, she expresses a near wish that she could die and never be lonely again—and then immediately says she thought of Hepzibah Pyncheon (in *The House of Seven Gables*), who also longed for the peace of death but stayed, for the sake of her brother, until "kind angels took both of them home, and it seemed almost a lesson, given us to learn." In the same letter she says she was thinking of Austin when she dropped off to sleep and had a dream. In the dream she was in another world, "bright and fair," and heard a voice say, "there shall be no more tears, neither any crying"; there were many people singing "who in their *lifetimes* were parted and separated, and their joy was because they never should be so anymore."[90] There is another reference, different from the others in that, although written in the body of a prose letter, it is really verse. It says in symbolic language and in a more extreme form what many of the above quotations suggest—that Emily unconsciously regards Austin as a potential lover. In this letter she describes an early October day; the house is shut up against the cold, and there has been a killing frost. All these images, though here intended literally, become later on in her poems symbols of her barren and loveless lot. She next contrasts the bleak weather outside with the joyful day of Austin's anticipated return home, and says: "There is *another* sky ever serene and fair, and there is *another* sunshine, tho' it be darkness there—never mind faded forests, Austin, never mind silent fields—*here* is a little forest whose leaf is ever green, here is a *brighter* garden, where not a frost has been, in its unfading flowers I hear the bright bee hum, prithee, my Brother, into *my* garden come!"[91] The warmth of her affection for Austin is here presented to him as a garden ready for the arrival of the bright bee. The sexual implications of the imagery are obvious. Though the hospitable sky, forest, field, and garden of flowers, through their expansiveness toward the little bee and also their protectiveness, betray the underlying mother-child quality in the attachment, there can be no doubt that on a less archaic level there is also an unconscious genital component.

There is another line of approach to the exploration of the status of Austin as an unconsciously desired love object.

Emily frequently was the first one up in the morning, and it became her task—which she enjoyed—to awaken her sister and brother. In a line to Austin, already quoted, she said: "speaking of *getting up* . . . I miss 'my department' mornings."[92] Months later she repeated this theme: "there's nothing that I enjoy more than rousing these self-same beings [her mother and Vinnie] and witnessing their discomfiture at the *bare idea* of morning . . . A'nt you sorry for her [Vinnie]; she thinks of your sympathies often, and thinks they would all be hers."[93] Obviously Austin's sympathy for Vinnie reflects his own experiences of being awakened by Emily's hands. Keeping this in mind, one can surmise something of the origin of the following poem (no. 1670):

> In Winter in my Room
> I came upon a Worm –
> Pink, lank and warm –
> But as he was a worm
> And worms presume
> Not quite with him at home –
> Secured him by a string
> To something neighboring
> And went along.
> A Trifle afterward
> A thing occurred
> I'd not believe it if I heard
> But state with creeping blood –
> A snake with mottles rare
> Surveyed my chamber floor
> In feature as the worm before
> But ringed with power –
> The very string with which
> I tied him – too

When he was mean and new
That string was there –

I shrank – "How fair you are"!
Propitiation's claw –
"Afraid," he hissed
"Of me" ?
"No cordiality" –
He fathomed me –
Then to a Rhythm *Slim*
Secreted in his Form
As Patterns swim
Projected him.

That time I flew
Both eyes his way
Lest he pursue
Nor ever ceased to run
Till in a distant Town
Towns on from mine
I set me down
This was a dream —

There seems to be no other explication possible than the one given by Clark Griffith. The poem is a sex-fantasy expressing her dread of masculine sexuality. But, as Griffith makes clear, the worm-snake "is treated throughout as a splendid object, first wonderfully warm, then beautifully patterned, and always *ringed with power.*" And, as he points out, the poet reacts with "profound awe" and "undisguised wonder."[94] Unless one can believe that women are born with an instinctive knowledge of male sexual anatomy and physiology, the most reasonable conclusion is that Emily Dickinson learned about the erection of the penis from observing her brother. That she could write a poem like this, however, indicates how deeply repressed was the identification of snakes with phalli. It also tells us that the original discovery had an overwhelming impact upon her. Clinical experience supplies the rest of the explanation: unless her own libidinal responses were massively stimulated by her brother, thereby coming up squarely against the incest taboo, she would not have repressed the episode or, as the poem states, dreamed about it. And what would make such an encounter with Austin particularly frightening is that it would engender psychic reverberations of earlier forbidden wishes. These, of course, involve the problem that every human being attempts to solve—must solve —that is, how to possess exclusively the parent of the opposite sex and render harmless and noncompetitive the parent of one's own sex. This problem, the oedipal dilemma, with its only possible resolution being a firm identification with one parent or the other, is one Emily Dickinson spent her life trying unsuccessfully to solve.

Let me summarize at this point my analysis of Emily Dickinson's relationship with Austin. It appears that it consisted basically of three major components. First, Austin as Emily's child; second, Austin as Emily's sexual representative; and third, Austin as Emily's lover. Of the three, the first two seem to have exerted the most noticeable effect on her life.

One overriding concern should be borne constantly in mind as one threads the labyrinth of Emily Dickinson's maturational transformations; it is the fundamental raison d'être of the whole series of psychic maneuvers she was forced to call into play. This theme is the longing for a mother and for her own never fully secured femininity. Wherever one begins to examine it, the entire complex of her relationships is restorative and remedial with regard to these basic needs. In those aspects of her relationship with Austin which assigned him the role of the helpless, lonely child, motherless save for his "adoption" by his sister, Emily was finding the lost maternal love she sought by reflection, as it were, of her own behavior. This "regressive identification," in which a self-induced feeling of being loved is generated by means of an outpouring of affection upon a dependent "child" with which one identifies one's self, was a maneuver she resorted to several times throughout her life, most conspicuously with Austin, her nephew Gilbert, and, finally, with her own helpless and dying mother.

Similarly, the second aspect of her identification with Austin, in which she saw him (and reflectively herself) not as a helpless child but as a virile male attractive to women, allowed her a vicarious and innocent outlet for her desire that young women be her own sexual objects. But here again, the homosexual urge had its essential origins in the search for a loving mother; Austin constituted a means, consciously disassociated from herself, to that end.

The third aspect of her relationship, with Austin himself as love object, is related to a time when her identification with her mother was still a possibility. Emily survived her infancy: as far as we know, she was an active and physically healthy baby and obviously the growth of her intellectual powers, as manifested, for example, in the development of her early speech, was not impeded. This is proof that Mrs. Dickinson, however inadequate she was as the mother of a growing female child, was in some measure, at least, adequate to the needs of a very young infant. Emily's cultivation of older women throughout her life, which can be interpreted as a search for a surrogate mother, implies that she once experienced the security and warmth of a sheltering mother or mother substitute. Therefore, in the apparently fleeting glow of these early days, there must have been imbedded in the core of the poet's psyche some partial inner representation of what it means to be good, valuable, generous, *and* a female. She necessarily carried this fragile, psychological structure within her throughout the oedipal years, at which time the ordinary girl accepts herself as made in the same mold as mother, and father becomes the prototype of the object of the long libidinal explorations of adolescence which lead ultimately to marriage. In Austin's eyes, Emily was primarily a sister. He was devoted to her and exercised a masculine protectiveness toward her, just as he did toward her mother and Vinnie. In short, he loved her for what she basically was (probably, in her own dysphoric estimation, in spite of it)—that is, a female. Thus, the tenuous, positive feminine identifications stirred fitfully to life again in the warmth of his companionship; the positive side of the oedipal alternatives was strengthened a little. Tentatively, fearfully, guiltily, protected by the incest barrier, Emily reached out to the least frightening male she knew. In this sense, then, and to this small and uncertain degree, Emily temporarily resumed the faltering steps toward heterosexuality that her infantile rejection of her mother as model had halted years before.

Each of the roles played by Austin in the economics of his sister's complex psychological organization predominated or receded in response to the fluctuations of external circumstances, which called first one, then another, into play. There seems to have been a balance of power, as it were, among these identificatory modalities, sensitive to the needs of the moment and held together in a dynamic equilibrium. Yet these orientations, singly or combined, did not constitute pathways to "normality"; indeed, they could not even lead Emily Dickinson to an "abnormal" redoubt which would guarantee any real security, stability, or libidinal fulfillment. For several years, however, she made shift in her interpersonal transactions, partly by utilizing the channels through which she drew strength and hope from Austin. But Austin was growing up and had his own requirements. It was only to be expected that at some point his needs would have to take precedence over his sister's. With a half conscious and dreadful awareness, Emily seems to have perceived this fact vividly, and at times she articulated her presentiment of impending calamity. Ultimately, with the evolution of her attachment to Austin's future wife, a consuming desperation seized her. Both she and Austin were drawn ever more deeply into Susan Gilbert's stormy orbit, and the supporting psychological bond with her brother was thereby placed under disintegrating tension.

Chapter V THE EARL, THE MALAY, AND THE PEARL

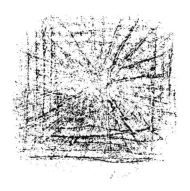

A new personality moved into Emily Dickinson's life in her late teens and early twenties, and her relationships with all other girl friends faded like stars before the morning sky. The new friend was Susan Gilbert, Austin's future wife.

Austin and Emily may first have met Susan Gilbert when she attended Amherst Academy for a term at the age of sixteen. But it was not until 1850, when Sue was nineteen and he twenty-one, that a serious interest on Austin's part began to develop. In the interval between 1847 and 1850 Sue had attended school in Utica, New York, living with an aunt in Geneva (by this time both her parents were dead). In 1850 she settled in Amherst, making her home with Harriet Cutler, an older sister. Mrs. Cutler had a strong sense of propriety and was eager to assure that Susan's behavior and outlook on the world be approved by those with whom she had social relations. From the death of Sue's sister Mary in childbirth in 1850 until 1853, Sue dressed in black, and one gathers from Austin's letters that Mrs. Cutler expressed an unequivocal disapproval of any activity that in her eyes was incompatible with the seriousness and dignity of the state of mourning. The early stages of Austin's courtship accordingly seem to have been carried on under some constraint, and it became almost a game with him and Sue to see how cleverly they could evade Mrs. Cutler's watchful and repressive eye. This early restrictiveness seems to have had a strong impress on the evolution of their friendship, which continued to be invested with a secretive air.

Susan was a many-sided and changeable personality. Austin complained that she tended to dissemble her feelings. Throughout the decades of their lives together, neither Emily nor Austin ever quite lost the feeling that there was something unpredictable about her. Undoubtedly Susan had a penetrating and lively intelligence, and it was said that in her matronly years "her presence filled the room with an ineffable grace and elegance" and that she appeared "easy, charming and sincere."[1] However, there seems also to have been a bitter and cutting side to her, which thrust out unexpectedly. There is evidence that Emily, and possibly Austin also, expected and demanded too much of her; and fearing to estrange them, she tried hard always to be the accepting, loving, and endlessly supportive person they wanted her to be. Perhaps her need for approval was great enough to cause her to suppress in face to face confrontation those thoughts and feelings that she sensed were not acceptable. Then, much later, in letters or in speech, under some peculiar provocation (or impulse toward greater honesty), she would give stinging expression to what she had previously held back. Both her anxiety to appear to be what others thought she ought to be and her occasional and impulsive flashes of bitterness are understandable in the light of her history.

Like Emily she was bereft of a mother, although her loss was through death when she was very young. Her father was an alcoholic ne'er-do-well, a disgrace to his sons and daughters. Susan was raised by various relatives who saw to it that she was well educated. As a young woman she looked toward an older brother for love and protection. She once wrote to this brother, Dwight: "I [feel] so keenly the loss of a Mothers love, and influence . . . Is it strange . . . dear brother, when I feel thus, that I should look to you, and find myself thinking of, and loving you as a Father."[2] Sometimes she was also forced to approach him for money when she incurred bills for medical care or other unexpected expenses. Probably she felt humiliated by her position and early developed a fierce pride and need to be independent. Austin described her (and himself) as "tall, proud, stiff . . . [and] so easily miffed."³ During their tempestuous courtship Susan made it clear that she would not be dictated to by Austin. She deliberately read a book he practically forbade. At times she lashed back at him venomously. He depicted one of their youthful quarrels: they would "speak words—& look, look, so cold, —so bitter, as hardly the deepest hatred could have prompted a pair as would the guiltiest wretch—& his most wronged victim."⁴ In compensation perhaps for her miserable childhood and broken family, Susan was ambitious of social position and eager to overcome her common background. One factor that may have influenced her decision to marry Austin was that the imperious and judgmental Edward Dickinson—wealthy lawyer, Congressman, and leading citizen of Amherst, so different from her own father —succumbed to her charm and indicated that he was willing to accept her as a daughter-in-law. One must take care not to be too severely critical of Sue's weaknesses and not to overlook the fact that living amidst Dickinsons was not an easy accomplishment. Only a very exceptional girl in Sue's position might have done a better job of steering a course among such subtly competing, demanding, and ambivalent personalities. And the fact that Austin did not think she compared unfavorably with his brilliant sister indicates that her affectional and intellectual endowments were real and considerable. Emily's lifelong devotion to her speaks to the same point. At the age of forty-five, Emily would refer to Sue as the "Only Woman in the World,"⁵ and five years after that would make the statement: "that Susan lives—is a Universe."⁶ There can be no doubt, then, that despite her double face, her superficial glitter, and her emotional lability, she possessed qualities that were durable and admirable. She seems to have been a warmhearted person, generous with her affection and possessed of considerable patience, forbearance, and loyalty.

From the fall of 1850, when Sue and Emily were both nineteen, until the summer of 1854, Austin and Sue were for the most part working or studying in different cities. The bulk of the correspondence reviewed in this chapter derives from this four-year interval and its attendant separations.

Austin first taught school for a term in Sunderland, then in

June 1851 began another year's teaching in Boston. Three months after his departure for Boston, Sue, bored with Amherst and uneasy at being supported by her brother-in-law, who apparently felt free to indulge his penchant for giving her unwelcome advice because he was supplying her room and board left for Baltimore, where she too taught school for a year. By July 1852 Austin and Sue, their teaching careers at an end, were both back in Amherst and seeing as much of each other as Austin could manage. By January 1853 the life of the town seems to have been brought to a near halt by the winter weather, and Sue, chafing at the lack of social activity, prepared to leave the following month for a visit with relatives in New Hampshire. While she was there, Austin moved to Cambridge to begin his law studies at Harvard. Except for short visits the relationship was sustained by letters until Austin's graduation in the summer of 1854, when he returned permanently to Amherst.

In the formative phases of his relationship with Sue, Austin "fell in love" in the full meaning of the phrase, with all its associations of blindness and heedlessness. His letters, first from Sunderland and later from Boston, are concerned with little else than his feeling for her. Although it is apparent that he was working hard, first as teacher and then as student, and, in Boston at least, having an active social life, his reports to Sue about these pursuits are very meager, and his voluminous letters are essentially outpourings of emotion. During his law school training he tried to send Sue at least two long letters a week and usually succeeded. He made every effort to keep his letters from falling under the prying eyes of Sue's relatives, sending them via circuitous routes and with envelopes addressed by others. He did not let his own parents in on the secret either, although Emily was aware of his attachment to Sue, and it was not long before his father suspected what was developing.

As has been shown, Emily Dickinson's enmeshment in her brother's life was intimate and inextricable. To understand precisely how shattering a blow Austin's marriage was to her, it is essential to examine the nature and development of the commitment Austin, Sue, and Emily had to each other. Only then can one appreciate the powerful cross currents in which she was caught.

During these years of separation and Austin's epistolary effusions, Sue and Emily, together in Amherst, became increasingly close companions. In fact, the increasing temperature of Austin's affection for Sue was matched by Emily's, degree for degree.

Emily seems to have been troubled by doubts that her growing fondness for Sue was fully acceptable to the other girl. It can perhaps be taken as a hallmark of their entire relationship that in her earliest extant letter to Sue, written just as Sue was reunited with her sister Martha, Emily speaks of her own "unwelcome face." She writes: "Were it not for the *weather* Susie—*my* little, unwelcome face would come peering in today—I should steal a kiss from the sister."[7] This suggests that Emily could never decide certainly what Sue was thinking or determine in a given instance whether or not and to what degree her own thought and behavior was congenial to Sue.

A year after writing the previously quoted letter to Sue, Emily begins another with similar doubts: "Will you forgive me, Susie, I cannot stay away."[8] A month later the theme appears again: "Will you let me come dear Susie—looking just as I do . . . Oh Susie . . . I love you just as dearly as if I was e'er so fine, so you wont care, will you?"

Later on in the same letter, after having given oblique expression to her covert anger and more direct vent to her depression and impatience at not hearing more often from Sue, Emily writes: "Susie, forgive me, forget all what I say." She advises Sue to occupy herself with other interests, "as if I had never written you all these ugly things. Never mind the letter Susie, I wont be angry with you if you dont give me any at all . . . Only *want* to write me," she begs, "only sometimes sigh that you are far from me, and that will do, Susie!"[9] Emily seems to have some inkling that Sue may feel that her emotional demands are exorbitant, and she hastens to assure Sue that she is actually willing to settle for mere crumbs of affection.

Susan apparently tried to reassure her, writing that if she ever got back to Amherst she would love Emily more than ever. Emily replies: "*Will* you 'love me more if ever you come home'? —it is enough, dear Susie, I know I shall be satisfied . . . Never mind the letter, Susie; you have so much to do [Sue was teaching school in Baltimore]; just write me every week *one line,* and let it be, 'Emily, I love you,' and I will be satisfied!"[10]

Sue seems to have attempted more reassurance, and in her next letter Emily, still doubtful, replies, "thank you . . . dear Susie, that you never weary of me, or never *tell* me so."[11]

The vehement emotionalism of Emily's outpourings to Sue almost necessitated a reply in kind if Sue was not to appear by comparison relatively cool and uncommitted. That she could not or was unwilling to bring her communications to the often frenzied pitch of Emily's utterances may have been partly responsible for Emily's uncertainty as to where she stood with Sue.

Emily's frustration at Sue's apparent reserve, combined perhaps with a dim awareness of something abnormal and even dangerous in her own intensity, is occasionally perceptible, as in the following: "Oh Susie, I often think that I will try to tell you how very dear you are, and how I'm watching for you, but the words wont come, tho' the *tears* will, and I sit down disappointed —yet darling, you know it all—then why do I seek to tell you? I do not know; in thinking of those I love, my reason is all gone from me, and I do fear sometimes that I must make a hospital for the hopelessly insane, and chain me up there such times, so I wont injure you."[12] The phrase "I must chain me up there" is perhaps not unrelated to the poet's gradual transformation into an entrenched recluse hidden behind closed doors.

Her need for Sue is as desperate as is her anxiety that through too great importunity she might drive Sue away. Therefore, she alternately exacts an immediate and loving response from Sue and then denies or modifies her demand. "And when shall I have a letter," she asks rhetorically, "when it's convenient, Susie, not when tired or faint—*ever!*"[13]

Again a dim awareness that there may be some incongruity or impropriety in her longing for Sue manifests itself: "Sometimes when I do feel so, I think it may be wrong, and that God will punish me by taking you away; for He is very kind to let me write to you, and to give me your sweet letters, but my heart wants *more*."[14]

Her uneasy sense of the excesses to which her longing for Sue is pushing her keeps reappearing: "How I do count the days [until Sue's return]—how I do long for the time when I may count the *hours* without incurring the charge of Femina insania! I made up the Latin."[15]

Emily's desire for Sue at length becomes unappeasable by mere letter writing; physical closeness and contact is essential if Emily is to be at rest. "When I seek to say to you something not for the world, words fail me. If you were here—and Oh that you were, my Susie, we need not talk at all, our eyes would whisper for us, and your hand fast in mine, we would not ask for language."

In the same letter, after telling Sue that it is necessary to express her love for friends *now* because the day will come when death will part them, Emily pleads: "Susie, forgive me Darling, for every word I say."[16] She appears to disclose here an awareness that underlying her evocation of death as rationale for her excessive ardor are less admissible impulses. What appears to be generating the fear that God will take Sue from her is her suppressed anger at Sue's less than satisfying response, reenforced, probably, by long-latent death wishes toward her mother displaced to Sue. Thus she can neither mitigate her longing for Sue, which she realizes has transgressed the bounds appropriate to a relationship with a prospective sister-in-law, nor stress too strongly her death fears for Sue as a justification for her intensity. Both sets of feelings approach the inadmissible, the latter because of their unconscious connection with long-buried rage responses stimulated anew by her evident sense of impending abandonment. Her fear of losing Sue, and a sense of rivalry toward those who justifiably claimed some of Sue's attention, culminated in an attitude of exclusive possessiveness. Its jealous beginnings are apparent in the first letter Emily wrote after Martha and Sue were reunited: "Dont forget all the little friends," she entreats Sue, "who have tried so hard to *be* sisters, when indeed you *were* alone!"[17]

Emily would no doubt have experienced much more trepidation in advancing her claim to Sue's attention if she had been fully aware of Austin's growing possessiveness toward her friend. It is clear, however, that Sue did not and could not share Austin's letters with Emily; neither could she share Emily's letters with Austin. Uncomfortable as her position must have been, she could only try to moderate as best she could the intensity of the wooing that besieged her from both quarters. Her struggles along these lines, however, seem only to have increased the insecurity of both her suitors, who reacted by redoubling their efforts.

The massively emotional nature of Austin's infatuation with Sue, which was mentioned a few pages back, and its sudden onset are characteristic of transference reactions, that is, those reactions in which the present realities of the situation have more to do with setting off the emotional charge than they do with providing the actual combustible substance. In reading Austin's love letters to Sue it becomes apparent that he insufficiently recognized her as a person in her own right. His overwhelming desire for her and his blind optimism overrode all her uncertainties, many of which were grounded in a clear recognition of certain fundamental incompatibilities between them. Austin's letters indicate his strong need to have Sue see things the way he saw them. He was blind to differences in their outlooks and resisted all her efforts to tell him that she found it difficult to commit herself to their relationship as wholly as he. He would see in Sue only a reflection of his own headlong passion: they must feel alike and think alike in all things. Very early in their relationship Austin composed for Sue an allegory of his devotion which adumbrated his future incapacity to accept those individual needs and tastes of Sue's that were at variance with his own.

The allegory involves a retelling of the story of Narcissus, who died "in the vain attempt to possess his image reflected"* in the water. Austin likens himself to Narcissus and transforms Sue into a "transparent soul" in which he beholds his own "spirit image" reflected. Self-love is perhaps the most characteristic attribute of the ephemeral love affairs of adolescents and young adults. Love lasts as long as the beloved reflects back the flattering image. If such narcissistic requirements play too large a part in the attraction of one partner for the other, the love relationship inevitably falters. Austin's need to see Sue as an extension of himself was strong.

Several years after the previous letter was written, when his passion was in full flower, he wrote to Sue explaining that for him to thank her for her letter would be like thanking himself. Because "you write," he tells her, "because your heart finds pleasure in it—I know it—for our hearts have *met* & read each other

---

* Letter from Austin to Susan, 1851, Houghton Library, Harvard University. This letter exists in several fair copies that are somewhat varied. Also in Houghton Library, in Box 7 of the Dickinson Family Papers, is a series of letters, most of them previously unpublished, which Austin wrote to Susan in 1853-1854, usually from Cambridge. Most of these letters are in the form of rough drafts, and the exact order of their composition is unknown. Passages from these letters are quoted in this chapter by permission of the Harvard College Library. Published sources are given in the notes for a few excerpts that have appeared elsewhere.

—& the spirits have no longer—to look but in *one* heart to have seen both—it seems Sue, as if we were almost but one person—or at least exact counterparts so entirely are all our minutest—most fleeting and yet *formless* longings realized to each of us in the other."

During their frequent and protracted separations Austin devised ingenious ways to replenish and keep alive this compelling sense of identification. As early as 1850 the couple agreed that at a given hour on nine consecutive nights they would eat separately a chestnut dedicated to the other's health. Later, in Boston, Austin wrote Sue that he dreaded the weeks and months of their coming separation but consoled himself that "we shall think of each other as much as though we were continually together. We will read our Bibles at the same hour & we'll pray for each other —every night and every morning—We'll keep a record of our every day's experiences—for each other—Sometimes we'll walk off alone at the same hour & we'll fancy we are together . . . & sometimes we'll [?] down to sleep at the same hour and be dreaming together." Thus Austin sought to overcome the attenuating effect of separation on his sense of fusion with Sue by binding her to him, if not spatially, at least temporally.

Austin sensed that his projected image of Sue might not bear a close and objective scrutiny: He tells Sue that one does not pull up roses by the roots to find the secret of their beauty, dissect the throats of nightingales to find their song, nor analyse the colors of a rainbow in terms of the physics of light. One had best simply enjoy roses, bird songs, and rainbows, for too thoughtful examination destroys joy and beauty. Similarly, it is best, he says, that he and Sue not "analyze that secret influence which has drawn you & I together & made us one . . . we only know that the sun *does* shine . . . & that we *are* happy in each other's love . . . let us be content . . . lest in vain search seek *how* it is—lest it be not." Earlier in the same letter he cautioned, "you let me tell you one thing Sue—that the passion for analyzing you speak of, is a very dangerous one to happiness."

However, it is not my purpose to push this argument to extremes. There is nothing unusual in such striving as Austin's for intensified contact and identity except the inventiveness of his methods and arguments. What these passages do suggest is that Austin's hunger for Sue tended to involve a one-sided quest for the fulfillment of his own inner needs, to the partial exclusion of that maturer kind of affection which is founded on the genuine interest of two persons in each other and which is firmly rooted in reality. Austin's motivations, to a large extent, were unmodified by any objective evaluation of Sue's actual suitability as a wife, and to that extent he pursued her with unswerving intensity. For several years, possessing Sue became the only important motive of his life. When Sue encouraged him in his affection, he rose to heights of bliss. But if she raised a doubt that their relationship might not be all he wished, he plunged into the greatest perturbation and anxiety.

One of the serious differences they had was on the matter of religion. Sue seems to have been more than a little self-righteous and complacent in her own faith, and she found it difficult not to hold against him Austin's relative skepticism and lack of commitment in religious matters. When she raised his unsatisfactory position and his sinful proclivities as a possible obstacle to their eventually marrying, he became frantic:

> Oh Sue, this beautiful, beautiful sunny day—when I ought to be so happy—& when I *am* so *miserable*. What shall I do? No one to talk with me—no one to advise me—oh a world for one friend, one friend, one that I could open all my heart to—to whom I could tell every secret thought—& who would tell me my duty—How I wish I could bury my head in your lap, & ask you to pray for me—for you feel God hears you—& He won't me—for I go to Him every night and every morning, it is my silent prayer through the day, & I ask Him to enlighten my mind—to direct my thoughts—to show me His will—to correct my wrong views—& to give me right ones—& I read the Bible more than we read together—but I cant, I cant think as you do—and so you will reproach me again—& call me an obstinate sinner—or an ungrateful monster—and *am* I? God answer me & is it the doubt of the stoniest heart—the doubt of the necessity of a religion so stern, so uncompromising as yours—a religion that is consigning all my companions about me—the kindest noblest spiritual fellows—honest—truth-loving & truth serving—to an Eternity of helpless misery—because a different star lightens their way from yours—or the doubt that God could have formed the human Soul— only to destroy it! Oh Heaven show me—& Heaven help me, for I cannot see—I cannot help myself—

> Fast day Sue, and as I sat in Church this afternoon—the first time I was ever in a church on Fast day afternoon—who of all that congre-

gation knew what was going on in one heart there—the suffering it
was bearing up against—the agony of despair that was wringing it—
How calmly they all looked! How calmly the minister prayed for all
who needed help—Heavens! was *his* Soul ever moved! Did he ever
know what suffering was! & shall I too be calm again!

Your last letter Sue, has almost killed me, *Did* you mean all you
said? & may I never write you again one word upon that only subject that I hope to God is only for a time to separate us? till I can
write just *your* words will it cast me from you Sue, *now*! Oh why is
this. Has God permitted me to set you in my heart & watch you &
cherish you there, till you have grown into its every fiber—become
a part of it, only then to tear you thence—& leave me mangled,
bleeding—dying - - - Oh Sue—I love you with a love that has almost
driven me wild—I have centered everything in you—every hope—
every aspiration—I've given you everything I have—all I am—& all
I can make myself—& *will* you forsake me now—will you forsake
me for only loving you too much? will you not cling to me till you
have shown me something better than you I ought to live for! Will
you give me up—Have you not told me that God has assured you
in your heart—that you are right—& I wrong—Have you not told
me too that He had promised to set all right who asked Him—& am
I not asking Him—will I not continue to ask Him! & will He not
bring us together then in our belief & thrust & faith - - -

Will you bid me leave you now? Will you hope for me no longer—
Can you not remember when you had not given your own heart to
God! & did it all seem as easy & plain to you then as it does now—
Did not your pious mother—your pious sisters tell you it was a
simple thing to come to Christ & lay your burdens at His feet—& did
you find it so! Was the way plain to you then! Did the same light
that was so bright to them lighten your way?

Did you know where to go—& what to do! Will you tell me it is
only my *will* keeps me back—& if it is not—will you reproach me for
not doing what you tell me of myself I cannot? Do I not believe in
God—Do I not bow before the author of my being & do I not
acknowledge His power—& worship Him for His goodness! Do I
not know my own weakness—my own unworthiness of the many
daily blessings of which He is the constant giver—Am I not ready to
serve him in whatever He may command—& yet am I so wicked
Sue—you can't love me *Am* I as wicked as you say, Sue—Oh I'm
sick—I want to go home—I want to see Vinnie & Emily & father &
mother & see if they'll notice me—if they will speak to me—if I shall
not find the doors of my home closed on me—See if things *are* all as

they seem to me today or if I am only in a bad dream—Did I dream that letter of yours Sue? Did I dream those words that have made my hours of yesterday & of today—what they are and were—Nothing can help me now & I'm not dreaming. The sun is shining—I am sitting at my table—I'm in my day dress—my thoughts are coherent—I can remember being in church this morning—& again this afternoon—& no night has intervened—& no sleep has come to my eyes—Or did I misinterpret them? Did you mean them as a continuation of the idea you suggested at our Tuesday evening's Boston conversation—that there is a doubt if we ever marry? Oh Sue—then I want no longer to live—I've nothing to live for—this world has no charm for me without you—Then why have I ever seen you—why ever loved you—why ever listened to loving words from you—Has your love been given to me only as a mockery! My hopes been lifted so high only to be cast lower down—

Tell me again you love me, Sue, tell me you *will* love me—tell me what love you have for Earth shall be mine—tell me God will bring us together in our religion—Tell me to be calm again—to study, to trust, to pray—tell me you will never leave me—but for God—or my star of hope has set—a blight has overspread my youth and a darkness overshadowed my morning's Sun—the chill touch of Autumn has come upon me in the "April hour" of my life & the flower of my Spring has faded in its earliest blossoming—

I'm faint when I ought to be strongest & old while I'm yet young. Are you surprised, Sue, to read such a letter from me? Then you have not known how deeply an occasional reproach—an occasional doubting expression has sunk in my heart—then you have not known all the passion that has lain there.[18]

As can be inferred from this letter, Sue had the upper hand, and she maintained it to the end. Austin dared not criticize her or demur in anything too strongly for fear of alienating her. Emotional necessity dictated that he must win her at all cost, and he was well aware that Sue was not likely to lose her head over him. Consequently he felt impelled to treat her with the greatest tact and circumspection and to take pains always to present himself in such a light as to evoke her approval. Very early in their friendship he described Sue's attitude toward him as being characterized by "stately indifference," "unapproachable dignity," and "rigid formality." Although it may be argued that initially Sue's posture was to some degree due to the admonitions of Mrs. Cutler, it seems clear that in the later years of the courtship, when Sue was doubtless acting on her own, she frequently adopted very similar attitudes. Sue's air of condescending superiority was at its most pronounced when her sensitivity regarding her religious convictions was pricked. At such times Austin was torn between his fear of increasing her touchiness on the subject and his need not to appear to be truckling to her. Sue took Austin's aloofness toward religion quite personally; even the slightest adverse comment about her faith was a criticism of herself. A glimpse of the way she berated Austin for his indifference to the most important thing in her life can be gained from this excerpt from one of Austin's letters: "I sincerely wish I could write you tonight that I thought of it [i. e., religion] to the result I know you would rejoice to hear of me. Yet you don't expect it 'you know I shall turn away from your sheet to live on as indifferently to the great truths of religion as though this world was bond & limit of our Souls longing'—I don't believe you meant quite this, Sue." In the preceding paragraph he assured her: "I have thought of this a great deal—I shall think of this more—& I promise you to think more seriously on the subject which this [i.e., Sue's letter] urges upon my attention. I have always thought of it more or less." Austin, fearing that he might lose Sue because of his religious doubts and "wickedness," here tries to assure her that he is concerned about religion. But he is forced to hedge because in reality he was not convinced as Sue was convinced. Thus, in another place, we find him pledging himself to subdue his predilection for skepticism and even capitulating to Sue's request that he no longer attend the services of a Unitarian minister whose sermons he enjoyed:

I promise you—my dearest—to omit no means in my power to become what you say I ought—I won't take the opposite side again—as I always have—& strengthen myself again to belief in which I have been brought up—& in which everyone of my dear friends—have placed their hope—for the sake of arguing—& I won't go to Unitarian meetings, though it's a good deal of a sacrifice for me to give up that man I like so much—& I don't believe he could hurt me—but you don't want me to hear him—I'll read the Bible & pray & try—& if I am wrong, I'll *hope* God will show me my error though it seems sometimes Sue—as if I had no access to God—as if He didn't hear my prayers at all—yet I know He *has* heard them for I have prayed for you and He has given you to me.

As a budding lawyer, Austin appears to have been proud of his mind and of his capacity to muster a telling rational argument. It is not difficult to imagine his frustration, therefore, when Sue proved impervious to his demonstrations, scorned his opinions, and even refused to discuss her views with him on the level of objective reason. His exasperation, always well controlled, can occasionally be detected:

> But to very few has He given it to love & be loved as to you and I— nor to but few to have *suffered*—more—than we have—yet for this very suffering is our love the richer—from the more perfect sympathy it finds in us—I had perhaps better not enlarge however on the theological view of the matter—for I know very well you have but little respect for my opinions therein—& would be almost inclined to consider it heterodox because it had come of itself into my head— Don't dislike this last sentence—will you—Sue? for I meant no trifling with your feeling that I am so very wrong—& you sometimes seem to think I am—though I do think you are a little uncharitable towards me—Sue—for I *feel* so much better than you say I am.

In addition to an air of religious self-righteousness and moral superiority to Austin, Sue occasionally exhibited a maddening tendency to withdraw; at these times Austin became bewildered:

> We hardly had a pleasant time last evening did we, Sue, hardly as pleasant as usual! Or was it all my fancy? & now do you know that I had an idea from your manner of speaking of my coming in the afternoon—& the evening before at your door—that perhaps you had some reason why you had as leave I wouldn't come last night? Though you wouldn't mention it from fear it might be unpleasant to me—that you spoke of it a little cooly—& that you seemed a little indifferent to me when I was *with* you? My presence didn't seem to make you happy—nor anything I could say . . . & it troubled me— made me unhappy very—for *your* happiness—your happiness in me—is now my very life—all I care for all that makes life pleasant all that makes it tolerable—all my soul's desire—take that from me— and what have I left.

Austin, of course, had no idea Emily's letters to Sue were rivaling his own in passionate intensity. If he had, he might have understood why Sue was not always able to concentrate on their relationship to the extent that he desired. Also, the exorbitance of his demands for unfaltering adoration perforce made Sue appear reserved. Here, too, in his excessive need for reassurance, Austin was like Emily. Sue's frequent failure to match Austin's enthusiasm continued to unnerve him.

"Are we lovers!" he exclaimed, echoing a question of Sue's,

Perhaps I am a very foolish child Sue but last evening troubled me—troubled me—I want to forget it—I wish it had never been—last evening or Friday evening—you *didn't* seem glad to see me—nor to have me with you—nor sorry to have me leave you—& we didn't talk at all of what was in my thoughts or of what I *wanted* to talk [about?] *Is* it all my imagination—& *am* I foolish & childish—then tell me so—& I will try never to have you say the same again.

Emily also had little sense of security as far as the dependability of Sue's affection and companionship were concerned. For her, young men, of course, including Austin, were apprehended as the biggest threat. "What would become of me when the 'bold Dragon' shall bear you both away," she asks Sue, referring to Sue and Martha, who by this time had become a constant companion, "and leave me here alone . . . I could have wept bitterly over the only *fancy* of ever being so lone."[19] After this remark, Emily's thoughts lead directly to the death theme, as though loss of Sue were to be equated with death.

Even in her dreams Emily fears to lose Sue: "Vinnie and I talked of you all last evening long, and went to sleep mourning for you," she writes, "and pretty soon I waked up saying 'Precious treasure, thou are mine,' and there you were all right, my Susie, and I hardly dared to sleep lest some one steal you away."[20]

Even before Austin was seriously considering a proposal of marriage, Emily anticipated the event, if not with Austin with some other man. She writes to Sue regarding Sue's journal: "I want you to get it bound . . . so when he takes you from me, to live in his new home, I may have *some* of you. I am sincere."[21]

From the beginning of his ardent friendship with Sue in 1850, when he was twenty-one, through his courtship and his engagement, and until his marriage in 1856—a period of at least six and a half years—Austin had to struggle to contain his emotions within the limits permitted by his circumstances. Even after his engagement to Sue, when the couple were reunited in Amherst, two years were still to elapse before they married. As their intimacy grew, Austin became, understandably enough, increasingly impatient. After all he was a lusty young man, given generally to

CHAPTER V

buoyant spirits and with a tendency to be headstrong and rebellious. His fantasies turned increasingly and ever more yearningly to scenes of marital bliss. "Do I not love you," he asks Sue, "when all my dreams are only of how I can make your life happier & sweeter—Do you not *know* I love you Sue with as strong a passion as ever glowed in a man's breast." The passion in his breast led him to suggest repeatedly that the distant date of their wedding be advanced even if some of the niceties of the occasion had thereby to be foregone. "Oh Sue," he writes, "It seems to me tonight I'd sacrifice a great deal of my ideal of externals—to be married now to have you by me now—to have those long months —as many as since our hearts have known each other—affixed instead of prefixed to our lives as we are planning them *now*—I want you more than I can tell." Then in the next paragraph, indulging in a bit of emotional blackmail to pressure Sue into acceding to an earlier marriage, he tells of a young friend of his who has just died leaving a grieving widow and two small boys. The point, of course, is that one should marry early because one cannot be certain of a satisfyingly prolonged married existence. "Death has never come so near to me as this winter," he writes, "One from the table where I sat has been taken—one from the circle in which I visited most—and there has been another—the name fails me now but the fact is with me—and who next—is it my next door neighbor whom the consumption has been these two years—slowly wasting—or is it me—in the flush of youth and strength." There is no evidence that Sue was much moved by this plea, Austin's depiction of friends dropping around him on all sides perhaps being weakened by the fact that he could not recall so much as the name of one of them.

On occasion Sue gave him an opening to express the dismay his reluctant celibacy was causing him. Without her, he says,

Life would be without the slightest object—I could do nothing—could care for nothing—could hardly live for anything—But the good God who has allowed only so high an ideal to fill my heart as you realize to me—has given me you . . . That sentence [from Sue's letter] 'every new day we are together makes the tie painfully stronger' was *just* what I was feeling—and painfully was just the word to express it—the tie that binds us is almost *too* painfully strong—for separation . . . You have not known yet darling just how purely & tenderly & delicately I love you . . .

200

The last four words of the following phrase are scratched out but are still legible. It reads, ". . . & you cannot till we are married." Apparently the words were too open to a construction other than the spiritual one he wanted to convey—one that disclosed some of his, in his and Sue's eyes, less creditable preoccupations.

Austin's fear of being too outspoken is frequently indicated in the lines he writes and then crosses out and rewrites. What ultimately appeared as "I wish I could kiss you before I leave you—but that is not yet—I can only say good night and a sweet sleep, my beautiful Sue" was originally cast in the following more erotic and somewhat jumbled form: "I wish I could kiss you before I leave you—let you press my lips to yours as you lie sweetly sleeping." The fantasy of kissing Sue in her bed, sleeping yet responding, obviously too boldly revealed what was on his mind.

On the occasion of the marriage of a common friend who spent his first wedded night with his bride in a hotel, Austin expressed his disapproval that an event that ought to be so privately sacred should be so publicly exposed. "When we are married," he reassures Sue tenderly, "our earliest married love shall consecrate our *home*—our first days and first weeks shall be at our own, our dear—long hoped for home—where our true life shall begin— then first will we kneel together and pray God's blessing upon us whose cup has filled so full of Joy—there will we receive our first calls." As if having gone too far, he immediately reassures her, "You shall still be Sue & I will still be Austin." And next follows a line originally reading: "And we will move right along as naturally—as though it had always been as it is"; Austin crosses this out and substitutes the vaguer "& shall be real then—with God's blessing—all the dreams we are dreaming now."

Even less delicate than the suggestion that he has needs that might move along "naturally" (that is, presumably, sexually) is the faint imputation that he believes Sue may have such needs. In reassuring Sue that he will devote his life to the furtherance of her happiness, he writes that there will exist "Not a wish of yours but a corresponding wish of mine to fulfill it. Not a dream of yours but a like dream of mine to gratify it—not an endearing word I would love to whisper to you but you would love to listen to . . ." And here he runs into trouble, for he next writes: "Not a caress of love to complete my dream but you would love to receive." Immediately "you would love to receive" is marked out, and the safer and less explicit "it would crown yours" is substituted.

Following their engagement, Austin became bold enough to use the words wife and husband. "How long I have loved you & how much! And now what a love binds us together forever forever—God's & each others. Such a flowing out from my heart as I feel toward you—Such a delight in feeling that you, *you*—want that I can be with you & keep you with me always that you are to be my *wife* & I your *husband.*"

Any acknowledgment from Sue that in any measure she feels toward Austin as he feels toward her brings forth a torrent of blissful words:

> . . . for I love you as you love me—I didn't know quite how nearly or how dearly till those few most precious months so lately ours—which told more than any words that I *satisfied* you—that my affection was your heart's longing—oh my *dear* Sue—what months those were! The first kiss of affection between two human beings—the first time my lips ever touched anothers—when the last—the choicest treasure I had guarded so long—*always*—I gave to you & I was all yours.

And he talks of "the mysterious power that has made you & I one—to think of all the joy that every new day is bringing us nearer to."

The joy that every new day brought nearer was nevertheless slow in coming. He reminds Sue that it has been four years "since the first fair dawning in our hearts of a consciousness we met something in each other sweeter than we met elsewhere—And not less than fifteen moons now since we have only known that the Sun of our love was not in its meridian splendor by its constantly increasing brightness." Perhaps one may legitimately ascribe a touch of exasperation to the question with which he concludes this passage about the ever-rising sun of their love: "When is it to culminate!"

In another letter he identifies Sue with the sun in a passage of unconsciously erotic imagery: "You are the light and you the genial warmth that have made the closed germ within me to expand and send up its tender shoot—& you the sweetest influence that is to cherish it to its perfect flower."

While Austin's desire for Sue was becoming ever more full-blooded, Emily's was reaching a new pitch of fervency. Despite her qualms about Sue's acceptance of her love, Emily's possessiveness and fear of displacement in Sue's affections were driving her to increasingly extravagant protestations of adoration.

From January 1852 until July, when Sue returned from Baltimore to Amherst, Emily's language becomes more and more passionate. In January she writes of the dragging months and anticipates the time when "Bounding o'er them all—I meet the glad July—and have you in my arms—Oh Susie—you *shall* come."[22] A few weeks later she mourns: "Oh my darling one, how long you wander from me, how weary I grow of waiting and looking, and calling for you; sometimes I shut my eyes, and shut my heart towards you, and try hard to forget you because you grieve me so, but you'll never go away, Oh you never will." A few lines later she exclaims: "I dont know how I shall bear it [if spring arrives before Sue] . . . Oh it would surely kill me!"[23]

After Sue wrote reassuring Emily of her devotion, Emily replied: "But what can I do towards you?—*dearer* you *cannot* be, for I love you so already, that it almost breaks my heart—perhaps I can love you *anew,* every day of my life, every morning and evening—Oh if you will let me, how happy I shall be!"[24]

A month or so later she tells of her impatience: "I sit here with my little whip, cracking the time away, till not an hour is left of it—then you are here! . . . joy now and forevermore! . . . 'Tis only a few days, Susie, it will soon go away, yet I say, go now, this very moment, for I need her—I must have her, Oh give her to me!"[25]

Emily tells Sue of her way of passing the time in church. "When [the minister] said 'Our Heavenly Father,' I said 'Oh Darling Sue' [meaning, *oh heavenly mother?*]." Rather than praise the Lord, Emily praises Sue: "when he read the 100th Psalm, I kept saying your precious letter all over to myself . . . when they sang . . . I made up words and kept singing how I loved you."[26]

By May Emily is proclaiming the full extent of her dedication: "Susie,—I shall think of you at sunset, and at sunrise, again; and at noon, and forenoon, and afternoon, and always, and evermore, till this heart stops beating and is still."[27]

Sue, while contending with Emily, was at the same time bearing the brunt of Austin's headlong vehemence, and her attitude as reflected in his letters betrays a need to draw back as if in self-protection. His sister Vinnie was sensitive to the fact that others might find his fervor oppressive, and she let Sue and Austin know that in her opinion he *was* a bit demanding. Austin then writes Sue, after having pledged himself to fulfill a promise and to give her anything else within his power that she could ask for,

> And need I ask you after this sentence, Sue, if that remark of Vinnie's—almost unkind unfair towards me—I think—though I know not intentionally so—need I ask you if that is working unpleasantness in you still? I *know* I need not Sue—I know you know me too well—& know me too long—for have you in all our intercourse ever seen the germ of an overbearing disposition in me? Have I not always been careful and tender of you? Have I not always counted it my completest joy to feel I was making *you* happy! Have I ever asked you to yield an opinion or liking or plan to me? & will I ever? Have I ever asked you to make any sacrifice for me—for do I not want to make them all myself—& for you! *No* Sue, I *know* that remark isn't bothering you.

Vinnie's remark, if it did not trouble Sue, troubled him, and in another letter, brooking absolutely no dissent, he asserts his objections to it:

> For I am *not* overbearing—not *too* exacting—I think I can understand you in the feeling which—expressed as it was—made that evening what it was—I think you feel entirely sure of my love—that I love you with all the love I am capable—but yet it doesn't lead me towards you in all my ways—all my acting expression of it just up to your ideal—isn't that it? Don't you have a feeling that if I love you as much as I say I do—that isn't quite so much in love as you had imagined—not quite the joy you had dreamed. At any rate that's my idea—& if it's yours—I don't think strange at all—for we haven't begun to enjoy each other as we *shall*.

Here Austin seems to have missed the point. It does not appear that he is falling short of Sue's ideal by default, as he thinks, but by excess. Telling Sue that they "haven't begun to enjoy each other as we *shall*" seems expressive of *his* frustrations, but one questions if this is Sue's concern. Yet Austin sensed Sue's reservations and worried about them: "I want to tell you", he writes,

> what troubles me what troubled me yesterday—what spoiled my

visit last night—what has worried me today—what has *worried* me! what has swept over my heart like the wasting Simoon over the desert . . . cutting off every anticipated joy—every fair hope—every bright expectation every sweet promise—it is a feeling—a fear which you have spoken of as troubling *you* for everything you have had to do with me.

In his bewilderment at her response to him he tries touchingly to reassure her. The following is from the same letter in which he defends himself against the accusation of being "overbearing" and says that he believes Sue's reserve is due to some defect in him. He speaks of the "mighty barriers" to be broken down, old doubts, constraint, guardedness, and distrust:

A long dream to find *not* a dream—is it strange then—wouldn't it be strange if we could forget all that at once—all our preconceived notions . . . and meet each other in the easiest way—familiarly & simply & lovingly as we feel in our hearts we might meet & would love to meet? Seems to *me* it would—but we shall grow into it as we grow more thoroughly into the fullest knowledge & confidence in one another. It must be in a measure the result of growth—of time. I know I *love* you & love you so much—that I want to do nothing in my expression of it to you that shall in the slightest jar with the expression you would like—for I could refrain from a great deal or do a great deal—to retain your love entire & I had rather fall a little short in some ways than a little excessive in another that I am not quite sure will please you. I love to be near you—Sue—to look at you—I love to call you mine—I love to hear you report your love for me—I would love to sit all the evening close by your side with my arm around you to draw you closer—with your hand in mine—I would love to feel your head resting trustingly on my shoulder—sweetly assuring me that you would "lean" on me & me alone that it should be mine only to support you—to cherish you—to protect you from all the roughness—all the hardness all the chill of the world mine only to love you & make you happy and we might, unreservedly —like loving confiding children as we all really are—tell each other all our love—yet all the fear that in the slightest tinges it—every doubt that enters into it—confessing to each other all we confess to our most hidden selves.

Sue apparently tried to tell him what troubled her, at first indirectly, with hinting. She tells him of the unhappy experience of her brother-in-law's sister; he replies with masculine obtuseness:

How in the world could that Mrs. Bartlett have managed to have had a sad year & full of trials the first year of her married life? I certainly can't conceive—*ours* won't be so how can it what's going to trouble us shan't I love you every moment! & do all for you & forbear from doing all that the entirest love & sympathy can suggest? Shan't I call you my own Sue—& kiss you—& press you to my heart? *What trials* can we have! Let them come. They'll only make our love stronger & deeper—they'll bind us closer together—"the first year" a year of "fearful unhappiness"! Not ours—of constant happiness—we'll see.

Even as early as 1851, when Sue was still teaching in Baltimore, she was interested in Austin's reactions to the idea that to a woman what is called married bliss might be less than an unmitigated pleasure. At this time she sent Austin a letter from her friend Hattie Taylor in which Harriet extols the virtues of love yet, according to Austin's letter, says that "the idea of being married is perfectly repugnant to her." The feminine capacity for combining romantic raptures with a cool eye toward objective reality puzzles Austin: "How at one moment [she can] be all absorbed with a love that is pervading her whole being—and in the next—going through a practical analysis & description of the personal talents and means of the object of that love to a schoolmate is to me a little mysterious."

For all the closeness of Sue's and Emily's relationship, Sue seems to have revealed to Emily very little of the content and warmth of her letters from Austin. Nevertheless, by June 1852 Emily is writing to Sue, still in Baltimore, in a way that indicates a growing and uneasy preoccupation with thoughts of married life; one receives the impression that Emily is beginning to worry that Sue also may be turning her attention, more positively perhaps, in this direction. Emily tells Sue that she is longing for Sue's return to Amherst and says that the mere sound of Sue's name causes her to weep: "Not that the mention *grieves* me, no, Susie, but I think of each 'sunnyside' where we have sat together, and lest there be no more, I guess is what makes the tears come." She tells Sue, "I . . . wished for you, and Heaven," heaven, in this context consisting of "those unions . . . by which two lives are one." Emily then inquires if Sue entertains fantasies of love: murmuring her beloved's name into her pillow or in daydreams walking by his side. In the following lines Emily reveals the extent of her own horror of the sexual side of marriage:

> ... to the *wife,* Susie, sometimes the *wife forgotten,* our lives perhaps seem dearer than all others in the world; you have seen flowers at morning, *satisfied* with the dew, and those same sweet flowers at noon with their heads bowed in anguish before the mighty sun; think you these thirsty blossoms will *now* need naught but—*dew*? No, they will cry for sunlight, and pine for the burning noon, tho' it scorches them, scathes them; they have got through with peace— they know that the man of noon, is *mightier* than the morning and their life is henceforth to him. Oh, Susie, it is dangerous, and it is all too dear, these simple trusting spirits, and the spirits mightier, which we cannot resist! It does so rend me, Susie, the thought of it when it comes, that I tremble lest at sometime I, too, am yielded up."[28]

No doubt these apprehensions of Emily's struck a sympathetic chord in Sue, augmenting her own anxiety. Austin was a more than ordinarily sensitive man. Either Sue told him or he ultimately divined what was troubling her. Here is the way he dealt with her fears of his sexual needs. He says that he has noticed that something in the past troubled Sue and guesses that it was

> the thought of giving yourself away to me—does it now [trouble you], Sue? Does it ever seem to you you could live happier—better— unmarried—or married to some of the many others whose hearts you have unwittingly won? Is there anything in the "mere relation of wife that gives you sometimes gloomy thoughts"—and if there is can I not say something that will relieve them—can I not say that you may live just exactly as you are happiest in living—just as free from care, and responsibility to me—as you please just like a girl always if so you are happiest—that I will ask nothing of you take nothing from you—you are not the happier in giving me—that your happiness & your life are above everything else with me—that everything I can do for you—everything I can sacrifice for you—it will be my life to do—Don't ever be discouraged, Sue, in thinking of "a man's requirements"—I ask nothing but your love—just the love you are giving me now—& I offer in return all I am—& all I can accomplish—without reserve—without qualifications. Be happy then Sue & be mine too.

In his zeal to reassure her he even resorted to a measure for which Sue felt he had scant aptitude—theological arguments. "Is there anything debasing in human love," he wonders, "does it not rather exalt & refine & purify our nature above all else—Has not God planted it in us." Some of the ensuing lines are scratched out for rephrasing, but since they are still legible they are given here in parentheses.

> (Did not Christ teach that the love of a man for his wife should be paramount—) And does He not wish us to exercise it—would He have given us this highest desire of the soul (& set before us the objects of this desire & bid us pass them by and heed them not—) & set before us the means of gratifying it—& bid us use them not—to hunger on & eat not to thirst on & drink not—to live on—& love not! No Sue, He has given us meat for our hunger—& drink for our thirst—& love for our loves.

It is not possible to say whether Austin was successful in his efforts to reconcile Sue to the physical intimacy of wedded love before (or after) their marriage. However, Austin's letters suggest that her anxieties were a recurring motif in their premarital association and a source of pain to Austin: "Are those tears, Sue, that you feel a little reluctance—as the day seems nearer to trust yourself entirely to me as your only happiness? Oh Heavens don't *don't* you be unhappy—Sue—Let *any*thing be *my* fate—but only happiness for you. It will kill me if *you* suffer."

Some time during the year Austin was in Cambridge Sue explained some of her scruples, to Austin's temporary relief: "And it made me happy Sue," he writes, "for even the little explanation you gave me of the origin and nature of those 'doubts' I asked you about—for I think I found in it the clue to the whole." His overriding optimism even managed to change Sue's frequent depressed moods into a virtue:

> I could take your wish that you were "always gay for my sake" Sue —& your "wonder if you shall ever be fit for my choice treasuring["]—& oh how *many* pages could I write you of how *more* than worthy you are of the choicest treasuring the human heart can give, of how if you were gay I shouldn't love you so much—*I don't like gaiety*—only now and then—I like *you*—just as you are—sober—thoughtful—noble—loving—deeper & truer than any gay girl ever dreamed of—I don't like gay girls . . . Don't ever want to be different for my sake, Sue . . . you are a little inclined, to find the dark shades now Sue—I know—it isn't strange—but when I get with

you—I am so much inclined to find the bright, we shall just balance & between us get just the right shade—shan't we?

At times Austin seriously doubted that Sue could love him. Yet her love was so necessary to his equilibrium that possession of her without her passionate commitment to their union would not do. If she could not give this commitment, he was prepared—or at least he let Sue believe he was prepared—to give her up. "For if I am the cause of all your despondency & gloom," he writes, "If your heart does not recognize in me its rightful keeper—if it does not find its peace in *me*—if it turns away—& feels its home is not yet reached then, Sue, the sooner I know it the better—then let us think no longer of ever marrying." And again, *"Never think of marrying me Sue—without loving me—only because you have promised to—for it would be a terrible thing for you and I."* He can never decide if Sue's reluctance resides in some shortcoming in himself or in some mysterious peculiarity of hers. "Tell me," he urges, "if you think these occasional fearful doubts that over-shadow you come from a distrust inborn in your own character & would come to you in your love for any other—or if it is from something in *me particularly*—some defects in my character that every now & then oppress you by their glaringness." Sue's strange hesitations and withdrawals caused Austin agonies of uncertainty:

You "wonder if you shall *always* love me as you do now"—Sue—*Do* you wonder Do you doubt if you shall always love me—that expression troubles me my dear girl . . . What do you mean, Sue, when you say you fear you shall never be married! Anything? Have you any definite presentiment that we are not to continue to love each other. Don't hold such things before me, Sue, if they are not *real* to you—for you don't know how they trouble me—when nothing *else* in the world can—I could never give you up my dear Sue—I couldn't live without you—perhaps it is wicked—I presume you will think it is—but I can't help it—I positively had rather never existed than [be] doomed to live without your love . . . I tremble Sue when I think of it how dependent my happiness my very existence is upon you . . . If there is anything in those doubting expressions you occasionally use—anything definite—real—won't you tell me & not let me suffer for any vain fears of losing all at last—*Let* me know the worst—if there is a worst—I presume you will say that I am very foolish . . . But it is the foolishness of the man who has hung his life upon a single thread.

One guesses that the impossibility of getting Austin to accept some of her insecurity and uncertainty as an unalterable fact might have driven Sue to some desperate attempts at explanation. Confronted with what seems to be one of these efforts of Sue's, Austin does not know what to make of it and says that he is at a loss to know how to respond to her letter. He says that Sue wrote him "In a strain so pure, so solemn, so like a warning teacher" [as if Sue] "desired to prove to me the necessity & blessedness of a religious life—and yet so anxious for me—your words impressed me somehow *strangely,* Sue—more indeed—they startled me." The ensuing lines, crossed out, are interesting because they suggest the magnitude of Sue's perturbation: "They seemed like the words of one just bidding adieu to the scene of this vain unsatisfying world to whom was even now revealed the greatness & glory & grandeur of Eternity—than of a young strong woman—just entering upon life."

With Sue Austin strove for an impossible love purged of all selfishness, demandingness, and mean "animal" promptings. An exalted, unworldly love such as, he says, is rare enough even in poetry; and when, indeed, such love is encountered in verse by the average lover, it is "even then passed by as imaging nothing to be found in the heart of man—& nothing commending itself even for its own pure beauty to his gross nature." But Austin's "gross nature," too, had its own demands, try as he might to suppress them; and at the times when they were most urgent, his self-esteem suffered and he felt unworthy of Sue. Though he worried about Sue's periodic lack of responsiveness to him, it is apparent that one of the qualities that made her so desirable to him was her "purity"—a quality which in himself he knew was of dubious reliability. Probably this consciousness of impulses originating in his lower nature, as he thought of it, was partly responsible for his feeling that he "had no access to God—as if He didn't hear my prayers at all." He prayed that he might suppress all carnal thoughts about Sue, but he did not have much confidence in the success of these efforts. "I love you too dearly, Sue, to be away from you a moment," he writes, "but the day is not far distant if you will keep loving me—so that I can keep studying—which is to bring us—if I am only good—all our hearts desires—which is to make us each other's before the world—as we are now before God—'If I am only good'—but this troubles me Sue—

and not exactly that either." The letters tell of episodes of extreme despondency, significantly occurring at times when he was not doubting that he had won Sue's affection. Sometimes he

"could eat nothing all day, I could hardly breathe—I was so oppressed by a sort of choking sensation—I continued along somehow—till the meeting bells rang—and then dropped into the first church I came to . . . I went back to my room again—alone and with a sick heart—knowing nothing what to do—& doing about as much. I could neither read, think nor sleep, though I had slept none on the night before. I laid my paper before me & commenced writing home—just as I felt—once for a moment I lost myself & the tears burst out.

Earlier in the same letter he admitted to having felt even worse the evening before: "It seemed to me yesterday morning when I got up as if I *should die*—as if I was already dead & enduring the misery of an after state."

In another letter he speaks of an affectionate letter of Sue's that was "so pure":

it made me feel my own impurity—& selfishness—& unworthiness so deeply—it completely broke me down & humbled me—I know you love me, Sue, & yet I feel today so unworthy of it—so as if I ought not to have won it—you deserve a better man than I am to keep your heart—Sue it is too rich—too pure for me—I am astonished every day at the new wealth I discover in it—& I tremble at the thought you have given me so much . . . How shall I repay it! I have nothing but myself to give you—& think it but a paltry gift compared with yours to me—but I pray God every night to make it greater—to make it worthy of you.

The theme of his relative unworthiness crops up in many letters, generally after his expressions of gratitude for Sue's love, as in the following: "How I wish I were more for your sake—how I wish I could give you in myself a greater gift—all I *can* give you, Sue, is yours." Probably such feelings are universal in men whose fantasies have conspired to overinflate the merits and uniqueness of the beloved. Austin, however, has even more extreme feelings: at times it appears to him that his campaign to possess Sue is rooted in something basically criminal. In one letter he complains of being depressed, of being the victim of "an old spiritual malady," and says that the day is

one of those days when I feel wicked & worthless & useless. When

I feel, Sue, as if I had no right to *you* & as if I ought not to *have* you
—as if I had done almost murder in even trying to gain your love
—as if a wrong I could never atone for—& these loving words before
me—which you have written & sent to me I feel as if I had *stolen*
—as if they were not meant for me—& I had no business with them
—one of those days when my prayers seem unheard—and my way
dark—when I wish I might [next follows a line, given here in
parentheses, which Austin scratched out] (die & no one care & no
one know it) pass out of existence—& no one care & no one know it
—& in death make amends for every wrong of my life. It is a blue
day with me, Sue, I needn't tell you more—but when I come home
I'll tell you partly what makes it. So don't worry & don't puzzle
about it my dear Sue I beg of you. Don't let me add to my sins
that of having given *you* an unhappy moment.

I love you, Sue, most fondly most tenderly—but you seem so pure
& so good & so generous. I feel today as if I committed almost sacrilege in holding your love for my own. If I could only be sure you
knew just what I am.

Tension generated in Austin through his relentless efforts to
suppress every element of his attraction to Sue that fell short of
his spiritual ideal and that appeared to him unworthy of her may
be what lay behind some of the constant and varied physical
complaints that plagued him during the year he lived in Cambridge. There is no evidence that the rigors of law school caused
any of Austin's psychosomatic symptoms. Austin took his studies
in stride, and he never once mentions having any particular concern about them. Yet he had recurrent neuralgia, palpitations,
choking sensations, feelings of suffocation, and frequent severe
headaches. One of the reasons he so strongly urged an earlier
marriage than the one initially planned was that he was uncertain
whether his physical vigor would last long enough for him to
enjoy it. In one letter he speaks of his anticipatory fantasies of
married life and expresses the hope that he will be able to participate in them when they become reality: "How I love to paint
the outlines of all these and a thousand more sweet pictures—for
the future to fill up for us—as it will if God spares our lives and
my health." At times, like his sister Emily, he felt on very shaky
ground: "Is there seen then no such a thing on Earth as unmixed
happiness—Is it not always shadowed by a fear it may not last—
Is there not something whispers to us Earth is not the place for

complete happiness? That if we rest our trust—how it may be dashed in pieces!"

According to a letter in which the word "requirements" figures prominently (compare Sue's phrase "a man's requirements," meaning a man's sexual needs), when Austin thinks of "the one joy that is to come," that is, sexual union, he experiences an intensification of his headache. "I believe now," he writes Sue,

> you answer to every aspiration of my heart—& I believe the more you know of *me* the more fully you will find all your own hearts —not requirements—some softer more delicate word if there was one—met in me . . . We were *born* to love each other . . . What a heaven, Sue, in such great love as ours! I can't *think* of it. Such joy intoxicates my Soul—almost bewilders me.

> I want to write a great deal more Sue—I mustn't write anything— my heart overflows toward you—but I can't write tonight—I've got too severe a headache . . . I've longed to see you all the afternoon— & I long to see you now to talk with you—to show you more of my heart—to tell you how perfectly you satisfy it—how it is my highest desire to be able to feel that I am making you happy—

> So you will excuse this letter—will you my dearest Sue—beautiful visions are floating through my mind of the one joy that is to come—but I can't tell you of it tonight—& mustn't look on them myself—their exquisite beauty pains me—

> Another time—another only because my headache's too bad to allow me to go on.

The guilt feelings associated with fantasies of sexually possessing Sue, the feeling that the mere wish to so possess her is akin to robbery, murder, and sacrilege, the fear that as retribution for such a wish one may die—all these reactions support the idea, put forward earlier in this chapter, that Austin's consuming absorption in Sue was basically a massive transference reaction. This means that for Austin's unconscious Sue promised the fulfillment of the hungers of childhood. Austin said that Sue was the only girl he ever loved, ever kissed, and that he had never received tenderness from anyone. But he was of course leaving out of consideration the days of infancy. Austin seems to have been seeking to establish with Sue the identical unqualified, unconditional, all-encompassing love that his sister Emily searched and longed for—that is, by means of Sue he sought to find his way back to a good mother, the pure, giving, accepting madonna, once so vitally needed. Now, however, the roles were reversed; he was the powerful, steady, selfless protector, and the woman was the vulnerable, wilful, imperious child. He was also, however, a sexually aroused adult male, not an immature, helpless organism whose diffuse sensual impulses were appeasable solely through the warmth of a maternal breast and embrace. The attachment to that early semblance of security appears to have remained unduly prominent in all the Dickinson children, and probably this is why none of them ever left home. It may also help explain Austin's inner struggles in his courtship of Sue, why he chose a woman who was obviously sexually phobic, and why a love relationship seemingly begun most auspiciously, with total commitment and passion on Austin's part, led to a marrige of great disenchantment and bitterness.

To some degree all men marry their mothers and all women their fathers. The exact degree, however, is a matter of the greatest importance. When, as in Austin's case, the beloved woman's real psychological constitution is almost totally obscured by the radiance emanating from a symbolic investiture borrowed from the man's distant past, the sexual impulses of maturity must necessarily appear incongruous and almost inadmissible. But human beings who take on the quality of symbolic figures have a unique power and fascination. It appears to have been this projection to Sue of their childhood mother images which magnetized Austin's and Emily's whole souls and made her the dominant goal of their lives. And because she was endowed by Austin with other and more than her real qualities, no other woman could conceivably ever take her place; he must attain her or die. Or so he thought. For this reason the fear that he might possibly fail to win her brought him at times to a state of extreme tension.

Parting with Sue after one of his visits home was agony. On one such occasion, Austin, writing from Cambridge, found his present circumstances "a little too dark—after so bright an hour in Amherst—I was too blue—after so much pleasure—I couldn't make anything seem natural here—nor right—I was lonesome & sober Monday night & Tuesday—& I didn't sleep—nor eat the world seemed hopeless & blank & cold—& I was wretched enough." This excerpt is given because it suggests that parting with Sue was capable of bringing on feelings of derealization in

Austin similar to those Emily felt under the same circumstances, of which I shall speak in a later chapter. His inability to make anything seem "natural" and the blankness of the world support this interpretation. Sometimes, however, it was Sue herself that seemed unreal to him: "it seems an age since Saturday morning & everything about my home and you seem dim and fanciful—as it always seems when I am not with you." These feelings of attenuation are possibly signs of a sense of inner emotional impoverishment that do not ordinarily occur in an adult when he is separated from a loved person upon whom he is dependent in a realistic and nonsymbolic way. They do, however, frequently occur when the loved one represents the universe of infantile nurturant experiences.

Sometimes the sense of derealization of the world reached such a pitch of intensity as to justify the designation pathological, if Austin is reporting his experiences accurately and not exaggerating. In the following passage lines marked out in the original are given in parentheses. "It is lonely & spiritless even beyond my expectations here without you" he writes Sue,

> very much as it used to be when I came home from Boston last year—(everything seems mechanical—) as if the *Soul* was gone— (and every motion was from no impulse but merely mechanical— as if men were only machines just going from habit—as if there doesn't seem to *be* anything—& I wonder what men are living for) and only a lifeless body was left me—(as if the village was deserted—) Everything seems to move on (as by machinery—) mechanically—just as it was left—(when the animating principle left —as if urged by no impulse—Spirit) I wonder what men are living for—& yet I suppose in reality the world is just as large—& just as important as it was two days ago—& the difference is only in me.

Such a perception of himself and the world, with its emphasis on the mechanical, is reminiscent in a milder way of the experience depicted in one of his sister's great psychological poems: "After great pain, a formal feeling comes."

To return again to Emily: all aspects of her relationship to Sue —her self-doubts, her tense possessiveness, and her extreme assertions of affectionate longing—resembled exaggerations of her previous feelings toward other girl friends. Beginning very early in her teens, these impulses appear to represent a need to fend off the terrors of adolescence and of growing up to adult responsibilities; as such, they were an abnormal extension of latency-age patterns. In this sense, then, they would not properly be designated as homosexual. Fed by the hormonal fuels of greater physical maturation, however, similar attitudes toward Sue begin, in Emily's early twenties, to burn with a consuming ferocity that leaves no doubt that Sue has become—consciously or otherwise—a sexual object.

Yet the relationship had other facets that one must not overlook. There is evidence of a fear-inspired withdrawal toward childhood that would avoid the perilous terrain Emily sees looming on the horizon. Thus, in January 1852, we find Emily attempting to deny the girls' maturity, calling Sue "my dear earthly child."[29] The next month Emily tells Vinnie she doesn't care to be young; to be old, say thirty, doesn't seem too sad. At twenty-two she writes Austin: "I wish we were children now. I wish we were *always* children, how to grow up I dont know."[30] And, in the same year, again to Austin: "Oh for the pleasant years when we were young together, and this was *home—home!*"[31]

Just before Susan returned to Amherst, Emily wrote her that she had one "thought," one "prayer," which was that she and Susan "in *hand* as we e'en *do* in heart, might ramble away as children, among the woods and fields, and forget these many years, and these sorrowing cares, and each become a child again."[32]

Sometimes it is only Emily who must remain a child; it is all right if Sue grows up, provided that she play the role of protector with regard to Emily. This mother-seeking quality in Emily's longing comes through clearly in the following: "Oh Susie, I would nestle close to your warm heart, and never hear the wind blow, or the storm beat, again. Is there any room there for me, or shall I wander away all homeless and alone?"[33] Several months later this side of the relationship again comes into prominence: "I do love to run fast—and hide away from them all; here in dear Susie's bosom, I know is love and rest, and I never would go away."[34]

Later, echoing the words of the biblical Ruth (the faithful younger woman) to Naomi (the forsaken older woman), Emily reassures the orphaned Susan: "You wont cry any more, will you, Susie, for my father will be your father, and my home will be your home, and where you go, I will go, and we will lie side by side in the kirkyard."[35]

Emily feels sometimes that only Sue, like an understanding parent, is a reliable source of comfort: "I know I was very naughty," she says childishly, "to write such fretful things . . . but I thought my heart would break, and I knew of nobody here that cared anything about it."[36]

Sue gave Emily a peculiar security; when she left town Emily felt frightened and estranged from reality. She writes: "Your absence insanes me so—I do not feel so peaceful, when you are gone from me—All life looks differently, and the faces of my fellows are not the same they wear when you are with me . . . the world looks staringly."[37]

Sue's wavering affection and ambivalence continued sporadically to stir up the smothered resentment in Emily's personality, the residue of her early deprived relationship with her mother. Whenever this hidden rage was stirred to life, thoughts of death came with it.

In one letter to Sue, after mentioning certain always-present household chores, Emily says: "but you, I have 'not always,' *why* Susie, Christ hath saints *manie*—and I have *few,* but thee—the angels shant have Susie—no—no no!" A few lines later we see the source of these disguised death wishes: "sometimes I shut my eyes, and shut my heart towards you, and try hard to forget you because you grieve me so [by your neglect], but you'll never go away, Oh you never will."[38] Remember also in this context Emily's fear that she must chain herself up in an insane asylum "so I won't injure you" because "in thinking of those I love, my reason is all gone from me."[39]

These ideas of death haunted her and obtruded unexpectedly in her letters to Sue. For example, Emily writes: "I have not asked you if you were cheerful and well—and I cant think why, except that there's something *perrennial* in those we dearly love, immortal life and vigor [here she denies the fear]; why it seems as if any sickness, or harm, would flee away, would not dare do them wrong . . . But, dear Susie, *are* you well."[40] Similarly, in anticipating the joy it will be to have Sue with her again, she says: "and when you come if we all live till then, it will be *precious,* Susie."[41]

The feeling that she will lose Sue to death or a young man, that

Sue will be taken from her because of her "idolatry," obsesses her: "And now how soon I shall have you, shall hold you in my arms [Sue was returning after having been away almost a year]; you will forgive the tears, Susie." And she continues with an intimation of doom, "But I think of each 'sunnyside' where we have sat together, and lest there be no more, I guess is what makes the tears come."[42]

Superstitiously, she is afraid to be too pleased at Sue's return lest Sue die. "I shall not count the days. I shall not fill my cups with this expected happiness, for perhaps if I do, the angels, being thirsty, will drink them up . . . God is good, Susie, I trust he will save you, I pray that in his good time we once more meet each other [Sue and Emily were both healthy and Sue was expected in one month!] but if this life holds not another meeting for us, remember also, Susie, that it had no *parting* more . . . neither death, nor the grave can part us, so that we only *love*!"[43] Here she makes explicit her need to believe that by focusing on and stressing love she can overcome "death," that is, her own simmering, destructive impulses born of her desperation and frustration.

She warns Sue to be more heedful of the danger: "How soon [friends] will go away where you and I cannot find them, *dont* let us forget these things, for their remembrance *now* will save us many an anguish when it is *too late* to love them!"[44] Such "anguish" follows upon the guilt one feels after having relaxed ones' loving long enough to allow a death wish to reach consciousness.

Six days before Sue's return Emily writes: "We are *three* next Saturday, if *I* have *mine* and heaven has none."[45]

Austin, meanwhile, was well aware that he was becoming overwrought to a dangerous degree. He speaks of loving Sue "too well" and longs for a less stressful relationship:

> I used to think, Sue, that the next moon—or the next after—or at farthest the third would look down upon us *calm* lovers—that all this passion, this intensity, this never abating constancy of love would subside into a peaceful—quiet *consciousness* of each other's love— I used to think that after a little while when we had seen each other a little longer & had each other in each other's arms a little more often . . . we should begin to feel growing in us an affection—*not like* but *more* like that we see between *other* lovers."

Clearly the "never abating constancy" was wearing him out, a fact which he realized: "I love you Sue up to the very highest strain my nature can bear—the least tension would snap my life threads—as brittle glass—more—you could not ask—more man could not give—Love *me,* Sue—*Love* me—for its my life."

Even though he is now almost convinced that Sue reciprocates his feelings, he nevertheless is subject to overwhelming fits of despondency.

> I am sober today—Sue—sober—It's dark out & gloomy & God sends such sober thoughts to me—& it is not a *rare* thing for me to be sober—I wonder how it is that one so young—naturally so hopeful —so buoyant, surrounded with so much to please—& delight—should incline to look on life so tremblingly earnestly . . . I have sat here since I came in Sue, & thought of you & your love for me —how *dearly* I love you—& of life—its shortness—its uncertainty— of myself—till I have cried almost like a child—I can hardly keep the tears back now—I have covered my face with my hands & so prayed—prayed to God to come to me—to let me lean on Him.

If one is to take seriously a passage in another letter, one must conclude that Austin was indeed driven to the breaking point, for he appears to be telling Sue that he believes he is haunted: "I don't forget though those spiritual rappings in my room all last night—at the head of my bed—& resumed for a few minutes a short time ago near my sitting place. And if my Grandmother Dickinson is at me in that way I must be very unhappy & miserable again as soon as possible." It is hard to know what to make of these lines. The tone is a little jocular and might suggest that the passage refers to some private amusement the couple shared. Yet the fact that after it was written the name "Dickinson" was squeezed in after the word "Grandmother" would suggest that Austin intended something more specific than simply that ghosts were after him, in which case "Grandmother" alone would have been adequate since both his grandmothers were dead. But I will not push the argument too far. There is ample evidence in other letters that Sue's vacillations had driven Austin to desperation, as the following passage shows. Austin apparently wrote it after one of Sue's protestations of love or perhaps after she had agreed to marry him. "Oh Sue," he writes,

God has heard the daily morning and evening prayer which for more than a year I have prayed . . . at last we understand each other. Life is *not* a dream. What a world is before us! I am overwhelmed with my emotions—I can't write—I haven't slept—all the night has a crowd of strange tumultuous feelings made wild riot in my heart—O my God—I am worthy of nothing—thou hast granted me everything—I tremble in my very joy—But I thank thee—I thank thee—& pray that thou will continue thy care over me—support me—calm me—for my shattered nerves are ready to snap.

When love and longing and sexual conflicts prove insupportable, there is always the illusion that one may cut the Gordian knot of adult dilemmas by a regressive escape into childhood, a notion that had a wide appeal in the midst of nineteenth-century repressions and a temptation, as has been shown, that attained almost irresistible strength in Emily. And one is not surprised, under the circumstances, that it had its allure also for Austin, whose beloved Sue, he knew, could "satisfy every desire of my soul—every need of my spirit—every aspiration of my being," though he might well be uncertain of her capacity to fulfill a "man's requirements." At the threshold of marriage and its responsibilities, Austin cannot bring himself to accept the reality of what is before him, and thoughts of the dependency of infancy take possession of his mind, as the following passage indicates. Passages marked out by Austin are given here in parentheses.

How strange it seems that I must be a man—& have a man's responsibility—& discharge a man's duty—& that I may have a home of my own—& of my own choosing—that I may be *married,* as other men are! I never used to think I should be married . . . I never really believed I should grow old—& I *don't* in my *feelings*—I am just as youthful there as ever I was—& I don't believe but I always shall be—(I have always all the feelings of a child) I would love to be a child always—(always have a father & mother to go to—always looking forward to, but never entering the dusty, toilsome arena of the man's strifes—& a man's victories—) to have a child's pleasure, & a child's freedom from care—a child's father & mother to go to & to depend upon . . . Oh that Paradise of childhood is a *charmed* period.

In another letter he speaks of childhood as a time of wonder and awakening "when we are just beginning to breathe the delicious atmosphere of love—when as yet nothing has caused us to distrust those sweet dreams that come so thickly to us"; and he concludes regretfully, "but the years are past when I may be a child."

And on a day when he feels in particularly good "animal health & spirits," he writes, "I feel almost like 'old times' as the phrase is—where everyone is supposed far back in the dim remoteness of his past—when the years were long & full to him & the world young—& before he had learned that the sky is not always bright & the sun doesn't always shine & that there are nights & darkness—clouds & storms—that it is not always summer," and so forth.

If Austin, Emily, and Vinnie had ever truly escaped their dependency and left the confining arms of Edward Dickinson's solicitude, one would be inclined to regard these passages as mere flights of nineteenth-century romantic rhetoric, which in part, of course, they are. But strong needs to be sheltered continued to be dominant throughout all their lives, and Sue's as well. In fact it strikes one at times that perhaps one of Sue's major motivations in marrying Austin was to seize for herself at last the secure and stable home her shiftless father had never been able to provide for her and to gain in Edward Dickinson, as the head of this extended household, a strong and protective man such as her father had never been. For the orphaned Sue also, in these years, was preoccupied with the largely imaginary freedom from care of childhood. In reply to one of her letters, Austin says that he might choose to comment on any one of her themes: "I could take the third [sentence]—your thoughts of 'your earliest childhood days before you were a woman' & that they will never come again." Austin recognized the inherent appeal for Sue of his respected, genteel, relatively wealthy family and emphasized all she would be affixing to herself if she married him. Especially he emphasizes that Sue, in marrying him, will be gaining parents. He is glad, he tells her, that she is happily anticipating using "the 'dear name of father again on earth' & that name you are to call *my* father—& then he will be *our* father! Do you know can you imagine how much *more* than delight it gives me to know that I am making you happy." And the same idea is expressed in another letter, in which Austin rejoices in Sue's stopping for "tea at our house—& talk with father & with mother—you couldn't *possibly* have written me anything pleasanter than that. How glad I am I have *just* such a father & such a mother for you to love & to love you!" Austin then says that he will inform his parents of his engagement to Sue on the following Thanksgiving because "I wish father to bless you once as his new dear child before he goes away to Congress. I want them to *know*—so that their love can be growing for you as something of theirs—yes, Sue, a father & mother & me too! & will it be a 'brimming cup'!" It was a particularly strong point which Austin did not fail to stress that the frequently remote and formidable Squire Dickinson had taken an unusual fancy to Sue. He says that he was delighted that his father had delivered a package to Sue and "met you as he did—& wanted you to go to tea with him—for I know he must be perfectly aware that you are his new chosen child—though he has never ever in the least way spoken of you to me—nor I to him & I believe that if it had been for him to choose instead of me it would still Sue have been his choice for me."

By the time Austin and Sue were known to be engaged Sue had been more or less adopted by the Dickinson family. Edward Dickinson welcomed her with rare warmth and Emily with avidity. Vinnie, however, remained undecided about Sue, and the two women seem never to have been congenial. Vinnie seems not to have trusted Sue, and later in life the relationship became one of enmity. There exists no record of what Mrs. Dickinson thought of Sue. As in other matters, her opinions were not preserved.

In addition to Emily's inclinations to regard Sue as a love object and at the same time as a sheltering mother, both of which orientations gave rise when thwarted to death wishes, there was yet another mode by which Emily related to Susan. She identified with her, a fact previously discussed in relation to Emily's long latency period. "[We] please ourselves," Emily confided to Sue, "with the fancy that we are the only poets, and everyone else is *prose*."[46] In a passage previously alluded to in reference to Emily's willingness to skip young adulthood, she told Sue: "I tell her [Vinnie] I dont care if I am young or not, had as lief be thirty, and you, as most anything else."[47] The phrase "and you" is a curious allusion to her readiness to identify herself with her admired friend.

When her nascent sense of identification with the lively Susan was disrupted, Emily tended to feel empty and incomplete: "I remember you, Susie, *always*—I keep you ever here, and when *you* are gone, then I'm gone—and we're 'neath one willow tree. I can only thank 'the Father' for giving me such as you, I can only pray unceasingly, that he will bless my Loved One, and bring her back to me, to 'go no more out forever.' "[48]

Emily deeply wanted to share Sue's life and spoke of "mingling our lives together."[49]

In the paragraph preceding the extraordinary passage in which Emily confides to Sue her view that woman's fate in marriage is to be the victim of masculine sadism and domination, she makes it clear that she expects Sue to agree with her. "How dull our lives must seem to the bride . . . but to the *wife,* Susie . . . our lives perhaps seem dearer than all others in the world."[50] The "our lives" suggests that Emily is here again emphasizing her and Sue's likeness to each other.

Later, when Emily was assisting Austin's and Sue's clandestine communication with each other, one senses her identification with both of them: "I love the opportunity to serve those who are mine . . . I think of you and Austin—and how it pleases you to have my tiny services."[51] By this time it was perhaps becoming clear to Emily that she was losing out in her pathetic rivalry with Austin. A grieving awareness that it was only through identification with Sue that she could achieve erotic fulfillment comes through clearly in the following lines: "to be sure your life is warm with such a sunshine," she writes Sue, "helps me to chase the shadows fast stealing upon mine . . . I want to have you gather more sheaves of joy—for bleak, and waste, and barren, are most of the fields found here, and I want you to *fill* the *garner.*"[52]

Sue's teaching career was at an end in the closing days of June 1852, when Emily wrote her last letter to her in Baltimore. The letter evinces an overwrought vehemence of anticipation at Sue's impending arrival in Amherst. "Susie, will you indeed come home next Saturday, and be my own again, and kiss me as you used to? . . . I hope for you so much, and feel so eager for you, feel that I *cannot* wait, feel that *now* I must have you—that the expectation once more to see your face again, makes me feel hot and feverish, and my heart beats so fast." Together with this esurient longing, a note of apprehension creeps into the letter:

"then I feel so funnily, and wish the precious day would'nt come quite so soon, 'till I could know how to feel, and get my thoughts ready for it." Finally, there is a clear implication of confusion of sexual roles, which, to some extent, may explain the note of caution: "Why Susie, it seems to me as if my absent Lover was coming home so soon—and my heart must be so busy, making ready for him."[53]

Sue resided in Amherst uninterruptedly for the next six months, so, of course, Emily's written outbursts came to an end. Lacking further letters, one can only surmise how Emily translated her epistolary fervors toward Sue into their day-by-day transactions with each other and how Sue parried Emily's efforts to make of her an all-loving and dedicated mother substitute. Because Emily's fantasies were so boundlessly fulfilling and her needs so patently exorbitant, the living confrontation with Sue can only have been disappointing. The first two weeks may have been the most difficult for Sue and the most painful for Emily; after that Austin returned from Boston and remained in Amherst for the next seven months.

The letters Emily wrote to him before his return suggest something of the means employed by Sue and Emily to resolve the stresses of the triangle: Sue emphasized the importance of Austin, and Emily defensively identified ever more closely with Sue. "Susie talked much of you," she writes Austin, "and of her lonely life when you were gone away, and we said you would soon be here, and then we talked of *how* soon."[54] And again: "Susie and I walked together all last Tuesday evening, talking of you and the visit, and wishing you were here, and would not go away again."[55]

When Austin returned home, his presence no doubt acted as a buffer between the two girls and provided Sue the opportunity to indicate to Emily that, whatever the strength of her sisterly devotion to Emily, her future expectations were becoming firmly crystallized about the person of her brother.

Thus, by November, Jane Hitchcock, Lavinia's best girl friend, writes to a friend of hers: "Austin D. and Sue Gilbert are constant, and the gossips say constantly together."[56] It is not clear how Emily is spending her time during these months. There are no remaining letters for this period save one brief and rather silly note to Sue telling of some of her father's political guests. There is also no evidence of sleigh rides and candy pulls and the constant stream of young men who were frequent visitors at the Dickinson home the previous year. It seems plausible to conclude that as Sue and Austin spent more time together Emily felt increasingly isolated and lonely.

Susan, of course, was painfully aware of the covert competition for her attention between Austin and Emily, and this may account for the sense of depression and weariness that one can detect in her letters to her brother Dwight and to a former boy friend, Edward Hitchcock, Jr. To her brother she sends a New Year's greeting from "plain humdrum old Amherst among the hills."[57] And to Hitchcock: "I hope [a snowstorm] will give some new life to the town, for we are as quiet, as if the Plague had ravaged the streets—*nothing* doing—no visiting—no gossiping—no lectures—no sociability—no railroad—all is still enough. You would be homesick *here,* I am sure—even if it is home."[58]

That Emily was depressed also at this time is indicated by a note she sent to Emily Fowler on January 13. Vinnie was in Boston, and Sue at this time apparently was not available to comfort her. She writes: "I fear you will be lonely this dark and stormy day, and I send this little messenger to say you must not be. The day is long to me, because I have no Vinnie, and I think of those today who never had a Vinnie, and I'm afraid they are lone." She then speaks of the snow and, by contrast, summer, then of the *eternal* summer of paradise—thus easily do her thoughts trace out a thread of associations that lead to the death theme. She concludes her letter by saying she happened to open Vinnie's Bible and found these words: "Blessed are they that mourn—Blessed are they that weep, for they shall be comforted."[59]

Sue was soon chafing to get away again. By February she was off to visit relatives in New Hampshire, leaving Austin with a week or two more to spend in Amherst before departing for law school; and, perhaps significantly, she left without saying good-bye to Emily. As Sue's coach pulled away, Emily "ran to the door . . . I ran out in the rain, with nothing but my slippers on, I called 'Susie, Susie,' but you did'nt look at me; than I ran to the dining room window and rapped with all my might upon the pane, but you rode right on and never heeded me. It made me feel so lonely that I could'nt help the tears . . . oh Susie, Susie, I must call out to you in the old, old way—I must say how it seems to me to hear the clock so silently tick all the hours away, and bring me not my gift—my own, my own!"[60]

Though Sue's comments speak of boredom with "humdrum" Amherst, it seems likely that a more pressing motivation for her New Hampshire trip was to escape the suffocating love that emanated from Emily and that saturates the letter quoted above. Whether Sue was overwhelmed by the burning and voracious need embodied in this letter or repelled and made hostile by it, the fact is that she chose not to respond. Dismayed and desperate, Emily ten days later writes again to Sue, still hoping to hear from her. A day or two later, still not hearing, Emily learns that Sue has written to Austin, that on his arrival in Boston a letter from Sue awaited him. In her second letter since Sue's departure Emily writes sentimentally, obviously hoping to make Sue feel guilty for her negligence: "I know dear Susie is busy, or she would not forget her lone little Emilie, who wrote her just as soon as she'd gone to Manchester, and has waited so patiently till she can wait no more, and the credulous little heart, fond even tho' forsaken, will get it's big black inkstand, and"—hurl it at the faithless Susan in an outburst of rage at her abandonment?—no, but "tell her once again how well it loves her."

The efforts Emily is expending in controlling her furious anger at Sue are apparent in the very next paragraph: "Dear Susie," she says sweetly, for she dares not risk more complete rejection by letting her feeling show too plainly, "I have tried so hard to act patiently, not to think unkind thoughts, or cherish unkind doubt concerning one not here . . . Why dont you write me, Darling? Did I . . . say anything which grieved you, or made it hard for you to take your usual pen and trace affection for your bad, sad Emilie?" *Bad,* sad Emilie. Why "bad"?—because importunate, demanding, jealous, and, above all, filled with suppressed hatred and destructiveness in reaction to Sue's indifference in the face of her longing for tenderness. Though Austin has not yet left and Vinnie and her parents are with her, Emily feels alone without Susan: "Dear Susie," she continues, "it is harder to live alone than it was when you were in Baltimore . . . I grow impatient, and cannot brook as easily absence from those I love."

It should occasion no surprise that this letter, whose surface reasonableness and sisterly affection conceals a depth of lonely bitterness, ends with thoughts of death. "I . . . stand and watch the West, and remember all of mine—yes, Susie—the golden West, and the great, silent Eternity [which] . . . will open it's everlasting, arms, and gather us all—all."[61] These are not only death wishes directed toward herself and toward those from whom she craves an impossible love: Framed in a religious fantasy in which she only half believes is the wish that the safe and tender refuge unattainable here may be granted them all in a life beyond the grave.

The extent to which Emily Dickinson was caught up in her brother's courtship of Susan is indicated by the effort she made to cement their relationship. That as one side of a triangle she should seemingly defeat her own purposes is not, upon examination, as paradoxical as it first appears. She probably dimly sensed that underlying her desire to possess Susan was the unconscious fantasy of reuniting with a loving mother, and with this intuition would come also the realization, again probably only very slightly conscious, that the wish was incompatible with reality. However, by advancing Austin to Susan as a legitimate lure, she might succeed at least in enmeshing Susan within the family circle and thereby ensuring a lasting, if limited, access to her; the only alternative would be to lose her altogether. It seems to have been these considerations that allowed her to participate in a strange and clandestine series of transactions between Austin and Susan.

For some reason that is not entirely clear because of gaps in our biographical information, it seemed desirable to Austin and Susan that they keep secret the growing intimacy of their relationship. To some extent, Emily was party to their subterfuges, from which she seems to have derived a certain satisfaction and sense of identification with the lovers. It is possible that by thus enlisting her as an ally Sue and Austin sought to clarify and emphasize her position in relation to them; that is: *they* were the loving couple soon to be united, *they* were bound by the ties of love that included only two. Emily might help smooth the path for them, run interference for them, and help Sue make nuptial plans, but the point they must have been making clear was that she was a bystander only, a mere witness. It was not to remain a triangle; Austin and Sue were a betrothed couple, and Emily, though accepted as a loving relative, must remain essentially an outsider.

Rationally, Emily appears to have accepted this view of things; it is doubtful, however, if emotionally she ever gave up her claims to Susan. Nevertheless, when Austin began his series of little deceptions, designed apparently to circumvent Sue's relatives and his own, Emily did her part. She addressed envelopes to Sue which Austin took to Cambridge with him. Later they were filled with Austin's letters to Sue and apparently mailed in covering envelopes to distant places, where they were removed from their covers and remailed, this time to Susan. Thus, with the addresses in Emily's handwriting, Austin's letters, by these circuitous routes, were ultimately delivered into Sue's hands. There is an allusion in one letter from Austin to Sue suggesting that Sue was upset because someone had found out that they were corresponding: "I shall enclose in an Envelope to Emily—& try that—I am very sorry it has happened so—but you must remember that I send in the best & most ingenious ways I can."[62]

Emily was pleased to be helpful: "One thing is true, Darling [she writes to Sue], the world will be none the wiser, for Emilie's omnipresence, and two big hearts will beat stouter, as tidings from *me* come in."[63]

Vinnie seems not to have been the only one who was suspicious of Sue's motives. Austin and Sue were frequently the object of rumors and speculations regarding the nature of their true relationship. As has been mentioned earlier, Sue's sister Mrs. Cutler, with whom Sue lived, was sensitive to what the neighbors thought. For this reason Austin was forced to conduct the initial strategies of his courtship with the greatest circumspection. This circumstance appears to have established a certain style in his relationship to Sue which persisted after it had ceased to be beneficial: the couple to some extent brought the gossip down upon themselves by what may have been only a mildly mischievous deviousness which others—including posterity—might easily interpret as furtiveness.

For example, here is Austin communicating one of his plots:

I will call for you at what hour this afternoon you may mention— you shall say you are going to spend part of the evening with the girls [i.e., Emily and Vinnie]—& after making a half hour or so with them—I will undertake to accompany you home—& find a carriage tied near by our door which we will avail ourselves of for half an hour or an hour—as we please—before walking down Amity Street. Choose as you will—I have no choice further than that the shadowy tent of evening seems kindlier & pleasanter to such as we than the broad open day.

The same impression of deliberate subterfuge comes through in another fragment: "How strangely it will seem to me not to see you tonight—& what will father think to find me at my office now when I haven't been there before a solitary evening this winter—I'm afraid he'll pair this with your being gone & draw conclusions—he wouldn't be displeased with them—but it isn't best for everybody to be quite sure of everything right away—& I must be a bit shrewd."

That Austin and Sue exceeded what Mrs. Cutler thought proper is certain; it is equally certain that the couple thought they were getting away with something. "I hope it will be as bright a day as today," writes Austin, "so we can be outdoors almost all the time. *I want one stroll* with you across the fields—& one walk down to the bridge . . . I wonder if Mrs. Cutler would let you go to Montague with me—after tea if I should ask you or if she continues to think 'there are *some* bounds to propriety'—& that such a ride wouldn't be included—tell Mrs. Cutler there's more going on than has entered her *dreams*."

No doubt the occasion most damaging to Sue's reputation—at least as far as posterity is concerned—took place on her visit to Boston in 1853. She arrived at the Revere House Hotel on Wednesday, March 23, and was met there by Austin. Emily wrote to Austin the next day: "I did 'drop in at the Revere' a great many times yesterday. I hope you have been made happy. If so I am satisfied. I shall know when you get home."[64] This suggests that Emily knew what her brother and his fiancée were about, but certain of her later responses, including those to the gossip that became rampant in Amherst, reveal that at this time she felt that the meeting was entirely innocent. Later Sue wrote Mrs. S. C. Bartlett, a relative of her sister, that she and Austin chatted in the parlor, no doubt a public place and as such perfectly proper. She did not tell Mrs. Bartlett the whole story, however, for upon her return to Amherst Austin inquires of their visit, "Had your imagination drawn for you hours more delicious than those Wednesday afternoon & evening hours? *Could* lovers desire more?" Obviously the visit consisted of more than an hour or two in the hotel lobby. And did they simply chat as Sue had indicated? Austin has this to say about it: "Those hours, Sue, let us never forget . . . those sweet kisses you, leaning over me imprinted upon my forehead—our parting that night—how warmly you let me press you to my heart—& how passionately you clung around my neck—& held my lips to yours . . . I never shall doubt that the deepest, strongest love of earth has been given me." Clearly they did not spend *all* those afternoon and evening hours in a public place; also it appears doubtful that they were chaperoned. In another letter Austin writes: "It's well we had those hours at the Revere House—we needed them—they'll do us good assure us"; and on another page:

> I thought over those precious, precious hours of just a week before . . . I thought them all over, Sue, all your loving words & all your endearing caresses—how trustingly sweetly—like an innocent child you laid your head upon my bosom—& slept in my arms—how you held me close to you & kissed my lips—& my forehead . . . I thought this all over Sue . . . how much those hours meant to us—Sue! How much more they made us love each other than we ever had before—how much they disclosed in us to love we have never known before—those hours Sue made us inseparable—we must always love now. We needed this time Sue for we have been both a little inclined to allow doubts & fears to trouble us—a little inclined to be not quite certain that it was all right that we had promised ourselves to each other—a little wanting confidence that we entirely satisfied each other's needs—but while we may remember Wednesday night—Sue—will a doubt come to us again?—Will a fear cross us—shall we distrust our fully meeting each other's every desire! We *can't,* Sue, we *know* we love each other—*love* each other—there's no greater word—it's all there in that—love each other—oh—Sue—a *world* couldn't buy those hours from me—they'll sweeten every moment of my life—I thought of your dear letter of Thursday night—and read it again before I went to sleep—as I shall *every* night—as regularly as—my Bible in the morning . . . I've been happier—Sue since you were here than ever before—for I feel now so sure you love me—& must love me—I can study better—for I know it's for you—there's no doubt now.

How is one to explain this puzzle? Sue seems to have been the very model of reserve and propriety, a girl with many uncertainties and reservations regarding sex and one almost oppressively pious and self-righteous. Yet for all that, one could not be blamed for concluding from the foregoing letter that she went to Boston, had a clandestine rendezvous with Austin, and gave herself to him without a scruple. It is true that there are certain details in Austin's letter that do not quite fit in with this interpretation. A man who has sexual intercourse with a woman is unlikely to recall as the thing that most impressed him that the woman clung passionately around his neck or leaned over him and imprinted kisses on his forehead. Also, Austin's reading Sue's letter just after the affair and coupling it with reading the Bible strikes a jarring note when one recalls that both Austin and Sue would probably have regarded sexual intimacies as a serious sin.

On the other hand, devout, church-going girls with marked sexual frigidity have been known to participate in such liaisons under certain provocative circumstances. To what extent such circumstances existed for Sue will be discussed later. It can be said here, however, that at the very least Sue's behavior, if it was not acquiescent or seductive, was calculated to test Austin's self-control to the limit of endurance. For she clearly presented herself to him under conditions of privacy and supposed anonymity, she behaved affectionately and erotically, and she met him at the hotel of her own free will. And she made the fatiguing journey from New Hampshire to Boston to be with him—Austin had little to do but wait for her to arrive and arrange for them to be together. If it was a question of seduction, the seduction was Sue's, in spite of all her later reservations and self-righteous posturing. In meeting Austin in this way, Sue placed her own reputation in serious jeopardy, which, considering the social prominence of the Dickinsons, the moral strictness of Edward Dickinson, and the control he exerted over the lives of his offspring, might well have given her some uneasy moments with regard to her aspiration to become a member of his family. That Amherst and Cambridge gossips were only too ready to make the most of any irregularities and that Sue was in fact troubled by what they were saying about her is indicated in a number of Austin's letters in which he attempts to reassure her that their detractors are lowly scoundrels to be ignored with lofty disdain. "My ideas of propriety I know are different from some others," he tells her in one of these letters,

You have heard what you have—& I can't help it now—we'll be

more careful in future—about the slightest appearance of anything that could give foundation for further remarks—for the motley crowd that thickens with the darkness—& finds its faces lighted—& its coarse words—speed to dark rooms—beneath the surface of the ground where no light shines out to tell of the vile haunts and pursuits . . . I don't think the rumors will last long—Sue . . . so long as nature is as it is—the poor will delight in reviling the rich—the ugly in slandering the beautiful—& the vulgar in low remarks about the pure—& because it is nature I care not for it . . . We cannot save our bodies from worms—we cannot save our characters from foul mouths—no one would believe an improper word between you & me . . . it's a fact that no two people can be much with one another —ride together & walk together—without being talked about by low people in a low way . . . "tell me again, I love you" Sue & "will take care of you"—you *know* & God knows *too* well I love only you —ever & only you.

The temperature of Austin's moral indignation as expressed in such purple prose and his phrase concerning "low remarks about the pure" seems out of place indeed if the letter (which is not dated) was written *after* an assignation at the Revere Hotel, in which case it would tend to raise doubts that Austin and Sue's meeting was anything but perfectly innocent. Be that as it may, the Revere rendezvous—before the rumors or after them, "pure" or furtively sexual—was a remarkably risky encounter, seems out of character for Sue, and indicates that, since she saw Austin alone and was willing to indulge in extensive caresses, her motivation was at an urgent level. There exist some reasons, discussed below, for believing that Emily contributed to the recklessness of Sue's flight into Austin's arms.

Austin and Sue's relationship continued to be the subject of considerable gossip in Amherst despite, or perhaps because of, their secretiveness. A month after Austin and Susan met surreptitiously in Boston, Austin's father seems to have become suspicious. Austin writes Sue: "*Father* there has been 'inquiring if you saw me in Boston.' I thought I wrote home about it—if I did'nt I *meant* to—just enough to make the thing plain & matter of course."[65] And, almost two months after the undisclosed encounter, Emily is still reassuring Austin: "The stories are all still, Austin. I dont hear any now, and Susie says she dont care now the least at all for them . . . they are very low—of the earth."[66]

These "low" stories "of the earth" can only mean one thing: the gossips were saying that Austin and Sue were having an illicit affair, and it is clear from Emily's reaction that at the time she wrote this letter she was convinced the stories were unfounded.

There would be no particular point in exploring the matter if it did not shed some light on Emily and her effect on her brother and future sister-in-law. An observation familiar to every psychiatrist is the very common situation in which heterosexual relationships are utilized unconsciously as a defense against threatening homosexual impulses. Typically, heterosexual coitus is engaged in by an unmarried couple who have hitherto regarded such behavior as entirely foreign to the moral standards of one or both of them. The situation develops in this way: If a homosexual temptation becomes impelling enough and opportunity practically unavoidable—the classic example being the case of men confined for long intervals aboard ship—the result may be a so-called homosexual panic. When such a situation arises in which there are no members of the opposite sex available, an incapacitating anxiety state ensues. The panic is dramatically relieved, however, when an opportunity for heterosexual intercourse presents itself. At such times the "normal" relationship is entered into compulsively—not for pleasure, but for reassurance of one's normality. Moral scruples go by the boards. The victim, horrified at the emergence of formerly repressed and abominated urges toward his own sex which the combined circumstances of heterosexual deprivation and homosexual opportunity have revived, behaves in this extremity as if he had no superego strictures with regard to the opposite sex. Or he may believe that he is choosing the lesser of two moral evils and remain completely unaware of any sense of guilt, though this may return in full force when the homosexual crisis has subsided. Thus, it appears likely that the imperiousness of Emily's passionate attachment to Sue precipitated such anxiety and tension in Sue that it drove her to Austin for relief.

It might be argued that Sue went to Boston to see her fiancé simply because she loved him and wanted to be with him. Moreover, any intimate situation which may have developed might be regarded as something that simply came about spontaneously and that neither of them had foreseen. To the first point, that

Sue went to Boston out of love, it can be said that to a certain extent this was undoubtedly the case. But, as is demonstrated by Austin's letters, Sue's need for him seems never before to have been so compelling as to override seriously the strictures of prudence, in spite of the fact that they both delighted in evading the purview of Mrs. Cutler and his family. Some further explanation seems necessary to account for Sue's abandoning her caution at this point. The second objection, that the compromising situation happened "accidentally," is one that a psychiatrist at least would find difficult to accept. Persons who place themselves in dangerous circumstances "in all innocence" generally, upon closer examination, are discovered to have had a quite clear idea of the likely consequences of their behavior, although they may have managed to keep the knowledge hidden from themselves through denial or repression. That Austin would have received Sue under the circumstances also seems natural enough. He was anything but sure of Sue, and, as will be shown later, he had become somewhat uneasy about her relationship with Emily. That he would castigate himself for his weakness later is also to be expected. Unlike Sue, whose father was an alcoholic ne'er-do-well, Austin had as the major moral influence in his life his unbending and high-principled father. Also, Austin's mother symbolized the religious attitude, however little personal force she exerted, and he could have had no doubts about her reaction to an illicit affair. With Emily, Austin shared a puritan conscience, but he was a young man in love living away from home and possessed of a strong rebellious streak—remember that Emily said of him "you always did what you wanted to, whether 'twas against the law or not."[67]

If Austin defied his conscience in this instance, he later must have felt at times that his sins were in vain as far as stabilizing his relationship with Sue was concerned. Following her Boston visit, she apparently wrote him of her strong doubts whether she really loved him after all. In a grieved and deflated mood, Austin replies: "I read under the sting of these lines that told me that . . . while you sat by my side—& pillowed your head upon my bosom & felt my arm around your neck & my lips on your cheek & my heart beating in its great love for you—Even there & then —you were doubting—*doubting*—questioning if after all you had any love for me . . . [then] let us think no longer of ever marrying—let our past be only as a dream that is soon forgotten . . . no one shall know that you have ever given yourself to me—except those of whom you yourself have told—for *I have never lisped it.*"[68]

The day following the one on which the foregoing was written Austin attended church, probably to please Sue, but he derived no spiritual uplift from his efforts: "I tried as hard as I could to find something in the sermon—but I could'nt & gave it up—& went thinking of myself, of you."[69]

At the same time, Sue is writing to her brother that her funds are low and giving as her excuse for returning to Amherst via Boston (and thereby incurring considerable extra expense) that her eyes were troubling her: "I was afraid to come home, without seeing a physician—I consulted one of the best oculists in the city."[70] Should anyone remain adamant that these subterfuges and deceptions cannot possibly be indicative of Sue's and Austin's engaging in a sexual encounter in Boston, let him consider what other probable causes can be adduced for the agonies of guilt which Austin now experienced. Sue, herself a member of the church for almost three years, is obviously urging Austin to repent and perhaps blaming him for what happened in Boston. In this context, let me quote from a letter given in full earlier in this chapter. Austin replies: "Oh Sue, this beautiful, beautiful sunny day—when I ought to be so happy—& when I *am* so *miserable* . . . I cant, I cant think as you do—and so you will reproach me again—& call me an obstinate sinner—and an ungrateful monster—and *am* I?" Recall that he tells her that he attended church again and that he wondered: "who of all that congregation knew what was going on in one heart there—the suffering it was bearing up against—the agony of despair that was wringing it." His guilt reaches a climax with these words: "your last letter Sue, has almost killed me—*Did* you mean all you said? . . . *Am* I as wicked as you say, Sue? Oh I'm sick—I want to go home—I want to see Vinnie, & Emily, and father and mother and see if they'll notice me—if they will speak to me."[71]

Whatever conclusions one draws from Susan's apparent inconsistency with regard to her rendezvous with Austin at the Revere Hotel, one thing is perfectly clear. She did not fall into Austin's embrace in capitulation to any demand of his. Throughout their courtship one element is pervasive: Sue's capacity to keep Austin on the defensive. Austin's overweening need to capture Sue and bind her permanently to him and to his family made him vulnerable. Any aspect of his character, therefore, that might be considered by Sue a defect provided her with the necessary leverage to bend him to her will. If she turned a cool ear on his religious views, for example, he, in his anxiety, sought to modify them to suit her better. If he strongly urged something that did not evoke her own enthusiasm, she had only to suggest that Austin was "overbearing" and he was ready to sacrifice everything for her. In order to persuade her to marry him he seems to have found it necessary to promise that he would not make demands on her, even to the point of assuring her that she had no obligations whatever to fulfill his "requirements" if it was not her inclination to do so. "All your fancies for love life and for married life," he writes her,

> I want you to find fulfilled—& with me—any plan of daily life and of our entire life that may have formed itself and dwelt pleasantly in your thoughts—I want should be carried out—any little spice of romance that may please you—as you approach—as you enter—and as you advance in married life I want you to indulge in—to put no restraint even upon any inclination because I may call you mine—nor ever hesitate in doing or refraining from whatever presents itself to you for your being so dearly cherished by me—I want you to feel free as ever you did—free to come and go—& see & do when & who & what you will & have no fear that it will displease me.

These are the words of a man who feels he has no bargaining power, who wants something so badly that he will pay any price. On the other hand, the impression of Sue that comes through in these letters is that very early she sensed she might gain complete control of the relationship and subsequently either deliberately or intuitively saw to it that in every encounter her position was strengthened. Her power over Austin stemmed from her relative coolness and lesser commitment, in contrast to his single-mindedness and compulsiveness. For these reasons and because of Austin's chivalrous character, one can rule out the hypothesis that Sue trysted with Austin because he demanded that she "prove her love" to him. If Sue had to prove her love, it appears that it was not Austin to whom she felt compelled to prove it but Emily.

Six months after the Revere incident Austin seems not to have recovered from his sense of remorse. Vinnie was visiting him in

Boston in January 1854, and they attended a soirée together with some friends. Here is Austin's reaction: "In front of us those fiddlers stood in white cravats—& fidelled—& drummed—& fifed —& at every pause the people clapped their hands—& the more they clapped the sicker I grew—till they asked me what was the matter . . . if I was sick—& I told them no—Life seemed sad to me."[72]

Six weeks after Sue's visit to Boston the rumors rife in Amherst are beginning to affect Emily and Vinnie, and apparently doubts about Sue have risen in their minds. When Austin visits Amherst, he observes that both his sisters are somewhat disagreeable to him—Emily, in particular, seems pointedly to have ignored him much of the time. Also, there seem to have been some sharp words, for Vinnie later apologizes to her brother: "I think Emilie & I were in the fault some what. I thought she ought not to say what she did the last morning & tried to prevent it, but she felt you must know it,"[73] and a week later in another note she makes it clear that Sue was the focus of contention. Now, however, Vinnie repudiates the gossip: "I saw *Sue* this afternoon, & everything is right between us now . . . I confess I did wrong to suspect her, but some times I feel rather depressed."[74]

Sue now settled in Amherst for six more months before leaving for a visit with relatives in New York. By this time, through the agency of Sue's meeting with Austin, it is increasingly clear to Emily that her assigned position is on the periphery of her brother's love life and that she must feel and behave toward Sue as though they were sisters. It is not possible to say to what extent Austin feared that Emily might be undercutting him with regard to Sue; there are suggestions during these months, however, that Emily is trying to reassure both him and herself. She draws closer to Sue, but in a more domestic, feminine way: "Did Susie write you," she asks Austin, ". . . how she came to stay with me? And how we sewed together, and talked of what would be? We did sew and talk together, and she said she should tell you what a sweet time we had."[75] One can clearly discern here Emily's need to remain included in the triangle, and it is equally clear that the basis for doing so has shifted in the direction of an attempt at closer identification with Sue. Following the statement just quoted, Emily says: "Emmons asked me to ride yesterday afternoon, but I'd promised to go somewhere else, so he asked me to

go this week, and I told him I would."[76] At this time the modified relationship with Sue seems to be strengthening Emily,
allowing her to attempt a few tentative, small-scale heterosexual
experiments of her own, a fact which, incidentally, she takes
great pains to emphasize in her letters to Austin. It is interesting
to observe that generally when she mentions Emmons the
thought follows close upon some reference to Sue. Thus, in her
June 9, 1853, letter to Austin, she reassures him concerning the
remarks being circulated in Amherst about him and Sue. Two
lines later in the same paragraph she says: "I rode with Emmons
last evening, and had a beautiful ride."[77] And again one encounters the same sequence from Sue to Emmons: "Father went
home with Sue. I think he and mother both think a great deal
of her, and nobody will make me believe that they dont think she
is their's, just as much as Vinnie or you or me. Perhaps I am
mistaken, but I can most always tell anything that I want to.
Emmons brought me a beautiful bouquet of Arbutus, last evening . . ."[78]

Austin seems to have been reassured by these references to his
sister's association with a young man, no matter how unenthusi-
astic her interest might be. She writes Austin: "I am glad you are
glad that I went to ride with Emmons. I went again with him
one evening . . . and had a beautiful ride."[79]

Her first reference to riding with Emmons was made in a letter to Austin dated February 6, 1852: "I have been to ride twice
since I wrote you . . . and last evening with *Sophomore Emmons,*
alone."[80] On the same day she was writing to Sue: "Oh my darling one, how long you wander from me, how weary I grow of
waiting and looking, and calling for you . . . Only *want* to write
me, only sometimes sigh that you are far from me, and that will
do, Susie!"[81] Her cultivation of Emmons perhaps was not a deliberate subterfuge, but had Austin had access to her prim and
brief notes to Emmons, he would have realized that the chance
that Emily's affection for Emmons might blossom into a love
affair that would remove Emily from his and Sue's orbit was
slight indeed.

Following Sue's Boston meeting with Austin and the attempt
of the trio—Austin, Susan, and Emily—during the following
months to keep their relationships on a more balanced and nor-

mal footing, Emily shows increasing signs of depression, preoccupation with death, and the emergence of neurotic symptoms.
Sue also appears subdued. She is working very hard on her
trousseau—Emily and certain of Sue's relatives think too hard.
Four days before Austin is to return to Amherst for the Thanksgiving holiday (1853), Emily writes him that she herself feels
tired "and a little disconsolate" and that "Susie is all worn out
sewing. She seems very lonely without you, and I think seems
more depressed than is usual for her."[82] It seems plausible that
the second thoughts that Sue expressed to Austin following their
Boston encounter are still active in her as she prepares her apparel
for her wedded life. It may be that Austin's imminent return to
Amherst has something to do with her low spirits at this time.

Adding substance to this view is the similar reaction of Sue
and Emily to a two-week hiatus in Austin's correspondence after
his return to Cambridge. Their common alarm and fantasies of
the possible perils preventing his writing suggest how close to
consciousness in both of them was the half-serious conclusion
that his departure from Amherst might go a long way toward
solving their interpersonal difficulties. Emily writes: "It's quite
a comfort, Austin, to hear that you're *alive* . . . and when I tell
you honestly that Vinnie and George Howland would have
gone to Northampton yesterday to *telegraph* to you, if we had'nt
heard yesterday noon, you can judge that we felt some alarm. We
supposed you had either been *killed* . . . for the sake of your
watch, or had been very sick and were at present *delirious* and
therefore could not write. [Sue and I were] each feeling perfectly sure that you were not in this world."[83]

Evidence of Emily's mood at this time is her December letter
to Emily Fowler, who had recently married. Perhaps it is justifiable to attribute the sadness of this message in part to her feeling
that this loss of another friend to a man was a precursor of her
impending loss of Sue to Austin. "And now five days have gone,
Emily, and long and silent, and I begin to know that you will
not come back again. There's a verse in the Bible, Emily . . . it's
a little like this—'I can go to her, but she cannot come back to
me.' I guess that isn't right, but my eyes are full of tears, and I'm
sure I do not care if I make mistakes or not."[84]

In January 1854, Susan left Amherst again to visit her relatives
in New Hampshire. At this time Vinnie and Edward Dickinson

were also away and Emily had to attend church alone. Though her preoccupation with death was already of long standing and her dislike of strangers had become almost a fixed attitude, one may nevertheless legitimately question whether these characteristics were crippling enough or uncongenial enough to her personality as a whole to constitute symptoms of emotional illness. However, as her brother's courtship progressed and her relationship with Sue underwent its succession of turbulent readjustments, psychological patterns began to emerge that are distinctly pathological. Though the letter she writes to Sue presents her beginning agoraphobia in a humorous way, the very real terror of her predicament is clearly evident:

> I'm just from meeting, Susie, and as I sorely feared, my "life" was made a "victim." I walked—I ran—I turned precarious corners— One moment I was not—then soared aloft like Phoenix, soon as the foe was by—and then anticipating an enemy again, my soiled and drooping plumage might have been seen emerging from just behind a fence, vainly endeavoring to fly once more from hence. I reached the steps . . . How big and broad the aisle seemed, full huge enough before, as I quaked slowly up—and reached my usual seat! In vain I sought to hide behind your feathers—Susie—feathers and *Bird* had flown, and there I sat, and sighed, and wondered I was scared so, for surely in the whole world was nothing I need to fear—Yet there the Phantom was, and though I kept resolving to be as brave as Turks . . . it did'nt help me any . . . Mr. Carter immediately looked at me—Mr. Sweetzer attempted to do so, but I discovered *nothing,* up in the sky somewhere, and gazed intently at it . . . During the exercises I became more calm, and got out of church quite comfortably. Several roared around, and, sought to devour me.

Ultimately, "our gate was reached . . . I clutched the latch, and whirled the merry key, and fairly danced for joy, to find myself *at home!* How I did wish for you—how, for my own dear Vinnie."[85]

As the security Emily once thought she had found in Sue gradually crumbled, leaving her anxious and feeling unprotected, Sue also began to appear apprehensive and increasingly unsure of the wiseness of her decision to marry Austin. Her lack of enthusiasm for the coming event is evident in her letters. To her brother Francis she writes: "Why don't you write to me Frank and congratulate me, that I have found some one who is going, by and by, to encumber himself with me?" She then advances her fiancé's merits in these less than glowing terms: "I see no reason, viewing the subject as I try to, without prejudice, why you won't like Austin . . . he is strong, manly, resolute— understands human nature and will take care of me . . . we shall have a cozy place some-where, where the long-cherished wish of my heart to have a home where my brothers and sisters can come, will be realized." The only expression of affection included in this prospect of married bliss is contained in her tepid designation of Austin as "the man I love well enough to marry."[86]

Earlier Austin revealed that he was aware of Sue's ambivalence. He wrote to her that there was something "indefinite" in her attitude toward him: "I never *did,* and don't *now think,* we understand one another, but [felt we were moving on] in the same pleasant, though somewhat indefinite way . . . it is a queer thing in you Sue, that the undercurrent of your feelings so clearly discernible in all your notes, is never apparent in your conversation."[87]

Austin was looking forward to his graduation from law school in July 1854 and to completing his bar examinations at about the same time. After these hurdles were passed, the way was open to begin making definite plans for his marriage. In early June he writes to Sue that he would prefer marrying that fall rather than waiting until spring, that he is planning a trip to Cincinnati and Chicago to find a good location for a law practice, and that as soon as he decides on a city he will settle down and work out with Sue the details of their future life together.

On June 26 Austin passed his bar examinations and on July 19 he was graduated from the Harvard Law School. He was now in a position to support himself and take on the responsibilities of a husband. At precisely this time Susan became ill and took to her bed for several weeks with an ailment diagnosed as "nervous fever." As Sue recovered, Emily assured Austin that his fiancée's appetite was improving and followed with the seemingly unrelated thought: "I think it's rather a serious thing to be an affianced being—I dont want to frighten you—still, when I think it over, it seems no trifling matter."[88]

Even without the diagnosis of "nervous fever," Emily's juxtaposition of Sue's illness and the seriousness and fearfulness of being engaged would lead one to suspect that a substantial psychological component contributed to Sue's collapse just at this time. One's heart goes out to Sue. Her family are scattered, her mother is dead, her father a disgrace. She was brought up as well as her relatives could manage but had no stable home life. Her acceptance by the Dickinson family must have seemed to her at first a piece of the most extraordinary luck. In place of the worthless Mr. Gilbert she now had the honorable Edward Dickinson as a surrogate father—the leading citizen of the town, a relatively wealthy lawyer who lived in a "mansion," a former state senator, and now a Congressman. Moreover, the redoubtable Squire Dickinson, who was not easily pleased, was quite taken with her. Passing this stringent test, she was assured entrance into the family circle. In Austin she found as good a prospective husband as a girl of her station could wish for. Vinnie always had reservations about Sue but, in general, liked her and for many years accepted her as a sister. If Emily had been an ordinary woman, Sue's life might have been the Cinderella story she perhaps at first anticipated. Instead, however, Sue was torn between the affection and gratitude she felt toward Austin and her fascination and apprehension in the face of his strange and brilliant sister with her obscure and insistent emotional demands. The pressure she felt must have been enormous. As Austin relinquished his plans for moving west and Emily became increasingly dependent and despondent, Edward Dickinson's possessiveness came to the fore, and it must have seemed at times to Sue that she was getting ever more deeply enmeshed in a trap from which there was no escape. We know from her poetry how strong were Emily's feelings of imprisonment. Even Vinnie, still in her teens, was already beginning to despair of ever marrying, perhaps because her mother seems not to have been pleased by any of her boy friends. "I am tired of receiving wedding cards," Vinnie wrote bitterly at the age of nineteen, "they come from some where, every day." A few lines earlier in this same letter to Austin she remarked: "I've been thinking lately how easily I could become *insane*. Sometimes I feel as though I should be."[89]

When Susan was well enough to travel she fled the Dickinson homestead, or rather was "hurried off,"[90] apparently on the advice of her physician, and went to New York to recuperate. Writing to her brother Dwight of her convalescence, she informs him of her relatives' explanation of her collapse and of her disagreement with their views: "I believe Hattie and Mr. Cutler think I made myself sick serving, but *I* know I did not. Imprudence in other respects was the immediate cause doubtless but I have felt for a year that I was not well and whether careless or not I should have been sick . . . I was very far from strong when I left Amherst . . . but I bore the journey finely and have felt better ever since. Indeed now I am quite well except a weakness naturally consequent upon my confinement to the bed so long."[91]

Once away from the pressures of Amherst, Sue made a rapid recovery. But Emily, back home, was well embarked on her lengthening retreat from life. While Sue was still ill, Emily refused an invitation to visit her friend Abiah: "I thank you Abiah," she writes, "but I dont go from home, unless emergency leads me by the hand, and then I do it obstinately, and draw back if I can. Should I ever leave home, which is improbable, I will . . . accept your invitation . . . but dont expect me. I'm so old fashioned, Darling, that all your friends would stare."[92] It is obvious that Emily is beginning to think of herself as peculiar, out of step with the times and with her former circle of friends, and as an object of curiosity to her contemporaries.

In the meantime Sue, after spending some weeks visiting in New York, moved on to Michigan to visit her brothers and there stayed several months. In late August Emily writes to her, and we learn that they have not written each other since Sue left Amherst several weeks before.

Thro' Austin, I've known of you, and nobody in this world except Vinnie and Austin, know that in all the while, I have not heard from you. Many have asked me for you, and I have answered promptly that you had reached there safely, and were better every day, and Susie, do you think, H. Hinsdale came to our house several days ago; came just to ask for you, and went away supposing I'd heard from you quite often. Not that I told her so, but spoke of you so naturally, in such a daily way, she never guessed the fact that I'd not written to you, nor had you thus to me.

Emily says that she was irritated by some "little thing" Sue did but that when they meet they will "try and forgive each other." Though Emily minimizes Sue's dereliction, its effect on Emily went deep and made life empty for her: "I do not miss you Susie—of course I do not miss you—I only sit and stare at nothing from my window, and know that all is gone—Dont *feel* it—no—

any more than the stone feels—that it is very cold." As in her letter to Abiah, she perceives that she is different from others: "I ... wonder what I am and who has made me so." She concludes the letter with the kind of excessive ardor that may have contributed to the hysterical anxiety of Sue's "nervous fever" and that even now may be the chief reason for Sue's staying away and failure to write. She says: "It's of no use to write to you— Far better bring dew in my thimble to quench the endless fire— My love for those I love—not many—not very many, but dont I love them so?"[93]

The breakdown in communication between the two girls seems, surprisingly, to have been initiated by Emily, though of course she was the first to attempt to heal the breach. Apparently Sue asked Austin what the meaning of Emily's silence was. Austin answered:

> As to your deprivation of "Spiritual converse" with my sister—I Know Nothing—I was aware that you had been in correspondence for some time, but had never had an intimation that the correspondence was at an end ... you will not suspect me of having interfered with your epistolary intercourse with her—Her choice of friends and correspondents is a matter over which I have never exerted any control.[94]

It is apparent that Susan believed that Austin told Emily not to write. Sue's questioning Austin in this way suggests that she was attempting to learn whether Austin suspected that Emily's influence was a factor in her recent flight. Clearly, Susan is aware of the Sue-Austin-Emily triangle and wonders if Austin, too, is aware and jealous.

Austin escorted Susan to Michigan, where it took a little time for her to settle down to a normal frame of mind. "Such a turmoil have I been in," she writes a relative four or five months after leaving Amherst, "ever since I was sick last Summer."[95]

What appears to be Emily's next letter to Sue cannot be placed for certainty in this sequence because it is dated solely through the handwriting, which is of this year. However, the content fits only with the events of these months, and the estrangement of the previous letter is probably the same which pervades this one. "We differ often lately, and this must be the last," Emily writes Sue,

You need not fear to leave me lest I should be alone, for I often part with things I fancy I have loved,—sometimes to the grave, and sometimes to an oblivion rather bitterer than death—thus my heart bleeds so frequently that I shant mind the hemorrhage . . . Sue—I have lived by this. It is the lingering emblem of the Heaven I once dreamed, and though if this is taken, I shall remain alone, and though in that last day, the Jesus Christ you love, remark he does not know me—there is a darker spirit will not disown it's child.[96]

The "lingering emblem of the Heaven I once dreamed" may plausibly be equated with the "Delinquent Palaces" of poem no. 959 (that is, lost maternal love), and appears to refer here to Sue's waning affection or virtuous repudiation. What Emily seems to be saying is that she willingly would renounce God Himself, heedless of damnation, should He deny her this all-important love. Afterward she would go about her affairs indifferent to the fact that her life, now rendered meaningless, was ebbing away as through an open wound.

Toward the end of this letter she seems to acknowledge that it was her effect on Sue that drove Sue from her—that her excessive love caused Sue's illness and occasioned the estrangement. "Few have been given me," she writes, "and if I love them so, that for *idolatry,* they are removed from me," Emily has no choice but to accept the loss and continue on her way alone.

The brave acceptance did not last, however, and by December Emily is sinking into a deeper despondency. "Susie," she writes,

it is a little thing to say how lone it is—anyone can do it, but to wear the loneness next your heart for weeks, when you sleep, and when you wake, ever missing something, *this,* all cannot say, and it baffles me. I would paint a portrait which would bring the tears, had I canvass for it, and the scene should be—*solitude,* and the figures—solitude—and the lights and shades, each a solitude. I could fill a chamber with landscapes so lone, men should pause and weep there; then haste grateful home, for a loved one left . . . In all I number you. I want to think of you each hour of the day.[97]

Sue remained in Michigan two months more, returning to Amherst in February 1855. In January Emily was preparing for a trip to Washington with Vinnie to visit their father; she was in Washington, not Amherst, when Sue returned and did not see Sue again until at least another month had gone by. Emily was depressed and thinking obsessively of death, and since, as noted, she was increasingly inclined not to leave home, it seems likely that she undertook the trip only at her father's insistence. An episode of depression Emily suffered when she was a young girl had been alleviated by a trip to Boston. Perhaps her father, seeing her declining into a lonely misery, arranged this trip hoping for a similar salubrious result.

Emily's January 1855 letter to Sue makes it clear that Sue still is not answering her letters. "I am sick today, dear Susie," she writes,

> [but] I have not been sick eno' that I cannot write to you. I love you as dearly, Susie, as when love first began . . . and it breaks my heart sometimes, because I do not hear from you. I wrote you many days ago—I wont say many *weeks,* because it will look sadder so, and then I cannot write . . . I miss you, mourn for you, and walk the Streets alone—often at night, beside, I fall asleep in tears, for your dear face, yet not one word comes back to me from that silent West. If it is finished, tell me . . .

These dark thoughts lead to thoughts of death: "you are my precious Sister, and will be till you die, and will be still, when Austin and Vinnie and Mat, and you and I are marble—and life has forgotten us!" She tells Sue that she will put aside her chores when Sue comes so as to be free to visit with her, and this thought again leads to the idea of the permanent putting away of life's activities: "I'll get 'my spinning done,' for Susie, it steals over me once in a little while, that as my fingers fly and I am so busy, a far more wonderous Shuttle shifts the subtler thread, and when *that's* web is spun, *indeed my* spinning will be done."[98]

Next Emily writes Sue, now in Amherst again, from Washington. She says that she has not been well since her arrival in Washington, that "all is jostle, here—scramble and confusion," yet admits that "I'm gayer than I was before." Considering the theme of death which pervades this letter, one may take her statement as indicative of the depth of despondency she felt before leaving home. To see Sue again, Emily says, she would give up all the pomp and protocol of Washington. "Will you write to me," she begs, "why hav'nt you before? I feel so tired looking for you, and still you do not come. And you love me, come soon—this is *not* forever, you know, this mortal life of our's."[99] In a letter to Mrs. Holland a few weeks later, the theme of death again obtrudes in a context that makes its introduction quite gratuitous.

She writes, "It seems to me many a day since we were in Spring-field [visiting the Hollands]." Emily recalls an incident there and says the details "seem as vague—as vague; and sometimes I wonder if I ever dreamed—then if I'm dreaming now, then if I *always* dreamed, and there is not a world, and not those darling friends, for whom I would not count my life too great a sacri-fice. Thank God there is a world, and that the friends we love dwell forever and ever in a house above." Seemingly realizing these feelings of a depersonalized, vague world and her thoughts of heaven are inappropriate, she apologizes: "I fear I grow in-congruous, but to meet my friends does delight me so that I quite forget time and sense and so forth."[100]

There are no surviving letters from Emily to anyone from March to October 1855, but judging from her last known let-ter to Jane Humphrey, written on October 16, Emily's despair and morbidity have outlasted her Washington excursion. "Only the loss of friends," she writes Jane, "and the longing for them—that's all, tonight Jennie, and I keep thinking and wishing, and then I think and wish, till for your sakes, who stray from me, *tears* patter as the rain." Toward the close of the letter, Emily tells Jane of preparations the Dickinsons were then making for moving to the mansion that Edward Dickinson had just pur-chased, and again the theme of death forces its way into the context with no pretext of appropriateness: "We shall be in our new house soon; they are papering now, and—Jennie, we have *other* home—'house not made with hands.' Which first will we occupy?"[101]

At this time Sue also was preoccupied with houses—and other matters. A letter she wrote to her brothers sometime in May, despite its cool tone, suggests indirectly some of the emotional turmoil in the Dickinson family. Sue wrote:

Austin's Father has over-ruled all objections to our remaining here and tho' it has been something of a sacrifice for Austin's spirit and rather of a struggle with his pre-conceived ideas, I feel satisfied that in the end it will be best and he will be fully rewarded for his filial regard . . . in the course of the Summer Austin will have a pleasant house in process of erection on the lot just west of [the Dickinson mansion]—For the sake of going at once, into our own home all complete, we have decided to defer our marriage till another Spring.[102]

Biographers generally hold Edward Dickinson responsible for his son's failure to leave Amherst, and they attribute to excessive possessiveness the pressure he put on Austin and Sue to stay. Actually Edward Dickinson spent little time with his family and was off on business trips or out to public meetings most of the time. It was certainly his idea that each of his children be sent away for part of their schooling, and Emily's remark that her father was "too busy with his Briefs—to notice what we do"[103] does not convey the picture of a man dependent upon his children. Austin, therefore, probably did not settle next door primarily to meet some emotional need of his father.

Austin and Susan did not marry for another fourteen months. Sue's other explanation for deferring their union—to await the construction of their house—is even less plausible. After all, Austin had already been courting Sue for five years and was now fully prepared to support a family. What, then, was the true explanation for Edward Dickinson's insistence that the couple give up their plans for relocating, and why did the headstrong Austin acquiesce? The answer is probably threefold—one factor being Sue's lack of enthusiasm for marriage. The other reasons undoubtedly involved the disturbed condition of Austin's sister and mother—Emily and her deepening despair and increasingly withdrawn and phobic behavior, and Mrs. Dickinson and her gradually developing depressive illness.

It should be recalled that in Emily's October letter to Jane Humphrey she speaks of her copious tears for lost friends and ponders on which house she will next reside in—the new mansion or the house in the skies "not made with hands." The question was resolved the following month when the Dickinsons moved back to the large and gloomy house in which Emily had spent her first ten years.

Two months after the move, Emily writes Mrs. Holland, and it is apparent from the letter that the transition has been difficult for Emily and even more so for her mother. Though there is a degree of fantasy and burlesque in the letter, these qualities cannot hide the disturbed and unhappy state of Emily's feelings. The train of thought moves from her pleasure at hearing from the maternal Mrs. Holland again, to Vinnie's being asleep, to past times when Emily and Mrs. Holland were together, and then—precipitantly—death comes to the fore again. What appears to bind these disparate associations together is a mood of estrangement, a feeling of unreality that probably reflects an increasingly disturbed psychological state.

Church is done [Emily says], and the winds blow, and Vinnie is in that pallid land the simple call "sleep." They will be wiser by and by, we shall all be wiser [a reference, of course, to Death]! While I sit in the snows, the summer day on which you came . . . seem fabulous as *Heaven* seems to a sinful world—and I keep remembering it till it assumes a *spectral* air, and nods and winks at me, and then all of you turn to phantoms and vanish slow away. We cannot talk and laugh more, in the parlor where we met, but we learned to love for aye, there, so it is just as well. We shall sit in a parlor "not made with hands" unless we are very careful!

After a brief return to a lighter mood, Emily comments on her mother: "Mother has been an invalid since we came *home,* and Vinnie and I 'regulated,' and Vinnie and I 'got settled' and still we keep our father's house, and mother lies upon the lounge, or sits in her easy chair. I don't know what her sickness is, for I am but a simple child, and frightened at myself." Mrs. Dickinson remained ill for over four years, suffering what appears to have been an incapacitating depression. Emily's worries about her mother and the extra responsibilities devolving upon her through her mother's incapacity no doubt contributed their share to her own eventual collapse.

In this same letter Emily gave some indications of her awareness that all was not well psychologically with herself. Though she described the family's move two months before with humor and imagination, she nevertheless admitted to a feeling of continued disruption: "I am out with lanterns, looking for myself. Such wits as I reserved, are so badly shattered that repair is useless." She signs the letter "from your mad Emilie."[104]

A few weeks before this letter to Mrs. Holland was written, Austin joined the church, most likely at Sue's urging. This left only Emily outside the circle of those "accepting Christ." Until then she and Austin had been "the lingering *bad* ones,"[105] while all the rest of her family and friends had flocked to the revivals and experienced conversion. Now, in still another way, she was standing alone.

There are no surviving letters from Emily after the January 1856 one to Mrs. Holland until April, when she writes to her cousin John Graves in answer to a letter from him. John had recently become engaged, and apparently spoke of this as well as of his job as principal of a school. Emily writes: "I am glad you have a school to teach—and happy that it is pleasant." Apparently John's letter contained some humor; she says, "[I was] amused at the *Clerical Civility*—of your new friends—and shall feel—I know, delight and pride, always, when you succeed." The point in quoting these remarks, uninteresting in themselves, is to indicate that her cousin's letter was not a pessimistic, dysphoric one. And how does Emily reply? First, she tells him she is writing from her garden and that it is a sunny, warm spring Sunday. But no sooner does she embark on her theme than the letter becomes full of premonitions of decay: "You remember the crumbling wall that divides us from Mr. Sweetzer—and the crumbling elms and evergreens—and *other* crumbling things— that spring, and fade, and cast their bloom within a simple twelvemonth." Then follows a descriptive line or two on blue skies, birds, and bees, after which the gloomy refrain is taken up again: "then there are *sadder* features—here and there, *wings* half gone to dust, that fluttered so, last year—a mouldering plume, an empty house, in which a bird resided . . . We, too, are flying—fading, John—and the song 'here lies,' soon upon lips that love us now—will have hummed and ended."[106] A strange letter indeed to send to a man enthusiastically embarking on a new job and looking forward to his marriage!

The same month Emily copies out and sends to Mary Warner a ten-stanza poem, "My Boy," by the Reverend John Pierpont. The subject of the poem is a father's anguish at the death of his young son; Emily apparently sent it to commemorate the death of Mary's younger sister three years previously. The poem is meant to inspire confidence in an afterlife of whose existence we know Emily herself was never entirely convinced. One suspects that the poem's appeal to her resided less in its sentimental hopefulness than in its lugubrious imagery, which resembles that in some of her own poems on death. The following stanza is an example:

> I know his face is hid
> Under the coffin lid,
> Closed are his eyes; cold is his forehead;
> My hand that marble felt –

> O'er it in prayer I knelt,
> Yet my heart whispers that, he is not there!

The accompanying letter says, "I send the verses of which I spoke one day—I think them very sweet—I'm sure that you will love them."[107]

In the meantime, arrangements for Austin's and Sue's wedding are being formulated. Sometime in the spring Sue again left Amherst for New York and from there wrote to her New Hampshire relatives of a change in her plans. She says that her aunt, "a sort of foster Mother" of hers, insisted that Sue be married in the aunt's home in Geneva. Of course, this arrangement precluded Emily's attendance at the wedding, for by now her phobia at leaving home had reached crippling proportions. As it turned out, none of the Dickinsons saw Austin married. Their reaction can be inferred from Sue's comments in this letter. "The decision [to be married in Geneva] made great shaking among the old plans . . . but for reasons I cannot explain, both for prudence and prolixity, it was adviseable, and almost an inevitable plan."

Sue's weary resignation is evident here too: "I shall have a quiet wedding," she says, "a very few friends and my brothers & sisters a little cake—a little ice cream and it is all over—the millionth wedding since the world began."[108]

On July 1, 1856, in Geneva, New York, Austin and Susan were married. For the remainder of the year there is little news of Emily. In September Mrs. Dickinson's condition was such that a water cure in Northampton seemed indicated, and her daughters remained home and kept house. What Emily's state of mind was at this time can only be conjectured. One letter to Mrs. Holland, dated about a month after Austin's wedding (though possibly written earlier), shows the embryonic beginnings of certain characteristics that became prominent features of Emily's letters of 1858 and later. The letters lose their informal, spontaneous character. They become increasingly mannered and stylized. Biblical quotations become ever more frequent, as do cryptic utterances that even the recipients probably had difficulty deciphering. And death becomes an overriding preoccupation.

The letter to Mrs. Holland is full of longing for death and release and there are suggestions of suicidal inclinations. "Don't tell, dear Mrs. Holland," Emily begins, "but wicked as I am, I read my Bible sometimes, and in it as I read today, I found a

verse like this, where friends should 'go no more out'; and there
were 'no tears.'" That she longed for this deliverance is explicit
in the next line: "and I wished as I sat down to-night that we
were *there*—not *here*." Suicide must have crossed her mind as
at least a possibility; she continues, "And I'm half tempted to
take my seat in that Paradise of which the good man writes, and
begin forever and ever *now*." In the next paragraph she speaks
of the fading joys of this life, which, if they were permanent,
would be heaven enough. Then she continues with her death-
theme: "I'm so glad you are not a blossom, for those in my garden fade, and then a 'reaper whose name is Death' has come to
get a few to help him make a bouquet for himself, so I'm glad
you are not a rose—and I'm glad you are not a bee, for where
they go when summer's done, only the thyme knows, and even
were you a robin, when the west winds came, you would cooly
wink at me, and away, some morning!" The next paragraph expresses the hope that Mrs. Holland will linger on earth as long
as Emily does so that together they can "seek the new Land."
She concludes, evidently somewhat aware of the incongruity of
what she is saying, "Pardon my sanity, Mrs. Holland, in a world
*in*sane." Then she asks that Mrs. Holland continue to love her,
"for I had rather *be* loved than to be called a king in earth, or a
lord in Heaven."[109] Following this letter to Mrs. Holland there
is a period of about two years for which there exist no letters.

On December 12, 1856, two days after her twenty-sixth birthday, Emily cuts out of the daily newspaper an advertisement for
tombstones.

On December 29 Vinnie writes to Joseph Lyman, an old sweetheart, then in New Orleans. Vinnie's letter broke a silence of two
years duration on her part and was provoked, Lyman assumed,
by his few trivial remarks to her included the previous summer
in a letter he wrote to Emily informing her of his engagement
to Laura Baker. Lavinia's letter, as quoted by Lyman to his
fiancée, is as follows:

> My Dear Joseph—I remember & love you still & have long longed
> to tell you so but I've been too full of care . . . I wonder if I shall
> ever see your face again—I'm glad you are happy—Im glad you are
> to be successful there where you most desire success—I'm glad you
> have found a life-companion who pleases you. I wish I could see
> you *once more* before you are married. Our Early Love seems to me

a sweet dream, I have forgotten all the bitter. Joseph Lyman, how would you & I appear were we to meet suddenly? . . . I wish we were all children again & lifes battle not begun. I remember how we parted on that April Day so long ago. You asked me who I will marry, Joseph. I wish I knew. I have some dear friends. I have promised to decide *the* question before winter is all gone. Perhaps I may give them all up. I shall always love to hear from you, Joseph, & trust you will be *good* & prosperous. God bless you! Joseph, Good bye Vinnie[110]

There is a distraught quality powerfully projected by these few lines. Lavinia speaks of a longing for childhood and an escape from "lifes battle." She seems apprehensive about the future: whether she will ever see Lyman again and whether she will ever marry. She says she has been "full of care." Richard Sewall points out the letter's tone of "unmistakable tenseness."[111] In his view Lavinia's anxiety may most readily be explained by assuming that she was severely troubled by the news of Lyman's proposed marriage to another woman. "She answered bravely Joseph's blunt questions about her marriage plans," writes Mr. Sewall, "and wished she could see Joseph *'once more'* before he is married." He emphasizes that on a later occasion Lavinia repeated this wish and concludes: "perhaps she never quite gave up hope."[112]

If, however, one recalls that five years had elapsed since Vinnie last saw Joseph, that she was only eighteen when he left Amherst, that she had had at least two serious beaux since that time, and that it took her about six months to respond to the notice of his engagement, the inevitability of Mr. Sewall's explanation appears doubtful. A more likely source of the strain noticeable in Lavinia's letter is the situation at home, which causes her to be "full of care."

Emily also congratulated Lyman on his engagement. Whether she wrote immediately after receiving Lyman's announcement in the summer or at the time of Lavinia's letter is not known, although Lyman lumped both letters together in his phrase "these beautiful letters."[113] In either case one concludes that Emily's letter aroused in him no suspicion of her turmoil. A shadow of this turmoil is perceptible, however, in the passage he sent his fiancée. Emily advanced the expected expression of joy at the news and saluted the approaching sexual union. Her pathetic aversion to any such union for herself, however, comes through clearly in her gratuitous denial of the feeling; marital bliss is no less heavenly, she tells them, "tho' the Angels do not so."[114] Austin and Susan and Joseph and Laura were entering a phase of life that seemed as alien and unnatural to Emily as she imagined it would be to the pure spirits in heaven. It was not to be long now before she would be proclaiming through dressing in white, her kinship to these spirits—the perpetually impending, frigid, virgin bride.

Austin's marriage brought crashing down forever all Emily Dickinson's poorly grounded hopes for her own sexual fulfillment. For Emily, the Austin-Susan-Emily triangle was, in essence, a revival of the old oedipal dilemma, now grossly magnified and frighteningly distorted. It was impossible for Austin and Emily both to possess Susan. Austin's need for Sue involved more than the love of a mature man for a woman. Powerful impulses rooted in childhood gave his romantic ardor a driven quality and made it heedless of reality. This is the love that would overleap all obstacles, shove aside every objection, brook no opposition, and *tolerate no rivals*. It was inevitable that Emily would lose in her competition with him. All the psychological advantages were on his side.

Emily's vulnerability came about through split identifications (with both Austin and Susan) superimposed on her peculiar ego structure, which was rendered defective through the mother-want of childhood. She had wished desperately to identify with Sue—the least pathological of her modes of relating to Sue. But her ego weaknesses brought about an intensity of identification that was unbearable. Her image of Sue became fused narcissistically with Emily's own self-image. Emily wrote: "Where my Hands are cut, Her fingers [meaning Sue's] will be found inside"[115]—an extraordinary insight revealing that in the depths of her being Emily felt herself to *be* Sue. But her psychological organization was so lacking in harmony and unity that she could also feel equally profoundly that her being was masculine, akin to Austin's. Caught in the intensified oedipal tensions of Austin's courtship, she was unable to stabilize her position, a failure fatal to her chances for a normal life.

To some extent Emily was invited by Austin to invest more of herself in him and Susan than was safe for her. To a much greater extent Sue seems also to have fostered this investment. Her weak and diffuse commitment to Austin in itself encouraged Emily to attempt to win Sue for herself. And Sue even half-deliberately may have encouraged Emily's excessive ardor, for certainly Emily's approval would have advanced Sue's chances of being admitted to the Dickinson family. It would be a mistake to underestimate the importance to a poor but genteel orphan girl of the security, wealth, respectability, and social position that would come automatically with marriage to Austin. Sue, the youngest of a large but scattered family, had lived in many homes but had none to call her own. She seems to have allowed both Austin and Emily to persuade her that she loved them. But it is abundantly clear from their letters that Sue's feelings never came close to matching theirs in intensity.

As Sue and Austin drew closer together, Emily was increasingly excluded. Thus two sources of the essential maternal love, from the paucity of which she suffered all her days, were withdrawn from her. From Susan the maternal love had come directly, from Austin, reflexively; in mothering him she had, through identification with him, mothered herself. Austin's marriage rendered her role as his "mother" unnecessary and impossible—Sue was now permanently at Austin's side.

Besides the disruption of the surrogate mother element, which was so important in the relationship of the two girls, Sue's defection meant a profound drop in Emily's self-esteem. The emotion that caused Emily to regard herself as "Susan's Idolator" was partly self-love. Emily's self-image as a woman was defective and repudiated until she saw it in the mirror of Susan, an admirable woman of her own age so like herself in many ways. No more intense attachment exists than the one that enables us to think well of ourselves, repairing our self-esteem and transfiguring our defects. The narcissism in Emily's love of Susan was highly unstable. The emergence of defects and weaknesses in Sue would fan into flame the ever-smoldering self-disgust Emily felt for herself as a woman. Sue's unfaithfulness in favor of Austin would have stripped Emily of all the pleasure in her femininity which Sue had brought her and caused a return of bitter self-rejection.

Each supporting bond severed imperiled further Emily's precarious balance. Much in Austin's and Sue's attitudes contained the implicit promise to Emily that their marriage would bring a partial restoration of the haven of childhood. For example, it was a keystone of Austin's suit that in addition to a husband Sue, in marrying him, would acquire parents; Sue was to be Edward Dickinson's "chosen child," an additional sibling. This fantasy of a return to childhood, which was elaborated by Emily with Austin's and Susan's help and which Emily found so seductive, evaporated upon their marriage. Such playing house was precluded by the real responsibilities of their new existence.

Also, Austin's joining the church at this time meant the loss of another kind of support. His occasional self-image as a wicked, impure, and unworthy person, aggravated by Sue's pious reprehension, linked him with Emily, who evaluated herself in much the same terms. With Austin's conversion, Emily found herself standing alone in her "wickedness."

All these considerations—the ruthless exclusiveness of Austin's passion, Sue's wavering commitment, the willingness of the couple to subordinate their marital relationship to the larger complexities of Edward Dickinson's family, and Emily's own excessive needs and vulnerabilities—all of these factors seemed to conspire against her. For Emily Dickinson they constituted a whirlpool of forces into which she was being drawn to near destruction by the dark and silent tides of childhood.

The old masculine identification with Austin added impetus to her drive toward Sue as a love object. Her sometime sense of fusion with Sue revived and intensified the repressed incestuous interests she had once had in her brother. Such a multiplicity of incompatible forces can exist only at the expense of divisions and splits in the structure of the ego. As her poems reveal, Emily's ego was like an opal, rent by fissures and fractures, brittle, never coalescing into a unity, reflecting first this, then that fracture-surface in a play of iridescent light.

Emily tried desperately to merge with Sue so that at least a vicarious fulfillment would not be denied her, as she began to look forward to Susan's marriage with certain illusory hopes. In her unconscious fantasy Austin's sexual possession of Susan represented the consummation of the erotic element in the relationship of the two women. Moreover, on a more primitive psychic stratum, the poet could anticipate through her identification with her brother the symbolic attainment, in the person of Susan, of the longed-for mother. Also, the poet's love for Austin contained unconscious erotic elements derived partly by displacement of her infantile longing for her father, which arose with compensatory force when her mother failed her. This means that in this one grand coup of Austin's marriage lay the poet's imaginary repossession of both mother and father in their representatives, Susan and Austin, as well as the fantasy of attaining fulfillment of her own deeply inhibited bisexual longings. Through the interplay of psychodynamics such as these, bearing little relation to the world of adult reality, Emily Dickinson unconsciously looked to the marriage of her brother to establish the emotional equilibrium which had so long eluded her. Both the erotic elements in her ties to him and her seemingly conscious physical attraction to his wife may have undergone repression through Emily's entrenched fears of maturity and of leaving the state of childhood "innocence." In spite of this, however, the preparation for the impending marriage would have fanned both repressed and overt feelings into flame and engendered in Emily a heightened state of sexual readiness for which, after the withdrawal of Austin and Susan, no object existed. Thus the poet's air castle collapsed in the marriage of Susan and Austin. Instead of further consolidating her important position in the Austin-Susan-Emily triangle (which also represented the father-mother-child triangle), the event, as was inevitable, firmly displaced and excluded her. Instead of further enhancing her intimacy with her brother and his wife, the marriage fixed an outer boundary past which she dared not venture. She was now the abandoned child again, suffering in complete revival the pain and rage of her earlier deprivations.

Emily Dickinson was to discover in misery that actual frustration cannot be overcome through dreams. Nevertheless, the needs of the moment dictated that she cling to the contrary conviction because she saw no other possible way out. Ultimately the opalescent intelligence and sensitivity of her ego could no longer withstand the forces that were breaking it apart from within. Many of her poems constitute fragments of the topography of a psychotic breakdown. Years before, as if in dread anticipation of the abyss of loneliness into which Austin's marriage would plunge her, Emily had written that her misery might drive her to paint "a portrait which would bring the tears, had I canvass for it, and the scene should be—*solitude,* and the figures—solitude—and the

lights and shades, each a solitude. I could fill a chamber with landscapes so lone, men should pause and weep there."[116]
  The following poem (no. 280) is one of these landscapes:

I felt a Funeral, in my Brain,
And Mourners to and fro
Kept treading – treading – till it seemed
That Sense was breaking through –

And when they all were seated,
A Service, like a Drum –
Kept beating – beating – till I thought
My Mind was going numb –

And then I heard them lift a Box
And creak across my Soul
With those same Boots of Lead, again,
Then Space – began to toll,

As all the Heavens were a Bell,
And Being, but an Ear,
And I, and Silence, some strange Race
Wrecked, solitary, here –

And then a Plank in Reason, broke,
And I dropped down, and down –
And hit a World, at every plunge,
And Finished knowing – then –

Chapter VI A PORCELAIN LIFE

Crumbling is not an instant's Act
A fundamental pause
Delapidation's processes
Are organized Decays.

'Tis first a Cobweb on the Soul
A Cuticle of Dust
A Borer in the Axis
An Elemental Rust –

Ruin is formal – Devils work
Consecutive and slow –
Fail in an instant, no man did
Slipping – is Crashe's law.

—no. 997 (about 1865)

Until now I have been focusing mainly on Emily Dickinson's growing awareness that Austin and Susan could never provide the fundamental security she needed. She had come at last to realize that, with their marriage, the deep participation she desired in the inner lives of both of them was to be forevermore precluded. Acceptance of this fact had various effects: loneliness, depression, tension, and fear, among other responses.

But additional disturbances—less obviously ascribable to the

259

transactions of Austin's love life and other external events—had for some years been rising to the surface of Emily Dickinson's thought and behavior from that hidden "fracture within" of whose existence she had been aware since childhood. These more mysterious and insidious manifestations of something deeply awry—justifiably termed *symptoms,* in view of the obscurity of their precipitating causes, as opposed to simple direct reactions—must be added to the picture of the poet's agony at the loss of Austin and Susan in order to encompass the full extent of the imbalance that preceded her collapse.

In a major psychiatric illness there are disturbances of feeling and thinking that appear at the peak of the disorder—the break with reality. Emily Dickinson's poems present most powerfully and completely these overwhelming subjective experiences, the ravaging climax of her anguish. How they do this is the subject of the next chapter. There are also premonitory symptoms which precede breakdown by years and even decades. In this chapter I will delineate these more objectively evident, more slowly developing, and less dramatic features of Emily Dickinson's gathering illness as they are discernible in her letters. It is clear that the first appearance of these symptoms preceded the loss of Austin and Sue by a considerable period.

Though my purpose is to chart the increasing imbalance of Emily Dickinson's personality that led to her collapse in her late twenties, it is useful to refer to letters written long after the crisis to fill in the picture of the first symptoms. The early letters indicate clearly the existence and nature of these symptoms. Later ones furnish additional knowledge of their many facets and implications. What justifies the citation of letters in seeming disregard of chronology is the fact that the signs of pathology under examination had their roots in the poet's early life, changed little through the years, and became with time chronic, almost characterological, components of her life-style.

As noted, the disturbances that were prominent features of the earliest mother-child relationship caused Emily Dickinson to enter childhood itself with an emotional deficit. With each succeeding phase of development her psychological equilibrium grew more and more precarious. In every crisis of maturation she chose the wrong path. Or, rather, the path her diverted quest for a secure love and an inner stability forced her to take led directly away from the goals she sought. She rejected her mother and identified herself with the males in the family. She evaded the exigencies of adolescence and avoided heterosexuality out of fear. She sought outside her home for the templates of maturation that her family should have provided. Conversely, she sought to find in the bosom of her family the gratification of those needs that can only be fulfilled in the outer world. Her position vis-à-vis the community and her generation became ever more untenable. The forces that enmeshed her in the relationship of Austin and Susan swept her to a final impasse from which there was no egress save through major realignment of the partitions and chambers of her personality. This necessarily involved a new beginning: a rebuilding, brick by brick, on a different plan and on a new scale—hence the collapse of the existing psychic structure.

Emily Dickinson wished to remain a child, but inevitably one reaches an age when this role becomes incongruous. The innocent humorousness, childlike spontaneity, precocious wisdom, and sexual undifferentiation of her girlhood personality could not have survived her twenties without becoming grotesque. These qualities, fixed features of Emily Dickinson until she was well into her twenties, were, for all their deceptive charm, evidence of an arrest in psychological growth. They were also, however, the exoskeleton that held her psychic structure together. The circumstances of Emily Dickinson's life pressed for a radical revision of personality. As she tried to grow, fissures in the supporting framework of her attitudes and orientations kept appearing. From early adolescence through young adulthood, the forces of growth, under terrific pressure, groped vainly for a possible channel, until eventually the constricting and supporting husk shattered. Before this occurred, though, the blocked energies, transformed by frustration into something dark and devious, had begun to create a strange psychic edifice of their own.

The following are the chief symptoms which first became manifest in the period of Emily Dickinson's life preceding her breakdown: depression, anxiety, estrangement, avoidance of gratification, extraction of pleasure from privation, preoccupation with death, withdrawal from social intercourse, agoraphobia, fear of loss of emotional control, preternatural awareness of the mind's unconscious depths (symbolized by the "sea" images in her poems and letters), weakness of ego boundaries, and night fears; each will be discussed in turn. These are the undramatic but ominous harbingers of chaos that preceded by years the mighty dislocations of the poems. As Emily Dickinson herself observed: "Fail in an instant, no man did / Slipping – is Crashe's law" (no. 997).

The slipping may have begun as early as her thirteenth year, when Sophia Holland's death precipitated the depression which the poet called a "fixed melancholy."[1] Her letters to Abiah Root, Jane Humphrey, and Austin over the next few years all speak periodically of low spirits[2] in such a way as to suggest that depressions were a common occurrence. Almost any circumstance— illness, the beginning of a new year, religious doubts, separation from her family—was sufficient to trigger a mood of deep and troubled sadness. Happiness was a rare and not-to-be-expected phenomenon. Thus, after a visit to her beloved Aunt Lavinia, Emily writes, "I am visiting in my Aunt's family & am happy. Happy! Did I say? no not happy, but contented."[3] She habitually uses the word "desolate" in describing her feelings, and as early as her twenty-first year she begins to think of the dead with something akin to envy. Upon the death of a neighbor's daughter she writes Austin, "I dont know but they [the dead] are the happier, and we who longer stay the more to be sorrowed for."[4] Two years later a change is noticeable. "Do you want to hear from me, Austin?" she asks her brother, "I'm going to write to you altho' it dont seem much as if you would care to have me. I dont know why exactly, but things look blue, today, and I hardly know what to do, everything looks so strangely."[5] Here, depression verges on a different reaction. The strange look of familiar things may be interpreted as a minor estrangement from reality— technically, the phenomenon of *derealization,* of which more later.

It might reasonably be argued that because Emily Dickinson was a poet, a celebrant of the emotional life paying special attention to fluctuations of feelings, these lines, quoted more or less out of context, are simply eloquent expressions of the ordinary "blues" that everyone experiences from time to time. Indeed, their prognostic significance can only be appreciated when one takes into account the fact that a few years after they were written the poet's world disintegrated as she was caught in a prostrating depressive illness. Because "slipping is Crashe's law," one may legitimately regard at least some proportion of these dysphoric moods as premonitory and examine them seriously as such.

Next in frequency of occurrence to depression, a symptom common to almost every kind of mental perturbation, comes anxiety, another nonspecific feeling state. Anxiety as a concomitant of Emily Dickinson's early years—indeed of her entire life—appears to have been almost unrelenting. Its many faces are recognizable as the necessary and constant accompaniment of each of the other symptoms examined in this chapter, and it would serve no purpose to belabor such an obvious fact. It might, however, be helpful to point out the various levels of anxiety that were her most frequent companions.

Given the nature of Emily Dickinson's inner conflicts and her unmet needs in the areas of sexuality and dependency, it is only to be expected that she would tend to regard the fulfillment of all the strongest desires and goals of her life as being just barely possible. One catches many glimpses in her early letters of a protracted state of apprehension associated with this uncertainty about such essential questions. Deeper still, the basic anxiety that was the result of her childhood loneliness and sense of lovelessness with regard to her mother continued unabated, of course, and the hostility this generated was a major determinant of her appraisal of the world as a hollow and alien place. That is to say, her own reactive anger projected onto the environment caused the environment to take on a hostile mien which in turn then stimulated a renewed and derivative anxiety.

Another and more internal source of deep tension was her awareness of a serious threat to the integrity of her ego organization. The constant pressure of instinctual demands which were opposed both to reality and to the prohibitions of her conscience generated an anxiety that incessantly spurred the formation of ever more costly and crippling defenses. These defenses, for example her withdrawal from society, while ameliorating anxiety of one sort, created their own problems, which eventually became themselves a source of anxiety. Moreover, Emily Dickinson's awareness of weakened ego boundaries, to be discussed later, brought with it a conscious fear of insanity, perhaps the most primitive and pervasive of all the anxieties with which the ego has to grapple.

In addition to these complex and obscure sources of anxiety,

there were habitual fears that were evoked with seeming directness by environmental circumstances. One of Emily Dickinson's
characteristic attitudes was to anticipate future evils and to fear
that present circumstances were likely to worsen. Although this,
too, had roots deep in the unconscious, it must have appeared to
her as a quite rational reaction to threatening external possibilities. One such anxiety occurred when the poet felt inadequate to
some demand of the environment, another in the context of her
religious doubts, and a third with regard to her awareness of the
transitoriness and undependability of her own and her loved
ones' lives.

A few quotations will serve to show the intensity of her dread
in the face of some ordinary trials of life. For example, though a
superior student, she dreaded examinations. She writes Abiah:
"I am already gasping in view of our examination, and although
I am determined not to dread it I know it is so foolish . . . I will
distress you no longer with my fears, for you know well enough
what they are without my entering into any explanations."[6]

In her early teens, in the midst of religious conflicts, she writes
Abiah of her state of chronic anxiety: "I feel that I am sailing
upon the brink of an awful precipice, from which I cannot escape
& over which I fear my tiny boat will soon glide if I do not receive
help from above."[7]

Later, after Austin's marriage, and in a similar mood she tells
Samuel Bowles: "In such a porcelain life, one likes to be *sure* that
all is well, lest one stumble upon one's hopes in a pile of broken
crockery."[8]

I have mentioned the experience of estrangement and derealization. Emily Dickinson developed this symptom when parted
from those she loved—especially Sue and Austin.

In 1853, three years before Austin married Sue, Emily writes
to Sue: "your absence insanes me so—I do not feel so peaceful, when
you are gone from me—All life looks differently, and the faces
of my fellows are not the same they wear when you are with me.
I think it is this, dear Susie; you sketch my pictures for me, and
'tis at their sweet colorings, rather than this dim real that I am
used, so you see when you go away, the world looks staringly,
and I find I need more vail."[9] Literally, she is saying that without
Sue all life looks (at Emily) differently; the world looks (at her)

staringly. Of course, life and the world are doing nothing of the kind; Sue's absence does not make Emily an object of increased curiosity to others. It can only be her perception of "life" and the "world" that is changed, that is, Sue's parting alters her so that she distorts the way she sees and interprets the environment. The actual meaning of these phrases, then, becomes "all life looks [to me] different(ly)"; "the world looks [to me] staring(ly)." The ambiguity in this passage as to what is perceived as having changed—the inner self or the outer world—is intrinsic to the state of *estrangement*. In reality the subject of estrangement has suffered an interior impoverishment. With the physical absence of beloved persons there seems to occur a decay in the vividness and warmth of their inner mental representations. The victims of the disturbance suffer, therefore, not only from losing the gratifications of immediate contact with the friend from whom they are separated. In addition, the friend in a sense ceases emotionally to exist for them. They cannot hold him vividly and satisfyingly alive in their inner world of human relationships and so feel emptied and isolated. The symptom of estrangement is a frequent precursor of psychotic severances from reality. When psychosis occurs, the emptying out from the personality of the internal images of all meaningful relationships depletes the vital reservoirs of feeling and responsiveness. Perceptions now impinge on the eyes and ears of a vacuum. When nothing living stirs within, the perceptions themselves are cold, clear, and detached—without emotional coloring. The outer world consequently appears altered and seems inhospitable, coldly alien, or hostile, and there is a sense of a diminution of its normal emotional resonance with the inner movements of the personality.

Emily Dickinson seems to have been referring to incipient symptoms of estrangement when she wrote Austin, "I hardly know what to do, everything looks so strangely."[10] Clearly, here she means everything looks so *strange*.

Several months after this letter to Austin, Emily writes similarly of her loneliness to Mrs. Holland: "I thought of you all last week, until the world grew rounder than it sometimes is, and I broke several dishes."[11]

A synonym for estrangement, derealization, emphasizes that in this symptom external surroundings and the happenings of one's life are divested of some of their sense of reality. Thus, when

Emily writes Mrs. Holland from Philadelphia, where she has gone on a trip apparently arranged by her father following the deterioration of her relationship with Sue, she says: "It seems to me many a day since we were in Springfield, and Minnie and the *dumb-bells* seem as vague—as vague; and sometimes I wonder if I ever dreamed—then if I'm dreaming now, then if I *always* dreamed, and there is not a world . . . Thank God there is a world, and that the friends we love dwell forever and ever in a house above. I fear I grow incongruous . . . I quite forget time and sense and so forth."[12]

In addition to depression, anxiety, and feelings of estrangement, other embryonic symptoms appeared in the years preceding Austin's marriage. Although they did not come to full development until after Emily Dickinson had made herself both a poet and a recluse, a survey of their small beginnings as evinced in the youthful letters helps to illuminate the emerging defenses and reaction patterns which her inner conflicts evoked and which determined the outlines of her later life. One of the most prominent features of the poet's mature personality was her deliberate avoidance of pleasure. She avoided many sources of potential satisfaction, giving as her reason her reluctance to develop a vulnerability to eventual loss. For example, she writes the Bowleses in 1858: "I am sorry you came, because you went away. Hereafter, I will pick no Rose, lest it fade or prick me."[13] And again, after an Amherst couple moves to Chicago she writes the wife by way of farewell: "Good night, dear Mrs. Haven! I am glad I did not know you better, since it would then have grieved me more that you went away."[14]

In 1860 she similarly writes Kate Anthon: "Why did you enter, sister, since you must depart?"[15] The same idea recurs frequently: "I think it sad to have a friend," she tells the recently widowed Edward Dwight, "it's sure to break the Heart so."[16] And, in a later letter to the Reverend Dwight she wonders "why a love was given—but just to tear away."[17]

Clearly, the lingering pain Emily Dickinson felt from her dependence on an unreliable mother made her determined not to be vulnerable again. Henceforth her love investments were to be tentative and cautious.

Her first statement of this position, which suggests in addition a dawning masochistic trend, occurs in an 1852 letter to Abiah Root written when Emily Dickinson was twenty-one. She writes: "I always try to think in any disappointment that had I been gratified, it had been sadder still, and I weave from such supposition, *at times,* considerable consolation; consolation upside down as I am pleased to call it."[18] The idea is developed into an overriding philosophy of life in her poems, in one of which she says of the "Banquet of Abstemiousness" that it "Defaces that of Wine" (no. 1430).

Her willingness to suffer to save others from suffering appears early, in a letter to Austin written in her twenty-first year. At the time Austin was suffering from facial neuralgia. She writes: "I do wish it was *me,* that you might be well and happy, for I have no profession, and have such a snug, warm home that I had as lief suffer some, a great deal rather than not, that by doing so, you were exempted from it. May I change places, Austin? *I* don't care how sharp the pain is, not if it dart like arrows, or pierce bone and bone like the envenomed barb."[19]

Generally speaking, a conspicuous willingness to suffer and a predilection for frustration rather than gratification are complex symptoms rooted in (among other things) an unconscious commitment to the expiation of guilt feelings. Also, as everyone has noticed, from such self-inflicted pain and deprivation a surprising volume of covert satisfaction and even pleasure can, at times, be wrung. The important role of this "consolation upside down" in the creation of Emily Dickinson's poetry will be examined in a later chapter. Here let it suffice merely to mention its existence and that of the sense of guilt from which it arose.

The sporadic depressions, anxieties, and estrangements that played a large part in Emily Dickinson's emotional life prior to her nervous breakdown are dwarfed by a symptom that manifested itself with inexorable persistence. This was her preoccupation with the theme of death.

As early as her fifteenth year, after she had been sent by her parents to Boston to recover her health and improve her spirits, she evinces an unusual intensity of interest in the subject in a letter to Abiah Root. She tells Abiah that since being in Boston she has "both seen & heard a great many wonderful things" and proceeds to list them, beginning: "I have been to Mount Auburn

[cemetery]." A few passages later she quotes Edward Young's
Night Thoughts: "Pay no moment but in just purchase of its
worth & what it's worth, ask death beds. They can tell." After a
few lines expressing her religious doubts and pleading with
Abiah to visit her, the death theme appears again: "There have
been many changes in Amherst since you was there. Many who
were then in their bloom have gone to their last account & 'the
mourners go about the streets.'" The body of the letter is followed
by a long postscript in which a discussion of the warm weather
leads again to the same theme: "There were over 100 deaths in
Boston last week, a great many of them owing to the heat."[20]

And recall the interesting intrusion of the death theme in an
1847 letter to Austin, previously quoted: "Did you think that it
was my birthday—yesterday?" Emily asks him; "I don't believe
I am *17*. Is. Jacob. Holt [a dying neighbor] any better than when
you wrote last & is there any hope of him?"[21] For Emily each
"happy birthday" was primarily just another milestone on the
journey to the grave, as the sequence of associations here indicates.

A little over a year later, in a Valentine's Day letter to her
cousin telling of the gaiety in Amherst, she observes that in
another year "the present writers of these many missives [that is,
the Valentines]"[22] may be dead. The idea of death is introduced
out of context by means of the flimsiest of transitional passages.
What appears to be underscored here is her inner pressure to talk
about the subject and her willingness to introduce it in the most
inappropriate contexts.

Another inappropriate and strained introduction of her concern with death occurs in an 1850 letter to Jane Humphrey.
Emily says: "Did you know that Payson had gone to Ohio to live?
I was so sorry to have him go—but everyone is going—we shall
all go—and not return again before long."[23] Here, an ordinary
change of residence of an acquaintance becomes the springboard
for her most obsessive theme.

Apparently Emily Dickinson's family were aware of her peculiar interest in mortality, though its significance as a symptom
may not have been evident in her youth. Thus, Emily writes
Austin: "Vinnie tells me *she* has detailed the *news*—she reserved
the *deaths* for me."[24]

Emily realized that she often brought up the subject of death
inappropriately and acknowledged this propensity in an 1852

letter to Jane Humphrey. "I think of the grave very often," she writes, "and how much it has got of mine, and whether I can ever stop it from carrying off what I love; that makes me sometimes speak of it when I dont intend."[25]

It has been advanced as a rational explanation of Emily Dickinson's fascination with the theme of death that her thoughts were naturally so directed because of the early demise of friends—that she was not particularly absorbed in the subject of death per se, but that she was concerned with the loss of specific individuals who had been or might be taken from her by death. In fact, she herself offers this explanation to T. W. Higginson: "Perhaps Death—gave me awe for friends—striking sharp and early, for I held them since—in a brittle love—of more alarm, than peace."[26] However, if one examines her responses to the deaths of Sophia Holland and Leonard Humphrey, both of which were exceedingly intense reactions, it becomes clear that what afflicted her most profoundly was the fact of mortality itself and the precariousness of all life, including her own, rather than the concrete loss of a particular person. Though the death of Sophia Holland when Emily was thirteen precipitated a "fixed melancholy" which lasted for more than a month, the poet a few years later had forgotten the loss of her little chum; for when Leonard Humphrey died when Emily was nineteen, she wrote Abiah Root: "I never have laid my friends there [that is, in the grave], and forgot that they too must die; this is my first affliction."[27] Similarly, three years after her tears for Humphrey had dried, she wrote to her brother after learning of B. F. Newton's death: "Oh, Austin, Newton is dead. The first of my own friends."[28] Death itself always had a tremendous impact upon her. However, the dead themselves seem merely to have been the vehicles through which this obsession attained its grip on her imagination.

Throughout her life Emily Dickinson displayed an avid interest in death scenes. She thirsted for details; it was important to her to learn just how the dying felt in the face of imminent dissolution.

The first evidence in her correspondence of this eventually pressing need appears in a letter she wrote after the death of Newton to his minister, who was a complete stranger to her: "tell me if he was willing to die, and if you think him at Home, I should love so much to know certainly."[29]

In some obsure way death stimulated her. After Frazer Stearns was killed in battle she wrote the news to her Boston cousins. In its wealth of concrete details the letter indicates her eagerness in gathering and conveying the precise circumstances of death. "His big heart," she tells the cousins, "[was] shot away by a 'minie ball' . . . Just as he fell, in his soldier's cap, with his sword at his side, Frazier rode [as a corpse] through Amherst . . . He fell by the side of Professor Clark . . . lived ten minutes in a soldier's arms, asked twice for water—murmured just, 'My God!' and passed! Sanderson . . . made a box of boards in the night, put the brave boy in, covered with a blanket . . . They tell that Colonel Clark cried like a little child . . . Nobody here could look on Frazer . . . The doctors would not allow it . . . you must come next summer, and we will mind ourselves of this young crusader."[30]

Upon the death of a relative she asks the same cousins to return the favor: "you must tell us all you know about dear Myra's going." A note of—triumph?—seems to creep in to her questioning: "Was Myra willing to leave us all? I want so much to know if it was very hard, husband and babies and big life and sweet home by the sea [that is, all those prizes of life that Emily lacked]. I should think she would rather have stayed."[31]

And after Dr. Holland's death Emily writes his widow: "I am yearning to know if he knew he was fleeing—if he spoke to you. Dare I ask if he suffered?"[32]

After Charles Wadsworth died Emily wrote his friend J. D. Clark: "I hope you may tell me all you feel able of that last interview."[33] Then, when Mr. Clark himself died, she directed her investigations to *his* death in a letter to his brother: "I am eager to know all you may tell me of those final Days."[34] And again: "and though we cannot know the last, would you sometime tell me as near the last as your grieved voice is able?"[35]

The same request is made of Helen H. Jackson's widower, a man Emily met only once: "[Will you] tell me a very little of her Life's close?"[36] she inquires. And, at the same time, she writes Forrest Emerson: "Should she [a friend of Mrs. Jackson] know any circumstances of her life's close, would she perhaps lend it to you, that you might lend it to me?"[37]

Her anxiety that her loved ones may be taken from her recurs again and again, and she frequently reminds her friends that life is transient. In an 1854 letter to Sue she asks, apropos of nothing,

"Did you ever think, Susie, that there had been no grave here [meaning in her immediate family]?"[38] And again to Sue: "And [if] you love me, come soon—this is *not* forever, you know, this mortal life of our's."[39] And to the Hollands: "this world is short, and I wish, until I tremble, to touch the ones I love."[40] And, at the close of an 1858 letter to Sue, death again appears as a non sequitur: "Good night . . . Since there are two varieties, we will say it softly—Since there are snowier beds, we'll talk a little every night, before we sleep in these!"[41]

One of the clearest examples of the intrusive appearance of the death obsession without benefit of a justifying context occurs in an otherwise gay letter of thanks to Mrs. Haven sent upon receipt of some notes and a gift. Emily speaks of missing her friends and of her feelings upon passing the house where they formerly lived. "Your house has much of pathos," she says, "to those that pass who loved you . . . I shall miss the clustering frocks at the door, bye and bye when summer comes, unless myself in a *new* frock, am too far to see. How short, dear Mrs Haven!" The letter then concludes with this poem: "A darting fear – a pomp – a tear – / A waking on a morn / to find that what one waked for, / inhales the different dawn."[42]

The death theme owed its burgeoning to many springs. New England puritanism and nineteenth-century romanticism were both obsessed with death in their own particular way, and both, of course, impinged on Emily Dickinson incessantly from every quarter of her culture. It is important to realize also that the standard of public health in the twentieth century (in which communicable diseases are well controlled, dangerous epidemics are thought of as the exclusive property of undeveloped countries, early death is a rarity, and longevity is the rule) renders it difficult for us to appreciate the impact on our nineteenth-century ancestors of the omnipresence of death and the very real and constant menace it presented every day of their lives. *Emily Dickinson's Home,* by Millicent Todd Bingham, provides an impressive review of the many frequently fatal diseases, today all but unheard of, which were prevalent in nineteenth-century Amherst. For Emily Dickinson's preoccupation with death Mrs. Bingham finds just excuse. She cites the incessant dramatization of illness and death by the newspapers, Mrs. Dickinson's anxieties, the tendency for colds to develop into more serious or fatal illnesses, and the frequent deaths of young people. "Furthermore," Mrs. Bingham reminds us, "the Dickinson orchard adjoined the burying ground where the final rites took place. Every funeral procession must pass their house. The wonder is, not that Emily as a young girl thought and often wrote about death, but that any buoyancy of spirit remained."[43]

The religious influences, the literary ones, and repeated actual confrontations with death undoubtedly made their contributions to Emily Dickinson's preoccupation with mortality. But it should be apparent that these forces, in their convergence on the poet, found fertile psychological ground. Austin's letters to Susan exhibit no such preoccupation with death, and it is significant that Vinnie reserved the report of deaths for Emily. Moreover, as I have shown, the way she introduced the subject in her letters—abruptly and often irrelevantly—suggests that her conscious ruminations were stimulated as much by inner emotional disposition as by external impressions.

What exactly were these inner emotional sources? Probably the three most prominent were: (1) fears of abandonment; (2) projection of anger; and (3) guilt feelings toward her mother. These three interrelated matters will be discussed in turn.

Emily Dickinson has told us that from the dawn of consciousness she felt herself a mourner among the children, cast out, one ever searching for her "Delinquent Palaces" (poem no. 959). She identified herself with the motherless Eve, banished from Eden and condemned to death.[44] I have interpreted this self-concept of one fallen from grace and high estate as arising from a sense of maternal abandonment, and I have related it to her admission that she felt she "never had a mother."[45] René Spitz's classical study[46] of European orphanages has shown that the deprivation of maternal love in infancy and early childhood may be a life-threatening situation. Babies lacking the cuddling, tender warmth, and passionate physical contact of a loving mother, even though they are adequately cared for in all other respects, frequently waste away and die. Such infants appear to sense the absence of something vital to their welfare, they become apathetic, immobilized and withdrawn, and they refuse to eat. If they have ever received an adequate mother's affection and are deprived of it through separation or death, they at first react with fear and rage and only later settle into a listless despair. Emily Dickinson's early nurturant experiences were undoubtedly disturbed. As a result, a primitive insecurity seems to have been mixed with the mortar of her psychological foundations. The entire course of her life reveals her exaggerated needs for parental protection. Thus, one of the sources of her preoccupation with death seems rooted in the infantile equation: abandonment equals death. Never feeling safely loved, she never felt safe at all; she was a frail, defenseless atom in a vast and uncaring universe.

Moreover, the ever-present threat of death through rejection and exposure was probably augmented by her inability to give vent to her intense hostility. That she had such feelings is proven by some of her poems, a notable example being "My Life had stood – a Loaded Gun" (no. 754). She had ample reason to be full of rage and destructive propensities. Unloved by her mother, abandoned by her girl friends, devalued as a female, discouraged in her literary aspirations, importuned to accept a religion that offered her no haven, she felt herself a seething volcano. Her uncertain tenure in her own eyes with regard to the place she held in the hearts of her parents caused her to subdue her will, conceal her feelings, and in general submit to the requirements of her father's autocratic rule, which brooked no insubordination. However, echoes of sadistic anger can be perceived when circumstances made it possible for her to clothe her destructive rage in the guise of humor or when family prejudices—for example, toward the Irish—sanctioned a vocal intolerance tinged with cruelty.

As an example of the hostile humor whose heaviness betrays her suppressed and underlying earnestness, there is the following excerpt from a letter to her uncle, Joel Norcross, written when she was nineteen. The "mock" anger of the letter was occasioned by her uncle's failure to reply to a previous letter. "I call upon all nature to lay hold of you," she writes, "let fire burn—and water drown—and light put out—and tempests tear—and hungry wolves eat up—and lightning strike—and thunder stun—let friends desert—and enemies drawn nigh and gibbets *shake* but never *hang* the house you walk about in! My benison not touch—my malison pursue the body that hold your spirit! . . . Had you a pallid hand—or a blind eye—we would talk about coming to terms—but you have sent my father a letter . . . at any rate I shall kill you . . . You can take Chloroform if you like—and I will put you beyond the reach of pain in a twinkling." There follow next inquiries about symptoms of decline, then she continues: "I only thought I'd inquire—no harm done I hope. Harm is one of those things that I always mean to keep clear of—but sometimes my intentions and me dont chime as they ought . . . Now when I walk into your room and pluck your heart out that you die—I kill you . . . but if I stab you while sleeping,"[47] and so forth.

The same straining after humor, using as vehicle a string of sadistic fantasies, occurs in a letter to Jane Humphrey written the same year. Jane had temporarily "deserted" Emily and she writes, "Gone *how*—or *where*—or *why*—who saw her go . . . hold—bind—and keep her—put her into States-prison—into the House of Correction—bring out the long lashed whip—and put her feet in the stocks—and give her a number of stripes and make her repent her going!"[48]

Perhaps related to this transformation of anger into humor is the delight she took in accounts of accidents as reported in the *Springfield Republican*. "Who writes those funny accidents," she asks Dr. Holland, the editor, "where railroads meet each other unexpectedly, and gentlemen in factories get their heads cut off quite informally?"[49]

For Emily Dickinson, sensitized as she was to rejection, the failure of a friend to write or call on her can only have been perceived by her as a betrayal of trust, a failure to care enough, and thus an injury calling forth the anger of the spurned and the excluded. However, she was aware of the excessiveness and unreasonableness of her demands for loyalty and affection. She knew that giving explicit vent to her exaggerated disappointment and wounded self-esteem would have made her appear ridiculous or unbalanced and that such behavior would only further alienate those whose love she craved. She chose the safe way; she swallowed her rage or attempted to convert it into amusing sadistic extravaganzas which gave her feelings partial outlet. One other way open to her was to deflect her anger to objects approved by her family for the purpose.

Austin, as Boston schoolmaster to a class of Irish pupils, was an exacting disciplinarian who did not shrink from corporal punishment. Emily greatly enjoyed her brother's comic account of incidents which revealed his harshness as a taskmaster. "How it made us laugh," she writes him, "Poor little Sons of Erin . . . I fancy little boys of several little sizes . . . then I set them all to shaking—on peril of their lives that they move their lips or whisper—then I clothe you with authority and empower you to punish . . . [Sue and I] should enjoy the terrors of 50 little boys and any specimens of *discipline* in your way would be a rare treat for us . . . I suppose you have authority bounded but by their lives, and from a remark in one of your earliest letters I was led to conclude that on a certain occasion you *hit the boundary line!*"[50]

That Emily shared Austin's attitude toward discipline is indicated in a letter to Sue written six months later, when Sue was teaching in Baltimore. "You must be faint from teaching those stupid scholars," she writes Sue, "I hope you whip them Susie—for *my* sake—whip them *hard* whenever they dont behave just as you want to have them!"[51]

Each member of the Dickinson family reacted characteristically to Austin's severity toward his pupils. Edward Dickinson was pleased that the Irish boys "had found their master" in his son. Gentle Mrs. Dickinson worried lest Austin be too enthusiastically savage with them. And Emily remarked, "So far as *I* am concerned I should like to have you kill some—there are so many now, there is no room for the Americans . . . Wont you please to state the *name* of the boy that turned the faintest . . . I dont think deaths or murders can ever come amiss in a young woman's journal."[52]

The intensity of dissimulated and displaced aggression one senses beneath the fun in these excerpts provides an insight into the poet's meaning when in her poems she refers to herself as a volcano. Magmas of fury flowing beneath the superficial strata of her personality erupted—not in fears of death for herself such as arose from her sense of abandonment—but in death wishes and sadistic fantasies toward others. These impulses would be sensed most keenly in connection with those she felt closest to, for they were in a position to cause her the most pain by their indifference. Recall her awareness of something dangerous in herself in her remark to Sue: "in thinking of those I love, my reason is all gone from me, and I do fear sometimes that I must make a hospital for the hopelessly insane, and chain me up there such times, so I wont injure you."[53] Here is a direct linkage between the fear of hostile impulses escaping control and a concern for the life of others.

A third psychodynamism reenforcing the death obsession involves guilt over Emily's rejection of her mother. As with her fears of abandonment, the concern here is again for her own life. The unconscious connection between her repudiation and contempt for her mother and her fears of death is to be found in the guilty expectation of punishment for a breach of filial piety and loyalty. "Honor thy father and thy mother" was a much stressed commandment in nineteenth-century New England, and Emily Dickinson had inherited a Calvinistic severity of conscience. She could not hope to flout it as she did without serious emotional repercussions. The wages of sin is death or, as in Emily Dickinson's case, the living in the presence and threat of it for a lifetime.

These three psychodynamic patterns—the fear of abandonment, the projection of anger, and the fear of retribution—in addition to the many external influences, are perhaps the major contributors to Emily Dickinson's fascination with death. There are doubtless additional facets to this persistent and variously determined symptom: there is space here only to suggest something of its complexity and dimensions.

Another symptom was Emily's gradual withdrawal from the social life of the town, a trend well under way before the marriage of Austin and Sue and consummated in the almost total isolation achieved some ten or so years later. As early as her seventeenth year, Emily was showing signs of a preference for her own company and a tendency to withdraw from her social circle. On one occasion at this time most of the girls at her school went to a menagerie; she preferred to remain behind and "enjoyed the solitude finely."[54]

By her twenty-first year she had become convinced of the dissatisfactions and frustrations of face to face interviews. Thus, in 1851 she writes Abiah: "Oh there is much to speak of in meeting one you love, and it always seems to me that I might have spoken more, and I almost always think that what *was* found to say might have been left unspoken."[55]

Another of her attitudes which encouraged withdrawal was the idea that friends deplete one. She expressed this view clearly to Austin in 1851: "if you talk with no one, you are amassing thoughts which will be bright and golden for those you left at home—*we* meet our friends, and a constant interchange *wastes tho't* and feeling, and we are then obliged to *repair* and *renew*—there is'nt the brimfull feeling which one gets *away*."[56]

The next year she is more firmly convinced than ever of the superiority of isolation: "I have the old *king feeling* even more than before, for I know not even the *cracker man* will invade *this* solitude."[57]

By 1853 her preference for being alone is beginning to take on the aspects of a phobic avoidance of others. "I sat in Prof Tyler's woods," she writes Austin, "and saw the train move off, and then ran home again for fear somebody would see me, or ask me how I did."[58]

Because the Dickinsons were faithful subscribers to many newspapers and periodicals, Emily Dickinson's biographers frequently attribute to her an interest in external affairs and current events for which her letters give little support. Her relative lack of interest in all town affairs (save deaths) is made explicit in a letter to Austin: "I'm telling all the news, Austin . . . You know it's quite a sacrifice for *me* to tell what's going on."[59]

By her twenty-fourth year her anxiety at leaving the shelter of her home unaccompanied is becoming almost incapacitating. In January 1854, in a letter that makes a joke of her apprehensiveness, she tells Sue something of what it cost her in emotional poise to attend church alone: "I walked—I ran—I turned precarious corners," and so forth,[60] a passage quoted at length in the preceding chapter. In the face of these vignettes of an advancing agoraphobia, it is difficult to see how anyone can maintain that Emily Dickinson's retreat into isolation was void of neuroticism.

Two months after the foregoing letter to Sue, Emily writes Austin of a similar occasion: "I went to meeting five minutes before the bell rang, morning and afternoon, so not to have to go in after all the people had got there."[61]

Four months later she makes her declaration to Abiah that she is developing a strong disinclination to leave home: "I don't go from home, unless emergency leads me by the hand,"[62] and so forth, a passage quoted previously. The reason Emily gives for not going to Abiah's is that she is peculiar in some way and would attract unfavorable attention.

The same year, in a letter to Mrs. Holland, Emily indicates that as long as she is accompanied by someone she can depend on for emotional support, in this case Vinnie, she is still able to leave home.

By 1859, however, it has become an ordeal even to meet visitors to her home. To her cousin Loo she writes: "you are one of the ones from whom I do not run away!"[63] About the same time she tells Mrs. Holland: "some one rang the bell and I ran, as is my custom."[64]

In time Emily enlisted the aid of relatives and certain friends to protect her from having to face those with whom she felt fearful. Thus, she writes her cousins, recently deprived through death of their mother's shelter, of her relief in knowing they were being looked after. She writes: "I thought that flown mamma could not, as was her wont, shield from crowd, and strangers, and was glad Eliza was there. I knew she would guard my children, as she has often guarded me, from publicity."[65]

As the years passed the habit of withdrawal became unshakable. Though forced by her anxiety to reject others, Emily nonetheless could not bear that those she cared for should disappoint her when she wanted to see them. "Odd, that I, who say 'no' so much, cannot bear it from others," she writes cousin Loo, who has changed her plans for visiting Amherst, "Odd, that I, who run from so many, cannot brook that one turn from me."[66]

The next year (1862) she writes the cousins of her panic at the prospect of the commencement tea—the annual social event hosted by Edward Dickinson as treasurer of Amherst College—"I am still hopeless and scared, and regard Commencement as some vast anthropic bear, ordained to eat me up."[67]

There is no doubt that her inability to withstand the emotional strain of meeting others face to face, especially some of her close friends, caused her considerable pain and guilt—additional proof that her withdrawal was an uncongenial and alien symptom and not a deliberately and freely chosen way of life. Rather early in her retreat her family could not accept her refusal to see their intimates, as is indicated in an 1862 letter Emily sent to Samuel Bowles following one of his visits: "Because I did not see you, Vinnie and Austin, upbraided me . . . Did I not want to see you?"[68]

When visitors came for whom she felt affection, Emily attempted to gain as close contact with them as possible short of actual confrontation. She eavesdropped on their conversation: "to hear your voice below [is better] than News of any Bird,"[69] she writes Mr. Bowles. Similarly she would enter rooms immediately vacated by the departing guest. Thus, in 1879, she writes Samuel Bowles: "I went to the Room as soon as you left, to confirm your presence."[70]

Clearly, her inability to be gracious to those she cared for pained her, and she feared her friends would misconstrue her feelings. For example, she expressed keen remorse for having sent Maria Whitney a note in lieu of seeing her in person: "[I was] sure you would never receive us again. To come unto our own and our own fail to receive us, is a sere response."[71] However, her extreme emotional constriction in the presence of others—probably an excessive girding against a feared loss of emotional control—seems to have rendered what interviews she did have barren of all feeling save anxiety. This is suggested in a note to Mrs. Holland following a visit: "When you had gone the love came. I supposed it would. The supper of the heart is when the guest has gone."[72] In other words, the poet remained unconscious of any positive feelings during Mrs. Holland's visit. Later, with the object of those feelings withdrawn, it was safe to experience— even savor—them in full force. There was now no danger that they would find alarming and incongruous expression in direct behavior. That Emily Dickinson avoided others through doubts of her ability to maintain appropriate emotional control is suggested by her remark to T. W. Higginson on the occasion of his first visit with her. "Forgive me if I am frightened," she told him, "I never see strangers & hardly know what I say."[73]

A similar lack of security with regard to her control of her thought processes is evinced in a letter to her uncle written in 1858. "I hardly know what I have said," she apologizes, "my words put all their feathers on—and fluttered here and there."[74]

She was more explicit about the devastating effect of her own verbalizations upon herself in a late letter to Joseph Chickering. "I . . . have no grace to talk," she writes, "and my own Words so chill and burn me, that the temperature of other Minds is too new an Awe."[75] She terminates the letter with the unusual complimentary close "Earnestly," which here may be taken to mean: *please* do not ask to see me again. Words "chill and burn" when they carry a charge of violent emotion. The expression of one's strong feelings is generally tolerable to others provided the outburst is in context, appropriate to the circumstances, and not lacking some measure of control. Also, it is a truism that the expression of feeling normally affords a relief of tension which tends to restore one's emotional equilibrium. Emily Dickinson would not have shrunk from personal contact if these had been her experiences. Clearly, then, communion with others did not afford her the relief that is the usual aftermath of the ordinary expression of emotion, and thus she regarded the chilling and burning effect of her communications with dread as something to be avoided. Moreover, we normally reserve the pouring forth of our deeper feelings for a person with whom we have some special rapport, one with whom we feel an emotional resonance of understanding and sympathy. We do not, as Emily Dickinson apparently felt in danger of doing, express our intemperate rages and desires to the indifferent and the lukewarm and thus find that "the temperature" of these "other Minds," being so alien, strikes us with "Awe" at the abyss which separates us from them. One is forced to conclude that Emily Dickinson, in addition to having emotional reactions of unusual intensity, lacked normal emotional control, that she was well aware of this weakness, and that it was one of the determining factors which caused her to seclude herself. In addition, the tendency for her words to break loose as though they had a life of their own means that the content of her thought and the feelings that accompanied it erupted from the deeper levels of her personality. Just as her private obsession with death intruded into the alien context of her letters, so other deeply personal preoccupations threatened to burst forth in driven and convulsive utterance in her social transactions. She was, therefore, not so much afraid of others as afraid of herself in their presence.

One source of her fear seems to have been an awareness of a serious ego defect—the inability to contain impulses and consequently to behave and converse appropriately. The result of such a weakness is to leave one dangerously open to the incursion into consciousness of mental processes that are ordinarily relegated to the unconscious. When these emerge into awareness they menace rationality and make conventional behavior almost impossible. This is the plight of the borderline psychotic. The condition is accompanied by just such anxiety and dread of exposure as was displayed by Emily Dickinson. "In all the circumference of Expression," she writes friends after having refused to see them, "those guileless words of Adam and Eve never were surpassed, 'I was afraid and hid Myself.' "[76] Adam and Eve hid themselves when their simple consciousness was split into the separate awareness of good and evil and when, according to tradition, they recognized moral implications in their sexual proclivities. Emily Dickinson, therefore, appears to be explaining that she conceals herself because she is shamefully aware of unacceptable impulses within her, and one may reasonably infer that she alludes here to erotic impulses that she would prefer to repress.

Emily Dickinson clearly recognized the exactions and perils of overinvolvement in the deeply introspective life. She writes to Maria Whitney: "Your sweet self-reprehension makes us look within, which is so wild a place we are soon dismayed."[77] And, in a prose fragment: "there are Apartments in our own Minds —that we never enter without Apology."[78] The wild reaches of the unconscious also have their allurements—perhaps their chief danger—as the following implies: "Paradise is no Journey because it . . . is within—but for that very cause though—it is the most Arduous of Journeys—because as the Servant Conscientiously says at the Door We are out."[79] When one loses oneself in the interior abyss, it may be said that one is out to the reality that knocks upon external perceptions. When this state is protracted and one is unable to withdraw voluntarily from its snare, one has fallen into psychosis; the rational processes of the mind founder in an ocean of affect and chaotic impulse. "A Word is inundation, when it comes from the Sea—Peter took the Marine Walk at the great risk,"[80] says Emily Dickinson in reference to a book which she says stirred her to awe as would a "starlight Night." The words that inundate invite the unconscious—this is the risk that accompanies the "Marine Walk," perhaps the necessary accompaniment of esthetic creation.

Although Emily Dickinson "never saw a moor and never saw the Sea," as one of her most famous poems (no. 1052) assures us, the image of the sea haunted her from her youth and always had a special and symbolic meaning for her. She used it variously to refer to death, immortality, eternity, and the vast emotional expanses of art and consciousness, all subjects that struck reverberations deep within her. The image is thereby related to that substratum of mental life the unconscious and to her uncanny awareness of its tides. She seems also to have used the symbol to express the sensation of merging with the world in a blurring of the sense of her separate existence. Such a loss of ego boundaries, whether in reference to the outer world or the inner, normally unconscious one, produces what Freud designated an "oceanic feeling."[81] Some access to the unconscious appears to be a necessary prerequisite for artistic creativity of the highest order. Too deep an immersion in its chaotic energies and conflicting impulses, however, sweeps one into psychosis. The genius, therefore, must take great care to preserve his balance.

An early indirect reference to the sea relevant to this discussion occurs in a letter to Abiah written when Emily was only fifteen. It involves her inability to accept the religious convictions of her friend and her consequent anxiety. "I feel," she writes, "that I am sailing upon the brink of an awful precipice, from which I cannot escape & over which I fear my tiny boat will soon glide if I do not receive help from above."[82]

A similar usage occurs in another letter written four years later. "You are growing wiser than I am," she tells Abiah, "and nipping in the bud fancies which I let blossom—perchance to bear no fruit, or if plucked, I may find it bitter. The shore is safer, Abiah, but I love to buffet the sea—I can count the bitter wrecks here in these pleasant waters, and hear the murmuring winds, but oh, I love the danger!"[83] Abiah was conventionally and evangelically religious, not one to indulge in "vain fancies." The "wrecks" here, therefore, may refer to those who do not avail themselves of religious guidance and who, instead, pursue their own daydreams, sometimes to destruction. The relationship discernible here between the fantasy life and the "sea" suggests that on one level Emily is already aware that her imagination springs from a mighty and dangerous reservoir.

The next appearance of the symbolic use of the sea image is a half-serious equating of drowning with being abandoned by a loved one. This is interesting in view of the fact that the onset of psychosis is frequently accompanied and perhaps precipitated by the impending severance, real or imagined, of a love relationship. The image is the central figure of a fantasy: "I am on the blue Susquehanna paddling down to you," she writes Abiah, "I am not much of a sailor . . . and I am not much of a mermaid, though I verily think I shall be, if the tide overtakes me . . . I don't believe you care, if you did you would come quickly and help me out of this sea; but if I drown, Abiah, and go down to dwell in the seaweed forever and forever, I will not forget your name, nor all the wrong you did me! Why did you go away and not come to see me?"[84]

In the rough draft of a letter to her still unidentified lover, the mysterious "Master," the symbol of the sea takes on the meaning of earthly wandering. The sea is a condition lacking in gratification and replete with pain. She writes "Master": "Each Sabbath on the Sea, makes me count the Sabbaths, till we meet on shore."[85] "Shore" seems to signify heaven. In other contexts the shore is earthly existence and the sea is death or eternity. Thus, she writes of her aunt's terminal illness that she fears that last year's was the aunt's "last inland Christmas" and asks, "Does God take care of those at Sea?"[86] What links death and psychosis is the clinical observation that the psychological disruption of personality in psychotic states is feared and experienced by the victim as a kind of death—the dissolution of one's personality as one has come to know it. Whether "sea" is death or empty aimlessness, therefore, on another level it has the additional meaning of the inundation of consciousness by unconscious mental life—which is psychosis.

The sea as representative of solitude and withdrawal—the defensive position of the beleaguered and retreating ego—occurs in a letter to Kate Anthon. Here it is indicated that only love can penetrate the barriers of withdrawal. "I am pleasantly located in the deep sea," she tells Kate, "but love will row you out if her hands are strong."[87]

In an 1860 letter written to Mary Bowles, probably after her third stillbirth, the symbolic sea means overwhelmed by death, mourning, or anxiety. "If you are at sea," Emily writes, "perhaps when we say that we are there, you won't be as afraid—The waves are very big, but every one that covers you, covers us, too."[88] Probably in the same year, she sent Mr. Bowles the anguished poem "Two swimmers wrestled on the spar," in which one of the "swimmers"—probably an aspect of the divided self

—drowns "With eyes, in death, still begging, raised / And hands – beseeching – thrown!"[89]

The image of the sea seems to have reached obsessive proportions in 1860. Approximately quoting Isaiah, Emily comforts Susan Phelps following the breaking of her engagement: "When thou goest through the Waters, I will go with thee."[90] Here water means nearly overwhelming vicissitude.

Two years later she writes to Samuel Bowles, seemingly asking for assistance or support of some kind: "Are you willing?" she asks, "I am so far from Land."[91] And, in another convulsive letter to "Master" written in the same year, we find her in the posture of one suffering rejection by a loved one. She couches her desperate need for reconciliation in oceanic imagery: "Oh how the sailor strains, when his boat is filling—Oh how the dying tug, till the angel comes."[92] As in her early letter to Abiah and the later one to Kate, only love can prevent her drowning.

In this year (1862) of great poetic outpouring and equally great psychological travail, she writes to Samuel Bowles: "Forgive the Gills that ask for Air—if it is harm—to breathe!" And she encloses in the letter a poem beginning: "Should you but fail at—Sea."[93] The theme of the poem is that should Bowles ever suffer what she is suffering she would "harass God" until He intervened to save her friend. The gasping "Gills" are apparently drowning for want of a love essential to life. Again, the relevance to the psychotic severance of love relationships is apparent.

Two years later the image persists. Emily writes Sue from Cambridge, where she has gone for eye treatment, that she is "At Centre of the Sea";[94] that is, probably, in the doldrums of despair and loneliness. Six months later, following the death of Sue's sister, Emily writes by way of consolation: "I live in the Sea always and know the Road. I would have drowned twice to save you sinking, dear, If I could only have covered your Eyes so you would'nt have seen the Water."[95] The idea that sightlessness preserves one from facing the "Water" of death reflects the psychosomatic component of Emily's own eye difficulty, for which she was under treatment at the time of this letter.

A few months later she sends Sue the verse: "An Hour is a Sea / Between a few, and me – / With them would Harbor be."[96]

Here again, "sea" is equivalent to separation, being without a "Harbor," that is, isolated from loved ones.

The next year, in replying to Higginson's mention of "Immortality," she says "That is the Flood subject. I was told that the Bank was the safest place for a Finless Mind."[97] As some subjects are too vast for human comprehension, so, on another level, Emily Dickinson's mind could not "swim" in the sea of lost ego boundaries.

Six years later she wishes her cousin, Perez Cowan, "Power" and "Peace" and adds "To multiply the Harbors does not reduce the Sea."[98] This seems to contrast the little securities and loving shelters of life with the vast chaoses of death, eternity, and isolation.

After the death of her mother and the unexpected death of her little nephew Gilbert, the sea again signifies death, the emotions that death brings, and the riddle of immortality. "I cannot tell how Eternity seems," she says upon the death of Mrs. Dickinson; "It sweeps around me like a sea."[99] And with the loss of Gilbert: "the Fathom comes!—the Passenger [Gilbert] and not the Sea, we find surprises us." Gilbert has leaped across "the Mystery" which his survivors "slowly ford."[100]

The "oceanic feeling" is not always unpleasant or frightening. The same indefiniteness of ego boundaries that presages psychotic confusion may, under other circumstances, lead to a feeling of expansiveness as the ego enlarges, as it were, to include new territory within its wavering perimeter. Thus, while Emily Dickinson acknowledges the painful tenuousness of the borders of her sense of self, from another perspective she rejoices in the heightened esthetic sensibility such a weakness sometimes brings with it. She speaks of her response to literature: "If I feel physically as if the top of my head were taken off, I know *that* is poetry."[101] And, similarly, when she experiences love for Judge Lord, she writes: "the exultation floods me. I cannot find my channel—the Creek turns Sea." In this same love letter to Lord she expressed her desire for fusion with him, fusion being a psychological capacity *only* of the ego whose boundaries are inordinately fluctuant. She writes: "Incarcerate me in yourself."[102]

I shall have more to say regarding the sea symbol in its relationship to the fluidity of Emily Dickinson's ego boundaries when I discuss in the following chapter her use of the symbol in her poetry. For the present suffice it to say that the permeable character of those boundaries, her openness to the instinctual life of fantasy, and her deficient emotional control, are all aspects of her vulnerability to psychosis. If, in addition, one considers the stresses of her adolescent years and all that losing Austin and Susan meant to her, it is not surprising that she had to find a way of life for herself that protected her from further travail as far as this was possible. A life of reclusiveness must have seemed her only option.

Another effect of her withdrawal from the world was that it softened that cruelest of realities—death—by keeping it at some remove from her and veiled. Instead of the loss of social intimacy, the death of a friend to Emily Dickinson meant the cessation of written correspondence. For this reason she could almost pretend that he was still living and that a letter might still arrive. In a letter to Maria Whitney, written after Mrs. Dickinson's death, Emily wrote, "I was never certain that mother had died, except while the students were singing [at the funeral services being conducted downstairs]. The voices came from another life." How much more uncertain must she have been when a friend died whom she had not seen for twenty years. Earlier in the same letter to Maria she had written: "You speak of 'disillusion.' That is one of the few subjects on which I am an infidel."[103] Emily Dickinson retained her illusions through her various methods of controlling and avoiding reality.

That her avoidance of physical proximity to her friends and the confinement of her relationships to letters rendered death unreal to her is clear from many of her comments. For example, after Charles Wadsworth died she told his friend, "I do not yet fathom that he has died—and hope I may not till he assists me in another World."[104] And after Judge Lord's death she wrote her Norcross cousins, "I hardly dare to know that I have lost another friend."[105] Not only death but also painful partings of other kinds were attenuated and nullified by this manner of reducing them to an ink and paper existence. When one of her epistolary friends moved to New York she wrote him, "We dare not trust ourselves to *know* that you indeed have left us. The Fiction is sufficient pain."[106] The implication is that life becomes almost as harmless as fiction if lived only through letters. Even with Sue Emily tried to soften her losses by evading firsthand knowledge that Sue had left her. Thus when Sue departed for her customary autumn visit to her sister in New York, Emily did not see her off. "Without the annual parting," she writes, "I thought to shun the Loneliness that parting ratifies."[107] Such a mediating of life through letters is in essence an almost magical way of achieving absolute command over what may or may not befall one. It represents the last desperate effort of an ego that feels excessively vulnerable to the onslaughts of life and that seeks to narcotize its anxiety through an illusory omnipotence.

Nevertheless, on a deeper level Emily Dickinson realized that happiness for herself, as for other human beings, was to be found only in flesh and blood relationships. "I thought that nature was enough / Till Human nature came" begins one poem (no. 1286); and after Judge Lord's death she writes: "Till the first friend dies, we think ecstasy impersonal, but then discover that he was the cup from which we drank it, itself as yet unknown."[108]

Those who hold that Emily Dickinson's withdrawal was a matter of preference rather than anguished reluctance fail to appreciate her terrible suffering. Though she affected an arrogant disdain of the world, she longed for human companionship—her poems reveal with what loneliness. One can gather some idea of the fastness of her phobic prison by the fact that at times she was unable even to see Susan, her "sweet Sister,"[109] to whom she wrote two years before her death: "Be Sue—while I am Emily —Be next—what you have ever been—Infinity."[110] Yet, "I must wait a few Days before seeing you," she once wrote Sue, "You are too momentous. But remember it is idolatry, not indifference."[111]

Night fears plagued Emily Dickinson when she was left alone, and they reflect another aspect of her dependence for emotional security on the presence of her family. In 1859 she made a self-mocking reference to Mrs. Holland regarding this symptom, and three years later, in an eerie passage to her cousins, conveyed its real terror and sexual undercurrents. To Mrs. Holland: "I am somewhat afraid at night, but the Ghosts have been very attentive, and I have no cause to complain. Of course one cant expect one's furniture to sit still all night."[112] The letter to the cousins reads: "The nights turned hot, when Vinnie had gone, and I must keep no window raised for fear of prowling 'booger,' and I must shut my door for fear front door slide open on me at the 'dead of night,' and I must keep 'gas' burning to light the danger up, so I could distinguish it—these gave me a snarl in the brain which don't unravel yet, and that old nail in my breast pricked me."[113]

Certain stigmata of psychosis are discernible in the syntactical looseness of the latter quotation. Here her thoughts have put their feathers on and flown headlong. The run-on sentence, the apparently meaningless quotation marks around "dead of night" and "gas" are concrete traces of the still unraveled "snarl in the brain" of which she speaks. The crashing through into consciousness of uprushing instinctual impulses that were formerly repressed is evident in the thinly veiled wish for sexual violation, which, from a conscious standpoint, her ego finds appalling. The "prowling 'booger' " against whom she guards with such desperation may invade the house if the front door slides open, but it is obviously not burglary she fears. The thought that clearly terrified her is that the imaginary intruder's real design is to seek out her person. Though any intruder would have that entire large house at his disposal, she nevertheless is concerned only with securing the windows of her little bedroom and bolting her door and keeping the gas lights burning so that she may see her attacker. To detect a realistic, rational basis for such fears is difficult indeed. She was, after all, a not very attractive, reclusive spinster whom her would-be rapist would scarcely have had occasion even to see, much less lust after, prior to his gaining her room. What one sees in this passage, therefore, is the emergence from the unconscious of her own previously suffocated sexual longings, now defensively disowned and projected to a threatening, fantasy male. It is of great interest and significance that this letter, which eloquently discloses the thought disorder, weakened impulse control, and inability of the ego to maintain repression —each a hallmark of the psychotic state—should have been written in the very middle of the three-year period that marks the climax of the poet's creative productivity. Of her 1,775 poems, 681 were composed in the interval 1862-1864, well over one-third of her creative output, which spanned, if one includes her juvenilia, thirty-six years. The light shed by the disproportionate and frenzied concentration of creative activity during the early

1860's on the relationship between genius and insanity will be discussed subsequently in reference to the love poetry.

The Dickinson family seem effectively to have suppressed most of the details concerning the poet's breakdown. If Emily Fowler was correct when she wrote, "these worthy people of Amherst have all knowledge in common,"[114] most of what they knew has failed to come down to us. That unsavory gossip could on occasion be suppressed in Amherst is suggested by the lack of present information regarding Emily's second cousin, Harriet Montague, and the behavior that caused her to be suspended from the communion of the church. "Miss Montague is still suspended," writes Mary Shepard in 1845, "not because of her sin, but because there was so much suspicion manifested in her returning. I suppose she is insane."[115] Certainly if Harriet had a nervous breakdown it was almost as hushed up as Emily's. Also, despite the gossipy Amherst biddies, little evidence remains of Lavinia Dickinson's "love affair" (not even the man's identity) or Mrs. Dickinson's protracted illness in the later 1850's. The poet herself expressed the attitude of her family when she remarked: "Lunacy on any theme is better undivulged."[116] The letters, diaries, official records, and newspapers which constitute biographers' chief sources have little to tell us on the subject of Emily's illness. Probably the first serious disturbance began in late 1856, when Emily was twenty-five years old, following Austin's marriage in July of that year. Austin's wedding came and went and in the few scraps from his sister's hand for the rest of that year there is no mention of it. For the following year, 1857, there is complete silence unbroken by letter or poem. It may be that in this year Emily was unable to write. The next year there seems to have been a partial remission. Then, in the fall of 1861, when she was thirty, there was a recurrence of old symptoms and an outbreak of new ones, all of which gradually subsided over the next four or five years. After 1856 there is observable a great change in the tone of Emily's letters. They are now less spontaneous and less colloquial. They are mannered, aphoristic, and disjointed. They plumb more deeply. They show evidence that they have been carefully chiseled and polished. A pointed wit has replaced the diffuse and charming humor of earlier days.

By 1861, Emily Dickinson was nearing the peak of her creativity, writing poems under the pressure of almost constant "inspiration." She was flooded with ideas at this time, jotting them down on any scrap of paper handy, including the edges of newspapers, candy wrappers, and the insides of used envelopes.

Her psychological states, including the stages of the breakdown through which she had recently passed, became in part her subject matter. At this point let us turn to the poetry for further elucidation of the varied manifestations of that illness.

Chapter *VII* A PLANK IN REASON

Crash's Law

One will inevitably misunderstand and trivialize much of Emily Dickinson's life and poetry if one fails to grasp the full intensity of her suffering and the magnitude of her collapse. For this reason let me state at the onset my thesis that the crisis Emily Dickinson suffered following the marriage of her brother was a psychosis.* The proof of this consists in the poet's description of psychological states that occur only in psychosis and in explicit statements in prose and verse which can scarcely be interpreted in any other way.

One such statement, already quoted, occurs in a letter to her cousins. Here Emily Dickinson speaks of having a "snarl in the brain which don't unravel yet,"[1] the phrase being embedded in a paragraph remarkable for its tense and nightmarish quality. What can this "snarl in the brain" be but a delusion which the poet herself recognizes as such? A complex of powerfully obsessive thoughts obtaining a strangle hold on one's mental life might conceivably constitute a "snarl in the brain." This and a state of psychotic confusion seem to be the only two conditions

---

* It is useful to think of the various "neuroses" and "psychoses," including the many "schizophrenia" subgroups, not as fixed states, but as representing points on a

which would justify such a description. The rest of the paragraph, however, rules out the neurotic obsessive state. The intense fear, the poet's shutting herself up in her room, her need to keep all the gas jets burning to light up the imaginary danger —these are not the concomitants of neurotic obsessive-compulsive states. Can there be serious doubt that here Emily Dickinson is disclosing the fact that she has undergone a psychotic episode? Certainly the poems support this conclusion.

In poem no. 280 (about 1861), "I felt a Funeral, in my Brain," the poet describes an experience of gradually increasing depression which finally becomes overwhelming to such a degree that it seemed to her "That Sense was breaking through." Finally there comes the line "And then a Plank in Reason, broke, / And I dropped down." She is here saying that she suffered a prostrating depressive illness which culminated in a loss of rationality.

It has been argued that the "I" in Emily Dickinson's poems does not refer to herself but, as she said, to a "supposed person." But the poem depicts not an event, which can easily be invented, but an experience. We must ask ourselves whether anyone, even a poet, can portray a feeling state that he has not himself undergone. And if one grant that this is possible, what could possibly motivate a person to attempt to express what he never felt? It may be replied that Emily Dickinson knew what ordinary depressions were and may even have had some acquaintance with severe neurotic ones and that, drawing on such experiences, she could imaginatively have extrapolated and projected the psychotic intensification of depression that is expressed in the poem. However, the intense depersonalization expressed in the phrase "I thought – / My Mind was going numb" and the sense of estrangement conveyed by the image of the universe resonating

---

continuum from a hypothetical completely "normal" extreme to a hypothetical completely disorganized extreme. An individual's position, which may continually shift along the scale, is determined by the degree to which his thought, feeling, and behavior are disorganized by stressful life situations. "Neurosis," nearer the "normal" end, implies hampering and rigid ego defenses, a strong capacity for repression, and the maintenance of contact with what is ordinarily called reality. "Psychosis" involves a diminished capacity for repression, an uneasy and potentially disorganizing openness to unconscious processes, and weak, unstable, or extreme defenses which, to varying degrees, call for a sacrifice in reality contact. Though points as they approach the disorganized end of the scale are traditionally and loosely called "illnesses," the present state of psychiatric knowledge does not justify regarding either neurosis or psychosis as a disease entity.

with the poet's projected despair like a mighty tolling bell convey an intensity of disintegration and a confounding of inner experiences with outer reality which reflect a profound insight into the specific pain of the psychotic state. Where could this insight have come from if not from Emily Dickinson's own inner life? The simplest and most natural explanation is that in this poem Emily Dickinson is talking about herself, that she is describing a real experience which actually happened to her, and that, in the line "And then a Plank in Reason, broke," she is revealing that she had been the victim of a psychological crisis that was not an ego-sparing and relatively benign neurosis, but a reason-disrupting, prostrating psychosis.

Poem no. 937 (about 1864) gives further support to this conclusion in the perfection of its description of a psychotic thought disorder. The poem reads:

> I felt a Cleaving in my Mind –
> As if my Brain had split –
> I tried to match it – Seam by Seam –
> But could not make them fit.
>
> The thought behind, I strove to join
> Unto the thought before –
> But Sequence ravelled out of Sound
> Like Balls – upon a Floor.

Here, directly and without equivocation, the poet discloses her awareness that her thinking has become disordered. Her mind feels "split"; she has an urgent need to reestablish the broken continuity of her intellectual processes. She vainly invokes conscious effort to correct and order the play of mental operations that ordinarily proceed spontaneously and effortlessly. Thought now follows thought without the usual connecting links, seemingly arbitrarily and incoherently. She strives to join one idea to another, but all sense of logical sequence is gone and she is unable to restore it by an act of will. The final two lines are obscure and one cannot be certain what image the poet had in mind. The obscurity may even be deliberate and meant as a graphic demonstration of the ambiguity and confusion produced by the deranged mental functioning.

A popular interpretation is that the "Balls" upon the "Floor" create an image of confusion—with balls of yarn dropped and rolling in all directions and becoming hopelessly entangled, rather like a "snarl in the brain." But balls of yarn do not unravel; they unwind, and they make no sound, which in the poem is said to be unraveled of sequence. "Sequence ravelled out of Sound" therefore may possibly mean that the regular patterns of thought construction and their vocal expression became disrupted, lost their normal rhythm, and trailed off into silence like the sound a ball makes when dropped on a floor: the ball strikes the floor, bounces in ever-diminishing oscillations until the sounds of impact crowd together, lose their intensity, and dwindle into silence. Whether or not either reading is correct, the intent of the poem is clear; it confesses that the poet reached a point at which she was no longer in command of her thought processes.

The foregoing references—the snarl in the brain, the broken plank in reason, and the cleavage in the mind—appear to be sufficient justification in themselves for concluding that the crisis in Emily Dickinson's life was a psychosis. With this conclusion as guide I will examine, solely as psychological documents, other poems, my aim being a deepened understanding of the poet's inner life.

In the preceding chapter, beginning with the simplest non-specific depressions and anxieties, I traced in her letters the emotional repercussions of Emily Dickinson's life situation and inferred the progression of these reactions to ever more highly elaborated, idiosyncratic, and crippling symptoms. It is not surprising that the poems, intrinsically more self-revelatory than the letters, provide further evidence of the same psychological trends. Although many of the poems reflect commonplace emotional states, others clearly communicate anguished and broken reactions to markedly adverse situations. These portray the ego in collapse, crushed between irreconcilable opposing forces: on one side, prodigious inner needs, on the other, unyielding environmental facts. These poems have almost no existing prose counterparts. They uniquely reveal a height of turmoil and phychic disintegration only obscurely adumbrated in the remainder of our biographical sources.

In my analysis no effort will be made to review the poems in the chronological order of their composition. Instead, they will be arranged in a sequence that corresponds to the gradually developing clinical picture of an actual psychotic illness. What justifies this approach is the fact that it is the only way to render the process understandable. Also, for my purposes, the chronology of composition is more or less irrelevant: A large percent of Emily Dickinson's poems could not have been written at the time the poet was living through the circumstances they depict. Obviously, a person depressed to the point of immobility, or one whose thought processes are unable to follow a rational sequence, cannot write a coherent poem. Emily Dickinson's poems are, almost without exception, perfectly coherent. Therefore, the poems evoked by her illness must largely have been written in retrospect. Moreover, there is no reason to believe that in composing the poems delineating her breakdown the poet necessarily followed the same order in which the symptoms actually presented themselves. A further reason for disregarding chronology is that the creation of most of the poems under consideration occurred within a two- or three-year period—not a long interval in a psychiatric illness.

What I shall attempt is a reconstruction of the phases of Emily Dickinson's illness from the point of view of its phenomenology. The underlying dynamics leading to the illness have been covered in preceding chapters. Here I am concerned only with the form the illness took and the sequence of clinical appearances it presented—that is, the way the poet herself felt her illness, comprehended it, and recorded it.

Psychosis, or the breaking down of the sense of reality, consists in the encroachment upon consciousness of desires, memories, fears, and former states of the personality that are ordinarily unconscious—the eruption of unconscious life into the field of consciousness and the confusion and disorganization that ensues.

Let me start with the early harbingers of illness as well as with certain premonitions and predispositions of the poet that existed before her emotional and psychic disturbance became manifest. A precarious psychological state at this time, though subjectively intense, would not have been such as to command the attention of others. It appears unlikely, for example, that Emily Dickinson's parents, in the early stages of her illness, would have been aware of its potential seriousness. For the same reason, many of the poems reviewed and interpreted in the next few pages may not impress one as unduly ominous.

As I have noted, Emily Dickinson's earliest distress consisted of simple depression. Her letters and poems indicate that her illness began with feelings of sadness that gradually increased in intensity. Some cherished dream had to be relinquished and was replaced by a feeling of despair. She mourned the loss of her hopes with accumulating vehemence and desolation. Probably it was in the later phases of this period of deepening melancholy that the earliest prodromal manifestations of her breakdown occurred.

The early stages of her depression were deceptively mild. In poem no. 111 (about 1859) the poet contemplates the joy and friendliness of nature and asks herself why she has feelings of sadness: "Wherefore mine eye thy silver mists . . . ?" In no. 353 (about 1862) she describes the deliberate forcing of a smile, the careful preparation of a happy facade for the purpose of deceiving others and hiding the misery inside. The same kind of smiling depression is presented in no. 514 (about 1862), in which she speaks of a woman's smile as being painful to see because one knew that it was erected to disavow and conceal a mortal wound.

Depressive reactions foreboding a psychotic outcome are almost invariably accompanied by feelings of remorse and guilt and a sense of unworthiness sometimes so all-encompassing that suicide may seem to be the only appropriate recourse. In poem 744 (about 1863) the poet tells of being haunted by guilt at the memory of "Departed Acts," and she calls her condition the "Adequate of Hell." The poem goes on to speak of the soul's past as being illuminated with a match, as if it were something unwholesome and sinister, hidden in a cellar. The same theme appears in poem 753 (about 1863), in which the poet speaks of quailing before the accusations and disdain of her soul, which she finds more painful to endure than "a finger of Enamelled Fire." Again in no. 1598 (about 1884) "Conscience" is represented as seeking her pillow at night, questioning " 'Did you' or 'Did you not' " and threatening damnation and hell, "the Phosphorus of God."

Either in her depression or in the subsequent phase of impending reality severance with its attendant panic, Emily Dickinson seems to have contemplated suicide. Such a measure is, of course, familiar to everyone as a consequence of depression. It is less well known that self-destruction may commonly be resorted to as a final desperate effort to escape the terror that accompanies a threatened personality disintegration in psychosis. The Dickinson poems that deal with the suicide theme are exclusively depressive in nature. If such a means of deliverance occurred to her at the height of her break with reality, she did not record the fact.

A kind of romantic languor invests certain of the early suicide poems. In no. 50 (about 1858) she writes as one who, having decided to die, contemplates the things she will miss and wonders what will be the reaction of her environment, including her family, to her death.

In no. 51 (about 1858) she describes a cemetery. She says that when she passed by it as a girl she did not know the year of her death. The implication is that she now knows when this event will take place. The poem concludes with a message to a female loved one to the effect that the poet will wait for her in the grave and will welcome her when the beloved herself dies.

In another poem, no. 146 (about 1859), the poet wonders if anyone would care if "On such a night" a "little figure" (presumably herself) should slip from its chair and lie "Too sound asleep." She then paints a picture of the busyness of life and reflects that all activities and aspirations have a common goal— the "little knoll" in the graveyard. None of these poems have great power and they seem to represent a sentimental toying with the idea of self-destruction at times of mild depression.

Perhaps, as no. 1692 (undated) suggests, the poet once actually attempted suicide. Here she speaks of the difficulty of asserting one's "right to perish" because the "Universe" will do all it can to thwart the effort.

A common theme of nineteenth-century romanticism is the fantasy of the reunion of sundered lovers beyond the grave. In no. 277 (about 1861) Emily Dickinson considers the implications of not awaiting a natural death. What if she should kill herself, she asks ("burst the fleshly Gate"), to be with her beloved? The reward, according to the poem, consists in being beyond the reach of the pains and frustrations of earth, whose clamor would then be meaningless to her.

More somber and suggestive of an earnestness lacking in the poems are some of the prose comments on the theme of suicide. In an 1877 letter Emily alludes to Austin's unhappiness in his marriage, speaks of his insomnia, and concludes shrewdly, "Sorrow is unsafe when it is real sorrow."[2] What worries her seems to be her belief, drawn from her experience of years before, that grief is a menace because it makes the thought of suicide enticing. Similarly, following a long silence on Higginson's part after his wife's death, Emily grew worried and wrote, "I cannot resist to write again, to ask if you are safe? Danger is not at first, for then we are unconscious, but in the after—slower—Days."[3] And to her cousin Louise Norcross she expresses consolation for some sorrow and implies that once she too had felt an impulse to die, "when rallying requires more effort than to dissolve life, and death looks choiceless."[4] And in the following undated fragment, the designated experience in which "Life stands straight," though not clearly grief, must be that or some similar reaction of profound shock or dismay, for its menace is similar. "'Tis a dangerous moment for any one," she writes, "when the meaning goes out of things and Life stands straight—and punctual—and yet no contents come."[5]

Fortunately for American letters, Emily Dickinson braved out her despair and did not destroy herself to escape the frightful anxieties of psychological disorganization. To conceive and carry out a plan for self-destruction presupposes a certain degree of organization and available energy. The poems testify that when the poet's crisis came she was too prostrated by it to be able to implement such an escape, even if that is what she had desired. The early stages of her depression were apparently not unbearable. But the depressive symptoms gradually became mixed with more malignant psychic processes.

The earliest subjective experiences of an impending psychotic episode may be transient and minor breaks with reality that occur suddenly and persist only for a few seconds or minutes. These minor estrangements and depersonalizations are almost invariably concomitants of severe depressive states and in themselves do not necessarily presage a psychosis. Yet every psychotic episode probably gives advance notice of its imminent arrival through increasingly severe and protracted experiences of estrangement and depersonalization, such as I have noted in Emily Dickinson's letters. The poet has also given numerous vivid descriptions of them in her poems. For one lacking her expressive genius the essence of these experiences is extremely difficult to convey in words.

Paul Ferdern, a close friend and pupil of Freud, was one of the first psychoanalysts to concern himself with these phenomena. Regarding the experience of depersonalization, he wrote, "we all know the earnest, and always somewhat uncanny, complaints with which severe cases of depersonalization describe their condition or rather their changing condition. The outer world appears substantially unaltered, but yet different; not so spontaneously, so actually, near or far; not clear, warm, friendly and familiar; not really and truly existing and alive; more as if in a dream and yet different from a dream. At heart the patient feels as if he were dead; and he feels like this because he does not feel. His feeling, wishing, thinking and memory processes have become different, uncertain, intolerably changed. And yet the patient knows everything correctly, his faculties of perception, of intellect, and of logic have not suffered at all . . . time, place and causality are recognized and properly applied in finding one's bearings, but they are not possessed spontaneously and self evidently."[6] When Emily Dickinson wrote: "I heard, as if I had no Ear," and "I saw, as if my Eye were on Another," and "I dwelt, as if Myself were out" (poem no. 1039, about 1865), she was probably recollecting an experience similar to the ones described by Federn.

The merging of Emily Dickinson's depressive symptoms into episodes of severe estrangement is clearly traceable. Although she seems at times to have thought that her despair dropped upon her with catastrophic suddenness, the letters and the poems reveal an insidious onset. The depressed moods she has recorded swelled gradually from mild loneliness and melancholy to crushing agony and frustration. The onset of a relentless state of estrangement seems to have been a feature of the depths of this depression.

The psychoanalyst Marguerite Sechehaye described the symptom of estrangement in her interpretive supplement to the *Autobiography of a Schizophrenic Girl*. The body of the book was written by Madame Sechehaye's patient Renée following her recovery after years of intensive full-time care in the therapist's home. Madame Sechehaye writes, "Renée's introspection reveals that the earliest disturbing subjective symptom bears uniquely on the perception of reality. Suddenly objects become enormous, cut off, detached, without relation to one another; space appears limitless . . . Normally the world of objects is perceived on a relative scale, each thing in its allotted space, coordinated by angles of vision. Each object is perceived in its relation to another, and in relation to the ground on which it stands. Further, a utilitarian function is attributed to seen objects: a chair is used to sit on. [In states of estrangement] objects no longer appear in inter-individual relationships. The spaces separating and arranging them on different planes are eliminated. This is why each object appears as a whole in itself, cut away, detached, larger than life, and why space seems limitless, without depth or control, without the successive planes lending a third dimension . . . In proportion as Renée loses subjective self-awareness, she increasingly localizes her feelings in things. The boundaries separating the inner world of thinking from the outer world of reality shade off, then fade out. Objects are alive, they become threatening, they sneer, they torment her."[7]

Renée describes one of her own experiences of estrangement thus: "One day, while I was in the principal's office, suddenly the room became enormous . . . Everything was exact, smooth, artificial, extremely tense; the chairs and tables seemed models placed here and there. Pupils and teachers were puppets revolving without cause, without objective. It was as though reality, attenuated, had slipped away from all these things and these people. Profound dread overwhelmed me, and as though lost, I looked around desperately for help. I heard people talking but I did not grasp the meaning of the words. The voices were metallic, without warmth or color."[8] When Emily Dickinson writes, "I clutched at sounds – / I groped at shapes – / I touched the tops of Films – / I felt the Wilderness roll back / Along my Golden lines" (no. 430, about 1862), she appears to be describing an experience very much like Renée's. The poem projects a desperate need to hold onto reality, which has become tenuous and impoverished. The sounds and shapes of the active, real world are slipping through her fingers; her senses no longer put her in contact with the living world, now hazy and without substance. The familiar environment, transformed and estranged, becomes an uninhabited wasteland. In four lines the poet has given us a powerful recreation of an experience of intense estrangement.

Emily Dickinson's repeatedly used symbols, the sea and the volcano, were eminently appropriate for expressing the encroaching menace of her mental illness. The inner transformations that lead to the breakdown of rational thought and reality contact generate two fears: (1) that one will lose control over one's erotic and destructive impulses; and (2) that one's unique and separate mental existence will undergo disintegration in a psychic death. The first of these is related to the "volcano poems," the second, to those concerned with the sea.

It has been stated previously that a psychosis is a process in which instinctual and repressed elements of the psyche, ordinarily unconscious, burst into consciousness, destroying the integrity of the personality. Environmental stresses combined with constitutional predispositions precipitate this breakthrough. It results in the ego's yielding its autonomy before the pressures of previously subjugated destructive and sexual impulses to such an extent that the ego no longer controls them, at which point they erupt into waking life like burning lava. In the most benign of the "volcano poems" (no. 1748, undated) the poet remarks, in images of a slumbering volcano, on the inscrutable reticence of nature, which keeps its plan for destructiveness a secret. Then she speculates upon the possible reasons why human nature cannot do the same. In poem no. 1705 (undated) she wryly remarks that she need not travel to view a volcano—that one may be contemplated at home. It has been said that in this poem she alludes to her father's red hair and fiery personality, but other "volcano poems" suggest a degree of potential destructiveness that she would have been unlikely to ascribe consciously to her father. For example, no. 175 (about 1860) states that great inner pain and destructiveness ("Fire, and smoke, and gun") may be long concealed, and the features of one's face may not for some time betray the violence that smolders within. The final stanzas of this poem reveal uncertainty regarding the security of this control. She asks: What if the forces of creativity and the nurturing of life ("Vineyard") are overthrown? Can there afterwards be a resurrection of sanity and peace?

The inner potential for bursting controls, symbolized by Vesuvius, is recognized in poem no. 601 (about 1862) as characteristic of a passionate few. "Natures this side Naples" remain unaware of the latent upheaval that others conceal within themselves.

Another poem, no. 1677 (undated), expresses the same general idea:

> On my volcano grows the Grass –
> A meditative spot –
> An acre for a Bird to choose
> Would be the General thought –
>
> How red the Fire rocks below –
> How insecure the sod
> Did I disclose
> Would populate with awe my solitude

Emily Dickinson believed that if her family knew how little her calm exterior revealed the true state of turmoil within her and how brittle her control really was, they would have consigned her to a solitude complete except for "awe."

In addition to the "volcano poems," many others testify that Emily Dickinson found her psychic equilibrium extremely difficult to maintain. No. 530 (early 1862) may be interpreted as expressing the idea that the instinctual drives and pressures of the unconscious are impossible to contain: the fire "You cannot put . . . out," the flood "You cannot fold" and "put in a Drawer" in that poem can be regarded as symbols of erotic and destructive impulses. In no. 576 (about 1862) the poet reflects on the comforts that religion might have offered her had she retained her childhood faith. She then proceeds to describe her intense feelings of insecurity and imbalance:

> And often since, in Danger,
> I count the force 'twould be
> To have a God so strong as that
> To hold my life for me
>
> Till I could take the Balance
> That tips so frequent, now,
> It takes me all the while to poise –
> And then – it does'nt stay –

The poet's disturbance, manifested by gradually increasing depression, fears that latent forbidden impulses were in danger of imminent eruption, and the feeling of precarious psychological equilibrium, ultimately took on aspects of a more serious disorder. As has been mentioned, one of the ego characteristics of the potential or borderline psychotic is that he, unlike the normal or neurotic person, has an awareness of the unconscious forces that underlie his illness. That is to say, the forces are no longer unconscious. Indeed, his consciousness is flooded with material that his previous relatively stable state had repressed, and such a situation is the hallmark of a psychotic illness.

The "sea poems," in contrast with the "volcano poems," are not related to fears that one's potential violence might evade control and endanger others. Here the anxiety is related to an inner threat to one's self—to one's psychic integrity. In the normal personality in the waking state there exists a feeling of continuity of bodily and mental reactions and relations that we think of as our inner selves. One's thinking processes—memories, sensory impressions—and one's characteristic reactions and relationships with others—in short, all the conscious and preconscious operations of our psychological lives—are enveloped and integrated within this feeling of personal continuity. The rest of the world is separate and distinct from ourselves. There exists a feeling of a frontier at which the heterogeneous external world stops and our personal, integrated inner world begins. Psychoanalytic terminology speaks of an "ego boundary" separating us from all that is not ourselves. It is important to note that this feeling of the circumscribed extension of our inner life into time and space and its impenetrability and separateness is an *ego* feeling; it does not invest the unconscious operations of the id—the primitive drives and all the memories and experiences that have been repressed from awareness or have never been conscious. The inner core of the feeling of one's unique existence and physical and mental discreteness therefore excludes one whole area of psychic life—the unconscious.

The ego feeling is so much taken for granted by the healthy personality that one's attention is rarely directed to it. It permeates all that transpires in one's waking mind with the unreflecting certitude that these are *my* thoughts, *my* waking consciousness. A sense of separateness from the external world of these inner operations is felt with great security. It is taken for granted that what is outside is real and not a part of one's self. The major premise of our rational lives is based on this elementary distinction between self and non-self—on the intactness and maintenance of this certain feeling of having a securely bounded ego. As Paul Federn says, "The basis of sanity is correct and automatic recognition of this breach between subjective mental individual experiences in the world and the knowledge of the status of the world that actually exists. Sanity means dealing with the world and with one's self with the faculty of distinguishing clearly between them."[9] When Emily Dickinson says, "A Plank in Reason, broke," and she felt herself dropping into a chasm of "Finished knowing," she appears to be describing the sensation of one experiencing a sudden loss of ego boundaries—the "plank" that supports one's conscious and rational psychological life gives way and plunges one into an awful abyss in which the external world and the inner unconscious, both equally "not me", have become difficult to distinguish from one another.

To be submerged, drowned in a vast sea, lost, alone, hopeless— this is the subject of many Dickinson poems. The sea, a most important and frequent symbol, is used to represent many different experiences, for example: the loss of one's self in death (no. 30, about 1858); the separation from security and safety and the sense of being isolated from others (no. 48, about 1858, and no. 905, about 1864); the feeling of being lost in a vast, uncharted, unknown expanse (no. 52, about 1858); the exultation of escape from the mundane and limiting—the afflatus of creativity (no. 76, about 1859); the loss of one's individual identity through absorption or fusion with another person (no. 162, about 1860); a complete abandonment of one's self through erotic passions (no. 249, about 1861); or the buffeting of violent emotions (no. 368, about 1862). These divergent experiences, all appropriately symbolized in various ways by images of the sea, are depicted as pleasurable when the self is imagined as merging with a larger, security-providing, beneficent reality, and as unpleasurable when the larger reality in which the self is immersed carries the connotations of loneliness, isolation, or turbulent chaos. The common denominator in all these "sea poems," however, regardless of the pleasurability of the feeling, is the poet's experience of a diffusion of herself—of the blurring of her own boundaries until she becomes lost in the infinite or expands into infinity herself.

One may recognize in these poems the weakening of ego

boundaries that has been discussed earlier as a prerequisite of psychosis. Just as Emily Dickinson's "volcano poems" depict the pressure of emotional forces within the personality—the threat of eruptive violence versus the effort to control and repress these forces—so the "sea poems" depict other predispositions for the same process of psychotic breakdown. In these latter poems the danger with which the poet is concerned is not that presented to others through her latent destructiveness, but that which is felt as a threatened dispersal of the integrity of her own personality.

It should be pointed out that not every experience of a loosening of ego boundaries is indicative of serious mental disorder. Normal persons may have the sensation when thrilled by any of the arts—especially, perhaps, music. The experience may be found in the contemplation of nature—a starry night, for example, or a startling panoramic view. "Breathtaking" is a word often applied to pleasurable experiences in which the ego undergoes a sudden expansion. A partial loss of ego boundary occurs also at the moment of orgasm. Perhaps this is one reason that some persons, aware of a psychotic propensity within themselves, will avoid sexual intercourse; being frightened of their increasing inability to distinguish the processes within their own minds from what is happening in the outer world, they become fearful of anything that weakens their already enfeebled sense of psychic separateness.

Emily Dickinson both courted and feared this experience of ego expansion and weakeneing of psychological boundaries. She recognized true poetry because it evoked this reaction: "If I feel physically as if the top of my head were taken off, I know *that* is poetry."[10] Yet her "sea poems" are often full of dread. It would appear that she was well aware that unless one kept one's guard up the unconscious was likely to trespass. Poem no. 520 (about 1862) is an interesting demonstration of this insight:

> I started Early – Took my Dog –
> And visited the Sea –
> The Mermaids in the Basement
> Came out to look at me –
>
> And Frigates – in the Upper Floor
> Extended Hempen Hands –
> Presuming Me to be a Mouse –
> Aground –upon the Sands –

But no Man moved Me – till theTide
Went past my simple Shoe –
And past my Apron – and my Belt
And past my Boddice – too –

And made as He would eat me up –
As wholly as a Dew
Upon a Dandelion's Sleeve –
And then – I started – too –

And He – He followed – close behind –
I felt His Silver Heel
Upon my Ancle – then my Shoes
Would overflow with Pearl –

Until We met the Solid Town –
No One He seemed to know –
And bowing – with a Mighty look –
At me – The Sea withdrew –

The poet here says that she started out casually and "visited the Sea"—in other words, she focused her attention on her deepest and most inward psychic processes. "The Mermaids in the Basement" then came out to look at her—that is, psychic curiosities and fantasy creatures appeared—and the poem indicates that she was not alarmed by this sudden appearance. "Frigates in the Upper Floor," presuming her to be stranded and in trouble, offer her rope so she can come aboard. The "Frigates" may be interpreted as representing the ego defenses that are alarmed by this dallying with the unconscious. They offer her a solid deck of reality before she is engulfed. The poem relates how the poet ignores the warnings and in her innocence is almost submerged before she realizes what is happening. She becomes aware of the possibility of imminent drowning—inundation by the unconscious and the instinctual drives, especially, in this poem, the erotic ones: "the tide . . . made as He would eat me up." The ego defenses are at last heeded and the poet beats a panicky retreat from the unconscious. She returns to reality, "the Solid Town" so unlike the fluid fantasies of the id.*

* Clark Griffith, in *The Long Shadow: Emily Dickinson's Tragic Poetry* (Princeton, Princeton University Press, 1964), pp. 18-24, offers an excellent analysis of the poem's erotic implications. My identification of the personality components with which the poem deals is perfectly compatible with his interpretation.

With the sea representing the vast unconscious (in terms of "infinity," "immensity," "tremendousness," and so on) and drowning in it representing the loss of one's psychic integrity in psychosis, the image of the boat becomes an appropriate means of delineating the ego which rides separate and distinct upon the surface of the id.

A strange little poem (no. 107, about 1859), possibly expressive of this ego-id relationship, speaks of a little boat seduced to its destruction by a seemingly gallant sea. The poem gives no clue to what catastrophe the poet had in mind—perhaps consciously she was merely referring here to a dashed hope. In no. 30 (about 1858) it is clear that the little boat represents a life; it sinks beneath the waves of death, but from an angel's vantage point its destination is heaven. In no. 48 (about 1858), the poet is "at sea," troubled and questioning and telling her soul that "Land" may still exist.

None of these and similar poems taken individually can be given a definitive interpretation. However, in the context of the poet's entire oeuvre plus all available biographical information, they reflect her preoccupation with that fragile craft—her conscious rational mental life—riding on a vast, formless, elemental power—the unconscious instinctual drives. Even when the theme takes the form of the soul's confrontation with eternity, it seems likely that the terms of the problem—survival or dissolution, life or death, haven or desolation—reflect not only the poet's philosophical speculations but also, on another level, her uneasy awareness of the precariousness of her sanity.

It may appear paradoxical that the same symbol—the sea—can refer equally to two seemingly opposite psychic states. On the one hand, it denotes the miseries of trackless isolation, on the other (as in poems 249, 212, and 162), to the union with the beloved. However, there is no real contradiction. One's sense of individual identity is lost when unconscious material (which is devoid of ego feeling) is projected to the external world. This causes the world to appear strange and alien and produces a feeling of uncertainty as to what is within and what without. A sense of separate existence can be lost equally when the tenuousness of the ago boundaries allows a fusion of one's identity with that of another person.

Clinical experience offers frequent examples of this phenomenon. In such *folie à deux,* the victims, most frequently a mother and daughter, experience themselves as one person. They so confound their past and present lives that neither knows for certain whether any single event has befallen herself or the other. So intimate is this fusion that when hospitalization brings about a separation each may feel that she herself has died, and it is a therapeutic necessity to arrange frequent meetings to reassure each other of the other's (and therefore her own) continuing existence.

Of course this extreme situation is the end point of certain compelling needs that in other persons merely tend in the direction of the psychological union with another. The full-blown psychotic process of fusion can occur only when both individuals have an irresistible impulse to merge, an impulse which seems to reflect a need for a security and strength that neither can find alone. When Emily Dickinson writes (no. 284)

> The Drop, that wrestles in the Sea –
> Forgets her own locality –
> As I – toward Thee –

she reveals a susceptibility to the kind of total immersion of identity described above. Though the word "wrestles" suggests an opposing impulse to retain separateness, the sum effect is an impression of the poet's readiness for intense identification and her awareness of ego boundaries that were at times unduly fluid.

Such fluidity or flexibility of ego boundaries, though psychologically perilous, may from the viewpoint of an artist be of inestimable value. Creative artists, without necessarily being psychotic, characteristically have an intuitive grasp of unconscious dynamisms without being overpowered by the unconscious forces —the raw instincts, conflicts, and forbidden impulses. The creative artist with his ego still rational, intact, and in contact with reality can tolerate a certain amount of inspection of this dangerous and ordinarily prohibited territory. It is as though his ego were more tolerant, more flexible, less easily alarmed than those of the ordinary person or the neurotic, whose egos maintain a constant rigid guard against the id. The artist, in contrast, appears to be able to turn to the dark places of his own mind for material for his art and bend the inner enemy to his own purposes.

Emily Dickinson's poetry affords us an outstanding example of the artistic use of psychodynamic insight, much of which was undoubtedly a combined product of extraordinary poetic gifts and intrepid self-confrontation. Some of it, one suspects, was also the result of her experience of, and reflections upon, the flooding of her personality by unconscious processes during a psychotic illness. The "sea poems," in conveying a sense of immersion in a vast and foreign element, probably to some degree derived from this aspect of her experience.

Poem no. 1225 (about 1872), though not one of her "sea poems," suggests that the poet was aware of processes within herself that even an artist has no business knowing.

> It's Hour with itself
> The Spirit never shows.
> What Terror would enthrall the Street
> Could Countenance disclose
>
> The Subterranean Freight
> The Cellars of the Soul –
> Thank God the loudest Place he made
> Is licensed to be still.

The poem says that the deepest self-knowledge must be hidden from the view of others. It is obvious from the context that the kind of self-knowledge referred to is not the self-awareness that a realistic person builds up through self-observation and ordinary introspection. It is not a continuous process but instead a kind of insight that occurs only at intervals: the spirit's "Hour with itself." The poem says that the knowledge is felt as a burden ("Freight") and associated with dark, hidden, buried, and perhaps unwholesome things (symbolized by the words "Subterranean" and "Cellars of the Soul"). The poet reacts to what she encounters at these times as to something overwhelmingly impelling and commanding of attention; she calls it the "loudest Place" that God has made. The poem concludes with the observation that should this knowledge be made known to others they would be appalled. What would most likely thus "enthrall" and terrify "the Street"? Most probably those propensities of the dark and troublesome side of human nature associated with sexuality, madness, and murder as they are manifested as agents of the unconscious. The poet herself, one suspects, was enthralled by them and terrified as well.

Another poem (no. 1203, late 1871) reveals Emily Dickinson's awareness that one's past experiences are never dead and buried once and for all. Instead the influence of the experiences remains alive within us and is capable of exerting an effect on the present. Sometimes, according to this poem, a recurrence of memory induces pleasure, sometimes disgrace. The final stanza, "Unarmed if any meet her [the Past] / I charge him fly / Her Faded Ammunition / Might yet reply," might be paraphrased in psychodynamic terms thus: Should the past be revived as one's defenses —that is, repressions—become inoperable ("Unarmed"), one would be confronted with a dangerous situation best avoided ("I charge him fly"); for the past and influences of the past are invested with the potentiality for violence, capable of destroying the present. The poem offers a clear exposition of the hazardous state of one whose consciousness is faced with a return of the repressed, a situation that obtains most painfully during the early stages of a psychotic illness.

Emily Dickinson's awareness that a glimpse into the hidden depths of personality should be avoided because it exposes one to the danger of being overwhelmed is also expressed in poem no. 1182 (1871), similar to that above. It compares "Remembrance" (by which we may understand all the stored residues, conscious and unconscious, of one's past experience) with a house that has a "Rear," a "Front," a "Garret" containing "Refuse" and a "Mouse," and "the deepest Cellar." Paraphrased, the poem reads: Some memories can be reviewed openly and publicly ("Front" of the house), others are more private—perhaps reserved for one's family or one's self ("Rear" of the house). Other memories are inconsequential and trivial and like refuse accumulate in stored nooks in the mind ("a Garret"), where they may be allied with discreditable memories akin to vermin and unclean things ("a Mouse"). The "Garret" and "Mouse" are Emily Dickinson's symbols for what in psychoanalytic terms would correspond to the suppressed and the denied. These are contents of the mind that are preconscious, that is, they are accessible to consciousness should one choose to focus attention on them. However, because of their unpleasant nature the personality tends to avoid dwelling on them and in a sense denies their existence.

Then there is the deep and hidden abyss of the mind whose contents are to be guarded against lest they overwhelm one

". . . the deepest Cellar / That ever Mason laid – / Look to it by its Fathoms / Ourselves be not pursued." This stanza refers to the unconscious and the most deeply buried and fearful things of the past, which must remain unconscious if the repressed is not to return and overtake one in psychosis.

Emily Dickinson has written several other poems in which aspects of the personality are likened to a house with many compartments, but none more strikingly reveals her awareness of the stirring of disavowed memories and threatening unconscious propensities than the one beginning "One need not be a Chamber – to be Haunted" (no. 670, 1862). Here she tells us that the psyche has "Corridors" that are "Haunted" with a ghost that is more to be feared than any real "Assassin"—that is, the unconscious may threaten to overflow into consciousness in psychosis, bringing with it a feeling of terror and imminent dissolution.

Evidence of Emily Dickinson's unusual awareness of psychic processes that ordinarily go unnoticed by the mass of mankind can be found on almost every page of her writings. One might justifiably assert that such observations constitute a major portion of her subject matter. Moreover, her formulations of her other major themes—death, love, and nature—in addition to the philosophical and externally descriptive characteristics they possess, are almost invariably colored and livened by psychological insight. This penetrating subjectivity lends depth and fascination to her work regardless of the ostensible subject matter. It would appear, however, that these qualities were dearly bought at the expense of emotional balance and inner security. The ego flexibility and tolerance of the artist that enriched and deepened her poetic gifts appears also, in Emily Dickinson, to have been an ego weakness carrying with it a perilous vulnerability to psychic disorganization.

A weakened ego in thrall to unconscious processes, depression, estrangement, and depersonalization, anxiety that violent impulses could no longer be contained, and feelings of being adrift in a void—these predispositions and premonitory symptoms inexorably ushered in the psychotic climax. In poem no. 1123 (about 1868) she writes:

> A great Hope fell
> You heard no noise
> The Ruin was within

Oh cunning wreck that told no tale
And let no Witness in

A cherished dream has evidently collapsed and now lies in silent ruins within the poet's mind, unsuspected by her environment. The next stanza tells of her difficulty in understanding her loss:

The mind was built for mighty Freight
For dread occasion planned
How often foundering at Sea
Ostensibly, on Land

Here again the mind is likened to a ship which feels itself in imminent danger of being swallowed up by a sea of emotions evoked by the crash of her hopes.

Despair now becomes complete and overwhelming and the poet's ego undergoes increasing disorganization. In poem no. 378 (about 1862) she describes the condition of utter psychological collapse:

I saw no Way – The Heavens were stitched –
I felt the Columns close –
The Earth reversed her Hemispheres –
I touched the Universe –

And back it slid – and I alone –
A Speck upon a Ball –
Went out upon Circumference –
Beyond the Dip of Bell –

At this point the "Plank in Reason" broke. The poem tells us that happiness and religious reassurance (heaven) were denied her and that there seemed no way out of the dilemma that faced her. Even the familiar consolations and pursuits of ordinary life ("Earth") became distorted and psychologically unavailable. The whole universe appeared to evade her perception and opened out into an enormous void. She felt alone, stranded, the only discrete speck of consciousness upon a planet ("Ball") that swam in nothingness. Then her consciousness itself eddied out into the void and was lost to itself and submerged too deeply in infinity and boundlessness to be summoned by any signal from reality ("Beyond the Dip of Bell").

Probably when Emily Dickinson wrote her cryptic letter to

T. W. Higginson saying she "had a terror—since September—I could tell to none,"[11] she was alluding to a recurrence or foreboding of an illness such as this. Anyone who has once witnessed this terrible sundering of the personality's connection with reality will never forget it. When the severance is relatively sudden, as appears to be the case with Emily Dickinson, and not a gradual slipping away, the experience is probably the most terrifying one that can befall a human being. Contrary to general belief, the person undergoing a psychotic break with reality frequently realizes that he is the victim of a catastrophic alteration—not only of the world but of himself as well. He knows that everything seems changed, that his home and family and friends look different and seem to behave strangely; and, especially early in the illness, he may know that it is he himself and not the world that is no longer familiar. As the process of disorganization continues, the world appears more and more alien. Initially, only the person's curiosity may be aroused by intermittent false observations of minor and mysterious alterations in familiar things. A book, for example, may appear on the mantle when the person is certain that he just put it on the end table, or the cat may have a strange and *knowing* look on its face that is somehow disturbing. Soon, however, curiosity gives way to anxiety, which increases as the feeling of strangeness begins to pervade everything in the environment. The person may then fly to someone loved and trusted for protection and beg like a child to be soothed and comforted. In the ambience of a strong and warm personality the uncanny fears may disappear and the world may resume its former comfortable aspect. However, if the refuge he is trying to find becomes impossible because the loved one has also shared in the general alteration, his anxiety gives way to terror. The loved and trusted person may well act accepting and sympathetic, but the sufferer now senses his behavior only as acting. The feeling that the friend or relative is now somehow sinister is reinforced by the very "perfection" with which the friend goes through the expected and familiar gestures, now experienced as studied or simulated. Later all the family and friends begin to seem like imposters or robots and only the shell of the real world seems to remain. As with Renée, Madame Sechehaye's patient, everything that is perceived may come to seem suspended in a great vacuum. The feel-

313

ing of immense space may alternate with the feeling that all one observes is two-dimensional, like a motion picture that is plotless, meaningless, and flat.

The fear that is evoked at the onset of a psychotic breakdown is not due solely to the apprehension that one is suddenly in a new and unfathomable world. Such feelings are augmented by uncertainty, adumbrated in Emily Dickinson's "volcano poems," about one's ability to control bodily reactions and physical movements. The fear arises that one may do everything that one most dreads doing. The repressive powers of the ego are breaking down. Aggressive, destructive, and erotic impulses, formerly forbidden to consciousness by the conscience and sense of propriety, now command the center of awareness. Because such proscribed and denied impulses have, during health, remained unconscious, they have never been invested with the ego feeling that allows one to recognize one's inner thoughts and other mental operations as one's own. For this reason, they are perceived as an encroachment from outside, and the afflicted person feels in the control of an external and invisible power. A woman, for example, may feel that she is about to kill her beloved children despite all her efforts to prevent the terrible deed. In her desperation to safeguard them she may hide or discard all knives and scissors in the house. Or she may rush from the house or beg her family to tie her up or lock her in a room out of reach of her children.

The dread of impending loss of control may become unbearable. To ward off the dreaded act a person may throw himself violently into some substitute activity—anything, however unreasonable it may appear, to escape the demands of a destructive demon that seems to have taken hold of him. A man, for example, may attempt to exhaust himself breaking up furniture or smashing windows. Or he may get into his car and drive at top speed without having any destination in mind. Frequently, as a last resort, the victim may injure himself, sever his radial arteries or shoot himself, rather than be forced (as he experiences it) to injure his loved ones. Such persons fear their own murderous potentialities so greatly that they seek a jail cell or enter a seclusion room in a mental hospital with the greatest avidity. It is impressive to witness the relief such patients exhibit when they realize that external controls will be substituted for the inner ones they believe they have lost or are in danger of losing. (Fortunately those patients who actually lose control are few, and of those few a still smaller percentage are actually dangerous to others.)

Not uncommonly, victims of incipient ego breakdown are, despite their panic, rational and perfectly oriented to the environment. Hallucinations and systematized delusions are secondary effects of the primary breakdown and may appear only later as the illness progresses, or they may never appear—the broken ego boundaries may seal over, as it were, and the psychotic reaction subside. The answer to the question whether Emily Dickinson's breakdown included these dramatic derivatives of the primary loss of reality or whether she made a rapid recovery without progressing to them will be considered in later pages.

To summarize my hypothesis so far: Emily Dickinson's writings, taken in the aggregate, point to a break with reality that was the culminating point of a prodromal depressive reaction. With the abandoning of certain cherished hopes the depression deepened in severity until the poet was prostrated. Then, mingled with these feelings of hopeless misery, episodes of estrangement and depersonalization intervened, along with fears of losing impulse control. All these symptoms probably increased in duration and intensity until the breaking point was reached and the poet succumbed to a psychotic illness.

It would perhaps be appropriate to conclude this discussion of the prodromal period of Emily Dickinson's breakdown with a psychiatric analysis of one of her poems. Written when she was thirty-one or so, the following poem (no. 410, about 1862) recapitulates metaphorically the above summary:

> The first Day's Night had come –
> And grateful that a thing
> So terrible – had been endured –
> I told my Soul to sing –
>
> She said her Strings were snapt –
> Her Bow – to Atoms blown –
> And so to mend her – gave me work
> Until another Morn –
>
> And then – a Day as huge
> As Yesterdays in pairs,
> Unrolled it's horror in my face –
> Until it blocked my eyes –

My Brain – begun to laugh –
I mumbled – like a fool –
And tho' 'tis Years ago – that Day –
My Brain keeps giggling – still.

And Something's odd – within –
That person that I was –
And this One – do not feel the same –
Could it be Madness – this?

A "day" of extreme distress ended in a "night" of release or relief. Perhaps Emily Dickinson is referring here to an actual day on which a painful event had taken place. However, if the word is a metaphor, which is perhaps likely, it may stand for her entire waking life over a considerable period. Day is ordinarily a time when one confronts the material realities of one's life, as opposed to night, a time when one retreats through activities of progressively smaller scope and increasing subjectivity, ending finally in sleep. In this sense the "day" of the "terrible" "thing" may be the experience of confronting the altered and strange world of pre-psychosis with its attendant terrors. "Night" then is the release— the growing numb, the trance-like states, the stupors that Emily Dickinson tells of in so many places, all of them equivalent to the escape from reality and pain into sleep and dreaming.

To paraphrase the first three lines then: My first relief from the dreadful chaos of insanity had come. I retreated into myself and withdrew from the alien world, grateful that I had survived the experience.

In the next three lines the poet has a dialogue with her "Soul"— that is, her inner psychic self, her ego. She tells her soul to sing. For Emily Dickinson, to sing means to celebrate her poetic gift, to release her feelings in poetry. This is what she meant when she wrote to T. W. Higginson: "I had a terror—since September—I could tell to none—and *so I sing,* as the Boy does by the Burying Ground—because I am afraid."[12] However, her soul replies that she cannot express her feelings in song because her strings and bow are destroyed. The analogy here is to a frail violin, the broken instrument that accompanied the singing. (Emily Dickinson used the image of a violin in another poem, no. 635, about 1862, where she speaks of impatiently attending to some household duty so that she will be free to return to her poetry: to "take up my little Violin." The musical instrument probably represents all the equipment of sentiency, emotion, thought, intelligence, and craftsmanship that, in proper combination, are necessary for the creation of poetry.)

In line 7 of "The first Day's Night had come," she says that she sought occupation in repairing her poetic apparatus: "And so to mend her – gave me work." A patient in the state of convalescence or remission from a psychotic illness frequently evinces a compulsion to be kept busy, to seek the employment of his talents and skills. Such mental and physical activity appears to be a way of exercising the functions of the ego, of combatting the illness and regaining strength by putting one's energies into some task that occupies consciousness, as though to divert such energy away from unconscious processes. That Emily Dickinson discovered this method of self-therapy is attested to by several poems. In no. 443 (about 1862), for example, she says, "we do life's labor . . . With scrupulous exactness – / To hold our Senses – on"; and in no. 786: "Severer Service of myself – / I – hastened to demand . . . I worried Nature with my Wheels – / When Her's had ceased to run."

Line 8, "Until another Morn," tells us that Emily Dickinson's efforts to work off a recurrence of the ordeal that wracked her on the "previous day" were not successful and another "Morn" arrived—that is, according to my interpretation, another experience of psychotic "reality" came about.

The third stanza divulges what the new episode brought: "a Day as huge" as two of the preceding "days," in other words, an estrangement doubled in intensity and duration, an experience of a world much more alien or deeply altered, more threatening than before. Its "horror" "unrolls" before her, just as in poem no. 430 "a Wilderness roll[ed] back." It now seems clear that the "day" of stanza 1 was not one of stress merely because of some event. Painful happenings in the real world may render a particular day lastingly memorable as one of great tragedy or intense suffering, but they do not cause it to "unroll its horror" in one's face. The image of unrolling suggests that what is terrifying is not something that chances to take place—a combination of circumstances—but something that has been prepared in advance and has been lying latent. Once it begins to manifest itself, the process is a continuous confrontation of some duration, like a series of frightening pictures on a vast scroll that unwinds itself before one's eyes little by little. Again, this would seem an appropriate figure for the distorted perception of reality which occurs as the repressed returns in an incipient psychosis.

The last line of stanza 3, "Until it blocked my eyes," relates probably to a late feature of Emily Dickinson's illness—her eye difficulties, the discussion of which will be reserved for a later chapter.

The effects of this second experience of ego breakdown are described in the last two stanzas. Note that the first line of stanza 4 reads "My Brain," not *I*, "begun to laugh." The line portrays a division within the personality. Her reactions here appear to be fractionated; her sense of an integrated and harmonious self whose feelings and responses are invested with a sense of unity no longer seems to exist. The "horror" causes one portion of the ego's awareness to react with terrible inappropriateness while another portion splits away and watches the performance as though objectively. There is no mirth in hysterical laughter. It represents a loss of control, a diffuse motoric discharge that expresses disorganization.

Line 2 of stanza 4 describes a loss of control over the power of speech. Her words are no longer clearly articulated and she "mumbled – like a fool." Patients newly psychotic frequently mumble in an ineffectual compromise—first, to comply with the demands of social intercourse, which expects one to converse and answer questions, and second, to hide the fact that they themselves recognize that what they say is often bizarre or incoherent. It may appear incredible and shocking that Emily Dickinson with all her verbal gifts for a time could have suffered such a state, yet it is difficult to imagine an adequate alternative explanation for these lines.

The second two lines of stanza 4 tell us that this second terrible "day" was "Years" ago, but the sense of inner division and inappropriate affective response has continued, albeit somewhat diminished in intensity (giggling now in place of outright laughing). The "Years" need not be taken literally any more than the "day" or "night," for all of these words may be metaphors. Moreover, the sense of time may be involved equally with the sense of space during periods of estrangement. The déjà vu phenomenon, experienced by everyone at times, is an estrangement of time. Modifications of the déjà vu experience are characteristic of many pathological psychic conditions. Therefore, "years" may allude to the sense of temporal remoteness attached to the experience the poet is describing, and this may have little to do with the actual length of time that has elapsed since those experiences.

The final stanza expresses the poet's concern, based on an awareness of a profound inner alteration of herself, that she may be insane. Her former self and her present self "do not feel the same." The ego feeling that invests the operation of her mental life has been altered and the processes themselves lack unity and coordination. The poet's final question—can this be madness?—indicates that she was well aware of what was happening to her.

Beyond the Dip of Bell

With immersion in psychosis, Emily Dickinson's fears of psychic dissolution and loss of control were swallowed up in the numb and disorganized condition that subsequently enveloped her. The gathering waves of suspense and anxiety had broken, releasing her to a strange kind of peace or indifference. "When madness comes," wrote a patient who had been through a similar experience, "a strange anaesthesia follows. A sleep akin to death . . . a state which is neither death nor living; lethal, mysterious—evil perhaps to some, but only to those who do not know the blind, intolerable horror that comes from seeing something which cannot be borne—nor escaped."[13] Emily Dickinson, in one poem (no. 305, 1862) called the condition "Despair" and contrasted it with a former state of "Fear," the one as different from the other as "the instant of a Wreck – / And when the Wreck has been." Following the psychological catastrophe: "The Mind is smooth – no Motion – / Contented as the Eye / Upon the Forehead of a Bust – / That knows – it cannot see."

The sensations and events that immediately follow the collapse of the personality are suppressed and forgotten by many patients during their period of convalescence. Probably much that happened during those first terrible weeks or months—that interval when "the Mind is Smooth" and impotent as a sightless eye—eluded recapture by the poet as she improved. The record she left in the poems most likely represents her recollctions of the earliest days of her recovery, after the acute disorganization had begun to yield to reparative forces. Probably all that she was able to portray were the remnants of the retreating illness, yet one must find her picture of psychic devastation awesome.

As her ego approached the extremity of disintegration and surrendered its hold on reality and reason, any one of a number of possible psychotic configurations of behavior might have assumed command. As it happened, judging by her description, the passing of the crisis left Emily Dickinson in a state most closely resembling the catatonic. The prodromal estrangements, depersonalizations, and sensations of mental numbness no doubt intensified until they coalesced to form the appearance of acute catatonia with its machine-like motility alternating with immobility, trances, apathy, muteness, and inaccessibility.

Poem no. 310 (1862) contrasts ordinary endurable suffering with anguish that is overwhelming. The poet states that human beings are impatient and complaining when beset by the former but "Give Avalanches – / And they'll slant – / Straighten – look cautious for their Breath – / But make no syllable – like Death – / Who only shows his Marble Disc – / Sublimer sort – than Speech." One might venture an interpretive paraphrase of these lines as follows: Given a degree of psychic pain barely sublethal (that is, enough to cause one to "slant," but just short of being utterly prostrating), the person quickly assumes the superficial appearance of recovery—he "straightens." But in reality he is not the same. His human responsiveness seems to have suffered a suspension through fear, to have lost its effortless and spontaneous functioning, which now requires conscious exertion for its maintenance (the victim must "look cautious" for his "Breath"). He is no longer able to complain, protest, or communicate his altered condition, but is rendered silent and verbally inaccessible—he can "make no syllable." One can comprehend what has befallen him only through awed contemplation of his muteness, just as one forcibly realizes the finality of another's death only when confronted with a tombstone (death's "Marble Disc"). Such reticence as exhibited by those so afflicted and by the headstone is more eloquently expressive than words of the true state of things.

It is true that one has only to look at a patient exhibiting the entranced stare and silent, somnambulistic manner of the acute catatonic to realize how far from human contact his illness has removed him. The feeling of being a nonsentient, empty husk, lacking inner vitality and moving about as an automaton or puppet, is a universal experience of catatonic patients. This may be what Emily Dickinson was expressing when she wrote (poem no. 272, 1861):

> I breathed enough to take the Trick –
> And now, removed from Air –
> I simulate the Breath, so well –
> That One, to be quite sure –
> The Lungs are stirless – must descend
> Among the Cunning Cells –
> And touch the Pantomime – Himself,
> How numb, the Bellows feels!

Since air symbolizes all that is necessary for life, "removed from air" therefore may mean deprived of love or lacking in essential human relationships, or without hope—characteristic deficiencies of the psychotic's world. The final line of the poem, "How numb, the Bellows feels!" reads in an alternate version "How cool – the Bellows feels!" which even more extremely suggests the uncanny breathing of an animated corpse.

The same life-in-death quality is developed in poem no. 396 (about 1862) which, in addition, indicates that the psychological extremity followed upon overwhelmingly intense or unduly protracted psychic pain:

> There is a Languor of the Life
> More imminent than Pain –
> 'Tis Pain's Successor – When the Soul
> Has suffered all it can –
>
> A Drowsiness – diffuses –
> A Dimness like a Fog
> Envelops Consciousness –
> As Mists – obliterate a Crag.
>
> The Surgeon – does not blanch – at pain –
> His Habit – is severe –
> But tell him that it ceased to feel –
> The Creature lying there –
>
> And he will tell you – skill is late –
> A Mightier than He –
> Has ministered before Him –
> There's no Vitality.

Here the "Despair" of poem no. 305 becomes "Languor," with

emphasis on torpor and enervation, a state said to be "More imminent than Pain." "Pain" here means an inimical transaction with the external world—the organism's agonized response to damaging outer forces. But when the hostile circumstances are perpetuated relentlessly, one's capacity to react may finally be lost. There is then a surfeit of pain; the mechanisms of response are exhausted. At this point the inner alteration occurs, and intrinsic re-equilibration on a lower level of reactivity takes place. "Pain's Successor" is delineated in the poem as a morbid state mercifully divorced from external conditions, less acute than pain and more likely to persist. Consciousness has now lost its focus and the cutting edge of reality is either no longer clearly defined or obscured altogether, "as Mists – obliterate a Crag." The victim has slipped beyond the reach of human assistance, and all the succoring resources of the environment ordinarily able to assuage suffering (symbolized by "Surgeon") are helpless in the face of this deathlike indifference and inertia.

The observation that the gravest emotional blows do not produce grief, but stupor, occurs several times in the poet's letters—some indication of the wonder with which Emily Dickinson regarded the phenomenon. In a variant of a passage to Higginson she wrote, "A breathless Death is not so cold as a Death that breathes."[14] Could a more fitting phrase be found for the cessation of feeling and the blocking of thought of a sudden catatonic reaction than "a Death that breathes"? Two prose fragments express the same concept: "Anguish has but so many throes—then Unconsciousness claims it";[15] and "Stolidity is more terrible than sorrow, for it is the stubble of the soil where the sorrow grew."[16] The later quotation is especially powerful in its evocation of blackened and cauterized fields, deprived of all capacity for productive growth, as a metaphor for the stunned and prostrate soul that has ceased to function under the onslaught of unbearable psychic pain.

Certain catatonic manifestations appear to have a defensive function and represent a more or less conscious withdrawal from a too painful reality. This aspect of the syndrome is apparently alluded to in the last line of poem no. 761 (about 1863):

> From Blank to Blank –
> A Threadless Way
> I pushed Mechanic feet –

To stop – or perish – or advance –
Alike indifferent –

If end I gained
It ends beyond
Indefinite disclosed –
I shut my eyes – and groped as well
'Twas lighter – to be Blind –

The poet's shrinking from further contemplation of her plight, her reluctance to ponder its ultimate extremity and her acceptance of hopelessness are amply conveyed in the lines "I shut my eyes – and groped as well / 'Twas lighter [that is, less burdensome] – to be blind." Again one finds blindness employed as a symbol for the psyche's sealing itself off from reality and its retreat into a self-contained isolation. The metaphor appears frequently in Emily Dickinson's thoughts and assumed a highly concretized form in her later eye disorder. The figure is mentioned here only to alert the reader to its recurrence, and to point out the prominence of blindness as a symbol in Emily Dickinson's poetry.

More germane to the present discussion is the poem's evocation of certain hallmarks of the catatonic state, for example, the vacillating or aimless wandering about ("Threadless Way") that patients display. The manner of the wandering, suggesting an unconscious automaton under a mechanical pressure to keep up a futile motility, is concisely conveyed by "I pushed Mechanic feet." It is important to note also the apathy in the words "To stop – or perish – or advance / Alike indifferent." Clinically, apathy may bear a superficial resemblance to the psychomotor retardation of profound depressions. Actually the two states not only are experienced differently by the patient but have profoundly divergent prognostic implications. Apathy is perhaps the more ominous symptom, indicative of a greater degree of psychological disorganization. The patient immobilized in the nadir of depression is suffering intensely and is therefore still affectively alive—that is, still in contact with feelings. Although he is outwardly inert, it cannot be said of him that "There's no Vitality" (poem no. 396), which phrase appropriately summarizes the apathetic state.

Poem no. 599 (early 1862) stresses the defensive function of a catatonic trance, which constitutes a psychogenic imperviousness to an intolerable reality.

There is a pain – so utter –
It swallows substance up –
Then covers the Abyss with Trance –
So Memory can step
Around – across – upon it –
As one within a Swoon –
Goes safely – where an open eye –
Would drop Him – Bone by Bone.

By means of trance, reality itself is rendered unreal and therefore unmenacing. The ego is thus safeguarded against further disruption, and certain of its functions (memory and orientation are the ones cited in the poem) can proceed almost normally. One of the features that enables one to differentiate between organic brain disease, in which brain tissue is physically damaged, and the functional psychotic disorders, such as the one under consideration here, is the presence or absence of disturbances of memory and orientation. In cases of organic damage memory loss and disorientation in time and place are the rule. In the functional psychoses such impairments are rare.

In a somewhat more advanced stage of catatonic withdrawal, the somnambulistic appearance of the patient may be succeeded by the picture of perfect immobility. The patient may stand or sit like a statue—silent, staring, seemingly unable to will—unresponsive to any stimulus. Poem no. 1046 (about 1865) probably describes such a situation, although it contains at the close almost a premonition of recovery:

I've dropped my Brain – My Soul is numb –
The Veins that used to run
Stop palsied – 'tis Paralysis
Done perfecter on stone

Vitality is Carved and cool.
My nerve in Marble lies –
A Breathing Woman
Yesterday – Endowed with Paradise.

Not dumb — I had a sort that moved –
A Sense that smote and stirred –
Instincts for Dance – a caper part –
An Aptitude for Bird –

Who wrought Carrara in me
And chiselled all my tune
Were it a Witchcraft – were it Death –
I've still a chance to strain

To Being, somewhere – Motion – Breath –
Though Centuries beyond,
And every limit a Decade –
I'll shiver, satisfied.

Emily Dickinson seems here to say that the normal operations of her intellect have ceased, that she is devoid of thought ("I've dropped my Brain"). Also, she is equally drained of feeling, there is an emotional vacuum ("My Soul is numb"). She feels as if all her physiological processes are suspended; the very circulation of her blood has ceased ("The Veins that used to run / Stop palsied"). She has become rigidly immobile and insentient, caught in a depth of paralysis akin to petrifaction and beyond the ordinary capacity of flesh ("'tis Paralysis / Done perfecter on stone / Vitality is Carved and cool / My nerve in Marble lies"). She then compares her present condition with her former state, before (to quote poem no. 1123 again) "A Great Hope fell." She not only felt alive then, she was ecstatically happy ("a Breathing Woman / Yesterday – Endowed with Paradise"). The "Yesterday" must be taken metaphorically to mean sometime in the past. Actually, as has been demonstrated, Emily Dickinson's breakdown was most probably immediately preceded, not by great happiness, but by inexorable anxiety and depression. "Yesterday," however, she was not mute and she possessed an animated demeanor ("Not dumb – I had a sort [meaning a manner of acting] that moved"). Also at that time her emotions were vivid and had forcible impact on herself and others ("A Sense that smote and stirred"). She was capable of uninhibited physical expressions of joy and fun ("Instincts for Dance [sexuality?] – a caper part – / An Aptitude for Bird").

The fourth stanza finds the poet wondering who or what it was that transformed her and reduced her to her present frozen and silent inertia ("Who wrought Carrara in me / And chiselled all my tune"). She reflects that if it were merely the result of "Witchcraft" or "Death" there might yet be grounds for hope that somewhere in some future existence life might again be attainable.

The final stanza states that if she could only be sure in some future time, no matter how remote, that there exists a possibility for "life" again, she could bear the present calamity, content to suffer and wait.

One of the earliest indications that a severely ill psychiatric patient is beginning to reintegrate occurs when he expresses a belief that a favorable outcome of his illness might just be within the realm of possibility. A hint of such a faint hope is detectable in the final line of the poem. But such flashes of optimism may be chimerical, and there may be many false starts before any real gains can be maintained. In the meantime the ray of hope may fade into a gloom perhaps deeper than before for having been momentarily relieved. The despair in poem no. 510 (early 1862), for example, is unassuaged by any sanguine tremor:

> It was not Death, for I stood up,
> And all the Dead, lie down –
> It was not Night, for all the Bells
> Put out their Tongues, for Noon.
>
> It was not Frost, for on my Flesh
> I felt Siroccos – crawl –
> Nor Fire – for just my Marble feet
> Could keep a Chancel, cool –
>
> And yet, it tasted, like them all,
> The Figures I have seen
> Set orderly, for Burial,
> Reminded me, of mine –
>
> As if my life were shaven,
> And fitted to a frame,
> And could not breathe without a key,
> And 'twas like Midnight, some –
>
> When everything that ticked – has stopped –
> And Space stares all around –
> Or Grisly frosts – first Autumn morns,
> Repeal the Beating Ground –
>
> But, most, like Chaos – Stopless – cool –
> Without a Chance, or Spar –
> Or even a Report of Land –
> To justify – Despair.

In examining this poem it becomes evident that one would be hard pressed to discover only a heightened emotional response to a painful situation. The condensation of meanings is tremendous, and the poem defies complete explication. Its tenuous imagery can be interpreted as depicting a psychological transformation in metaphors of physical sensations and symbolic locations.

On one level the sensations signify a loss of psychic vitality and integrity, and on another they suggest a sense of spiritual damnation. The place, a church, whose clamorous bells are announcing noon, provides a discordant background for the movement of the benumbed and isolated soul. The two in contrast—the church with its connotation of bustling communal activities, funeral ceremonies, and promises of salvation and peace; and the poet's soul with all its damning fire and ice locked within it—reveal the complete estrangement of the one from the other, the individual woman from her human environment.

The state is distinguished from death only because the subject can still stand. To the rest of the world it is day, and yet to her it seems like midnight—in other words, the farthest extreme from "noon," Emily Dickinson's symbol for love, human warmth, fulfillment, happiness and heaven. Peripheral sensation only is still intact; she knows she is not benumbed by extreme cold because her skin registers a warm breeze—the "Frost," therefore, is an inner cold that has brought about an anesthesia of the spirit. Her "Marble feet" are said to be equal to keeping a "Chancel, cool." Why a chancel? Perhaps because a chancel is always in the ecclesiastical "east" of a church, regardless of true location, and "east" is a symbol related to "noon." East is the direction of sunrise and therefore suggests promise, hope, glory, and approaching light and warmth (intellectual or affective). East is the cradle of "noon." It brings about the banishment of "night" (fear, loneliness, and so forth) and it announces the arrival of day. By extension, then, the chancel is the most "warmly" located part of the church. But the poet's mere presence is sufficient to chill it. The phrase "Nor Fire" signifies that the poet is certain that the consumption of her vitality was not the result of excess or uncontrolled erotic or destructive passions. Nevertheless, salvation has become impossible. To summarize the first two stanzas: the present alienation did not come about through the loss of the body's physical integrity or through physiological malfunctioning or through uncurbed passions (designated by "Death," "Frost," and "Fire"). Yet the result appears to be due to something that combined features of all three ("it tasted, like them all"). Probably only a state of psychosis could exhibit such an extremity of disintegration and lack of control.

The next two stanzas develop the ideas already presented in the first two. The poet, transfixed in a strange, unnatural composure, feels herself akin to corpses, "Set orderly." She feels constrained, rigidly constricted, shorn of freedom, spontaneous action, and free choice ("As if my life were shaven, / And fitted to a frame"). Her ordinary bodily processes are encumbered too and have taken on a mechanical quality. She "could not breathe without a key."

The final two stanzas resemble so closely other passages from poems that have already been cited that detailed discussion is redundant. Let it suffice to point out that here again one encounters the intense estrangement, isolation, hopelessness, desirelessness, and immobility that characterize catatonic states.

There are a great many fragmentary descriptions of isolated catatonic symptoms to be found throughout Emily Dickinson's poems, but only one compact poem, no. 341 (early 1862), provides both a summary of the major symptomatology and a general outline of the course of the entire acute phase of the poet's illness.

> After great pain, a formal feeling comes –
> The Nerves sit ceremonious, like Tombs –
> The stiff Heart questions was it He, that bore,
> And Yesterday, or Centuries before?
>
> The Feet, mechanical, go round –
> Of Ground, or Air, or Ought –
> A Wooden way
> Regardless grown,
> A Quartz contentment, like a stone –
>
> This is the Hour of Lead –
> Remembered, if outlived,
> As Freezing persons, recollect the Snow –
> First – Chill – then Stupor – then the letting go –

Here again a precipitating stress ("great pain") has brought about the substitution of a compulsive, rule-bound, extrinsic mode of behavior for a spontaneous natural inner one ("a formal feeling comes"). The responsive sensory apparatus is suspended in a deathly stolidity ("like Tombs"). The emotional life is thus slowed and encumbered like rusted machinery, as if some great interval of time had elapsed since it last tried to function (the "Heart" is "stiff"). There has also occurred such a complete loss of affective and meaningful contact with the human environment that time has lost its meaning. Even the events that engendered the catastrophic pain have lost their vividness and appear almost to have happened to somebody else or to have occurred in some infinitely remote past (the "Heart questions was it He, that bore, / And Yesterday, or Centuries before?").

The second stanza is an epitome of the clinical appearance of catatonia. Here, perfectly delineated, is the automatized ("Wooden"), apathetic wandering, indifferent alike to direction, survival, or obligation ("Ground, or Air, or Ought").

A loss of emotional pliancy and an induration of human sensibility has occurred and is conveyed in metaphors from the inanimate world; there is a sense of leaden inertia and of crystalline rigidity and coldness: "a Quartz contentment, like a stone," prevails and it is the "Hour of Lead." The retrospective viewpoint of the poem is explicit in the final lines, together with a suggestion that certain areas of the experience described may have been forgotten. The onset of the catatonic state ("First – Chill – then Stupor – then the letting go") is compared with death by freezing, which culminates in a final "letting go" of consciousness. With reference to the psychosis, what is ultimately relinquished is not so much consciousness but a portion of reality. In either case what can be "Remembered, if outlived" is the gradual loss of self-awareness and contact with the environment through the dissolution of the ego. In the person literally freezing the ego simply ceases to function and cannot, of course, recall anything which happens following the onset of coma. In the psychosis also memory usually fails, at least partially because the ego has become disintegrated and consequently experience loses its coherence, making it, like a dream, difficult to recall. Such confused impressions as result are invariably difficult to recapture, and frequently there is complete amnesia for them; one recalls only "Stupor"—then a "letting go."

The question now arises: What psychological events, if any, ensue following the stupor and the letting go? Emily Dickinson's poems cannot be expected to provide a complete answer to this question. Judging from her account, her memory of the acutely disturbed stages of her illness ended with the onset of complete catatonic immobilization. Her power of recall seems only to have been resumed after the stage of immobility receded, leaving an interval of forgetfulness between.

Occasionally an exceptional patient will be able, upon recovery, to reconstruct the pattern of unrealistic thought that accompanied this phase of profound withdrawal. Through such individuals an insight may be gained into the defensive function of catatonic rigidity, and it is frequently discovered that the inability to move spontaneously is directly related to the patient's fears of what he might do should he not be immobilized. Environmental stresses and frustrations and a concomitant weakening of repression first bring about an awareness of one's own potential ferocity and capacity for retaliatory violence, which in turn gives rise to fears of losing self control. Emily Dickinson's "volcano poems," seen as adumbrations of her eventual breakdown, strongly suggest her concern with the destructive-erotic elements of her personality and her anxiety about restraining them. As the fear of losing control increases, greater effort is expended to counteract the dangerous propensities. The patient, divided now against himself, becomes locked in mortal self-combat. The ego appears to consolidate its various energies into massive attempts to subjugate the powerful urge to vent the barely containable rage incited by the frustrating circumstances. Fear of one's self, fear of what one might do should one embrace these wild sectors of the personality take complete possession of consciousness.

Lara Jefferson, a patient who wrote a memoir of such an illness, felt as if she were battling another person within herself as she attempted to control her violence: "I must awaken myself—for no one else can do it. But I do not know how. There is only a shadow remaining of the person I used to be . . . If the person whom I used to be could not prevent the birth of the person I have become, there is not much chance that the latter more powerful creature will be controlled by the ghost of the person whom she succeeded." Later, she says of this new self, "So the monster was out . . . and the fierce hatred exulted that it had possessed itself of a massive and powerful body. And the thing that was in me was not I at all—but another—and I knew that no power on earth but a straight jacket could hold her . . . But the nurse could not see any deeper than the deadly calm of the exterior—nor that when my self-control went, it would go out like a flood . . . All my energy was being expended to hold the thing down till I could be tied."[17]

As the patient feels giving way within him his power to subjugate this dangerous "other self," he first looks, as Lara Jefferson did, to external controls for reassurance. If these seem to be unavailable or inadequate, he may join the monster within and actually become violent. More commonly, his terror eventually invokes the mechanism of self over-control with a resulting immobilization. The replacement of one's own conscious volition by this involuntary inhibitory pattern may be what is experienced by patients and described by Emily Dickinson as "letting go."

That this possibility of resolving an inner schism occurred to Emily Dickinson is suggested by poem no. 642 (about 1862). Here she expresses the insight that a potential division within herself and a warring of the opposing sectors of her personality may eventuate in a peaceful, impregnable, and unconscious state. The defensive function of such a calamity is clearly set forth:

> Me from Myself – to banish –
> Had I Art –
> Impregnable my Fortress
> Unto All Heart –
>
> But since Myself – assault Me –
> How have I peace
> Except by subjugating
> Consciousness?
>
> And since We're mutual Monarch
> How this be
> Except by Abdication –
> Me – of Me?

Such a poem as this seems to be surveying future possibilities and to be written from the standpoint of one contemplating possible alternatives. The opposite maneuver from "abdicating" from one's self is, as has been noted, to combine forces with one's self —that is, to embrace the violent spirit actively instead of attempting to dissociate one's self from it. A phase of increased motoric discharge and excitement may then replace the previous immobility and stupor. In this state, the coalition unites conscious

331

mentation and the previously unconscious destructive impulses, which, until the psychotic breakthrough, were held separate from each other by the partitions of sanity. One's violent proclivities, newly discovered and claimed by the conscious personality, may now be wielded as an instrument of aggression against the frustrating and threatening external world. Such a conscious acceptance of impulses previously maintained in an unconscious state does not, of course, imply a greater integration of personality. On the contrary, when psychosis brings such a relationship about, the subjective experience is of a divided self in which two elements seemingly foreign to each other cooperate side by side without merging into a unity. In poem no. 754 (about 1863), Emily Dickinson refers to herself as a "Loaded Gun," long standing unused. Eventually the gun is discovered and claimed by its "Owner," who henceforth hunts and kills and defends himself with it. What the poem appears to be describing are two aspects of the same personality—the directing, executive, volitional function (the "Owner") and the aggressive, destructive, and erotic impulses (the "Gun"). Here both appear as segments, split apart from each other, of the same personality, which lacks normal integration. Subjectively, the individual experiences these parts of his personality as dissociated. Nevertheless, as this poem indicates, under certain conditions the two may operate together synergistically, not like the harmonious processes of an individual organism but more like two distinct persons who have decided to form a temporary alliance while maintaining their separate identities.

In the series of poems I have been considering, there are references to another aspect of Emily Dickinson's illness that has only been touched upon. One finds it expressed in such phrases as "A Plank in Reason, broke" and "I dropped my Brain" and "The Mind is Smooth – no Motion." This is the symptom of thought disorder. At the height of her illness, Emily Dickinson was subjectively aware of disturbances in her intellectual functioning. The implications of poem no. 937, "I felt a Cleaving in my Mind," give strong support to the hypothesis that there occurred something more than the retardation in tempo of thought processes that is characteristic of profound depressions. In addition to this disturbance, there must have been also a disjunction in the train of associations that ordinarily link one thought with another.

At this point one is confronted with a paradox; for, when reading the majority of the poems and letters, one is immediately struck by the esthetic control of the writing. That Emily Dickinson had, at least at one period of her life, a thought disorder symptomatic of a psychotic illness there can hardly be any doubt. Several poems confess it explicitly and define unmistakably the blocked and disjunctive features that one encounters so frequently in the clinic. Why is this incoherence not more evident throughout the poet's writings?

The simplest explanation, of course, is that all the manifestations of her illness were acute and of short duration and were followed by complete recovery. However, this is probably not the case. Although the catatonic character of the acute breakdown eventually gave way to other, and in a sense, milder manifestations, Emily Dickinson seems to have remained a more or less disturbed woman for the remainder of her life.

A more plausible explanation resides in the "metaphorical" character of psychotic thought and its resemblances to poetic thought. Also, the more one studies the verbalizations of the "insane" the more one is aware of underlying meaning. The surface of such thought may seem irrelevant or inappropriate to the occasion and lacking in continuity. Yet, on a deeper level, on the level of metaphor—one might almost say of poetry—there is meaning. Given Emily Dickinson's facility in the manipulation of symbolism and imagery and the complexity and subtlety one expects of her writing, it might easily happen that occasional autistic utterances would pass as poetic obscurities or be supplied with meanings that made sense to the individual reader. Certainly, one justifiably impressed with the extraordinary qualities of the poet's mind would not be quick to brand an elusive passage autistic. If one is unable, after much reflection, to succeed in extracting meaning from such a passage, prudence leads one to assume that one has simply missed the point, and in the great majority of instances this indeed will prove to be the case. What appears incomprehensible at first reading will often, after some pondering, become clear and take its logical place within the context. The author Helen Hunt once wrote to Emily Dickinson:

"This morning I have read over again the last verses you sent me: I find them more clear than I thought they were. Part of the dimness must have been in me."[18] The cautious reader must many times share Helen Hunt's experience.

Early in this century, when the poet's heirs and editors were gradually releasing her work to the public, it was a commonplace of literary criticism to attack various poems as incomprehensible and to ascribe this obscurity, usually, to carelessness, faulty technique, or a straining after originality. With time and study most of these poems have proved to be the coherent result of highly developed craftsmanship and exquisite sensitivity to sound and language. Nevertheless, a few poems are still being cited for their obscurity and apparent incoherence. Are these the few that failed to escape a degree of psychotic contamination? What can one say, for example, of such a poem as no. 42 (late 1858):

> A Day! Help! Help! Another Day!
> Your prayers, oh Passer by!
> From such a common ball as this
> Might date a Victory!
> From marshallings as simple
> The flags of nations swang.
> Steady – my soul: What issues
> Upon thine arrow hang!

Is the poem incoherent, unfathomable, autistic, as some writers have believed? At first glance it may seem so. Yet it has a strange and forceful emotional expressiveness that causes one to wonder to what extent it owes its power to those very qualities to which one may be tempted to assign pejorative adjectives. After diligent scrutiny, one seems to discern a connecting thread linking lines and binding the whole poem into a unified statement. The question is, is the thread really there or is one supplying it?

The thought the poem appears to express is that there are tremendous potentialities latent within every dawning day. The poet, overwhelmed with the magnitude of the yet undisclosed possibilities, is afraid lest she prove inadequate to cope with them. In her anxiety she cries for help and asks for the prayers of a "Passer by." Why a passer-by? To emphasize that the day to come is precisely an ordinary day and not one on which some specific intimidating event is anticipated. Because nothing particular is expected, support may be asked of any casual stroller—

in other words, any other human being who, after all, is faced with the same impending unknowns as herself. The phrase "common ball" possibly means *ordinary bullet* and refers to the day —"common" reinforcing the idea that there is nothing exceptional about it and "ball" meaning that if aimed and fired correctly it may effect certain definite and possibly crucial results —for this day may be like the bullet that turns the tide of a war and designates the victor. Through such simple "marshallings" (continuing the battle metaphor) as the ordinary day, nations have been founded. At first the poet tries to brace herself against the eventualities of the external day. But the consequences of this bullet, this marshalling, depend largely on what she herself does with it. The vast exterior potentialities, then, are transformed in the final line into the arrow of the soul. The responsibility for effecting some gain through this day rests with herself. The anxiety is not fear of what might befall one but fear that one may fail to make the most of one's opportunities.

Clark Griffith finds this poem unintelligible and considers it "too distraught to be expressive—a poem put together on the outskirts of sanity, and at a time when the poet's sense of sequence had ravelled perilously close to the breaking point."[19] My purpose is not to disparage Mr. Griffith's opinion but to show how easily a plausible significance can be imputed to an obscure figurative statement. It may be an impossible task at times to determine whether or not one is reading a coherent meaning into something that on a conscious level is incoherent and autistic. This is frequently true when the utterance in question is couched in metaphorical language.

It is even more difficult to find incontrovertible indications of distorted thought processes in Emily Dickinson's letters. One reason for this is that they—at least her mature ones—are almost as metaphorical as the poems. Another is that many statements that are meaningless to us undoubtedly, in the context of the poet's life, made perfect sense and were clear to the recipients of the letters. In every personal letter there are private passages meant only for the eye of the recipient which allude to shared experiences that it was not necessary to define explicitly. Probably most of the obscurities in the letters are of this nature. Whether this is true of all of them is difficult to say.

To indicate something of the reservations one has in deciding

whether a given passage in a letter is intelligible and appropriate to the occasion and to the recipient, consider the first two
paragraphs of a letter written to Mrs. Samuel Bowles in the summer of 1861. These lines are more or less typical of the poet in
her late twenties or early thirties.

> I do not know of you, a long while—I remember you—several
> times—I wish I knew if you kept me? The Dust like the Mosquito,
> buzzes round my faith.
> We are all human—Mary—until we are divine—and to some of
> us—that is far off, and to some [of] us—near as the lady, ringing at
> the door—perhaps that's what alarms—I say I will go myself—I
> cross the river—and climb the fence—now I am at the gate—Mary—
> now I am in the hall—now I am looking your heart in the Eye![20]

Are these passages appropriate and coherent? At a century's
distance and isolated from the flux of the daily New England
circumstances in which they were originally embedded, they can
readily be rationalized. One has no trouble discerning the links
between thoughts, and it seems natural to suppose that the occasional opacity is a result of a narrowly personal meaning whose
relevance to Mrs. Bowles is rooted in a context of life which she
shared with the poet but which excludes us.

On second thought, though, one wonders to what extent the
lines did communicate something to Mrs. Bowles with clarity.
Is there not here a wild leaping from abstraction to fantasy and
back again? The words and images that occur to the poet often
seem to dictate the thought—rather than the more rational re-
verse process. Instead of being chosen because they are the best
words to express the concept, the words selected seem sometimes
to be determined by personal associations or by linguistic relationships in which words are related to each other as words.
For example, the word *human* here seems immediately to have
set off an association with its opposite, *divine*; and this purely
verbal connection seems to have determined the direction of the
rest of the paragraph. The arbitrary verbal connection seems employed here as a pretext to disguise what is essentially a non
sequitur intrusion into the letter of the poet's underlying personal
preoccupation with the theme of death. The thoughts of psychotic
patients often make the leap from intelligible communication to
autistic ruminations in just this way. Some characteristic of a

word—its sound perhaps—calls forth an association with another word of similar sound. The second word, more closely tied to the patient's inner emotional life, leads to a train of thought divorced from the present circumstances. The observer, unaware of the connecting link, is mystified by what seems to be a disjunctive succession of unrelated ideas.

But do not poets function in just this way—playing with words as words, juxtaposing them on the basis of sound and structure, concerning themselves as much with patterns as with logic? Herein lies another difficulty. When the victim of psychosis is a poet, it may be a practical impossibility to separate the manipulation of language that is part of his craft and talent from that which is an expression of the looseness of his psychic organization. In fact, it is quite possible that the two approaches to language— the inventive and the defective—at times work hand in glove.

Let me return to the intrusion, mentioned above, into the poet's communications of ideas that seem inappropriate to the occasion—another common sign of psychotic thought processes. For example: The first paragraph in the letter to Mrs. Bowles says that Emily Dickinson has had no letter or news of her for a long time and that she wonders if Mrs. Bowles still remembers her warmly. The next remark, alluding to "the Dust," implies that the possibility that death has struck frequently disturbs the poet whenever her faith is taxed by a long separation from one she loves. Paraphrased, the letter begins: I have not heard from you for so long a time that I feared you might be dead. There seems to have existed no realistic grounds for Emily Dickinson to have had such a fear for Mrs. Bowles at this time. The lines must therefore represent an expression of the poet's own obsession with the thought of death. The degree to which one allows one's inner anxieties to dominate the center of the stage depends ordinarily on the extent of one's emotional control and on one's sense of what is fitting in terms of a particular interpersonal relationship. If these private matters overleap the bounds of propriety and the degree of intimacy understood to exist in the relationship, the communication indicates impaired judgment and control. All we know of Emily Dickinson's relationship with Mrs. Bowles supports the impression that her expressed doubt of Mrs. Bowles's continued existence might not have been congenial to Mrs. Bowles, who doubtless did not feel that the character of her relationship with the poet would allow her to respond in a similar vein. The expression of death fears here may then be interpreted as one aspect of a thought disorder. There seems to be a weakened hold on the conventional proprieties of the situation and an overriding inability in Emily Dickinson to modify the expression of her inner needs to conform to these social strictures. The content of the communication also may suggest a disturbance in mentation: separation and death are very frequently equated by persons whose thinking has become unrealistic through psychosis. Such persons have intense fears that the beloved one no longer exists whenever he is not physically present. There seems to be an attenuated form of this delusion in many of Emily Dickinson's letters.

Theodora Ward in *The Capsule of the Mind* draws the conclusion, based on her appreciation of the relevance and coherence of Emily Dickinson's writings, that the poet could never have been psychotic because, as Mrs. Ward says, "the insane cannot explain themselves."[21] The hypothesis that Emily Dickinson did indeed undergo a psychosis will probably be rejected by the large numbers of people who share Mrs. Ward's views regarding insanity. Her opinion, however, is necessarily in contradiction to the experience of anyone who has had the opportunity to become well acquainted with an extensive variety of psychiatric patients. Yet the parading of such experience by a psychiatrist to bolster his assertion that psychotic patients can and frequently do—very elegantly and persuasively—"explain themselves" carries little weight. Great efforts in this direction have accomplished little by way of modification of the popular stereotype of the unreflecting and mindless madman that one suspects is at the heart of Mrs. Ward's statement. What appears to be needed is direct acquaintance with those not uncommon patients who have recovered from psychotic breakdowns and who are able to reflect upon their past experiences and describe them accurately and understandably.

Since it is rarely convenient for the layman to share the psychiatrist's experience, even if he were desirous of doing so, and since it is difficult to persuade otherwise those who lack clinical familiarity with the psychotic process and hold to the image of mental illness presented by tradition, perhaps a helpful alternative for the psychiatrically uninitiated would be to acquaint them with an account of a psychosis written by a recovered patient.

There are many such accounts in the professional literature. Several long excerpts from one of them[22] are included in the following pages. Pertinent to the formation of a realistic conception of the role of psychosis in Emily Dickinson's life are certain observations one would ask that the reader make in reading the ensuing passages. The first thing to notice is the intellectual control manifested by the patient in her writing. Though she had three hospitalizations for serious "schizophrenic" reactions, her thought processes following her recovery are perfectly coherent and to the point. Notice also that the patient did not lose the capacity for self-observation during the height of her disturbance and see how able she is to recall her experiences and to convey them intelligibly. One should observe also that this patient is disclosing in a striking way a partial awareness of the dynamics that underlie her illness. A psychosis reveals to its victim secrets that for the rest of us are closely guarded and inaccessible to consciousness. This quality is perhaps most prominent in the passages the patient devotes to her mother.

The patient is a social worker, thirty-six years old at the time of her breakdown. She was hospitalized for six months and received the diagnosis of schizophrenic reaction, catatonic type. After her discharge she managed at home for another six months, then had to be rehospitalized. She remained in the hospital for three months, was out again for six months, and then in again for fourteen months. She is the mother of three children. Prior to her breakdown she had decided to divorce her husband and was aware of a feeling of emotional deprivation with regard to him. She was of an active and outgoing temperament and says of herself, "I had always had an adequate number of friends and had never had any difficulty in making close friends." She had many intellectual interests and enjoyed reading and writing poetry. Certain of her pathological experiences—for example, her feeling of merging into a vast sea and her sensitivity to light, to which she assigned a symbolic value—are slightly reminiscent of those Emily Dickinson suffered.

Following her separation from her husband the patient felt intense loneliness. "I sought compensations for this increasing isolation," she writes.

I seemed to be torn from my moorings and alienated from my former self, because I had temporarily lost my normal investment in other interests . . . I made desperate efforts to break the over-attachment [to her lover], and thought finally that I had succeeded. I found the best corrective was writing poetry and intellectual work which enabled me to fight off feelings of incipient depression. Creative activity was intensified but finally became compulsive and overabsorbing. I was not able to maintain a normal extroverted relation to my children, or to switch my attention at will to practical details of living. I experienced a sudden feeling of creative release before my illness, was convinced that I was rapidly attaining the height of my intellectual powers . . . I began to write compulsively and at the same time was aware that I was developing schizophrenia. I found later among the disorganized notes which I had carefully hidden away, a number of passages that were quite lucid as well as others that were incoherent—full of symbolic sexual content. I also felt that I was embarking on a great Promethean adventure. I was filled with an audacious and unconquerable spirit. As panic mounted, I grew afraid of being alone, had an intense desire to communicate . . . Shortly after I was taken to the hospital for the first time in a rigid catatonic condition, I was plunged into the horror of a world catastrophe. I was caught up in a cataclysm and totally dislocated . . . Part of the time I was exploring a new planet (a marvelous and breath-taking adventure) but it was too lonely, I could persuade no one to settle there, and I had to get back to the earth somehow . . . During some of the time that I was dislocated in interplanetary space, I was also having vivid fantasies in connection with water, and these afforded me considerable relief. Water represented conservation of life, in contrast to its destruction by fire. Water fantasies had started one or two days after admission to the hospital. I suddenly felt I had been plunged into a sea, was drowning and struggling for breath . . . [The patient was given sedative treatments in tubs and wet packs, which stimulated these fantasies. The patient clearly remembers reciting passages of Swinburne to herself:] "I will go back to the great sweet mother / Mother and lover of men, the sea. / I will go down to her, I and none other, / Close with her, kiss her, and mix her with me; / Cling to her, strive with her, hold her fast" . . . (pp. 678-680)

The patient says,

It was not I who wanted to go back to the sea, because I myself was the sea, or maternal principle . . . though I seemed to be almost pulled apart in a disintegrating universe, I felt there must be some way I could hold things together . . . I was unable to think coherently or plan any action, but I had to use my poetic imagination instead, for poetry could be counted on not to lead me astray . . . Occasionally during subsequent periods of disturbance there was some distortion of vision and some degree of hallucination. On several occasions my eyes became markedly oversensitive to light. Ordinary colors appeared to be much too bright, and sunlight seemed dazzling in intensity. When this happened, ordinary reading became impossible, and print seemed excessively black . . . pp. 680-681)

The patient describes her early days of extreme disorganization and her delusions accompanied by fear, her perceptual distortions, and her erroneous inferences from accurate perceptions.

I also had a sense of discovery, creative excitement, and intense, at times mystical, inspiration in intervals when there was relief from fear . . . A different and less terrifying sense of menace [than that experienced in relationship to certain nurses] was experienced occasionally in relation to men toward whom I was attracted, i.e., doctors and male attendants on the staff. A feeling of conscious attraction would be replaced suddenly by a feeling that the other person possessed special and vaguely threatening power . . . Pleasantly toned rape fantasies were also prominent in my first illness, but these also contained an element of fear aroused by apprehension of aggressive or threatening qualities in the particular individual about whom these fantasies were constructed. Before onset of illness, I had become acutely aware of a great need to be protected and taken care of by a man in an absolutely secure relationship . . . During the terrifying first weeks of my illness I went through an experience of separation from my mother which was traumatic in intensity. The feeling I had was about as acute as it would have been had my mother died in the ordinary course of events. I had always dreaded the thought of my mother's death and during my illness I felt that I had lived through this event in advance. I would subsequently be able to react normally, but not to feel a terrible sense of loss for someone on whom I had leaned too heavily. The pain of the separation experience I attribute to the fact that my viewpoint was changing, my own ideas were developing, and the area in which I could communicate with my mother in the future would be somewhat more restricted. I was also becoming more sharply aware of our dissimilarities in personality and temperament. (p. 681)

The separation experience did not prevent me from wishing, at a later stage of the first illness, that my mother were dead. This wish was connected with a fantasy in which I saw myself as the undisputed female head of a household, with sole power to make decisions and to exert authority in regard to feminine functions. I did not find these fantasies particularly disturbing but regarded them as natural . . . In spite of the suffering and tension of the first episode, it was also a time of inspiration and renewal which helped to counteract the difficulties of my situation. My capacities for aesthetic appreciation and heightened sensory receptiveness, for vivid grasp of the qualities of living, and for imaginative empathy were very keen at this time. I had had the same intensity of experience at other times when I was perfectly normal, but such periods were not sustained for as long, and had also been integrated with feelings of well being and happiness that were absent during the tense disturbed period. (p. 684)

Truth and love were abstract central themes which held my interest during the period of onset and recurred directly or symbolically in consciousness during non-rational phases. I was particularly struck during the onset panic with the "inspired" nature of simple and ordinary truths. I was reading a good deal of poetry at this time . . . (pp. 688)

The patient then quotes a few lines by Robert Hillyer on time-honored truths and by Emerson on love.

Truth, unlike love, was both wonderful and terrifying at the same time. It was sometimes overwhelming, sometimes cruel. In lines of my own I wrote: "Truth can be comfortless and cold / Ice in the hand and hard to hold / Or hotter than a match's flame / Who touches it is seared with pain" . . .

Light symbolism was a dominant feature of the first illness. The sun was the mystical symbol of life and of truth, particularly intellectual illumination. The sunlight was dazzling and blinding—prolonged exposure was dangerous. I felt I had been subjected to an excess of light—that what I was enduring was the utmost violation, an "intellectual rape," the rape of the mind by truth . . . I was afraid that my eyes would be damaged by the light [the patient would stare at the sun] and that I would become blind.

Light in general was a less violent symbol than the sun—it stood
for moral insight or inner illumination. Blindness was symbolized
spiritual blindness . . . I found later during more rational periods that
isolation due to intellectual stimulation was particularly difficult to
bear and seemed to be most threatening to nervous stability. This
type of inspiration, accompanied by a very rapid flow of ideas, produced a craving for social communication. When this craving was
inevitably thwarted, the frustration served to heighten the nervous
tension that was already present because of mental overstimulation.

Poetic inspiration, on the contrary, seemed to be of different
character. It represented a closer synthesis of emotion and intellect.
Poetic conception and poetic expression produced feelings of integration and well being . . .

The inspiration that was perhaps strongest of all after remission
of the first episode was reflected in a renewed devotion to science
. . . My approach to science was mystical and philosophical as well
as rational. A poem which I wrote before my second illness . . .
closed with the following stanzas:

> And he who loves the ways of earth
> And loves the life that's lived thereon
> Shall gaze enraptured at the point
> Uncounted angels dance upon
>
> With keen uncompromising knife
> Shall cleave the flesh, lay bare the bone,
> Shall heal the sick, sustain the weak,
> No terror turning him to stone
>
> Whose visionary patient eyes
> Look deeper than the utmost dream
> Beneath the chaos of disguise
> To where the heart of order lies.

(pp. 688-689)

Among the personality changes the patient noticed in herself
during the interval of years which included the psychosis were the
following:

I lost a sense of excessive dependency on other adults; a sense of
personal separateness and isolation replaced a former capacity for
identification with other individuals and with groups. (p. 689)

The point in presenting at such length these passages written
by a recovered psychotic patient is not to imply that the dynamics
of her illness and Emily Dickinson's were essentially similar.

343

Rather it is to persuade the reader that there exists no inherent implausibility in the idea that Emily Dickinson could have undergone a psychosis such as I have proposed while at the same time developing into a great poet. The social worker patient was stimulated to write verse during her psychosis. Following her first psychotic break with reality she produced poems that, though not indicative of outstanding talent, were coherent and meaningful. There is no reason to believe that had she possessed the intellectual and verbal gifts of Emily Dickinson she would have been prevented by her psychosis from exercising her creative faculty in the production of genuine art.

Taking into consideration the many isolated fragments of prose and poetry cited in this and the preceding chapter which pertain to the symptoms of Emily Dickinson's nervous breakdown, I will now integrate them according to clinical experience in an attempt to reconstruct her illness as it might have appeared to an eyewitness.

The first sign noticeable to Emily Dickinson's family that something is seriously wrong would be her gradual preoccupation and increasing withdrawal from them and from the world outside. They speak to her at meals and it is with difficulty that she pulls her attention back to what they have said. She asks them to repeat their remarks and apologizes for having been thinking of something else. They ask her if she is worried about something and she denies that this is so. She is clearly shutting them out of her real concerns. They sense this and worry that despite her disclaimer something is wrong. She appears tense, sad, lonely. They become aware that the intervals spent in her room are increasing daily until she is absent from family activities for hours and eventually whole days at a time. Their discreet inquiries as to how she has been spending the time are met with evasions. Her face appears pale and expressionless; her former vivacity is replaced by a distant stare, a mysterious unmotivated smile, a toneless voice. They find scraps of writing that reveal an inner agony. When these are brought to her attention, she dismisses their importance with a transparent rationalization. They notice that she no longer reads and that she prefers to stare out the window looking at nothing for long periods of time. She refuses to leave the house and will not receive visitors regardless of the closeness of her previous relationship with them.

Now it should be recalled that Mrs. Dickinson from 1855 to 1860 was not herself, suffering from some illness which removed her from society for these years. She was fifty-one years old in 1855 and possibly undergoing an involutional or menopausal reaction accompanied by depression. In Jay Leyda's listing of Dickinson family physicians[23] there is a conspicuous gap for this interval, and there exists no item in family correspondence or elsewhere that can provide a clue as to the identity of the physician who cared for Mrs. Dickinson during this protracted illness. It seems likely that at the time of the first symptoms of his wife's illness Edward Dickinson called on a local doctor from Amherst or Northampton. As the illness prolonged itself, however, and Mrs. Dickinson failed to recover, specialists from outside western Massachusetts were no doubt consulted, among whom may have been physicians who concentrated their practice on the area of mental and emotional disorders. Be this as it may, by the time his daughter exhibited the early symptoms of a breakdown, Edward Dickinson need not have delayed calling for medical advice, having an already developed access to the appropriate physicians through his efforts to obtain help for his wife.

Before the physician is called, however, Vinnie and Austin attempt to be helpful and to ascertain the cause of the strange alteration that has come over their sister. Closer to her than her parents, they take her aside and express their concern and beg her to unburden herself to them, while Edward Dickinson waits anxiously in the background praying that Emily will not sink into the same inertia and despondency that grips his wife. Vinnie spends long hours in her sister's room, and Austin manages to get Emily to take an occasional ride with him into the country, and Sue comes over to do her part. To all their worried inquiries and their pleas that she allow them some glimpse into what is troubling her, Emily presents an impassive face whose only expression is remoteness. Occasionally she utters some words whose significance eludes them. They discuss these infrequent verbalizations among themselves and speculate as to their intent. They urge her to be clearer and to enlarge upon her meaning, and she either stares at them silently or murmurs something equally puzzling or strange.

Sometimes she sheds silent tears and wears a worried, troubled look. She mutters something to herself whose import is self-disparaging or self-accusatory, although again her family cannot fix the content and she refuses to share with them the cause of her disquietude.

The physician at last comes and she attempts to evade his visit. Austin and Vinnie reason with her and attempt to persuade her of the necessity of talking with the doctor. When arguments fail they beg her, for their sakes, to let him examine her. She is deaf to their arguments and their anguish alike. Finally Edward Dickinson, in great perturbation and sorrow, brushes them aside and declares that she has no choice. She must see the doctor—something is seriously wrong and she must submit. She is led to the parlor weakly resisting and looks as if she is in a trance. The physician is kind and patient. At first she is perfectly mute, sitting as if unaware of his presence, neither responding to his questions nor glancing in his direction. The family have withdrawn, leaving them alone. The calm and professional manner of the physician used to dealing with such cases accomplishes what her relatives' overwrought tenderness has failed to do, and she begins haltingly to give him some idea of the state of her mind and feelings. She feels dead, she says, or like a puppet without any feelings. The world appears strange and she feels shut away from others, as if enclosed in a transparent vacuum. The doctor inquires if she has ever had the experience of hearing voices that she knew were really imaginary but that nevertheless sounded real to her ears. She admits that on occasion she has had this terrifying experience—that the voice has told her she must kill herself because she is a wicked person. Sometimes there is more than one voice—a medley of voices all murmuring something directly pertaining to her. The voices are not intelligible but one thing is certain: they have a disapproving, indignant tone, as though they were reproaching her for some dreadful and undisclosed sin. They cause her to want to hide, but there is no way to escape their obscure and insistent accusations. The physician asks her to guess what crime the "voices" appear to believe she has committed. She replies that she thinks they are accusing her of doing something to injure her mother or of having sexual feelings toward her brother or his wife. These thoughts are intolerable to her, and she sometimes feels that she must kill herself because this is the only way to escape their constant torment. The physician presses for further information, though he has

learned enough to make his recommendations. At some point
he recognizes that he may have intruded too far and that his
patient has retreated again into herself. She darts a look at him
in response to further questions, as if startled out of a reverie at
the sound of his voice. He can no longer keep in psychological
contact with her. As if in response to a magnetic attraction, her
attention is pulled away to her innermost thoughts, and she
seems to become unaware of his presence and of her surroundings.
She appears oblivious to his bidding her good-by. In the adjoin-
ing room he speaks in a subdued voice to Edward Dickinson,
Austin, Vinnie, and Sue, who have been anxiously awaiting his
diagnosis. He asks whether Emily has been reading a great deal
prior to her illness, and when they acknowledge this he tells
them that a prevalent cause of mental breakdown is too great an
absorption in fiction and other imaginative literature. The excessive reading and writing of poetry is especially harmful for
persons of nervous temperament, he tells them, and the agitation
of the emotions produced by this habit frequently results in
mental breakdown. The physician then offers his opinion that
Miss Dickinson is suffering from a mysterious affection of the
nervous system; in fact, one might go so far as to call it a mild
attack of insanity characterized by unrealistic feelings of guilt
and worries concerning the health of her mother. He has some
reasons for believing that improperly regulated sexual impulses
have played a part in reducing the brilliant young woman to her
present condition. A delicacy and a deference to Edward Dickinson's social position restrains him from confiding this to the
family. He recommends that the patient be maintained under
very close surveillance for her own safety. In conformity with the
generally optimistic attitude held by the medical profession of
the day toward psychological disorders, he reassures them that it
is not unlikely that with time the patient may achieve a full
recovery. All books should be withheld from her, however, and
all poetry writing, daydreaming, and other solitary pursuits
should be discouraged. Instead she should be urged to take up
her share of the housekeeping and cooking, so far as this is possible, get plenty of fresh air, nutritious food, and so forth. He
will leave them a prescription or two for some medicine to calm
the patient and to help her to sleep better. If she fails to improve
under this regimen, they must summon him and he will insti-

tute more vigorous measures. Hospitalization may then have to be considered.

Following the physician's visit the family attempt with difficulty to put his recommendations into practice. They persuade Emily to bake some rye bread, which they proceed to enter in a competition at the cattle show. When it receives a second prize, they are disappointed at her indifference, and are unable to persuade her to accept her award in person. Their attempts to get her to socialize a little also fail. She will not attend church and even refuses to take any more rides with Austin. She becomes more withdrawn than ever and after a slight improvement seems to be suffering a relapse. An overt hostility toward her mother becomes apparent, and Vinnie and Austin see to it that one of them is always present to act as a buffer between the two unhappy women. Emily does not say much but glares with unmistakable hatred at her complaining and helpless mother.

One day Emily fails to arise in the morning, and Vinnie discovers that she has become more withdrawn than ever. She stares mutely at Vinnie and seems no longer to comprehend what is being said to her. Her physical motions have gradually become more rigid. She dresses herself in a confused and mechanical way and needs help to find her clothes and put them on. Her gait is stiff and somnambulistic, and she appears to be listening to inaudible sounds issuing from remote distances. She would not move from the lounge for hours at a time if Vinnie or Austin did not persistently intrude into her psychological isolation. The doctor comes again and confirms their fears that Emily is indeed worse and must be hospitalized. The MacLean Asylum in Somerville is an excellent sanitarium for such cases, he tells them. The patients there are all from well-to-do New England families; it is a private institution from which Irish immigrants and other undesirable elements are excluded. The atmosphere is pleasant; the superintendent and his wife treat the patients like members of their own family; there are parties for the patients and work to keep them busy and games to while away the hours and distract them from their worries. The improvement rate is encouraging—most patients go home recovered after only a few months.

Emily by now is unable to resist or even to understand what the physician is proposing. But the idea of such a separation is more than Edward Dickinson and his family can bear. When told of the doctor's recommendation that Emily be sent away to a hospital for a while, Mrs. Dickinson wrings her hands and weeps and blames herself for not having been a better mother to Emily. Aware of her daughter's shyness with strangers and her dependency on Vinnie and Austin, Mrs. Dickinson fears that Emily will regard her trip to Somerville as proof that she is a burden to them and is no longer wanted at home. Mrs. Dickinson cannot bear to send Emily away—not even for her own good. Emily must stay at home with her. With Vinnie and Austin's help they can make Emily better. Besides, what would it do to Edward's political career and the confidence others had in him as a lawyer if it were revealed that he had an incompetent wife at home and a daughter in an asylum in Somerville? No, she may have been an impediment to the fulfillment of her husband's ambitions in the past, failing him in so many ways by her timidity and her unwillingness to meet people or to accompany him on his business trips. But now she will not allow her inadequacies and weakness to stand in his way. If Emily is the way she is because of her—as Emily herself at times seemed to think—then Emily's place is at home with her, where she will do her best, despite her own infirmities, to look after her daughter. Of course, Vinnie and Sue will help.

Faced with his wife's distress and self-accusations at the prospect of Emily's being sent away for treatment and fearful that the plan, if carried out, would bring about a worsening of Mrs. Dickinson's melancholia, Edward Dickinson must make a difficult decision. He wants to do what is best for his daughter, but not at the expense of his wife's precarious stability. Also it goes against his grain to allow any of his family to escape his own immediate influence and supervision. Moreover, he is as aware as anyone of his daughter's unhappiness when she is among strangers and the intensity with which she clings to her home and family and all that is reassuring and familiar. The doctor did not know Emily before her breakdown; therefore, his recommendations have to be evaluated in the light of her family's awareness of her peculiar sensitivity and her unique emotional responsiveness. What succeeds with the majority of patients may not be at all salutary with Emily, who is unlike other young women. In the end, Edward Dickinson makes his decision that Emily remain in Amherst under the care of her sister and her brother's wife. If it is possible for her to again become the person she had been, then home of all places offers the best chance that this should come about, despite the physician's recommendation.

Weeks of anxious care follow weeks of unrelenting watchfulness. The trance-like state, the apathetic detachment give way to unreasonable terrors and horrible nightmares. Emily insists that all doors and windows be kept locked at all times. Her father and brother assure her that she is safe and everything is locked, but she is not easily satisfied. She makes them accompany her to each door and window to reassure herself that the house is impregnable. She is afraid to sleep alone, and Vinnie moves into Emily's room with her. The lights must not be dimmed at night and each room must contain a lighted lamp. As the weeks pass Emily at last begins to improve. She sleeps better and appears less nervous. She begins to take an interest in her plants again. Her obsession with housebreakers and burglars begins to relax its hold on her mind, and she is able from time to time to enter into household conversation. She still seems confused occasionally, but now recognizes when she has said something irrational. She displays an awareness that she has passed through an interval of illness that in retrospect seems like a week's or month's long nightmare. Her sense of humor shows signs of returning and she begins to laugh a little at some of her strange ideas and she wonders where they came from.

Mrs. Dickinson also begins to show signs of improvement. More energy appears to be at her disposal, and although still complaining and full of self-pity, she is less self-disparaging and begins to occupy herself with the household chores that formerly had been her chief absorption. Edward Dickinson, Vinnie, Austin, and Sue begin to feel a sense of relief. There are many indications that the Dickinson household is returning to normal.

Day by day Emily continues to brighten. The utter inaccessibility and remoteness that characterized the depth of her breakdown many months before, when she gave up entirely all verbal communication, have gradually diminished and there ensues an increasing vivacity of communication. Her eyes liven, her face becomes ever more animated, she gives an impression of unbounded alertness and energy. Her verbal productions seem alive with new, original ideas and colorful and startling figures of speech. She appears as one inspired. There is also an atmosphere

about her of knowing a choice and sumptuously gratifying secret
—an air of covert and uncommunicable satisfaction. There is a
hectic quality to all of this and her family immediately sense it.
Though she is immeasurably improved over her previous state,
there is still something unnatural about her elation and they are
disturbed. Emily begins to write poems again, in a manner quite
unlike her previous pedestrian attempts at rhyme and meter.
Vinnie observes her jotting down phrases and lines on any scrap
of paper handy and in the midst of chores and activities ordinarily far removed from the composition of poetry. She notices
that her sister's euphoria seems to alternate with anxiety and
tension, and is concerned because, for all her new and apparently
free-flowing responsiveness and openness to her surroundings,
Emily still shows a distinct preference for her own thoughts and
her own company and appears more than ever to have relinquished all direct contact with Amherst society. And sometime,
at about this stage of her recovery from her psychological prostration, Emily confides to the astonished Vinnie that she is in
love and that the man loves her in return.

Vinnie and Sue ponder the significance of this latest seeming
aberration. They find Emily unapproachable on the subject.
Hers is a private ecstasy; she is offended by any intrusion and
especially by the attitude of skepticism with which they appear
to regard her beloved. The two women shake their heads and
find it difficult to fathom how Emily, who has retained intact
all her profundity, her intellectual brilliance, and her sense of
fun, can on this one subject remain so unrealistic, so lost in fantasy. Sometimes they doubt their own judgment and wonder if
somehow the man in question has declared his love for Emily as
she has said.

As the months go by Emily again appears to be sinking into
despair. Vinnie speculates with some alarm that either the man
has written that he no longer cares for Emily or Emily is beginning to realize that she has deluded herself and that the man was
not really in love with her after all. Vinnie, however, is fearful
of broaching the subject. She can only express her affection and
loyalty to her sister in the little domestic ways she knows and
attempt to convey to Emily that everything will be all right
and that she will always be there for Emily to lean on. Emily
begins to complain of intolerable pain in her eyes, and for many

months her eye problems become the focus of her waking life. With the passing of years she settles into a weary depression, avoiding strangers, keeping out of bright light because of her sensitive eyes, and reading a great deal.

It is now the closing years of the 1860's. Emily is almost herself again after nearly ten years. She is open to communication with all her family on all but a few subjects. On these they continue to respect her privacy, as they have always done. Gone, however, are the ebullient spirits of her early twenties. Gone also are the strange and inspired words that at times caused an almost palpable aura of light to radiate from her every gesture and expression. Departed is the intensity and excited energy with which she jotted down her ideas as well as the rapt concentration she could devote to her own thoughts, almost oblivious of what was taking place around her. Vinnie and Austin have nearly lost now the genius created in their midst, seemingly by a strange mental pertubation. But they have almost regained their sister—a little more subdued perhaps, a little less outspoken, a little more inflexible in her idiosyncratic need for a special attire, a special life—which more than compensates them for the departed creature of fiery creativity that had for a time taken her place.

The account above is, of course, a fantasy, but it encompasses the essential facts of Emily Dickinson's mental illness. Something rather similar to it in reality must have confronted her family, and it seems likely, in view of their personalities, that they may have reacted in ways resembling those here imagined.

Of this crisis of 1857-1864 three main phases can be distinguished. The poet clearly recognized them herself, as in the poem "The Soul has Bandaged moments," to be examined shortly. Her own designations for them exactly parallel the technical ones. In prosaic terminology there were the phases of (1) ego breakdown, (2) manic restitution, (3) constrictive reorganization; or, in the poet's terms, the Soul's (1) bandaged moments, (2) moments of escape, (3) retaken moments.

In the stage of *ego breakdown* the poet experienced an inundation of uncontrolled erotic and hostile impulses escaping from repression, and she feared that she was going mad. This stage seems to have been ushered in by the collapse of her unconscious hopes of fulfillment in her brother's marriage.

In the stage of *manic restitution* the inadmissible impulses

toward Austin and Sue appear to have been projected and displaced upon a less interdicted love object—the unattainable "beloved"—thus the fear and guilt were reduced and were allowed
expression through the poetry.

In the stage of *constrictive reorganization* came the realization
that this solution was also illusory and doomed to frustration. The
agitation and exuberance of the previous stage were then replaced
by depression, guilt feelings, over-control of all impulses, and
repudiation of the instinctual life. The creative drive, hampered
by inhibitions and obsessive doubting, fell away.

The clarity with which Emily Dickinson perceived and recorded these changes in herself seems almost miraculous. Poem
no. 512 (early 1862) contains all that has been inferred, and much
more, about the morphology of her illness:

> The Soul has Bandaged moments –
> When too appalled to stir –
> She feels some ghastly Fright come up
> And stop to look at her –
>
> Salute her – with long fingers –
> Caress her freezing hair –
> Sip, Goblin, from the very lips
> The Lover – hovered – o'er –
> Unworthy, that a thought so mean
> Accost a Theme – so – fair –
>
> The soul has moments of Escape –
> When bursting all the doors –
> She dances like a Bomb, abroad,
> And swings upon the Hours,
>
> As do the Bee – delirious borne –
> Long Dungeoned from his Rose –
> Touch Liberty – then know no more,
> But Noon, and Paradise –
>
> The Soul's retaken moments –
> When, Felon led along,
> With shackles on the plumed feet,
> And staples, in the Song,
>
> The Horror welcomes her, again,
> These, are not brayed of Tongue –

For "Soul," we may substitute ego.

CHAPTER VII

The Soul is bandaged—therefore *wounded,* kept from bleeding (losing integrity and ability to contain impulses) by flimsy gauze dressings (ego defenses). The Soul is too frightened to stir (catatonic rigidity). The "Fright" represents the escape of repressed impulses, seen to be erotic in the caressing and kissing, and hostile in their degradation of a "Theme so fair" (the marriage of Austin?).

In the middle part of the poem the impulses and the ego are participating in an uneasy relationship. The ego is highly energized and barely able to contain the impulses within safe channels of expression. The doors are burst (inhibitions swept away), the Soul dances (libidinous motoric release) "like a Bomb" (invested with destructive potentialities). As the Bee to his Rose, the Soul is borne "delirious" (heedless of reality) toward "Noon and Paradise" (sexual consummation).

In the final part, the Soul's flight is over, the plumed feet are shackled (depression, acceptance of the strictures of reality). The Soul is a "Felon" (oppressed with a sense of guilt) being led to imprisonment (the years of seclusion), and the song is stapled (the creative drive is bound and immobilized by inhibition).

That these three phases were not entirely separate and distinct but tended in reality to interpenetrate and alternate with each other is evident from the letters and the sequence of the poems. The fact is stated outright in the poem's penultimate line—"The Horror welcomes her, again"—which tells us that for some time after the poet retreated indoors the repressed fears and desires continued to threaten her sanity.

The poems cannot represent gross exaggeration or accounts of imagined emotion, for the poet's biography and letters support the view that her anguish was real and substantially as the poems describe it. Most of us have something of the abnormal in us, some emotional scar, a trace of having broken a little in some time of pain. And most of us would suffer anything rather than admit the fact, even to ourselves. The convulsions of the spirit found in Emily Dickinson's poems are only the culminating manifestations of processes incipient in all of us. Although one may be fortunate enough never to undergo the extremities which befell her, most of us who read her poems recognize ourselves in them. Therein lies the difficulty. Many persons, not aware that the "insane" can be intelligent, warm, suffering, introspective, creative, lovable—in short, *human*—take the greatness of the poetry as proof that Emily Dickinson never did break down. The madman for them is an alien, bestial monster—a creature from outer space. Readers with this misconception remain in fearful opposition to the least suggestion that anything that initiates a resonance deep within themselves can be a product of madness.

As for the proposition that the poet is guilty of romantic inflations of feeling, there can be no doubt that human beings, collapsing under great psychic pressure, actually exhibit the precise reactions Emily Dickinson describes in her poems. Although it is not impossible that she may have derived this knowledge as Freud did—largely through observation of others, especially her mother, and analytic genius—the prominence of such psychological themes in her writing overwhelmingly suggests that they had a more profoundly personal significance to her. And if, as is here hypothesized, Emily Dickinson actually underwent catatonic agonies of psychological disorganization and later attempted to record them objectively, she could scarcely have done so without employing language that would inevitably appear immoderate to those unacquainted with these states.

Chapter VIII MANSIONS OF MIRAGE

When Austin and Susan married in 1856, Emily Dickinson was a terrified and lonely girl standing at the brink of an abyss. No purpose for her existence revealed itself to her, no possible sexual or social role, no bridge to the future. The emptiness that seemed to stretch before her, devoid of warmth, solace, or meaning, was unbearable to contemplate. Psychological collapse then turned her gaze inward—to a vista no less inhospitable and appalling. But following psychosis, which dissolves and throws into flux many of the supporting rigidities of the inner self, a rebuilding commences; a new organization of personality and a different view of life begin to come into being. Emily Dickinson, through the redistribution of psychic resources and through new growth, had by the end of 1862 made herself a great poet. During the six years between Austin's marriage and the poet's creative apogee in 1862 there occurred, in addition to Emily Dickinson's psychotic experience, other interior events of great interest. One of these was her famous and mysterious love affair.

As Emily Dickinson approached her thirties she underwent an ecstatic and tortured love relationship with a man. Two letters, distraught and pathetic, but clearly love letters, were found in rough draft among her papers after her death. The first one dates from her thirty-first year (1861), the other a year later. These are the famous "Master" letters addressed to a man still unidentified. (Another letter written in her twenty-eighth year is also addressed "Dear Master." It is tender and intimate in tone but perhaps no more so than many other letters to friends; it seems questionable whether it would be considered a love letter if the later "Master" letters did not exist.) The year preceding the first passionate and anguished "Master" letter marked the beginning of the creation of a long series of love poems. The poems and letters taken together constitute the esthetic distillate of an experience that Emily Dickinson regarded as the crucial and climactic one of her life.

Before examining the love poems and letters, however, it is necessary to consider the emotional atmosphere which prevailed from Austin's marriage to the time these documents came into being.

From 1856 through 1862 Edward Dickinson did remarkably little traveling; the same is true of the rest of the family, including Austin. This is understandable, of course, in view of Mrs. Dickinson's prolonged illness (probably a severe menopausal depression) and, as I have postulated, Emily's breakdown and subsequent tenuous equilibrium. Austin and Susan, after a brief honeymoon in Geneva, New York, returned to Amherst to the still unfinished home which Edward was building for them beside the mansion. Austin was soon busy with his law practice and, like his father, with myriad community activities. Many evenings and weekends Austin must have devoted to these causes, which required him to be away from home often. Although Austin's absences might have increased the time Sue spent with Emily, Sue soon dedicated herself to the development of her social connections and seems early to have established herself as an elegant and prestigious hostess.

Following Austin's marriage there is practically no word of Emily for the remainder of 1856. In October her bread received a second prize at the cattle show. Emily was no doubt desperately in need of encouragement at this time, and it would be surprising if Vinnie, as a member of the judging committee, had not used her considerable charm and persuasiveness in the interests of her dispirited sister; Vinnie was hardly impartial when family interests were at stake. At any rate Emily seems never to have appeared at the exhibition nor to have collected her prize of seventy-five cents.

Emily possibly wrote no letters or poems during 1857—at least none survive for that year. It is significant too that she seems not to have met Ralph Waldo Emerson when he lectured in Amherst on December 16, 1857, and was an overnight guest at Sue's. Emily must still have been too disturbed for social activities at this time; otherwise, in view of her admiration and affinity for Emerson's writing, the absence of any comment in any letter at any time on a meeting that would surely have been eminently memorable is strange indeed.

Edward, in these six years, made occasional trips to the nearby towns of Northampton, Springfield, and Hadley—all within a day's drive. Once, in 1857, he made a brief trip to Boston, and he went again in 1861, when his wife, now recovered, accompanied him. It was then generally considered in Massachusetts that he had given up his political ambitions permanently. This was not so, of course, but the fact that it was widely believed is indicative of the degree to which his home life now required his presence and attention.

These were years without outward crisis or event, and our biographical sources, including family letters, give little direct information concerning the condition of the Dickinsons' personal relationships with each other. We do know that in 1858 Emily began writing poetry in earnest, producing a surprising amount for that year. With Austin and Sue occupied in their different ways, Emily, who by now rarely visited outside the family, must have had many hours of solitude; the bulk of her creative output in these years attests to this fact. Her relationship with Austin and Susan still continued, of course. Her once breathless participation in the affairs of her brother and his fiancée she resigned for a gentler and outwardly less feverish intercourse. The months of convalescence following a psychotic collapse characteristically are reduced in social interaction; there is also a tendency toward increased introverted behavior and apathy toward one's environment. Probably Emily was more withdrawn after her breakdown than before, but with time she again established something of the old intimacy with Susan and began making frequent visits to the house next door, especially when friends she particularly liked—Kate Scott and Samuel Bowles, for instance—were there.

In view of her deeper needs as expressed in her lifelong letters to Susan, it is obvious that Susan continued to represent a mother figure to Emily as well as a peer with whom she could identify. Emily confided in Sue as she had before her breakdown and shared her first poetic efforts with her. After Emily accepted the brutal fact that her earlier demands for love from Susan and Austin were exorbitant and could not be fulfilled, she seems to have resigned herself to a lesser role in their lives and accepted, almost comfortably for a time, the role of intimate guest in their household. Her hunger for the protective, selfless devotion of a mother was as vehement and unsatisfied as ever, but she had learned through bitter disappointment that toning down her demands made certain small gratifications possible, which was a great deal better than nothing—the only alternative.

Emily's earliest surviving letter to "Master," written probably in the spring of 1858, carries the impression that she was already feeling emotionally close to (though perhaps not yet deeply in love with) him. This is also the year of Emily's serious commitment to poetry, and a total of fifty-two poems are ascribable to that year. With her deepening attachment came more poetry, and for this reason some writers regard "Master," whatever his identity, as the spark which ignited the poet's creative energies. The spring of 1858, except for the continuing worrisome state of her mother, must have been a relatively halcyon time for Emily. Austin and Susan were firmly settled in next door, and if the atmosphere in the mansion became too oppressive, she could always escape to their house for relief and companionship, being accepted almost as a member of Sue's family. Her writing, too, was going well, and in the background was the comforting presence of "Master," whom she loved and who appeared to love her in return. In May she even felt unconstrained and confident enough to accompany some friends on an outing to Roaring Brook. The year continued in this rather quiet and undramatic way until its end, the only evidence of latent turbulence occurring in a few strained and queer letters to some of her friends. Among these are the one to her uncle, Joseph A. Sweetser, which has a cryptic and ominous undertone;[1] the August letter to Samuel Bowles, which is tense and constricted and unlike anything she wrote before 1857;[2] a September letter to Sue whch has a peculiar choppy tenseness and tone of suppressed hysteria, setting it apart from every preceding letter to Sue;[3] and the November letter to Dr. and Mrs. Holland, which is both death-ridden and flippant.[4] The only crisis evident for this year was Austin's episode of typhoid fever in October, which might have had something to do with the immoderate insistence on the death theme in this last letter. Even excluding this one from consideration, the other letters indicate, at the least, a profound alteration in Emily's stance toward those closest to her. Some of the warmth and a lot of the spontaneity has gone out of her writing style; the letters also reveal the continuing existence of an inner disquiet.

In 1859 Emily surpassed her previous poetic output with ninety-four poems. She continued to visit Austin and Susan, even when they had guests, and there were some gay and convivial times. Sometimes Emily played the piano, improvising melodies, and stayed so late that her father, irritated and with lantern in hand, had to come and escort her home.

In February both Mrs. Dickinson and Emily (possibly with Sue's help) could manage well enough without Vinnie to enable her to make a visit to Boston, although Emily on this occasion admitted that she felt frightened with Vinnie away. In March there was another seemingly inappropriate letter to Mrs. Holland,[5] but there is little else to reveal Emily's state of mind during that year. In August, Mrs. Dickinson must have been considerably better, for she made, with her husband and Vinnie, an excursion to Mt. Holyoke. Emily did not accompany them.

Beginning in 1860 Carlo, a large dog, the sole pet Emily Dickinson ever had, is mentioned in the letters. Carlo seems to have accompanied Emily on all her rambles, and it is clear that she became very fond of him. It seems likely that he may have been acquired by Edward Dickinson to provide Emily with a constant source of security and an antidote for her night fears.

Emily seems to have increased her visiting during this year, especially to the home of the Reverend Edward S. Dwight, for whose wife Emily felt a tender and childlike devotion. The year seems to have started well. Mrs. Dickinson had recovered sufficiently for Austin and Susan to feel free enough of cares at home to make a trip to Boston. In a March letter Emily mentions that she is not feeling well.[6] Mrs. Dwight was ill at this time also, and Emily's strong tendency to fuse identities with those she particularly loved may have caused her to be concerned about her own health through identification with Mrs. Dwight, certainly one of Emily's mother figures. Aunt Lavinia was also ill at this time and died in April. In August, Edward Dwight resigned his job and moved away from Amherst.

In September Edward Dickinson went to Worcester for the Bell-Everett Convention and was nominated for lieutenant governor, an honor which he declined. Perhaps he was uncertain of the stability of his wife's recovery and hesitated to upset her by accepting a position which would mean new demands on both of them and an increase in the time he would have to spend away from home. Perhaps, too, with the loss of Aunt Lavinia and the moving of Mrs. Dwight—both women having been sources of maternal affection for her—Emily was less secure and balanced than earlier in the year.

In October an event occurred which was to have a profound and multileveled impact on Emily: Susan became pregnant. The antagonisms between Austin and Susan, which all but destroyed their marriage a few years later, appear to have sprung up at this time. Austin was upset about Sue's pregnancy. Possibly he blamed her for her condition and was angry at her because he did not want children, or possibly he was full of anxiety and felt that by getting pregnant Sue had put her life in jeopardy. Whether for these reasons or some other, it is clear that Austin regarded his wife's pregnancy with serious misgivings and no happy anticipations of fatherhood. When Sue was three months into her pregnancy, Austin told Jane Hitchcock, whose brother was in Europe and missing his children, that "if he had three children [as had Jane's brother] he believed it would cause him to start for Europe immediately & stay as long as he could." When Jane replied that he was in no position to understand a father's feelings, he answered that "he considered himself fortunate"[7] for that. The bitter and almost rude tone of Austin's comments to Jane indicates that he felt intensely unhappy about Sue's approaching motherhood.

As Sue's condition began to be obvious, Emily's psychological state became more distraught. Probably early in 1861 Emily wrote the second two letters to "Master"—both of them poignant and full of suffering and tortured affection.[8] War fever was rampant in Amherst at this time, but if this affected her in any way there is no evidence of it. Rather, she seems as always to have been deeply preoccupied with the inner reverberations of her interpersonal life.

Samuel Bowles developed a painful and protracted, but not life-endangering, ailment in the spring. Emily wrote a queer letter to Mrs. Bowles in August.[9] On September 11 Mrs. Dwight died. Emily wrote Susan that the summer had been a particularly painful one for her.[10] In October Edward again went to Worcester and again declined the nomination for lieutenant governor. The same month, though she seems to have been excessively concerned about his health, Emily refused to see Samuel Bowles when he visited the mansion. On December 19 Mrs. Bowles had a son, the first live baby after three stillbirths. During this year, full of intense and obscure emotional turmoil for her, Emily wrote eighty-six poems. It was also the year of her "terror—since September."[11]

I do not believe that the Civil War, Samuel Bowles's sciatica, or the possibility that her father might be called away to be lieutenant governor had a great deal to do with Emily's "terror." Surely the comment must refer to her fear that she was experiencing a resurgence of her psychosis. These other concerns may have added to her distress and increased her vulnerability to that calamity, but they cannot have been the decisive precipitating conditions. The death of Mrs. Dwight also, though a serious loss and therefore a contributing stress, seems not likely to have been at the core of the "terror." The same is true, for reasons that will be apparent later, of conflicts in her relationship with "Master."

Susan's pregnancy had come to term in June, at the beginning of that summer which Emily said had brought her so much suffering. Sue was in her thirty-first year—an advanced age, by nineteenth-century standards, at which to embark for the first time on childbearing. Even today, with greatly improved obstetrical techniques, the maternal death rate at age thirty is about 10 percent greater than at age twenty. A century ago it was undoubtedly considerably higher. Susan, Austin, and Emily must often have thought of Sue's older sister Mary, who had died in childbirth a few years before. They must also have thought of the three dead babies which were the products of Mrs. Bowles's labors. There can be little doubt that a factor contributing to Emily's distress that summer was their dreading anticipation, month after month, of Susan's lying-in.

For two or three years Emily had enjoyed Austin's home and the security she must have felt with these relatively approachable and responsive surrogate parents. But Susan's pregnancy, in addition to the physical dangers it involved, entailed for Emily more obscure and less realistic threats.

Susan became pregnant in late 1860. Emily's poetic output was at that time just reaching its stride. Susan's baby was born in mid 1861; Emily wrote a total of eighty-six poems that year. As Susan's baby prospered and grew, Emily became increasingly disturbed, her "terror" beginning in September of that year. The next year brought the high water mark of her genius with the prodigious outpouring of 366 poems. Emily was deeply identified with Susan; in the light of her remark "Where my Hands are cut, Her fingers will be found inside"[12] it is not surprising that the climax of her creative life followed so closely on the climax of Susan's reproductive life.

When Emily first became aware that Susan was going to have a baby, what must have been her feelings? Recall now Emily's hostile feelings toward Austin and Susan. Remember that earlier Susan had rejected Emily in favor of Austin; consider also Emily's voracious hunger for a loving mother—a need Emily had deluded herself into believing could be satisfied through Susan. The rage that boiled over, expressing itself in Emily's equation of a "Bliss" with "Murder" (poem 379) and her statement "Had I a mighty gun / I think I'd shoot the human race" (poem 118), was the buried, infantile fury of early childhood revived again with Susan as its object now instead of the original rejecting mother.

As Sue became preoccupied with her changing body, with the life stirring within her and with her private fears, she, like the majority of expectant mothers in their first pregnancy, probably became introspective and self-absorbed. Emily, sensitive to any turning away of Sue, would have been reminded of her earlier losses. At the age of two, remember, Emily had been sent away from home when Lavinia was born, and thereafter, on the deepest levels of her personality, an expected birth meant for her a threatened rejection, the loss of love and a symbolic starvation.

Sue's motherhood, therefore, conjured up all over again many of those terrible emotional conflicts evoked five years before by Sue's marriage.

Following the baby's birth Emily did not immediately visit next door but sent this poem (no. 218) instead:

> Is it true, dear Sue?
> Are there *two?*
> I should'nt like to come
> For fear of joggling Him!
> If I could shut him up
> In a Coffee Cup,
> Or tie him to a pin
> Till I got in –
> Or make him fast
> To "Toby's" fist –
> Hist! Whist! I'd come!

Stripped of its playful language, what message does this poem really convey? Just this: I do not wish to visit for fear of harming the baby in some way. If I could get him out of sight and secure him fast or give him to the cat (Toby), I would come at once. The deeper impulse beneath the clever words is clear enough; the poem is a message full of murderous aggression toward the infant.

Martha Dickinson Bianchi in one of her sentimentalized and idealized biographies of her Aunt Emily, surprisingly enough confirmed this interpretation when she divulged that Emily was resentful of the time Susan devoted to the new baby.[13] Also, it was at this time that Emily began to ask Sue's advice regarding her poetry, as if she were making a last-ditch stand to compete with the baby for Sue's attention. She wants to be a good poet to please Susan and Austin, she tells them: "Could I make you and Austin—proud—sometime—a great way off—'twould give me taller feet." She then follows this remark with the rueful recollection that just a short while before her sister-in-law was *"just-Sue,"* instead of being, as now, "Nest" to the "Ring dove,"[14] Sue's pet name for the baby. Emily once confessed to a friend that, in her, love and jealousy were inseparable: "You see we keep a jealous Heart—That is Love's Alloy."[15]

The love alloyed with darker feelings was certainly much in evidence in January 1862 after Mrs. Bowles finally succeeded in producing a live baby and Emily wrote: "Shall you be glad to see us—or shall we seem old-fashioned—by the face in the crib? ... We have very cold days ... and I think you hear the wind blow ... Dont let it blow Baby away."[16] And in another letter to

Mrs. Bowles, the tone of sibling jealousy strikes almost a threatening note: "Dont love him so well—you know—as to forget us—We shall wish he was'nt *there*—if you do—I'm afraid—shant we?"[17] It seems evident that the withdrawal of Susan toward the terminal phases of her pregnancy and during the first months of her motherhood inflicted a crushing privation on Emily. Six months after Sue's baby's birth Emily wrote Louise Norcross, "Odd, that I, who run from so many, cannot brook that one turn from me."[18] The ostensible stimulus for this remark was the postponement of a visit from the cousin, but one suspects that Emily's raw sensitivity to exclusion was preconditioned through her renewed loss of Sue.

If Emily could feel such ill-disguised hatred toward Mrs. Bowles's baby, think how incomparably more virulent must have been her feelings toward Sue's baby and, before his birth, toward Susan herself. After all it was Sue who was to blame for bringing this rival into the world, behaving thus like Emily's natural mother, who in Emily's view had defrauded her of the love she craved. Sue's pregnancy, therefore, must have created deep sympathetic vibrations in the archaic strata of Emily's mind. These old resentments, stirring to life again in this way, greatly augmented Emily's realistic fears for Sue's life just prior to the baby's birth. Of course her anger at Sue, excessive, inappropriate, and self-defeating as it was, had to be repressed. Such emotions cannot be annihilated or extinguished, however; they seek expression in other forms.

In view of Emily's habitual dwelling upon death, it is inconceivable that in these circumstances the old obsession did not intensify tremendously. And given her death wishes toward Susan and her intense identification with her, not only would guilt have been inevitable but, following that, a fear that as Susan neared her crisis Emily herself would, and deserved to, die. Of course it was physical death which menaced Sue; the disaster that threatened Emily was the psychic death of another episode of psychosis—and, beyond that, the possibility that her poems, the fruit of all her creative agony, might be stillborn. When the fog of pain and medication first passed from before Sue's eyes, she must have first asked of her child, "Is he alive? Is he breathing?" When Emily sent Higginson a sample of her poetry the next year, she did not ask him if it was accomplished, original, expressive, or publishable. She inquired, "Are you too deeply occupied to say if my Verse is alive? . . . Should you think it breathed . . ."[19]

What all this adds up to is that Emily's great creative outpouring, which subsided as rapidly as it began, was for her, on the deepest level, the psychological equivalent of Susan's pregnancy; that the secret horde of poems which swelled in volume so rapidly in 1862 in her dresser drawer was not just metaphorically the offspring of Emily's brain but, from the viewpoint of her most unconscious and primitive emotions, her real and only child. Thus, in this strange way, she tried to satisfy one aspect of a deeply felt need, the need fully to be Susan, to experience all that Susan experienced, to secure wholly and permanently the sense of femininity which had always eluded her. Having a baby of her own was desperately important to Emily Dickinson. In the year of Susan's confinement she tried persistently and inappropriately to get Mrs. Bowles to name her son "Robert" after Robert Browning, with whose recently deceased wife, Elizabeth Barrett, Emily felt closely identified. Even after the child was named Charles, the poet referred to him as "Robert."[20]

But there were other facets to Emily Dickinson's need than her desire to be a mother. The heightened sexual readiness and desire, engendered throughout her brother's courtship, whose forbidden objects were Susan and Austin, remained frustrated. The complete development of a sense of womanliness requires more than the establishment of an inner femininity and more than the experience of giving birth, both of which Emily vicariously achieved through her psychological fusion with Sue. To be thoroughly female requires also a relationship with a male. A woman feels herself most to be a female through contrast with a male in intimate and loving union with him. The *production* of the poems was a symbolic giving of birth; the *content* of a large percent of them reflects the need for a love relationship with a man.

In the chronological flow of Emily Dickinson's poetry, as in her letters, the love theme breaks into the sequence *sforzando,* seemingly unheralded by intimations or antecedents. Having explored the various maturational false paths and successive cul de sacs which marked the evolution of Emily Dickinson's emotional life one may well be astonished that the wavering inner journey

should culminate so decisively in what has generally been regarded as a subtype of the conventional adult love affair. How, it
may be asked, could the poet at one stroke nullify all her previous
uncertainties and reservations and circumvent all her desperate
struggles to achieve closure in her sexual identity? How is it possible that almost at a bound she appears to have developed the
capacity to respond to the physical and emotional importunities
of a man as a mature and integrated woman—she who a short
time before dreaded so to depart the safe harbor of childhood?

Such questions as these, as will be seen, take one to the very
door of the forge of Emily Dickinson's creativity. Before attempting to answer them, however, let me try to place the matter in
perspective, first by fixing the salient features of Emily Dickinson's love affair as she interpreted and recorded it and, second, by
consulting certain conclusions of leading Dickinson critics which
pertain to the love poetry.

Viewed from a little distance, the love story has the form of a
great peak with precipitous slopes leading down on either side.
Love grows imperceptibly at first, and even as the great height of
recognition is reached, the poet is not aware until it is too late that
the other side of the watershed and the long decline into loneliness is all that remains before her. For Emily Dickinson, love, like
poetry, did "pile like Thunder to it's close / Then crumble grand
away / While Everything created hid" (poem 1247). The tremendous climax of love, its fading into remembered glory, and
the final sinking to despair and death constitute the topography
of Emily Dickinson's love affair. In her poetic vision of the
experience, the heightened dramatic intensity and tendency to
attach cosmic significances to the event are characteristically
nineteenth-century and romantic. Though the lyrics in which she
enshrined her passion are concise, their aggregate outline is extravagant and almost Wagnerian; the love poems, in their fusion
of love and death form a kind of puritan *liebestod*.

Seen in detail and close up, the love story, though lying in dis-
connected fragments throughout the poems, reveals its peculiar
features. Certain points having to do with circumstances, emotional responses, and meaning are consistent and sufficient to convey the unique transactions of the relationship.

As one reads love poem after love poem, the first cluster of
characteristics to be apparent shows that Emily Dickinson re-

called her love affair as a supreme climactic event, that its duration was very brief indeed, and that it passed decisively and irrevocably. Her lover expressed his affection unobtrusively, according to one poem (no. 1053), and she responded nonverbally with a glance: "It was a quiet way – / He asked if I was his – / I made no answer of the Tongue / But answer of the Eyes." Despite the lack of outward show, the emotional resonance was profound. Her recognition by her lover became her coronation day (poems 356 and 508). It was a "moment of Brocade" and a "drop of India" (poem 430), both of which metaphors convey brevity and circumscription. At that moment, "Heaven" came near her door, stimulated her hopes, then immediately withdrew (poem 472). Her "One Blessing" was a bliss so scantily allotted to her that it was like a flood being served to her in a bowl (poem 756). It was as though she were "Born – Bridalled – Shrouded" all in a day's time (poem 1072). Poem 322 likewise confines the experience to a short interval: "A Day at Summer's full." It occurred on a day on which she hoped (poem 768). Poem 470 repeats the idea that it was like a new birth into life, and poem 508 compares it to a baptism. The experience was an "instant's Grace" (poem 359) that unfitted her for the "Contented-Beggar's Face" she had worn only an hour before. Her love "touched" her and it was as though, fleetingly, she had brushed a "Royal Gown" (poem 506). Her lover's avowal was a "Best Moment," given as a stimulant for despair and then immediately withdrawn, leaving a sense of dazzled emptiness (poem 393).

Part of the significance of this ephemeral event was that it consecrated her for all time and elevated her to a state that she compared with royalty, as the many references to coronations, baptisms, and other sacraments indicate. The moment also brought her completion—it was the finished errand "We came to Flesh – upon" (poem 443) and it was her "Reward for Being" (poem 343). Her lover was, himself, "Existence," and she tells him that her life had been a "Paradise fictitious / Until the Realm of you." Her loss of him constituted him a "confiscated God" (poem 1260). The finality and exclusiveness of her commitment to her lover is conveyed powerfully in the lines "He put the Belt around my life – / I heard the Buckle snap" (poem 273).

Finally, the joy of the occasion was shortlived—it was a "Wine" that "Came once a World"; the lovers "breathed – / Then dropped the Air" (poem 296). She says of her lover, "So fleet thou wert, when present – / So infinite – when gone" (poem 788). And she tells him that the moment of his love marked the high tide of her soul.

The evanescence, uniqueness, and impossibility of repeating the moment of fulfillment are all attributes which are conveyed explicitly in the following poem (no. 978), as well as the important point that the poet was not fully aware of what was really happening to her until later:

It bloomed and dropt, a Single Noon –
The Flower – distinct and Red –
I, passing, thought another Noon
Another in it's stead

Will equal glow, and thought no More
But came another Day
To find the Species disappeared –
The Same Locality –

The Sun in place – no other fraud
On Nature's perfect Sum –
Had I but lingered Yesterday –
Was my retrieveless blame –

Much Flowers of this and further Zones
Have perished in my Hands
For seeking it's Resemblance –
But unapproached it stands –

The single Flower of the Earth
That I, in passing by
Unconscious was – Great Nature's Face
Passed infinite by Me –

None of Emily Dickinson's metaphors of brevity can be taken literally, of course. The "single noon" represents the entire interval of her rapport with her beloved. Whether that was a matter of hours, weeks, or months one cannot say. All that can be justifiably concluded is that Emily Dickinson, for dramatic and emotional purposes, is stressing the idea that the duration of her happiness in love was painfully short.

The 1861 "Master" letter and some of the poems convey the suggestion that the man did not take her protestations of love or her pain at their mutual renunciation seriously. In poem 296 she says, "You said it hurt you – most – / Mine – was an Acorn's Breast – / And could not know how fondness grew [in a man's heart]." In the letter she asks him what it would take to convince him of her passion and her pain at their separation: "One drop more from the gash that stains your Daisy's bosom—then would you *believe*?" After trying to assure him that she does indeed wish "with a might I cannot repress" that she could be with him, she complains: "You make me say it over—I fear you laugh." Later she says, "You say I do not tell you all," and she paraphrases him as saying "tell [me] of the want." She answers this question thus: "you know what a leech is, dont you[?]," meaning that her longing for him is draining her life's blood. Her letter implies that "Master" asked her what she thought he could do about the situation, and she replies, "I dont know what you can do for it— thank you—Master." Then she asks him what he would do if the situation were reversed, and "you cared so for me."[21] She then begs him to walk with her in the meadows an hour and asks him if he thinks anybody would really disapprove if they did.

The next "Master" letter suggests that in addition to the man's not taking her seriously, he now appears to be critical and somewhat rejecting. "Oh, did I offend it[?]" she begins. She explains that she would have sheltered him in her "childish bosom—only it was'nt big eno' for a Guest so large." She admits she frequently blundered and may have affronted the man's superior taste and troubled or teased his finer nature. Must she go unpardoned, she asks, and gives as her excuse for failure to meet his requirements that she is ignorant of "majesty" and "patrician things" and that even the wren on the nest knows more than she dares to know. Tell her her fault, she pleads, "punish, dont banish her—shut her in prison, Sir—only pledge that you will forgive— sometime—before the grave." She begs not to be turned away: "Wont he come to her," she asks him, "or will he let her seek him, never minding so long wandering if to him at last . . . Master —open your life wide, and take me in forever."[22] An 1861 poem (no. 235) also implores forgiveness in similar language:

> My Sovereign is offended –
> To gain his grace – I'd die!
> I'll seek his royal feet –
> I'll say – Remember – King –

Thou shalt – thyself – one day – a Child –
Implore a *larger* – thing –

What is it that the poet has withheld from her master that causes him to smile condescendingly at her passion? The apology for not having sheltered him in her bosom and for not daring to learn as much as a nesting wren knows supplies the answer. The wren on her nest has learned to be a functioning female; it seems patent that Emily Dickinson has withheld her sexuality from her lover and that he is offended and doubts the sincerity of her expressions of affection.

Poem 861 appears also to be a response to "Master's" doubts that she really loves him. "Split the Lark – and you'll find the Music," she assures him, it is all there reserved for him, "Scarlet Experiment! Sceptic Thomas! / Now, do you doubt that your Bird was true?"

That the lover's physical desire for her touched off profound sexual reservations is indicated in a number of poems. In poem 251 she remarks that she would climb over the fence to get at some forbidden strawberries except that God would disapprove if she stained her apron. In poem 213 she advances the idea that both man and woman might be demeaned should "the Harebell loose her girdle / To the lover Bee," and she wonders if the "Bee" would lose his holy awe of the flower if she yielded to him. In poem 340 she equates "Bliss" and "Abyss" and questions whether she will not soil her shoe if she steps in bliss. The theme apparently appears again in "He showed me Hights I never saw" (poem 446), which continues:

> "Would'st Climb" – He said?
> I said, "Not so."
> "With me" – He said – With me?"
> He showed me secrets . . .
> "And now, Would'st have me for a Guest?"
> I could not find my "Yes" . . .

Poem 275 further reinforces the impression that her lover employed the ancient masculine argument that if she truly loved him she would give herself to him. "Doubt Me! My Dim Companion!" the poem begins. She goes on to say that she has poured her life out to him stintlessly and asks what more any woman can give. "Say quick, that I may dower thee / With last Delight I

371

own!" That her offer excludes sexual intercourse is made clear in the second stanza, where she says that her spirit is already his and that she has "ceded all of Dust I knew." We know from her previous comparison of herself with the wren that what she knows of "Dust" (that is, the flesh) is very little. One motive she gives for withholding herself in this way recalls the question of the harebell—that is, if she conferred these favors, her lover might lose interest in her: "To lack – enamor Thee – / Tho' the Divinity – / Be only / Me." (poem 355). Her rejection of the physical overtures of her lover is the theme of another poem (no. 643): "I could suffice for Him, I knew," it begins as though for self-reassurance,

> He – could suffice for Me –
> Yet Hesitating Fractions – Both
> Surveyed Infinity –
>
> "Would I be Whole" He sudden broached –
> My syllable rebelled –
> 'Twas face to face with Nature – forced –
> 'Twas face to face with God –

Her uncertainty that she "could suffice for him" is made explicit in poem 751, "My Worthiness is all my Doubt." She fears perhaps that she "should insufficient prove / For His beloved Need," and calls her misgiving "the Chiefest Apprehension / Upon my thronging Mind." In another place she remarks that God gave her a "Crumb" but that she "dare not eat it – tho' I starve" (poem 791), and she concludes that she is quite contented with her meager portion.

The obtrusive fact about her lover, of course, is that he was inaccessible. Tradition has it that he was married, and there are several poems which lend support to this view. In poem 398 she says that even the most impenetrable physical obstacles could not keep the lovers apart. What does accomplish this feat, however, is an insubstantial but absolute principle: "tis a single Hair – / A filament – a law – / A Cobweb – wove in Adamant – / A Battlement – of Straw." In poem 485 she remarks upon the effort it takes to set her hair and make her "Boddice gay – / When eyes that fondled it are wrenched / By Decalogues – away." Presumably the commandment that forbids closer contact here is "Thou shalt not commit adultery" (although in several other places Emily Dickinson admits her tendency to break the first commandment through her idolatry of those she loves). Though ultimately she decided that the prudent course to pursue was one of renunciation, the poet finds the soundness of the motive does not lessen the pain: "Denial – is the only fact / Perceived by the Denied," she says, and asks, "What Comfort was it Wisdom – was – / The spoiler of Our Home?" (poem 965).

Law, the ten commandments, and wisdom all dictated that the lovers go separate ways. The poet says that these abstract proscriptions made her lover infinitely unreachable. In poem 240 she tells the distant moon and stars: "There is one – farther than you – / He – is more than a firmament – from Me – / So I can never go!" She feels excluded from heaven and begs the angels to give her another chance: "Dont – shut the door!" she pleads (poem 248). In poem 319 she tells how her dream of love recedes unrealized like a bee evading a schoolboy, leaving him "Staring – bewildered / at the mocking sky." In poem 400, "A Tongue – to tell Him I am true!" she indulges the fantasy of hiring a boy to "run / That Interdicted Way" to her lover with the message that she is still faithful. In poem 498 she expresses envy of the seas on which her lover sails, the stagecoaches he rides in, the fly on his windowpane, and the hills "That gaze upon His journey – / How easy All can see / What is forbidden utterly / As Heaven— unto me!" She would be "Noon" (a symbol for the consummation of love) to him if it were allowable, "Yet interdict – my Blossom – / And abrogate – my Bee." In poem 640, Emily Dickinson says she can neither live, die, nor rise to heaven with her beloved. The best that is permitted to them is to "meet apart" (that is, through correspondence and by the enshrinement of each in the other's heart) with "You there – I – here – / With just the Door ajar / That Oceans are – and Prayer – / And that White Sustenance – / Despair."

A large number of poems treating of a great sorrow attest to Emily Dickinson's grief and despair following the mutual renunciation. A striking example is Poem 236, which follows. It has an unusually large number of italicized words in it, which suggests that in her distress the poet was straining to express more than her unaided words could utter.

If *He dissolve* – then there is *nothing – more –*
Eclipse – at *Midnight –*
It was *dark – before –*

Sunset – at *Easter*
Blindness – on the *Dawn –*
Faint Star of Bethlehem –
Gone down!

Would but some *God – inform* Him –
Or it be *too late!*
Say – that the pulse *just lisps –*
The *Chariots wait –*

Say – that a *little life –* for *His –*
Is *leaking – red –*
His little Spaniel – tell Him!
Will He heed?

At times her anguish is modified by another feeling toward her lover—disappointment. For, as is clear from a number of poems, he did not *hallow* their supreme moment quite as she did. In poem 203, "He forgot – and I – remembered," she compares her lover's denial of her to Peter's denial of Christ: "Jesus merely 'looked' at Peter – / Could I do aught else – to Thee?" And, in poem 261, she suggests that her beloved was not moved by her poems: "the sole ear I cared to charm – / Passive – as Granite – laps My Music – / Sobbing – will suit – as well as psalm!" The underlying message of poem 238, "Kill your Balm – and it's Odors bless you," is: no matter how badly you treat me I will continue to love you.

Still another subtheme of the love poetry is the poet's hope that what is denied her in this relationship on earth will be granted her in heaven. Many poems treat of this celestial marriage, all more or less along the same lines as the final quatrain of "There came a Day at Summer's full" (no. 322). Here the poet says that the lovers swore fidelity on their crucifixes and gave no other bond: "Sufficient troth, that we shall rise – / Deposed – at length, the Grave – / To that new Marriage, / Justified – through Calvaries of Love."

With the perspective of time Emily Dickinson began to evaluate her lost beloved with more objective eyes; the result was that her image of him waned in stature. As early as 1862, in poem 388, "Take Your Heaven further on," a tone of lofty disdain toward

him is apparent. Be gone with your paltry physical paradise, she
seems to say, she will occupy herself henceforth with the heaven
of God. The poem is imbued with an almost bitter rejection and
an air of moral superiority toward a lover who is depicted here
as an insensitive bungler.

> Take Your Heaven further on –
> This – to Heaven divine Has gone –
> Had You earlier blundered in
> Possibly, e'en You had seen
> An Eternity – put on –
> Now – to ring a Door beyond
> Is the utmost of Your Hand –
> To the Skies – apologize –
> Nearer to Your Courtesies
> Than this Sufferer polite –
> Dressed to meet You –
> See – in White.

A poem dated a year later may be interpreted to mean that her
renunciation of her lover was motivated by conscience and fidelity
to an ideal and that these superior moral considerations dwarfed
in importance the significance of her love relationship. The latter
half of the poem reads: "Renunciation – is the Choosing / Against
itself – / Itself to justify / Unto itself – / When larger function – /
Make that appear – / Smaller – that Covered Vision – Here."
(no. 745).

With the passing of another year the love affair at times appears
in retrospect a little shrunken and alien, like a garment whose
style has become dated: "We outgrow love, like other things,"
she observes (poem 887). Another poem, no. 747, may possibly
refer to something other than her dwindling estimation of her
lover, although its sentiment is consistent with the poems that
express negative feelings toward him.

> It dropped so low – in my Regard –
> I heard it hit the Ground –
> And go to pieces on the Stones
> At bottom of my Mind –
>
> Yet blamed the Fate that flung it – *less*
> Than I denounced Myself,
> For entertaining Plated Wares
> Upon my Silver Shelf –

A somewhat earlier poem, also inexplicit with regard to its referent, observes that "We see – Comparatively" and that what seemed of such towering importance yesterday "This Morning's finer Verdict – / Makes scarcely worth the toil." Thus, mountains are seen in this new perspective to be, in reality, mere molehills. The poet goes on to speculate that perhaps the seeming cruelty of the God who enjoins upon us such painful sunderings is actually a kindness "to spare these Striding Spirits / Some Morning of Chagrin – / The waking in a Gnat's – embrace – / Our Giants – further on." (poem 534).

Finally, the poet reaches a point where she can hardly believe that she could ever have longed so for something that at last appears to her entirely unworthy of her interest:

> Art thou the thing I wanted?
> Begone – my Tooth has grown –
> Invite some minor Palate
> That has not starved so long –
> I tell thee while I famished –
> The mystery of Food
> Increased till I abjured it
> And dine without Like God –
>
> (Poem 1282, 1873)

This, then, is the story the poems and letters tell. The poet became acquainted with an unattainable (probably married) man and, by a process almost imperceptible to herself, came to love him with a consuming intensity whose vehemence she did not fully realize until after they had parted. The man, perceiving her attraction and ignoring his prior commitments (presumably out of passion), indicated to the poet that he loved her also. The poet was flooded with rapture and imagined herself elevated to the status of a queen. She felt baptized into a new life, revitalized, exalted, fulfilled—completely the man's wife in every way but legally and sexually. His simple recognition almost contented her. The man, however, ultimately became importunate—wished to consummate their love in physical intimacy. The poet, having many sexual reservations and fears, was alarmed and refused to allow this, reminding the man of the strictures of morality—of his obligation to his wife. There followed a scene of anguished parting whose only consolation was the hope of an eventual reunion in heaven after death. Later, the man revealed that he was offended, and he accused the poet of feigning or exaggerating a love she was, in reality, too inexperienced to feel. He then retreated from the relationship, and the poet, fearful that she had lost his affection, pursued him with avowals of her love and reminders that they would be together in paradise. She desperately tried to explain that her refusal to submit to his sexual demands was not a reflection on the sincerity or depth of her love. The "Master" letters indicate the extent of her desperate need of her lover and the fact that "Master" now clearly had the upper hand. There followed months, perhaps years, of despair for the poet, who felt that her one chance for happiness had eluded her. The pain subsided and soon she began to take a new look at her relationship with her beloved. The abject humiliation of the "Master" letters was superseded by a posture of regal dignity and scorn. "Master" then tended to be regarded as wholly unworthy of her and as an altogether inferior creature whom her love had invested with a kingly aura. This attitude, however, continued to alternate with one that anticipated the lovers' eventual reunion in heaven. As much as ten years later Emily Dickinson still regarded her blighted love affair as the summit of her life. The theme in her poetry dwindled in prominence at the same time that her total poetic output declined. The letters and poems indicate that her preoccupation with her love faded, and more philosophical ruminations and other relationships, mostly epistolary, replaced it. Seventeen years later she had found a new "Master" in Judge Lord, to whom she expressed an undesperate, self-possessed, and warm, though similarly ambivalent, affection.

Emily Dickinson's love poetry has stimulated more curiosity and speculation with regard to the identity of her lover than it has critical analysis and appreciation. Indeed, it is difficult to find a commentator who enthusiastically admires the love poetry. Clark Griffith, for example, calls it "thin and brittle," "drably unoriginal," says that it has a "somewhat mechanical quality," and concludes that "the love theme was surely Emily Dickinson's weakest" and that it "has received an acclaim that is all out of keeping with its intrinsic value."[23]

Richard Chase, though somewhat less harsh, is in general agreement. Emily Dickinson, he says, "would not be of great eminence, surely, if her reputation depended solely on her love poems."[24] Henry Wells also, in commenting on the love poetry, remarks, "This is not the Emily Dickinson who will last best . . . The great Emily is not here."[25] And, finally, Charles Anderson concludes his review of the love poems thus: "In spite of some freshness of phrasing and an occasional haunting image, these poems tend to fritter themselves away in a series of exclamations."[26]

One of the objections these men have to the poems is that they lack genuine erotic passion. Griffith calls the emotion of the poems "a contrived passion, a passion that the poet borrowed from an eminently public literary convention," and he suggests that possibly "from time to time [Emily Dickinson] ground out a set of love lyrics, for no better reason than her belief that this was the accepted thing—the conventional thing—for poets of the age to do."[27] Chase believes that these poems are more concerned with the increased status being loved brings to the woman than with her emotional investment with the man. "Her love poems," he says, "show a persistent impulse to establish lover and loved in a kind of legalized hierarchy, instead of picturing the ecstatic fusing of souls or weeping at the swift passage of time."[28] Wells observes, "In her use of two of the most important reservoirs of inspiration for the lyric [religion and love], Emily unhappily stood at considerable disadvantage . . . In the usual sense she writes very few hymns either of praise or of passion . . . Passion she hardly experienced as by far the greater number of the masters of poetry and art have experienced it." He goes on to say that Emily Dickinson metamorphosed her love into something intangible, something idealistic and metaphysical, and that "some of her best poems on love remain remarkably noncommital on the subject." When, however, the love affair is rendered in more human and mundane terms, he seems to be saying, the poems are less convincing: "Where Emily is franker and fuller in her love poems, she tends to lose the finest distinction of her poetic imagination, to forfeit her originality, and to fall back to some extent upon current romantic taste." Wells concludes that Emily Dickinson's best love poems are those which envision her reunion with her lover in heaven: "They are, then, elegies as well as love poems, and songs of death as well as of passion . . . They are not love poems in the manner of Sappho, Catullus, Villon, or Burns, but in a manner Emily made peculiarly her own."[29] Anderson seems to agree that erotic passion is not Emily Dickinson's strong point: "it can be said that in her poetry spiritual ecstasy burns with a purer incandescence than amorous joy, and it creates better poems."[30]

These writers agree that the poems are weakened by the fact that the figure of the beloved man lacks presence. The love poems of Shakespeare, Donne, and Elizabeth Barrett Browning, says Griffith, "ordinarily provide two centers of interest—provide a sharp sense of time, but also a sharp sense of the loved one . . . whom time bears away—Miss Dickinson's habit is to subordinate the loved one to mutability." The poems of Emily Dickinson, he says, seem addressed to "disembodied personages . . . without much substance or identity."[31] Chase makes the same observation: "The lover is rather ghostly," he writes; "Very little appears to happen to him; she possesses him and the experience he brings her, and she makes the 'marriage' an integral part of her life."[32] Citing the poem "There came a day at Summer's full," Chase says that it is "somewhat weakened by a running analogy between the lovers and various phenomena associated with the Christian religion which tend to give a remoteness, an intangibility to the lovers and their feelings."[33] And Anderson, referring to the same much-admired poem, says, "The situation involving the renunciation is so obscure the reader is not able to share in the anguish, nor for that matter are the lovers." Anderson then advises the reader to regard "both lover and beloved as poetic figures, and [to read] the individual poems as images of love rather than as aspects of a narrative."[34] In another place, Anderson remarks that "in all the bridal poems . . . the bridegroom is conspicuous by his absence."[35] Rebecca Patterson also makes the same observation: "there is no man—no real man—anywhere in the poems."[36]

Reducing these critical demurers to their basic objections, one is faced with the following conclusions: the love poems of Emily Dickinson are unlike those of other poets; her portrayals of erotic passion are unconvincing; her lover is lacking in individuality and solidity; the love relationship is attenuated to a hope for future paradisaical fulfillment; some of the poems appear to be derived less from experience than from reading.

It may strike the reader as odd that the poet Yvor Winters called "one of the greatest lyric poets of all time"[37] should fail so miserably in the area considered the special province of lyric poets. Yet it is not necessary to concur in the poor regard with which the critics quoted above view the love poems to realize that their reservations, being so much in agreement, have a basis in fact. The attentive reader must agree that Emily Dickinson's love poems do not resemble, say, the positive assertions of Juliet, who was sure of her love, secure in her feminine passion, uninhibited by conventional propriety, unintimidated in the face of sexuality. Emily Dickinson's lover is not a flesh and blood Romeo, say the critics, and the poet seems never to have approached him closely enough to have touched his flesh or felt the pulsing of his blood. The poets with whom she is unfavorably compared had consummated sex lives. Compared with theirs, Emily Dickinson's bridal lyrics appear to be not so much love poems as the airy embodiments of unfulfilled longing.

Although Thomas Johnson believes that Emily Dickinson's lover was the Reverend Charles Wadsworth, what he has to say about the poet's relationship with the clergyman would apply as well to any other of her male friends placed in the role of renounced lover. Johnson writes: "to [Emily Dickinson] it was a basic necessity that he [Wadsworth] continue in all ways to be exactly the image of him that she had created. For her he must be both immediate and afar, acutely desired yet renounced, a physical being to be seen and touched if only by handclasp after long intervals, yet a counselor to be longed for and reached by letter . . . The 'bridal' and renunciation poems have meaning when interpreted as a part of Emily Dickinson's lifelong need for a preceptor, a muse whom she could adore with physical passion in her imagination . . . one doubts that their communications touched upon poetry or that he was aware that her creative energies stemmed from the spell which he had unaccountably induced. One imagines that she gained her inspiration from the relationship that her imagination projected."[38]

Certainly this view does much to explain the remoteness of the lover's poetic image: Emily Dickinson adored her "Master" *with physical passion in her imagination*; he had *unaccountably induced* the outpouring of her poetic genius; her inspiration flowed from a love affair *that her imagination projected*. In other words, according to Johnson, there never was anything in reality resembling the agonizing, intense, frightening, and all but consummated love relationship depicted in the poetry. Johnson does not offer to explain why Emily Dickinson had a need for such a remote lover or why, since in his view the danger can never have been imminent, so many poems portray intense sexual anxiety. If Emily Dickinson was simply fabricating a love affair around the person of a distant and highly respectable clergyman, why do her poems not resemble more closely those of Elizabeth Barrett Browning in projecting an affair that was unmarred by such unromantic apprehensions? And unless the "Master" letters are to be taken as literary exercises which Emily Dickinson never intended for any real person, one finds it difficult to reconcile them with Mr. Johnson's suggestion that the lover was the decorous Wadsworth. For it is clear from the letters that "Master" was piqued at the poet's refusal to surrender herself to his sexual needs.

Here we are faced with a dilemma. If "Master" existed and was close enough to Emily Dickinson frequently enough to feel he might proffer offers of sexual intimacy with her, why does he appear so insubstantial and unindividualized in the verse? If, on the other hand, he was a veritable stranger except for letters and a man of conventional and stringent moral standards—both of which descriptions fit Wadsworth—how does one explain the "Master" letters and the poet's uneasy preoccupation with sexual matters? Rebecca Patterson solved this problem by asserting that the lover was, in reality, a woman. This hypothesis would explain the lack of a distinct masculine image in the verse, while at the same time it would account for the sexual fears and reservations. The "Master" letters alone, however, are sufficient to explode this theory. In them it is clearly stated that "Master" has a beard; the relationship the letters picture is that between a small fragile, immature female and an older, parental, kindly, somewhat formidable male.

In order to reconcile the lover's unreality with his very real sexual menace, it is necessary simply to assume that Emily Dickinson had a compelling need to elaborate a love fantasy while at the same time she was desperately insistent that it remain just that, and that the lover, mistaking her intentions, presumed to offer an invitation to sexual intimacy which, bursting the framework of her dream, produced in her feelings of dread, revulsion, and moral indignation. The man's real needs, his individual personality, and the circumstances of his life were not of any genuine emotional interest to the poet, according to this view. Therefore, they did not find their way into the poetry. His personal attributes were largely irrelevant to her overriding need, which, as Johnson says, was to elaborate an imaginary relationship employing the living man as a mere scaffold for the constructions of a dream. Her pain at her "lover's" irritability and offended pride and her fear that he might dismiss her from his mind indicate another need in addition to the necessity of maintaining the semblance of a total but ill-starred love. This second need is that she remain unconscious of her lack of authentic commitment to the relationship. Her agony following the renunciation, despite the fact that there seems to have existed in reality little to renounce, had to be real. In fact her agony *was* real, but as will be indicated later, it had its roots elsewhere than in her relationship with the interdicted lover.

It cannot be overstressed that it was her lover's presumed unattainability that was his chief attraction; this was the major attribute that qualified him for the role her emotional needs dictated he play. Many poems, in a general way, attest to her insight that this was indeed the case. The theme is rendered explicitly in poem 239, written in 1861, the first two stanzas of which are as follows:

> "Heaven" – is what I cannot reach!
> The Apple on the Tree –
> Provided it do hopeless – hang –
> That – "Heaven" is – to Me!
>
> The Color, on the Cruising Cloud –
> The interdicted Land –
> Behind the Hill – the House behind –
> There – Paradise – is found!

Another poem written in the same year (no. 257) begins "Delight is as the flight" and states that "flight / Were Aliment."

The first lines of poem 801, "I play at Riches – to appease / The Clamoring for Gold," may be interpreted as meaning that a fantasy of love may be employed as a substitute for a real love relationship. The poem goes on to say that the poet comforts herself for the love that is lacking with the thought that through her emotional "poverty" she is able to derive a greater appreciation of the value of love. The poem concludes with the lines "I know not which, Desire, or Grant – / Be wholly beautiful." The theme of poem 815 is that the luxury of simply imagining a confrontation with her beloved is so satisfying in itself that "for a further Food / I scarcely recollect to starve / So first am I supplied." The mere remembrance of feasting on her lover's face "A Sumptuousness bestows / On plainer Days."

Poem 1057 presents the same idea, a little differently—that what one loses consequently grows increasingly important.

> I had a daily Bliss
> I half indifferent viewed
> Till Sudden I perceived it stir –
> It grew as I pursued
>
> Till when around a Hight
> It wasted from my sight
> Increased beyond my utmost scope
> I learned to estimate.

If it is legitimate to apply this poem to Emily Dickinson's love affair, it can be taken as a reflection of the fact that only after the renunciation was a fait accompli did the lover take on his tremendous importance; as soon, that is, as he was safely distant, it became possible to elaborate the romantic dream. Poem 1071 speaks to the same point

> Perception of an object costs
> Precise the Object's loss –
> Perception in itself a Gain
> Replying to it's Price –
>
> The Object Absolute – is nought –
> Perception sets it fair
> And then upbraids a Perfectness
> That situates so far –

That the lover took on imaginary qualities of grandeur and preciousness once it became safe for her that he do so is suggested by poem 1083.

> We learn in the Retreating
> How vast an one

Was recently among us –
A Perished Sun

Endear in the departure
How doubly more
Than all the Golden presence
It was – before –

The idea that the "fruit perverse to plucking" is sweetest haunted Emily Dickinson and, as those excerpts indicate, became a favorite poetic theme. Poem 1209 begins "To disappear enhances" and makes the observation that when a thing of no value is withdrawn from us forever we, rendered "impotent to cherish," "hasten to adorn."

Let me now turn back to the questions raised earlier by the love poetry and the "Master" letters. How was it possible that Emily Dickinson could move so emphatically and swiftly from her former uncertainties of sexual identity and orientation directly into the arms of a man? For years Emily Dickinson held desperately to latency-age interpersonal social patterns through dread of adulthood and inability to quell the turmoil of her repudiated femininity. By what psychological alchemy could she be suddenly enabled to abandon herself to a grand heterosexual passion? The answer is to be found in the idealistic and spiritualized passion of the poems, their paucity of true erotic feeling, their sexual apprehensiveness, the literary and derivative quality of some of them (from a poet who is other wise preeminently original), and in the insubstantiality of the lover. Suggestive also are: the critical complaint that the poems are unlike Shakespeare's, Donne's, or even Elizabeth Barrett Browning's; the frustration and apparent chagrin of "Master"; the poet's repeatedly expressed view that fantasy surpasses reality; the stress she placed on the ineligibility of her lover; and her determination to convince herself that she had the best part of love. Speaking also to the same point are her later refusal to marry the widowed Judge Lord and the entire virginal course of her life following her renunciation of "Master." All these considerations must be taken as evidence that in fact Emily Dickinson never did accomplish the leap from adolescent erotic tentativeness to mature womanly capacity. The story of Emily Dickinson's love affair as it is told in the poems cannot be accepted at face value. Her poetic record and the "Master" letters taken together indicate a different reality behind the poems. It is not valid to conclude, however, that because this is so the love story is merely a species of fiction. The truth appears to be that it falls midway between the extremes of fact and fantasy.

The question remains to be answered: What was the function of "Master" in the poet's psychic economy if he was not a complete and real love object?

In the initial effort to grapple with this problem it may be helpful to turn again to the third "Master" letter. Here, as in many other instances in which Emily Dickinson writes to older men and women, the poet places herself in the relation of child to adult. "Master—open your life wide," she pleads, "and take me in forever . . . I will never be noisy when you want to be still. I will be your best little girl."[39] This suggests that "Master" is, on one level at least, the embodiment of the protective, all-powerful parent. The poet's love for him resembles that of a child for its mother or father, intensely dependent and protection-seeking and based on the sense of her own relative frailty and diminutive stature. The search for a loving parent is a current that continually undermines Emily Dickinson's life in its several phases, and one should not be surprised to find it contributing a measure of energy to her thrust toward "Master." However, one cannot read Emily Dickinson's love poems without realizing that the need to be cared for as a dependent child plays only a small part in the total structure of her relationship with the beloved man.

It is clear that the passion of the poems is frequently smothered by sexual dread and constrained by inhibitions which tend to channel the flesh and blood encounter of the lovers into a postponed, rarefied, and heaven-oriented commitment. Nevertheless, it is apparent from the "Master" letters and from a perhaps small percentage of the poems that intense erotic emotions were present on the poet's side of the relationship. For example, to "Master" she writes that if it had been God's will she would have been allowed to "breathe where you breathed—and find the place—myself—at night . . . I wish with a might I cannot repress—that mine were the Queen's place."[40] Also, the poem "Wild Nights" (no. 249) is a good example of heightened erotic stimulation. Colonel Higginson, in preparing this poem for publication, expressed qualms "lest the malignant read into it more than that virgin recluse ever dreamed of putting there."[41] The poem is reprinted here again so that the malignant may judge for themselves the nature of the fantasies that occupied the virgin recluse.

> Wild Nights – Wild Nights!
> Were I with thee
> Wild Nights should be
> Our luxury!
>
> Futile – the Winds –
> To a Heart in port –
> Done with the Compass –
> Done with the Chart!
>
> Rowing in Eden –
> Ah, the Sea!
> Might I but moor – Tonight –
> In Thee!

If Emily Dickinson had been devoid of erotic stirrings, she would have felt indifference to sexual encounter, not dread, and her relationship with "Master" would have had the character of a friendship.

Clinical psychiatric experience attests to the truth of this observation. Most commonly, sexual fears and inhibitions are in reality disguised expressions of strong underlying sexual impulses and are related to uncertainties regarding one's ability to keep these impulses reigned in and within bounds that one considers appropriate and safe. To lack such covert urges is for the most part to be free of anxiety.

When I speak of strong erotic passion underlying her reservations, I may seem here to be contradicting a previously made assertion that Emily Dickinson never achieved the psychosexual maturity to respond fully to a man. It should be pointed out that human beings, of every age and at every stage along the psychological continuum to full emotional maturity, experience erotic feelings toward others. It is the way these feelings are integrated into the person's behavior and interpersonal relationships that determines his capacity for an adult love relationship. Without a doubt, Emily Dickinson was possessed of intense erotic emotions. Their primary stimulus, however, seems not to have been the one she was aware of and she therefore managed to keep it at a distance—the interdicted lover. To attain a plausible psychological explanation of Emily Dickinson's love affair, one must regard it as representative of a massive displacement of emotion generated in quite another context than in her relationship with "Master" and projected beyond the bounds of its origin to this man she initially regarded as safely distant and inaccessible.

What was the real situation that evoked passions so threatening and inadmissible that Emily Dickinson was driven to this desperate defensive maneuver? The marriage of Austin and Susan, of course. Emily exclaimed of "Master," "Ah, what a royal sake / To my necessity – stooped down!" (poem 195). What exactly was her necessity? The tremendous need for someone to provide her with love and emotional support, but even more important, the need for a person who could serve as the object of that welter of overwhelming and unsatisfied emotions which had been generated by the Austin-Susan-Emily triangle.

Rage at her abandonment and all the heightened libidinal expectations aroused by Austin's courtship were the emotions which she had to discharge somehow. And the rage was not mere anger but was enormously intensified, one must recall, through the addition of revived feelings of deprivation associated with her father and mother, of whom Austin and Susan were unconsciously representative. Emily, as abandoned child, was furious, and containing wrath of such virulence, she was dangerously vulnerable to prostrating depression. If the murderous rage cannot be satisfied outright (as it cannot, usually), there are only two recourses: it can be repressed—that is, turned toward the self, which means depression and death-obsession—or the rage can be totally nullified through satisfaction of the frustrated needs which provoked the anger in the first place. The choice was made for Emily Dickinson when Samuel Bowles, or Charles Wadsworth, or whatever male acquaintance was destined for this role as "Master," offered his strength and sympathy and opened the floodgates upon himself. The release brought the poet a wave of anguish and ecstasy that dispersed itself in the creative tide that reached its crest in 1862, never afterward to be approximated.

Emily Dickinson had made the momentous discovery that the organization and symbolic intensity of poetry relieved and channeled her pent-up feelings to a degree afforded by no other avenue open to her. In this poet, creativity and psychic disorganization came within a hair's breadth of each other. The delusion expressed in her letter to the Norcrosses that a prowler was going to break in and rape her reveals a fearful, unconscious desire approaching awareness, and is a sign the instinctual life was overwhelming the forces of control. Distorted memories or childhood fantasies of sex play with Austin may also have revived and escaped from the repression of her disintegrating ego. When she struggled to keep her sexual conflicts out of awareness, they came back in the disguished fantasies and fears of sexual assault: " I must shut *my* door for fear *front* door slide open on me at the 'dead of night' " (italics added);[42] in other words it was not the plundering of the house she feared but someone who would seek *her* out within her own bedroom. For what purpose? The fear reveals the hidden wish. The terrifying nightmare of the worm in her room, "Pink, lank and warm," that became a snake "ringed with power" (poem 1670) may have dated from this time. Her defense against such primitive and taboo fantasms was to weld them to wishfulfillment daydreams fabricated around a distant "beloved."

The Reverend Charles Wadsworth would never have made the sexual advances ascribed to the man of the poems. His being the model would have necessitated her imagination's being inflamed indeed, and her "Master" letters, if he were the recipient, could not help but have struck him as the overheated effusions of a woman suffering from hysteria. It is a little easier to believe that some other of the poet's male friends, perhaps Samuel Bowles, actually gave her cause to think that he had a romantic interest in her. However, even Mr. Bowles—good friend of Austin and the pious Dr. Holland—though apparently not above occasional infidelities to his wife, is not likely to have made the proposals of the man of the poems under the only circumstances in which Bowles saw Emily, that is, in the homes of her relatives. What she possibly did, therefore, was to invest her daydreams with the vividness of projected feelings, thereby creating, as a form of *pseudologia fantastica,* the substance of her love poetry.

Pseudologic fantasies involve by definition the communication to others of imaginary experiences in the guise of real happenings. They differ from other fantasies in being essentially elaborations of forgotten memories of actual events which have been retained in the unconscious. The real characteristics of the repressed experiences give to the pseudologic fantasy an air of almost irresistible credibility. Yet they differ also from delusions in that the subject knows they are not true.

Helene Deutsch in *The Psychology of Women* describes a teen-age patient she once treated who bears certain striking resemblances to Emily Dickinson at the time with which this chapter deals. Dr. Deutsch says of this patient:

> She is an attractive girl, intelligent and of ardent temperament. She does not lack opportunities for amorous relations, but always avoids them with the greatest reserve. A high school boy of about 17, rather unattractive, whom she knows only by sight, becomes the hero of her erotic fantasies. These have an extremely passionate character —consuming kisses, ardent embraces, sexual ecstasies, the young girl's imagination creating everything that reality can give to a sexually mature woman. She becomes so absorbed in this fantasy that in her seclusion she leads a life full of joys and sorrows; her eyes are often swollen with tears because her lover turns out to be tyrannical, covers her with abuse, and even beats her; then, overflowing with love, he brings her flowers that actually she buys herself. She manages to get a picture of him and on it she writes a loving dedication in her own hand, distorted for the purpose. She has dates with him in forbidden places, they become secretly engaged, etc. For three years she keeps a detailed diary about all their imaginary experiences; when her lover goes away she continues her relations with him by writing him letters that she never mails, and to which she replies herself . . . Her descriptions are so convincing that no one doubts the truth of them, even though the innocent boy has denied having any relations with her.

As we have said, this girl had every opportunity to experience in reality what she invented pseudologically. But she had several motives for preferring the latter course . . . In her choice of "lover" she was determined by her unconscious attitude toward her brother . . . The regressive nature of adolescent fantasies is manifested in the fact that as a rule the real objects that are chosen strongly resemble earlier objects—that is to say, father or brother . . . our pseudologic girl tries to center her longing on a real object, but succeeds only partially. She chooses one object after the model of her brother, but she is incapable of a real love relation. The kind of relation she wants must be imaginary, not real. The girl strictly avoided every opportunity to become acquainted with the hero of her fantasies. She preferred the fantasy; in it her brother, to whom she was unconsciously faithful, and her real object could merge. In her childhood she had had various real experiences with her brother that were preserved in her unconscious and that at a given moment were revived with all the force of a fresh experience. The old experience was attributed to the new object, and former reality endowed the present love fantasy with a real character.[43]

The patient thus described by Dr. Deutsch was quite conscious that she herself wrote the love letters and that the events recorded in her diary were not true. In spite of this awareness the concealed burden of reality carried by the fantasies gave them a verisimilitude that strongly impelled even the subject of them toward a belief in their reality.

To what extent is the foregoing applicable to Emily Dickinson's love poems? The *emotional* reality that invests the poems overbalances the fictitious elements they contain and impresses upon most readers a conviction that the poems record authentic happenings. The poems which convey sexual fears and suggest that the man introduced an urgent and unwanted sexual element into the relationship are so atypical of love poetry in general and so much in accord with the same theme as it appears in the "Master" letters that one is impelled to believe that Emily Dickinson drew closer to "Master" than Dr. Deutsch's patient approached her "lover." The precise nature of "Master's" role is impossible to decide on the evidence available. With her desperate need to project her feelings safely beyond the confines of her family, it would not be surprising if the poet ascribed to him a degree of emotional involvement far out of proportion to his actual interest. She then might easily mistake Samuel Bowles's avuncular affection or even Charles Wadsworth's pastoral solicitude for much deeper feelings. Hyperalert to any signal from the man she "loved," she might find every glance and vocal inflection fraught with meaning and misinterpret them as guarded expressions of his love. Under the pressure of her own heightened susceptibility and sexual tension, she may have attributed equally vehement feelings to him and fled from him in fear.

If "Master" gave her *no cause whatever* to believe he desired her (which, however, seems unlikely from the poet's letters to him), the love poetry would be less pseudologic and more akin to frank delusion or even *psychose passionelle*. This latter condition, also called Clerambault's syndrome or pure erotomania, leaves the intellectual functions and most of the personality relatively intact. The disordered thought processes are confined almost exclusively to the mistaken belief, found usually in a married woman, that a man other than her husband is in love with her. The woman believes that circumstances make it impossible either for him to express his attachment, except by slight hints, or for her openly to reciprocate. Silvano Arieti's description of the disorder and his observation that "this love becomes the purpose of the existence of the patient, and everything in her life revolves around it,"[44] is not incompatible with what we know of Emily Dickinson.

It should be emphasized that the issue in qustion here is not the psychological necessity and dynamics of the poet's engrossment in her "Master." These seem clear enough. What is in doubt is the degree of her departure from reality as manifested by the love poetry. A delusion implies a greater degree of reality severence than does *pseudologia fantastica,* and it is evident that once before Emily Dickinson was pushed beyond the limits of rationality. In either case, however, the underlying defensive mechanism would be the displacement of forbidden feelings to a safely distant object.

The point, important for American literature, is that threatening personality disintegration compelled a frantic Emily Dickinson to create poetry—for her a psychosis-deflecting activity. In her poetic outpouring her yearning, projected and modified as indicated, now became entirely conscious, although its real origin of course remained hidden from her. It was then safely sealed and contained within the structure of the poems and rendered practically guilt free through the guise of an intense but ordinary love affair. Thus through poetic creation she had intensified her identification as a woman through psychic fusion with Sue, achieved a vicarious motherhood through this symbolic gestation, and satisfied, in fantasy, some of her libidinal needs. "My Wars are laid away in Books," she said (poem 1549).

Though a second psychotic breakdown seems to have been deflected, the displacements, symbolic realizations, and illusions which palliated her pain did not in the end replace reality. As the fruitful crisis passed, depression gradually took its place. The deceptive gifts of lover, child, and femininity, like all products of magic, lost their luster, faded and, over the course of the next

half dozen years, vanished altogether. Early in 1862 Emily sent
Sue a poem (no. 299)* which indicates that she already foresaw
this resolution:

Your – Riches taught me – poverty!
Myself, a "Millionaire" [a]
In little – wealths – as Girls can boast –
Till broad as "Buenos Ayre"
You drifted your Dominions –
A Different – Peru –
And I esteemed – all – poverty –
For Life's Estate – with you!

Of "Mines" [b] – I little know – myself –
But just the *names* – of *Gems* [c] –
The *Colors* of the *Commonest* –
And scarce of Diadems –
So much – that did I meet the *Queen* –
Her glory – I should know –
But *this* – must be a *different wealth* [d] –
To miss it – beggars –so!

I'm sure 'tis *"India"* – all day –
To those who look on you [e] –
Without a stint – without a blame –
Might I – but be the Jew!
I know it is "Golconda" –
Beyond my power to dream –
To have a smile – for mine – each day –
How *better* – than a *Gem*!

At least – it solaces – to know –
That there *exists* – a *Gold* –
Altho' I prove it, just in time –
It's distance – to behold!
It's far – far – Treasure – to surmise –
And estimate – the Pearl [f] –
That slipped – my simple fingers – thro'
While yet a Girl – at School!

* My interpretations of several obscure references in the poem are indicated in the
text by letters in brackets: (a) "Millionaire," as is known from a letter to Kate
Anthon (*Letters,* II, 365, no. 222), means a woman who is loved and probably alludes here to "Master's" love for Emily; (b) "Mines" refers here to husbands, or
persons bound to one permanently and conceived of as inexhaustible sources of
affection; (c) the *"names — of Gems"* refers to casual acquaintanceships with admired individuals; (d) *"different wealth"* is evidently the possession of a baby;

Sue had Austin and her baby to love and be loved by—the riches that emphasized by contrast Emily's poverty. And what did Emily have? A cache of great poems in her drawer that she was never assured lived or breathed and that remained there, not to see the light of day until after her death. She possessed a fine mind and a rare talent, but none of the primitive and fundamental gratifications that she longed for and that constitute the goal of all our inescapable instincts. A longing to be loved, to be comfortable in herself, and to nurture young exists in every woman, and the thwarting of these impulses produces an aching emptiness for which intellectual achievements and fantasy can only partially compensate.

For Emily, Austin's home was a constant reminder of all she lacked. Her first reliable biographer, George Whicher, summed up her life and work in these words: "The fact everpresent to her consciousness was that what she most asked of life had been denied her."[45] With her soul, as she said, against the windowpane, she looked often toward the house next door.

Her letters from 1862 to 1866 continue at intervals to provide glimpses of her depression and difficulty in regaining her equilibrium. In March 1862, she wrote Samuel Bowles a letter in which she playfully yet strangely referred to herself throughout as "Austin,"[46] thereby overtly revealing her identification with her brother. In May 1863, she wrote her Norcross cousins that agitated and dreadful letter to the effect that she had "a snarl in the brain which don't unravel yet"[47] and spoke of an anguish of long standing which still tormented her. In September 1864, she wrote Sue, "Do not cease, Sister. Should I turn in my long night I should murmur 'Sue.' "[48] The long night continued, and in May 1865 she told Sue, "I live in the Sea always."[49] Her last trips before her irrevocable withdrawal from society were made in 1864, when she lived for seven months in Cambridge, Massachusetts, with the cousins and in 1865, when she spent six months with them. Both visits were ostensibly made to obtain treatment for her eyes. Her letters, however, give the impression that the eye difficulty was only one symptom closely related to and aggravated by the poet's emotional responses to her situation.

(e) those who look on Sue all day are Austin and the baby; (f) "Pearl" may refer to several early friends who died, to the renounced "Master," or to Sue and Austin themselves.

The creative furor which produced 366 poems in 1862 subsided. By 1863 her productivity had fallen off; that year brought
141 poems. The following year saw 174 new poems. By 1865 the
number had dwindled to 85, by 1866, 36; and in 1867 the poet
reached the nadir of her creative life with only 10 poems ascribable to that year. These latter poems are generally impersonal;
they are either nature studies or philosophical reflections and they
are devoid of the strange and startling symbolism of the poems of
1861 and 1862.

It is surprising that the years 1864 and 1865 brought as many
poems as they did, for the letters from Cambridge are heavy with
depression and the poet's concern for her vision. By this time
Emily Dickinson may have realized that her passion for "Master"
was illusory—that it was a late manifestation of the attenuation
of reality contact that had afflicted her following Austin's marriage. Poem 1113 (1867) suggests that her major consolation at
this time was that she had again survived; the poem begins:
"There is a strength in proving that it can be bourne / Although
it tear."

Sue's riches continued to teach Emily what poverty was. In a
somewhat obscure poem of 1862 (no. 631) one thing stands out
clearly: Emily is comparing herself to a more fortunate woman.
The woman can only have been Sue. The first two stanzas are
as follows:

> Ourselves were wed one summer – dear –
> Your Vision – was in June –
> And when Your little Lifetime failed,
> I wearied – too – of mine –
>
> And overtaken in the Dark –
> Where You had put me down –
> By Some one carrying a Light –
> I – too – received the Sign.

The first line has been interpreted variously but undoubtedly
means "Ourselves were wed [to different men] one summer."
Though the poem indicates that the other woman's marriage was
in June, the reader will recall that Susan and Austin were actually
married on July 1. Susan, however, left Amherst to be married
in Geneva sometime in June and had written earlier that month,
"The last of June, if nothing mal-apropos occurs we shall be mar-

ried . . . in Geneva."[50] Doubtless, therefore, both Susan and Emily thought of Susan as a June bride.

"When Your little Lifetime failed" probably means *when you withdrew from me* or *when you failed me*. It cannot mean *when you died* (*failed* in other contexts is an Emily Dickinson euphemism for *died*) because this meaning is contradicted by the last two stanzas, which reveal the other woman's prosperity. In any case, when the woman withdrew and left the poet without the illumination of love, "Some one," undoubtedly "Master," discovered her and bestowed the "Sign" of a spiritual marriage upon her. The final two stanzas express the disparity in outcome between the two "marriages"; Emily's leads to deprivation and sterility, Sue's to abundance and life:

> 'Tis true – Our Futures different lay –
> Your Cottage – faced the sun –
> While Oceans – and the North must be –
> On every side of mine
>
> 'Tis true, Your Garden led the Bloom,
> For mine – in Frosts – was sown –
> And yet, one Summer, we were Queens –
> But You – were crowned in June –

The final coronation in June may commemorate the birth of Susan's son, Ned, born the June immediately preceding the poem's composition. Though fate, in time, did much to equalize their separate fortunes, at this time Sue's apparently completely fulfilled life made Emily feel all the colder and more barren by contrast. Her handwriting shows her impoverishment dramatically. The originality and richness of form apparent before 1862 is gradually replaced by stiffness and aridity—a garden sown in frosts.

The course of Emily Dickinsons illness and the symptoms it brought into play can be understood as a series of attempts to maintain or regain a precarious psychic equilibrium in the face of great inner and outer stress. Because of the early and continuing impoverishment of essential relationships, the demands of maturation and independent adulthood greatly exceeded her resources. She asked, in effect, not only Colonel Higginson but everyone she knew: "Could you tell me how to grow?"[51] She clearly could not find the answer herself.

Those readers who approach Emily Dickinson's love poetry expecting to find the outpouring of an unconstrained and romantic love emotion find to their disappointment that it exists only in those verses which are least her own. Since she never loved unreservedly according to the romantic ideal, it is understandable that she was unable to project into her poems that perfect fusing of souls—or that total dedication of one soul, requited or unrequited—that is the sine qua non of erotic verse. Perhaps the public acceptance these verses have gained, as opposed to the negative response of professional criticism, is in part due to the fact that a great many readers are themselves not as acquainted with the uninhibited and all-consuming heroic passions as they might wish. The view of a psychiatrist is of course subject to distortion because patients rarely consult him when their love lives are perfectly satisfying. Be this as it may, the profession as a whole is in general agreement that even in this day of permissiveness and toleration of a diversity of sexual behaviors there is still considerable unhappiness of this variety among us, and it is believed that it has its origin in the thwarting of maturational processes similar to those which tormented Emily Dickinson. Readers therefore may recognize in her poetry some of their own anxieties and reservations and find her ecstatic anguish speaking more intimately and realistically to their inner lives than the extroverted affirmations of poets who are more ostensibly healthy and satisfied in their love affairs.

For example, it is hard to imagine a more haunting evocation of an impossible love—the poet's love for "Master"—than the last two stanzas of poem 925:

> Most – I love the Cause that slew Me.
> Often as I die
> It's beloved Recognition
> Holds a Sun on Me –
>
> Best – at Setting – as is Nature's –
> Neither witnessed Rise
> Till the infinite Aurora
> In the other's eyes.

Chapter IX   SUNSET AT EASTER

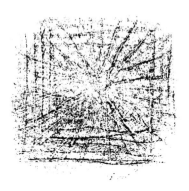

I have designated certain underlying impulses of Emily Dickinson's emotional life as bisexual. It is time to say more about
this peculiarity.

As has already been noted, when the poet's sense of her own
fundamental identity began to be based on her love and admiration of and desire to emulate the males in her family, her relationships with others took on a predominantly masculine
orientation. Then the active, assertive, persevering, and innova-
tive capacities of her personality tended to be liberated, for such
were the qualities she observed in these men. Irrevocably linked
in her mind with these "male" attributes was the tendency to
react to women as a male would and to regard them as the opposite sex. But Emily Dickinson's inability to grasp and maintain
a consistent, reliable, and single-faced sexual identity involved
oscillations back to the feminine position. When circumstances
brought about conditions strongly hostile to her "masculine"
proclivities, Emily Dickinson's tendency was either to lapse back
into the dependent, unassertive depressed posture of her mother-
identification or to embark on a shallowly rooted and tentative
heterosexuality borrowed temporarily from some admired girl
friend such as Susan Gilbert.

But in her creative states the opposing trends achieved an unstable synthesis in which both aspects of her personality—her need to be masculine and generative and her feminine need to be receptive and gestative—combined in the production of poetry. A psychic bisexualism frequently marks the great artist, whose mind showers forth a multitude of ideas which subsequently must undergo an internal and often protracted incubation before the creative product can be delivered. It has frequently been asserted that the man who cannot accept the presence of feminine components in his personality cannot become a productive artist. The converse of this observation has received less attention. Yet it follows that a woman who cannot accept the assertive, penetrative, and fructifying masculine principle in herself remains forever unpregnant of her talents.

I have already discussed the feminine side of Emily Dickinson's creativity, which became viable at the time of Sue's first pregnancy through her identification with Sue. It is the masculine contribution to this creativity that requires elucidation now.

Initially, I shall examine a poem which reveals a great deal about the way Emily Dickinson perceived intuitively the creative potential in herself as intimately linked both with masculinity and with aggression. Later, I shall explore the psychodynamic underground of Emily Dickinson's eye affliction. Through an analysis of this strange illness I hope to demonstrate something of the extraordinary intensity with which the poet cherished and subsequently mourned her deeply ingrained sense of maleness. Also, in the process of examining these residuals of her identification with the men in her family, I must speak again of the influence of her father, which manifested itself on more than one level in her poetry.

As I have indicated in previous chapters, Emily Dickinson, in common with many other poets and artists, had profound insight into the complexities of psychological operations, including the shadowy movements of the unconscious. Frequently she used her psychical discoveries as subject matter for her verse. Perhaps for this reason scholars without psychoanalytic knowledge or experience have found some of her poems opaque and frustrating to explicate.

In 1863 she wrote a brilliant and baffling poem: "My Life had stood – a Loaded Gun" (no. 754). It is significant that, as dated

by her editors, it was born in the retrospect of the creative outpouring that had reached its prodigious climax the previous year.
Dickinson authorities have grappled with its meaning but seem
not entirely to have grasped it. However, the seemingly arbitrary
images and the final knotty paradox may be found to yield
delicately and without force to psychoanalytic interpretation.

The complete poem is as follows:

My Life had stood – a Loaded Gun –
In Corners – till a Day
The Owner passed – identified –
And carried Me away –

And now We roam in Sovreign Woods –
And now We hunt the Doe –
And every time I speak for Him –
The Mountains straight reply –

And do I smile, such cordial light
Upon the Valley glow –
It is as a Vesuvian face
Had let it's pleasure through –

And when at Night – Our good Day done –
I guard My Master's Head –
'Tis better than the Eider-Duck's
Deep Pillow – to have shared –

To foe of His – I'm deadly foe –
None stir the second time –
On whom I lay a Yellow Eye –
Or an emphatic Thumb –

Though I than He – may longer live
He longer must – than I –
For I have but the power to kill,
Without – the power to die –

Among the questions that one would hope to answer are: What
is represented by the image of the loaded gun? Who or what is
meant by "The Owner" and "My Master"? Why is it specifically
the "Doe" that is hunted? In what sense can the killing discharge
of a gun be considered "cordial" and a volcanic eruption as
giving "pleasure?" And, skipping to the final stanza, what is
the meaning of this paradox? In what sense "must" the "Owner"

survive the "Gun?" And how can he if the "Gun" lacks the power to die? It is instructive to see how scholars lacking a psychoanalytic background have fared with these questions.

For example, Charles Anderson[1] sees the poem as a "ballad narrative" containing elements of "the tall-tale mode of western humor." He interprets the "Owner" as a masculine pioneer lover and eventual husband and the "Gun" as the man's frontier sweetheart and wife.

Stanzas 2 and 3, according to Anderson, portray the devotional aspects of their relationship with the focus on the wife, the man's "Joyous servant." The line "And every time I speak for Him" is interpreted as her vocal expression of love metaphorically conveyed in the image of the discharging gun. The "cordial light" denotes the affectionate glances she bestows on her husband. The "Doe" is not specifically interpreted as a symbol, but its general suitability to the romantic "troubadour" theme is pointed out.

Stanzas 4 and 5 are given over to what Anderson interprets as the protective role of the wife and "the service of love." He sees in the poem the implication that the love of husband and wife is not consummated in sexual intercourse—that the wife prefers to stand guard over her sleeping husband rather than sleep with him—and he calls this "a curious suggestion."

Anderson encounters his greatest difficulty in the final stanza, which he finds almost impossible to integrate into his interpretation. He says of these lines that they seem "to have little structural relation to the rest of the poem" and that if the poem is what he thinks it is—a combination of folk ballad, tall tale, and so forth —it is a "bold experiment even though it does not quite come off." In spite of this conclusion he nevertheless struggles to reconcile the final lines with previous stanzas. The "Gun" is now seen to represent the woman's mortal, physical organization and love, which may outlive her husband. However, in the immortal realm of heaven his soul will survive these fleshly attributes of his widow. The final two lines offer seemingly insurmountable obstacles. What Anderson calls the wife's "Gun-body" has "but the power to kill." This destructiveness in part is taken to indicate that the wife's physical body may cause the husband to be "too enamoured of the Eden of this life" for the good of his soul. But in this frame of reference the "power to kill" also has suicidal undercurrents, according to Anderson. The altruistic wife might resort to self-destruction to remove the threat her profane love presents to her husband's spiritual welfare. Though Anderson points out that according to the poem the woman's "Gun-body" lacks the "power to die," he follows this with the contradictory statement that the wife "must have the 'power to die' into heavenly love in order to become immortal." But it is just this ability that the poem explicitly states the "Gun" lacks. Obviously there is something wrong with this reading: either that or Anderson is quite right when he concludes that "judged by the highest poetic standards [the poem is] a failure."

Anderson's interpretation is in marked contrast to Thomas Johnson's[2] earlier and more inward-looking one and seems not to have been influenced by it. According to Johnson, the "Gun" represents the poet as a "physical entity," while the "Owner" is a function of her personality—it represents "the animating spirit within that creates or withholds creation at will." Johnson suggests that at the time the poem was written Emily Dickinson was able to appraise her poetic achievement with some objectivity and that she felt assured of her destiny as a poet. The poem, therefore, is a testimonial to her dedication to her art. Johnson apparently believes that all but the final four lines speak for themselves, and he does not interpret their individual symbols.

The final quatrain he explains thus: The poet acknowledges that she may outlive her inspiration. But to live deprived of this creative expression would be unendurable—the word *must* in the second line of this stanza being understood by Johnson as the poet's fierce conviction that such a fate is too dreadful to be thinkable. This would appear to be an entirely plausible reading of these lines. However, Johnson finds the final paradox difficult to resolve, and one is left with the feeling that he blurs the issues.

He points out that the body is "function only" and that in this it resembles the gun, which possesses only the function of killing. In other words, it would seem, both are mechanisms without spirit. Johnson appears at this point to abandon his former definition of the "Owner" as limited to the creative spirit or inspiration and now enlarges it to include all the functions of consciousness. The rest of his interpretation is very cryptic. The body, he says, is "powerless to summon death at will." Surely, this can only be true if the departure of the "Owner" left the body

devoid of consciousness and volition and reduced it to mere vege-
tative functions. In this case, Johnson's statement that the body
would find the loss of inspiration "more terrifying than death"
is inconsistent. An unconscious mechanism cannot be terrified.
But on the other hand, a conscious human organism *can* commit
suicide. Perhaps Johnson is suggesting that moral considerations
render the act impossible. But if moral considerations are germane to the essence of the poem, why are they not brought into
relation with the killing described in stanza 5?

And, for the sake of consistency, it would seem that if the
"Gun" represents the body, what is said of the "Gun" must also
be true of the body. Now the poem tells us that the "Gun" has
"but the power to kill, / Without – the power to die." Certainly
the body can kill, but this is not the body's single function in the
way that killing is a gun's single function. To specify this capacity
as the body's crucial attribute is peculiar indeed and out of keeping with the rest of the poem as explicated by Johnson.

There is no difficulty regarding the mortality of the "Gun"; the
"Gun," never having lived, cannot die. But even if one accepts
Johnson's view that the spiritless body cannot take its own life,
does it follow therefore that it lacks "the power to die?" If Johnson's explication is valid, the poet's analogy clearly collapses in
this stanza.

One other writer, Louise Bogan,[3] has touched upon this poem,
only to say that it "defies analysis." She praises it highly and
offers no explanation. Then she asks herself and the reader a
provocative and discerning question. May not the poem have
arisen, she says, "from some psychic deep where good and evil
are not to be separated?" The question is an important one. One
reason that this poem is frequently singled out is that readers
apparently sense that in some way it is of critical importance to
an understanding of Emily Dickinson's emotional and creative
modus operandi.

A psychoanalytic overview of "My Life had stood – a Loaded
Gun" suggests that two or three related psychodynamics pervade,
and perhaps determine, the imagery throughout. Therefore, before
analyzing the individual stanzas it might clarify the problem to
identify at the outset what appear to be the poem's overriding
themes. They are: (1) the fusion of sexuality and destructiveness,
(2) the oedipal constellation, and (3) the poet's acceptance of the

masculine components of her personality. The last two themes will be examined as they present themselves in the poem.

With reference to the first of the themes, it is apparent that despite the many differences between the Johnson and the Anderson interpretations they have in common an almost exclusive emphasis on the libidinal implications of the symbolism. Let us take another look at these symbols. The erotic element is indubitably there and, as will be shown, on more levels than is first apparent. But one must not overlook the rampant aggression that is fused with the sexual component in each of the symbols. The loaded gun, the volcanic face, the emphatic thumb-bullet—each is an agent of death. In every instance a wish to love, to be sexual, to be creative, is mated to its opposite—a furious propensity to destroy. Clearly, a psychologically plausible reading of this poem necessitates an acceptance of its pervasive violence. In activities fraught with destructiveness—hunting, killing, eruption, and revenge—the poem tells of the release, channeled but exuberant, of pent-up aggression. The question naturally arises: What circumstances prevailed before the outburst embodied in the poem took place? What was Emily Dickinson's life like when it stood in corners and all aggression lay dormant and concealed?

As has been pointed out previously, anyone who has worked in the field of psychiatry for any length of time has been impressed by the peculiar relationship that obtains between depression and anger. When intense rage reactions are denied, put down, suppressed, shut out of awareness—when there is no allowable outlet for anger—the most frequent result is depression. It is as though the aggression were turned in on the self, resulting in the self-disparagement and self-recrimination that are a feature of depressions. Therefore, if "My Life had stood – a Loaded Gun" depicts the discharge of hostile feelings, it might be profitable to recall the antecedent state of depression as presented elsewhere in the poet's writings. Emily Dickinson, in many poems, but most completely in poem 280, "I felt a Funeral, in my Brain," dated 1861, offered a graphic description of the prostrating despondency which beset her at intervals throughout the course of her life. In this powerful poem we are made to feel each tormenting increment of a gathering depression until vitality reaches a nadir, and reason gives way to a numb and psychotic state of reality severance.

We know from Emily Dickinson's biography and letters that she was almost formidably sweet and rarely showed any anger. A search of her correspondence reveals only one or two trivial instances of direct expression of anger. Generally she seems to have resembled her mother in this respect, who, according to the poet, even "frowned with a smile."[4] But there is plenty of anger apparent in the poems. Remember poem 118, in which she wishes for a "mighty gun" with which she would destroy the human race.

The letters, poems, and biographical data all indicate that during her psychotic breakdown Emily Dickinson's unconscious life forged into awareness accompanied by the fear that aggressive and libidinal drives would get out of control. This necessitated some extreme defense mechanisms, brilliantly portrayed in the poems. The poet experienced overwhelming depressions that safely immobilized her in states of trance-like apathy and depersonalization or permitted merely mechanical and purposeless movement in catatonic, automaton-like states. The acute phase of the breakdown, of short duration, lasted possibly several months. As she recovered, the drives to some degree found channeled release through the poetic skills she had previously developed and by means of the psychodynamic mechanisms that I have elucidated in previous chapters. Here I shall only recall that the previously repressed and forbidden erotic drives were contained and made permissible by a displacement to a noninterdicted and safely unobtainable love object. The aggression and hostility stimulated by her frustrated love needs also found their way into the poems. Here they generally took the form of bitter denunciations of God and demonstrations of the extent to which the poet felt wronged, denied, defrauded, and unappreciated. Some of her hostility also went into her overriding preoccupation with death and less obviously into the rigid agoraphobia which made her a prisoner in her father's house for at least the last fifteen years of her life.

If one keeps in mind the foregoing brief pathographical review, it is now possible to present a psychoanalytic interpretation of "My Life had stood – a Loaded Gun." Each stanza and its symbolism will be considered separately, and an attempt will be made to clarify through expanded paraphrases the intensely concentrated language of the poem. Although some of the figures may appear sufficiently clear as they stand, for the sake of continuity these easier passages will be included in the paraphrasing. Also included are those portions of interpretations by others previously cited which are pertinent to the present analysis.

The following interpretative comments are approximately arranged on a continuum of increasing psychological depth. That is, they begin with an attempt to approximate ideas and feelings that were most likely present in the poet's awareness as she composed the poem. Subsequent remarks proceed through transitional stages that probably were only partly conscious and incompletely grasped by the poet. Finally comes material that was most certainly repressed, the expression of which was inadvertent and unconscious.

> My Life had stood – a Loaded Gun –
> In Corners – till a Day
> The Owner passed – identified –
> And carried Me away –

"My Life had stood": My vitality lay unused, unexpressed, inactive. My potentialities for thought and intense feeling lay dormant.

"In Corners": These proclivities and personal abilities were stagnating, hidden away, unrecognized by myself or others, and not accessible to my own purposes.

"a Loaded Gun": I had within me all I needed for effective action and expression, especially of an explosive and aggressive kind.

Although there is no need to emphasize the point, it is possible to sense a lonely and depressive quality in the image of an abandoned gun standing forgotten in a corner. It is mentioned here because of the relationship touched on above between depression and repressed aggression. In this stanza, the poem suggests that depression as well as inactivity preceded the release described in the following stanzas.

"till a Day / The Owner passed": An unfamiliar aspect of my divided self suddenly came to my awareness.

The poem implies that the "Owner" had not recently been in evidence, that the "Gun" had stood in corners neglected by him for perhaps a lifetime. This may be taken to mean that an unconscious portion of Emily Dickinson's personality, or certain functions of her personality, had suddenly become accessible to consciousness and that this aspect of herself had previously been unknown to her or had been forgotten by her through the years.

"identified": This new aspect of myself claimed the dormant and repressed aggression within me as its own.

Notice that two separate entities previously unrecognized have emerged into consciousness. One is the "Owner"—those aspects, perhaps former ego states of the poet's now enlarged ego or consciousness, which are seen as strong enough to wield and control the newly emerging emotional forces. The other revived entity is the previously repressed—or overcontrolled—drives themselves, which now become the instrument of the poet's augmented personality.

"And carried Me away": My former incomplete personality was overwhelmed by the influx of these previously repressed functions and drives. These new portions of myself are very powerful and swept my old self off her feet.

The poem probably alludes to the period of heightened activity in 1861, when Emily Dickinson began to write poems at a furious rate. The new sectors of the poet's personality are masculinized: When Emily Dickinson emerged as a poet, it can only have been her identification with her active father and her poetic brother, Austin, that came to the fore—not her blighted identification with her passive and inadequate mother. In this stanza we find the poet embarking on what she fancies is a characteristically masculine adventure.

> And now We roam in Sovreign Woods –
> And now We hunt the Doe –
> And every time I speak for Him –
> The Mountains straight reply –

"And now We roam in Sovreign Woods": The active, aggressive, even grandiose aspect of my masculinized personality is now in full command of its emotional energies. I feel free to explore previously eschewed territory.

The "Sovreign Woods" may be the domain of poetry and literature on one level; on another, the habitat of love.

"And now We hunt the Doe":

Why "Doe"—the epitome of the gentle, passive, timorous, and feminine? Emily Dickinson could easily have found a word of masculine or neuter gender if all she wanted to convey was the idea of hunting in general terms. Consciously or otherwise she appears to be implying that it is particularly appropriate for the *male* "Owner" to hunt the *female* "Doe." One can hardly escape the fact that the only distinct object of aggression presented in the poem is conspicuously female. The "Doe," therefore, may stand for a woman in the poet's life who has incurred her enmity. Her frustrating and limited mother comes to mind, and the image may also apply to other rejecting female love objects. It is important, however, not to miss the fact that the "Doe" is not only the target of aggression but also a sexual object, as further examination of the symbolism will show. What we have here, then, is Emily Dickinson's idea of the relationship between the sexes. Heterosexuality is seen as an attack—sadistic, rapacious, potentially destructive—on the helpless female.

Perhaps this libidinal aspect of the symbol remained unconscious. It might be argued that on a more superficial level the "Doe" stands for the poetry itself. The animal is a thing of beauty characterized by delicacy, swiftness, elusiveness, wildness, hypersensitivity, and many other qualities that may justly be ascribed to Emily Dickinson's poems. And on occasion the poet did overtly liken her poetic efforts to an animal. Alluding to certain poets whom she admired, she said that it afflicted her to think of herself as "the only Kangaroo among the Beauty."[5] However, poems are not killed, but captured alive, and it is difficult to comprehend how a poem could be an object of hostility. Yet when aggression is fused and neutralized with the erotic drive, it can be turned to creative purposes. Consequently "We hunt"—not shoot—"the Doe." A fine distinction, but perhaps intended and significant.

"And every time I speak for Him – / The Mountains straight reply": The mountains echo the sound of my shooting.

The lines convey both the energy and decisiveness of the aggressive outburst and the grand sweep of its effectiveness. The "Mountains" may be the reacting world applauding the poet's work and resonating in sympathy. Perhaps the poet is saying her work might reverberate to the distant mountains, that is, the "giants" that Emily Dickinson admired—Emily Brontë, Elizabeth Browning, George Sand, George Eliot, and so on. She always longed for the recognition of these female literary figures, although by refusing to publish her work she denied herself access

CHAPTER IX

to them. It should be noted that mountains in Emily Dickinson's poems often are symbols of maternality and femininity.

In the speaking of the gun and the reply from the mountains one can also clearly distinguish latent genital connotations. The discharging gun suggests a masculine orgasm; the echo from the mountains a responsive orgasm from the female symbol. As will be pointed out later, on a more primitive oral strata the same symbols may stand for the child's relationship to the mother.

> And do I smile, such cordial light
> Upon the Valley glow –
> It is as a Vesuvian face
> Had let it's pleasure through –

When I give vent to my feelings, my surroundings are illuminated by a psychological truth from deep within me. I experience this explosive release as a pleasurable expression of my nature, as a volcano must enjoy disclosing its inner fires.

Anderson takes the *cordial* smile and volcanic *pleasure* almost literally and regards them as entirely benign symbols of the warmth of love. It would appear more likely that the light is cordial the way the slap of a panther may be playful while nevertheless inflicting a mortal wound. Or perhaps a better interpretation: cordial because it comes from the heart, red-hot and burning. It seems doubtful that the poet here means *friendly*. *Light,* meaning poetic truths, is what poets shed, as is indicated by another poem: "The Poets light but Lamps – / Themselves – go out" (no. 883). Therefore the "cordial light" means the heartfelt and earnest expression of emotion in the poetry—devastating emotion. "Vesuvian" signifies uncontrollable feeling or smoldering turmoil. Emily Dickinson never used the word in any benign sense— if indeed such exists. And the fiery "pleasure" is "let through," not frankly expressed. "Let through" suggests the deliberate release of something that ordinarily would be or should be held back. "Pleasure" in this context can be felt to take on a quality of sinister and illicit joy, reminiscent of that striking phrase (poem no. 379): "a Bliss like Murder." The pleasure let through, therefore, is the result of the satisfaction of a blood lust combined with the explosive erotic gratification of a sexual act here regarded as being as destructive as it is pleasurable.

There are clues to be found in the poet's writing that the "Loaded Gun" may not refer exclusively to the male organ but may encompass also the genital of the so-called phallic woman. What is represented by this term is a woman who has suffered a particular arrest in her emotional development. As a very young girl, such a woman wills, with the full force of her personality in both its conscious and unconscious aspects, not to be a female. The rejection of femininity is driven hard; the girl by her aggressive and daredevil behavior compels her male companions to accept her as one of themselves. She competes with them vigorously, hoping to surpass them in academic and athletic prowess and trying to convince herself that she is not their inferior in masculinity. She dresses like a boy if her mother will allow it and, undressed, convinces herself that her anatomical difference is illusory or temporary. She denies the lack of a penis. It is small but it will grow, she tells herself, observing the clitoris. Or somehow it is internal and will sometime appear. It is not uncommon for very disturbed girls of this kind to hallucinate the presence of a penis. On a deeper level of the girl's personality she knows that she is not a male. The knowledge evokes hostility and envy toward men as well as self-hatred.

The identification of the "Loaded Gun" with the illusory female phallus is expressive of an anatomical bisexuality that is in perfect accord with the psychological bisexuality found throughout the other stanzas. Certainly at first glance the gun and the bullet (the "emphatic Thumb") seem unequivocally male. Yet in Emily Dickinson's view the gun also is found in the fiery craters of volcanoes, which, according to poem 175, are "Usually so still – [but they] Bear within – appalling Ordnance, / Fire, and smoke, and *gun*." Surely, the volcano is the female genital: "The Solemn – Torrid – Symbol –/ The lips that never lie –/ Whose hissing Corals part – and shut" (poem 601). At least five "volcano" poems bear out this impression. The gun that smiles, then, must have a slitlike aperture and the "Vesuvian face" that lets its pleasure through adds additional female characteristics to the originally phallic image.

With this additional perspective on the symbolism let me turn back a moment to stanza 2. The replying mountains, as I have noted, are on one level accepting and sympathetic females. On another they may represent the responsive female sexual partner. More deeply yet, the mountains may be replying by giving milk— they are breast symbols. When the little gun speaks the mountains reply. Austin, the poem may unconsciously be saying, was favored over Emily by their mother—when he demanded love he got it. Emily, on at least four occasions, referred to her childhood as a time when she had been a boy. If she was a boy once, what happened to her? Little girls whose identification with their mothers is fraught with rejection and conflict often conceive the idea that they have been castrated by a rivalrous mother who herself has a hidden phallus. In this poem Emily endows herself with a phallus, and afterward all is exuberance. She is then, perhaps, loved like Austin.

The "cordial light" that glows on the "Valley" glows on terrain that has a distinctly feminine cast. If the mountains are maternal, the valley is female too. Again one sees the mixed eroticism and aggression burning for the mother. Can it be that the appreciation and fame Emily hoped to get from her writing (regarded in this context as the masculine activity of a phallic woman) represents unconsciously the longing for maternal love—more easily gained, she fancies, if one has made oneself a male? There is considerable evidence that Emily Dickinson resented being a woman. The poem says that the female genital is endowed with great destructive potential. This attitude can only have been borrowed from her view of her relationship with her mother, which Emily experienced as emotionally destructive. It seems that to be female, for Emily Dickinson, was to be maimed and second-rate. Such a self-view naturally begets rage and the impulse to destroy in retaliation. To be male, on the other hand, is to be cherished and accepted—the mountains then reply.

> And when at Night – Our good Day done –
> I guard My Master's Head –
> 'Tis better than the Eider-Duck's
> Deep Pillow – to have shared –

"And when at Night – Our good Day done – / I guard My Master's Head": My newly awakened aggressivity stands ever ready, even when the remainder of my personality relaxes its defenses. My masculine poetic faculty, while quiescent and not engaged in its work of fusing my aggression and eroticism into creative art, is rendered safe from external molestation by my newly found capacity for self-protective ferocity.

One might be tempted to take the "good Day" as in part ironic, because what is "done" is an interval that appears to have been one of violence, killing, and unbridled sensual pleasure. It may be "good," however, in the sense that it has been creative— if hunting the "Doe" can be equated with the constructive use of aggression—and that it has satisfied many pent-up needs.

" 'Tis better than the Eider-Duck's / Deep Pillow – to have shared": I would rather nurse in solitude my frustrated sexual longings, my rage, and my aggression and cherish the creative faculties that afford these emotions expression than be physically close to the object of this mixed love and hate.

The words "to have shared" can be seen to carry with them the implied words "with someone else." Obviously Emily Dickinson cannot consciously be talking of sharing a bed sexually with the "Owner" and "Master," who is not another person but a part of herself.

What about the "Eider-Duck's Deep Pillow"? One might easily dismiss the capitalized modifiers in this phrase as evidence of the poet's wish to heighten her image of voluptuous self-indulgence. Her purpose would be to sharpen the contrast with the sternness and asceticism of the "Gun's" dedication to duty. This explanation is not convincing. The poem is short and sparing of words. Making such a point of the ornithological source of the down stuffing would be empty elaboration if she were not attempting to suggest something more than mere physical luxury. Now it is characteristic of the eider duck that she lines her nest heavily with down plucked from her own body. The "Deep Pillow" therefore connotes the idea of a nest with its cozy security and maternal nurturing. No one familiar with Emily Dickinson's life history will deny that she sought persistently for these attributes. Again we must ask ourselves: Was she consciously disavowing her dependency needs in these words? And her dependency on whom? Her mother? Early in life she gave up expecting much maternal care from Mrs. Dickinson. And she put considerable effort into cultivating the affection of motherly women outside the home. Perhaps the most plausible hypothesis is that here she had in mind a relationship with a beloved woman that she has relinquished for the sake of her art. Several close friends in Emily Dickinson's life, but especially Sue, come to mind in this context.

Here let me proceed to another level of awareness. What has come alive in Emily Dickinson in this poem is her identification with her father—the original "Owner" of the "Gun." For purposes of analysis one must now dissect this aspect of the poet's personality into the elements from which it was derived—the father and the female child. Accordingly, on a deeper level one finds in this stanza intimations of the oedipal constellation. At night, the poem says, all is remarkably quiet in the bedroom and the bed; nothing happens. This is a denial of "normal" heterosexuality, particularly that between the parents. No one shares the father's bed, and especially not the daughter. Here is a disavowal of the girl's wish to take her mother's place. Instead of this wish the poet presents a picture of asexual devotion. At the same time there is a suggestion in the "Eider-Duck" symbol that the poet was aware that it should be Mother who shared Father's bed.

> To foe of His – I'm deadly foe –
> None stir the second time –
> On whom I lay a Yellow Eye –
> Or an emphatic Thumb –

Anything impeding the free creative expression of my erotic and aggressive impulses must brave the threat of my destructive wrath. (The "Yellow Eye" is, of course, the explosive flash at the end of the barrel of the gun, and the "emphatic Thumb" is the bullet.)

The metaphorical essence of the lines consists probably in the poet's stressing the great value her masculinized, aggressive, creative self has for her. And very understandably so—since it helped restore her to sanity. Thus any foe of "His," that is any foe of her creative self, was a threat to her mental and emotional life and would be dealt with emphatically. Her family to some extent must have sensed this and left her to her solitary pursuits.

To proceed to a more unconscious level: the Master's foe, his quarry, is women (the "Doe"). In the violence of the sexual act the penis, it is intimated, may destroy the female. Even the smaller hidden penis of the phallic woman (the "emphatic Thumb") is deadly. This imagery points up Emily Dickinson's fear of sexuality* and her shrinking from all direct human relationships. As a female she would fall victim to the lustful brutality of a male. As a homosexual woman with a "Vesuvian face" she herself would be the destroyer. Her only recourse in this dilemma was to avoid sexuality in any form—to her heterosexuality and homosexuality were equally threatening and dangerous.

> Though I than He – may longer live
> He longer must – than I –
> For I have but the power to kill,
> Without – the power to die –

"Though I than He – may longer live": Though my rage, hostility, and aggression may outlast those masculine components of my personality that bend my destructive impulses to creative purposes . . .

"He" represents the poet's masculine identification and possibly also a former ego state, both of which have recently been unconscious; they are therefore felt to be capable of re-repression and of again becoming unavailable—a not unfounded fear.

"He longer must – than I – / For I have but the power to kill": He *must* (a word of desperation, as Johnson implies) outlive me; it is necessary that this be so because the thought of my survival without him is too terrible to contemplate.

The poet here is expressing the fear that without those creative faculties which master the instinctual drives and find acceptable outlets for them nothing would remain but raw, unrestrained destructiveness and unregulated sexuality. Such a loss of control is possible in psychosis, a fate the poet had reason to fear might once more engulf her. Another, almost equally oppressive, alternative to the creative state (an alternative not mentioned in the poem) is the repudiation and stifling of all instinctual gratification in a kind of living death. This latter course is the one the poet seems actually to have taken.

"Without – the power to die": The instinctual erotic and aggressive drives are inextinguishable as long as the physical life of the body endures.

* Recall her jaundiced views on a woman's relationship to her husband, expressed forcefully in a letter to Susan written when she was twenty-one. She there described the typical wife as forgotten, bowed in anguish, thirsty, crying, pining, scorched and "through with peace." *Letters,* I, 209, no. 93 (early June 1852).

The drives can be channeled and sublimated and even expressed fairly openly under appropriate circumstances; or they can be overly controlled, suppressed, and repressed, in which case they will find expression in symptoms such as the poet's agoraphobia. But the drives cannot be killed.

One senses in this conclusion an effort on the part of the poet to curtail the unconscious "crazy" symbolism and to achieve closure on a more sane note. The poem has pursued the masculine identification in a sadistic fantasy—hunt, rape, orgasm, destruction of the female, and relaxed sleep. Following this orgy the poet is left to grapple with her conscience, and characteristically she thinks of death—the Puritan retribution for giving way to one's passions. After "accompanying" the penis on what she fantasies is a characteristic escapade, she detaches herself from the identification and turns loose her envious hostility toward men—in a thinly disguised death-wish whose ultimate victims would be Austin and Father. I can kill and he can die, she says. Consciously she could not have borne such a thought and would instead have turned this aggression on herself. Consequently: "He longer must – than I."

To sum up: Prior to the processes described in "My Life had stood – a Loaded Gun," the personality sectors employed in the poet's creative periods were dormant and the drives were stifled and forced to find outlet in depressive symptoms. They found release from repression, according to my interpretation, when the poet was struggling to gain a new psychic equilibrium in the aftermath of a psychotic episode. The "new" sectors of the personality were activated by the poet's acceptance of her masculine identifications and were never again wholly lost, although, as I shall show subsequently, there occurred increasingly arid periods when they were greatly diminished. Also, the emergence of the maculine elements, and with them previously repressed bisexual impulses, appears to have prevented the reestablishment of the degree of integrity characteristic of the poet's personality prior to her breakdown. Her convalescent personality, though enlarged and deepened, always remained to some degree disturbed. She seems never afterward to have functioned in a completely intact manner, and she was beset with many inner conflicts and irrational fears.

From the poem just analyzed, one tends to draw the conclusion, borne out by the study of numerous other poems, that Emily Dickinson's poetry does not so much represent the sublimation of love, as is generally supposed, as it does the sublimation of rage. Emily Dickinson had no difficulty expressing her kind of love— at least verbally. However, like her mother she seems not to have had any direct outlet for her aggression. And because she felt so cheated by fate, God, some of her friends, and her mother, she had a great deal of aggression to express. Her poetry offered her a vehicle for her unmet demands for love, her complaints of rejection, and her indignation at not having received at the hands of life what she felt was rightfully hers.

Her creative self emerged in 1860–1861, and by means of poetry she found relief from her frustrations. Until then she was a smoldering, potentially destructive volcano. Now she became a "Loaded Gun" with the resources within herself to bear her anger, neutralize it with erotic elements, focus it, and make it effective in a sublimated form. Her remarkable grasp of these processes provide the content for many of her most perfect poems. Among them surely is "My Life had stood – a Loaded Gun."

The perfect balance of feminine and masculine propensities that found its symbolic expression in the generation of poetry did not last; the precarious alliance of opposing tendencies was undermined by the constant environmental pressure exerted upon Emily Dickinson to resign herself to an exclusively feminine role, which in her milieu meant to be unobstrusive like her mother, domestic, unassertive, and subservient to her father and the realities of his practical life. Of course, intrapsychic factors, some of which will be examined in the following pages, also played their part. The net result was that the years following 1862 saw a decline in productivity from the 366 poems of that year to the 10 poems of 1867. As the creative process became increasingly strangulated, the poet more and more took on the features of a reluctant caricature of her shrinking and timorous mother. And it was during the early stages of this period of dwindling poetic virility and creative potency that the poet first worried about a curious malfunctioning of her eyes.

Thus, in her middle thirties, Emily Dickinson suffered for a protracted period from photophobia and ocular pain. She consulted a physician, who recommended that she temporarily discontinue all reading and writing, an injunction to which she did not scrupulously adhere. Her eyes bothered her for a period of approximately two years, after which she seems not to have had any further difficulty.

The matter would be of no importance if it were not for the fact that concern for her vision has been advanced as the explanation for the emotional turmoil of her letters and poems. Yet, as has been demonstrated in the foregoing chapters, it is perfectly clear that a grave psychological upheaval was in progress in the poet many years before her eyes began to give her trouble. Therefore, rather than consider her emotional reaction to her ophthalmic symptoms a separate crisis in her life, as her biographers tend to do, it should prove more enlightening to integrate this anxiety into the already existing pattern of stress and suffering as one of its later manifestations.

We do not know the degree to which Emily Dickinson's eye affliction had an organic basis. However, there is reason to believe that it was slight and that whatever physical pathology was present was emphasized by the intense emotional investment the poet had in her eyes and by her irrational expectations of blindness.

In the following pages I will attempt to establish the proposition that Emily Dickinson's eye disorder was a psychosomatic affliction. Second I will inquire into the possible meaning that psychogenic photophobia would have had for the poet as this can be inferred from her writings and her biography.

In his notes to the *Letters,* Thomas Johnson says that Emily Dickinson "made a trip to Boston on 4 February 1864 to consult Henry W. Williams, M.D." He then makes an inference that has been accepted by most subsequent writers: "He [the ophthalmologist] must have prescribed a course of treatments requiring his supervision, for late in April she went back to stay, remaining until 21 November."[6] When scrutinized, this statement proves a provocative one—a consultation regarding an eye ailment eventuates in treatment three months later. It is hard to imagine any but a psychogenic symptom-picture being handled in so casual a manner. Dr. Williams was a highly competent specialist, whose book *Recent Advances in Ophthalmic Science* reads almost like a present-day text. Had a serious eye disorder been apparent, it seems unlikely that he would have allowed it to go unattended for three months. Probably he was unable to demonstrate any pathology and advised the poet to return in three months' time if her symptoms continued to trouble her.

In a letter to Thomas W. Higginson, Emily Dickinson wrote: "I was ill since September, and since April, in Boston, for a Physician's care—He does not let me go, yet I work in my Prison, and make Guests for myself."[7] Here are two more bits of evidence for my hypothesis. For five or six months (from September to February) Emily Dickinson has been suffering with her eyes, and in all that time her usually over-solicitous family were either unaware of the fact or they were not sufficiently impressed by her ailment to see that she got medical attention. Also it is apparent that she is using her eyes—she writes to Higginson that she makes "guests" (poems) for herself. And in recalling the home of the cousins with whom she stayed during this time, she wrote: "I think of your little parlor as the poets once thought of Windermere,—peace, sunshine and *books*."[8] Apparently she did some reading while she was there.

Again she writes, alluding to her illness: "I wish to see you more than before I failed."[9] Emily Dickinson frequently used the expression "to fail" in referring either to death or to a state of general physical illness or debility. The tone of this statement does not appear to make the phrase applicable to a self-contained ocular difficulty. But it would be an appropriate way to imply a more generalized condition such as a depressive or obsessive reaction.

The fact that Emily Dickinson wrote "the Physician has taken away my Pen"[10] does not prove that the proscription against writing necessarily indicated his concern for her eyesight. In the 1860's the reading and writing of poetry was unquestioningly accepted as one of the causes of nervous breakdown. If Emily Dickinson were depressed, beset with guilt feelings, obsessed with an anxious need to find ultimate purposes and meanings in existence, a nineteenth-century physician might well have advised her to stop ruminating and occupy herself with more practical matters, such as the daily household chores.

Consider this: She writes to her sister-in-law, "For caution of my Hat, He says, the Doctor wipes my cheeks."[11] This suggests that the patient is weeping and that the physician has the role of consoler. It *could* mean that eye medication is overflowing from her eyes or inducing lacrimation during a treatment, but for a physician to apply medication without removing the patient's hat would be an extraordinarily odd procedure.

That the eye disorder was part of an overall depressive picture is indicated by a statement to her sister: "I feel no gayness yet. I suppose I have been discouraged so long." And the presence of guilt feelings is clearly discernible in her comment on her cousins: "to see the 'Ravens' [the cousins] mending my stockings, would break a Heart long hard."[12] Acts of kindness toward patients suffering from depression involving repressed and self-directed hostility often exacerbate the depression by increasing existing feelings of unworthiness.

She speaks of her physician thus: "The Doctor is very kind."[13] Yet only a counselor or a psychiatrist need be "very kind." An ophthalmologist would more commonly be very patient or very skilled or very persevering.

To her sister Vinnie she writes: "The Doctor says . . . I 'cannot yet walk alone.' "[14] Again the implication is that the patient needs someone to lean upon and that the problem is one of emotional insecurity and lack of confidence.

A reduced self-esteem incongruous if the ailment were a circumscribed ocular one comes through in the following excerpt from the same letter: "Thank you all for caring about me when I do no good. I will work with all my might, always, as soon as I get well."

Then there is this odd bit: "The Doctor . . . wants to see me Sunday."[15] Sunday seems an unlikely day for a follow-up visit for a chronic eye problem. It suggests that Emily Dickinson was a special patient seen during off hours—a plausible arrangement if treatment sessions were largely taken up with counseling.

She writes to cousin Loo: "This is my letter—an ill and peevish thing, but when my eyes get well I'll send you thoughts like daisies."[16] It is obvious that Emily can see to write—her eyes only prevent her from being pleasant and expressing herself beautifully.

When Emily Dickinson returned home to Amherst, things did not go well for her and she longed to return to Boston: "what it would be to see you and have the doctor's care—that cannot be told . . . I wish I were there, myself . . . When I dare I shall ask if I may go, but that will not be now."[17] This longing for the doctor's care suggests that her dependency on him was emotional

—which is understandable if his primary role regarding her was a psychotherapeutic one. That she would be so eager for further treatments of a physical nature seems doubtful. In these lines we can again glimpse the attitude of her family, especially her father, which seems to have been one of skepticism regarding the efficacy or need of further treatment. That Edward Dickinson would set himself above medical authority in the matter of an undoubted eye disorder seems unlikely. That he would be dubious of the value of some type of long drawn out and expensive therapy which was essentially counseling for an emotional problem is more understandable.

Another fragment of evidence that the doctor's order to cease writing was necessitated more by his patient's psychological condition than by the condition of her sight has recently come to light. In a letter which exists only in a copy made by the recipient, Emily Dickinson says, "Some years ago I had a woe, the only one that ever made me tremble. It was a shutting out of all the dearest ones of time, the strongest friends of the soul—*BOOKS*. The medical man said 'avaunt ye tormentors,' he also said 'down, thoughts, & plunge into her soul.' He might as well have said, 'Eyes be blind,' 'heart be still.' "[18] It is possible to interpret the physician's recommendation as evidence that he believed her eye trouble was only a portion of a more diffuse psychological difficulty and that it was the nature of her ponderings and broodings and the exacerbating effect of books on obsessive thought processes that made them "tormentors"—not that reading was injurious to her eyes. What the doctor may have said to her would go something like this: "If you are to recover your health and overcome these feelings of despair, you must stop reading. These books are upsetting you, and even Shakespeare and the Bible, if read with too much intensity, can disturb the mental faculties. You must stop thinking about death and other morbid things; get them off your mind and become interested in sewing and other womanly occupations. Assist your cousins around the house, see what you can do about helping with the meals and so forth. And remember, no deep books, and no more dwelling on morbid thoughts." This would seem a more plausible explanation of those words of the physician, "down thoughts, & plunge into her soul," than to conclude that he was apprising her of the hazards of eyestrain.

At one point in this peculiar illness, Emily Dickinson writes: "I cannot write in bed."[19] Can this eye ailment, which ultimately vanished without leaving the least residuum, have been so severe as to necessitate her taking to her bed?

Guilt feelings continue to crop up. To Vinnie, who is apparently doing Emily's share of the work at home, she writes: "Do not get tired, Vinnie, or troubled about things—all I can do, leave till I come . . . dont work too hard . . . I can sweep, next Fall."[20] And again: "it wont be long, Vinnie,—You will be willing, wont you, for a little while."[21] Here Emily is begging Vinnie's permission to stay in Boston a little longer. The wording suggests a tacit mutual acknowledgement that whatever Emily's ocular difficulty is it is not sufficient to explain her profound incapacity.

In another letter Edward Dickinson's attitude toward further therapy is made explicit: "I had promised to visit my Physician for a few days in May, but Father objects because he is in the habit of me."[22] I submit that Edward Dickinson would not have objected to his daughter's getting necessary ophthalmological treatments.

An alternate explanation is that Emily herself now no longer wishes to leave home and is invoking her father to bolster her resistance to the importunities of the Boston cousins. Either way, the seriousness of the eye disorder is invested with a dubious air.

That the degree of Emily Dickinson's ocular distress was directly related to the state of her emotions is most clearly revealed in a letter to her cousins after she returned to Amherst: "You persuade me to speak of my eyes, which I shunned doing . . . The eyes are as with you, sometimes easy, sometimes sad . . . The snow-light offends them, and the house is bright." She then says that for the first few weeks at home she did nothing but tend her plants and "chop the chicken centers when we have roast fowl . . . Then I make the yellow to the pies, and bang the spice for cake, and knit the soles to the stockings I knit the bodies to last June. They say I am a 'help.' Partly because it is true, I suppose, and the rest applause. Mother and Margaret [the servant] are so kind, father as gentle as he knows how, and Vinnie good to me, but 'cannot see why I don't get well.' This makes me think I am long sick, and this takes the ache to my eyes."[23]

It is clear that the family, sensing her feelings of uselessness and of being a burden to them all, are making every effort to be encouraging and loving and patient. They give her little chores to do and make a fuss over the great help she is. This is the spontaneous response evoked by the severely depressed patient and is probably the least therapeutic attitude the family could adopt. Emily Dickinson here recognizes the emptiness of the "applause," and in guilt and introjected anger she suffers a worsening of her symptoms. The family say they "cannot see why I don't get well." If Emily had a demonstrable eye disease stubbornly resistant to treatment, they would scarcely make such a statement, for it presupposes some knowledge of the pathological process, which, as laymen, they of course lacked. A plausible paraphrase of their remark might be: "We are all happy to have you home. You are no trial at all to us. We don't see how you can feel useless and burdensome and unhappy here where we all love you." It is understandable that a remark of this import would take "the ache to [her] eyes."

Inevitably the relatives of a depressed person lose their patience and become exasperated because she *will* not cheer up, although they hide their response owing to feelings of guilt. In the light of this line of thought, the phrase "this makes me think I am long sick" suggests that Emily Dickinson sensed the carefully concealed reproach underlying all the reassurance. It is important to note that her eye pain is directly evoked by her reaction to the words of her family—they are overly solicitous, they covertly rebuke her, she feels an intensification of her feelings of uselessness and "this takes the ache to my eyes." It would be rare to find such a clear-cut sequence in illnesses that are predominantly organic.

Also if Emily's mysterious "terror—since September," about which she wrote Higginson, reflected a dread of blindness—an explanation which is widely accepted today—why was it, as a respectable enough calamity, a fear she "could tell to none"?[24]

Admittedly, the evidence for a psychogenic disturbance is circumstantial. But what evidence is there that she had a serious eye disease? She consulted an ophthalmologist. She complained of photophobia—the discomfort caused by the snow light and the brightness of the house—and she complained of bilateral eye pain. These are the commonest ocular complaints of persons who are suffering from intense emotional conflicts unaccompanied by any physical pathology. Emily Dickinson never had any recurrence of her eye trouble and she never had to wear glasses—in fact her vision seems to have been remarkably good. In describing the brightness of a neighborhood fire years later, she wrote: "And so much lighter than day was it, that I saw a caterpillar measure a leaf far down in the orchard."[25]

A two-year illness, photophobia, bilateral ocular pain, no impairment of visual acuity either during the illness or afterward, no cosmetic deficiency, good general physical health—it is hard to find a real eye disease that corresponds to this picture. This fact, together with a consideration of all the evidence of severe emotional dislocations to be found in the poems and letters and in the poet's style of life impel one to the conclusion that Emily Dickinson's eye disease was in some measure an expression of her emotional life and needs to be evaluated as such.

There is a bit of evidence that Emily Dickinson was emotionally ripe for the development of a psychogenic eye disorder before her symptoms began. It consists of the following poem (no. 327), dated by her editors "c. 1862":

> Before I got my eye put out
> I liked as well to see –
> As other Creatures, that have Eyes
> And know no other way –
>
> But were it told to me – Today –
> That I might have the sky
> For mine – I tell you that my Heart
> Would split, for size of me –
>
> The Meadows – mine –
> The Mountains – mine –
> All Forests – Stintless Stars –
> As much of Noon as I could take
> Between my finite eyes –
>
> The Motions of The Dipping Birds –
> The Morning's Amber Road –
> For mine – to look at when I liked –
> The News would strike me dead –
>
> So safer Guess – with just my soul
> Upon the Window pane –
> Where other Creatures put their eyes –
> Incautious – of the Sun –

Note that Emily Dickinson's eye treatments began in 1864 and continued through most of 1865. She did not go to Boston for her first consultation with Dr. Williams until February 1864, that is, many months *after* she composed this poem on blindness. One is tempted to explain the startling "coincidence" that she anticipated her eye disease by concluding that the poem is evidently misdated and that actually it was written a year or two later, when the poet felt that she had sufficient reason for her attention to be centered on her eyes. But in the *Letters* Thomas Johnson states that the poem was included in a letter to T. W. Higginson written in August 1862. This fact alone is almost sufficient proof that the poet's eye complaints were of a psychological nature. And even if the poem had been written later, one would still be left with the strong impression that its preoccupation with total blindness was unwarranted by whatever organic pathology might have been present, since obviously, in view of her later perfect vision, any physical disorder must have been minor. Dr. Williams was one of the country's leading ophthalmologists and he would have reassured her that her symptoms were not calamitous. Had the poem been written at the height of her ocular discomfort, therefore, the implication would still remain that her reaction was unrealistic and that consequently it was exaggerated by emotional determinants.

I shall now assume, therefore, that the psychological nature of Emily Dickinson's eye difficulty has been established as being at least worthy of consideration and will proceed to examine the possible significance such a disturbance might have had in the poet's life.

Photophobia reaches its greatest intensity with reference to the sun. Emily Dickinson complains about the glare reflected from the snow that causes the house to be painfully bright; if this is so, then the direct confrontation of sunlight would be even more distressful to her. The most acute aversion in her phobia would therefore have been the direct sight of the sun, a fact of considerable psychoanalytic significance.

Although multiple symbolic meanings may accrue to any object, the relevance of the sun as a symbol to many patients consists in its unconscious identification with the figure of the father. Freud's friend Karl Abraham was one of the first psychoanalysts to investigate the underlying meaning of photophobia, and he had occasion to analyze a number of patients with this complaint.

423

In all of them he found the train of associations to lead ultimately from the light of the sun to the gaze of the father. Also it has long been evident that psychogenic constrictions of the range of sight and anxious shrinking from normal use of the eyes represent, among other things, fears of being observed as well as unconsciously determined defenses against an urge to look at forbidden things. With these clinical observations in mind—the frequent identification of the sun with the father, fears of being seen, and the repression of a temptation to observe what one's conscience instructs not be observed—I shall proceed to examine Emily Dickinson's use of the sun symbol in her poems. Later, I will attempt to demonstrate evidence of an inner conflict involving the poet's need to conceal herself and her unconscious impulse to expose that which it is prohibited to view.

It is beyond question that in the majority of Emily Dickinson's poems in which the image of the sun is anthropomorphized, the symbol is consciously and explicitly masculinized. For example, the sun is referred to as "He" and the poet speaks of "His Yellow Plan," "His Eye," "His Head" (all poem 591); "His Golden Will" (poem 766); "His interests of Fire" (poem 1278); "his Scarlet shelf" (poem 1136); and she compares sunset to the death of a "Peacock" (poem 120). Although one may find examples of feminine suns in nineteenth-century literature with which she was probably familiar, she seems not to have been influenced by them or by her favorite poet Shakespeare's "and Juliet is the sun."*

That she frequently endowed the sun not only with masculine attributes but with many of the qualities of her own father also is evident. Edward Dickinson was a punctual, busy lawyer. For years he was the first one up in the morning and he aroused his family by ringing a bell. In poem 888 the sun emerges from "His

---

* Of the 221 poems that mention the sun (that is, those which contain the words *sun, sundown, sunrise, sunrise's, sun's, suns, sunset, sunset's, sunsets,* and *sunshine*), 186 contain no suggestion whatever of gender. Of the remaining 35 poems, 32 explicitly give the sun's gender as masculine, and in two more masculinity is clearly implied. In only one poem (no. 666, "Sunset – reviews her Sapphire Regiment") is there an explicit imputation of femininity. It may be important to note, however, that in this single exception to the rule the sun is not conceived of as a single feminine object. It is the entire spectacle of sunset, of which the sun is only a part, that is feminized.

amazing House" and, like a conscientious milkman, deposits "a Day at every Door."

Emily Dickinson said once that her father was "too busy with his Briefs—to notice what we do."[26] His absorption in serious professional concerns precluded fantasy and poetry; his life was all *"real life."*[27] Like him, in poem 591, the sun has a "Yellow Plan" which keeps him "Busy with Majesty." According to the poem, the vagaries of the terrestrial atmosphere are not allowed to impinge on his momentous affairs.

Edward Dickinson was the axis of his daughter's world. She considered him her major source of strength and security. After his death she remarked: "Home is so far from Home, since my Father died";[28] and she said that she was "accustomed to all through Father."[29] Thus when we read in poem 591 that it is the function of the sun to "bind Astronomy, in place," the relevance to Edward Dickinson is clear.

Another characteristic of Mr. Dickinson was his unrelenting industry. "He never played,"[30] declared Emily. Thus in poem 1447 the sun is a "laborious Boy – / Who must be up to call the World."

And the sun, like her father, has the will to enforce his authority. When, in poem 1190, the "Fog" challenges him for the "Government of Day," the sun takes down his phallic "Yellow Whip" and asserts his supremacy.

That the poet endows the sun with male physical attributes is suggested by other poems. In poem 204, for instance, the poet draws an analogy between the rising of the sun and a man's dressing himself: "A little purple – slipped between – / Some Ruby Trowsers hurried on." It would appear that the masculine morning fears to be caught naked.

Another poem (no. 152) assigns an active male role to the sun in its relation to the "Hills," a familiar female symbol in Emily Dickinson's poetry:

> The Sun kept stooping – stooping – low!
> The Hills to meet him rose!
> On his side, what Transaction!
> On their side, what Repose!

The stanza seems unconsciously to portray the prevailing Victorian view of the woman's participation in sexual intercourse as an essentially passive one.*

Probably Emily Dickinson's most unequivocal and unflattering identification of the sun image with the sexually rapacious and domineering male is to be found in that famous letter to Sue, written twelve years before Emily had any trouble with her eyes. She writes that she and Sue have been "strangely silent" upon the subject of marriage, that they have "touched upon it, and as quickly fled away, as children shut their eyes when the sun is too bright for them" (that is, Emily Dickinson shuts her eyes to a too dazzling aspect of reality—sexuality). She goes on to compare the wife to a flower, the husband to the sun. The flower-wife at noon is "bowed in anguish before the mighty sun." Yet, she says, wives will "cry for sunlight, and pine for the burning noon, tho' it scorches them, scathes them . . . the man of noon, is *mightier* than the morning" (that is, the sexually active husband is overwhelming to the woman, in contrast to the tender and considerate fiancé). She calls such a relationship "dangerous" and confesses her great fear of sexual intercourse with a man: "It does so rend me, Susie, the thought of it when it comes, that I tremble lest at sometime I, too, am yielded up."[31] One wonders where else she could have developed such a view of the marriage relationship except through her interpretation of the parental one. Her adjectives here call to mind similar ones she used to describe her father; to her he was "so mighty a man"[32] and "His Heart was pure and terrible."[33]

As a woman has only one father, so the sun is unique. Emily Dickinson recognizes this quality in a quatrain (poem 1550) written eight years after her father's death:

> The pattern of the Sun
> Can fit but him alone
> For sheen must have a Disk
> To be a sun –

There is often a suggestion of phallic imagery in Emily Dickin-

---

* It should go without saying that most of Emily Dickinson's poems lend themselves to a commonsense, nonabstruse interpretation. The level of meaning examined throughout this chapter is generally one that was beneath the poet's level of awareness. It is assumed that the reader will not conclude that the psychoanalytic meaning is the only one.

son's lines on the sun. Here the "Disk" is the sun with its shining corona—the "Yellow Whip" of poem 1190 that subdues the rebellious. The same impression is gained from poem 1079, which stresses the rising and the falling of the sun: "The Sun went down," begins one stanza, "The Sun went up," another, while the poet looked on and was "present at the Majesty," witnessing the sun's coronation. The activity of the sun suggests the processes of erection, a phenomenon of which the virginal poet was well aware, at least unconsciously, as is proven by poem 1670, in which she recounts a dream. The poem says that she found a worm in her room "Pink lank and warm." Later "A thing occurred / I'd not believe it if I heard / But state with creeping blood / A snake with mottles rare / Surveyed my chamber floor / In feature as the worm before / But ringed with power."

In poem 1178 she beseeches the sun to "Shine thy best – / Fling up thy Balls of Gold / Till . . . every Crescent hold." Note that the sun's light is caught and held by a "Crescent." A crescent represents that quantity of light sent from the sun which fills up to varying degrees the darkness of a body which in itself does not contain or emit light. The crescent here is an unconscious symbol for the woman—the target for and vessel of the rays discharged from the sun. The image of the crescent appears in another poem (no. 508) which tells of the poet's being claimed by her beloved: "Called to my Full – The Crescent dropped – / Existence's whole Arc, filled up, / With one small Diadem." Later I shall discuss the significance of the "Diadem."

Insofar as the sun is the male symbol, that which is illuminated can be regarded as impregnated with light—the crescent that gradually broadens and becomes full. Thus "morning" and "day" also may be regarded as female symbols because they are susceptible of being filled with sunlight. These symbols also will be discussed more fully later on.

Observe how often Emily Dickinson in her poems peers with fascination at the processes of the sun. The following examples demonstrate this tendency. In poem 121 the time is daybreak, when "Watchers hang upon the East," awaiting the moment "The East / Opens the lid of Amethyst / And lets the morning go." The morning in this context is synonymous with the sun in a highly energized image. It may plausibly be argued that the lid of amethyst has some intrinsic psychological relationship to the previously mentioned "Ruby Trowsers" of poem 204, which are clearly sex-linked accouterments. The vigor with which the sun is expected to leap when the lid of dawn is lifted seemingly has its phallic counterpart in poem 304, in which "The Day . . . sprang before the Hills / Like . . . the Light / A Sudden Musket – spills." Here the figure seems to delineate the male orgasm. In poem 425 the poet asks: "I can look – cant I / When the East is Red?" as if there were some implied impropriety in her behavior. In another poem (no. 480) she explains that she looks because she is powerless to do otherwise: "The Sunrise – Sir – compelleth Me – / Because He's Sunrise – and I see."

Thus it is clear that the poet consciously and habitually presents the sun as a masculine object that powerfully allures and magnetizes. In some of the poems, however, the elaboration of certain parallel metaphors embodying the same basic idea suggests, as one would expect, something beyond the masculine identification. The associational channels that connect these metaphors can be seen to provide access to a psychological stratum more deeply unconscious than the one on which the identification sun = father predominates. Poem 121, cited above, establishes the topography of these connections clearly. The complete poem reads as follows:

> As Watchers hang upon the East,
> As Beggars revel at a feast
> By savory Fancy spread –
> As brooks in deserts babble sweet
> On ear too far for the delight,
> Heaven beguiles the tired.
>
> As that same watcher, when the East
> Opens the lid of Amethyst
> And lets the morning go –
> That Beggar, when an honored Guest,
> Those thirsty lips to flagons pressed,
> Heaven to us, if true.

In this poem the watcher impatient for the advent of dawn, the famished beggar, and the thirsty desert-wanderer far removed from any stream at which he might slake his thirst are all three presented as equivalent metaphors for the soul longing for "Heaven." Only the "Watchers," however, seems to have been drawn from the oedipal level, that is, only this image is evidently related to the sun symbol with unconscious roots in the little girl's curiosity about and sensual fascination with her father. The other two figures—the starving and the parched—must have their origin in an earlier level, in a time when "thirsty lips" were once pressed to maternal "flagons." Poem 121, then, takes images drawn from two distinct psychic levels—the oedipal and the oral —and renders them equivalent. We are thereby provided with a key through which access can be obtained to one of the deeper significances of the sun symbol in the mind of Emily Dickinson.

Therefore, before one goes too far in emphasizing Emily Dickinson's anxiety-ridden preoccupations with male sexuality, certain reservations must be indicated. It is a basic psychoanalytic postulate that those symbols which carry heavy psychological freight have superimposed referents, that is, they stand simultaneously for different things, depending upon the psychic level under scrutiny. Necessarily, though, a common channel of meaning connects the various aspects of the symbol. On the oldest strata of personality are impressed the traces of the mother-infant attachment and the first life-giving and life-sustaining experiences of love. Because Emily Dickinson never fully overcame her need to resolve what was conflictual and unsatisfied at this level, almost all her symbols have roots in the disrupted mother bond. The father relationship exists on a more recent psychological level. It is well, therefore, to keep in mind that, although Emily Dickinson's writing displays an almost exclusive emphasis on the sun's masculinity, the warmth and light she most deeply desired were not basically masculine. The child whose need for a mother's love exceeds the supply turns ultimately to the father —not for a father's love (that is, the care expressed by a father in his role as benign representative of the larger world and as tender mediator between that world and his children) but for the love the child failed to get from the mother. The father becomes a substitute for the mother (instead of a supplementary source of support), and the child then develops all the fantasies and fixations and symbolic representations that can be elaborated from the personality and physical characteristics of the father. In the sun symbol, therefore, the symbolic elaboration of the image of the father most likely functions somewhat as an eclipse behind which blazes still the unrivaled preoedipal mother. In a woman like Emily Dickinson with strong dependency needs, all symbolic representations, including those which involve the father, will be permeated with a quality of orality. An example of this is poem 121, which, in addition to the sun imagery cited above, expresses in oral imagery (starving and thirsting) the longing for the heaven of maternal love, a hunger which there is every reason to believe underlay all of the poet's searching, regardless of her ostensible object. To repeat, then, not only is the sun a symbol of the mother, one must even say that the father himself has become most profoundly a symbol of the mother. Emily Dickinson remained a predominantly oral personality whose major fixations were to the oral stage; she craved a dependent existence enfolded in a protective love.

To return to my thesis: The image of the sun in Emily Dickinson's poetry most proximately signifies the father, personally and anatomically, just as it may for persons in psychoanalysis. Furthermore, I believe that Emily Dickinson's photophobia is, on one level, related to repressed forbidden impulses involving sexual attraction to and curiosity about her father, with accompanying fears and guilt feelings. Of course we know that such impulses are universal in daughters; therefore, it is necessary to show why in Emily Dickinson they should lead to such an extreme defensive maneuver.

The following poem (no. 232) is instructive and may be interpreted as expressing a facet of the early father-daughter oedipal relationship:

The *Sun – just touched* the Morning –
The *Morning* – Happy thing –
Supposed that He had come to *dwell* –
And Life would all be *Spring!*

She felt herself *supremer* –
A *Raised – Etherial Thing!*
Henceforth – for Her – *What Holiday!*
Meanwhile – Her wheeling King –
Trailed – slow – along the Orchards –
His *haughty – spangled* Hems –
Leaving a *new necessity!*
The *want* of *Diadems!*

The Morning – *fluttered – staggered* –
Felt feebly – for Her *Crown* –

Her *unannointed forehead* –
Henceforth – Her *only* One!

If one assumes that the unconscious meaning of *"Sun"* here is *Father,* the hidden drama of the poem becomes amenable to analysis. The feminized "Morning," here of course representing the female child, mistakenly believing the Sun has claimed her as his own, is inflated with self-importance. Her happiness is short-lived, however, and after a brief period she makes the painful discovery that her possession by the Sun was illusory and that he has moved on (presumably to something more mature—possibly "Noon"). What was it the little girl expected of her father, here designated a *"Diadem"* and referred to as "a *new necessity"*? It seems clear that the girl has made the discovery that she *is* a girl, that is, that she lacks a crown—a corona—such as is possessed by the Sun-King. She is thus faced with her incompleteness. "The Morning – *fluttered – staggered –* / *Felt feebly –* for"—the penis that was not there? The poem concludes with the implication that the loss was irrevocable and that the poet resigned herself to it.

Emily Dickinson wrote other poems whose theme is the loss or inaccessibility of crowns, pearls, and other gems in which the unconscious meaning appears to be related to feelings of castration. The following (no. 245) is typical:

I held a Jewel in my fingers –
And went to sleep –
The day was warm, and winds were prosy –
I said " 'Twill keep" –

I woke – and chid my honest fingers,
The Gem was gone –
And now, an Amethyst remembrance
Is all I own –

As we know from clinical experience, some little girls do not accept their "deposed" state with the readiness implied in these poems, and neither, it appears, did Emily Dickinson. That she continued to entertain unconscious fantasies of possessing the attributes of masculinity, including the anatomical ones, is clear from "My Life had stood – a Loaded Gun" and other poems. She rejected the idea of her "inferior" station and, as her symbols suggest, seems to have regarded her genital femininity as a wound. Whatever meaning one ascribes to the following poem (no. 379) on a conscious level, the unconscious meaning involves a revulsion against femininity, rage at castration, and a fierce possessiveness with regard to the penis:

> Rehearsal to Ourselves
> Of a Withdrawn Delight –
> Affords a Bliss like Murder –
> Omnipotent – Acute –
>
> We will not drop the Dirk –
> Because We love the Wound
> The Dirk Commemorate – Itself
> Remind Us that we died.

The "Dirk" that she would not drop may represent both the illusory penis of the phallic woman and the coveted genitals of her father.

A somewhat similar poem (no. 951) presents—unconsciously, in nature symbolism—the poet's feeling that the female genitals are like a blighted garden. She infers the previous existence of a phallus from the evidence of a "Gash" and a "stain" (that is, menstrual blood):

> As Frost is best conceived
> By force of it's Result –
> Affliction is inferred
> By subsequent effect –
>
> If when the sun reveal,
> The Garden keep the Gash –
> If as the Days resume
> The wilted countenance
>
> Cannot correct the crease
> Or counteract the stain –
> Presumption is Vitality
> Was somewhere put in twain.

In still another poem (no. 1233) she cries out in despair: "Had I not seen the Sun / I could have borne the shade."

Probably if the poet had not lacked a loving and admired mother after whom she could model herself, this psychological alignment with the male role would not have taken on the character of a dominant undercurrent in her psychical life. This is what happened, however, and her position in regard to men became a competitive one noticeable in her jealous possessiveness toward her girl friends, her rivalry with Austin for the affections of Sue, and in the apparent pleasure she derived from bewildering males with her superior intelligence. "All men say 'What' to me, but I thought it a fashion,"[34] she told poor Col. Higginson, one of her most hapless and unsuspecting victims. One has only to recall her tactics in repeatedly seducing him into submitting his self-important and inept literary advice to appreciate this need to "castrate." For years she adopted the pose of his "pupil" and called him "Master," but whenever he took the trouble to point out the ways in which *he* thought her verse could be improved, she "innocently" responded by sending him poems which utterly repudiated his every suggestion.

In several of the "sun" poems one fancies one can obtain glimpses of a vendetta against men, including her father. The setting of the sun as a trope signifying death is a commonplace in poetry, but Emily Dickinson invests it with an unusual vehemence in which death occurs through exsanguination. She associates the ruddy hues of sunset with bleeding, and the phenomenon thereby takes on the appearance of an act of violence, as in "Soft as the massacre of Suns / By Evening's Sabres slain" (poem 1127). Elsewhere she calls sunset the "Evening Blood" (poem 223), and in still another poem (no. 658) she describes it as a red sea with fleets of red ships and "Crews – of solid Blood." This association of cutting, bleeding, and death with the image of the sun perhaps betrays unconscious fantasies of eventual revenge and triumph over her father and other males. It also may remind her of the fate of her own blighted identification with her father and of aspects of her self-concept as a castrated "man."

As has been frequently pointed out, Emily Dickinson's poems metaphorically equate fulfillment in love with a capacity for unflinching vision in the face of an intense celestial illumination. Conversely, darkness and blindness are associated with the idea of renunciation. For example, in a poem (no. 63) that speculates on the relation between earthly privation and heavenly reward, she exclaims: "If night stands first – *then* noon / To gird us for the sun, / What gaze! / When from a thousand skies / On our *developed* eyes / Noons blaze!" In a poem (no. 188) whose theme is the superiority of a supportive fantasy to a depressing reality, the poet requests "a picture of the sun" so she can "make believe [she's] getting warm." In the effort to forget a renounced beloved, she says (poem 47): "Heart! . . . You may forget the warmth he gave – / I will forget the light!" In poem 638 love again brings warmth and light; the sexual nature of the imagery is evident: "To my small Hearth His fire came – / And all my House aglow / Did fan and rock, with sudden light – / 'Twas Sunrise – 'twas the Sky." Again she ponders the security love would bring, deemed "Certainties of Sun – / Midsummer – in the Mind" (poem 646). The attempt to convey the ecstasy of love to one who has not experienced it is as vain as if "a Hand did try to chalk the Sun / To Races – nurtured in the Dark" (poem 581). She expresses the idea that reality is unnecessary when one's fantasy is complete, vivid, and permanent: "What need of Day – / To Those whose Dark – hath so – surpassing Sun – / It deem it be – Continually – / At the Meridian?" (poem 611). In these and in many other instances Emily Dickinson equates love, fulfillment, and security with the possession of an abiding sun—the possession of a male lover patterned after her father or the establishment of his attributes within her own personality. But, again, one must not forget that these heterosexual tendencies were tenuous and relatively superficial and that a more fundamental undertow existed beneath them: the search for mother.

And here is what Emily Dickinson has to say regarding the absence of love. One of her favorite ideas is that one can only appreciate a thing when one lacks it, as, for example, thirst reveals to us the essence of water. The assertion that ecstasy is best perceived from the vantage point of suffering is expressed in terms of vision and the sun: "To learn the Transport by the Pain – / As Blind Men learn the sun!" (poem 167). The pain of losing the beloved is described in similar terms: *"Sunset –* at *Easter – / Blindness –* on the *Dawn"* (poem 236). This enhancement through loss is again conveyed in visual terms: "The Blind – esteem it be / Enough Estate – to see" (poem 355). "Renunciation" is defined as "The putting out of Eyes – / Just Sunrise" (poem 745). The inaccessibility of the beloved causes a "Chasm" in the poet's life, and she declares, "When Sunrise through a fissure drop / The Day must follow too" (poem 858). When she blames her environment for separating her from her lover, she says, "They took away our Eyes" (poem 474).

This emotional investment in the faculty of sight and the extent of the poet's multiplication of its associations with the possession and the loss of her love object is persuasive evidence that Emily Dickinson's worries about her eyes had profound unconscious roots.

I come now to one more link in the chain tying the poet's eye problem to her emotional life. This involves the defensive function of her photophobia. That it served this function is suggested by the poet herself. After describing a state of abject hopelessness, she says: "I shut my eyes – and groped as well / 'Twas lighter – to be Blind" (poem 761)—that is, it eased her burden to withdraw from the contemplation of the source of her misery.

What caused Emily Dickinson to fear that she would be deprived of her vision? Why could she not bear the gaze of the sun and why did she consider it dangerous? "A Toad, can die of Light" (poem 583), she says. But she is not a toad. Certainly she had read in Matthew, her favorite book of the Bible, "If thine eye offend thee, pluck it out." Did her eye offend her conscience that she should psychologically pluck it out? The answers to these questions involve the residuals of her oedipal experiences.

In the oedipal period, Emily Dickinson, like all female children, turned to her father as a source of sensual love. It is a vestige of this phase in her development that is prominent in many of the "sun" poems in which the father symbol is aggrandized. The oedipal attraction for her father, renounced through fear of maternal retaliation and the loss of what little maternal affection was available, lingers also in her propensity for envious contemplation of his sexual life and the physical organs that make it possible. On several occasions the poet speaks of lightning, a phenomenon which clinical experience demonstrates is related to the sun image by its frequent use as symbol of the father. It is this linkage of the sun with lightning that provides the clue necessary to answer the question: What caused Emily Dickinson to hide from the sun's gaze?

She relates the symbols of sun and lightning explicitly. "Omnipotence" (a quality with which the infant girl endows the father), she says, does not introduce himself to us in words: "His lisp – is Lightning – and the Sun" (poem 420). Lightning is also

"The awful Cutlery / Of mansions never quite disclosed / And never quite concealed / The Apparatus of the Dark / To ignorance revealed" (poem 1173). The phallic connotations of lightning are more clearly evident in poem no. 1593, where it is linked with the image of a snake, the only animal which terrified Emily Dickinson, in the phrase "The Doom's electric Moccasin." The connection between the phallic lightning and blindness is also made explicit in poem 1129: "Truth," she says, is "Too bright for our infirm Delight," and like lightning, which to children must gently be explained away, "The Truth must Dazzle gradually / Or every man be blind." One sees in these examples some of the roots in infantile curiosity of the forbidden impulse to discover the male "Apparatus of the Dark," probably one of the determinants of Emily Dickinson's avoidance of the light and of her difficulty with her eyes. But the fear of lightning, snakes, and the rays of the sun has deeper roots than these.

A benign resolution of the oedipal attachment to her father was not possible for the poet; this involves an acceptance of being female, and the woman's role as it was exemplified in her family caused her to disclaim it for herself. Her pathetic cultivation of motherly women outside her family and her compulsive identification with Susan came too late; the sexual structures of her mind were set as in a crystal with its flaws and inclusions. One such inclusion was her identification with the males in her family. This unconscious adoption of a masculine perspective pervaded her life, although she never became an outwardly aggressive, defiantly competitive woman. Instead, in a kind of reaction formation, she became increasingly shy and shrinking—possibly an angry caricature of her mother's timid submissiveness. But, in the secrecy of her unconscious, she cherished the masculinity in her nature and she reveled in it symbolically in some of her poems. Psychoanalysis has made us familiar with the fact that women who deny their femininity fear the loss of their maleness, that is, they fear castration.

What has this to do with Emily Dickinson's fears for her eyes? Not only is the eye a receptive organ, it penetrates as well. Emily Dickinson says it can "accost – and sunder" (poem 752). In short, it can, by unconscious mechanisms, be erotized and invested with a significance totally inappropriate to it—it can become a substitute phallus for a woman who finds it crucial to deny that, anatomically or otherwise, she is a man's inferior.

It would be important to know what circumstances precipitated Emily Dickinson's concern for her eyes, here interpreted as a fear for the preservation of what she unconsciously imagined was the only worthwhile part of her—her illusory, creative masculinity. What impulses or behavior would have caused her to fear her father's gaze and shrink from his castrative retribution?

In view of the fact that Emily Dickinson's eye trouble succeeded her renounced love affair, one answer that springs readily to mind is as follows: Victim of a profound father attachment, the poet reacted to her love for another man with the dreadful conviction that she was betraying her father, who would strongly condemn her unfaithfulness. Consequently, she developed an intense sense of guilt and shrank from his disapproving scrutiny.

Though plausible at first glance, this hypothesis is untenable on closer inspection. A woman caught up in a deep heterosexual commitment is ipso facto accepting her womanhood. Though she may under certain circumstances develop strong guilt feelings because of her love affair, it is absurd to imagine that the punishment she might unconsciously anticipate and dread would take the form of castration, which necessarily carries the implication that she has rejected the feminine role. Moreover, for reasons that have already been given, it is apparent that Emily Dickinson's "love affair" was in itself a defensive maneuver, alleviating fear and anxiety and assuaging guilt rather than provoking these feelings.

For a more cogent interpretation of the significance of Emily Dickinson's fears for her vision, one must again return to the oedipal constellation, here inverted. The girl's identification with her father endows her with a spurious masculinity. Because of this, *his* love objects become *her* love objects; and with her sensual impulses augmented by the sadistic ones that have been exaggerated by the mother's rejection, she turns toward the mother and her representatives as her prey—with "Loaded Gun" she hunts "the Doe." These impulses are then repressed because of fears of the father's retaliation, for, after all, the mother is *his* property. The image of the snake in the garden seems to have been adopted by Emily Dickinson to convey these unconscious

437

fears. She tells us that "when [she was] a Boy" she never saw a snake "Without a tighter breathing / And Zero at the Bone" (poem 986). She regards the snake as "summer's treason" and declares, "Sweet is the swamp with its secrets, / Until we meet a snake" (poem 1740). The alluring swamp, related to the garden image, is the female genitals, enticing to her until her father appears. This fear of the snake is not for Emily Dickinson simply a fear of male sexuality per se. For her, as for the oedipal boy, the snake is the great deterrent to her encroachments upon the swamp —the female love object (ultimately, that is, the desired mother). Not long before she wrote these lines she reexperienced these long forgotten impulses toward her mother, this time in the guise of her attraction to Susan.

The year 1862 saw the high point of Emily Dickinson's capacity to convert her psychological terrors into artistic productivity. In 1863 and 1864, the years that marked the beginning of the poet's concern for her eyes, began the striking decline in poetic output. It appears that poetic expression had by then proven an inadequate defense mechanism to cope with the psychic torrents it had to channel, and the excessive pressures were henceforth converted into nonproductive symptoms such as emotional constriction and the ocular complaints. By 1865 the poetic faculty had become a mere sluice compared with the wild cataract of 1862. Because in Emily Dickinson's mind her creativity was intimately linked with a sense of herself as the possessor of a certain psychological virility, as her creative power subsided she lapsed into self-depreciation, diminished self-esteem, and depression. The loving "mother" she coveted in Sue and for whom she had competed so desperately with Austin had been relinquished anew to another male—Sue's infant boy. If she was ever to fear emasculation as the result of her daring to usurp masculine prerogatives, she must now have felt that this punishment for her guilt had indeed descended upon her. Loveless, excluded, almost burned out as a poet, and reduced to the status of a queer, hypochondriacal, and depressed old maid, she may well have felt "castrated." The plucking out of her eyes as the terrible consequence of sexual transgression—a doom antedating Oedipus Rex—seems to be the deeper meaning of Emily Dickinson's ocular complaints. And, one must remember, all the vicissitudes of her relationship with Sue took place under the blazing eye of Emily's father.

From this perspective, therefore, the dread of looking at the sun can be seen to involve far more than disavowed infantile temptations to voyeurism with regard to the males in her family (and generalized later, of course, to other males). Of greater significance is the sun as an externalized puritan conscience in the apotheosized image of father. Vinnie once said that she and Emily were so afraid to displease their father that they would not fail to heed his admonitions even after his death. He was the final judge of their behavior, and they were uneasy lest he hear anything in a letter or in the "kitchen talks" of the brother and sisters that might meet with his disapproval. Similarly, the sun as ultimate judge appears in poem 1372, where it "estimates" both the unruly weed and the "conscientious Flower."

That Emily Dickinson felt exposed and vulnerable we can infer from her withdrawal from contact with men and women; that the feeling induced a need to conceal herself is suggested by her lines (poem 891):

> In Cave if I presumed to hide
> The Walls – begun to tell –
> Creation seemed a mighty Crack –
> To make me visible –

The fact that Emily Dickinson saw to it that her poetic outpouring never came to the attention of even her closest relatives during her lifetime points up still another aspect of her fear of exposure. Quite probably she sensed on some level of consciousness that her poems divulged the deeply forbidden impulses that are the subject of this chapter. When the poet asked Higginson to help her improve her poetry, she confessed to something that sounds almost like guilt feelings over her writing, and it is perhaps significant that she phrased the idea in terms of the sun's surprising her in the act. She said that it pained her to be grotesque and awkward in an art in which others were beautiful; these are her words: "but if caught with the Dawn—or the Sunset see me—Myself the only Kangaroo among the Beauty, Sir . . . it afflicts me."[35] The remark is an illustration of the concept that formal beauty is essential to art partly because it is a means of legitimatizing the otherwise unacceptable propensities expressed in it. It seems more than a coincidence that it is the discovery by the magnificent sun of her inadequacies and her presumptions that the poet dreads.

CHAPTER IX

Suppose a man her equal in sensitivity and intelligence had come into her life, could he have resuscitated her repudiated femininity? I raise the question in view of the love poems she addressed to her more or less nonexistent male lover. Some poems suggest a negative reply. In a poem whose theme is the futility of bemoaning the irreparable, she says that her regret "Were useless as next morning's sun – / Where midnight frosts – had lain!" (poem 205). Since the garden signifies the female genitals, the statement at an unconscious level expresses her doubt that anything can alter the damage of castration. It also implies that the advent of a man's warmth and love ("next morning's sun")— originally the father but now any of his representatives—would be too late to thaw her frozen emotional capacities.

She wavered in her view, however, as is indicated by other poems. Consider the following (poem 925):

> Struck, was I, nor yet by Lightning –
> Lightning – lets away
> Power to perceive His Process
> With Vitality.
>
> Maimed – was I – yet not by Venture –
> Stone of stolid Boy –
> Nor a Sportsman's ruthless pleasure
> Who mine Enemy?
>
> Robbed – was I – intact to Bandit –
> All my Mansion torn –
> Sun — withdrawn to Recognition –
> Furthest shining – done –
>
> Yet was not the foe – of any –
> Not the smallest Bird
> In the nearest Orchard dwelling
> Be of Me – afraid.
>
> Most – I love the Cause that slew Me.
> Often as I die
> It's beloved Recognition
> Holds a Sun on Me –
>
> Best – at Setting – as is Nature's –
> Neither witnessed Rise
> Till the infinite Aurora
> In the other's eyes.

In this moving poem the poet beholds the possibility that the salvation of her womanhood through her love for a man might slip through her fingers. She fully acknowledges her condition as a woman, though the admission causes her to regard herself as deprived of "Vitality," "Maimed," "Robbed," "intact [only] to Bandit." All her "Mansion" is "torn" and *her* "Sun" is "withdrawn to recognition," its "furthest shining done."

The fourth stanza represents a denial of her belief that her state is the recompense for her own aggression and guilt, and she specifically disclaims any hostility in herself, saying she was no one's foe (least of all her father's). In fact, so harmless is she that even the smallest birds are unafraid of her.

The piercingly beautiful eight lines beginning "Most – I love the Cause that slew Me" suggest potentialities for heterosexual love that, because her male beloved was distant, inaccessible, and largely imaginary, were never to be realized. She feels he "recognizd" her, however, and for a brief interval, after he persuades her to accept her proper function as a woman, she is warmed by a masculine tenderness similar to her father's in her childhood. She no longer needs to hide her eyes from the solar light, although, as another poem confesses, she is deeply pained by "a Setting Sun – / Where Dawn – knows how to be" (poem 944). But the fact is that her lover never materialized; her rejection of womanhood was perhaps too deeply ingrained for him to have been anything more than a dream, her need for a mothering woman too overriding. Her fantasy gradually faded, she relinquished much of her claim to Sue, and the eyes, no longer in danger, ceased troubling her.

Elizabeth Browning's life represented to Emily Dickinson all she longed for. The male-envying woman, made physically complete through an identification with her husband and through his gift of a child, can begin to accept her womanhood. Emily Dickinson seems desperately to have wanted this solution for herself despite her fears. She managed only to convince herself (and half the world) that she had a lover who was out of reach. A decade hence she "adopted" Sue's little boy Gilbert, who stirred her to abundant outpourings of maternal affection derived probably from her identification with him. His death at the age of nine prostrated her and left her emotionally ravaged.

First mother, then father, then their representatives, then the virile thrust of creativity, then her proxy motherhood—each in turn dissolved when she turned to them for the meaning of her existence. A short poem (no. 546), interpretable on different levels —oral, phallic, and genital—epitomizes her emotional hungers:

> To fill a Gap
> Insert the Thing that caused it –
> Block it up
> With Other – and 'twill yawn the more –
> You cannot solder an Abyss
> With Air.

Chapter X OUR PRACTICAL SISTER

Following her second series of eye treatments, Emily Dickinson, in 1865, returned home, never to leave again. She retreated into a seclusion that was almost airtight as far as the neighbors and Amherst social life in general were concerned, although she seems to have remained accessible to some of the neighborhood children and to Austin's children—Ned, Martha, and Gilbert.

The years after 1865 were without event except for deaths—her father's in 1874, Samuel Bowles's in 1878, Charles Wadsworth's and her mother's in 1882, little Gilbert's in 1883, and Judge Lord's in 1884, to mention some of her deepest bereavements. She continued to cultivate new friendships, however, though only through letters, and she corresponded frequently with a surprising number of people, most of whom were never to lay eyes on her. Susan continued her active social life and, through her and Austin, Vinnie met new people; and it was through Vinnie's reports to her sister that these new acquaintances took on reality for Emily. Throughout the years until her death, Emily sent wine, fruit, poems, and flowers to friends she never saw.

One such friendship developed between the Dickinson sisters and a young college professor, David Todd, and his wife, Mabel Loomis Todd, who was to become Emily Dickinson's first editor.

The Todds came to Amherst in 1881 and were attracted immediately to Susan and Austin. Mrs. Todd was impressed by their charm, wealth, and handsome style of life. Though at first almost overwhelmed by Susan's brilliance, she liked and admired Austin immediately and thought him strong, dignified, good-looking, and a bit odd.

Soon after, when the Todds had become almost members of Sue's family, Vinnie issued them an imperious invitation to come to the mansion "at once."[1] Sue tried to discourage the young couple from seeing Vinnie, possibly out of a possessiveness toward them, going so far as to picture Vinnie and Emily to the Todds as unscrupulous seductresses who might attempt to lure the young man away from his wife. The Todds accepted the invitation anyway, Mabel sang and played the piano, and Emily listened from upstairs. Sue's friendship with the Todds cooled after that, although Austin continued to be fond of them, especially Mabel, toward whom he was gallant and tender. Though Mabel never did see Emily, she sang and played often for her, wrote to her, and made several bird and floral paintings for her. Emily in return sent rare and beautiful flowers from her conservatory, books, jam, and other gifts and even wrote to Mabel's parents as though they were old friends.

After the deaths of the elder Dickinsons, Vinnie and Emily continued to live in the large house, looked after by two house servants. They became dependent on their cook and housekeeper, Margaret, to such an extent that when Margaret was ill the neighbors felt it necessary to send them food. Vinnie from time to time went riding with Austin in his carriage or sleigh; Emily, of course, did not. The house during these last years of Emily's life was dark and shuttered.

Susan and Austin, in the 1870's and thereafter, had an increasingly conflict-ridden relationship. Austin found it necessary to work extremely hard to meet the expenses of Sue's style of life and her lavish entertaining. Her position as social leader of Amherst was, by the 1880's, undisputed, though Austin's part in her teas and soirées seems to have been perfunctory and performed against his will. Sometimes he would not even put in an appearance at these social events, and he and his wife for the most part tended to go their separate ways. Sue had become exclusive, snobbish, and extremely class-conscious, a side of her that was uncongenial to Austin. When Gilbert died, Austin was heartbroken and Mrs. Todd wrote in her diary that "Gilbert was . . . the only thing in his [Austin's] house which truly loved him, or in which he took any pleasure."[2]

The beginning of Emily's final illness occurred in the fall of 1883, and she was never completely well again. She was confined to her bed with "Nervous prostration"[3] for a time, then rallied somewhat. In June of the next year she became unconscious; a physician was called and she received the diagnosis "revenge of the nerves."[4] In October she had another attack. She continued to be very ill and in June 1886 had yet another episode. Her "nerves" probably had little to do with her condition, although in view of her past breakdown and her strange manner of life the physician should not be too much condemned for ascribing the illness to a "nervous" (that is, emotional) cause. Actually she was suffering from kidney failure and, probably, the secondary complication of elevated blood pressure.

Austin and Vinnie were deeply worried, and Austin would steal away an hour at a time to sit with Emily and confer with Vinnie. Meanwhile Sue was preoccupied with her own family, writing to Martha, now away at school in Farmington, and worrying about Ned, who was already, at twenty-four, showing signs of congestive heart failure, although Susan did not know this, believing that exertion gave him "asthma."[5] On February 13, 1886, while Austin sat with the dying Emily, Sue, next door, gave a party. She seems not to have been greatly concerned about Emily; possibly she was unaware of the seriousness of her illness. Emily at this time was too feeble even to read and write. On March 10 Sue gave another party, which Austin left to spend time with Emily. By now he must have been aware that she could not live much longer.

In early May, Emily became unconscious again, had a convulsion, and developed paralysis—apparently as a consequence of a cerebral hemorrhage. She survived for two and one half days in this condition, dying at 6 P.M. on May 15. Vinnie, exhausted, was thin and pale after the many weeks of caring for her sister. The funeral arrangements were made by Susan according to Emily's wishes. Her tiny figure was dressed in robes of white and placed in a white coffin that was carried out the *back* door of the mansion by six Irish workmen known to the family. The men carried the coffin through fields to the cemetery; the select group of guests attending followed on foot. Emily's grave was beside her father's and mother's. It was a beautiful spring day.

Austin did not long outlive Emily. He died in 1895 and was followed in three years by his unfortunate Ned, who used to take Vinnie for rides when his father was not available. The final years of Vinnie's life in that echoing, shuttered, empty mansion were desolate, with only her enemy Sue next door, by way of family, and only her cats to love and be loved by, and with all the subtle ties to her strange and irreplaceable sister forever broken.

And what exactly were those subtle ties? I have heretofore said little about Lavinia Dickinson's personality and about her deeper relations with Emily. It is time now to bring them to light as the final chapter of Emily Dickinson's emergence as a poet.

Although Lavinia must have been subject to many of the same psychological pressures that molded Emily, there were distinct differences between them. In her teens and early twenties Vinnie was a sexually attractive, saucy coquette; in her middle years she was the hard-working, organizing, practical, and protective manager of her father's household; later, in the final decade of her life, she appears as an aggressive and furtive crone—demanding and self-centered, with a malicious streak. Emily's shyness, interpersonal delicacy, sensitivity, and introspectiveness were never Vinnie's. And Emily had nothing of Vinnie's robust self-assertiveness, shameless mercenariness, and earthy physical gusto.

Vinnie reacted to the privations and tensions of her maturation in her own way. But the distorting stresses imposed on her by the peculiarities of her parents were probably roughly similar to those with which Emily struggled. Vinnie too gave up hope of ever marrying, but not because of the same inner forces that beset Emily. Vinnie, in changing from a charmingly warm and fun-loving girl to a termagant, followed different internal lines from those that led Emily from the spontaneous, humorous, and troubled adolescent of the 1850's to the orphic and constricted recluse of the later years.

It is a striking fact, though, that all three Dickinson children in a general way followed the same overall life pattern. Each manifested in his or her youth a superabundance of personal liveliness and social magnetism, each suffered a crisis of disappointment in early maturity. The brother and sisters, all to varying degrees, ended up somewhat queer, lonely, at odds with the environment, and apart from the community, toward which they developed a defensive hauteur. This inexact parallelism in their life trajectories argues for the existence of common psychological shaping forces acting upon personalities of dissimilar constitutional fiber. However, too little is known of Lavinia Dickinson's inner life—far less than is known of Emily's or even Austin's—to make possible an exact and detailed analysis of her character.

There were some character traits, though, that the sisters obviously had in common. Both in their youth were noted for their quick tongues and sense of humor. They tended to be critical of their neighbors. Each was proud of the other—Vinnie of Emily's intelligence and Emily of Vinnie's looks. There was a minimum of rivalry between them. Both were unusually fearful of adulthood, tending to cling to childhood and dependency upon parental support. Both became spinsters. Both betrayed an envy of men, both took on some of the qualities of their father—Emily his diligence and perseverance, Lavinia his aggressiveness and nerve. Both identified with aspects of their mother—Emily with her fearfulness, shyness, and masochism, Lavinia with her domestic role. Both relegated their mother to a position of inconsequence —Lavinia by usurping most of her functions, Emily by direct emotional rejection. Both girls stood in awe of their remote and dominating father. Both were absorbed in Austin and his activities.

In their middle years they restricted their activities to the home, Emily, of course, more than Lavinia. Lavinia's poor opinion of the neighbors became increasingly tinctured with spite; Emily feared them and withdrew from all contact with them. Neither sister adjusted her attire or coiffure to the changing styles; they dressed in the fashions of their youth to the end of their lives. Both adopted peculiarities of dress—Lavinia sporadically (for example, the fantastic yellow shoes, blue flannel dress, and long black mourning veil of her court appearance of 1898) and Emily continuously, in her white dresses. Both on occasion could jettison the truth without compunction; for example, Emily told T. W. Higginson that her father did not want her to read any book except the Bible and Lavinia lied during the court hearing.* On

---

* Lavinia gave a tract of land to the Todds in gratitude and compensation for Mrs. Todd's editing of Emily's poetry. Later she changed her mind and maintained that she had not understood the document she had signed which deeded the

this occasion Mrs. Todd wrote, "She perjured herself right along for an hour. It was apalling to see a person lie so composedly."[6]

Though Lavinia never underwent the kind of acute psychological breakdown that her sister suffered, she seems gradually to have developed habits of suspiciousness, parsimoniousness, deviousness, and mild antisocial behavior that can justly be called symptoms. In her own way she gave evidence of a disturbance of personality almost as grave as Emily's, though she was far less incapacitated. There is even a hint in Lavinia's unkind treatment of a young male cousin of the same residuals of early maternal deprivation in the form of a peculiar and probably unconsciously metaphorical emphasis on food that are found in the oral symbolism of Emily's poetry.

Emily's childhood deprivations were probably also repeated in the evolution of her sister, although the fact that Lavinia was not a poet and did not record the secrets of her inner life leaves us with a paucity of evidence to that effect. It will be recalled, however, that following Vinnie's birth Mrs. Dickinson was so ill as to necessitate Emily's being sent away from home. Newborn Vinnie, who remained, of course, with her mother, appeared sickly; thus both mother and daughter were a cause of concern. As I have suggested elsewhere, Mrs. Dickinson's physical infirmities may have been supplemented by a postpartum depression, in which case Vinnie's failure to thrive, as is so often the case, reflected the infant's anxious, instinctive perception of her mother's self-absorption and emotional remoteness. In view of these suggested indications, there exists at least the possibility that an insufficiency of maternal love was an aspect of Lavinia Dickinson's infantile experience.

Practically nothing is known of Vinnie's childhood beyond the fact that she was subject to croup—an ailment encountered frequently in the insecure offspring of anxiety-ridden mothers. A comment of the aging Lavinia to Mrs. Todd, "A saddle horse & the sea were the only playthings I valued!"[7] suggests the existence of an athletic bent congruent with her sturdy build and the physical energy she was later to demonstrate in her housekeeping. Although, in her youth at least, Vinnie seems to have been almost

property to the Todds. During the hearing held to decide the matter Vinnie adopted the role of rustic innocent duped by urban sophisticates. The court ruled in favor of Lavinia.

as voracious a reader as her sister, her very lively and romantic interest in boys probably limited the time she spent pursuing intellectual interests. It was perhaps in this regard more than in any other way that Lavinia and Emily in their adolescent years differed from each other.

Vinnie appealed to boys and received several offers of marriage. She was short and had luxuriant chestnut hair, both of which features she shared with Emily. Unlike Emily, however, she was markedly pretty and not at all shy. No doubt her outgoing personality, combined perhaps with an affinity for physical activities such as horseback riding, made her a congenial companion. The unusual and repellent aggressiveness and outspokenness of her later years are in fact simply exaggerations of traits that in her youth, when she retained a measure of softness and malleability, gave her personality a challenging quality that boys probably found attractive.

But even when she was a girl Vinnie's directness at times unsettled her friends. Joseph Lyman, a beau of her teen years, commenting on the failure of their romance to achieve fulfillment, said, "Vinnie might have done something with me if she had not done just as Laertes and Polonius told Ophelia *not* to do."[8] Apparently Vinnie's mistake was being too openly affectionate and lavishing her companionship on Joseph too unreservedly. "Keep you in the rear of your affection, / Out of the shot and danger of desire," Laertes told Ophelia, and Polonius added, "Be something scanter of your maiden presence." However, Lyman on occasion found Vinnie's wiles quite pleasantly seductive. "She sat in my lap," he recalled fondly after their relationship was over, "and pulled the pins from her long soft chestnut hair and tied the long silken mass around my neck and kissed me again & again. She was always at my side clinging to my arm . . . Her skin was very soft. Her arms were fat & white and I was very, very happy with her."[9] On another occasion he wrote how well he remembered the way Vinnie "used to take her little red ottoman and with almost childish grace come and set it close by my chair on the left side of me and lay her arm across my lap and put the book she was reading up against me and look from its pages into my face & read to me—and then follow me out at the front door with Austin and say 'Don't be gone very long Joseph' and meet me at the front door when I came back."[10]

CHAPTER X

One result of Vinnie's unabashed coquetry was to tax Joseph's self-restraint. Also, some doubt may possibly have crossed his mind that his arousal in the face of her blandishments was entirely outside her naive awareness. Thus we find him reassuring himself that Vinnie is simply childishly trusting and not deliberately arousing him: "Vinnie forgot everything except that within the two arms of her lover she found the softest, sweetest sleeping place *she* ever saw; and the perfect confidence she reposed in my self controll & the unclouded faith she put in my essential honor & nobleness more than balanced the 'frailty' . . . The very blindness of her love had honored & ennobled it. She confided in me as if I had been above human frailties."[11] That Vinnie loved blindly even as a teen-ager is of interest, since it was this very quality of imperviousness to uncongenial realities that in later life brought her campaign for the recognition of her sister's poetry to a successful conclusion.

One must take these passages with a grain of salt. They are from letters Lyman wrote to his fiancée, and it seems clear that he is attempting to demonstrate his irresistibility to women and to persuade her that she therefore has made quite a catch. Possibly he is here exaggerating Vinnie's ardor, as in other passages; to establish his emotional detachment from his relationship with Vinnie he emphasizes her limitations of intelligence and character. What these quotations do establish, certainly, is that the anguished, baffled groping after a sexual identity that obsessed Emily was no part of the experience of Vinnie. Vinnie was secure in her status as a female. This is not to say necessarily that she preferred being a woman—there is evidence that she did not—but that she accepted it for better or worse. One must therefore conclude that at a critical phase of childhood and to an extent that cannot possibly be true of Emily she gazed upon her mother and *assented*: Yes, I am like her; yes, I will grow to be more like her —for whatever her limitations I accept her and I love her—we are similar.

To explain why this all-important affirmation was possible for one sister and not for the other requires biographical information that is unattainable. It also involves a knowledge of constitutional propensities and vulnerabilities that are unique to individuals and that in part decide what the psychological consequences of environmental circumstances will be.

A glance at Emily's and Vinnie's daguerreotypes suggests that whatever their experiences the sisters started life with different textures of body and mind. The portraits of Vinnie, one dating from her late teens and the other from her thirties, clearly disclose strong bone structure, full neck muscles, sensual eyes and mouth, and a harmonious interrelationship of features that as a whole create an impression of sturdy mesomorphic handsomeness. Emily's photograph, taken in her teens and the only one we have of her, reveals that she possessed a skeletal structure of a delicacy that imposed no sculptural and comely prominences on the flesh. The outline of her face is vague, with a small chin; the eyes are large, and their gaze seems veiled, tender, and yet somehow judgmental—a face that derives its basic character not from the skull or musculature but from the nervous system. The contrast of Vinnie's portraits with Emily's is the difference between a lioness and a doe. No matter how one nurtures and trains two such dissimilar creatures one can cause them to be alike only in certain gross respects.

It seems that Mrs. Dickinson's anemic personality almost sufficed for Lavinia's development because her intrinsic need was not so great as her sister's. It is also possible, however, that psychological factors in Mrs. Dickinson militating against her effective nurturing of the older daughter in the first months of her life were not as strongly operant two years later in the case of the younger. One can say with certainty only that the myriad factors involved in Lavinia's relationship with her mother contributed to the daughter's acceptance of her mother as a sexual model.

As Vinnie grew older, her early identification with her mother must have been strengthened as it became apparent to the family that she, like her mother and unlike Emily and Austin, was not intellectually gifted. Joseph Lyman gives the baldest appraisal of Vinnie's ability, but what he says openly can be inferred from the letters of Emily, Austin, and Vinnie herself. "Vinnie was not very noble or accomplished," writes Lyman, "She could hardly be called 'a woman of superior merit.'"[12] And in another place he writes: "Vinnie hasn't brains at all superior," although he does concede that, compared with Emily, she "talks more human like."[13] Throughout his life Austin believed that Vinnie existed on a different and lower plane from him and Emily—that he could fathom Emily's mind, a feat in his view forever beyond

Vinnie. Near the end of his life he wrote Colonel Higginson, "My sister Vin . . . had no comprehension of her sister."[14] And Mrs. Todd wrote, "For Vinnie he [Austin] seemed to have a half humorous, half-absurd feeling not to be compared to his real attachment to Emily."[15]

Emily herself seems always to have been amused at Vinnie. Her letters are full of vignettes in which Vinnie appears in a sympathetic but comical light. "Vinnie is at the instrument [piano]," she writes at age twenty, "humming a pensive air concerning a young lady who thought she was 'almost there'—. Vinnie seems much grieved, and I really suppose *I* ought to betake myself to weeping; I'm pretty sure that *I shall* if she dont abate her singing."[16]

When family letters to relatives needed to be written, Emily tended increasingly to assume the role of spokesman for her mother and sister, both of whom disliked to write. No doubt part of their disinclination was based on their fear of ridicule from Austin and Emily—the littérateurs of the family. The following is a passage from an early letter of Vinnie's that captures some of her unpretentiousness and humor and also some of her anxiety lest her letter not meet with Austin's approval:

> Why, Amherst was never so gay before. What do the good people think the town is comming to. They must foresee certain destruction, in the end. Jennie & I have come to the conclusion, that you are celebrating these *feasts,* games &c, in honour of our absence, for what else can it be? . . . I've allways had a great aversion to writing, I hope, by constent practice, the dislike will wear away, in a degree, at least. Oh! dear, was ever any thing more unfortunate! two wretched blots have I made, & these, added to the other deformities of this sheet, render it quite unfit for inspection . . . I suppose you know the conditions, on which, I send this, that no one shall see it. Dont forget it! Write soon & dont ridicule this will you?[17]

Like all the Dickinsons, Vinnie was addicted to admonitions regarding her relatives' health. For example, she tells Austin: "I dont like to have you so nervous. Cant you in some way prevent it? It will injure you I'm afraid."[18] To some passage such as this Austin responded disparagingly, and Vinnie replies, "You are a pretty young man I should think to 'poke fun' at my good advice. I wont give you any more, not I."[19] She generally responded to Austin and Emily's amused condescension without getting unduly ruffled, but occasionally it becomes apparent that her relative inferiority was a source of dismay to her, as in this snappish retort to Austin's complaints about her handwriting: "If you cant read my writing, Austin, perhaps twill do no good to say any thing to you. I really dont understand your inability to read what has always been called *plain*. I think you must be growing blind."[20]

Sometimes her brother and sister tended to exclude her from the intimacy of their relationship. When this occurred Vinnie was not slow to alert them to the fact: "Vinnie says she thinks you dont pay much attention to her,"[21] Emily tells Austin. And Vinnie herself writes to him regarding the scarcity of his letters to her: "We hav'nt been zactly so intimate lately & we used to be & while I think the fault on your part entirely, I am going to be very noble & 'let by gones be by gones,' " but, she adds emphatically, "Direct the next letter to me."[22]

Vinnie strove for the good opinion of her brother and sister and was pathetically thrilled when she received their praise: "It pleased me exceedingly that you liked my music," she writes Austin, "You dont know how much your favor encouraged me. I shall practice with a great deal more interest now than before."[23] However, Vinnie had to acknowledge the intellectual primacy of Austin and Emily and never tried to compete with either of them. She seems to have accepted herself and her limitations and to have derived great personal satisfaction from their attainments and triumphs.

Emily in turn seems not to have envied Vinnie her good looks; they were for Emily a source of pleasure and pride. For example, when Emily was seventeen she wrote her brother that she had told her friends at school about Vinnie: "All the girls are waiting with impatience to see her & to about a dozen I have given her dimensions. Tell her she must look her prettiest or they will be disappointed for I have given a glowing account of her."[24] Though with no thought of outdoing Vinnie, Emily seems at times to have tried to resemble her, especially in ways that were pleasing to Austin. Thus she writes Austin of a particular calico dress, "Vinnie has one, I think I would like to have one. You used like her's, I remember."[25]

In spite of this absence of overt rivalry one might reasonably expect that Emily concealed resentful feelings regarding her sister's assets and the favorable notice they attracted. An impetus for such envy and jealousy was Emily's displacement from home after her sister's birth. This episode coupled with Emily's pervasive sense of having been defrauded of adequate maternal nurturance in childhood would make such feelings comprehensible. Lavinia's acceptance of the feminine role suggests that she secured a larger share of mothering than Emily. It follows from these considerations, therefore, that close scrutiny of Emily Dickinson's life and writings would be expected to reveal a dissimulated rivalry with Vinnie.

When all the letters and poems and all the other sources of biographical information are sifted, however, no trace, explicit or covert, of such a feeling comes to light. Nor is there any suggestion that Emily held conscious hostile feelings toward Austin or he toward either of his sisters. This absence of inter-sibling competition is especially remarkable in view of Emily's very clearly expressed resentment of Mrs. Bowles's new baby and her fear that she would be forgotten as the baby took up more and more of Mrs. Bowles's time. Recall also that Emily felt rejected when Sue's first child was born. In view of these intimations of strong feelings of jealousy with regard to parent figures, how is one to explain this lack of rivalry with regard to Vinnie and Austin?

The answer to this riddle lies in the emotional remoteness from their children maintained by Edward and Emily Norcross Dickinson. The mother withdrew into herself and into her endless, petty preoccupations with housekeeping and local gossip. The father was absorbed in his law practice, his political activities, and all the innumerable community services he performed to such an extent that he was only vaguely aware of the "real lives" of his son and daughters. Emily Dickinson said that she never had a mother; it might almost as justifiably be said that, as far as emotional intimacy is concerned, she never had a father either. It is this fact—the affective distance of the Dickinson parents—that explains the lack of rivalry among their children.

Anna Freud, in her study of infants and young children separated from their parents and living in residential nurseries in England during World War II, observed that under conditions of parental deprivation children turn to their companions as their love objects. Emotional contact with other children in such circumstances, writes Miss Freud,

> is precociously stimulated and developed. Under normal family conditions contact with other children develops only after the child-mother relationship has been firmly established . . . Love and hate towards them [that is, siblings] are usually not developed directly, but by way of the common relation to the parents. So far as they are rivals for the parents' love, they arouse jealousy and hate; so far as they are under the parents' protection and therefore "belong" they are tolerated and even loved. Under institutional conditions the matter is completely different. At the time when the infant lacks opportunities to develop attachment to a stable mother figure, he is overwhelmed with opportunities to make contact with playmates of the same age. Whereas the grown-ups in his life come and go in a manner which inevitably bewilders the child, these playmates are more or less constant and important figures in his world.[26]

Something akin to this mutual interdependence of peers may have been the lot of the Dickinson children in the days of their childhood, accounting for the peculiar bonds that later joined them. Emily's comment with reference to Vinnie that "She has no Father and Mother but me and I have no Parents but her"[27] confirms Anna Freud's observations.

Another of Miss Freud's observations may cast some light on the difference in life-style between Lavinia and Emily. "The basic emotional needs of the institutional child," writes Miss Freud,

> are, of course, the same as those of the child who lives at home. But these needs meet with a very different fate. One important instinctual need, that for early attachment to the mother, remains as we know more or less unsatisfied; consequently it may become blunted, which means that the child after awhile ceases to search for a mother substitute and fails to develop all the more highly organized forms of love which should be modeled on this first pattern. Or, the dissatisfaction may have the opposite effect: the dissatisfied and disappointed child may overstress his desire to find a mother, and remain continually on the lookout for new mother figures whose affection he might gain. These are the infants who change their allegiances all the time, are always ready to attach themselves to the latest newcomer, and are at the same time exacting, demanding, apparently passionate, but always disappointed in whatever new attachment they form.[28]

The child who reacts to maternal deprivation with a failure to develop "all the more highly organized forms of love" most clearly resembles Lavinia; the child who continually searches for mother substitutes reminds one of Emily.

Lavinia Dickinson shared another characteristic with her sister —her clinging to home and childhood—that suggests that the two women suffered from a similar insecurity in their formative years. The child who feels basically safe and secure is not subject to crises of anxiety in the face of separation from his parents. A pervasive confidence is built into the child who is truly loved— an inner certainty that the world outside his home is basically benign and is safe enough for self-reliant exploration. Vinnie, though she seems not to have shared the sexual uncertainties that further shackled Emily, nonetheless clung to home with a tenacity almost as constricting and compulsive as her sister's.

Five months after Austin's marriage, Vinnie wrote a harried letter to Joseph Lyman—her first to him in two years—alluding to worries at home and excusing herself for not writing sooner to congratulate him on his engagement, giving as her reason that she was "full of care." Adult responsibilities generated anxiety in Lavinia, as they did in Emily, and Lavinia's reaction was similar to her sister's under the circumstances: "I wish we were all children again," she writes Lyman, "& lifes battle not begun."[29] Over a year later, in a less intense letter, she repeats the regression theme to Lyman: "How queer it will seem to know that you are married! . . . but I guess we—we would be children again for a little while if we were together."[30]

Decades later and about six months after her mother's death, when Lavinia was a crusty harridan in her fifties, she wrote Mrs. Todd: "Keep fast hold of your parents, for the world will always be strange & homesick without their affection."[31] Eight months later she wrote: "What joy to be with a real Father & Mother. I rejoice you have such a possession."[32] And a little over a month later she repeated the remark: "I still envy your possession of Father & Mother. Realize the joy to the full for memory is poor substitute for reality. I *know* what *each* means."[33]

Adults, if they have had trusting childhoods and are emotionally healthy, do not long for the protection of their mother or father, even if they do not marry and have children of their own. And they do not cling closely to their brothers and sisters. It is ordinarily a sign of emotional health for siblings in their later years to continue to maintain warm bonds of affection with one another, provided that there is a minimum of possessiveness in their relations. Even a certain detachment from one's grown-up brothers and sisters is not unhealthy. But too much clinging and dependency usually indicates that certain aspects of the personality have not matured sufficiently for a complete life in the larger world outside one's home. A person's unwillingness to let go of a parent or sibling suggests that he is motivated less by a dedication to the welfare of the loved relation than by anxiety that his own dependency needs will go unmet. The Dickinson family as a unit represented to its members a protection against the world. Lavinia, though to a far less degree than Emily, sacrificed an autonomous life for the illusory security of a protracted childhood. Vinnie's longing for Austin while he was away at school reflects in a paler hue the intense need Emily had to keep her brother close. To repeat Anna Freud's observation, the child whose parents are emotionally withdrawn regards his peers as his love objects. Thus Lavinia, at nineteen, writes Austin: "Oh Austin how I wish you were here. It is so lonely without you. I dont think I shall ever get used to your being away. I miss you more & more every day."[34] The quotation could almost be one lifted from a letter of Emily's.

The anxiety Emily felt for the safety of members of her family when they were away from home was shared by Lavinia. Although the predominating theme in this anxiety is a need to keep the loved one within reach, ambivalence is always present, and the suggestion of unconscious hostility should not be overlooked in the familiar fantasy of some harm's befalling the loved one. Both feelings are easily sensed in this passage from Vinnie to Austin: "I've just heard of that frightful rail road accident on the New York way & it makes me feel so sad that I want to sit right down & ask if you are safe. When I hear of such things I feel a desire to cling closer, closer to my dear friends lest I should loose some of them, & you know I've none to spare."[35] The difference between Miss Freud's nursery children and the Dickinsons is that the former had *no* parents for whose love they competed, while Austin, Emily, and Lavinia, though unduly thrown back upon their own resources, experienced some degree of parental affection, insufficient though it was for their total needs. They were, therefore, in competition with each other to a lesser degree than the average child, but more so than the nursery children. What rivalry did exist, however, evidently went underground—partly because of the pressures exerted by the puritan milieu to contain aggression and partly because the children looked to one another for support to such a degree that they feared to alienate one another. For them survival itself seemed to depend on maintaining the sheltering presence of affectional bonds.

There is evidence, some of which has already been cited, that Emily did entertain certain unconscious rivalrous feelings toward her brother, for Emily rejected the very idea of being, like her mother, a mere woman. Lavinia, while accepting the unalterable fact, cannot have reacted to her feminine identification with a great deal of self-esteem. Nineteenth-century New England was a man's world. Austin was the undisputed pride and joy of both parents. That some of the overt spitefulness manifested by Lavinia in later life was related to an earlier envy of Austin—his pre-eminent position in the family and his masculine prerogatives—is suggested strongly by an incident in which the aged Lavinia displayed an astonishing degree of seemingly deliberate cruelty toward a young male relative, Wallace H. Keep, most probably an unconscious symbol of Austin.

In 1890 the young man and his mother paid a visit to his cousin Lavinia, who insisted they stay for lunch. When the food appeared, however, it was apparent that only Lavinia and the boy's mother were to dine. As the boy wrote later:

> Before they were seated I was assigned to a seat not far from the table where I could *see* what they were eating and be heard if necessary . . . Nary a bite to eat nor a sip to drink was offered me! . . . I longed to have a taste of the good things, but the best Lavinia would do was to ask me to come *after* I had had my supper the next Saturday evening and she would give me some apples and pears. Just why she chose to discriminate so painfully against me and my youthful appetite I could not understand.[36]

Later as a lonely college freshman away from home, the boy visited Lavinia weekly: "her chief topic concerned my boarding place and if I was getting 'good nourishing meals.'" The boy sensed Lavinia's lack of real concern for him, however, and refers to her professed anxiety about his nutritional needs as "insincere." Can it be that Lavinia, in her big home with its cellar amply stocked with pears and apples, is gloating over her hoard of food;

that the essential love-hunger that haunts Emily's poetry in images of orality is here in the case of the less imaginative sister taking a grossly concrete and nearly mad form? It almost seems as though Lavinia were saying revengefully to the young cousin: I am the withholding mother and you the child; I have all the love I need; the tables are turned; now *you* shall see what it is like to starve. It is difficult not to see in this extraordinary relationship an inverted reflection of Lavinia's furious childhood conviction that her brother, because he was a male, was receiving at her expense what it was emotional starvation to be denied.

Lavinia seems always to have had more direct access to her aggression than Emily to hers, although age appears to have loosened Lavinia's control and caused it, as in the episode described above, to appear in a raw and unsublimated form as almost overt sadism. When she was young and pretty Lavinia's hostility emerged in the form of social satire—her comical and devastating "take-offs," which consisted of imitations by speech and gesture of the foibles of her teachers and neighbors. Even in her last years, when she was exceedingly perverse and insincere, she continued to be an entertaining, if exasperating, companion. Mrs. Todd, though one of the victims of Vinnie's wiles, nevertheless wrote, "Lavinia was a brilliant exponent of ancient wit and comment not involving any superfluous love for her fellow man . . . I could not help a liking for the fierce denunciations which sprung forth from Vinnie's nimble tongue."[37]

What bespoke an unpleasant sourness and misanthropy in Lavinia as Mrs. Todd knew her had been, in Vinnie's girlhood, a delightful antidote to the oppressive sternness and grim religiosity of her school life. What in Emily became an excessive shyness and aloofness with regard to the community was in Lavinia from the first open combat. She was not easily intimidated by anyone— in this she was like her father—and even in her high school days in an extremely decorous and solemn atmosphere she relieved the sobriety by her humorous and irreverant burlesques of her teachers. Her school chum Jane Hitchcock wrote: "Fortunately she still retains her ability to 'take off' people . . . I assure you it is a real comfort. And now and then we have a good laugh together."[38] No frailty escaped Vinnie's merciless eye. A little of the flavor of this side of her can be perceived in a letter to her brother written when she was eighteen, in which she describes a hypochondriacal neighbor: "Mrs James' lungs are all tied up in a knout & she haint got nothin to hitch her breath on to & her vitals are struck. This is a true statement Austin, the poor lady really thinks she does suffer & 'if it had'nt a been for [Dr.] Gridley she'd a went' that time."[39]

Unlike Emily's self-dramatization, which served to consolidate her threatened sense of identity as a person and as an artist, Lavinia's penchant for theatrics was deeply involved, as in her take-offs, in a close (albeit antagonistic) interaction with others. Vinnie possessed in addition an almost operatic tendency to heighten the emotional potentialities of an opportune moment— a characteristic that seems psychologically akin to her talent for mimicry and to her sister's ability to turn genuinely incapacitating phobias to account in the making of her own legend. An example of such not-fully-conscious heightening of a situation can be seen in Lavinia's pose as a naive provincial during her courtroom interrogation in her lawsuit against the Todds. Her bizarre attire on this occasion and even her "perjury" (Mrs. Todd's designation) may not have been fully deliberate efforts to advance her unjust cause, as Mrs. Todd believed, but rather the result of a childish psychology that automatically denied the existence of inconvenient realities and spotlighted those aspects of a situation that served egoistic aims.

The same "hysterical" trait in Vinnie, though with very different objectives, is delineated in a letter of Emily's telling Austin about a severe dog bite sustained by Vinnie. Vinnie's behavior under the circumstances assured that her plight would receive exclusive and immediate attention: "she looked so faint I thought somebody had killed her," writes Emily, "Her hand pained her so much that she fainted constantly."[40] Enough instances of such spontaneous, self-serving histrionics have come down to us to support the tentative conclusion that Lavinia and Emily were psychodynamically similar in this regard. However, the habit of obscuring and repressing certain aspects of a situation through dramatic heightening of other aspects took quite different forms in each of the sisters. In Lavinia, as I have said, this aptitude was employed largely for the perpetration of her aggression.

Lavinia, for whatever reason—perhaps because she was personally more secure—had less need than Emily to appear loving and agreeable. Consequently, she depended less on circuitous channels for the venting of anger and frustration. Like her father, she frequently felt that she was justified in her wrath, and on these occasions she had no difficulty in venting her anger. An excerpt from one of her letters to Austin, written when she was twenty, establishes this fact. It should be pointed out that no instance ascribed to Emily of such a propensity to attack has ever come to light. Vinnie writes:

> Sue was here this afternoon & told us a long story that Mrs Sweetser had told Harriet about us this morning. I . . . hope to get out again tomorrow & then Mrs Luke [Sweetser] will get such a lecture from me as she never heard, I guess. She says we dont treat the Newmans with any attention & that Mrs Fay has talked with her about it & all such stuff. I shall first go to Mrs Luke & give her a piece of my mind, then Mrs Fay another piece & see what effect will come of it. Mrs Sweetser has interfered with my business long enough & now she'll get it, I tell you. I'll bring up all past grievances & set them in order before her & see what she'll say for herself. I hope to start by 11 oclock in the morning to deliver my feelings. I *certainly shall*. She has watched me long enough . . . & now I'll have a stop put to such proceedings, I will indeed.[41]

It is impossible to imagine the gentler Emily reacting in this pugnacious way even in circumstances in which she felt as justified in anger as Vinnie did here. Millicent Todd Bingham, in commenting upon another of Vinnie's letters, points out that the matter of angry feelings constitutes a fundamental difference between Lavinia and Emily. Mrs. Bingham writes,

> Vinnie's remark, that Sue's silence had made "Emilie very unhappy & me vexed," is another illustration of the temperamental difference between the sisters. Although, as she [Emily] said, "it breaks my heart sometimes because I do not hear from you," Emily was not irritated by Sue's failure to answer her letters; she tried to excuse her as she had done once before when Sue was teaching in Baltimore. Preferring to pretend that a snowstorm had held up the mail, Emily explained that ". . . I am so credulous and so easily deluded by this fond heart of mine."[42]

Vinnie's comment that Emily became depressed under the same circumstances which provoked Vinnie to anger reflects the fact that depression is often anger turned against oneself when other needs dictate that it not be discharged toward its actual object. One questions Mrs. Bingham's contention that "Emily was not irritated." Mrs. Dickinson and Emily, who rarely became openly angry, suffered depressions; Vinnie, who flared up like a bonfire, never, as far as is known, had a depression. Her occasional sharp attacks of the blues were not the consequences of introjected anger that her need for love or her conscience prohibited from direct expression; rather they derived from her sense of impotence and exasperation in the face of unsympathetic and overly controlling parents. Thus, at nineteen, she writes Austin: "Mother has been sick for two days & Father 'is as he is,' so that home has been rather a gloomy place, lately. You are at home so little, that you see only the sunshine & none of the clouds, but clouds there are & very black ones sometimes, which threaten entirely to obscure the sun."[43] And two months later she writes: "I've been thinking lately how easily I could become *insane*. Sometimes I feel as though I should be. Emilie & I had cards from Mr. White, too. I am tired of receiving wedding cards, they come from some where, every day."[44]

The latter quotation, in addition to indicating that Lavinia's low spirits were psychodynamically different from Emily's depressions, raises the question of Lavinia's spinsterhood, for it conveys the impression that the reason she feels she is being driven "insane" is related to the frequent reception of announcements of marriage. One might reasonably conclude from this that Lavinia feels completely blocked from marriage herself and that the happier example of others only serves to remind her of the hopelessness of her own position. The passage suggests also that opposition to the full unfolding of her heterosexuality is causing Lavinia intense frustration, which indicates that the drive itself was strong. Certainly there is nothing to support an assumption that Lavinia had the kind of sexual conflicts and inhibitions that crippled Emily. Moreover, it is questionable to what extent the taking on of the spinster role itself is indicative of a less than normally uninhibited capacity for marriage. Psychiatric experience tends to impose on one the impression that any woman, regardless of her protestations to the contrary, can marry if she really wants to, provided she is not a thoroughgoing physical and mental gorgon. Lavinia, pretty and attractive to boys, was attracted by them. Why then did she never marry?

Vinnie herself in later life told Mrs. Todd (according to Mrs. Todd's daughter Mrs. Bingham) that Edward Dickinson together with his wife and Austin conspired to keep Emily and Lavinia single. "He [Edward Dickinson] did not like to have students come to see the girls," reported Mrs. Todd. Also: Emily "was repressed, and had nothing to do with young men. Vinnie was pert and flirted if she wanted to. The father and mother would not let young men come [to the home] for fear they would marry. They [Mr. Dickinson and Austin] were men that could manage the world if they wanted to, and wouldn't have any foreigners in their family. They didn't want a strange young man in the family."[45] (Brackets and enclosed words are Mrs. Bingham's.)

To believe that both of the elder Dickinsons, with Austin's support, would deliberately have prevented the sisters from marrying strains one's credulity. There certainly exist severely disturbed fathers who because of intense incestuous wishes toward their daughters cannot bear to relinquish their rights to them to any other man. Sometimes, as a defense against the forbidden wish, the incestuous urge is overlaid by a violent revulsion to the thought of the sexual possession of the daughter by anyone. Elizabeth Barrett Browning's father seems to have belonged to this latter category. Such men make no secret of their determination to see to it that their daughters never socialize with men, never date, and never marry, and they are fanatical in their maintenance of the closest surveillance over the consequently very restricted comings and goings of their daughters. Now Edward Dickinson seems to have invited Emily, at least, to usurp certain of his wife's functions, and Emily placed considerable emphasis on her father's need of her with regard to certain small comforts with which she provided him. But as Emily said: "Father [is] too busy with his Briefs—to notice what we do."[46] Edward Dickinson's letters are full of admonitions to his wife and children, but in none of them is there the least suggestion that Mrs. Dickinson should do anything to keep young men away. The Dickinson girls may have been overly impressed with their father and therefore may have viewed other men unfavorably by comparison, but there is no reason to believe that he who spent so little time at home was wrapped up in them to the pathological degree suggested by Vinnie's statements to Mrs. Todd.

Vinnie's inclusion of Austin as one of the family determinants of her and Emily's spinsterhood may be valid on the level of the interplay of unconscious psychological forces, at least as far as

Emily is concerned. But on the level of overt and openly expressed behavior—the level at which their relationships were observable by Vinnie—the assertion that Austin opposed Emily's and Vinnie's marrying contradicts everything we know of Austin's personality. Austin in his youth and young manhood was an idealistic, fun-loving, boisterous, passionate, and rebellious romantic. He looked forward to a married existence that would be the pinnacle of happiness for him and his wife. It appears most unlikely that he would actively have denied his sisters what he so vocally and enthusiastically prescribed for himself. Though leaning in some respects and to an unusual degree on Emily, he had plans for his own life that were independent of her. He did not discourage her interest in young men; he introduced her to his classmates and was apparently pleased when she went riding with Emmons. For these reasons, one must reject Vinnie's accusation that her father and brother deliberately blocked her chances of marriage.

That leaves Mrs. Dickinson. Lavinia, writing in her diary at the age of eighteen with reference to one of her more ardent suitors, William Howland, notes in her laconic style: "Tutor Howland called twice, Great commotion on maternal side."[47] And another entry: "Walked with Howland, Displeased Mother *thereby*."[48] And again: "Howland & Jane called. Austin gone to Maria's funeral. Mother displeased again [at Howland's visit?] . . . Not happy."[49] By contrast, Edward Dickinson, as we know from a letter of Emily to Austin, "likes Howland grandly."[50] However, it would be a mistake to read much into these few brief and suggesive jottings from Vinnie's diary; they are far from being proof that Mrs. Dickinson consistently discouraged her daughters' attachments to young men. What does recommend the hypothesis that it was Mrs. Dickinson, not Edward Dickinson and Austin, who wished the girls not to marry is the indisputable fact of Mrs. Dickinson's abject dependency. Losing Lavinia to a young man through marriage meant, for Mrs. Dickinson, the loss of a companion, a domestic, and a household administrator. For she—as well as Emily—came increasingly to look to Lavinia for the performance of these functions.

In time the Dickinson household came to be considered almost exclusively Vinnie's domain. Though Emily was the older of the two, the mansion in later years was habitually referred to as

Lavinia's, as in one of Emily's letters: " 'Home—sweet Home'—
Austin's Baby sings—'there is no place like Home—'tis too—over
to Aunt Vinnie's."[51] And in a neighbor's note: "We turned up
Main Street and called at Miss Vinny Dickinson's."[52] Even the
piano on which Emily seems to have played at least as much as
Vinnie became "Vinnie's piano."[53] Austin's daughter's statement
with reference to Emily that Mrs. Dickinson's "gentle reign" had
been "increasingly enfeebled in spite of herself by the dominating
daughter"[54] seems even more applicable to Lavinia than to Emily.
In summary, what all these observations reflect is the vacuum left
by Mrs. Dickinson's inadequacies, which Vinnie, particularly,
came gradually to fill. But Mrs. Dickinson's gentle reign could
not have suffered such an eclipse if the mother herself had not
invited it. Feeling overwhelmed perhaps by the social and domestic requirements involved in being the wife of the town's leading
citizen, she abdicated her uneasy prerogatives to her daughter.
However, such a redistribution of family responsibility would
necessarily have increased not only her sense of inadequacy but,
as Lavinia became an ever more efficient manager, her undermining dependency as well. Of the three—Mr. Dickinson, Mrs. Dickinson, and Austin—only Mrs. Dickinson would have been really
threatened by the possibility of Vinnie's leaving home. Thus,
through some combination of guilt at leaving her timid and frequently ill mother, a need herself to continue under the protective
roof of her father, overestimation of her father coupled possibly
with the insight that a hostile, envious impulse toward males
might make a harmonious married life impossible, Lavinia Dickinson, one may speculate, chose to remain unmarried.

Here let me shift focus from the general motives of Lavinia's
life-style to the specific motive for her manifestly bogus explanation of her and Emily's spinsterhood. For what possible reason
would she impute such culpability to her father and brother?

To approach the problem one must emphasize that at the time
Lavinia made the remark to Mrs. Todd she was hoping momentarily for the acclaim of the world for her deceased sister's poems.
She was aware of the danger that the poems, because of their unconventionality and heedlessness of the poetic standards of her
time, might be regarded with condescension by some readers. For
this reason she was anxious that no trace of queerness in her sister's life be allowed to generate prejudice against the poems. She

had a need, therefore, to normalize Emily's life and find acceptable nineteenth-century explanations for its irregularities. She was of course acquainted with the dramatic deliverance of Elizabeth Barrett Browning and seems to have adopted the British poet's experience to serve as cover for Emily's embarrassing recluseness. Accordingly we are presented with a coalition consisting of father, mother, and Austin as a composite parent who proscribes marriage for his daughters, and an improbable, already married, and therefore offstage "Robert Browning" (such as Charles Wadsworth) as the would-be rescuer. Vinnie evidently was willing to sacrifice the esteem posterity might accord her parents and brother to safeguard the poetry and Emily from any imputation of eccentricity or abnormality. She seems to have fractionated the role of "Edward Barrett" to include father, mother, and brother for several reasons. First, she understandably may have shrunk from placing all the blame on her father. Second, she knew no one would believe a story which required that her self-abnegating mother be viewed as a despot. And third, she included all three together as the insurmountable obstacle to her sister's attainment of a normal life because, on a deeper level, she knew in her heart that it was the truth—true also for herself perhaps and certainly true for Emily.

If Vinnie and the other members of the family had agreed on and stuck with this story, even in its superficial sense, the world might have been willing to accept it. But the lack of agreement between Lavinia's and Austin's interpretations followed by Martha Dickinson Bianchi's multiple, divergent, and embroidered variations served to convince readers that the Dickinsons were hiding something from them.

To return again to more general themes: A supporting, if secondary, reason for Lavinia's remaining at home resided in Emily's ever deepening dependency on her. In their young girlhood it seems to have been the other (and more usual) way around—the younger sister in general relied on the older one. Emily in the beginning seems even to have taken the lead in the housework, if we are to believe Joseph Lyman. Lyman writes: "Em is an excellent housekeeper—Vinnie is sometimes afraid of soiling her little fat hands but can do very well when she chooses."[55] As time went on, however, Emily's deep dislike for ordinary woman's work became openly manifest; Vinnie after awhile overcame her first frivolous aversion, and became the domestic mainstay of the household.

By the time she was nineteen Vinnie was apologizing to Austin for the fact that her letters so frequently involved requests that Austin buy cloth or other household articles: "Perhaps you think I never write to you," she tells him, "except on business, but the folks make me do all the errands, else I should sometimes say some thing different."[56] Vinnie soon came to be regarded as the "practical sister"[57] who looked to the groceries, directed the servants, and enforced the doctor's orders. In late middle age, when her mother was a bedridden paralytic, Vinnie ran *everything*, as is indicated in a letter from Emily to Mrs. Holland: "Vinnie wants to write, but was it 'Atlas'' fault the World was on his Shoulders?"[58] And later, "Vinnie is far more hurried than Presidential Candidates . . . *they* have only the care of the Union, but Vinnie the Universe."[59] And again, "Vinnie is under terrific headway, but finds time to remember you."[60] No doubt Lavinia's burdens increased following the incapacitation of her mother, but there is no suggestion in Emily's letters that she assumed these responsibilities concomitantly with the onset of her mother's illness; rather, through her relatively prodigious energy and forcefulness of personality, she gradually overshadowed her mother and, without conscious rivalry, to a large extent displaced her. Vinnie sems to have been no more capable of preventing this dethronement of her mother in the domestic sphere than was Emily in the intellectual sphere. Vinnie had the assertiveness of the Dickinsons, Emily their perseverance and intelligence. Psychodynamics played their part; so no doubt did natural endowment.

Now consider again, in relation to Lavinia and Emily, Anna Freud's conclusion that siblings whose parents are remote tend to regard each other as love objects. Then, by superimposing this observation on the vivid image of Lavinia as matriarch, one can see to what a large extent Lavinia eventually came to represent for Emily not only the tender loving peer but the long missing mother as well.

The following quotations from Emily's letters span three decades, the first dating from an 1850 letter written when Emily was nineteen.

Vinnie you know is away—and that I'm very lonely is too plain for me to tell you—I am *alone—all* alone.⁶¹ (1850)

Vinnie is still at school, and I sit by my lonely window, and give bright tears to her memory.⁶² (1850)

The day is long to me, because I have no Vinnie, and I think of those today who never had a Vinnie, and I'm afraid they are lone.⁶³ (1853)

I would like more sisters, that the taking out of one, might not leave such stillness. Vinnie has been all, so long, I feel the oddest fright at parting with her for an hour, lest a storm arise, and I go unsheltered.⁶⁴ (1859)

Vinnie is yet in Boston . . . I am somewhat afraid at night.⁶⁵ (1859)

You are to have Vinnie, it seems, and I to tear my hair.⁶⁶ (1860)

[To Vinnie] I wept that you left me . . . I will try and share you a little longer, but it is so long, Vinnie.⁶⁷ (1860)

[To Vinnie upon Emily's departure for home from Cambridge following eye treatments] You will get me at Palmer, yourself. Let no one beside come.⁶⁸ (1864)

I have no Parents but her [Vinnie].⁶⁹ (1873)

[Of her bond with Vinnie] early, earnest, indissoluble. Without her life were fear.⁷⁰ (1883)

The older the two sisters grew the more the younger came to regard the older as her particular charge—almost her child. A touching instance of Lavinia's maternal solicitude toward Emily occurred on the occasion of an Independence Day fire that destroyed a large portion of the town. The family were in bed when the warning bells rang. A great conflagration, frighteningly close to the Dickinson's house, blazed in at the windows. Vinnie tiptoed into Emily's room and told her the kind of comforting lie one usually reserves for children; she tried to make Emily believe that the crashing buildings and exploding oil tanks were part of the holiday fireworks. "Don't be afraid, Emily," she whispered, "it is only the 4th of July." Then Vinnie took Emily by the hand and led her from her room, all the while reassuring her: "It's only the 4th of July." Of this incident Emily later wrote her cousins, "Vinnie's 'only the 4th of July' I shall always remember. I think she will tell us so when we die, to keep us from being afraid."⁷¹

As Emily's health failed toward the end of her life, Lavinia took stern parental measures to insure her getting the proper rest. "I was led resisting to Bed," writes Emily, "but Vinnie was firm as the Soudan."[72]

On the day of Emily's death Lavinia told a neighbor, "How can I live without her? Ever since we were little girls we have been wonderfully dear to each other—and many times when desirable offers of marriage have been made to Emily she has said—I have never seen anyone that I cared for as much as you Vinnie."[73] These words of Emily, prompted according to Vinnie by masculine attention, reveal what has been repeatedly emphasized throughout this book—that a protecting mother figure was of far greater importance to Emily than a husband.

As Lavinia aged she became increasingly eccentric. For example, she had always been fond of cats, and by the time she reached her late forties and early fifties the mansion crawled with them. As many lonely, childless women do, she babied them and talked to them. She hovered over her feline retinue with fierce maternal possessiveness and reacted like a lioness when anyone attempted to harm or disturb her "pussies."

Lavinia was inordinately suspicious and was convinced that her least doings were the object of every neighbor's fascinated and malicious interest. Accordingly, when Mrs. Todd first moved to Amherst and Vinnie began wooing her as possible editor of Emily's poems, she preferred that Mrs. Todd come to the mansion rather than that she go to Mrs. Todd's, giving as her reason that she might meet someone on the way. "If I go to you, I may encounter strangers,"[74] she wrote in a note. Later, when the work of editing aroused her curiosity, she would go to Mrs. Todd's to check up on her progress, always arriving late at night.

Mrs. Bingham recorded another instance of Vinnie's peculiar relations with others. As a child she was occasionally given an apple by Lavinia with the understanding that she "go far away to eat it for Miss Vinnie could not bear the sound of crunching."[75]

Lavinia's oddities are numerous and, considering that she was only sixty-six when she died, doubtless not to be ascribed to the cerebral degeneration of old age. Indeed they resemble closely the functional psychological quirks of her sister. When she gardened she dressed herself in old rags that horrified Mrs. Todd; the habit may be related to her extreme parsimoniousness. In spite of the fact that she was the heiress of a large estate she apparently lived in a perpetual panic of material insecurity. Not being able to support herself, should the unlikely need for this ever arise, she grasped at pennies as if she were uncertain of her next meal. When Mrs. Todd, for example, to whom Lavinia owed a great deal, brought her a Christmas present, Vinnie gave her in return "a broken blue plate."[76]

Lavinia's eyes failed and in the last years of her life she was unable to read. She refused to get glasses, however, had a servant read to her, and wrote letters and notes in a grotesque and illegible hand replete with misspellings and omitted letters. According to Mrs. Todd, "Sometimes she followed Emily's example, pasting on the envelope a printed address cut from a newspaper or from hotel stationery."[77]

Lavinia developed the idea that the black stockings then in fashion were poisonous to her feet. Because stockings of any other color were impossible to obtain in Amherst, she sent Mrs. Todd while in Boston on repeated errands to buy white ones.

Mrs. Todd records another of Lavinia's habits that was even more peculiar: "If she had more than one caller at a time, each was put in a different room to be entertained separately."[78] These aberrations of Lavinia strike one as being only a shade less extravagant than those of Emily.

Consider the implications of the fact that Vinnie, in the last two decades of her sister's life, constituted along with Austin a major filter through which the world reached Emily. From this viewpoint one can appreciate that Vinnie's skewed interpretations may have encouraged Emily's withdrawal by maintaining the poet's worst fears regarding the hostile and dangerous forces to be encountered outside the walls of the mansion. To counteract distortions in the image of the world that arise from one's own inner needs requires the constant corrective of interaction with the world as it really exists. This kind of direct confrontation with reality Emily lacked. Lavinia was her go-between and she was far from objective in her own appraisal of the situation outside. Austin also in his late middle age, with his disappointment in his marriage and in his career and his rancor at the world, can only have confirmed Emily's conclusion that she was better off in isolation. Of those close to Emily in the last decade of her life, only Sue continued to regard community life and socialization as a source of interest and gratification. But Sue, as she and Austin became increasingly estranged, became persona non grata as far as Lavinia was concerned, which made it difficult for her to provide any corrective to the crabbed views of Lavinia and Austin.

Most writers have accepted Lavinia's foibles and limitations, her crotchets and bizarrerie, without feeling a need to explain them away. The manifestation of very similar qualities in Emily, however, has in general been met with incredulity and a determination, on the part of many writers, to show that the evidence can be interpreted in such a way as to leave Emily untouched by blemishes of eccentricity or perverseness. The difference in scholarly approach to the two sisters has thus tended perhaps to exaggerate their differences and obscure certain profound resemblances. That Lavinia and Emily Dickinson were constitutionally quite different is beyond doubt. But in the general outlines of their lives, they were remarkably alike, although Emily's genius tends to obscure the warped and stultified sequelae of their upbringing, which one can discern with such objective clarity in Vinnie, who lacks the blinding nimbus.

The cardinal role played by Vinnie was, of course, that of surrogate mother to her sister. I have said earlier that Sue, Mrs. Holland, Mrs. Bowles, and Mrs. Dwight—to name only the most obvious—also stood in this relationship to Emily. Lest the reader murmur at this multiplicity of mothers, I would remind him of the pervasiveness of the derivatives of this mother-hunger throughout the poet's work and the infantile dependency of her way of life. Moreover, the adult who continues to search blindly and unconsciously for an emotional fulfillment whose day is forever passed can never be satisfied. The time when Emily Dickinson's needs could have been met was during the first few years of her life. The mother-infant relationship she missed is unique in its combination of features: its physical and emotional unity, its innocent and uninhibited eroticism, its nurturant and protective qualities, its completeness, dependency, exclusiveness, and intensity. After the first years of life are passed, reality no longer holds the possibility of duplicating these boons within the limits of one relationship. In the case of a woman, some of them may be recaptured in her relationship with her husband, some with her children, and others with her mother and other woman friends. The woman who has successfully gone through all the phases of psychosexual maturation no longer craves the possession of these qualities within the limits of one supremely dependent relationship. But one must have experienced the full satisfaction of the earlier need if one is to move on to its maturer—and, in a sense, more attenuated—forms. Emily Dickinson was forever groping after this first unsatisfied infantile phase. That is why so many different women came, in her unconscious, to signify aspects of the mother figure.

Lavinia could no more be a complete mother to Emily than Sue could. In Emily's relationship with Sue there was a strongly erotic component that was either acknowledged consciously or else came very close to being conscious. Sue seemed to hold out a promise of physical closeness and caressing; for Sue there was no one like Emily—Emily was the preferred child—until she was displaced by Austin, and later by Austin's son. Mrs. Holland was the experienced, guiding, comforting mother, the mother who offered in her person a model for warm and generous maternalism. Mrs. Bowles was predominantly the oedipal mother—that is, Emily's identification with her seems to have been based on their relationship to the same beloved male, Mrs. Bowles's husband Samuel, one of the few men who seems to have struck in Emily a spark of physical attraction. Distant, imaginary mothers Emily found in her conception of the personalities of Elizabeth Browning, Emily Brontë, and George Eliot—women who in fantasy were cast in the role of the mother as teacher, as intellectual guide, or as admiring audience. And what fragments of this scattered and composite mother image did Lavinia provide?

She was the "practical" mother, the mother who saw to it that the pantries were stocked, the clothes washed, the beds made, the food cooked, the supplies ordered, and the social obligations met. She was also the protecting mother—the bulwark against the indifferent or hostile world—and the emissary mother who conducted for Emily by proxy any of those necessary negotiations with the outside world that could not be avoided. She was almost invariably there, she was dependable, and she made few demands. In the long run she was perhaps the most satisfactory of all Emily's mother substitutes. Following Emily's death a neighbor observed that it was fortunate that Lavinia had outlived her sister: "Perhaps there is a Providence in Emily's thus being taken as she could not very well be left alone."[79] Others have observed that it was largely Lavinia who made the prodigy that was Emily Dickinson possible. While he lived, Edward Dickinson guaranteed economic and material security—but generally and remotely, like an able head of state. Austin, next door, was a nearer, but often absent, protector, his own troublesome family competing for his time and attention. Mrs. Dickinson, shrinking, worrisome, and ineffectual, herself had always to be taken by the hand and led through life by a stronger personality. Thus, as buffer against all the innumerable little confrontations and transactions that made up the intimate and prosaic fabric of the family's daily routine—encounters with visitors, vendors, seamstresses, physicians, and even servants (each of which at times was capable of inspiring in Emily the profoundest dread)—there was only Vinnie. Her father and mother preceded Emily in death. Austin, as I have said, was preoccupied with the burdens of his own home. Without Lavinia it appeared to the neighbors that Emily could not have survived. The poet probably would have agreed with them. The sanctuary in which she cerebrated and created was a nest fashioned and guarded by Vinnie. After Emily's death Vinnie exhibited and championed the offspring of her sister's spirit with grandmotherly pride. Readers have smiled at what has been deemed an overly proprietary attitude toward an oeuvre whose genuine quality Vinnie could not even begin to understand. Absurd as it may seem, her attitude was almost that it was *her* poetry. And yet from one viewpoint she was right. By her rigid maintenance of the conditions necessary to its creation, Lavinia Dickinson, unknowingly and instinctively, almost as much as Emily, became the medium by which it came into existence.

As Mrs. Bingham in *Ancestors' Brocades* makes clear, the prime mover behind the initial publication of Emily Dickinson's poetry was Lavinia. Certainly Vinnie was very fortunate to stumble upon an editor of Mrs. Todd's caliber to undertake the skilled and difficult task of preparing the manuscripts for the printer— a task of which Vinnie herself was entirely incapable. But it was Vinnie's aggressiveness and determination to see the poems in print that led her to Mrs. Todd. If Vinnie had not been driven by what was almost a compulsion to see her sister's poems acclaimed by the world, they would probably still be a part of the "compost of old newspapers and clipped magazines, the dust of neighbor's attics, the grime of birth, marriage, and contractual records, the diaries and tombstones of dead friends"—what Jay Leyda called "the mould of Amherst."[80]

When Lavinia discovered the hoard of manuscripts following her sister's death, she first looked to her sister-in-law to prepare them for publication. Sue agreed but procrastinated. Two years passed amidst the rising tides of Vinnie's impatience. Sue's eventual attitude was that the task was impossible. She gave two incompatible reasons for not readying the poems for the printer: one, the poems held no general interest for the reading public (in this she was agreeing with T. W. Higginson's opinion that the poems were unfit for publication); and two, she dreaded the publicity that publication of the poems would bring upon the family. Her advancement of two such contradictory explanations for her two-year delay suggests that there was yet another reason. The third and real explanation probably resided in some inhibition within herself—some unresolved ambivalence that thwarted her efforts to deal effectively with the mass of manuscripts.

Vinnie, now exasperated and desperate, took the poems to Mabel Loomis Todd and eventually had some of them published. Sue was not consulted in this venture, having been excluded both by Vinnie and by Austin, with whom Sue's relations by this time were very strained. Vinnie seems to have felt guilty about undercutting Sue in this way, although it was of course to a large extent Sue's fault that she had no part in the publishing venture. Uncertainty regarding the legal ownership of poems given by Emily to Sue aggravated the situation. When Sue accepted money for the publication in a magazine of some of her material, she was in effect inaugurating a competition with Vinnie and with Mrs. Todd, who was trying to edit and publish the poems discriminatingly and systematically. Sue's undisguised conviction that she was Vinnie's intellectual superior, her refusal to defer to her husband's wishes in these and other matters, and the priority she assigned her daughter's social career, seemingly at the expense of advancing Emily's posthumous interests—these factors, combined with Vinnie's guilt feelings, served to make Sue Vinnie's hated enemy.

Austin was hardly more helpful than Sue in forwarding the publication of the poetry. He seems not to have been much involved with the poems; his opinion of them—if he had one— was never fully expressed. He seems not to have cared whether the poems were published—in fact he may have preferred that they not be. His role with regard to Mrs. Todd's labors was not that of mover but of regulator, advisor, governor, and arbitrator. He provided none of the impetus toward publication and at times, through vacillations and postponements, appears actually to have hindered the process.

Thus, both Sue and Austin seem to have had an obscure but stubborn resistance to the public distribution of the poetry. Indeed, they seem to have shared Emily's own ambivalence—none of the three would destroy the poems yet neither Emily, Susan, nor Austin could bear to turn them over to the scrutiny of strangers. Possibly it was because Austin and Susan saw more deeply than Vinnie into the nature of Emily's psychological problems and realized that the poems betrayed them that they could not act. Vinnie, of course, knew of her sister's breakdown; it was possibly to conceal this knowledge that Vinnie made up her naive stories involving a tyrannical father and a possessive brother who drove away boy friends. But Vinnie may never have achieved any real insight into the sexual ambiguities of her sister's personality. According to Austin "My Sister Vin . . . had no comprehension of her sister, yet believed her a shining genius."[81] Therefore only Vinnie, who everyone agreed did not understand either Emily or her poems, was sufficiently free of crippling inner reservations to see that the poems were given to the world.

Austin's bitterness and reluctant cooperation in the editing and publication of Emily's poems and letters suggests that he had become aware of Emily's inappropriately intense and erotically tinged mother-daughter fixation upon his wife. Before he allowed his sister's ardent early letters to Sue to be published, he scratched out the name Sue and substituted a variety of other feminine names. He also made frequent changes of the words "she" and "her" to "he" and "him." No plausible explanation of this peculiar behavior surpasses in credibility that which makes Austin privy to the difficulties Emily had in establishing an unwaveringly feminine sexual orientation. Vinnie had only to minimize her sister's eccentricities and conceal the fact of her nervous breakdown—both serious enough handicaps if one is hoping that literary critics will take seriously and appraise favorably poetry that in its day seemed crazy enough in its unconventionality. Austin had in addition the reputation of his wife to consider and the good name of the entire Dickinson family—for in nineteenth-century Amherst any suspicion of homosexual tendencies was enough to bring down upon a whole family the stigma of mental and moral degeneracy.

Vinnie's qualms had another counterpart in the notorious reticence of Emily's cousins Fanny and Loo Norcross. When Mrs. Todd was gathering material for a volume of Emily's letters, the Norcrosses displayed great agitation lest any eyes but their own read certain passages. After giving Mrs. Todd their expurgated versions of the letters, they refused to allow her to check the printer's proof against the original letters, though they had brought the letters with them to Mrs. Todd's home. Mrs. Todd was highly irritated at their behavior, which seemed silly and unnecessary to her. Since Emily had lived for two protracted periods with the Norcrosses during the depressed convalescent phase of her breakdown, it seems likely that the expunged passages contained details of this illness which the Norcrosses were eager to hide. Largely because of Mrs. Todd's impatience with the cousins and her unflattering estimation of them, they have come down to us as a couple of empty-headed and short-sighted nincompoops. Emily's tender affection for them and her intense feelings of gratitude for their care during her eye treatments indicate that there must have been more to them than Mrs. Todd saw. Probably they looked foolish because of their fear of disclosing anything to Mrs. Todd that would be prejudicial to their beloved and admired relative. It should be remembered that one of the most revealing prose glimpses of Emily's symptomatology (the "snarl in the brain" passage) occurs in a letter to the Norcrosses —a passage that must have been relatively innocuous since it passed those careful censors.

Thus the Norcrosses probably shared Vinnie's need to protect Emily's reputation from the stigma of mental illness. But they, like Vinnie, lacking the acuteness, depth, and opportunity for observation that Austin and Sue possessed, probably had no inkling that a more pervasive disturbance antedated and succeeded the acute phases of the nervous breakdown.

Mrs. Todd's impressions of Austin, Vinnie, and Sue have done much to form and color our conception of their personalities, just as the version of Emily's personality they wished to make public formed and colored Mrs. Todd's (and consequently posterity's) view of the poet. Mrs. Todd and others, including Austin himself, assert that Austin and Emily were particularly close, that they largely excluded Lavinia, who played second fiddle to both of them. This intimacy was limited in one important respect, however: Emily seems rarely to have sent Austin any of her poems or asked his opinion of them. The most important thing in Emily Dickinson's life was undoubtedly her poetry, yet from this Austin seems largely to have been excluded or to have excluded himself. When Vinnie discovered the huge cache of poetry manuscripts in the dresser drawer, only Sue, who had been the recipient of more poems than any other person (Emily is known to have sent her at least 276 poems) and whose critical opinion Emily respected, would have had no reason to be surprised. Emily never shared her poems with Vinnie because Vinnie was incapable of understanding them. Sue, therefore, might well have been exasperated by Austin's and Vinnie's claims that they had been especially close to Emily's mind and heart, for Emily involved Sue intimately in her creative activity, even including her in some of the poems. Perhaps Sue legitimately had more claim to the poems than either Austin or Vinnie. But Sue and Vinnie were rivals for the affection of Emily—the question was who was the "real" sister. The superiority of Vinnie's legal claims to the poetry and Sue's estrangement from Austin weakened Sue's position, although morally she seems to have felt she should have had more to say than she did about the ultimate fate of the poems. However, Sue's antagonism toward Vinnie combined with her need to impress others with her own brilliance and sophistication may, if the poems had been left with her, have resulted in their oblivion even if she had succeeded in throwing off her inhibition with regard to publication: for Sue had to flaunt her superiority to Vinnie, and to accomplish this she assumed for the benefit of editors and publishers a lofty view toward the poems—a view in keeping with the contemporary critical trend, which saw the poems as deficient in technical skills and devoid of general interest. Sue, in her defense of the poems, was not willing to run the risk of appearing gauche. Vinnie, by contrast, refused to recognize that the poems were anything but perfect. Sue was willing to capitulate to current opinion for the sake of what others would think of *her*. Vinnie really did not care what people would think of her—her blind faith in her sister's poems overrode everything else. Here an absolute triumph for Emily would be an absolute triumph for Vinnie. Sue knew that she had been intellectually, and in some ways emotionally, closer to Emily than Vinnie. But Vinnie had a primitive identification with Emily that Sue lacked—Vinnie knew she was *family*. Emily was Vinnie's sister and Austin's sister and Sue was an outsider. Both women ultimately came to regard one another as monsters, each believing herself to be wholly right and the other wholly wrong. But with Sue's own needs and her weaker legal position, it was a foregone conclusion that she must bow out of the whole matter of publication.

It is an interesting irony that the person who knew least about the poems was in the long run the most right about them. No doubt if Vinnie had really plumbed the depths of the poetry and realized their revelations she would have shared the debilitating ambivalence of Austin and Sue, and the poems might never have seen the light of day. Austin would never have seen to it that his sister's poetry was published. What little assistance he did give Mrs. Todd was half-hearted and desultory. Sue would have let the matter fade into oblivion. But Vinnie's ignorant and unreasoning certainty that every scrap from her sister's hand constituted a revelation of genius was decisive. Had Mrs. Todd not been available to prepare the poems for publication, Vinnie could not have rested until she had found someone else to perform this service. Atlas to the end, she bore the burden of her sister's legacy solely upon her shoulders.

Vinnie died in 1899, of heart disease. She was probably willing to part with life, which by then had grown intolerably lonely, and she had achieved at last the satisfaction of seeing some of her sister's poems in print—her ultimate ambition. When fifty-seven years after Emily's death, Martha Dickinson Bianchi died without having had children, Emily Dickinson's branch of the family came to an end. Flesh and blood generation had proved less viable than those children of the mind and heart—her poems.

EPILOGUE

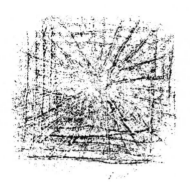

The widely accepted view that Emily Dickinson's mother was a benign cipher who exerted a negligible influence upon the poet's personality is a fallacy that must be abandoned. As I have attempted to demonstrate, it was largely because Mrs. Dickinson was the kind of person she was that her daughter became the kind of woman she became. The crippling impact upon the daughter of what were crucial maternal deficiencies relative to the child's most vital needs can scarcely be overestimated, for the disruption of the earliest mother-child bond created an imbalance that hampered and haunted Emily Dickinson throughout her life. Her scathing references to her mother are the straws that indicate the direction of the wind. Such bitterness and disappointment as they reveal can only have arisen from the cruelest and most damaging infantile experience, and the ramifications of this experience led Emily Dickinson into ever more painful and insoluble psychological dilemmas. No other circumstance in Emily Dickinson's life can have had as profound an effect on her as those unhappy early transactions in the Dickinson nursery, and no person can have influenced her growing mind and heart more decisively and pervasively than that colorless, self-abnegating, and "harmless" woman who is so easily overlooked in the biographical records.

This book has concentrated all along on the damaging consequences of Mrs. Dickinson's inability to be the kind of parent
her daughter needed. Moreover, it has emphasized the obstacles
that hindered the processes of identification with the mother and
has shown that, when a reluctant identification was finally accomplished, it involved those aspects of Mrs. Dickinson that the
daughter experienced as fear-ridden, helpless, constricted, and
unfulfilled—an identification that allowed all of Emily Dickinson's tendencies toward withdrawal, isolation, and self-rejection
to come to full flower. In short, I have been following the poet's
lead, placing Mrs. Dickinson in a negative light. This concentration on the baleful side of the mother's influence was necessitated by two considerations. First, the ramifications of this side
of the poet's interaction with her mother are by far the most
important for an understanding of the poet's peculiar life-style.
And second, the introduction of the more benign and minor aspects might have confused the already complex pattern of relationships I was attempting to clarify. The mother bond had
immediate and long-range effects other than the injurious ones,
however. It is time to add a few words about them.

The last decade or so of Emily Dickinson's life brought certain
marked psychological changes. For a considerable period following the sudden death of her father in June 1874 she suffered intense grief. As late as October of that year she still could not
think of him without tears. Thus, she wrote Samuel Bowles, in
apology for the briefness of her letter, "The Paper wanders so
I cannot write my name on it."[1] And the following Easter found
her still preoccupied with her bereavement; she confessed that
save for an unexpected Easter greeting from a friend "the rising
of the one we lost would have engrossed me to the exclusion of
Christ's."[2]

During this painful year, her forty-fourth, dormant psychological forces were again set in motion. As she tried to grapple
with the awful fact of her father's removal and to achieve some
inner resolution of the profound dependency she had formerly
satisfied through him, certain rigid inner patterns began to thaw.
The role of mourner among the children, of the abandoned child
shut off from parental affection, was rendered untentable by her
father's death. A process of revision became necessary.

The year 1875 brought with it two events that, breaking in

upon the poet's mourning for her father, accelerated the processes of growth and brought about a radical redistribution of her emotional investments. The first was the sudden paralysis of her mother following a stroke. This occurred on June 15, precisely one year after Edward Dickinson's death. The other was the birth of Sue's second son, Gilbert, on August 1. The former event stimulated a latent emotional predisposition in Emily Dickinson and, in combination with the latter, offered her ample scope for the development of this hitherto unsuspected aptitude—the capacity to be maternal.

There is no evidence that prior to 1875 Emily Dickinson ever took much interest in young children. Her surviving notes to Sue's first child, Ned, are not motherly but comradely; they reveal insight into the child's mind, but they display no sign of the brooding tenderness that was to develop later with regard to Gilbert. True maternalism was a facet of Emily Dickinson's personality that remained embryonic prior to 1875, and ultimately it was her mother's serious illness that provided the conditions necessary to its growth.

Until her death seven years after the onset of her paralysis, Mrs. Dickinson rested in a chair or lay in bed, a helpless invalid with a wandering mind, sometimes unable to so much as lift a glass of water to her lips. In the third year of her suffering she sustained a fractured hip, despite which she survived four more years, a continuous and grueling care. Her nurses were Emily and Lavinia, who tended her faithfully from morning until night. She was not easy to care for, and as a neighbor remarked of her, "She was no comfort to any one, unless it was a comfort to work hard for her."[3] As it happened it *was* a comfort to work hard for her—at least Emily found it so.

During that long illness the estrangement of the years seemed to dissolve, and Emily, to her astonishment, experienced something very like the love she had long sought so vainly. As she explained it, "We were never intimate Mother and Children while she was our Mother—but Mines in the same Ground meet by tunneling and when she became our Child, the Affection came."[4] She referred to her ailing mother as "the one we have cherished so softly so long"[5] and observed that as her mother declined she "achieved in sweetness what she lost in strength."[6]

With their roles reversed—Mrs. Dickinson as the dependent

one and Emily as the protector—"the Affection came." With this release of affection, which was intensely sheltering and motherly, Emily could also turn toward others with a more tender regard. When Gilbert was born just after Mrs. Dickinson became Emily's "child," he was greeted by an aunt who had recently been enabled to develop maternal feelings in abundance. With the overflow of her new-found love for her mother she embraced Gilbert and grew to love him as she had never loved Ned and his sister Martha. The sibling rivalry had given way to protecting and mothering.

Thus, in the winter of 1877, she called in a neighbor boy to show him a butterfly that had emerged from its chrysalis in her conservatory. The boy remembered for many years her delight and eagerness in sharing this beautiful occurrence with him.

Another example of her autumnal tenderness toward children occurred in 1880. At that time a solicitor for a children's charity asked to be allowed to publish some of her poems. Though by this time adamant in her determination never to submit her poems to print, she nevertheless was moved to produce three fair copies for the man's publication, later explaining this uncharacteristic gesture: "The name of 'Child' was a snare to me."[7]

Emily greatly enjoyed this new side of herself, as a remark made in 1882 makes clear. "[Mother] ate a little Supper I made her with such enthusiasm," she wrote, "I laughed with delight."[8]

During these years of service to her mother Emily became a doting aunt to little Gilbert. She particularly enjoyed his innocent rebelliousness and insouciant imperviousness to his mother's and Vinnie's demands for better behavior. She delighted in his childish sayings and repeated them in letters to her friends like the proud parent she felt herself to be. Gilbert's charm and undiscriminating friendliness did much to reconcile the two households, which prior to his birth had undergone a period of increasing estrangement and animosity whose focal points were Vinnie and Sue. It is not surprising in view of the intense identification of the poet with her brother and his wife that in time Emily came to regard Gilbert as her own and to refer to him as "our child."[9]

The loss of her mother and Gilbert within the same year was one of the cruelest blows fate ever dealt her. The death of Mrs. Dickinson "crushed"[10] Vinnie and "benumbed" Emily, who wrote, "Plundered of her dear face, we scarcely know each other, and feel as if wrestling with a Dream, waking would dispel."[11] She must have felt astonished that the woman to whom she had once alluded in the phrase "I never had a mother"[12] had grown to mean so much to her. Speaking of Mrs. Dickinson's funeral, she wrote, "As we bore her dear form through the Wilderness, Light seemed to have stopped."[13] The poet believed that her mother had developed a finer nature and had become more loving during her seven-year ordeal. "She was scarcely the aunt you knew," she told her cousins. With persistent sorrow had come tenderness; "a larger mother died than had she died before."[14] However, it seems doubtful that Mrs. Dickinson's helplessness could have increased her capacities to the extent that Emily maintained. More likely the reversal of roles had made it possible for Emily to see qualities in her mother to which she had previously been blind. Surely she is the one who really changed. That is, the "Affection came" because the identification of daughter with mother, so long and so tragically delayed, at last became possible. In the course of her daily ministrations, Emily suddenly found within herself one of love's unsuspected wellsprings from which she could lavish upon her "child" quantities of devotion. The missing "something" (of poem 959), of which she had always felt bereft, now returned to her. Thus, in caring for her mother, she recovered, by reflection back upon herself of her own newly released maternal tenderness, something of the "Delinquent Palaces" and lost "Dominions" of childhood.

Gilbert's death at the age of eight, less than a year after her mother's death, seems to have triggered the onset of the poet's own decline. On the night the little boy died, Emily, apparently frantic with apprehension, deliberately disregarded the fixed agoraphobic defenses she had maintained for many years. She left the mansion, crossed the expanse of lawn between the two homesteads, in what perturbation one can only imagine, and entered Sue's house for the first time in fifteen years to bid her last good-bye to her beloved "son." The price she paid for defying her neurosis was great. She developed an incapacitating pain in the back of her head and began to vomit—nauseated ostensibly by the odor of disinfectants. Nevertheless, she remained at Gilbert's bedside until the child was dead. Finally she collapsed and was very ill and confined to her bed for the next two months. Her physician's diagnosis was "Nervous prostration."[15] Austin also was overwhelmed and was treated by his physician two days after Gilbert's death for a "malarial attack."[16]

In the few years remaining to her following Gilbert's death she did not fail to remember his little friends, as if in cultivating her relationship with them she could feel a little nearer to the child she had lost. She sent them cakes each Christmas and to one of them she wrote, "Missing my own Boy, I knock at other Trundle-Beds."[17]

Caring for her mother had taken up a great deal of her time and energy, and as was to be expected, the belated identification with her mother, while it fostered the development of greater domesticity and womanliness in the poet, did nothing to stimulate her flagging creative drive. Emily Dickinson continued sporadically to write poems for the rest of her life, but the fruitful agitation of her early thirties never appeared again.

The twilight excursions into a more fully evolved femininity and maternalism must have had an intense bittersweet quality for the poet—a fleeting taste of the mature gratifications she had missed. With the deaths of her mother and Gilbert even these newly awakened dispositions were deprived of their objects. It is small cause for wonder that she survived their loss by only four years.

Did Emily Dickinson owe anything else to her mother beyond these brief and belated glimpses of another side of life—a life that might have been—in addition to the heritage of frustration and loneliness, and her resentment, her distrust of her own sex, and her despair?

The answer is: almost everything that makes Emily Dickinson of interest to us today. Her debt to her mother is of incalculable magnitude. For it is beyond question that Mrs. Dickinson unwittingly provided her daughter with the conditions necessary for the development of her peculiar gifts. Without such a mother Emily Dickinson could not have become the poet we know. It was Mrs. Dickinson's failure as a sufficiently loving and admirable developmental model that set in motion the series of psychological upheavals which were unmitigated misfortunes for Emily Dickinson *the woman*. These maturational impasses consigned her to a life of sexual bewilderment, anxiety, and frustration by impairing those processes of psychic growth which would have made the roles of wife and mother possible. With reference to Emily Dickinson *the artist,* one cannot speak of misfortunes at all. For, amazing as it may seem, Mrs. Dickinson's inadequacies, the sequence of internal conflicts to which they gave rise, and the final psychotic breakdown all conspired in a unique way to make of Emily Dickinson a great and prolific poet.

Emily Dickinson's psychic imbalance and eventual collapse allied themselves on the side of her genius. However much it hampered her evolution as a woman, the blockade she reached in her emotional maturation and the various symptoms to which it gave rise appear, one and all, to have been conducive to the exercise of her poetic talent. Even the plunge into irrationality and perceptual and affective chaos, once the acute catastrophe had subsided, became fuel for the poetic fire. Not in one dimension only, but in several, Emily Dickinson's psychopathology was friendly to her creativity. And, as I have emphasized, the wellsprings of this productive disturbance go back to her "nonentity" of a mother. Let me survey the features of this maternal bequest that for another woman would have been unqualified afflictions but that for the artist and poet were blessings in disguise.

First, Emily Dickinson's inability to solidify her self-image as a woman made her awkward and uncomfortable in her efforts to establish congenial relationships with either men or women. Ultimately her anxiety in social situations joined with her progressively constricting agoraphobia, and she was compelled to withdraw from the social scene altogether. The vacuum in her life which resulted from the impoverishment of relationships brought intense loneliness and a store of unoccupied hours. This vacuum was of immense importance to her development as a poet, because it afforded her freedom from time-consuming and distracting social responsibilities that she could not otherwise have avoided. Thus she had ample time to steep herself in the Bible and in the works of Shakespeare and many nineteenth-century poets and writers. Her family recognized the intractability of her phobias, and eventually she was excused from social occasions, even from the annual commencement teas at which her parents played host to the elite of Amherst. Probably by this time she had learned how to exploit her symptoms for her own purposes—her phobic fear of face to face encounters becoming for her what the conventional "headache" is to other women. In this way her symptoms curtailed the drain on her time and energy that was detrimental to her creative life.

Second, the loneliness that followed upon her isolation from even the most potentially sympathetic of her neighbors and friends came to invest letter writing with an almost sacramental importance. Bearing the full burden of her need for understanding, love, and companionship, letters assumed a prominence in her life far beyond their usual role for more ordinary personalities as a mere addendum to direct contact. Also, increasing awareness of her psychological difference from others gradually made her more guarded, and her early prolix exuberance was superseded by a defensive care and caution in her written utterance that moved her in the direction of ever more conscious craftsmanship. These two factors—the increased emphasis on written communication and the tendency toward allusion and away from explicit statement—very likely paved the psychological way for the symbolic and metaphorical expression of poetry.

For Emily Dickinson writing was more hazardous than speech, and she exercised great tact in composing letters. "We bruise each other less in talking than in writing," she told her cousin, "for then a quiet accent helps words themselves too hard."[18] Thus the *emotional* need to find the word that says neither too much nor too little, is neither too dull nor too cutting, served as forerunner of the *esthetic* need to find the word that speaks with maximum incisiveness and suggestiveness. The letters seem to have been the forward guard of her poetry, and in them she weighed her words and practiced the rhythms and verbal convolutions that appear later in the poems. There is nothing careless or even spontaneous in the ordinary sense of that word in her mature letters; they are for the most part carefully calculated and exquisitely chiseled works of deliberate art. What began probably as an emotional need to balance what one revealed with what one hid grew through genius into a style richly suggestive and oblique.

In addition to isolating her physically from others and thereby greatly emphasizing the importance of written communication, Emily Dickinson's psychiatric symptoms necessarily increased her awareness of inner mental processes, which in turn added another dimension to her poetry.

One of the fascinations of Emily Dickinson's poetry is its capacity to look inward and throw a spotlight into the obscure recesses beyond consciousness. The person in whose behavior irrational compulsions and ill-defined fears play a part frequently develops his capacity for introspection. Probably there is no circumstance more effective in leading one to a realization that there exists a dark, unconscious continent in one's self than to be afflicted with a fear of something in which one's rational faculties recognize no danger. Only to the extent that one can maintain that all one's affective responses are appropriate and reasonable and that all one's acts are free of compulsion can one relegate the concept of an active unconscious to the category of fantasy. Emily Dickinson was confronted with too much in her own reactions to make her doubt that consciousness was not the totality of mental operations. She did not understand herself, she was driven to wonder about the strange, uncontrollable quirks that shut her away from others, and she strove to discover their roots. Much of the power of her poems emanates from her self-explorations and psychological discoveries, neither of which perhaps would have occurred had she been an entirely sound personality, the offspring of a hearty and security-providing mother.

Her emotional turmoil and inability to adapt herself to a ready-made social role generated an impulse to examine and characterize all her feeling states. Many poems appear to be efforts to delineate or fix particular responses—to sort out, one by one, from a welter of emotions, sensations, and impulses, each individual reaction, as if by this painstaking inventory to arrive at a resolution of her existential perplexity. Any diminution of this need to characterize and analyze the motions of the inner life would to that extent, one imagines, have superficialized the poetry.

Even Emily Dickinson's experience of the psychotic state itself —ordinarily the gravest of psychological misfortunes—appears to have added its increment to the enrichment of her art. When "a Plank in Reason, broke" and she plunged through into an acute psychotic episode, she suffered what all persons do when the partitions separating conscious and unconscious mental operations give way. Previously repressed and alien impulses, ideas, and affects flood the ego. The littoral reaches of the mind open up, revealing a pelagic depth. Like a not uncommon type of patient, Emily Dickinson preserved her capacity to observe herself during the cataclysm and to record her experiences in her memory. Later, her artistic transformation of the strange material that erupted from the depths within her mind added a sometimes unearthly and startling power to her poetry that it doubtless would not have had save for this interval of disorganization. It is as though her ego, in order to ward off being overwhelmed, was driven to clothe the recently unconscious intrusions in symbols, much as if she were dreaming while awake.

Emily Dickinson, by her late twenties, was a woman of extraordinary sensitivity, had a superior command of language, was widely read, and possessed a very high general intelligence. She was also thoroughly familiar with the verse forms, meters, and rhyme schemes of the Protestant hymnal and for several years at least had been practicing manipulating these forms in her poetry. With the onset of an acute psychotic reaction precisely at the time these technical skills were ripening, her competent poetic talent was kindled into inspired flame by the uprush of unconscious material and the ego's need to channel and find symbolic expression for it. Poems such as "My Life had stood – a Loaded Gun" and "In Winter in my Room," for example, fall just short of autism in the obscurity and strangeness of their symbols, and they yield their meaning only to the kind of interpretation that renders intelligible dreams and schizophrenic communications.

To turn to another aspect of the matter: there can be no doubt that psychoses and neuroses are frequently powerful motivators. It is proverbial that obstacles insurmountable to men in their right minds are as nothing to the fear-crazed, those beside themselves with rage, and the "inspired." Similarly, insofar as a man is driven by unconscious forces, he is to that degree impervious to those strictures of reality that curtail the timid exertions of the majority. Consider the immense fund of energy spent singlemindedly by Emily Dickinson in the pursuit of poetry—to the exclusion of those physical and emotional needs and gratifications that are important goals for the rest of us.

She herself explained that she "sang" because she was afraid, just as boys whistle when they pass cemeteries. Boys whistle in such circumstances, it can be assumed, for purposes of selfencouragement and to counteract the terrifying expectation of the resurrection of ghosts from graves. The cemetery Emily

488

Dickinson was passing was the graveyard of the repressed that once again was stirring to life. The provocative effects of a fear of impending disorganization and loss of control appear to have brought about a defensive need to organize, contain, and channel the emerging images and emotions. One way she discovered to cope with these phantoms from the id was to subject them to rule—the rules of poetry.

As she wrote in one poem commemorating a friend's death, "I run it over – 'Dead,' Brain, 'Dead.' / Put it in Latin – left of my school – / Seems it dont shriek so – under rule" (poem 426). The formal structures of poetry seem to have served as "Latin" to these most unruly and overwhelming emotions. Thus the poetry provided an intellectual framework in which dangerous emotions, upon reflection and in retrospect, could be manipulated, ordered, and contained symbolically, and thereby she was afforded at least an illusion of control over a rampant and disturbed inner life.

At times, however, the emotion that she poured into poems seems to have been not merely a remembered feeling but the very one that gripped her at the moment of composition. Remarkable as it may appear, the poetry seems frequently to have served as a *direct* outlet, affording the kind of relief that in ordinary people is achieved by weeping, outbursts of rage, and fits of hysteria. That Emily Dickinson believed she wrote poetry for the direct emotional relief of many kinds of feelings is clear, and this explanation, which she repeated in many different contexts, was the one motive she acknowledged.

Moreover, the writing of poems apparently eased her fear of death. To T. W. Higginson she wrote, "My dying Tutor told me that he would like to live till I had been a poet, but Death was much of Mob as I could master—then—And when far afterward —a sudden light on Orchards, or a new fashion in the wind troubled my attention—I felt a palsy, here—the Verses just relieve."[19]

When Higginson criticized her unorthodox poems, calling her "gait" "spasmodic" and "uncontrolled," the excuse she gave for her metrical and rhythmic irregularities was: "I am in danger."[20] It seems probable that the danger that would mold the structure of poetry might be an interior danger, a threatening pressure from one's own thoughts and impulses.

That Emily Dickinson believed poetry was essential to her very survival is suggested by a comment she made following the death of Judge Lord: "Abstinence from Melody was what made him die,"[21] she said. "Melody" here refers both to the music of poetry and to the softer, imaginative aspects of life.

When Emily Dickinson told Higginson that insofar as her evolution as a poet was concerned she "knew no tutor but the North,"[22] she indirectly acknowledged the debt owed to Mrs. Dickinson for the emergence of her talent. If the "North" taught Emily Dickinson to be a poet it was through the agency of her mother, who first introduced her to the "North," the poet's symbol for deprivation, loneliness, hardship, and death. As Emily Dickinson grew older, the cluster of associations attaching to the concept naturally enlarged to include her many other disappointments and losses, but it should not be lost sight of that the nucleus of this paradoxically fruitful sense of impoverishment was generated in her early years by the emotional inaccessibility of her mother. Emily Dickinson never cited a zest for living, a sense of ecstasy, or a feeling of fulfillment as the springboards of her creative outpouring. Instead she held the view that she "sang off charnel steps"[23] and that the poetic seed germinated in "Lybian" sand (poem 681), yielding fruit whose necessary condition of growth was the austerity of the desert.

In many instances the poet explicitly cited misery as the chief fountainhead of her creative life. A recurring theme is that suffering evokes the creative work, which in turn eases suffering. Poem 442 conveys the idea that Emily Dickinson's psychological distress made her a poet: "The Tyrian would not come / Until the North – invoke it." Here "Tyrian" (the precious royal purple dye) stands for the poetry. That Emily Dickinson's creativity arose from despair and isolation is the thought of the first lines of poem 773: "Deprived of other Banquet, / I entertained Myself." A similar idea occurs again in poem 850: "I sing to use the Waiting . . . To Keep the Dark away." The easing effect of giving expression to pent-up feeling is cited in poem 554: "We – tell a Hurt – to cool it." In poem 544, in which it is observed that "Some seek in Art – the Art of Peace," it is said of the "Martyr Poets" that they "wrought their Pang in syllable."

That the broken spirit requires work to heal itself is the idea behind "At leisure is the Soul . . . It begs you give it Work" (poem 618), and "Severer Service of myself / I – hastened to demand" (poem 786). Can it be doubted that when Emily Dickinson speaks of her therapeutic "work" she is referring to her poetic labors?

When the curative or palliative properties of society are denied one, work is all that is left for therapy for emotional suffering. "I am glad you are working. Others are anodyne,"[24] she tells a bereaved friend; and again she expresses the same thought: "I am glad you 'work.' Work is a bleak redeemer, but it does redeem; it tires the flesh so that can't tease the spirit."[25] "Work" for Mrs. Bowles, the grieving widow to whom Emily addressed this last, might have been some domestic chore. For Emily Dickinson it would have been the writing of poems.

One of the most interesting variations on the idea that Emily Dickinson wrote poems to relieve a psychological distress is the following: "I work to drive the awe away, yet awe impells the work."[26] What stimulated this particular insight was her grief and consternation following the death of Judge Lord.

Unconscious motivation, operating with greater urgency and with greater menace to the ego than is usual, played an important role also in Emily Dickinson's "love affair," which in turn might be considered the *ignis fatuus* that kindled a significant proportion of her creative effort. When Emily Dickinson first fell in love with a married man it was as though, to her external eye, the impediment of marriage did not exist. The psychodynamic basis for her choice of such a lover has been examined. Here the point to be made is that without her particular constellation of unconscious needs—needs involving Austin and Susan that, by this stage in her life, were grossly inappropriate (that is, psychopathological)—she would not have had such a love experience. For it was rooted in fantasy, displacement, and projection; it was a blind love unaware of the real impulses active beneath the surface of consciousness. Thus we are confronted with yet another way in which Emily Dickinson's psychosexual conflict indirectly facilitated her becoming a poet. Most women who become spinsters do not have a grand and hopeless passion to the commemoration of which they devote a goodly portion of their lives. To do so requires a very special set of interior needs and psychological structures. Fortunately for her art, Emily Dickinson was possessed of these peculiar prerequisites. Imagine the course of her life if she had been able to accept phlegmatically her deficient capacity to respond to the opposite sex and if she had been less regressively involved with Austin and Susan. She might then have settled into a bland resignation to her fate or perhaps, given her tendency to depression and overawareness of death, become morose and cynical. In either case it is difficult to conjecture what source her poetry, provided she wrote any under these circumstances, could possibly have drawn upon for the excitement, drama, passion, and anguish that were supplied by her illusory love affair.

In addition to having the effects already mentioned—the increased importance of written communication, the increased availability of material usually unconscious, the need to control potentially inundating feelings and ideas, the stimulation of symbol production, the frustrated love affair—Emily Dickinson's psychological travail, including the crisis reached in her acute breakdown into psychosis, befriended and fecundated her art in still another way. The phenomenology of her psychic distress (as distinct from its underlying dynamics) provided her with novel and impressive subject matter. The sensations and altered perceptions of the psychotic state provided the main substance for some of her most original and vivid poems, a good example being the catatonic-like psychomotor retardation of "After great pain, a formal feeling comes" (poem 341). This aspect of the relationship of her emotional disturbance to her poetry has been treated at length in Chapter VII. I need only mention here that depression, apathy, dread, estrangement, depersonalization, thought disorder, and many other phenomena of psychopathology discernible by introspection provided the basis for numerous poems.

All that is presented in the preceding pages is, of course, not to say that a disordered psychological life invariably enhances creative talent. But, in Emily Dickinson's case, a psychological catastrophe does appear to have been wrenched to constructive poetic purposes by an ego that was extraordinarily strong and well furnished in most other respects. It may not be going too far to surmise that lacking such serious psychic conflict Emily Dickinson might never have become more than a mildly interesting, sentimental, conventional poetess—that is, if she took time to write poetry at all. The violent disharmonies and unceasing restlessness of her inner life, which would have represented for most people a debilitating and unproductive dissipation of emotional energy, thus appear in her case to have contributed copiously to the transformation of woman into poet.

What, after all, do we find when we survey Emily Dickinson's subject matter? Death, renunciation, sexual conflicts, psychological distress, religious doubts, and love of nature. And each of these major themes can be shown to have taproots that extend down to her unsatisfying relationship with her mother.

The motifs of death and immortality in part reflect a longing for love deferred to heaven because it is judged unavailable in this life. Emily Dickinson spoke of George Eliot in terms that define her own youthful experience: "As childhood is earth's confiding time, perhaps having no childhood, she lost her way to the early trust, and no later came."[27] Herself losing the "early trust" with reference to her mother, Emily Dickinson wandered through life trying to replace it. She sought consolation in religion but, ostensibly hindered by an inability to accept certain doctrines, she was unable to avail herself of religious solace. Since Edward Dickinson did not join the church until middle age, it seems that religion in Emily Dickinson's mind must have been indissolubly associated with her mother, who was converted when Emily was still an infant. To the agnostic Judge Lord, whom she loved, the poet wrote, "It may surprise you I speak of God—I know him but a little, but Cupid taught Jehovah to many an untutored Mind."[28] Cupid taught Jehovah—in other words, Emily Dickinson could accept religious teaching provided the instruction came to her through the vehicle of love. On another occasion she expressed the same idea: "I am glad if you love your Clergyman," she wrote Mrs. Holland, "God seems much more friendly through a hearty Lens."[29] If her mother had been a heartier lens, Emily Dickinson might have been able to perceive a more benignant God, to the possible detriment of her poetry. After Dr. Holland's death Emily told his wife how impressed she was with Dr. Holland's conception of God: "*That* God," she said, "must be a friend—*that* was a different God—and I almost felt warmer myself, in the midst of a tie so sunshiny."[30] These disclosures would appear to justify the conclusion that one of the roots of Emily Dickinson's ambivalence concerning religion, which is an important recurring theme in her poetry, involves her childhood association of her mother's emotional inaccessibility with her mother's religious dedication. If Mrs. Dickinson had been able to generate greater warmth toward her daughter, Emily might then have associated religion with love and, like Austin and Vinnie, resolved her religious doubts and joined the church.

It is significant that the haunting omnipresence of a vague sense of bereavement that Emily Dickinson said clung to her from her childhood and that I have associated with her mother's inadequacies seemed to leave her temporarily when she came close to a conversion experience at the age of thirteen. It was as though the "lost dominions" of childhood—if found—would restore happiness. Thus, after Emily Dickinson hesitated on the brink of embracing her mother's religion with the feeling that she might have been acceptable as a member of the church and that she belonged there, she wrote, "I think of the perfect happiness I experienced while I felt I was an heir of heaven as of a delightful dream."[31] What made Emily Dickinson, able to get as close as this, hold back from the final commitment? Probably the acceptance of her mother's religion unconsciously meant to her falling back into a regressive and precarious dependence on her mother.

The reason Emily Dickinson gave for not "accepting Christ" was that she loved the "world" too much to give it up. It should be recalled in this context that of special importance to Emily Dickinson as a surrogate mother was Aunt Lavinia, Mrs. Dickinson's younger sister. After the poet's second or third bout of severe depression and her second "cure" at Aunt Lavinia's in Boston, Emily wrote, "I feel that the world holds a predominant place in my affections. I do not feel that I could give up all for Christ."[32] This was written after Emily's return from Boston, which certainly represented the wide world to her. In Boston she had been taken to museums and exhibits, had heard a performance of Haydn's *Creation,* and received her first taste of certain other big city wonders. It seems probable that if Mrs. Dickinson was representative of Christ, his church, and the forsaking of earthly pleasure, the more maternal Aunt Lavinia, despite the fact that she also was a religious woman, stood, in Emily Dickinson's unconscious, for the allurements of the world that the poet maintained she could not (but of course eventually did) give up.

Emily Dickinson's interest in nature, outdoors and in her

greenhouse, and the large place her naturalist observations played in her poetry may indirectly be related to the feeling of deprivation that stemmed from the maternal void, for the poet seems to have been driven to nature for consolation. Reminiscing perhaps upon the love relationship with "Master," an 1873 poem states, "I thought that nature was enough / Till Human nature came" (poem 1286). If one recalls that as a child Emily Dickinson had no mother but "Awe" to cling to in times of distress and was unable to derive comfort from the religion that she unconsciously felt to be an extension of her mother, it appears more than plausible that she drew on the natural world for solace. However, as might be expected, Emily Dickinson regarded nature also with a certain suspiciousness and ambivalence. Sometimes nature was the "Gentlest Mother" (poem 790), but at other times she became a "haunted house" and a "stranger" (poem 1400) that could never be fathomed.

Thus the psychological distress and sexual conflicts and all their derivatives—the renunciation of love and marriage, the preoccupation with death and immortality, the religious doubts, and even the poet's uneasy approach to nature—all can be seen as outgrowths of her feelings of maternal deprivation. Had Mrs. Dickinson been warm and affectionate, more intelligent, effective, and admirable, Emily Dickinson early in life would probably have identified with her, become domestic, and adopted the conventional woman's role. She would then have become a church member, been active in community affairs, married, and had children. The creative potentiality would of course still have been there, but would she have discovered it? What motivation to write could have replaced the incentive given by suffering and loneliness? If, in spite of her wifely and motherly duties, she had still felt the need to express herself in verse, what would her subject matter have been? Would art have sprung from fulfillment, gratification, and completeness as abundantly as it did from longing, frustration, and deprivation? Emily Dickinson did not think so. She cherished her "sumptuous Destitution" (poem 1382) because it stimulated compensatory fantasies that in turn fed her art. She welcomed protracted pain and disconsolation because they transformed transient joys into ecstatic moments, filling her with the pent-up feelings that could overflow into poetry. Too much pleasure and sympathetic recognition was a danger that she instinctively avoided, for it threatened to deplete her subject matter and lull the unsatisfied appetites that ignited her art. Critical appreciation could only be tolerated in sips; too much would have ruined her. This seems to be the reason T. W. Higginson's rejection "saved her life." If his critical verdict had been that the poems must be published, she might not have escaped becoming famous, with the result that the core emotion of her poetry—her responses to deprivation—would have vanished and she would have been finished as a poet.

Was not Emily Dickinson then playing a kind of Russian roulette when she sent her poems for Higginson's appraisal? Why did she take such a chance? For one thing, it was necessary to her that her obscurity be genuine, the result of unkind fate. She had to convince herself that she was really blocked, unappreciated, and shut out and that the condition was not of her own contrivance. On an unconscious level she must have been well aware that she was safe in writing to Higginson. She knew something of Higginson's taste—that it accorded with the taste of those other two literary men of her acquaintance—Josiah Holland and Samuel Bowles—to whom she showed her verse and who firmly advised her that the poems were too insubstantial to publish.

Even if she was not at that time familiar with Higginson's own commonplace verse, she had good reason to believe that it was not equal to that of Emerson, whose poems she had admired for some years. The question has often been raised why she did not see that Emerson was presented with her poems for his opinion when he was a house guest at her brother's next door. Emerson's poetry and Emily Dickinson's hold many characteristics in common, and it seems highly probable that he would have perceived her genius. Also, as a widely acclaimed and influential author, he could easily have brought her to the attention of a willing publisher. Instead of sending her poems fifty yards to the genius down the street, however, she chose to send them fifty miles to Higginson in Worcester. The most plausible explanation for not placing them at Emerson's disposal is that unconsciously she anticipated and feared a positive appraisal from him.

By her thirtieth year Emily Dickinson had become what could almost be considered a martyr to her art. That is, she had learned that she could suffer fruitfully, extracting artistic gains from deprivation. Yet her creativity, whose touchstone was emotional famine and pain, must itself have been a source of intense gratification. Thus as poetry gives rise to pleasure so pain gives rise to poetry. Or, as Emily Dickinson phrased it: "Power is only Pain – / Stranded [that is, woven into strands], thro' Discipline, / Till Weights – will hang" (poem 252). When Emily Dickinson said this she designated the prime mover—pain—behind her verse. Power (poetic) comes from pain (arising from the sense of loss rooted in her unhappy relationship with her mother and her mother's subsequent surrogates) stranded through discipline (a quality derived from her identification with her hard-working and conscientious father).

The foregoing raises an interesting question. If Emily Dickinson had to convince herself that she was the victim of a malignant and inescapable destiny in order to become a poet, is it not also possible that the image of her mother that she has handed down to us is similarly distorted, through unconscious forces, for the same purposes? That is, is it not likely that Emily Dickinson had a deep need to feel unloved, unappreciated, and rejected by her mother (and her mother's later representatives) in order to bring about the barren, arid, emotional climate that she intuitively realized was necessary for the flowering of her poetic fantasies? After all, Emily Dickinson had already reached middle age when she made those bitter statements about Mrs. Dickinson: "I had a mother"[33] and "I always ran Home to Awe when a child, if anything befell me. He was an awful Mother, but I liked him better than none."[34] Thus these remarks came a long time after Mrs. Dickinson's hypothesized maternal failure.

Though the question is probably not resolvable on the basis of the evidence left to us, it suggests the need for caution before one completely exonerates Emily Dickinson herself as an agent in the strained relationship between herself and her mother. However, in view of the stresses of Emily Dickinson's adolescent development, her intense and conflict-ridden relationships with her brother and his wife, and her eventual breakdown, one must accept the existence of a severe blocking of Mrs. Dickinson's maternal functions prior to the time the daughter was in a position to contribute anything herself to the schism unless one postulates some constitutional incapacity of the child to evoke an appropriate maternal response. The most plausible conclusion is that the primary deficiency did indeed reside in Mrs. Dickinson.

This is not to say that the daughter did not later exacerbate the existing disharmony and exaggerate it for her own psychological purposes. For one thing Emily Dickinson possibly disparaged her mother partly out of feelings of envy. No matter how much the poet may have unconsciously heightened the emotionally deprivative circumstances of her life, she was acutely aware of all the normal joys she was missing. Though she doubtless would have rejected an offer that exchanged her poetic faculties for the ordinary goals of married love and motherhood, she suffered real pain at the loss of these fulfillments. And Emily Dickinson could criticize her mother quite readily because she did not know from her own experience how difficult it was to be a perfectly adequate parent. Thus ignorance of the magnitude of the demands she made upon her mother and envy of her mother for having achieved all those prizes of life that were denied the daughter added their bit to Emily Dickinson's arrogance toward Mrs. Dickinson. If one then adds Emily Dickinson's need to see herself in the role of rejected child, one may form some conception of the extent to which Mrs. Dickinson's shortcomings may have been exaggerated. In the last analysis, however, it seems certain that the whole image of Mrs. Dickinson's failure, however overblown as a result of the daughter's neurotic and esthetic needs, sprang primarily from a genuine maternal deprivation syndrome that the daughter in no discernible way could have brought about herself.

Emily Dickinson could not have failed to experience guilt feelings for her explicit denigrating attitude toward her mother. One does not sneer at and depreciate one's mother to strangers as Emily Dickinson did to Higginson without suffering twinges of conscience. And this would hold especially true, one imagines, in nineteenth-century New England, where great emphasis was placed on honoring one's parents. Here again one sees a circular process inimical to the woman but kindly to the artist: feelings of rejection by the mother lead to hostility and bitter denunciation of the mother and what she represents. As a result, guilt feelings are engendered that in turn evoke a need for punishment that is partly satisfied through self-inflicted social deprivation brought about by means of neurotic symptoms. The ensuing loneliness and frustration then feed the art in ways that have been mentioned. The art in turn, providing its own compensatory and self-reinforcing gratification, demands further self-denial (the precious productive destitution), which is brought about by the perpetuation of the estrangement from and enmity toward mother, religion, God, and society. These hostile rejections in turn evoke more guilt feelings and further suffering and a continuation of the endless cycle. Emily Dickinson seems in this way to have been consigned to an affective desert from which she could not escape and which, on the crucially decisive levels of her mind, she paradoxically came to cherish as the most efflorescent of gardens.

Psychological calamities, decades of frustration, isolation, and loneliness all created a void that Emily Dickinson's talent rushed in to fill. Without this void there might well have been no poet. Her afflictions all had their point of origin in the circumstances and personality of Edward Dickinson's young wife in the early days of her motherhood. To this extent it may be said that Emily Dickinson was able to become a great poet because—not in spite of—her unobtrusive, ungifted, and unstimulating mother—the ultimate progenitress, therefore, of the verse. With a different mother Emily Dickinson may well have married and had children and in all ways have pursued a conventional life. Living in uninterrupted ignorance of her latent artistic gifts, there is no reason why she could not have had a placid life, unacquainted with the "North." Probably she would have been better off if Mrs. Dickinson had been abler. In that case the only impoverishment would be ours.

NOTES

INDEX OF FIRST LINES

GENERAL INDEX

NOTES

I. The Myths of Amherst

1. Jay Leyda, *The Years and Hours of Emily Dickinson* (New Haven, Yale University Press, 1960), II, 357.
2. Ibid., II, 65.
3. Millicent Todd Bingham, *Emily Dickinson's Home* (New York, Harper and Brothers, 1955), p. xv.
4. Yvor Winters, "Emily Dickinson and the Limits of Judgment," in *Emily Dickinson: A Collection of Critical Essays*, ed. Richard B. Sewall (Englewood Cliffs, N.J., Prentice-Hall, 1963), p. 40.
5. *Letters*, II, 474, no. 342a (T. W. Higginson to his wife, August 1870).
6. Ibid., I, 21, no. 8 (Emily to Abiah Root, September 25, 1845).
7. Ibid., I, 36, no. 13 (Emily to Abiah Root, September 8, 1846).
8. Ibid., I, 27-28, no. 10 (Emily to Abiah Root, January 31, 1846).
9. Ibid., I, 291, no. 159 (Emily to Austin, March 26, 1854).
10. Ibid., II, 348, no. 202 (Emily to Mrs. J. G. Holland, about February 20, 1859).
11. Ibid., II, 407, no. 264 (Emily to Louise and Frances Norcross, late May 1862).
12. Ibid., II, 424, no. 281 (Emily to Louise and Frances Norcross, late May 1863).
13. Ibid., II, 631, no. 581 (Emily to Susan Gilbert Dickinson, about 1878).
14. Ibid., III, 706, no. 721 (Emily to Mrs. J. G. Holland, August 1881).
15. Ibid., III, 792, no. 858 (Emily to Susan Gilbert Dickinson, about 1883).
16. Leyda, *Years and Hours*, II, 213.
17. *Letters*, II, 570, note to no. 481 (Emily to Mrs. T. W. Higginson, Christmas 1876). The phrase is from T. W. Higginson's letter to his sister, December 28, 1876.
18. Ibid., II, 473, no. 342a (T. W. Higginson to his wife, August 16, 1870).
19. Ibid., II, 476, no. 342b (T. W. Higginson to his wife, August 17, 1870).
20. Ibid., II, 476, note to no. 342b, reprinted from the *Atlantic Monthly*, 68 (October 1891).
21. Thomas H. Johnson, *Emily Dickinson: An Interpretive Biography* (Cambridge, Mass., Harvard University Press, Belknap Press, 1963), p. 53.
22. Ibid., p. 51.
23. John Crowe Ransom, "Emily Dickinson: A Poet Restored," in *Emily Dickinson: A Collection of Critical Essays*, p. 100.
24. Theodora Ward, *The Capsule of the Mind: Chapters in the Life of Emily Dickinson* (Cambridge, Mass., Harvard University Press, Belknap Press, 1961), p. 72.
25. Johnson, *Emily Dickinson*, p. 56.
26. Charles R. Anderson, *Emily Dickinson's Poetry: Stairway of Surprise* (New York, Holt, Rinehart and Winston, 1960), p. 294.
27. Ibid., p. 295.
28. Richard Chase, *Emily Dickinson* (New York, William Sloan, 1951), p. 8.
29. Millicent Todd Bingham, *Ancestors' Brocades: The Literary Debut of Emily Dickinson* (New York, Harper and Brothers, 1945), p. 86.
30. Allen Tate, "Emily Dickinson," in *Emily Dickinson: A Collection of Critical Essays*, pp. 19, 20.

31. Bingham, *Emily Dickinson's Home* p. xv.
32. Bingham, *Ancestors' Brocades,* p. 96.
33. Ibid., p. 128.
34. Ibid., p. 204.
35. Ibid., p. 192.
36. Ibid., p. 99.
37. Johnson, *Emily Dickinson,* p. 50.
38. Ibid., p. 46.
39. John Malcolm Brinnin, *Emily Dickinson* (New York, Dell Publishing Co., 1960), p. 13.
40. Clark Griffith, *The Long Shadow: Emily Dickinson's Tragic Poetry* (Princeton, Princeton University Press, 1964), p. 283.
41. David T. Porter, *The Art of Emily Dickinson's Early Poetry* (Cambridge, Mass., Harvard University Press, 1966), p. 2.
42. Ibid., p. xii.
43. Henry W. Wells, *Introduction to Emily Dickinson* (Chicago, Packard and Co., 1947), chap. 3.
44. Ward, *Capsule of the Mind,* pp. 53–55.
45. Bingham, *Emily Dickinson's Home,* p. 417.
46. Chase, *Emily Dickinson,* p. 116.
47. Ibid., p. 128.
48. Johnson, *Emily Dickinson,* p. 24.
49. Ibid., p. 248.
50. *Letters,* II, 474, no. 342a (T. W. Higginson to his wife, August 16, 1870).
51. Johnson, *Emily Dickinson,* p. 51.
52. Ibid., p. 83.
53. Richard Sewall, *The Lyman Letters: New Light on Emily Dickinson and Her Family* (Amherst, University of Massachusetts Press, 1965), p. 65.
54. Ibid.
55. R. P. Blackmur, "Emily Dickinson's Notation" in *Emily Dickinson: A Collection of Critical Essays,* p. 85.
56. Brinnin, *Emily Dickinson,* p. 10.
57. William Robert Sherwood, *Circumference and Circumstance: Stages in the Mind and Art of Emily Dickinson* (New York, Columbia University Press, 1968), p. 138.
58. Ibid., p. 152.
59. Ibid., p. 160.
60. Griffith, *The Long Shadow,* p. 207.
61. Ibid., p. 208.
62. Johnson, *Emily Dickinson,* p. 206.
63. Albert J. Gelpi, *Emily Dickinson: The Mind of the Poet* (Cambridge, Mass., Harvard University Press, 1965), pp. 112, 113.
64. Archibald MacLeish, "The Private World: Poems of Emily Dickinson," in *Emily Dickinson: A Collection of Critical Essays,* p. 160.
65. Martha Dickinson Bianchi, *The Life and Letters of Emily Dickinson,* (Boston, Houghton Mifflin, 1924), p. 51.
66. Ibid., p. 48.
67. Ibid., p. 16.
68. Ibid., p. 30.
69. Ibid., p. 42.
70. Ibid., p. 86.

71. Ibid., p. 81.
72. Leyda, *Years and Hours*, II, 77.

II. Earth's Confiding Time

1. *Letters*, II, 499, no. 379 (Emily to Louise Norcross, late 1872).
2. Ibid., II, 475, no. 342b (T. W. Higginson to his wife, August 1870).
3. Martha Dickinson Bianchi, *The Life and Letters of Emily Dickinson* (Boston, Houghton Mifflin, 1924).
4. Millicent Todd Bingham, *Emily Dickinson's Home* (New York, Harper and Brothers, 1955).
5. Clark Griffith, *The Long Shadow: Emily Dickinson's Tragic Poetry* (Princeton, Princeton University Press, 1964).
6. Thomas H. Johnson, *Emily Dickinson: An Interpretive Biography* (Cambridge, Mass., Harvard University Press, Belknap Press, 1955).
7. Ibid.
8. Richard Chase, *Emily Dickinson* (New York, William Sloan, 1951).
9. Ibid.
10. Bianchi, *Life and Letters*.
11. Anna Mary Wells, "Was Emily Dickinson Psychotic?" *American Imago*, 19 (Winter 1962).
12. Millicent Todd Bingham, *Ancestors' Brocades: The Literary Debut of Emily Dickinson* (New York, Harper and Brothers, 1945), p. 235.
13. *Letters*, II, 518, no. 405 (Emily to T. W. Higginson, January 1874).
14. Jay Leyda, *The Years and Hours of Emily Dickinson* (New Haven, Yale University Press, 1960), I, 315 (draft of a letter from Austin Dickinson to Susan Gilbert, early September 1854?).
15. *Letters*, II, 543, no. 442 (Emily to Louise and Frances Norcross, summer 1875).
16. Ibid., II, 355, no. 209 (Emily to Catherine Scott Turner [Anthon], late 1859?).
17. Ibid., II, 350, no. 204 (Emily to Mrs. J. G. Holland, March 2, 1859).
18. Ibid., II, 617, no. 562 (Emily to Otis P. Lord, about 1878).
19. Ibid., III, 777, no. 824 (Emily to Maria Whitney, May 1883?).
20. A. A. Brill, "Poetry as an Oral Outlet," *Psychoanalytic Review*, 18 (October 1931).
21. Leyda, *Years and Hours*, I, 28 (Catherine Dickinson to Edward Dickinson, May 12, 1835).
22. Ibid., I, 16 (Lavinia Norcross to Mrs. Edward Dickinson, December 6, 1830).
23. Ibid., I, 279 (Lavinia Dickinson to Austin Dickinson, July 1, 1853).
24. Ibid., I, 17 (Lavinia Norcross to Mr. and Mrs. Edward Dickinson, April 25, 1831).
25. Ibid., I, 21-22 (Lavinia Norcross to Mrs. Edward Dickinson, May 20, 1833).
26. Ibid., I, 22 (Lavinia Norcross to Mrs. Edward Dickinson, May 29, 1833).
27. Ibid., I, 21 (Lavinia Norcross to Mrs. Edward Dickinson, May 20, 1833).
28. Ibid., I, 22 (Lavinia Norcross to Mrs. Edward Dickinson, June 11, 1833).
29. Ibid., I, 22-23.
30. *Letters*, II, 475, no. 342b (T. W. Higginson to his wife, August 1870).
31. Ibid., II, 635, no. 593 (Emily to T. W. Higginson, February 1879).
32. Ibid., I, 254, no. 127 (Emily to Austin Dickinson, June 13, 1853).
33. Ibid., I, 180, no. 76 (Emily to Austin Dickinson, February 18, 1852).
34. Leyda, *Years and Hours*, II, 224 (obituary by Samuel Bowles, June 17, 1874).

35. Ibid., I, 180; from a letter published in *The Express,* September 27, 1850.
36. Ibid., I, 307.
37. Ibid., II, 226.
38. *Letters,* II, 528, no. 418 (Emily to T. W. Higginson, July 1874).
39. Ibid., II, 475, no. 342b (T. W. Higginson to his wife, August 17, 1870).
40. Ibid., I, 185, no. 79 (Emily to Austin Dickinson, March 2, 1852).
41. Leyda, *Years and Hours,* I, 202 (Lavinia Dickinson's diary, June 16, 1851).
42. Ibid., I, 240 (Lavinia Dickinson to Austin Dickinson, March 25, 1852).
43. *Letters,* I, 111, no. 42 (Emily to Austin Dickinson, June 8, 1851).
44. Leyda, *Years and Hours,* II, 18.
45. *Letters,* II, 486, no. 360 (Emily to Louise Norcross, spring 1871).
46. Ibid., I, 231, no. 108 (Emily to Austin Dickinson, March 18, 1853).
47. Ibid., I, 243, no. 116 (Emily to Austin Dickinson, April 16, 1853).
48. Ibid., I, 268, no. 139 (Emily to Austin Dickinson, November 8, 1853).
49. Leyda, *Years and Hours,* I, 248 (Lavinia Dickinson to Austin Dickinson, May 10, 1852).
50. *Letters,* I, 251, no. 125 (Emily to Austin Dickinson, June 5, 1853).
51. Leyda, *Years and Hours,* II, 142.
52. *Letters,* I, 65, no. 23 (Emily to Abiah Root, May 16, 1848).
53. Ibid., I, 190, no. 82 (Emily to Austin Dickinson, March 24, 1852).
54. Leyda, *Years and Hours,* I, 50.
55. Ibid.
56. Ibid., I, 56.
57. Ibid., I, 58.
58. Ibid., I, 62.
59. Ibid., I, 8.
60. Ibid., I, 30 (Edward Dickinson to his wife, September 7, 1835).
61. Ibid., I, 11.
62. Ibid., I, 3.
63. Ibid., I, 5.
64. Ibid., I, 6.
65. Ibid., I, 29.
66. *Letters,* I, 119, no. 45 (Emily to Austin Dickinson, June 29, 1851).
67. Leyda, *Years and Hours,* I, 14.
68. *Letters,* I, 152, no. 60 (Emily to Austin Dickinson, October 30, 1851).
69. Leyda, *Years and Hours,* I, 10 (Edward Dickinson to his wife, June 7, 1829).
70. Ibid., I, 10 (Lavinia Norcross to Mrs. Edward Dickinson, July 17, 1829).
71. Ibid., I, 4 (Edward Dickinson to Emily Norcross, April 29, 1828).
72. Ibid., I, 178.
73. *Letters,* II, 486, no. 360 (Emily to Louise Norcross, spring 1871).
74. Ibid., II, 551, no. 457 (Emily to T. W. Higginson, spring 1876).
75. Ibid., I, 277, no. 146 (Emily to Emily Fowler Ford, December 21, 1853).
76. Ibid., I, 210, no. 93 (Emily to Susan Gilbert, early June 1852).
77. Leyda, *Years and Hours,* I, 27 (Edward Dickinson to his wife, February 11, 1835).
78. Ibid., I, 52 (Mrs. Edward Dickinson to her husband, January 6, 1839).
79. Ibid., I, 52 (Edward Dickinson to his wife, January 8, 1839).
80. Ibid., I, 40 (Edward Dickinson to his wife, January 9, 1838).
81. Ibid., I, 87 (Edward Dickinson to Emily, June 4, 1844).
82. Ibid., I, 81 (Ann Sheperd to Mrs. C. M. Terry, September 15, 1843).
83. Ibid., I, 48 (Mrs. Edward Dickinson to her husband, April 3, 1838).

NOTES

84. Ibid., I, 40 (Edward Dickinson to his wife, January 9, 1838).
85. Ibid., I, 41 (Mrs. Edward Dickinson to her husband, January 12, 1838).
86. Ibid., I, 41 (Edward Dickinson to his wife, January 13, 1838).
87. Ibid., I, 41 (Edward Dickinson to his wife, January 17, 1838).
88. Ibid., I, 53 (Edward Dickinson to his wife, January 20, 1839).
89. Ibid., I, 47 (Edward Dickinson to his wife, March 18, 1838).
90. Ibid., I, 42 (Mrs. Edward Dickinson to her husband, January 21, 1838).
91. Ibid., I, 42-43 (Edward Dickinson to his wife, January 21, 1838).
92. Ibid., I, 24 (Lavinia Norcross to Edward Dickinson, April 5, 1834).
93. Ibid., I, 74 (Edward Dickinson to Austin Dickinson, April 14, 1842).
94. Rev. John S. C. Abbott, *The Mother at Home* (New York, American Tract Society, 1833), p. 5. Jay Leyda in *The Years and Hours of Emily Dickinson*, I, 23, says Edward Dickinson acquired the book in 1833.
95. Abbott, *Mother at Home*, p. 165.
96. *Letters*, I, 32, no. 11 (Emily to Abiah Root, March 28, 1846).
97. Abbott, *Mother at Home*, p. 122.
98. Ibid., p. 123.
99. Ibid., p. 125.
100. Ibid., p. 28.
101. Ibid., p. 30.
102. Ibid., p. 38.
103. Ibid., pp. 41-44.
104. Ibid., p. 121.
105. Ibid., p. 47.
106. *Letters*, III, 929 (prose fragment 117).
107. Abbott, *Mother at Home*, p. 148.
108. Ibid., p. 66.
109. Ibid., p. 158.
110. Ibid., p. 87.
111. Ibid., p. 88.
112. Ibid., p. 86.
113. Ibid., p. 68.
114. Ibid., p. 39.
115. Leyda, *Years and Hours*, I, 328.
116. Ibid., II, 224.
117. Austin Dickinson to Susan Gilbert, 1853. Unpublished letter in Box 7 of the Dickinson Family Papers, Houghton Library, Harvard University. Quoted by permission of the Harvard College Library.
118. Ibid.
119. Leyda, *Years and Hours*, II, 482.
120. Ibid., I, 291.
121. Ibid., II, 203.
122. Ibid., I, 48 (Edward Dickinson to his wife, late March 1838).
123. Ibid., I, 38 (Edward Dickinson to his wife, January 3, 1838).
124. Ibid., I, 40 (Edward Dickinson to his wife, January 9, 1838).
125. Ibid., I, 38 (Edward Dickinson to his wife, January 3, 1838).
126. Ibid., I, 44 (Edward Dickinson to his wife, February 16, 1838).
127. Ibid., I, 45 (Mrs. Edward Dickinson to her husband, February 20, 1838).
128. Ibid., I, 45-46 (Edward Dickinson to his wife, February 22, 1838).
129. Ibid., I, 38 (Edward Dickinson to his wife, January 3, 1838).
130. Ibid., I, 42 (Edward Dickinson to his children, January 17, 1838).
131. Ibid., I, 39 (Edward Dickinson to Lavinia Dickinson, January 5, 1838).

132. Ibid., I, 39 (Edward Dickinson to Emily, January 5, 1838).
133. Ibid., I, 42 (Edward Dickinson to Austin Dickinson, January 17, 1838).
134. Ibid., I, 86 (Edward Dickinson to Emily, May 19, 1844).
135. Ibid., I, 87 (Edward Dickinson to Emily, June 4, 1844).
136. Ibid., I, 43 (Edward Dickinson to his wife, January 21, 1838).
137. Ibid., I, 44 (Edward Dickinson to his wife, February 13, 1838).
138. Ibid., I, 44 (Mrs. Edward Dickinson to her husband, February 11, 1838).
139. *Letters*, II, 411, no. 268 (Emily to T. W. Higginson, July 1862).
140. Leyda, *Years and Hours*, II, 216 (Edward Dickinson to Austin Dickinson, January 20, 1874).
141. Ibid., I, 323.
142. *Letters*, I, 111, no. 42 (Emily to Austin Dickinson, June 8, 1851).
143. Ibid., I, 227, no. 106 (Emily to Austin Dickinson, March 12, 1853).
144. Ibid., II, 537, no. 432 (Emily to Mrs. J. G. Holland, late January 1875).
145. Ibid., II, 591, no. 518 (Emily to Harriet and Martha Dickinson, about 1877?).
146. Ibid., II, 404, no. 261 (Emily to T. W. Higginson, April 25, 1862).
147. Leyda, *Years and Hours*, II, 225.
148. Ibid., II, 226.
149. Ibid., II, 225.
150. Ibid., II, 227.
151. Letters, II, 526, no. 414 (Emily to Louise and Frances Norcross, summer 1874).
152. Ibid., II, 559, no. 471 (Emily to Louise and Frances Norcross, August 1876).
153. Ibid., II, 635, no. 593 (Emily to T. W. Higginson, February 1879).
154. Ibid., II, 404, no. 261 (Emily to T. W. Higginson, April 25, 1862).
155. Ibid., I, 10, no. 5 (Emily to Abiah Root, February 25, 1845).
156. Ibid., II, 528, no. 418 (Emily to T. W. Higginson, July 1874).
157. Bianchi, *Life and Letters*, p. 13.
158. Leyda, *Years and Hours*, I, 44 (Edward Dickinson to his wife, February 16, 1838).
159. *Letters*, I, 257, no. 128 (Emily to Austin Dickinson, June 19, 1853).
160. Ibid., II, 366, no. 223 (Emily to Samuel Bowles, early August 1860).
161. Ibid., I, 278, no. 148 (Emily to Austin Dickinson, December 27, 1853).
162. Ibid., III, 782, no. 833 (Emily to Mrs. J. G. Holland, summer 1883?).
163. Ibid., II, 404, no. 261 (Emily to T. W. Higginson, April 25, 1862).
164. Ibid., I, 245, no. 118 (Emily to Austin Dickinson, April 21, 1853).
165. Ibid., I, 239, no. 114 (Emily to Austin Dickinson, April 8, 1853).
166. Ibid., II, 508, no. 391 (Emily to Mrs. J. G. Holland, early summer 1873).
167. Ibid., III, 765, no. 807 (Emily to James D. Clark, mid March 1883).
168. Ibid., II, 617, no. 562 (Emily to Otis P. Lord, about 1878).
169. Ibid., III, 727, no. 750 (Emily to Otis P. Lord, April 30, 1882).

III. Of Shunning Men and Women

1. *Letters*, I, 6, no. 3 (Emily to Jane Humphrey, May 12, 1842).
2. Ibid., I, 18, no. 7 (Emily to Abiah Root, August 3, 1845).
3. Ibid., I, 7, no. 3 (Emily to Jane Humphrey, May 12, 1842).
4. Ibid., I, 9, no. 5 (Emily to Abiah Root, February 23, 1845).
5. Ibid., I, 22, no. 8 (Emily to Abiah Root, September 25, 1845).
6. Ibid., I, 38, no. 13 (Emily to Abiah Root, September 8, 1846).
7. Ibid., I, 90, no. 32 (Emily to Emily Fowler [Ford], early 1850?).

8. Ibid., I, 93-94, no. 35 (Emily to Jane Humphrey, April 3, 1850).

9. Ibid., I, 109, no. 40 (Emily to Emily Fowler [Ford], about 1851).

10. Ibid., I, 277, no. 146 (Emily to Emily Fowler [Ford], December 21, 1853).

11. Ibid., I, 14, no. 6 (Emily to Abiah Root, May 7, 1845).

12. Ibid., I, 16, no. 7 (Emily to Abiah Root, August 3, 1845).

13. Ibid., I, 34, no. 12 (Emily to Abiah Root, June 26, 1846).

14. Ibid., I, 38, no. 13 (Emily to Abiah Root, September 8, 1846).

15. Ibid., I, 59, no. 20 (Emily to Abiah Root, January 17, 1848).

16. Ibid., I, 71, no. 26 (Emily to Abiah Root, October 29, 1848).

17. Ibid., I, 84, no. 30 (Emily to Jane Humphrey, January 23, 1850).

18. Ibid., I, 105, no. 39 (Emily to Abiah Root, late 1850).

19. Ibid., I, 166, no. 69 (Emily to Abiah Root, about January 1852).

20. Ibid., I, 211, no. 94 (Emily to Susan Gilbert [Dickinson], June 11, 1852).

21. Ibid., II, 320, no. 180 (Emily to Jane Humphrey, October 16, 1855).

22. Ibid., I, 11, no. 5 (Emily to Abiah Root, February 23, 1845).

23. Ibid., I, 24, no. 9 (Emily to Abiah Root, January 12, 1846).

24. Ibid., I, 29, no. 10 (Emily to Abiah Root, January 31, 1846).

25. Ibid., I, 41, no. 14 (Emily to Abiah Root, late autumn 1846).

26. Ibid., I, 46, no. 15 (Emily to Abiah Root, March 14, 1847).

27. Ibid., I, 71, no. 26 (Emily to Abiah Root, October 29, 1848).

28. Ibid., I, 130, no. 50 (Emily to Abiah Root, August 19, 1851).

29. Ibid., I, 94, no. 35 (Emily to Jane Humphrey, April 3, 1850).

30. Ibid., I, 207, no. 91 (Emily to Abiah Root, about May 1852).

31. Ibid., I, 305, no. 173 (Emily to Susan Gilbert [Dickinson], about 1854).

32. Ibid., I, 104, no. 39 (Emily to Abiah Root, late 1850).

33. Ibid., II, 320, no. 180 (Emily to Jane Humphrey, October 16, 1855).

34. Ibid., I, 306, no. 173 (Emily to Susan Gilbert [Dickinson], about 1854.

35. Ibid., I, 128, no. 49 (Emily to Austin Dickinson, July 27, 1851).

36. Ibid., I, 9, no. 5 (Emily to Abiah Root, February 23, 1845).

37. Ibid., I, 17-18, no. 7 (Emily to Abiah Root, August 3, 1845).

38. Ibid., I, 23, 25, no. 9 (Emily to Abiah Root, January 12, 1846).

39. Ibid., I, 61, no. 21 (Emily to Austin Dickinson, February 15, 1848).

40. Ibid., I, 69, no. 25 (Emily to Austin Dickinson, June 25, 1848).

41. Ibid., I, 84, no. 30 (Emily to Jane Humphrey, January 23, 1850).

42. Ibid., I, 99, no. 36 (Emily to Abiah Root, May 7 and 17, 1850).

43. Ibid., I, 109, no. 40 (Emily to Emily Fowler [Ford], about 1851).

44. Ibid., I, 168-169, no. 70 (Emily to Susan Gilbert [Dickinson], January 21, 1852).

45. Ibid., I, 177, no. 74 (Emily to Susan Gilbert [Dickinson], about February 1852).

46. Ibid., I, 194-195, no. 85 (Emily to Susan Gilbert [Dickinson], April 5, 1852).

47. Ibid., I, 293-294, no. 161 (Emily to Emily Fowler [Ford], spring 1854).

48. Ibid., II, 321, no. 180 (Emily to Jane Humphrey, October 16, 1855).

49. Ibid., I, 63, no. 22 (Emily to Austin Dickinson, February 17, 1848).

50. Ibid., I, 102, no. 38 (Emily to Susan Gilbert [Dickinson], about December 1850).

51. Ibid., II, 430, no. 288 (Emily to Susan Gilbert [Dickinson], about 1864).

52. Ibid., I, 97-98, no. 36 (Emily to Abiah Root, May 7 and 17, 1850).

53. Ibid., I, 177, no. 74 (Emily to Susan Gilbert [Dickinson], about February 1852).

NOTES

54. Ibid., I, 174, no. 72 (Emily to Austin Dickinson, February 6, 1852).
55. Ibid., I, 183, no. 77 (Emily to Susan Gilbert [Dickinson], about February 1852).
56. Ibid., I, 214, no. 95 (Emily to Austin Dickinson, June 20, 1852).
57. Ibid., I, 210, no. 93 (Emily to Susan Gilbert [Dickinson], early June 1852).
58. Ibid., I, 211, no. 94 (Emily to Susan Gilbert [Dickinson], June 11, 1852).
59. Ibid., I, 241, no. 115 (Emily to Austin Dickinson, April 12, 1853).
60. Ibid., I, 229-230, no. 107 (Emily to Susan Gilbert [Dickinson], March 12, 1853).
61. Theodora Ward, *The Capsule of the Mind: Chapters in the Life of Emily Dickinson* (Cambridge, Mass., Harvard University Press, Belknap Press, 1961), pp. 45-46.
62. Ibid., p. 14.
63. *Letters,* I, 181, no. 77 (Emily to Susan Gilbert [Dickinson], about February 1852).
64. Ibid., II, 329-330, no. 185 (Emily to Mrs. J. G. Holland, early August 1856?).
65. Ibid., II, 373, no. 233 (Emily to an unknown recipient, about 1861).
66. Ibid., II, 449, no. 315 (Emily to Mrs. J. G. Holland, early March 1866).
67. Ibid., II, 491, no. 367 (Emily to Louise and Frances Norcross, October 1871).
68. Ibid., II, 622, no. 571 (Emily to Edward [Ned] Dickinson, about 1878).
69. Ibid., III, 738, no. 767 (Emily to T. W. Higginson, summer 1882).
70. Ibid., I, 57, no. 19 (Emily to Austin Dickinson, December 11, 1847).
71. Ibid., II, 463, no. 332 (Emily to Perez Cowan, October 1869).
72. Ibid., I, 103, no. 39 (Emily to Abiah Root, late 1850).
73. Ibid., I, 175, no. 73 (Emily to Susan Gilbert [Dickinson], February 6, 1852).
74. Ibid., I, 298, no. 166 (Emily to Abiah Root, about July 25, 1854).
75. Genevieve Taggard, *The Life and Mind of Emily Dickinson* (New York, Alfred A. Knopf, 1930).
76. *Letters,* II, 499, no. 379 (Emily to Louise Norcross, late 1872).
77. Ibid., II, 350, no. 204 (Emily to Mrs. J. G. Holland, March 2, 1859).
78. Ibid., II, 617, no. 562 (Emily to Otis P. Lord, about 1878).
79. Ibid., I, 58, no. 20 (Emily to Abiah Root, January 17, 1848).
80. Ibid., I, 62, no. 22 (Emily to Austin Dickinson, February 17, 1848).
81. Ibid., I, 146, no. 57 (Emily to Austin Dickinson, October 10, 1851).
82. Ibid., II, 475, no. 342b (T. W. Higginson to his wife, August 16, 1870).
83. Ibid., II, 460, no. 330 (Emily to T. W. Higginson, June 1869).
84. Ibid., II, 542, no. 441 (Emily to T. W. Higginson, July 1875).
85. Ibid., II, 548, no. 450 (Emily to T. W. Higginson, February 1876).
86. Ibid., II, 635, no. 593 (Emily to T. W. Higginson, February 1879).
87. Ibid., III, 664, no. 645 (Emily to Otis P. Lord, about 1880).
88. Ibid., I, 209-210, no. 93 (Emily to Susan Gilbert [Dickinson], early June 1852).
89. *Ibid.,* II, 315, no. 177 (Emily to Susan Gilbert [Dickinson], late January 1855).
90. Ibid., III, 753, no. 790 (Emily to Otis P. Lord, December 3, 1882).
91. Rebecca Patterson, *The Riddle of Emily Dickinson* (Boston, Houghton Mifflin, 1951).
92. *Letters,* I, 187, no. 80 (Emily to Austin Dickinson, March 7, 1852).

IV. The Bright Bee

1. *Letters,* II, 412, no. 268 (Emily to T. W. Higginson, July 1862).
2. Ibid., I, 257, no. 128 (Emily to Austin, June 19, 1853).
3. Ibid., I, 240, no. 114 (Emily to Austin, April 8, 1853).
4. Martha Dickinson Bianchi, *The Life and Letters of Emily Dickinson* (Boston, Houghton Mifflin, 1924), p. 13.
5. *Letters,* I, 4, no. 1 (Emily to Austin, May 1, 1842).
6. Ibid., I, 55, no. 18 (Emily to Abiah Root, November 6, 1847).
7. Ibid., I, 113, no. 43 (Emily to Austin, June 15, 1851).
8. Ibid., I, 118, no. 45 (Emily to Austin, June 29, 1851).
9. Ibid., I, 125, no. 48 (Emily to Austin, July 20, 1851).
10. Ibid., I, 137, no. 53 (Emily to Austin, October 1, 1851).
11. Ibid., I, 141, no. 54 (Emily to Austin, October 5, 1851).
12. Ibid., I, 143, no. 55 (Emily to Austin, October 7, 1851).
13. Ibid., I, 145-146, no. 57 (Emily to Austin, October 10, 1851).
14. Ibid., I, 150, no. 59 (Emily to Austin, October 25, 1851).
15. Ibid., II, 508, no. 391 (Emily to Mrs. J. G. Holland, early summer 1873).
16. Ibid., I, 155, no. 62 (Emily to Austin, November 11, 1851).
17. Ibid., I, 157-158, no. 63 (Emily to Austin, November 16, 1851).
18. Ibid., I, 160-161, no. 65 (Emily to Austin, December 15, 1851).
19. Ibid., I, 162, no. 66 (Emily to Austin, December 24, 1851).
20. Ibid., I, 170, no. 71 (Emily to Austin, January 28, 1852).
21. Ibid., I, 173, no. 72 (Emily to Austin, February 6, 1852).
22. Ibid., I, 225, no. 104 (Emily to Austin, March 8, 1853).
23. Ibid., I, 243, no. 116 (Emily to Austin, April 16, 1853).
24. Ibid., I, 248, no. 122 (Emily to Austin, May 7, 1853).
25. Ibid., I, 253-254, no. 127 (Emily to Austin, June 13, 1853).
26. Ibid., I, 276, no. 145 (Emily to Austin, December 20, 1853).
27. Ibid., I, 287, no. 156 (Emily to Austin, March 14, 1854).
28. Ibid.
29. Ibid., I, 289, no. 157 (Emily to Austin, March 16, 1854).
30. Ibid., I, 248, no. 122 (Emily to Austin, May 7, 1853).
31. Jay Leyda, *The Years and Hours of Emily Dickinson* (New Haven, Yale University Press, 1960), I, 288 (Austin to his sisters, December 6? 1853).
32. *Letters,* I, 240, no. 114 (Emily to Austin, April 8, 1853).
33. Ibid., II, 507, no. 390 (Emily to Frances Norcross, late May 1873).
34. Ibid., III, 742, no. 772 (Emily to Mrs. William F. Stearns, October 1882).
35. Ibid., III, 848-849, no. 949 (Emily to Susan, about 1884).
36. Ibid., I, 3, no. 1 (Emily to Austin, April 18, 1842).
37. Ibid., I, 174, no. 72 (Emily to Austin, February 6, 1852).
38. Ibid., I, 83, no. 30 (Emily to Jane Humphrey, January 23, 1850).
39. Ibid., I, 270, no. 141 (Emily to Austin, November 14, 1853).
40. Ibid., I, 8, no. 4 (Emily to Austin, summer 1844).
41. Ibid., I, 113, no. 43 (Emily to Austin, June 15, 1851).
42. Ibid., I, 290, no. 158 (Emily to Austin, March 19, 21, 1854).
43. Ibid., I, 161, no. 65 (Emily to Austin, December 15, 1851).
44. Ibid., I, 230-231, no. 108 (Emily to Austin, March 18, 1853).
45. Ibid., I, 286, no. 156 (Emily to Austin, March 14, 1854).
46. Ibid., I, 118, no. 45 (Emily to Austin, June 29, 1851).
47. Leyda, *Years and Hours,* II, 226 (eulogy to Edward Dickinson by J. L. Jenkins, June 28, 1874).
48. *Letters,* I, 237-238, no. 113 (Emily to Austin, April 2, 1853).

49. Ibid., I, 68, no. 24 (Emily to Austin, May 29, 1848).

50. Leyda, *Years and Hours*, II, 76 (Samuel Bowles to Austin, March 1863).

51. *Letters*, I, 100-101, no. 37 (Emily to Austin, October 27, 1850).

52. Ibid., I, 115, no. 44 (Emily to Austin, June 22, 1851).

53. Ibid., I, 231, no. 108 (Emily to Austin, March 18, 1853).

54. Ibid., I, 243, no. 116 (Emily to Austin, April 16, 1853).

55. Ibid., I, 117, no. 45 (Emily to Austin, June 29, 1851).

56. Ibid., I, 122, no. 46 (Emily to Austin, July 6, 1851).

57. Ibid., I, 200, no. 87 (Emily to Austin, April 21, 1852).

58. Ibid., I, 255, no. 127 (Emily to Austin, June 13, 1853).

59. Ibid., I, 300, no. 167 (Emily to Austin, summer 1854).

60. Ibid., I, 148, no. 58 (Emily to Austin, October 17, 1851).

61. Ibid., I, 113, no. 43 (Emily to Austin, June 15, 1851).

62. Leyda, *Years and Hours*, II, 30 (Samuel Bowles to Austin, July 8, 1861).

63. *Letters*, II, 426, no. 283 (Emily to Samuel Bowles, about 1863).

64. Ibid., II, 350, no. 204 (Emily to Mrs. J. G. Holland, March 2, 1859).

65. Ibid., II, 374, no. 233 (Emily to an unknown recipient, about 1861).

66. Ibid., II, 449, no. 315 (Emily to Mrs. J. G. Holland, early March 1866).

67. Ibid., II, 491, no. 367 (Emily to Louise and Frances Norcross, early October 1871).

68. Ibid., II, 366, no. 223 (Emily to Samuel Bowles, early August 1860).

69. Ibid., I, 309, no. 175 (Emily to Dr. and Mrs. J. G. Holland, about November 26, 1854).

70. Ibid., I, 140, no. 54 (Emily to Austin, October 5, 1851).

71. Ibid., I, 187, no. 80 (Emily to Austin, March 7, 1852).

72. Ibid., I, 235, no. 110 (Emily to Austin, March 27, 1853).

73. Leyda, *Years and Hours*, I, 171 (Emily Fowler to Austin, March 1850).

74. *Letters*, I, 98, no. 36 (Emily to Abiah Root, May 7 and 17, 1850).

75. Ibid., I, 67, no. 23 (Emily to Abiah Root, May 16, 1848).

76. Ibid., I, 27-28, no. 10 (Emily to Abiah Root, January 31, 1846).

77. Ibid., I, 30-31, no. 11 (Emily to Abiah Root, March 28, 1846).

78. Ibid., I, 82-83, no. 30 (Emily to Jane Humphrey, January 23, 1850).

79. Ibid., I, 86, no. 31 (Emily to Abiah Root, January 29, 1850).

80. Ibid., I, 309, no. 175 (Emily to Dr. and Mrs. J. G. Holland, about November 26, 1854).

81. Ibid., I, 87-89, no. 31 (Emily to Abiah Root, January 29, 1850).

82. Ibid., I, 5, no. 2 (Emily to Austin, May 1, 1842).

83. Ibid., I, 138, no. 53 (Emily to Austin, October 1, 1851).

84. Ibid., I, 158, no. 63 (Emily to Austin, November 16, 1851).

85. Ibid., I, 178-179, no. 76 (Emily to Austin, February 18, 1852).

86. Ibid., I, 132, no. 52 (Emily to Austin, September 23, 1851).

87. Ibid., I, 125, no. 48 (Emily to Austin, July 20, 1851).

88. Ibid., I, 150, no. 59 (Emily to Austin, October 25, 1851).

89. Ibid., I, 152, no. 60 (Emily to Austin, October 30, 1851).

90. Ibid., I, 155-156, no. 62 (Emily to Austin, November 11, 1951).

91. Ibid., I, 149, no. 58 (Emily to Austin, October 17, 1851).

92. Ibid., I, 113, no. 43 (Emily to Austin, June 15, 1851).

93. Ibid., I, 163, no. 66 (Emily to Austin, December 24, 1851).

94. Clark Griffith, *The Long Shadow: Emily Dickinson's Tragic Poetry* (Princeton, Princeton University Press, 1964) p. 180-181.

NOTES

V. The Earl, the Malay, and the Pearl

1. Jay Leyda, *The Years and Hours of Emily Dickinson* (New Haven, Yale University Press, 1960), II, 353 (Mabel Loomis Todd to her parents, October 2, 1881).
2. Ibid., I, 179 (Susan Gilbert to her brother Dwight, September 8? 1850).
3. Ibid., I, 266 (Austin to Martha Gilbert, March 27, 1853).
4. Ibid.
5. *Letters,* II, 546, no. 447 (Emily to Susan, about 1875).
6. Ibid., III, 659, no. 636 (Emily to Susan, spring 1880).
7. Ibid., I, 101, no. 38 (Emily to Susan, about December 1850).
8. Ibid., I, 168, no. 70 (Emily to Susan, January 21, 1852).
9. Ibid., I, 175, no. 73 (Emily to Susan, about February 6, 1852).
10. Ibid., I, 177, no. 74 (Emily to Susan, about February 1852).
11. Ibid., I, 181, no. 77 (Emily to Susan, about February 1852).
12. Ibid., I, 182, no. 77 (Emily to Susan, about February 1852).
13. Ibid., I, 184, no. 77 (Emily to Susan, about February 1852).
14. Ibid., I, 194, no. 85 (Emily to Susan, April 5, 1852).
15. Ibid., I, 208, no. 92 (Emily to Susan, about May 1852).
16. Ibid., I, 211, no. 94 (Emily to Susan, June 11, 1852).
17. Ibid., I, 102, no. 38 (Emily to Susan, about December 1850).
18. Parts published in Leyda, *Years and Hours,* I, 269 (Austin to Susan, April 7, 1853).
19. *Letters,* I, 168-169, no. 70 (Emily to Susan, January 21, 1852).
20. Ibid., I, 177, no. 74 (Emily to Susan, about February 1852).
21. Ibid., I, 203, no. 88 (Emily to Susan, late April 1852).
22. Ibid., I, 169, no. 70 (Emily to Susan, January 21, 1852).
23. Ibid., I, 175-176, no. 73 (Emily to Susan, about February 6, 1852).
24. Ibid., I, 177, no. 74 (Emily to Susan, about February 1852).
25. Ibid., I, 194, no. 85 (Emily to Susan, April 5, 1852).
26. Ibid., I, 201, no. 88 (Emily to Susan, late April 1852).
27. Ibid., I, 208, no. 92 (Emily to Susan, about May 1852).
28. Ibid., I, 210, no. 93 (Emily to Susan, early June 1852).
29. Ibid., I, 169, no. 70 (Emily to Susan, January 21, 1852).
30. Ibid., I, 241, no. 115 (Emily to Austin, April 12, 1853).
31. Ibid., I, 274, no. 144 (Emily to Austin, December 13, 1853).
32. Ibid., I, 211, no. 94 (Emily to Susan, June 11, 1852).
33. Ibid., I, 177, no. 74 (Emily to Susan, about February 1852).
34. Ibid., I, 193, no. 85 (Emily to Susan, April 5, 1852).
35. Ibid., I, 201, no. 88 (Emily to Susan, late April 1852).
36. Ibid., I, 202, no. 88 (Emily to Susan, late April 1852).
37. Ibid., I, 229, no. 107 (Emily to Susan, March 12, 1853).
38. Ibid., I, 175-176, no. 73 (Emily to Susan, about February 6, 1852).
39. Ibid., I, 182, no. 77 (Emily to Susan, about February 1852).
40. Ibid., I, 183, no. 77 (Emily to Susan, about February 1852).
41. Ibid., I, 203, no. 88 (Emily to Susan, late April 1852).
42. Ibid., I, 209, no. 93 (Emily to Susan, early June 1852).
43. Ibid., I, 210-211, no. 93 (Emily to Susan, early June 1852).
44. Ibid., I, 211, no. 94 (Emily to Susan, June 11, 1852).
45. Ibid., I, 215, no. 96 (Emily to Susan, June 27, 1852).
46. Ibid., I, 144, no. 56 (Emily to Susan, October 9, 1851).
47. Ibid., I, 175, no. 73 (Emily to Susan, about February 6, 1852).
48. Ibid., I, 195, no. 85 (Emily to Susan, April 5, 1852).

49. Ibid., I, 202, no. 88 (Emily to Susan, late April 1852).
50. Ibid., I, 210, no. 93 (Emily to Susan, early June 1852).
51. Ibid., I, 229, no. 107 (Emily to Susan, March 12, 1853).
52. Ibid.
53. Ibid., I, 215-216, no. 96 (Emily to Susan, June 27, 1852).
54. Ibid., I, 245, no. 118 (Emily to Austin, April 21, 1853).
55. Ibid., I, 248, no. 122 (Emily to Austin, May 7, 1853).
56. Leyda, *Years and Hours,* I, 257 (Jane Hitchcock to Ann Fiske, November 7, 1852).
57. Ibid., I, 259 (Susan to her brother Dwight, January 10, 1853).
58. Ibid., I, 259 (Susan to Edward Hitchcock, Jr., January 13, 1853).
59. *Letters,* I, 218, no. 98 (Emily to Emily Fowler, about January 13, 1853).
60. Ibid., I, 221, no. 102 (Emily to Susan, February 24, 1853).
61. Ibid., I, 222-224, no. 103 (Emily to Susan, March 5, 1853).
62. Leyda, *Years and Hours,* I, 262 (Austin to Susan, March 11, 1853).
63. *Letters,* I, 229, no. 107 (Emily to Susan, March 12, 1853).
64. Ibid., I, 233, no. 109 (Emily to Austin, March 24, 1853).
65. Leyda, *Years and Hours,* I, 272 (Austin to Susan, April 24? 1853).
66. *Letters,* I, 254, no. 127 (Emily to Austin, June 13, 1853).
67. Ibid., I, 270, no. 141 (Emily to Austin, November 14, 1853).
68. Leyda, *Years and Hours,* I, 268 (Austin to Susan, April 2, 1853).
69. Ibid., I, 269 (Austin to Susan, April 3, 1853).
70. Ibid., I, 269 (Susan to her brother Dwight, April 5, 1853).
71. Ibid., I, 269-270 (Austin to Susan, April 7, 1853).
72. Ibid., I, 293 (Austin to Susan, early January? 1854).
73. Ibid., I, 272 (Lavinia to Austin, June 16, 1853).
74. Ibid., I, 273 (Lavinia to Austin, May 6, 1853).
75. *Letters,* I, 258-259, no. 129 (Emily to Austin, June 26, 1853).
76. Ibid., I, 259, no. 129 (Emily to Austin, June 26, 1853).
77. Ibid., I, 253, no. 126 (Emily to Austin, June 9, 1853).
78. Ibid., I, 242, no. 115 (Emily to Austin, April 12, 1853).
79. Ibid., I, 260, no. 130 (Emily to Austin, July 1, 1853).
80. Ibid., I, 174, no. 72 (Emily to Austin, February 6, 1852).
81. Ibid., I, 176, no. 73 (Emily to Susan, about February 6, 1852).
82. Ibid., I, 272, no. 142 (Emily to Austin, November 21, 1853).
83. Ibid., I, 273-274, no. 144 (Emily to Austin, December 13, 1853).
84. Ibid., I, 277, no. 146 (Emily to Emily Fowler Ford, December 21, 1853).
85. Ibid., I, 283-284, no. 154 (Emily to Susan, January 15, 1854).
86. Leyda, *Years and Hours,* I, 293-294 (Susan to her brother Francis, January 6, 1854).
87. Ibid., I, 184-185 (Austin to Susan, Deember 11, 1850).
88. *Letters,* I, 299-300, no. 167 (Emily to Austin, summer 1854).
89. Leyda, *Years and Hours,* I, 253 (Lavinia to Austin, July 8, 1852).
90. Ibid., I, 318 (Susan to Edward Hitchcock, Jr., late September 1854).
91. Ibid., I, 311 (Susan to her brother Dwight, August 13, 1854).
92. *Letters,* I, 298, no. 166 (Emily to Abiah Root, about July 25, 1854).
93. Ibid., I, 304-305, no. 172 (Emily to Susan, late August 1854).
94. Leyda, *Years and Hours,* I, 316 (Austin to Susan, September 23, 1854).
95. Ibid., I, 323 (Susan to Mrs. Bartlett, mid-December? 1854).
96. *Letters,* I, 305-306, no. 173 (Emily to Susan, about 1854).
97. Ibid., I, 310, no. 176 (Emily to Susan, November 27-December 3, 1854).
98. Ibid., II, 315, no. 177 (Emily to Susan, late January 1855).

99. Ibid., II, 317, no. 178 (Emily to Susan, February 28, 1855).

100. Ibid., II, 319, no. 179 (Emily to Mrs. J. G. Holland, March 18, 1855).

101. Ibid., 320-321, no. 180 (Emily to Jane Humphrey, October 16, 1855).

102. Leyda, *Years and Hours*, I, 332 (Susan to Francis and Dwight Gilbert, mid May? 1855).

103. *Letters*, II, 404, no. 261 (Emily to T. W. Higginson, April 25, 1862).

104. Ibid., II, 323-324, no. 182 (Emily to Mrs. J. G. Holland, about January 20, 1856).

105. Ibid., I, 98, no. 36 (Emily to Abiah Root, May 7 and 14, 1850).

106. Ibid., II, 327-328, no. 184 (Emily to John C. Graves, late April 1856).

107. Ibid., II, 325-326, no. 183 (Emily to Mary Warner, about April 20, 1856).

108. Leyda, *Years and Hours*, I, 342 (Susan to Rev. and Mrs. S. C. Bartlett, May 19, 1856).

109. *Letters*, II, 329, no. 185 (Emily to Mrs. J. G. Holland, early August 1856?).

110. Richard B. Sewall, *The Lyman Letters: New Light on Emily Dickinson and Her Family* (Amherst, University of Massachusetts Press, 1965), p. 34.

111. Ibid., p. 55.

112. Ibid., p. 33.

113. Ibid., p. 36.

114. Ibid., p. 35.

115. *Letters*, II, 430, no. 288 (Emily to Susan, about 1864).

116. Ibid., I, 310, no. 176 (Emily to Susan, November 27-December 3, 1854).

VI. A Porcelain Life

1. *Letters*, I, 32, no. 11 (Emily to Abiah Root, March 28, 1846).

2. Ibid., I, 21, no. 8 (Emily to Abiah Root, September 25, 1845).

3. Ibid., I, 36, no. 13 (Emily to Abiah Root, September 8, 1846).

4. Ibid., I, 157, no. 63 (Emily to Austin, November 16, 1851).

5. Ibid., I, 255, no. 128 (Emily to Austin, June 19, 1853).

6. Ibid., I, 16, no. 7 (Emily to Abiah Root, August 3, 1845).

7. Ibid., I, 31, no. 11 (Emily to Abiah Root, March 28, 1846).

8. Ibid., II, 338, no. 193 (Emily to Samuel Bowles, late August 1858?).

9. Ibid., I, 229, no. 107 (Emily to Susan, March 12, 1853).

10. Ibid., I, 255, no. 128 (Emily to Austin, June 19, 1853).

11. Ibid., I, 264, no. 133 (Emily to Dr. and Mrs. J. G. Holland, autumn 1853).

12. Ibid., II, 319, no. 179 (Emily to Mrs. J. G. Holland, March 18, 1855).

13. Ibid., II, 334, no. 189 (Emily to Mr. and Mrs. Samuel Bowles, about June 1858).

14. Ibid., II, 337, no. 192 (Emily to Mrs. Joseph Haven, late August 1858).

15. Ibid., II, 365, no. 222 (Emily to Kate Anthon, summer 1860?).

16. Ibid., II, 384, no. 243 (Emily to Edward S. Dwight, December 1861).

17. Ibid., II, 389, no. 246 (Emily to Edward S. Dwight, January 2, 1862).

18. Ibid., I, 167, no. 69 (Emily to Abiah Root, about January 1852).

19. Ibid., I, 162, no. 66 (Emily to Austin, December 24, 1851).

20. Ibid., I, 36-38, no. 13 (Emily to Abiah Root, September 8, 1846).

21. Ibid., I, 57, no. 19 (Emily to Austin, December 11, 1847).

22. Ibid., I, 76, no. 27 (Emily to William Cowper Dickinson, February 14, 1849).

23. Ibid., I, 84, no. 30 (Emily to Jane Humphrey, January 23, 1850).

24. Ibid., I, 138, no. 53 (Emily to Austin, October 1, 1852).

25. Ibid., I, 197, no. 86 (Emily to Jane Humphrey, about April 1852).

26. Ibid., II, 423, no. 280 (Emily to T. W. Higginson, February 1863).
27. Ibid., I, 102, no. 39 (Emily to Abiah Root, late 1850).
28. Ibid., I, 236, no. 110 (Emily to Austin, March 27, 1853).
29. Ibid., I, 283, no. 153 (Emily to Edward Everett Hale, January 13, 1854).
30. Ibid., II, 397, no. 255 (Emily to Louise and Frances Norcross, late March 1862).
31. Ibid., II, 406, no. 263 (Emily to Louise Norcross, early May 1862).
32. Ibid., III, 713, no. 731 (Emily to Mrs. J. G. Holland, October 1881).
33. Ibid., III, 738, no. 766 (Emily to James D. Clark, August 1882).
34. Ibid., III, 778, no. 826 (Emily to Charles H. Clark, early June 1883).
35. Ibid., III, 779, no. 828 (Emily to Charles H. Clark, mid June 1883).
36. Ibid., III, 885, no. 1009 (Emily to William S. Jackson, mid August 1885).
37. Ibid., III, 890, no. 1018 (Emily to Forrest F. Emerson, late September 1885).
38. Ibid., I, 285, no. 154 (Emily to Susan, January 15, 1854).
39. Ibid., II, 317, no. 178 (Emily to Susan, February 28, 1855).
40. Ibid., II, 354, no. 207 (Emily to Dr. and Mrs. J. G. Holland, September 1859).
41. Ibid., II, 340, no. 184 (Emily to Susan, September 26, 1858).
42. Ibid., II, 346-347, no. 200 (Emily to Mrs. Joseph Haven, February 13, 1859).
43. Millicent Todd Bingham, *Emily Dickinson's Home* (New York, Harper and Brothers, 1855), pp. 179-180.
44. *Letters*, I, 24, no. 9 (Emily to Abiah Root, January 12, 1846).
45. Ibid., II, 475, no. 342b (T. W. Higginson to his wife, August 16, 1870).
46. René A. Spitz, "Hospitalism: An Inquiry into the Genesis of Psychiatric Conditions in Early Childhood," *The Psychoanalytic Study of the Child*, I (1845), 53-74.
47. *Letters*, I, 78-80, no. 29 (Emily to Joel Warren Norcross, January 11, 1850).
48. Ibid., I, 83, no. 30 (Emily to Jane Humphrey, January 23, 1850).
49. Ibid., I, 264, no. 133 (Emily to Dr. and Mrs. J. G. Holland, autumn 1853).
50. Ibid., I, 124-125, no. 48 (Emily to Austin, July 20, 1851).
51. Ibid., I, 144, no. 56 (Emily to Susan, October 9, 1851).
52. Ibid., I, 113, no. 43 (Emily to Austin, June 15, 1851).
53. Ibid., I, 182, no. 77 (Emily to Susan, about February 1852).
54. Ibid., I, 48, no. 16 (Emily to Austin, October 21, 1847).
55. Ibid., I, 131, no. 50 (Emily to Abiah Root, August 19, 1851).
56. Ibid., I, 141, no. 54 (Emily to Austin, October 5, 1851).
57. Ibid., I, 181, no. 77 (Emily to Susan, about February 1852).
58. Ibid., I, 254, no. 127 (Emily to Austin, June 13, 1853).
59. Ibid., I, 271, no. 141 (Emily to Austin, November 14, 1853).
60. Ibid., I, 283, no. 154 (Emily to Susan, January 15, 1854).
61. Ibid., I, 291, no. 159 (Emily to Austin, March 26, 1854).
62. Ibid., I, 298, no. 166 (Emily to Abiah Root, about July 25, 1854).
63. Ibid., II, 345, no. 199 (Emily to Louise Norcross, about January 4, 1859).
64. Ibid., II, 348, no. 202 (Emily to Mrs. J. G. Holland, about February 20, 1859).
65. Ibid., II, 367, no. 225 (Emily to Louise and Frances Norcross, mid September 1860).
66. Ibid., II, 386, no. 245 (Emily to Louise Norcross, December 31, 1861).
67. Ibid., II, 407, no. 264 (Emily to Louise and Frances Norcross, late May 1862).

68. Ibid., II, 419, no. 277 (Emily to Samuel Bowles, late November 1862).
69. Ibid., II, 419, no. 276 (Emily to Samuel Bowles, late November 1862).
70. Ibid., II, 589, no. 515 (Emily to Samuel Bowles, about 1877).
71. Ibid., III, 771, no. 815 (Emily to Maria Whitney, spring 1883).
72. Ibid., II, 452, no. 318 (Emily to Mrs. J. G. Holland, early May 1866).
73. Ibid., II, 473, no. 342a (T. W. Higginson to his wife, August 16, 1870).
74. Ibid., II, 336, no. 190 (Emily to Joseph A. Sweetser, early summer 1858).
75. Ibid., III, 758, no. 798 (Emily to Joseph K. Chickering, early 1883).
76. Ibid., III, 847, no. 946 (Emily to Mr. and Mrs. E. J. Loomis, autumn 1884).
77. Ibid., III, 793, no. 860 (Emily to Maria Whitney, summer 1883).
78. Ibid., III, 914 (prose fragment 21).
79. Ibid., III, 926 (prose fragment 99).
80. Ibid., III, 858, no. 965 (Emily to an unknown recipient, early 1885).
81. Sigmund Freud, *Civilization and Its Discontents*, vol. XXI in The Standard Edition of the Complete Psychological Works of Sigmund Freud (London, Hogarth Press, 1961), pp. 64-65, 72.
82. *Letters*, I, 31, no. 11 (Emily to Abiah Root, March 28, 1846).
83. Ibid., I, 104, no. 39 (Emily to Abiah Root, late 1850).
84. Ibid., I, 167, no. 69 (Emily to Abiah Root, about January 1852).
85. Ibid., II, 333, no. 187 (Emily to an unknown recipient, about 1858).
86. Ibid., II, 354, no. 207 (Emily to Dr. and Mrs. J. G. Holland, September 1859).
87. Ibid., II, 356, no. 209 (Emily to Kate Anthon, late 1859?).
88. Ibid., II, 361, no. 216 (Emily to Mrs. Samuel Bowles, 1860?).
89. Ibid., II, 363, no. 219 (Emily to Samuel Bowles, about 1860).
90. Ibid., II, 364, no. 221 (Emily to Susan Phelps, May 1860).
91. Ibid., II, 390, no. 247 (Emily to Samuel Bowles, about January 11, 1862).
92. Ibid., II, 392, no. 248 (Emily to an unknown recipient, early 1862?).
93. Ibid., II, 393, no. 249 (Emily to Samuel Bowles, early 1862).
94. Ibid., II, 434, no. 294 (Emily to Susan, September 1864).
95. Ibid., II, 441, no. 306 (Emily to Susan, about March 1865).
96. Ibid., II, 446, no. 312 (Emily to Susan, early December 1865).
97. Ibid., II, 454, no. 319 (Emily to T. W. Higginson, June 9, 1866).
98. Ibid., II, 503, no. 386 (Emily to Perez Cowan, about February 1873).
99. Ibid., III, 750, no. 785 (Emily to Louise and Frances Norcross, late November 1882).
100. Ibid., III, 799, no. 868 (Emily to Susan, early October 1883).
101. Ibid., II, 474, no. 342a (T. W. Higginson to his wife, August 16, 1870).
102. Ibid., II, 614-615, no. 559 (Emily to Otis P. Lord, about 1878).
103. Ibid., III, 794, no. 860 (Emily to Maria Whitney, summer 1883).
104. Ibid., III, 745, no. 776 (Emily to James D. Clark, late 1882).
105. Ibid., III, 817, no. 891 (Emily to Louise and Frances Norcross, late March 1884).
106. Ibid., III, 876, no. 989 (Emily to Joseph K. Chickering, July 1885).
107. Ibid., II, 512, no. 397 (Emily to Susan, autumn 1873).
108. Ibid., III, 817, no. 891 (Emily to Louise and Frances Norcross, late March 1884).
109. Ibid., II, 459, no. 328 (Emily to Susan, about 1868).
110. Ibid., III, 830, no. 912 (Emily to Susan, about 1884).
111. Ibid., II, 631, no. 581 (Emily to Susan, about 1878).
112. Ibid., II, 351, no. 204 (Emily to Mrs. J. G. Holland, March 2, 1859).

NOTES

113. Ibid., II, 424, no. 281 (Emily to Louise and Frances Norcross, late May 1863).
114. Jay Leyda, *The Years and Hours of Emily Dickinson* (New Haven, Yale University Press, 1960), I, 97 (Emily Fowler to Francis A. March, October 1, 1845).
115. Ibid., I, 94 (Mary Shepard to Lucius Boltwood, July 25, 1845).
116. *Letters*, III, 775, no. 823 (Emily to Mrs. J. Howard Sweetser, early May 1883).

VII. A Plank in Reason

1. *Letters*, II, 424, no. 281 (Emily to Louise and Frances Norcross, late May 1863).
2. Ibid., II, 581, no. 501 (Emily to Mrs. Jonathan L. Jenkins, late May 1877).
3. Ibid., II, 594, no. 522 (Emily to T. W. Higginson, early autumn 1877).
4. Ibid., II, 500, no. 380 (Emily to Louise Norcross, late 1872).
5. Ibid., III, 919 (prose fragment 49).
6. Paul Federn, *Ego Psychology and the Psychoses* (New York, Basic Books, 1952), pp. 40, 41.
7. Marguerite Sechehaye, *Autobiography of a Schizophrenic Girl* (New York, Grune and Stratton, 1951), pp. 110-115.
8. Ibid., p. 7.
9. Federn, *Ego Psychology*, p. 229.
10. *Letters*, II, 474, no. 342a (T. W. Higginson to his wife, August 16, 1870).
11. Ibid., II, 404, no. 261 (Emily to T. W. Higginson, April 25, 1862).
12. Ibid.
13. Lara Jefferson, "I Am Crazy Wild This Minute. How Can I Learn to Think Straight?" in *The Inner World of Mental Illness*, ed. Bert Kaplan (New York, Harper and Row, 1964), p. 30.
14. *Letters*, II, 611, no. 553 (Emily to T. W. Higginson, early June 1878).
15. Ibid., III, 922 (prose fragment 67).
16. Ibid., III, 927 (prose fragment 105).
17. Jefferson, "I Am Crazy Wild This Minute," pp. 8, 34.
18. *Letters*, II, 565, no. 476c (Helen Hunt to Emily Dickinson, 1876).
19. Clark Griffith, *The Long Shadow: Emily Dickinson's Tragic Poetry* (Princeton, Princeton University Press, 1964), p. 208.
20. *Letters*, II, 377, no. 235 (Emily to Mrs. Samuel Bowles, about August 1861).
21. Theodora Ward, *The Capsule of the Mind: Chapters in the Life of Emily Dickinson* (Cambridge, Mass., Harvard University Press, Belknap Press, 1961), p. 55.
22. "An Autobiography of a Schizophrenic Experience," *Journal of Abnormal and Social Psychology*, 51 (November 1955), 677-689. Quotations from this article are identified by page number in the text.
23. Jay Leyda, *The Years and Hours of Emily Dickinson* (New Haven, Yale University Press, 1960), I, xxx.

VIII. Mansions of Mirage

1. *Letters*, II, 335, no. 190 (Emily to Joseph A. Sweetser, early summer 1858).
2. Ibid., II, 338, no. 193 (Emily to Samuel Bowles, late August 1858?).
3. Ibid., II, 339, no. 194 (Emily to Susan, September 26, 1858).
4. Ibid., II, 341, no. 195 (Emily to Dr. and Mrs. J. G. Holland, about November 6, 1858).

518

5. Ibid., II, 350, no. 204 (Emily to Mrs. J. G. Holland, March 2, 1859).

6. Ibid., II, 360, no. 215 (Emily to Louise Norcross, March 1860).

7. Jay Leyda, *The Years and Hours of Emily Dickinson* (New Haven, Yale University Press, 1960), II, 19 (Jane Hitchcock to her brother Edward, December 7, 1860).

8. *Letters*, II, 373, no. 233 (Emily to an unknown recipient, about 1861); and II, 391, no. 248 (Emily to an unknown recipient, early 1862?).

9. Ibid., II, 377, no. 235 (Emily to Mrs. Samuel Bowles, about August 1861).

10. Leyda, *Years and Hours*, II, 38 (Susan to Emily, late October? 1861).

11. *Letters*, II, 404, no. 261 (Emily to T. W. Higginson, April 25, 1862).

12. Ibid., II, 430, no. 288 (Emily to Susan, about 1864).

13. Martha Dickinson Bianchi, *Emily Dickinson Face to Face: Unpublished Letters with Notes and Reminiscences by Her Niece* (Boston, Houghton Mifflin, 1932), p. 165.

14. *Letters*, II, 380, no. 238 (Emily to Susan, summer 1861).

15. Ibid., II, 592, no. 520 (Emily to Jonathan L. Jenkins, September 1877).

16. Ibid., II, 385, no. 244 (Emily to Mrs. Samuel Bowles, about December 20, 1861).

17. Ibid., II, 396, no. 253 (Emily to Mrs. Samuel Bowles, early March 1862).

18. Ibid., II, 386, no. 245 (Emily to Louise Norcross, December 31, 1861).

19. Ibid., II, 403, no. 260 (Emily to T. W. Higginson, April 15, 1862).

20. Ibid., II, 406, no. 262 (Emily to Mrs. Samuel Bowles, spring 1862).

21. Ibid., II, 373-374, no. 233 (Emily to an unknown recipient, about 1861).

22. Ibid., II, 391-392, no. 248 (Emily to an unknown recipient, early 1862?).

23. Clark Griffith, *The Long Shadow: Emily Dickinson's Tragic Poetry* (Princeton, Princeton University Press, 1964), pp. 149-151.

24. Richard Chase, *Emily Dickinson* (New York, William Sloan, 1951), p. 242.

25. Henry W. Wells, *Introduction to Emily Dickinson* (Chicago, Packard and Co., 1947), p. 240.

26. Charles R. Anderson, *Emily Dickinson's Poetry: Stairway of Surprise* (New York, Holt, Rinehart and Winston, 1960), p. 169.

27. Griffith, *The Long Shadow*, pp. 154, 155.

28. Chase, *Emily Dickinson*, p. 140.

29. Wells, *Introduction to Emily Dickinson*, pp. 239, 240, 244.

30. Anderson, *Emily Dickinson's Poetry*, p. 190.

31. Griffith, *The Long Shadow*, p. 162.

32. Chase, *Emily Dickinson*, pp. 158, 159.

33. Ibid., p. 243.

34. Anderson, *Emily Dickinson's Poetry*, p. 168.

35. Ibid., p. 179.

36. Rebecca Patterson, *The Riddle of Emily Dickinson* (Boston, Houghton Mifflin, 1951).

37. Yvor Winters, "Emily Dickinson and the Limits of Judgment," in *Emily Dickinson: A Collection of Critical Essays*, ed. Richard B. Sewall (Englewood Cliffs, N.J., Prentice-Hall, 1963), p. 40.

38. Thomas H. Johnson, *Emily Dickinson: An Interpretive Biography* (Cambridge, Mass., Harvard University Press, Belknap Press, 1963), pp. 79, 80.

39. *Letters*, II, 392, no. 248 (Emily to an unknown recipient, early 1862?).

40. *Letters*, II, 374, no. 233 (Emily to an unknown recipient, about 1861).

41. Thomas H. Johnson, ed., *The Poems of Emily Dickinson* (Cambridge, Mass., Harvard University Press, Belknap Press, 1963), I, 180.

42. *Letters*, II, 424, no. 281 (Emily to Louise and Frances Norcross, late May 1863).

43. Helene Deutsch, *The Psychology of Women* (New York, Grune and Stratton, 1944), I, 124-125.

44. Silvano Arieti, ed., *American Handbook of Psychiatry* (New York, Basic Books, 1959), I, 551.

45. George F. Whicher, *This Was a Poet* (Philadelphia, Albert Saifer, 1952), p. 271.

46. *Letters*, II, 398, no. 256 (Emily to Samuel Bowles, late March 1862).

47. Ibid., II, 424, no. 281 (Emily to Louise and Frances Norcross, late May 1863).

48. Ibid., II, 434, no. 294 (Emily to Susan, September 1864).

49. Ibid., II, 441, no. 306 (Emily to Susan, about March 1865).

50. Leyda, *Years and Hours*, I, 342 (Susan to Mrs. Ford, June 7, 1856).

51. *Letters*, II, 404, no. 261 (Emily to T. W. Higginson, April 25, 1862).

IX. Sunset at Easter

1. Charles R. Anderson, *Emily Dickinson's Poetry: Stairway of Surprise* (New York, Holt, Rinehart and Winston, 1960), pp. 172-176.

2. Thomas H. Johnson, *Emily Dickinson: An Interpretive Biography* (Cambridge, Mass., Harvard University Press, Belknap Press, 1963), pp. 138-140.

3. Louise Bogan, "A Mystical Poet," in *Emily Dickinson: A Collection of Critical Essays*, ed. Richard B. Sewall (Englewood Cliffs, N.J., Prentice-Hall, 1963), p. 142.

4. *Letters*, III, 929 (prose fragment 117).

5. Ibid., II, 412, no. 268 (Emily to T. W. Higginson, July 1862).

6. Ibid., II, 429, note to no. 287.

7. Ibid., II, 431, no. 290 (Emily to T. W. Higginson, early June 1864).

8. Ibid., II, 514, no. 400 (Emily to Louise and Frances Norcross, 1873?).

9. Ibid., II, 431, no. 290 (Emily to T. W. Higginson, early June 1864).

10. Ibid.

11. Ibid., II, 432, no. 292 (Emily to Susan, June 1864).

12. Ibid., II, 433, no. 293 (Emily to Lavinia, June 1864).

13. Ibid., II, 434, no. 294 (Emily to Susan, September 1864).

14. Ibid., II, 434, no. 295 (Emily to Lavinia, about 1864).

15. Ibid., II, 436, no. 297 (Emily to Lavinia, November 13, 1864).

16. Ibid., II, 438, no. 301 (Emily to Louise Norcross, early 1865).

17. Ibid., II, 439, no. 302 (Emily to Louise Norcross, early 1865).

18. Richard B. Sewall, *The Lyman Letters: New Light on Emily Dickinson and Her Family* (Amherst, University of Massachusetts Press, 1965), p. 76.

19. *Letters*, II, 440, no. 304 (Emily to Louise Norcross, March 1865).

20. Ibid., II, 443, no. 309 (Emily to Lavinia, May 1865).

21. Ibid., II, 443, no. 308 (Emily to Lavinia, mid May 1865).

22. Ibid., II, 450, no. 316 (Emily to T. W. Higginson, early 1866).

23. Ibid, II, 438-439, no. 302 (Emily to Louise Norcross, early 1865).

24. Ibid., II, 404, no. 261 (Emily to T. W. Higginson, April 25, 1862).

25. Ibid., II, 644, no. 610 (Emily to Louise and Frances Norcross, early July 1879).

26. Ibid., II, 404, no. 261 (Emily to T. W. Higginson, April 25, 1862).

27. Ibid., I, 161, no. 65 (Emily to Austin, December 15, 1851).

28. Ibid., II, 542, no. 441 (Emily to T. W. Higginson, July 1875).

29. Ibid., II, 591, no. 518 (Emily to Harriet and Martha Dickinson, about 1877?).

30. Ibid., II, 486, no. 360 (Emily to Louise Norcross, spring 1871).

31. Ibid., I, 210, no. 93 (Emily to Susan, early June 1852).

32. Ibid., I, 148, no. 58 (Emily to Austin, October 17, 1851).

33. Ibid., II, 528, no. 418 (Emily to T. W. Higginson, July 1874).

34. Ibid., II, 415, no. 271 (Emily to T. W. Higginson, August 1862).

35. Ibid., II, 412, no. 268 (Emily to T. W. Higginson, July 1862).

X. Our Practical Sister

1. Jay Leyda, *The Years and Hours of Emily Dickinson* (New Haven, Yale University Press, 1960), II, 375 (Mrs. Todd quotes Lavinia's note in an interview with Millicent Todd Bingham, 1931; Leyda dates the note early September? 1882).

2. Ibid., II, 411 (Mrs. Todd's Journal, November 11, 1883).

3. *Letters*, III, 802, no. 873 (Emily to Mrs. J. G. Holland, late 1883).

4. Ibid., III, 827, no. 907 (Emily to Louise and Frances Norcross, early August 1884).

5. Leyda, *Years and Hours*, II, 454 (Susan Dickinson to her son Ned, August 1, 1885).

6. Millicent Todd Bingham, *Ancestors' Brocades: The Literary Debut of Emily Dickinson* (New York, Harper and Brothers, 1945), p. 358.

7. Ibid., p. 22.

8. Richard B. Sewall, *The Lyman Letters: New Light on Emily Dickinson and Her Family* (Amherst, University of Massachusetts Press, 1965), p. 39.

9. Ibid., pp. 50-51.

10. Ibid., pp. 42-43.

11. Ibid., pp. 45-46.

12. Ibid., p. 42.

13. Ibid., pp. 51, 52.

14. Bingham, *Ancestors' Brocades,* p. 66.

15. Ibid., p. 12.

16. *Letters,* I, 110-111, no. 42 (Emily to Austin, June 8, 1851).

17. Millicent Todd Bingham, *Emily Dickinson's Home* (New York, Harper and Brothers, 1955), pp. 88-89.

18. Ibid., p. 202.

19. Ibid., p. 191.

20. Ibid., p. 203.

21. *Letters*, I, 174, no. 72 (Emily to Austin, February 6, 1852).

22. Bingham, *Emily Dickinson's Home,* pp. 148, 149.

23. Ibid., p. 237.

24. *Letters*, I, 63, no. 22 (Emily to Austin, February 17, 1848).

25. Ibid., I, 191, no. 83 (Emily to Austin, March 30, 1852).

26. Anna Freud and Dorothy T. Burlingham, *Infants Without Families* (New York, International University Press, 1944), p. 28.

27. *Letters*, II, 508, no. 391 (Emily to Mrs. J. G. Holland, early summer 1873).

28. Freud and Burlingham, *Infants Without Families,* p. 28.

29. Sewall, *The Lyman Letters,* p. 34.

30. Ibid., pp. 52, 53.

31. Bingham, *Ancestors' Brocades,* p. 8.

32. Ibid., p. 10.

NOTES

33. Ibid.
34. Bingham, *Emily Dickinson's Home*, p. 238.
35. Ibid., p. 282.
36. Bingham, *Ancestors' Brocades*, p. 28.
37. Ibid., p. 6.
38. Bingham, *Emily Dickinson's Home*, p. 90.
39. Ibid., p. 211.
40. *Letters*, I, 227, no. 106 (Emily to Austin, March 12, 1853).
41. Bingham, *Emily Dickinson's Home*, p. 358.
42. Ibid., pp. 268-269.
43. Ibid., pp. 238-239.
44. Ibid., p. 249.
45. Bingham, *Ancestors' Brocades*, p. 233.
46. *Letters*, II, 404, no. 261 (Emily to T. W. Higginson, April 25, 1862).
47. Leyda, *Years and Hours*, I, 216.
48. Ibid., I, 198.
49. Ibid., I, 199.
50. *Letters*, I, 134, no. 52 (Emily to Austin, September 23, 1851).
51. Ibid., II, 604, no. 542 (Emily to Mrs. J. G. Holland, early 1878).
52. Leyda, *Years and Hours*, II, 466.
53. Ibid., II, 451.
54. Martha Dickinson Bianchi, *The Life and Letters of Emily Dickinson* (Boston, Houghton Mifflin, 1924), p. 13.
55. Sewall, *The Lyman Letters*, p. 14.
56. Bingham, *Emily Dickinson's Home*, p. 234.
57. *Letters*, I, 213, no. 95 (Emily to Austin, June 20, 1852).
58. Ibid., II, 633, no. 589 (Emily to Mrs. J. G. Holland, early January 1879).
59. Ibid., III, 676, no. 667 (Emily to Mrs. J. G. Holland, about September 1880).
60. Ibid., III, 693, no. 692 (Emily to Mrs. J. G. Holland, spring 1881).
61. Ibid., I, 83, no. 30 (Emily to Jane Humphrey, January 23, 1850).
62. Ibid., I, 100, no. 36 (Emily to Abiah Root, May 7 and 17, 1850).
63. Ibid., I, 218, no. 98 (Emily to Emily Fowler, about January 13, 1853).
64. Ibid., II, 346, no. 200 (Emily to Mrs. Joseph Haven, February 13, 1859).
65. Ibid., II, 351, no. 204 (Emily to Mrs. J. G. Holland, March 2, 1859).
66. Ibid., II, 360, no. 215 (Emily to Louise Norcross, March 1860).
67. Ibid., II, 362, no. 217 (Emily to Lavinia, late April 1860).
68. Ibid., II, 435, no. 296 (Emily to Lavinia, November 1864).
69. Ibid., II, 508, no. 391 (Emily to Mrs. J. G. Holland, early summer 1873).
70. Ibid., III, 779, no. 827 (Emily to Charles H. Clark, mid June 1883).
71. Ibid., II, 643-644, no. 610 (Emily to Louise and Frances Norcross, early July 1879).
72. Ibid., III, 871, no. 979 (Emily to Mrs. J. G. Holland, spring 1885).
73. Leyda, *Years and Hours*, II, 471.
74. Bingham, *Ancestors' Brocades*, p. 7.
75. Ibid., p. 14.
76. Ibid., p. 245.
77. Ibid., p. 27.
78. Ibid., p. 298.
79. Leyda, *Years and Hours*, II, 472.
80. Ibid., I, xxiii.
81. Bingham, *Ancestors' Brocades*, p. 66.

NOTES

Epilogue

1. *Letters,* II, 529, no. 420 (Emily to Samuel Bowles, about October 1874).
2. Ibid., II, 538, no. 434 (Emily to Mrs. William Stearns, after Easter 1875?).
3. Jay Leyda, *The Years and Hours of Emily Dickinson* (New Haven, Yale University Press, 1960), II, 383.
4. *Letters,* III, 754, no. 792 (Emily to Mrs. J. G. Holland, mid December 1882).
5. Ibid., III, 746, no. 779 (Emily to Mrs. J. G. Holland, November 1882).
6. Ibid., III, 771, no. 815 (Emily to Maria Whitney, spring 1883).
7. Ibid., III, 682, no. 676 (Emily to T. W. Higginson, November 1880).
8. Ibid., III, 748, no. 782 (Emily to Mrs. J. Howard Sweetser, November 1882).
9. Ibid., III, 890, no. 1018 (Emily to Forrest F. Emerson, late September 1885).
10. Leyda, *Years and Hours,* II, 384.
11. *Letters,* III, 748, no. 782 (Emily to Mrs. J. Howard Sweetser, November 1882).
12. Ibid., II, 475, no. 342b (T. W. Higginson to his wife, August 16, 1870).
13. Ibid., III, 752, no. 788 (Emily to James D. Clark, late 1882).
14. Ibid., III, 750, no. 785 (Emily to Louise and Frances Norcross, late November 1882).
15. Ibid., III, 802, no. 873 (Emily to Mrs. J. G. Holland, late 1883).
16. Leyda, *Years and Hours,* II, 407.
17. *Letters,* III, 853, no. 956 (Emily to Kendall Emerson, Christmas 1884).
18. Ibid., II, 463, no. 332 (Emily to Perez Cowan, October 1869).
19. Ibid., II, 408, no. 265 (Emily to T. W. Higginson, June 7, 1862).
20. Ibid., II, 409, no. 265 (Emily to T. W. Higginson, June 7, 1862).
21. Ibid., III, 861, no. 968 (Emily to Benjamin Kimball, 1885).
22. Ibid., II, 491, no. 368 (Emily to T. W. Higginson, November 1871).
23. Ibid., II, 436, no. 298 (Emily to Louise and Frances Norcross, 1864?).
24. Ibid., II, 463, no. 332 (Emily to Perez Cowan, October 1869).
25. Ibid., II, 601, no. 536 (Emily to Mrs. Samuel Bowles, early 1878).
26. Ibid., III, 817, no. 891 (Emily to Louise and Frances Norcross, late March 1884).
27. Ibid., III, 700, no. 710 (Emily to Louise and Frances Norcross, about 1881?).
28. Ibid., II, 617, no. 562 (Emily to Otis P. Lord, about 1878).
29. Ibid., II, 576, no. 492 (Emily to Mrs. J. G. Holland, about March 1877).
30. Ibid., III, 713, no. 731 (Emily to Mrs. J. G. Holland, October 1881).
31. Ibid., I, 30, no. 11 (Emily to Abiah Root, March 28, 1846).
32. Ibid., I, 38, no. 13 (Emily to Abiah Root, September 8, 1846).
33. Ibid., II, 475, no. 342b (T. W. Higginson to his wife, August 16, 1870).
34. Ibid., II, 517–518, no. 405 (Emily to T. W. Higginson, January 1874).

INDEX OF FIRST LINES

Numbers in italics indicate complete text given on that page.

Poem No.

GENERAL INDEX

dressing in white, 12, 19, 34, 254; birth, 14; synopsis of life, 14–23; impression on classmates, 17; education, 17; religious conversion, 18; excursions, 19; seclusion, 19; friends, 22; impression on neighbors, 22; household responsibilities, 23; death, 23, 445; interest in death, 35; as "part demon," 37, 445; "disgust at everything & everybody," 37; lack of rapport with mother, 40; independence of thought and fantasy, 46, 74; infancy and early childhood, 48–52, 54; sent to aunt's as young child, 50; fear of father, 58, 59, 81; pleasant times, 83; enjoyment of brother and sister, 83; sense of humor, 83; estrangement from father, 85; dependence on father, 91; reactions to father's death, 91, 92, 480; competition with mother, 93, 94; self-appraisal, 94; authoritarian manner, 95; dependence on brother and sister, 99; "grand" gestures of assistance, 164; "my department mornings," 180; "old fashioned," 243; congratulates Joseph Lyman, 253, 254; appearance, 451; dependence on Lavinia, 466–468

Inner dynamics (see also specific psychodynamics, symptoms, etc.): "hugeness of core" and "awkward rind," 14; depression, 17, 18; fear of spiritual self-deception, 18; avoidance of others, 19, 20, 22; fears, 20, 46; voracious need, 21, 44, 98, 101 (see also Food and drink; "Oral" symbols); hypersensitivity, 24, 25; "ecstasy" a short lived emotion, 29, 32; crisis of 1862, 34; emotional impoverishment, 40, 43; sense of loss, 41, 42; sense of being shut out, 44; life style as "oral" dependent, 46, 47; desire to escape home, 52; views on marriage, 67; reaction to Sophia Holland's death, 72; resistance to publication, 75; religious conversion, resistance to, 78, 79; dreams of father, 91; competition with mother, 155, 156, 163, 164; overconcern with Austin's health, 157, 158, 159, 161, 162, 163; as Lavinia's "Father and Mother," 160, 455; identification with Austin, 168, 177, 178, 249, 256; feminine aspects of, 170; "chain me up there," 190; letters lose spontaneity, 251; self-rejection, 255; ego weakness, 256; psychotic illness, reconstruction of, 344–352

Dickinson, Emily Norcross (mother), postpartum illness, 16, 50; early experience of death, 16, 47, 48; education, 16; paralysed, 23, 481; characteristics of, 42, 53; de-emphasized by biographers, 42; depression, 49, 50, 64, 249, 251, 345; remarriage of father, reaction to, 49; religious conversion, 49; loss of domestic authority to Lavinia, 53; subservience to husband, 53, 54, 58; "unobtrusive faculties," 56, 66, 94; unwillingness to leave home, 63; need of reassurance, 68; dependence on husband, 69, 86; as disciplinarian, 71, 76; letter writing, 155, 156; death, 285, 286, 482; recovery from depression, 360; dependence on Lavinia, 464, 465

Inner dynamics: emotional rejection of ED, 2; relationship with ED, 40, 43; maternal failure of, 41, 42, 48, 49, 51, 101; reasons for failure, 47–49, 67; ED's inability to admire, 53, 54; tendency to provoke guilt feelings, 68; failure rationalized through Mother at Home, 80; ED's rejection of as model, 92, 93, 97, 101; loss of domestic authority to ED, 94, 155, 156, 163, 164; capacity to care for infant, 183; influence on ED's life and art, 479, 484, 485, 487, 490, 493, 495, 499; ED's belated affection for, 481–483; ED's envy of, 498

Dickinson, Gilbert (nephew), 182; death, 285, 482, 483; birth, 481; ED's affection for, 482

Dickinson, Lavinia Norcross (sister), education, 17; death, 478

Overt personal characteristics: left at home, age eleven, 68; "take-offs," 99; "I could become insane," 242, 462; nostalgia for childhood, 253, 456; contrasted with ED, 446, 448, 449, 451, 461; peculiarities of dress, 447, 469; similarities to ED, 447, 460, 471; interest in young men, 449; seductiveness, 449, 450; appearance, 451; humor, 452, 459, 460; aggression, 459–462 passim; "she fainted constantly," 460; "practical sister," 467; eccentricities, 469, 470; "no comprehension of her sister," 475

Overt family interrelations: insistence on ED's normality, 27, 466, 475; fear of father, 58; reaction to father's death, 90; as ED's protector, 99; dependence on ED, 99; distrust of

Ego: weakness, 127; boundary, loosening of, 282, 285, 303–305 passim, 307, 308, 311; boundary in normal persons, 305; defenses, 306, 354
Eliot, George, 97, 407, 493
Emerson, Ralph Waldo, 22, 358; ED's failure to consult, 496
Emily Dickinson's Home, 13, 271. *See also* Bingham, Millicent Todd
Emmons, Henry V., 116, 117, 119, 237, 238
Emotional control, fear of loss of, 301, 302, 314
Estrangement, 217, 249, 262, 264, 265, 292, 298–301 passim, 313, 314; in Austin, 214, 215
Examinations, anxiety at, 264
Eye, as phallic symbol, 436, 437
Eye disorder, 284, 318, 323, 393, 394, 415, 416; beginning of treatment, 416; relation to masculine identification, 94; ED uses eyes during, 417; writing proscribed during, 417; ED's dependency on physician, 418, 419; depression during, 418, 420, 421; books as "tormentors," 419; father's objection to further treatment, 420; vision unimpaired by, 421, 422

Face, as sexual symbol, 136, 408
Father-daughter psychodynamics, summarized, 101, 102
Father figure, ED's attraction to, 100; as obstacle to heterosexuality, 102; B. F. Newton as, 117
Father fixation, 100
Fear of being observed, 424, 439
Federn, Paul, 299, 304
Feminine identification. *See* Identification
"Five" (group of girls), 105, 106, 109–111 passim, 113, 125
Flight, from instinctual life, 151
Folie à deux, 308
Food and drink, as love symbols, 39, 40, 43–46 passim, 52, 133, 134, 139, 163. *See also* "Oral" symbols
Ford, Emily Fowler, 67, 106, 108, 109, 115, 116, 239
"Fracture within," interpretation of, 155
French, Daniel Chester, 22
Freud, Anna, 454, 455, 457, 467
Freud, Sigmund, 6
Fusion, 106, 118, 127, 285, 307, 308; in Austin, 193

Garden, as sexual symbol, 177, 440
Gelpi, Albert J., on ED's "morbidity," 35
Gilbert, Dwight, 186, 225, 242

Gilbert, Francis, 240, 241
Gilbert, Martha, 115, 118, 177, 178, 189, 191, 199
Gilbert, Mary, 185, 362
Girl friends, affection toward, 108
God, as parental ally, 78
Gossip, during Austin's courtship, 228, 231, 232, 233, 237
Gould, George, 116, 117, 119
Graves, John, 250
Griffith, Clark, 181, 306n, 335, 377–379; on ED's life, 29; on ED's psychological disturbance, 35
Groups, as characteristic of latency, 109
Guilt, 172, 218, 233, 235, 267, 272, 276, 296, 346, 420, 421; in *Mother at Home*, 76, 77; as motivator, 81; its contribution to the poetry, 498; inducement of, as expression of hostility, 82

Hallucination, 170, 315, 346
Harvard Law School, 241
Haven, Mrs. Joseph, 266, 271
Health, overconcern with, 157, 158, 159, 161, 162, 163
Heaven: as "oral" image, 45; as state of renewed relationships, 91; as equivalent to "Home" symbol, 135
Heterosexuality, 94; fear of or indifference to, 96, 100, 146; enhanced through Susan, 118–120, 238; obstacles to, 126, 128, 143; as defense, 150, 233; encouraged by Austin, 183; as attack on female, 407, 412; potential for, 441
Higginson, Col. Thomas Wentworth, 22, 89, 91, 124, 135, 155, 269, 279, 298, 313, 316, 322, 365, 385, 386, 395, 417, 423, 447, 474, 489, 490; attitude toward ED's poetry, 13; impressions of ED, 21, 22; awareness of abnormality, 32; marriage, ED's comment on, 52; requests ED's photograph, 88; ED's rejection of his advice, 433; "saved my life," 496
Hitchcock, Edward, Jr., 225
Hitchcock, Jane, 361, 459
Holland, Dr. Josiah Gilbert, 22, 271, 274, 360, 388, 493, 496
Holland, Mrs. Josiah Gilbert, 251, 252, 265, 266, 270, 271, 278, 279, 287, 360, 471, 472, 493
Holland, Sophia, 72, 262, 269
Holt, Jacob, 124, 268
Home, as symbol, 52, 131, 133, 134, 135, 136, 137, 145; of Eden, 159; of mother: as entombment, 52; as place of crisis, 98; clinging to, 159
"Home" and "Food" as psychological equivalents, 133, 135

Homosexuality, 103, 125, 138, 144, 147,
149, 150, 177, 182, 216; "normal," 109;
obstacles to, 126–128, 144; of latency,
127; "advantages" of, 127, 128; in poem,
145, 146; as defense, 178
Homosexual panic, 233
Houghton Library, 192n
Household chores, dislike of, 105
Howells, William Dean, normalizing of
ED, 26
Howland, William, 464
Humphrey, Jane, 106–109 passim, 111,
112, 115, 116, 173, 247, 248, 262, 268,
269, 274
Humphrey, Leonard, 269

Identification, 153; with Susan, 118–120,
222, 223, 224, 237, 254, 365, 366;
regressive, 182, 481, 482, 483
With mother, 54, 121; hindrances to,
54, 55; rejection of, 55, 92, 93, 97,
101, 121, 126, 167, 432
With other females, 117; piecemeal,
143
With males, 93, 94, 95, 102, 121, 138,
167, 171, 403, 406, 414, 433, 436,
437; relation of, to creativity, 94,
103, 121–123 passim, 144
With Austin, 165, 168, 169, 174, 177,
178, 249, 254, 256, 393; dangers of,
169, 170
"Idolatry," 113, 245, 287
Immaturity, compared with girl friends,
113
Immobility, 324, 325
Incest taboo, 101, 102
Incoherence, in poems, 334; in letters, 336
Indulgence, condemned in Mother at
Home, 80
Inner life, similar, of ED, Austin and
Lavinia, 447
"Insanity," poetry reading as cause of, 89
"Inspiration," 290
Instinctual life, flight from, 151
Irish, hostility toward, 273, 274, 275

Jackson, Helen Fiske Hunt, 22, 270, 333,
334
Jealousy, 160, 161. See also Sibling rivalry
Jefferson, Lara, 319, 330, 331
Jenkins, Rev. J. L., observation on Edward
Dickinson, 57, 58
Johnson, Thomas H., 10, 380, 416; on ED's
seclusion, 24; normalizing of ED, 25, 29;
acknowledgement of ED's disturbance,
32; on ED's "morbidity," 35;
interpretation of "Loaded Gun" (poem
754), 401–403

Jung, Carl Gustav, 121

"King feeling," interpretation of, 123, 277

Late hours, 146
Latency, 153, 154; definition of, 105;
characteristics of, 105, 107, 125
Lawsuit, Dickinson-Todd, 447n
Letters: cited out of chronology, justification
for, 260; as defense against death, 286,
287; loss of spontaneity of, 289; change in
tone of, 359, 360; as forerunner of poetry,
486
Leyda, Jay, 345, 474
Life and Mind of Emily Dickinson
(Genevieve Taggard), 100
Lightning, as masculine symbol, 435, 436
Lind, Jenny, 168
"Loaded Gun" (poem 754): Anderson
interpretation, 400, 401; Johnson
interpretation, 401–403; Louise Bogan
on, 402; aggression and violence in, 403.
See also Index of First Lines
Loneliness, 111, 112, 113, 125, 126, 159,
163, 257, 258
Lord, Judge Otis P., 93, 147, 285–287, 377,
490, 491, 493; ED's love for, 101; ED's
rejection of, 44, 100
Love: for father images, 34, 92, 93; as
teacher of religion, 493
Love affair, 356, 366, 367, 376, 377, 384,
491, 492; general outlines, 377, 384; as
elevation to royalty, 368; brevity of, 368,
369; moral obstacles to, 372, 373;
renunciation of, 373; fulfillment in
heaven, 374; disappointment in lover,
374, 375, 376; as projected feeling, 387,
388, 391
Love poetry, critical judgments of, 377–380;
popular acceptance of, 396
Lyman, Joseph, 252, 253, 254, 466; calls
ED "morbid," 33; friendship with
Lavinia, 449, 450, 456; appraisal of
Lavinia, 451
Lyman Letters, The (Richard Sewall), 33

MacLean Asylum, 348
MacLeish, Archibald, on ED scholars, 36
Males: indifference or hostility toward, 105,
107, 110–116 passim, 126, 129; as
rivals, 114–116 passim, 126, 199; relative
freedom of, 166; revengeful feelings
toward, 433; older, warmth toward, 116
"Man of morning . . . of noon," 120
"Mansion": description of, 16; return to,
17, 48, 64; ED's dislike of, 64
"Man's requirements," 207, 213, 220, 236

In this unusual biography, the product of seven years' intensive study, John Cody, a practicing psychiatrist, offers a fresh and persuasive interpretation of what made Emily Dickinson the person and poet she came to be. By approaching her poems and letters — a rich though cryptic record of her feelings and fantasies — as psychological documents, he is able to trace the undercurrents that permeate her poetry and to integrate the external signs of psychic disturbance, such as her reclusion, into a total view of her emotional development.

Emily Dickinson, according to Dr. Cody, experienced her mother as inaccessible, ineffectual, and self-abnegating, and thus suffered a twofold deprivation: an unappeasable longing for maternal affection and the absence of an adequate feminine model on which to pattern her own development as a woman.

The imbalance resulting from the mutual mother-daughter rejection and the entanglement in the stresses and crises of her brother Austin's courtship and marriage, the author demonstrates, led to a series of misplaced and frustrated love relationships culminating in a serious emotional and mental breakdown. The consequent upheaval of personality in an already technically competent craftsman, Cody shows, generated insights into the depths of the mind and spirit that greatly increased the richness and power of her art.

Dr. Cody, who is Medical and Administrative Director of the High Plains Comprehensive Community Mental Health Center, Hays, Kansas, is steeped in Emily Dickinson's writings. His study, which draws on previously unpublished family letters as well as on published sources, reveals a thorough knowledge of the Dickinson literature. His sensitive and compassionate interpretations illuminate the workings of a major creative personality as it dealt with psychological catastrophe.

2068